Oskar A Andersson

Proceedings of the Linnean Society of New South Wales

Oskar A Andersson

Proceedings of the Linnean Society of New South Wales

ISBN/EAN: 9783741169809

Manufactured in Europe, USA, Canada, Australia, Japa

Cover: Foto ©Thomas Meinert / pixelio.de

Manufactured and distributed by brebook publishing software
(www.brebook.com)

Oskar A Andersson

Proceedings of the Linnean Society of New South Wales

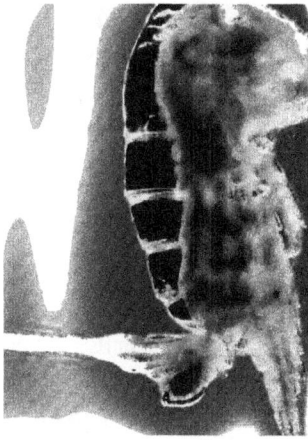

THE LINNEAN SOCIETY OF
NEW SOUTH WALES
ISSN 1839-7263

Founded 1874
Incorporated 1884

The society exists to promote the cultivation and study of the science of natural history in all branches. The Society awards research grants each year in the fields of Life Sciences (the Joyce Vickery fund) and Earth Sciences (the Betty Mayne fund), offers annually a Linnean Macleay Fellowship for research, and publishes the *Proceedings*. It holds field excursions and scientific meetings including the biennial Sir William Macleay Memorial Lecture delivered by a person eminent in some branch of natural science.

Membership enquiries should be addressed in the first instance to the Secretary. Candidates for election to the Society must be recommended by two members. The present annual membership fee is $45 per annum.

Papers are published at http://escholarship.library.usyd.edu.au/journals/index.php/LIN and access is free of charge. All papers published in a calendar year comprise a volume. Annual volumes are available to any institution on CD free of charge. Please notify the Secretary to receive one. "Print on demand" hardcopies are available from eScholarship.

Back issues from Volume 1 are available free of charge at www.biodiversitylibrary.org/title/6525.

The postal address of the Society is P.O. Box 82, Kingsford, N.S.W. 2032, Australia.
Telephone and Fax   +61 2 9662 6196.
Email: linnsoc@iinet.net.au
Home page: www.linneansocietynsw.org.au/

Cover motif: The copepod *Hemiboeckella searli* from Kobayashi et al., this volume.

Etymology of the Dragonflies (Insecta: Odonata) named by R.J. Tillyard, F.R.S.

IAN D. ENDERSBY

56 Looker Road, Montmorency, Vic 3094 (endersby@mira.net)

Published on 23 April 2012 at http://escholarship.library.usyd.edu.au/journals/index.php/LIN

Endersby, I.D. (2012). Etymology of the dragonflies (Insecta: Odonata) named by R.J. Tillyard, F.R.S. *Proceedings of the Linnean Society of New South Wales* **134**, 1-16.

R.J. Tillyard described 26 genera and 130 specific or subspecific taxa of dragonflies from the Australasian region. The etymology of the scientific name of each of these is given or deduced.

Manuscript received 11 December 2011, accepted for publication 16 April 2012.

KEYWORDS: Australasia, Dragonflies, Etymology, Odonata, Tillyard.

INTRODUCTION

Given a few taxonomic and distributional uncertainties, the odonate fauna of Australia comprises 325 species in 113 genera (Theischinger and Endersby 2009). The discovery and naming of these dragonflies falls roughly into three discrete time periods (Table 1). During the first of these, all Australian Odonata were referred to European experts, while the second era was dominated by Robin John Tillyard, an Australian-based entomologist who described 87 species and 21 genera. Tillyard also described Odonata from New Zealand, Fiji, and Papua New Guinea and, if ranks lower than species are included, 26 genera and 130 specific, subspecific or infrasubspecific taxa can be attributed to him.

All but two of his genera (*Anacordulia*, *Notoneura*) are still recognised, as are 52 of his species (40%). Thirty-seven (29%) of his species have been

Table 1. Description of the Australian species of Odonata

		Genera	Species
1770 -1906	European Era	57	116
1907-1958	Tillyard Era	35	114
1959 - present	Recent Era	21	95
		113	325

moved to another genus while 16 (12%) have fallen into junior synonymy. Twelve (9%) of his subspecies have been raised to full species status and two species have been relegated to subspecific status. Of the eleven subspecies, or varieties or races as Tillyard sometimes called them, not accounted for above, five are still recognised, albeit four in different genera, two are no longer considered as distinct subspecies, and four have disappeared from the modern literature. Watson (1969) lists the location of primary type material, and designates lectotypes where necessary, for all Australasian dragonflies described by Tillyard. This paper serves as an excellent checklist to the dragonflies which Tillyard named.

After reading mathematics at Cambridge University, Robin (sometimes Robert) John Tillyard (1881-1937) moved, for health reasons, to Australia where he taught science and mathematics at Sydney Grammar School (Baker 2010). After nine years he moved to Sydney University as a research scholar and then as the Macleay Fellow. For eight years he was head of Biology at the Cawthron Institute in Nelson, New Zealand and then he became the Australian Government's chief entomologist in the Division of Economic Entomology at the Commonwealth Council for Scientific and Industrial Research (CSIR). Baker (2010) gives details of his life, career, and influence on the study of Odonata.

This paper provides the etymology of each of the generic, and then species-group and lower, names for the Odonata which Tillyard described, excluding fossil species.

METHODS

In more recent times descriptions of new genera, species or subspecies have usually included an explanation of the etymology, sometimes including grammar and/or gender of new names. This was not the case in the nineteenth and early twentieth centuries when many Australian species were described.

All original descriptions of the taxa involved have been sighted. The following hierarchy has been used to analyse each entry:

(1) When the etymology is included it has been directly quoted;

(2) If the etymology is not quoted but the Greek or Latin roots are obvious (e.g. flavomaculata = yellow spots) then a search has been made of the type description for the terms which best match those roots;

(3) If no obvious characters are apparent, the roots are given with some speculation as to how they might apply

Direct quotations from references are given in single inverted commas and square brackets have been used for translations, clarifications and comments. Page numbers in the citations refer to the location of the actual quotation, not necessarily the original description. In some cases the clue to the etymology can be quite remote from the type description.

Brown (1956) and Williams (2005) were excellent sources for determining the probable construction of each genus and species name, if it had not been defined by the author. Greek roots were taken from Hionides (1977) and Latin roots mainly from Collins (2005) augmented from Simpson (1974). The abbreviations Gr. = Greek and L. = Latin.

Each entry is headed with the scientific name which Tillyard proposed followed, in square brackets, by the current name recognised by Theischinger & Endersby (2009) or Houston & Watson (1988). To conform with taxonomic priority, dates of issue are used in the references which contain original descriptions, rather than the cover date of publication. In the few examples where these differ the cover dates are given in square brackets following the citation.

ETYMOLOGY OF GENERA

Aeshna Fabricius 1775: 424

Æshna Fabricius, 1775 was published originally without citation of its derivation. Hemming (1958) records that Mr. R. A. Muttkowski had submitted a case for amending the "barbaric *Æshna* to *Æschna*, a *lapsus calami* being assumed". He argued *inter alia* that *Æshna* is not a Greek spelling and "Fabricius being a purist, as is evident from most of his generic names, the elision of "c" in *Æshna* suggests a typographical error".

In searching for possible derivations Muttkowski quoted αίσχρός = ugly and αίσχύνω = disfigured (after death), with a preference for the latter as the former would lead to *Æschrus*. Quoting the submission and other references, the Commission recognised that a certain amount of speculation was required in arriving at the derivation of the name. It declared that it was of the "opinion that since the original publication of *Æshna* Fabricius, 1775, 424-425, does not indicate clearly the origin of the word, it is not evident that there is either an error of transcription, a *lapsus calami*, or a typographical error present. It is, therefore, the opinion of the Commission that the original spelling, namely, *Æshna*, should be preserved".

However, -aeschna is retained as the stem of *Adversaeschna*, *Austroaeschna*, *Notoaeschna*, *Spinaeaschna*.

Agrion Fabricius, 1775: 425

Agrion was the name established by Fabricius (1775) to contain all of the Zygoptera. It is derived from Gr. άγριος = wild, and Fliedner (2006) suggests this was chosen because the insects live in the fields rather than domestic areas.

Anacordulia Tillyard, 1926: 161

[syn *Metaphya* Laidlaw, 1912]

'Closely allied to *Hemicordulia* and also to *Tetragoneuria.*' Gr. άνά = over, towards + *Cordulia* (q.v.).

Archipetalia Tillyard, 1917a: 450

'*Archipetalia auriculata*, n.g. et sp., is probably the most archaic Æschnine Dragonfly yet discovered, and appears to represent a type ancestral, in many of its characters, to *Austropetalia* of the Blue Mountains on the one hand, and to the three Chilian genera *Petalia*, *Phyllopetalia*, and *Hypopetalia* on the other. These five genera forming the tribe Petaliini, ...' Gr. άρχαϊος = ancient + Gr. πέταλον = petal, referring to the leaflike anal appendages of the males.

Austroagrion Tillyard, 1913a: 467

'they [*Pseudagrion cyane* and *Pseudagrion coeruleum*] are more of the *Agrion* build, and probably

represent one of the first asthenogenetic offshoots from that type.'
The derivation becomes L. australis = southern + Agrion (q.v.)

Austrocnemis Tillyard, 1913a: 456
'Characters of Agriocnemis Selys, but with closer venation, narrower wings, and remarkably long legs. It is with M. René Martin's approval, that I propose this new genus for his interesting species [Agriocnemis splendida], which is clearly not congeneric with other members of the genus Agriocnemis.'
The derivation becomes L. australis = southern + cnemis. Cnemis comes from Gr. κνήμη = shin or leg. Fliedner (2008) points out that it 'was used first in 'Platycnemis' [Greek: 'broad greave [i.e. armour for the leg]', an allusion to the widened tibiae in that genus]. But in many names it only means 'Coenagrionid or Platycnemidid dragonfly'.

Austrocordulia Tillyard, 1909a: 744
'Allied to Oxygastra Selys (Europe) and Syncordulia Selys (Australia)'.
L. australis = southern + cordulia which is the adjectival form of the Gr. χορδυλε = club or cudgel, alluding to the shape of the abdomen in the males of the genus Cordulia (q.v.).

Austrogynacantha Tillyard, 1908d: 425
'Though the two species of Karschia are of smaller size than the true species of Gynacantha, yet G. heterogena again is smaller still.' and 'I propose to found a new genus Austrogynacantha for the reception of the beautiful and remarkable species Gynacantha heterogena.' [see also Austrogynacantha heterogena].
L. australis = southern + Gynacantha, which is derived from the Gr. γυνή = woman + άκανθα = thorn, alluding to the spines on the ventral side of the 10th abdominal segment of the females in this genus.

Austrolestes Tillyard, 1913a: 410, 421-422
L. australis = southern + lestes where 'Greek ληστής = a robber or pirate, masculine (rarely used in the common gender). I have therefore treated Lestes and its derivations as masculine, though de Selys used feminine terminations with them'.
Tillyard (1913a) defines Austrolestes by 'Characters of Lestes Leach, and Selys, second section, with the important addition that the wings are not spread out horizontally in repose, but are completely folded back (as in most other Agrionidae). The genus Lestes contains a very large number of species, and has become somewhat unwieldy. De Selys himself

indicated a good point from which a subdivision might be made, when he divided the genus into two sections, distinguished by the form of the quadrilateral. In all the Australian species, together with a very few from outside Australia, the quadrilateral is of a very different shape from that of the more typical Lestes of de Selys' first section.'

Austropetalia Tillyard, 1916: 15
'This genus is very closely related to the Petalia-group of genera which inhabits Chili, viz.: - Petalia, Phyllopetalia, and Hypopetalia.'
The derivation becomes L. australis = southern +Gr. πέταλον = petal, referring to the leaflike anal appendages of the males.

Austrophlebia Tillyard, 1916: 22
'This genus is closely allied both to Telephlebia and to Austroaeschna.' Hence the concatenation of parts of the two generic names.
L. australis = southern + Gr. φλέβα = vein

Austrophya Tillyard, 1909a: 738
'Allied to Neophya Selys, and to Cordulephya Selys.'
See Austrosticta where the quotation from Tillyard says, in part, that the prefix Austro- (derived from the L. australis = southern) may conveniently be used to denote purely Australian genera. To this is added Gr. φύή = stature or growth, used in the name of its two allies.

Austrosticta Tillyard, 1908c: 765
'Allied to Isosticta Selys, from which it differs in the following important points: - ...' Tillyard (1916) defines: 'The prefixes Noto- and Austro- [L. australis = southern] may conveniently be used to denote purely Australian genera.' and he here applies it to the genus Isosticta, in spite of it mixing Latin and Greek roots. [Gr. ίσος = equal to + Gr. στικτός = spotted, tattooed].

Caliagrion Tillyard, 1913a: 468
The type of this genus is Pseudagrion billinghursti Martin. There is no etymological explanation in the type description; the only comment of relevance being 'Very distinct from Pseudagrion Selys, ...; but connected with this genus by the intermediate species Ps. ignifer Tillyard,' which is retained in Pseudagrion on venational and other characters.'
Gr. καλόσ = good + Agrion (q.v.)

Choristhemis Tillyard, 1910b: 334
'Greek χωρίς without, in allusion to the absence of membranule.' + Gr. θεμις = laws, decrees, ordinances,

judgements. Themis was also the Goddess of Divine Law, Order and Justice, a wife of Zeus. Fliedner (2006) points out that Hagen (1861) created eight names ending in *-themis* most probably choosing it to match other names of divine beings established in Odonata with its connotation of reflecting classification. He adds the nice comment that 'Being the goddess of order, Themis is a suitable patroness of taxonomists'.

Recognising that at the time of its inception, Odonata taxonomy comprised only the families Libellulidae, Æschnidae and Agrionidae, *-themis* is effectively a synonym for the Libellulidae of the time. Australian examples occur in the currently recognised families of Synthemistidae. Corduliidae and Libellulidae.

Cordulia Leach, 1815: 137
Leach (1815) introduces the genus name *Cordulia*, without explanation. It is the adjectival form of the Gr. χορδυλε = club or cudgel, alluding to the shape of the abdomen in the males of the genus *Cordulia*.

Dendroaeschna Tillyard, 1916: 42
From the type description: 'δένδρον, a tree' + *aeschna* (q.v.). The description is not specific in which character showed the dendritic character but a couplet leading to the monotypic *Dendroaeschna* in a key to the genera includes 'Basilar space reticulated'.

Hesperocordulia Tillyard, 1911a: 376
'This genus is intermediate between the two main divisions of *Cordulina* (s.str.), of which the typical genera may be taken to be *Somatochlora* and *Syncordulia*.' The derivation appears to be Gr. ἐσπέρα = evening + *Cordulia* (q.v.). Neither the type description, nor more modern texts, give any indication that this monotypic genus is crespuscular; to the contrary, the collector (Tillyard 1911: 378) is quoted 'On the wing, they are very active and mostly high out of reach. ... On some very good days I have taken four, but mostly only one or two.' Evening, therefore, is being equated with the west, as the distribution of the species is restricted to southwest Western Australia.

Lathrocordulia Tillyard, 1911a: 378
λαθραίος = furtive, clandestine + *Cordulia* (q.v.)
'Allied to *Syncordulia** ... (* It must be understood that I refer here to *S. atrifrons* McLach., which I assume is congeneric with the type *S. gracilis* Burm., of which no really reliable or sufficiently full descriptions are available.'

Lestoidea Tillyard, 1913a: 428
'Characters intermediate between those of the legions

Lestes and *Protoneura*.' [see also *Lestoidea conjuncta* Tillyard, 1913]. The genus is derived from ὠδης = Gr. adjectival suffix indicating resemblance, applied to *Lestes* (see *Austrolestes*).

Metathemis Tillyard, 1910b: 335
[junior synonym of *Eusynthemis* Förster, 1903]
' ... we can at once pick out a homogenous group of four characterised by the short anal appendages of the males, the absolute loss of the ovipositor in the females, and the generally rather shorter and less constricted abdomen. These are *S[ynthemis]* *brevistyla*, *S. virgula*, *S. guttata*, and *S. nigra*. ... These four species are also very much more closely allied to one another than any other two species outside them. I therefore propose to place them in a new genus, *Metathemis*, of which the type will be *S. guttata* Selys.'
Gr. μετά = with + Gr. θεμις = laws, decrees, ordinances, judgements. In this case *-themis* is inherited from *Synthemis* but, for its ultimate derivation, see *Choristhemis*, above.

Neosticta Tillyard, 1913a: 435
'Allied to both *Isosticta* and *Austrosticta*, but easily distinguished from both by the form of the male appendages, and by the much greater length of the superior sector of the triangle.' Gr. νέος = new + sticta being the common root of *Isosticta* and *Austrosticta*. -sticta comes from the Gr. στικτός = spotted, tattooed.

Notoaeschna Tillyard, 1916: 58
From the type description: 'Greek νότος, the South Wind. The prefixes *Noto-* and *Austro-* may conveniently be used to denote purely Australian genera. Before the 'æ'of *–æschna* the 'o' may be retained for euphony.'
and
'This remarkable dragonfly stands out as by far the most highly specialized of our entogenic Australian Æschninæ.'

Notoneura Tillyard 1913a: 431
'It is necessary to propose this new genus for the reception of the two Australian species, *Alloneura solitaria* Tillyard, and *A. cœlestina* Tillyard, inasmuch as a careful comparison with de Selys' definition of *Alloneura* (viz., that portion of his 'grand-genre' *Alloneura*, which he designated as 'Sous-genre' *Alloneura*) shows us that the two groups are evidently not congeneric. The two species mentioned are most closely related to *Nososticta*, and might be included in that genus, were it not for important differences in build and venation.' Gr. νότος, the South Wind +

4

neura, being the root of *Alloneura*, from which the species were excised.

Oristicta Tillyard, 1913a: 438, 439
Gr. ὄρος = mountain + Gr. στικτός = spotted, tattooed. 'It resembles *Isosticta* and *Nososticta* in the shortness of the superior sector of the triangle, and further resembles *Isosticta* in its elongated and slender abdomen.' The type is *Oristicta filicicola*, n.sp. 'This retiring and inconspicuous species was discovere by me not far from the summit of Mount Cook [Cooktown, Queensland]'

Pseudocordulia Tillyard, 1909a: 743
'This genus comes closest to *Syncordulia* Selys [= *Micromidia*], of the Australian Corduline genera, but may be easily distinguished from it by the fact that *Syncordulia* has the sectors of the arculus separated at their base, while the appendages of the male are very long.' Gr. ψευδής = false, deceptive + [Syn]Cordulia; false because it is not easily distinguished from the other cordulines.

Synthemiopsis Tillyard, 1917a: 463
'Characters intermediate between those of the Australian genus *Synthemis* and the Chilian genus *Gomphomacromia*.'
Synthemis [Gr. σύν = together with + themis (see *Choristhemis*)] + Gr. suffix οψιζ = outward appearance, indicating a resemblance of one genus or species to another.

Xanthocnemis Tillyard, 1913a: 465
'It is necessary to study this New Zealand species [*Xanthagrion zelandicum* Selys] here in conjunction with its Australian allies. A new genus is required for its reception, as it is clearly not congeneric with *Xanthagrion erythroneurum* Selys, the type of the genus *Xanthagrion*.' Gr. ξανθός = yellow + Gr. κνήμη = shin or leg. See *Austrocnemis* above for a discussion of –*cnemis*.

ETYMOLOGY OF SPECIES.

albescens, Argiolestes griseus Tillyard, 1913a: 414
[*Griseargiolestes albescens*]
L. albesco = becoming white. 'Specimens taken from February to May show a growth of very white pruinescence.'

albicauda, Synlestes Tillyard, 1913d: 239, 240)
[*Episynlestes albicauda*]
L. albus = white + L. cauda = tail of an animal. 'Appendages: superior, 2.7 mm., white, elongate,

forcipate, and also bifid at their basal third;' and 'They are, curiously enough, only betrayed by the distinct white tip of the abdomen, which, I soon convinced myself, is actually necessary to enable the sexes to discover one another.'

alcestis, Rhyothemis Tillyard, 1906c: 482
[junior synonym of *Rhyothemis braganza* Karsch, 1890]
Tillyard was of a generation that still capitalised a species' name if it were a proper noun. In Greek mythology, Alcestis was the wife of Admetus, who saved the life of her husband by sacrificing her own. Perhaps Tillyard followed the naming of *R. phyllis* which commemorated the daughter of Lycurgus, who committed suicide when Demophon, son of Theseus, did not return on the betrothal date.

alleni, Austrolestes Tillyard, 1913a: 425
[*Indolestes alleni*]
'I have dedicated this species to its discoverer, Mr. E. Allen, to whom I am indebted for much valuable help in the form of careful collecting of *Odonata* in the Cairns district.'

allogenes, Agrionoptera Tillyard, 1908f: 641
[*Agrionoptera insignis allogenes*]
'This species was described by me under the name *A. insignis* Rambur ... Since that description was published, I have sent specimens of my type-series to Dr. Ris, and he tells me that they are distinct from the type *A. insignis* Ramb., of Java.' The derivation therefore appears to be Gr. ἄλλος = another + γένεσις = origin (or genus in this context).

alpinus, Argiolestes Tillyard, 1913a: 418
[*Austroargiolestes alpinus*]
'Hab. – Ebor, N.S.W., altitude 4600-4800 feet; January, 1912.' and 'The males are very conspicuous, and easy to capture, as they sit poised on the long grass and sedge growing on the damp hill-slopes at the top of the watershed.' L. alpinus = pertaining to the Alps.

anacantha, Austroaeschna Tillyard 1908b: 735
'This species, to which I have given the name *anacantha* because of the absence of the large dorsal spike on segment 10 of the male, is very closely allied to *A. parvistigma* and *A. multipunctata* of the Eastern States.'
Gr. prefix ἀν = without + Gr. ἄκανθα = thorn

angeli, Austrogomphus Tillyard, 1913d: 234
[*Austrogomphus angelorum*]

The discussion in the type description includes the statements 'Taken by Messrs. F. and S. Angel, of Adelaide, to whom I am indebted for a series of five males and six females, taken between 1909 and 1912.' and '... which I have much pleasure in naming after its discoverers, ...'

Peterson (1993) argued that the specific epithet should be amended from *angeli* to the group masculine form *angelorum* as Tillyard (1913) 'had clearly named this species after two people (two brothers)'

angulicollis, Nesobasis Tillyard, 1924: 323
L. angulus = corner, angle + L. collum = neck. 'Prothorax with the pronotum strongly angulated postero-laterally.'

arbustorum, Austrogomphus Tillyard 1906a: 549
L. arbustus = planted with trees. 'It is also fond of flying in and out about the trees on warm still days.'

arenarius, Austrogomphus Tillyard 1906a: 551
[junior synonym of *Antipodogomphus proselythus* (Martin, 1901)]
L. harenarius = sand. 'This species is found along the sandy shores of the River Barron.'

argentea, Agriocnemis Tillyard 1906b: 192, 193
L. argenteus = of the colour of silver. 'Abdomen very thin, cylindrical. Colour: the true ground colour is a dull black, but this is completely covered in mature specimens by a beautiful silvery white bloom, which can be rubbed off with the fingers.' and 'When flying its wings are invisible, and it appears as a bright silver streak, darting in and out of the grass.'

aridus, Lestes Tillyard, 1908c: 764
[*Austrolestes aridus*]
There is no etymological explanation in the type description but the habitat details are 'Tennant's Creek, N,T.; common round the waterholes in September – April. Probably widely distributed in Central Australia.' Hence L. aridus = dry, arid

armiger, Austrogomphus Tillyard, 1913b: 578
[*Armagomphus armiger*]
L. armiger = bearing arms. 'The remarkable development of parallel spurs on segment 10 and the superior appendages seems to be a contrivance to enable the male to clasp the occipital ridge of the female, which, in this species, is not furnished with the usual tubercular processes by which this process is accomplished.'

asthenes, Telephlebia Tillyard, 1916: 42
[*Antipodophlebia asthenes*]
'This species [*Telephlebia asthenes*] is very different from *T. godeffroyi* by its hyaline wings without trace of bands, its short pterostigma, open venation, absence of membranule, very regular prolongation of subcosta, smaller size, and somewhat different coloration. It appears to be a specialized asthenogenetic offshoot from the main stock, and is one of the smallest *Æschninæ* known to me.' Tillyard (1917b) defines '*Asthenogenesis* (Gr. ἀσθενής, weak; γένεσις, begetting), the development of a successful line of descent by the adoption of weakness in structure.'

aurantiaca, Nesobasis Tillyard, 1924: 331
L. aurantiacus = orange. '... rest of frons orange; ... anteclypeus and labrum orange; ... Prothorax rich orange, ... Synthorax rich metallic green above, with a triangular orange spot in front of the base of each forewing; ... Abdomen: - Seg. 1 orange; seg. 2, orange with two basal black points ...; 3-6 with a narrow basal orange ring,'

aureofrons, Pseudagrion Tillyard, 1906b: 190
'Head - ...front, near the postclypeus, golden-yellow'
L. aureus = golden + L. frons = forehead, brow

aureus, Argiolestes Tillyard 1906b: 179
[*Austroargiolestes aureus*]
L. aureus = adorned with gold. 'It is easily distinguished from the other two Australian species of the genus [*Argiolestes*] by its brilliant orange thorax.'

auriculata, Archipetalia Tillyard 1917a: 457
'*Auricles* very large, bright yellow above, edged with dark brown outwards and posteriorly; underside brown.'
L. auricula = lobe of the ear, used to describe the ear-shaped processes on tergum 2 of some Odonata.

aurolineata, Metathemis guttata Tillyard, 1913b: 575
[*Eusynthemis aurolineata*]
L. aureus = adorned with gold + L. linea = a straight line. '*A pair of distinct antehumeral lines or rays on thorax*, gold or yellow, from 1.5 to 2.5 mm. in length. These are not present in the type-form.'

banksi, Isosticta Tillyard, 1913a: 434
[*Rhadinosticta banksi*]
'*Hab.* – Banks Island, Torres Strait. Four males and five females, taken by Mr. H. Elgner, in February, 1910.'

6

berthoudi, Hesperocordulia Tillyard 1911a: 377
'Taken by my friend Mr G. F. Berthoud, to whom I dedicate this species.' Tillyard (1908b: 721) gives further details of this collector 'I am much indebted to Mr. G[eorge] Berthoud, of the State Farm, Hamel [WA], for sending me a large number of specimens from Waroona (Murray District), thus linking together the northern and southern localities which I myself worked.'

bifurcatus, Austrogomphus Tillyard 1909b: 245
'Appendages: *superior* very remarkable; 1.6 mm., bases separated, straight, cylindrical, jet black, hairy, *strongly bifurcated*; the outer fork being the longer, fairly pointed, the inner somewhat shorter, very pointed. *Inferior* bifurcated, the two parts widely separated ...' L. bis = twice + L. furcatus = forked, branched.

brachycerca, Nesobasis Tillyard, 1924: 333
Gr. βραχύνω = shorten + Gr. κέρκος = tail of a beast 'Appendages excessively short; superiors only 0.2 mm. long, dark, sub-cylindrical, bluntly rounded at tips;'

brevicauda, Telephlebia goddefroyi Tillyard, 1916: 35, 36
[*Telephlebia brevicauda*]
'.. the shorter superior appendages of the male [*Telephlebia godeffroyi brevicauda*]' compared with *Telephlebia godeffroyi godeffroyi*
There is no specific etymological explanation in the type description but the discussion includes the statement 'It seems therefore extremely probable that the longer [superior] appendage is the more archaic form, and that the shorter [cf. *Telephlebia godeffroyi*] one of *T. brevicauda* has either evolved gradually from it as a more useful form, or has arisen as a sudden mutation, or, possibly, as the direct inheritance of an acquired character, in the Lamarckian sense.'

brisbanense, Agrion Tillyard 1917a: 478
[junior synonym of *Coenagrion lyelli* (Tillyard, 1913)]
'Type, ♂, in Coll. Tillyard. (Brisbane, a unique specimen, taken by myself on Kedron Brook, January 22ⁿᵈ, 1913).'

campioni, Nesobasis Tillyard, 1924: 306
'I also wish to thank Mr. Herbert Campion, Odonatologist in the British Museum of Natural History, for his valuable help in collecting together a complete record of the Odonata of these Islands [Fiji].'

canescens, Neosticta Tillyard 1913a: 436
L. canesco = to become white or hoary. 'More mature specimens show signs of becoming pruinescent-grey.'

chiltoni, Uropetala Tillyard 1921: 343
'I wish to dedicate this new species, whose description follows, to Dr [Charles] Chilton as a memorial of the excellent work which he has done, and is doing, in connection with the Cass Biological Station [University of Canterbury, New Zealand]'.

chrysoides, Argiolestes Tillyard, 1913d: 237
[*Austroargiolestes chrysoides*]
'*Meso-* and *metathorax* bright golden-yellow above, except for a narrow black border near prothorax, and a broad black patch above and surrounding interalar ridge;' Gr. χρυσός = gold + ὥδης = Gr. adjectival suffix indicating resemblance.

circularis, Pseudocordulia Tillyard, 1909a: 743
'Named from the exceedingly forcipate appendages, forming almost a complete circle.'

cladophila, Tetrathemis Tillyard 1908f: 648
[*Tetrathemis irregularis cladophila*]
'I have named it *T. cladophila* because of its great fondness for returning again and again to the same twig, even after being frightened away with the net.' Gr. κλάδο = branch, twig + φιλος = friend, loved.

claviculata, Synthemis Tillyard 1909a: 749, 750
[*Tonyosynthemis claviculata*]
'Named from the peculiar form of the appendages.' and 'Appendages: *superior* long, 3 mm. hairy, black, wide apart and slightly swollen at bases, then undulating and swelling out into a rather rounded and somewhat clubbed tip.' L. diminutive of clavis = cudgel.

coelestina, Alloneura Tillyard 1906b: 186, 185
[*Nososticta coelestina*]
L. caelestis = belonging to heaven. 'Superior appendages of ♂ pale sky-blue.' and 'I have named it *coelestina* [sic] because of the remarkable colour of the appendages.'

coerulescens, euphoeoides Diphlebia Tillyard, 1913d: 235
[*Diphlebia coerulescens*]
L. coerulescens = becoming blue [L. caeruleus = blue, and the suffix –escens (becoming). '*Abdomen* coloured as follows: ... 4-7 black *with a pair of conspicuous basal blue spots* (these segments are

Proc. Linn. Soc. N.S.W., 134, 2012

7

wholly black in type form [*Diphlebia euphœoides*])'. The context would seem to be that it becomes blue with respect to the type species, rather than indicating some temporal change.

coeruleum, Pseudagrion Tillyard, 1908b: 741
[junior synonym of *Austroagrion cyane* (Selys, 1876)]
'This species is very closely related to *P. cyane* Selys, of the eastern States. The males can be at once distinguished by the greater amount of blue on the abdomen of *P. cœruleum*; in particular, segments3 and 7-9.' L. caeruleus = blue, dark blue (esp. of the sea or sky).

comitatus, Austrogomphus Tillyard 1909b: 247
[*Hemigomphus comitatus*]
L. comitatus = retinue, a body of companions. The only reference in the type description that might allude to the specific epithet is 'It flies in small clearings in company with *Synthemis Olivei* Tillyard.'

comosa, Nesobasis Tillyard, 1924: 321
L. comosus = hairy. 'The frons carries a series of long, slender, light brown hairs, which project forwards in a regular row, their tips reaching well beyond the level of the anterior end of the labrum.'

conjuncta, Lestoidea Tillyard, 1913a: 429
L. coniungo = to join together. 'This unique and wonderful insect, ... is of the greatest phylogenetic importance, as it supplies the missing link between two very distinct groups or legions of the *Agrionidœ*, both of which have been claimed to be archaic. *Lestöidea* may be regarded as a form *asthenogenetically intermediate* between the less-reduced *Lestes* and the more reduced *Protoneura*.'

conspersa, Caliaeschna Tillyard, 1907a: 728
[*Dendroaeschna conspersa*]
L. conspersus = sprinkled, which probably refers to 'Meso- and metathorax rich dark chocolate-brown spotted with pea green. ... Colour of abdomen deep rich-chocolate-brown spotted with pea green.'

corniculata, Nesobasis Tillyard, 1924: 319-320
[*Melanesobasis corniculata*]
L.cornu = a horn + L. suffix –atus = provided with. 'The form of the appendages is generally similar to those of *N. flavilabris*, but the superiors are longer, 0.5 mm., only about one-sixth or less shorter than the inferiors, and they carry on the inner margin, just before the apex, a very distinct cornicle or tooth projecting inwards transversely;'

costalis, Planaeschna Tillyard, 1907a: 724
[*Austrophlebia costalis*]
L. costa = rib has given rise to the name of the costal vein in Odonata and other insect orders. 'Wings with a deep russet-brown colouration covering the lower half of the costal space up to nodus and all of it beyond, also all the subcostal and median spaces, except the basilar area.'

cyanitincta, Synthemis Tillyard 1908b: 725, 726
[*Austrosynthemis cyanitincta*]
'Rest of abdomen dark brown shading to black, each of the segments 3-7 carrying a pair of central dorsal spots, oval or suboval, of a beautiful very pale greyish-blue colour; those of 3-5 touching along the dorsal ridge, each spot crossed by a transverse black line in the supplementary carina; 8, a pair of large oval spots similar to those on 3-7, but more than half the length of the segment; 9, a pair of small round basal spots of the same colour.' and 'The pale blue colouring of the spots is remarkable, and I do not know of another species of the *Corduliinœ* which possesses it.' Gr. κυανοΰς = blue, azure + L. tingere = to dye. Mixing a Greek and a Latin root is an unusual practice which casts some doubt on this interpretation.

cyclops, Telephlebia goddefroyi Tillyard 1916: 36
[*Telephlebia cyclops*]
Although Tillyard (1916) does not disclose why he chose *cyclops* as a subspecies of *Telephlebia goddefroyi*, one of its prime distinguishing features is 'Front ... with a large black rounded blotch' perhaps reminiscent of the one-eyed giant.

dalei, Nannodythemis Tillyard, 1908e: 446
[*Nannophya dalei*]
Within the introduction to the type description, Tillyard (1908) states: 'I propose to name the Western Australian form *N*[*annodythemis*] *occidentalis*, and to give to the third species (that from the Wentworth Falls) the name of *N. Dalei* in memory of de Selys' great friend, the well-known British entomologist Mr. Dale; this name having already been applied by de Selys to this species on the label in his cabinet.'

divergens, Cordulephya Tillyard 1917a: 469
'superior appendages of ♂ distinctly divergent' L. dis = apart + L. vergere to bend, turn.

doddi, Austrogomphus Tillyard 1909b: 251
'A single male taken by Mr F.P. Dodd.' Frederick Parkhurst Dodd, an amateur collector of butterflies and beetles originally employed in a bank, moved from Victoria to Brisbane, Townsville and then

8

Kuranda, where he became known as the 'Butterfly man of Kuranda.

dorrigoensis, Neosticta canescens Tillyard 1913a: 437
'Race *dorrigoensis*. – On the Little Murray River, near Dorrigo, N.S.W., I met with this insect again, in November, 1911, and secured two males, for comparison.' + -ensis = L. adjectival suffix indicating place of origin.

eboracus, Argiolestes griseus Tillyard, 1913a: 413
[*Griseargiolestes eboracus*
'Race *eboracus* – A short series taken by me at Ebor and Dorrigo, N.S.W.'.-ακός is a Gr adjectival suffix indicating 'belonging to'.

elliptica, Pseudocordulia Tillyard, 1913d: 229
'Appendages: *superior* 1.5 mm., black, slightly forcipate; viewed from above, they form a slightly pointed oval;' Gr. ἔλλειψις = ellipse.

eludens, Nannophlebia Tillyard 1908f: 647
'I have named it *N. eludens* because of its peculiar elusive zigzag flight up into the air when disturbed from its usual rest on a favourite twig.' L. eludere = to evade.

euphoeoides, Diphlebia Tillyard, 1907b: 398
'The specific name is adopted on the suggestion of M. Martin so as to maintain the uniformity of the specific nomenclature in use for this genus.' This suggests that the root might be Gr. εὐφωνια = a pleasing sound + ᾠδης = Gr. adjectival suffix indicating resemblance.

fieldi, Austrosticta Tillyard 1908c: 766
'I wish to tender my heartiest thanks to Mr J.F. Field [of Tennant's Creek, N.T.] for the interest and keenness with which he undertook to supply me with specimens, and to his aboriginal servant, Billy, who wielded the net with the greatest sagacity and discrimination, and evidently handled the specimens with much care.'

filicicola, Oristicta Tillyard, 1913a: 440
L. filix = fern + L. incola = inhabitant. 'The whole of the rock is densely covered in ferns. Resting on these ferns, deep in shade, and drenched with the spray of the fall, I found this little dragonfly.'

flavomaculata, Austroaeschna parvistigma Tillyard, 1916: 49
[*Austroaeschna flavomaculata*]
There is no etymological explanation in the type

description but the discussion includes the statement: 'This very striking and beautiful subspecies is very different from the type-form [*A. parvistigma*] in appearance, owing to the yellow colouring and greater size of its markings.' In a table on p. 48 the characteristics of yellow spots and streaks on the thorax, and yellow abdominal spots, are given. Hence L. flavus = yellow, golden + L. macula = spot, stain.

fontanus, Argiolestes Tillyard, 1913a: 420
[*Griseargiolestes fontanus*]
L. fontanus = of a spring or fountain. 'The Dorrigo series were all found either settled upon or flying round the ferns which clustered on the steep, rocky sides of a small waterfall, about twenty feet high, in dense scrub. ... Two other males were also seen flying about dense vegetation near a waterfall,'

forcipata, Planaeschna Tillyard 1907a: 727
[*Dromaeschna forcipata*]
'Appendages: *Superior* 3 mm., depressed, forcipate, black; wide apart at bases.' L. forcipis = a pair of tongs, pincers.

fragilis, Ischnura Tillyard 1906b: 187
[*Aciagrion fragile*]
L. fragilis = fragile, easily broken. In discussing the genus *Ischnura* (in which he had provisionally placed this species) Tillyard gives the only clue to the specific epithet. '... the present species differs from other members of the genus *Ischnura* ...' and 'The typical characters of the genus as exhibited by *I. delicata* or *I. heterosticta* are (1) rather broad head and thorax, rather robust form, wings not remarkably slender, and well-rounded at tips;'

geminata, Notoaeschna saggitata Tillyard 1916: 59
[*Notoaeschna geminata* Theischinger, 1982]
'a very fine and long series taken by me at Guy Fawkes, N.S.W., is distinct enough to warrant a varietal name. I therefore propose for it the name var. *geminata* defined by the following characters:- ... Sagittate dorsal spots of abdomen much reduced, each being split into two geminate [paired] subtriangular halves separated by the black line of the dorsal ridge.' L. geminatus = doubled, twinned.

gomphomacromioides, Synthemiopsis Tillyard 1917a: 463
'General facies of the insect resembles that of *Gomphomacromia paradoxa* Br.' + ᾠδης = Gr. adjectival suffix indicating resemblance applied to *Gomphomacromia*.

hardyi, Austroaeschna Tillyard 1917a: 461
No information is given in the type description but the species is endemic to Tasmania and George Hurlstone Hudlestone Hardy was Acting Curator of the Tasmanian Museum, Hobart (1913-1917). In the type description of *Synthemiopsis gomphomacromioides* (Tillyard 1917a: 466) the author relates 'Mr G.H. Hardy, of the Tasmanian Museum, also captured a single male at Flowerdale Creek ...'

heterogena, Austrogynacantha Tillyard, 1908d: 423, 424
'In his unpublished MSS. De Selys has described a new species *Gynacantha heterogena* from a unique female in his collection.' and 'Doubtless de Selys felt, when describing the female, that its smaller size and very different markings and colouration might warrant the formation of a new genus to contain it; at least the name *heterogena* irresistibly suggests the impression it made on his mind. But it was not de Selys' way to propose a new genus for a unique female, which possessed all the more essential characters of the genus *Gynacantha* as defined by Rambur.' Gr. . ἕτερος = other, different + γένεσις = origin (or genus in this context).

heteroneura, Nesobasis Tillyard, 1924: 333
Gr. ἕτερος = other, different + Gr. νεύρον = nerve.
'This species differs from all others of the genus in having the origins of M_3 and M_5 placed further apart than usual, the distance between the two being equal to, or a little more than, the descending basal piece of M_S.'

hurleyi, Rhyothemis Tillyard 1926: 166
'This magnificent species, which I dedicate to Captain Frank Hurley, leader of the expedition to Lake Murray, resembles *Rh. severini* Ris., most closely in its scheme of colouration;' James Francis 'Frank' Hurley, OBE (1885 – 1962) was an Australian photographer and adventurer who participated in a number of expeditions to Antarctica and served as an official photographer with Australian forces during both world wars.

hyacinthus, Agriocnemis Tillyard 1913a: 457-458
[junior synonym of *Agriocnemis pygmaea* (Rambur, 1842)]
The flower *Hyacinthus* L. is an ancient Gk. name used by Homer, the flowers being said to spring from the blood of the dead Hyakinthos, a youth beloved by Apollo and accidentally slain by him. There is some resemblance in colour to the flower: 'Abdomen ... Colour, 1-7 bronzy-black above, greenish or yellowish underneath; 3-6 with a pair of pale yellow basal marks, very small; 8, basal two-thirds black, apical third and sides red; 9-10 bright red.'

hyalina, Telephlebia g. *goddefroyi* Tillyard, 1916: 34
[infrasubspecific variety no longer recognized in any form]
'The density of the brown bands on the wings is subject to much variation. ... At Ebor ... I found ... a form in which the band was extremely light and in places scarcely discernible. ... I propose to call this form variety *hyalina*.' Gr. ὕαλος = glass.

hybridoides, Diphlebia Tillyard 1912: 588
'In colouration, it resembles *D. lestoïdes*, but the shape of the abdomen is closer to that of *D. euphœoïdes*. The banding of the wings may also be considered as intermediate between the narrow milky band of *D. lestoïdes* and the deep, almost black, shading of *D. euphœoïdes*, which nearly covers the wing. For these reasons, I have proposed the name *D. hybridoïdes* for this species.' L. hibrida (hybrida) = a mongrel, cross.

ignifer, Pseudagrion Tillyard 1906b: 188
L. ignifer = fire-bearing. 'Head. – *Epicranium* black behind, front brilliant rust colour, crossed by a short black transverse line in the middle, and bordered below, next the clypeus, by a second black line. ... *Clypeus* and *labrum* brilliant rust-colour.'

ingentissima, Petalura Tillyard, 1908a: 717
Superlative of the L. ingens = enormous. *P. ingentissima* is larger than *P. gigantea* as seen in a table in Tillyard 1908a 'The expanse of wing in *P. gigantea* is ♂ about 110 mm.; ♀ about 120 mm. ditto *P. ingentissima* ♂ 151 mm.; ♀ 163 mm.'

insularis, Austrolestes Tillyard 1913a: 426
'Hab. – Banks Island, Torres Straits, taken by Mr. H. Elgner, February 16th, 1910.' L. insularis = pertaining to an island.

intermedius, Argiolestes griseus Tillyard, 1913a: 412
[*Griseargiolestes intermedius*]
'Race *intermedius* – A small series of three males and one female taken by me at Alexandra, Vic, December, 1906, are of intermediate form between typical specimens [*Argiolestes griseus* Blue Mountain Series] and the very distinct form *eboracus*.'

lineata, Aeschna brevistyla Tillyard, 1916: 62
[infrasubspecific variety no longer recognized in any form]
'Var. *lineata*, with the dorsal bands reduced to lines.' L. linea = a linen thread, string.

lyelli, Agrion Tillyard, 1913a: 450)
[*Coenagrion lyelli*]
'This very beautiful and conspicuous species was first discovered by me during a visit to my friend, Mr. Lyell, at Gisborne, Vic., in December, 1908.' George Lyell (1866-1951), naturalist, built up an enormous collection of butterflies and moths, at first from country areas near Melbourne and then from the Gisborne area and other States, donating it to the National Museum of Victoria in 1932.

maccullochi, Agriocnemis (Tillyard 1926: 161
[*Austrocnemis maccullochi*]
'This unique specimen is a fine discovery, and the species is dedicated to its captor, the late Allan R. McCulloch.' Allan Riverstone McCulloch (1885-1925) was a noted systematic ichthyologist, working at the Australian Museum, Sydney.

maccullochi, Anacordulia Tillyard 1926: 163
[junior synonym of *Metaphya tillyardi* Ris, 1913]
'... the species is dedicated to its captor, the late Allan R. McCulloch.'
In the introduction to the paper Tillyard also writes 'The collection of Dragonflies dealt with in this paper was made by the late Allan R. McCulloch of the Australian Museum, Sydney, during the period from November, 1922, to January, 1923, while exploring unknown regions of the central western part of Papua by boat and aeroplane, in company with Captain Frank Hurley.'

manifestus, Austrogomphus Tillyard 1909b: 241, 249
[junior synonym of *Antipodogomphus acolythus* (Martin, 1901)]
L. manifestus = clear, visible, evident. 'My friend, Mr. Allen, of Cairns, took [the female of] a very remarkable new species at Atherton, N.Q., in April, 1907,' Perhaps the meaning lies within the comparison with '*A. bifurcatus*, of which the female is not known. It [clearly = manifestly?] cannot be the female of that species, however, as the markings of head, thorax, and abdomen are entirely different.'

martini, Synthemis Tillyard 1908b
[junior synonym of *Synthemis leachii* Selys, 1871]
No acknowledgement of René Martin, the French odonatologist, but it is extremely likely that the species was named for him.

melaleucae, Austrogomphus Tillyard 1909b: 244
[*Austroepigomphus melaleucae*]
'All the other specimens I have, were taken, one or two at a time, in the teatree [*Melaleuca* sp.] bush

fringing the creek. The insect is very fond of sitting perched high up on a sprig of teatree, sometimes beyond reach of the net. If disturbed, it flies off with bewildering swiftness and settles on another bush. I have named it *A. melaleucœ* because of this habit.' (*Melaleuca* L. is named from Gr. μέλας = black + Gr. λευκόν – white, as the trees often have a black trunk and white branches due to the papery bark.)

melanosoma, Metathemis guttata Tillyard 1913d: 231
[*Eusynthemis guttata melanosoma*]
'Colouration of abdomen: ♂, almost completely black:' Gr. μέλας = black + Gr. σώμα = body.

metallica, Lathrocordulia Tillyard 1911a: 379
'Thorax dark brown, with grey downy hairs. On each side of dorsal ridge is a band of metallic green; sides also reflecting metallic green or rich steel-colour nearly all over.' Gr. μεταλλικός = metallic.

mimetes, Stenobasis Tillyard 1913a: 473
[*Archibasis mimetes*]
'Evidently rare, but probably often overlooked owing to the remarkable similarity between it and the commoner *Pseudagrion australasiæ*. I have named it *mimetes* because of this resemblance.' Gr. μιμητικός = imitative.

minimus, Argiolestes Tillyard 1908b: 735,736
[*Miniargiolestes minimus*]
L. minimus = superlative of parvus = small, i.e. smallest. While dimensions of the most common form are given, there is no comparison to show how it might be considered smallest. The sizes given for race *pusillus* are smaller than the type.

montana, Cordulephya Tillyard 1911b: 397
'The only known locality for *C. montana* at present is Medlow, Blue Mountains, N.S.W., where I took the type-male and female on January 19th 1910.' L. mons, montis = a mountain.

mystica, Austrophya Tillyard, 1909a: 740
L. mysticus = secret. Only a female specimen was available. '[The specimen is an aged one, somewhat damaged, and if there are other markings they have been obliterated.]' Perhaps the 'secret' is hidden in the obliterated markings.

nigra, Synthemis Tillyard, 1906c: 489, 491
[*Eusynthemis nigra*]
L. niger = black, dark-coloured. 'Abdomen Colour deep black ...' and in a key to the closely related

species of *Synthemis*: 'Abdomen almost entirely black'

nigrescens, Synlestes weyersi Tillyard 1917a: 473
'This subspecies is at once strikingly distinguished from the type-form by its dull colouration; but it does not differ from it morphologically sufficiently to warrant its elevation to full specific rank.' 'eyes black; epicranium, frons, clypeus, and labrum nearly black, ... antennae black ... thorax dull blackish ... abdomen blackish' L. nigresco, nigrescere = to become black.

nobilis, Argiolestes icteromelas Tillyard, 1913a: 410
'This fine race occurs on the Dorrigo Plateau, N.S.W., and especially at Ebor. ... It differs from the type-form not only in size, but in its very robust build, and in a much greater tendency towards pruinescence, giving the insect a much greyer appearance.' L. nobilis = known, of noble birth.

nymphoides, Diphlebia Tillyard, 1912: 590
From the type description 'It is one of the most beautiful and brilliant insects known to me, the blue of its body far out-rivalling the colour of *D. lestoides*, itself a brilliant insect. I have therefore chosen the name nymphoïdes (Greek νύμφη, a bride) in allusion to its beauty.' + ὡδης = Gr. adjectival suffix indicating resemblance.

oblita, Aeschna brevistyla Tillyard, 1916: 62
[infrasubspecific variety no longer recognized in any form]
'Var. *oblita*, with no markings at all on the dorsal part of the thorax.' L. oblittero = to cancel, blot out.

occidentalis, Austrogomphus Tillyard 1908b: 731
[junior synonym of *Austrogomphus lateralis* (Selys, 1873)]
'Hab. – Margaret River district [Western Australia]; very rare.' Thus L. occiduus = setting, sinking, hence western.

occidentalis, Nannodythemis Tillyard, 1908e: 452
[*Nannophya occidentalis*]
'Hab. – South-Western Australia' Thus L. occiduus = setting, sinking, hence western.

occidentalis, Synthemis macrostigma Tillyard 1910b: 354
[*Archaeosynthemis occidentalis*]
'I consider that the eastern and western Australian races [of *Synthemis macrostigma* Selys] are sufficiently distinct from one another, and from the

oceanic types, to warrant subspecific names.' Thus L. occiduus = setting, sinking, hence western.

olivei, Synthemis Tillyard 1909a: 747
[*Choristhemis olivei*]
'Dedicated to my friend, Mr. E.A.C. Olive, of Cooktown.'
Edmund Abraham Cumberbatch Olive established a business as an auctioneer, and horse and cattle salesman during the early days of the Palmer River gold rush and remained in Cooktown until his death in 1921. In his later natural history collecting he relied heavily on the knowledge and assistance of Aboriginal people (McKay 2000).

orientalis, Synthemis macrostigma Tillyard, 1910b: 354
[*Archaeosynthemis orientalis*]
'I consider that the eastern and western Australian races are sufficiently distinct from one another, and from the oceanic types [of *Synthemis macrostigma*], to warrant subspecific names'. Hence L. oriens = rising of the sun, eastern.

othello, Camacinia Tillyard 1908f: 640
Tillyard (1908) stated 'It is quite feasible that *C. othello* arose as a differentiation from the parent stock *C. gigantea*, which does not occur in Australia.' The primary character he cites is 'contraction and intensification of dark pigmentation on the wings.' Perhaps this led him to name the species for Shakespeare's Moor.

pacificum, Pseudagrion Tillyard 1924: 312
[*Nesobasis pacificum*]
'Habitat: - Waido Plantation' The type locality is on the island of Viti Levu, Fiji, which is in the Pacific Ocean.

pallida, Metathemis guttata Tillyard 1910b: 363
[infrasubspecific variety no longer recognized in any form]
'Specimens from the Illawarra District of New South Wales are of small size, and the male has a pale creamy or straw-coloured labium. I propose to name this var. *pallida*; it does not deserve subspecific rank.' From L. pallidus = pale, wan.

paludosus, Lestes Tillyard 1906b: 182
[junior synonym of *Lestes concinnus* Hagen, 1862]
L. paludosus = marshy, boggy. 'A single pair of this species was taken by me on the lagoons by the town [Townsville, Queensland].'

12

Proc. Linn. Soc. N.S.W., 134, 2012

papuense, Pseudagrion Tillyard 1926: 157
[junior synonym of *Pseudagrion cingillum* (Brauer, 1869)]
'The collection of Dragonflies dealt with in this paper was made by the late Allan R. McCulloch of the Australian Museum, Sydney, during the period from November, 1922, to January, 1923, while exploring unknown regions of the central western part of Papua by boat and aeroplane, in company with Captain Frank Hurley.

patricia, Phyllopetalia Tillyard 1910a: 699
[*Austropetalia patricia*]
'I propose to name it *Phyllopetalia patricia* in honour of my wife.'

prasinus, Austrogomphus Tillyard 1906a: 554
L. prasinus = leek-green or Gr. πράσινος = green. The head and thorax each contain green markings which give the specific epithet. '*A. prasinus* seems to be the least closely allied to the others [*A. arbustorum, A. arenarius*], and it is the only one whose colours are not pure yellow and black;'

pruinescens, Agriocnemis Tillyard 1906b: 191, 192
[*Ischnura pruinescens*]
L. pruinosus = frosty. 'Thorax - ... Meso- metathorax deep black, slightly metallic, a little bluish-grey bloom low down on the sides. *Underside* covered with bluish-grey bloom. ... Abdomen ... Colour: 1-2 dull black, bluish-grey bloom on sides of 1 and at base of 2,'

pulcherrima, Petalura Tillyard, 1913b: 583
'This very beautiful insect is intermediate in size between *P. ingentissima* Tillyard and *P. gigantea* Leach,' L. superlative of pulchra = beautiful, hence, most beautiful.

pulchra, Austroaeschna unicornis Tillyard, 1909c: 91
[*Austroaeschna pulchra*]
Martin (1909) described what he regarded as the male of *Austroaeschna unicornis*, but it was not. In the same work Tillyard (1909c) described *pulchra* as a new race of *A. unicornis*. The variability in *pulchra* is such that Tillyard's (1909) specimen does not warrant subspecific rank. Theischinger (1982) corrected the erroneous use of *A. unicornis*, recognising these specimens as *Austroaeschna pulchra*. The specific epithet comes from L. pulcher –chra = beautiful. There is no etymological explanation in Tillyard's (1909) type description, the only relevant comment, perhaps, being: 'le 9ᵉ avec une belle tache

dorsale centrale ...' [the 9th with a beautiful central dorsal spot].

pusillus, Argiolestes minimus Tillyard 1908b: 736
[*Archiargiolestes pusillus*]
'An extremely small race found in the southern districts, and differing considerably from the type.' L. pusillus = tiny.

refracta, Austrocordulia Tillyard 1909a: 744
'Named from the peculiarly bent or broken appearance of the appendages.' L. refractus = (perfect participle passive) of refringo = to break open, to break off

regalis, Agrionoptera Tillyard, 1908f: 645
[junior synonym of *Agrionoptera longitudinalis biserialis* Selys, 1879]
L. regalis = royal, regal. When comparing it with its close ally, *A. longitudinalis* from New Guinea, Tillyard states 'The species is peculiar in being an exception to the general rule that the Australian form is generally smaller than the closely allied form from Papua or the Malay Archipelago.' There is no other indication why it might be considered regal.

risi, Nannophlebia Tillyard, 1913c: 713
'Comparing them with types of my *N. eludens*, it was at once evident that they were a new and very distinct species, which I now propose to describe under the name of *Nannophlebia risi* n.sp., in honour of my friend, Dr. F. Ris' Friedrich Ris (1867 - 1931) was a Swiss physician and entomologist who specialised in Odonata. He was Director of a psychiatric clinic in Rheinau, Switzerland.

rubricauda, Agriocnemis Tillyard, 1913a: 460
L. rubrica = red earth + L. cauda = tail of an animal. 'Abdomen ... 7, brilliant red, with a touch of black at base; 8 - 10 brilliant red; ... Appendages: *superior* 0.2 mm., bright red,'

selysi, Nesobasis Tillyard, 1924: 327
No mention of etymology but obviously named for Michel Edmond de Selys-Longchamps. Baron Michel Edmond de Sélys Longchamps (1813 - 1900) was a Belgian liberal politician and scientist, regarded as the world's greatest authority on dragonflies and damselflies. His wealth and influence enabled him to amass one of the finest collections of neuropteroid insects and to describe many species from around the world.

selysi, Synlestes Tillyard 1917a: 473
No mention of etymology but obviously named for

Michel Edmond de Selys-Longchamps.

simmondsi, Nesobasis Tillyard, 1924: 321, 305
[*Melanesobasis simmondsi*]
'taken by Mr. Simmonds ...' 'Mr. H.W. Simmonds,
F.E.S., Acting Government Entomologist in Fiji'.
Hubert W. Simmonds (1877-1966), a prominent
Pacific entomologist, lived in Fiji for 47 years and
contributed greatly to the economy of the country
through his extensive travels in search of beneficial
insects for the control of a number of serious pests
in Fiji.

solitaris, Alloneura Tillyard 1906b: 184
[*Nososticta solitaria*]
'On nearly every day on which I went collecting I
secured one specimen, but only twice did I get a pair,
and once a male and two females in one day. This fact
suggested the name *solitaris*.' L. solitarius = alone.

spiniger, Synthemis Tillyard, 1913b: 573
[*Archaeosynthemis spiniger*]
L. spiniger = thorn-bearing. 'Appendages: ... The
superior carry a large inferior spine at bases.'

subhumeralis, Nesobasis Tillyard, 1924: 326
[*Nesobasis angulicollis*]
'*Synthorax* ... with a long and well-developed black
band running just below the humeral suture, so as to
isolate a narrow blue band on the upper portion of the
mesepimeron;'
L. sub = under + L. humerus = shoulder (from which
is derived humeral suture which runs from just in
front of the forewing to the edge of the mid-coxa.)

subjuncta, Metathemis brevistyla Tillyard 1913b:
574
[*Eusynthemis brevistyla subjuncta*]
L. subiunctus (subiungo) = to subordinate. 'It differs
from the type as follows: - (1) Smaller, more compact
build. (2) Much shorter *pterostigma* ... (3) Smaller
spots on abdomen.'

superba, Hemicordulia Tillyard 1911a: 371
L. superbus = exalted, brilliant, splendid. 'This
fine insect is easily the most distinct and beautiful
member of the genus. ... greater size, more brilliant
colouration'

tasmanica, Austroaeschna Tillyard, 1916: 50
'Type: ♂ unique, Hobart Museum (Hobart, February
1892). This peculiar species, which Mr. Robert
Hall, Curator of the Hobart Museum, kindly sent
me for study, is without doubt very distinct from all

other known species of the genus in possessing its
remarkable bifid inferior appendage, and the huge
tubercle or spine on segment 10. '

tasmanica, Ischnura heterosticta Tillyard 1913a: 451
'In Tasmania, this species is common, and appears to
reach its highest development in a form that seems to
me to deserve a racial name,'

tasmanica, Synthemis Tillyard 1910b: 346
'This species is the Tasmanian representative of
S[ynthemis] eustalacta, the latter not being found on
the island.'

tenuis, Argiolestes griseus Tillyard 1913a: 413-414
L. tenuis = thin, slender. 'A single male ... is of the
very slender build found in *A. fontanus* n.sp.'

tenuissimus, Lestes Tillyard 1906b: 180, 181
[*Indolestes tenuissimus*]
L. superlative of tenuis = thin, slender, i.e. thinnest.
'Abdomen extremely long and thin' and 'It is easily
distinguished from all other species of *Lestes* by its
extremely long abdomen.'

tindale, Austrolestes albicauda Tillyard 1925: 42
[junior synonym of *Indolestes alleni* (Tillyard,
1913)]
'As this form is probably a distinct race, I name it race
tindalei, after its discoverer.' Norman Barton Tindale
(1900 – 1993) was an Australian anthropologist,
archaeologist and entomologist who collected
prolifically in Australia and was associated with the
South Australian Museum.

torresiana, Ischnura Tillyard 1913a: 453
[junior synonym of *Ischnura heterosticta* (Burmeister,
1839)]
'*Hab.* - ... Banks' Island, Torres Straits (H. Elgner);
February 1910.'

tropicus, Synlestes Tillyard 1917a: 475
'Hab – Kuranda and Herberton, North Queensland.
Only two males known ...' Gr. τροπικός = tropical
alluding to the locations which are north of the Tropic
of Capricorn.

tryoni, Telephlebia Tillyard 1917a: 460
'I dedicate this very rare species to Mr Henry Tryon,.
F.E.S., Government Entomologist of Queensland to
whom I am indebted for the opportunity of studying
it.' Henry Tryon (1856-1943) became Queensland
government entomologist in August 1894 and
vegetable pathologist in 1901. His efforts to rear
cactoblastis to control Prickly Pear failed.

viridescens, Macromia Tillyard 1911a: 380, 381
L. *viridis* =green , with the suffix –*escens* = becoming.
'Thorax deep brilliant metallic-green all over, ...
Abdomen ... 1-4 brilliant metallic green'. There is no
obvious reason for the modifier 'becoming'.

vitiensis, Agriocnemis Tillyard, 1924: 338
[junior synonym of *Agriocnemis exsudans* (Selys,
1877)]
'taken by Mr. Simmonds on Waidoi Plantation [not
far from Navua on the Island of Viti Levu, Fiji] The
specific name, *vitiensis*, is a Latin adjective derived
from the Latin word for Fiji: *Viti* + -*ensis* = L.
adjectival suffix indicating place of origin.

vitiensis, Austrolestes Tillyard, 1924:310
[*Indolestes vitiensis*]
'Habitat: - Suva, Fiji Is., taken by Mr. H.W. Simmonds
on Dec 21ˢᵗ, 1919.' As for the previous taxon this
species was named for the Latin word for Fiji: *Viti* + -
ensis = L. adjectival suffix indicating place of origin.

xanthosticta, Metathemis nigra Tillyard 1913d: 230
[*Eusynthemis nigra xanthosticta*]
'Abdomen of male with segments 1-8 spotted with
yellow' Gr. ξανθός = yellow, golden + Gr. στικτός =
spotted.

ACKNOWLEDGEMENTS

Gunther Theischinger is thanked for advice on
the status of some infrasubspecific taxa, and for his
encouragement for my etymological searches. Two
anonymous referees provided useful comments which
improved the manuscript.

REFERENCES

Baker, R.A. (2010). Robert John Tillyard (1881-1937)
F.R.S. – an account of his life and legacy with special
reference to Odonatology. *Journal of the British
Dragonfly Society* **26**, 1-9.
Brown, R. W. (1956). 'Composition of Scientific Words:
A Manual of Methods and a Lexicon of Materials
for the Practice of Logotechnics'. (Smithsonian
Institution Press: Washington, DC.).
Collins (2005). 'Collins Latin Dictionary and Grammar'.
(Harper Collins: Glascow).
Fabricius, J. C. (1775) V. Vnogata pp. 420-427. In
*Systema entomologiae, sistens insectorum classes,
ordines, genera, species, adiectis synonymis, locis,
descriptionibus, observationibus.* (Flensburgi et
Lipsiae: Libraria Kortii).

Fliedner, H. (2006). Die wissenschaftlichen Namen
der Libellen in Burmeisters 'Handbuch der
Entomologie'. *Virgo* 9: 5-23. [available in English
translation at http://www.entomologie-mv.de/
9105%20aBurmeister%20Fliedner%20englisch.pdf,
accessed 11 April 2011]
Hagen, H.A. (1861). '*Synopsis of the Neuroptera of North
America with a List of the South American Species'.*
(Smithsonian Institution: Washington).
Hemming, F. (ed) 1958. 'Opinion 34 *Aeshna* vs. *Aeschna*'
pp. 78-81. In Opinions and declarations rendered
by the International Commission on Zoological
Nomenclature. Vol. 1 (B) London.
Hionides, H.T. (1977). 'Collins contemporary Greek
dictionary: Greek-English English-Greek'. (Collins:
London & Glascow).
Houston, W.W.K. & Watson, J.A.L. (1988). Odonata,
pp. 33-132. In Houston, W.W.K. ed., 'Zoological
Catalogue of Australia'. (Australian Government
Publishing Service: Canberra ,Vol. 6).
Leach, W. E. (1815) Entomology. In Brewster, D.
[ed.] 'The Edinburgh Encyclopaedia' Vol. 9: 57-
172. [Odonata p. 136, 137] (William Blackburn:
Edinburgh).
Martin, R. (1909) Aeschnines. In *Collections zoologiques
du Baron Edmund de Sélys-Longchamps, Catalogue
Systématique et Descriptif* **19**, 85-156.
McKay, B. (2000). Constructing a Life on the Northern
Frontier: E.A.C. Olive of Cooktown. *Queensland
Review* **7**, 47-65.
Peterson, M. (1993). A nomenclatural/conservation
note on an Australian dragonfly species (Odonata:
Gomphidae). *Sydney Basin Naturalist* 2: 16.
Simpson, D.P. (1974). 'Cassell's new compact Latin-
English English-Latin Dictionary'. (Cassell &
Company, London).
Theischinger, G. (1982). A revision of the Australian
genera *Austroaeschna* Selys and *Notoaeschna*
Tillyard (Odonata: Aeshnidae: Brachytroninae).
Australian Journal of Zoology Supplementary Series
87: 1-67.
Theischinger, G. and Endersby, I. (2009). 'Identification
Guide to the Australian Odonata'. (Department of
Environment, Climate Change and Water NSW:
Sydney).
Tillyard, R. J. (1906a). Descriptions of three new
species of *Austrogomphus* (Neuroptera: Odonata).
*Proceedings of the Linnean Society of New South
Wales* **30**, 547-554 [1905].
Tillyard, R. J. (1906b). New Australian species of
the family Agrionidae. (Neuroptera: Odonata).
*Proceedings of the Linnean Society of New South
Wales* **31**, 177-194.
Tillyard, R. J. (1906c). New Australian species of
the family Libellulidae. (Neuroptera: Odonata).
*Proceedings of the Linnean Society of New South
Wales* **31**, 480-492.
Tillyard, R. J. (1907a). New Australian species of
the family Aeschnidae. (Neuroptera: Odonata).
*Proceedings of the Linnean Society of New South
Wales* **31**, 722-730 [1906].

Tillyard, R. J. (1907b). New Australian species of the family Calopterygidae. *Proceedings of the Linnean Society of New South Wales* 32, 394-399.

Tillyard, R. J. (1908a). On the genus *Petalura*, with description of a new species. *Proceedings of the Linnean Society of New South Wales* 32, 708- 718 [1907].

Tillyard, R. J. (1908b). The dragonflies of south-western Australia. *Proceedings of the Linnean Society of New South Wales* 32, 719-742 [1907].

Tillyard, R. J. (1908c). On a collection of dragonflies from central Australia, with descriptions of new species. *Proceedings of the Linnean Society of New South Wales* 32, 761-767 [1907].

Tillyard, R. J. (1908d).On the new genus *Austrogynacantha* (Neuroptera : Odonata) with description of species. *Proceedings of the Linnean Society of New South Wales* 33, 423-431.

Tillyard, R. J. (1908e). On the genus *Nannodythemis*, with descriptions of new species. *Proceedings of the Linnean Society of New South Wales* 33, 444-455.

Tillyard, R. J. (1908f). On some remarkable Australian *Libellulinae*. Part ii. Descriptions of new species. *Proceedings of the Linnean Society of New South Wales* 33, 637-649.

Tillyard, R. J. (1909a). On some remarkable Australian Corduliinae, with descriptions of new species. *Proceedings of the Linnean Society of New South Wales* 33, 737-751 [1908].

Tillyard, R. J. (1909b). On some rare Australian Gomphinae, with descriptions of new species. *Proceedings of the Linnean Society of New South Wales* 34, 238-255.

Tillyard, R.J. (1909c) In Martin, R. (1909). Aeschnines. In 'Collections Zoologiques du Baron Edm. de Selys Longchamps' Vol XIX, 85-156. (Institut royal des Sciences naturelles de Belgique: Brussels).

Tillyard, R. J. (1910a). Studies in the life-histories of Australian Odonata. No. 3. Notes on a new species of *Phyllopetalia;* with description of nymph and imago. *Proceedings of the Linnean Society of New South Wales* 34, 698-708 [1909].

Tillyard, R. J. (1910b). Monograph of the genus *Synthemis* (Neuroptera: Odonata). *Proceedings of the Linnean Society of New South Wales* 35, 312-377.

Tillyard, R. J. (1911a). Further notes on some rare Australian Corduliinae. with descriptions of new species. *Proceedings of the Linnean Society of New South Wales* 36, 366-387.

Tillyard, R. J. (1911b). On the genus *Cordulephya*. *Proceedings of the Linnean Society of New South Wales* 36, 388-422.

Tillyard, R. J. (1912). On the genus *Diphlebia*. with descriptions of new species, and life-histories. *Proceedings of the Linnean Society of New South Wales* 36, 584-604 [1911].

Tillyard, R. J. (1913a). On some new and rare Australian Agrionidae (Odonata). *Proceedings of the Linnean Society of New South Wales* 37, 404-479 [1912].

Tillyard, R. J. (1913b). On some Australian Anisoptera, with descriptions of new species. *Proceedings of the Linnean Society of New South Wales* 37, 572-584 [1912].

Tillyard, R. J. (1913c). Description and life-history of a new species of *Nannophlebia*. *Proceedings of the Linnean Society of New South Wales* 37, 712-726 [1912].

Tillyard, R. J. (1913d). Some descriptions of new forms of Australian Odonata. *Proceedings of the Linnean Society of New South Wales* 38, 229-241.

Tillyard, R. J. (1916). Life-histories and descriptions of Australian Aeschninae; with a description of a new form of *Telephlebia* by Herbert Campion. *Journal of the Linnean Society (Zoology)* 33, 1-83.

Tillyard, R. J. (1917a). On some new dragonflies from Australia and Tasmania (Order Odonata). *Proceedings of the Linnean Society of New South Wales* 42, 450-479.

Tillyard, R.J. (1917b). 'The Biology of Dragonflies (Odonata or Paraneuroptera)' Cambridge Zoological Series. (Cambridge University Press: London, England).

Tillyard, R. J. (1921). Description of a new dragon-fly belonging to the genus *Uropetala* Selys. *Transactions of the Royal Society of New Zealand* 53, 343-346.

Tillyard, R. J. (1924). The dragonflies (Order Odonata) of Fiji, with special reference to a collection made by Mr. H. W. Simmonds, F.E.S., on the island of Viti Levu. *Transactions of the Royal Entomological Society London* 71, 305-346.

Tillyard, R. J. (1925). Odonata, Neuroptera and Trichoptera from Groote Eylandt. Gulf of Carpentaria. *Records of the South Australian Museum* 3, 41-44.

Tillyard, R. J. (1926). On a collection of Papuan dragonflies (Odonata) made by the late Mr. Allan R. McCulloch in 1922-3. with descriptions of new species. *Records of the Australian Museum* 15, 155-166.

Watson, J.A.L. (1969) Australasian dragonflies described by R.J. Tillyard, with the location of types and the designation of lectotypes. *Journal of the Australian Entomological Society* 8, 153-160.

Williams, T.W. (2005). 'A Dictionary of the roots and combining forms of scientific words'. (Squirrox Press: Norfolk, England).

.

16

The following corrections should be made to the previous paper - Endersby, I.D. (2012). Etymology of the dragonflies (Insecta: Odonata) named by R.J. Tillyard, F.R.S.

The author is grateful to Dr. Heinrich Fliedner for pointing out a number of philological errors and inconsistencies and for prompting further research.

Page 2
Methods (2) - For 'flavomaculata = yellow spots' read 'flavo-macul-ata = with yellow spots' *Æshna* For '*Spinaeaschna*' read '*Spinaeschna*'.

Page 3
Austroagrion, Austrogynacantha, Austrolestes, Austropetalia, Austrophya, Austrosticta - For 'australis' read auster (stem austro-) = south wind, hence south.

Austrocnemis - For 'australis' read auster (stem austro-) = south wind, hence south. For 'κνήμη' read 'κνημίς' = legging.

Austrocordulia - For 'australis' read auster (stem austro-) = south wind, hence south. For 'χορδυλε' read 'κορδύλη'

Austrophlebia - For 'australis' read auster (stem austro-) = south wind, hence south. For 'φλέβα' read φλέψ (stem φλεβ-)

Page 4
Cordulia - For 'χορδυλε' read 'κορδύλη'

Lestoidea – For 'ώδης' read '-ειδής'

Page 5
Synthemiopsis - For 'Gr. suffix οψις = outward appearance, indicating a resemblance of one genus or species to another' read 'Gr. όψις = appearance, used as a suffix to denote resemblance.'

Xanthocnemis - For 'κνήμη' read 'κνημίς' = legging

albescens - For 'albesco = becoming white' read 'L. albus = white + L. suffix –escens = becoming'

allogenes - Substitute 'ἀλλογενής (adj) = of another race'

Page 6
arbustorum - For 'arbustus' read 'genitive pl. of arbustum (noun) = coppice, shrubbery'

arenarius - For 'sand' read 'belonging to the sand'(adj.)

aurolineata - For 'aureus' read 'aurum = gold'. Add L. suffix -ata, -atus –atum = provided with.

Page 7
brachycerca - For 'βραχύνω' read 'βραχύς (adj) = short'

brevicauda - Add 'L. brevis = short + L. cauda = tail of an animal.'

brisbanense - Add L. suffix –ensis (neuter –ense) indicating place of origin.

canescens - For 'L. canesco = to become white or hoary' read 'L. canus = white, hoary + L. suffix – escens = becoming'

chrysoides – For 'ώδης' read '-ειδής'

claviculata - For 'clavis' read 'clava'. Add L. suffix -ata, -atus –atum = provided with

Page 8
comitatus – For ' L. comitatus = retinue, a body of companions' read 'L. comitatus is a participle of the verb comito = to accompany, hence accompanied'

CORRIGENDUM TO ENDERSBY pp 1-16.

conjuncta - For 'coniungo' = to join together' read 'coniunctus (adj) = linked with, associateded with'

corniculata - For 'L.cornu = a horn + L. suffix –atus = provided with' read 'Derived from corniculum, diminutive of cornu = a horn + L. suffix –atus = provided with.'

cyanitincta - For 'κυανοῦς' read 'L. cyanus = lapis lazuli + past participle of tingere = to dye' and delete the comment on a mixture of Greek and Latin roots.

Page 9
elliptica - Add '-τικός = concerning, pertaining to'

euphoeoides - Replace the explanation with 'An allusion to the Calopterygid genus *Euphaea* (Selys 1840), [but misspelled by Tillyard], as all three species known in that genus at the time were named for *Agrion, Lestes* and then *Euphaea*. *Euphaia* is a Greek female name, derived from the adjective εὐφαής = very bright + -ειδής = Gr. suffix indicating resemblance

flavomaculata - Add 'L. suffix -ata, -atus –atum = provided with'

forcipata - For 'forcipis' read 'forceps (stem forcip-)'. Add L. suffix -ata, -atus –atum = provided with.

sagittata - *saggitata* should read *sagittata*

Page 10
heterogena - For 'γένεσις' read 'adj. suffix derived from γένος = race, clan, family'

hyalina - For 'ὖαλος' read 'ὑάλινος (adj) = made of glass'

lineata - Add 'L. suffix -ata, -atus –atum = provided with'

Page 11
melaleucae - For 'Gr. λευκόν' read 'Gr. λευκός'

nimetes - For 'μιμητικός = imitative' read 'μιμητής = imitator'

montana - For 'mons, montis' read 'montanus (adj) = pertaining to a mountain or mountains'

mystica - mysticus is better translated as 'mysterious, enigmatic, baffling' which would be fitting for a species not easily detected or not easily determined.

Page 12
oblita - For 'oblittero' read 'participle of oblino = to smudge but also to efface' because the marks of the species are not seen in this subspecies'.

occidentalis - For 'occiduus' read 'adj. derived from occidens = the setting sun, (thus sunset, west), hence western'.

orientalis - For 'oriens read 'adj. derived from oriens = the rising sun, (thus sunrise, east), hence eastern'.

Page 13
papuense - Add L. suffix –ensis (neuter –ense) indicating place of origin.

pruinescens - For 'L. pruinosus = frosty' add '+ L. suffix –escens = becoming'

rubricauda - For 'rubrica' read 'ruber = red'

Page 14
subhumeralis - Add 'L. suffix –alis = associated with'

subjuncta - For 'L. subiunctus (subiungo) = to subordinate' read 'L.. subiunctus: past participle of subiungo = to subordinate'

REFERENCES

Add 'Liddell, H.G and Scott, R. (1869). 'A Greek Lexicon'. 6th ed., rev. and augm., (Clarendon Press, Oxford).

As a Modern Greek lexicon was used instead of an Ancient Greek one, changes to the diacritic marks should be made (Liddell and Scott 1869):

For:	Read	For:	Read
άγριος	ἄγριος	θεμις	θέμις
αίσχρός	αἰσχρός	ίσος	ἴσος
αίσχύνω	αἰσχύνω	καλόσ	καλός
άκανθα	ἄκανθα	κλάδο	κλάδος
άν	ἀν-	λαθραίος	λαθραῖος
άνά	ἀνά	νεύρον	νεῦρον
άρχαϊος	ἀρχαῖος	όρος	ὀρός
άσθενής	ἀσθενής	σώμα	σῶμα
έλλειψις	ἔλλειψις	φιλος	φίλος
έσπέρα	ἑσπέρα	φύή	φυή
έτερος	ἕτερος		

New Information on *Culmacanthus* (Acanthodii: Diplacanthiformes) from the ?Early–Middle Devonian of Southeastern Australia

CAROLE J. BURROW[1], GAVIN C. YOUNG[2]

[1]Geosciences, Queensland Museum, 122 Gerler Rd, Hendra Qld 4011 (carole.burrow@gmail.com); [2]Department of Earth and Marine Sciences, Australian National University, Canberra ACT 0200

Published on 25 June 2012 at http://escholarship.library.usyd.edu.au/journals/index.php/LIN

Burrow, C.J. and Young, G.C. (2012). New information on *Culmacanthus* (Acanthodii: Diplacanthiformes) from the ?Early–Middle Devonian of southeastern Australia. *Proceedings of the Linnean Society of New South Wales* **134**, 21-29.

A new articulated acanthodian from the Devonian Bunga Beds on the south coast of New South Wales is assigned to *Culmacanthus* sp., and reveals that this diplacanthiform has smooth dental plates on the occlusal surfaces of the lower jaws. Within the Acanthodii, this type of element was first identified in "*Gladiobranchus*" *probaton* from the earliest Devonian MOTH locality, Northwest Territories, Canada, and has now also been identified in "*Euthacanthus*" *curtus* (Lochkovian, Lower Old Red Sandstone, Scotland) and *Diplacanthus* spp. (Givetian, Scotland and Frasnian, Canada). The dental plates in *Culmacanthus* have the same morphology as those of "*Gladiobranchus*" *probaton* and "*Euthacanthus*" *curtus*. Reexamination of type specimens of *Culmacanthus* shows that its pectoral fin spines do not have long insertions, and the purported lack of prepectoral, admedian and prepelvic fin spines could be due to loss of the elements before burial rather than morphological absence.

Manuscript received 3 May 2012, accepted for publication 6 June 2012.

KEYWORDS = acanthodian, Bunga Beds, *Culmacanthus*, Devonian, southeastern Australia, taxonomy

INTRODUCTION

Exposures of Devonian sedimentary and igneous rocks along the southern coastline of New South Wales have been recognized since the mid-19th century (Young 2007). Detailed geological mapping by students of the Australian National University Geology Department during the 1970s led to discovery of fossil fish remains at several levels within the sedimentary sequence, including dark shales referred to the 'Bunga Beds', which preserve abundant plant remains and rare vertebrates, and have been interpreted as a deep freshwater lake deposit. Fergusson et al. (1979) assigned the Bunga Beds to a 'Flyschoid facies' within the Boyd Volcanic Complex, and suggested an age 'not older than Givetian' (late Middle Devonian). However, Hall (1959, 1960) had suggested an Early–Middle Devonian age, and recent comparisons of the plants and vertebrates with similar taxa occurring elsewhere also suggest an older (Eifelian, possibly Emsian) age (Young 2007, Young et al. 2010). Apart from acanthodians, other vertebrates in the Bunga Beds assemblage include the chondrichthyan *Antarctilamna prisca* Young, 1982, remains of a tristichopterid sarcopterygian (including partial skull and jaw remains, many scales, and a cleithrum from the shoulder girdle; see Young 2007:fig. 3a), and a single partly articulated actinopterygian named ?*Howqualepis youngorum* (sic) by Choo (2009). Acanthodians include the probable ischnacanthid described by Burrow (1996), the tail of a large acanthodiform acanthodian, and the diplacanthiform acanthodian described here. The Bunga Beds assemblage is unusual in that placoderm remains have not been found (Young 2007), even though phyllolepid placoderm plates with highly distinctive ridged ornament are well represented at other fossil fish localities (Pambula River) in sedimentary interbeds presumed to be higher (younger) within the Boyd Volcanic Complex (e.g. Young 2005).

Culmacanthus stewarti Long, 1983, the type species of *Culmacanthus*, comes from Late Devonian lacustrine shales at Mt Howitt, Victoria. Two additional species, *C. antarctica* Young, 1989 and *C. pambulensis* Young, 1989 are based on distinctive cheek plates from the Aztec Siltstone, Antarctica, and the Boyd Volcanic Complex (Pambula River), respectively. The Pambula River locality represents another sedimentary facies of the Boyd Volcanic Complex, and is some 60 km to the south of the Bunga Beds locality (Fig. 1). In this paper we describe a newly discovered acanthodian specimen showing distinctive dental elements. The same elements are identified in a previously undescribed specimen of the type species of *Culmacanthus*. We also reinterpret some other features of the type species.

GEOLOGICAL SETTING

The Boyd Volcanic Complex was defined by Fergusson et al. (1979) to include the 'Eden Rhyolite' and 'Lochiel Formation' of earlier authors. Previously the 'Eden Rhyolite' was interpreted as the basal unit of the Devonian sequence, which was unconformably overlain by two Upper Devonian formations, the 'Lochiel Formation' and the 'Merrimbula Formation' (e.g. Brown 1930; Hall 1959, 1960). More detailed mapping indicated a complex interfingering between the intrusive and extrusive silicic rocks and the basalts and associated sediments, and on this evidence the Boyd Volcanic Complex was named, and described in terms of eight facies associations (Fergusson et al. 1979). One of these ('Flyschoid facies') represented the 'dark coloured shales containing abundant *Lepidodendron clarkei*' recorded by Hall (1959:7) in the vicinity of Bunga Head. This sedimentary unit mapped as lying beneath the 'Eden Rhyolite', and the plant fossils establishing a Devonian age for strata that at some localities rest unconformably on folded Ordovician of similar lithology (Powell 1983; Young 2007). The outcrop of sediments and associated volcanics in the Bunga Head area is separated by some 20 km from the main outcrop of the Boyd Volcanic Complex, which extends from Tathra to the south through Pambula and Eden (Fig. 1).

Within this northern outlier, the Bunga Beds (finely bedded carbonaceous dark shales and sandstones) were first described from three separate exposures, with an apparent erosion surface separating them from the overlying volcanics (Hall 1969). The Bunga Beds are best exposed for about 9 km along the coast between Picnic Point and Goalen Head, where they are intruded by the Goalen Head Gabbro.

The northern sedimentary outcrop is the largest, and extends some 3 km inland (Rickard & Love 2000: fig. 1). Student mapping (Bucknell 1969; Scott 1972) established a range of sedimentary lithologies including black shale, siltstone, sandstone and conglomerate. Fergusson et al. (1979:fig. 15) indicated the sequence at Bunga Head to be some 200 m thick, based on the work of Scott (1972), and this thickness was attributed by Lewis et al. (1994) to the basin margin. Cas et al. (1990) illustrated measured sections of stratified volcaniclastic successions less than 40 m in coastal exposures. The published geological map (Lewis et al. 1994) closely follows the student maps of Bucknell (1969) and Scott (1972); the only other published map (Rickard & Love 2000:fig. 1) shows less detail of the sedimentary outcrop. Bucknell (1969) and Scott (1972) both recorded several plant fossil localities, but no fish. Plant fossils may be locally abundant, for example in the gravel quarry (Bunga Pinch Quarry) on the main Tathra–Bermagui Road about 2.5 km north of Lake Wapengo (examples figured by Young 2007:fig. 3d-f). This is about 2.5 km inland from the coastal outcrop on Bunga Beach that has produced, in addition to similar plant remains, the shark, sarcopterygian and actinopterygian fossils documented by Young (1982, 2007), Long and Young (1995) and Choo (2009). About 2.5 km to the north of Bunga Pinch Quarry along the Tathra–Bermagui Road black shales can be exposed in small gravel pits and road cuttings in the vicinity of the intersection with Hergenhans Road (Murrah 1:25 000 Topographic Map 8924-4N, second edition). This is the area that produced the acanthodians described by Burrow (1996), and also the new specimens described here (collected in February, 2008).

The detailed map of Bucknell (1969) suggests that the vicinity of the Hergenhans Road intersection (locality 1, Fig. 1) is at a similar stratigraphic level to the main *Antarctilamna* locality at Bunga Beach (locality 2, Fig. 1), whereas the Bunga Pinch Quarry (locality 3, Fig. 1) may be considerably higher stratigraphically. Bucknell (1969) and Scott (1972) mapped two east-west trending conglomerate bands separated by volcanics which evidently lie stratigraphically beneath the acanthodian fish localities, and showed a general dip of strata to the south-west with dips of up to 35°. Although the sequence is made complex by interbedding of volcanics (Cas et al. 1990), and faulting and folding (but the folds are moderate to gentle; Rickard and Love 2000), the general dip and south-easterly strike indicates that the Bunga Pinch Quarry locality is considerably higher in the sequence than the other fish horizons. Scott's (1972) detailed stratigraphic analysis was confined to the limited

22

Proc. Linn. Soc. N.S.W., 134, 2012

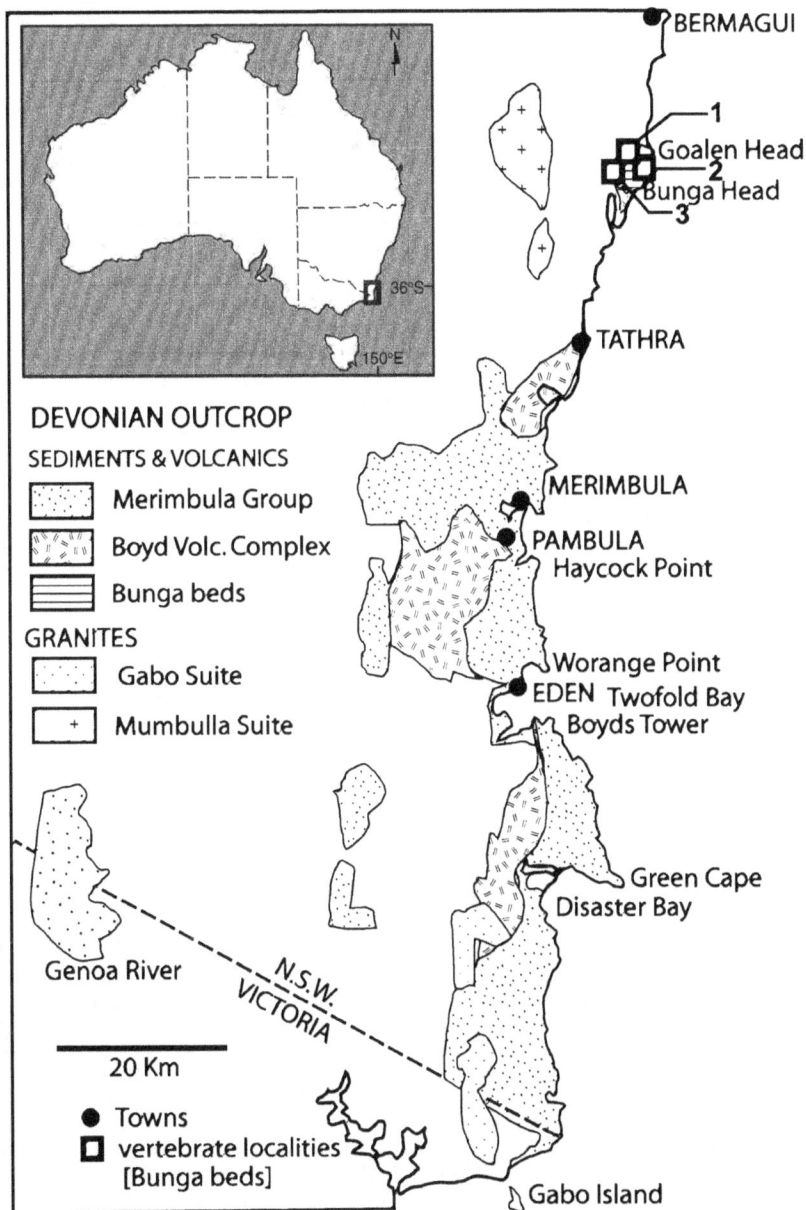

Figure 1. Generalised Devonian geology of the far south coast of New South Wales (after Young 2007), showing the three main fossil fish localities within the Bunga Beds discussed in the text: 1, Hergenhans Road intersection; 2, Bunga Beach; 3, Bunga Pinch Quarry.

Proc. Linn. Soc. N.S.W., 134, 2012

23

sedimentary sequence well exposed on the coast, but Scott (1972:45) also mentioned overlying 'arenites and coarse lutites' more than 450 m thick extending inland, and assuming a general dip of 35° to the SW, without folding or faulting, the Bunga Pinch Quarry locality could be perhaps more than 1 km higher than the other localities. This locality produced the undescribed tail of a large acanthodiform mentioned above. Note that the suggestion (Cas et al. 1990:160) that the fossil fish from the Bunga Beds are most likely marine is unsupported by any evidence.

MATERIALS AND METHODS

Bunga Beds specimens ANU V3374, V3375, 3376, and 3377 were collected in 2008 in a laminated black shale exposed in a road cutting on a road providing access to the beach on the northern side of Goalen Head, south of Bermagui, NSW. *Culmacanthus stewarti* specimen NMV P230281 was collected from Mt Howitt, Victoria by Ian Stewart in the 1990s.

Institutional abbreviations: ANU V, College of Science palaeontological collection, Australian National University; CMN, Canadian Museum of Nature collection; NMS G., National Museums Scotland, geology collection; NMV P, Museum Victoria palaeontological collection; UALVP, University of Alberta vertebrate paleontology collection.

SYSTEMATIC PALAEONTOLOGY

CLASS ACANTHODII Owen, 1846
ORDER DIPLACANTHIFORMES Berg, 1940
Diagnosis.
See Newman et al. (in press) for a revised diagnosis.

Family Culmacanthidae Long, 1983
Diagnosis
(revised). Diplacanthiform acanthodian lacking prepelvic and admedian spines; paired pinnal plates and anterior lorical plate ornamented with flat sinuous narrow ridges; large cheek plate with the same ornament, plus sensory lines, extending from just behind eye almost to scapulocoracoid; two or three anterior circumorbital plates ornamented with spiky tubercles; lower jaws each have a short ossified plate with a high dorsally-directed process near the posterior end; scapulocoracoid tall and slender with a narrow posterior flange; pectoral fin spine not attached to dermal plates; anterior and posterior dorsal fin

spines of equal length, twice the length of the pelvic fin spines and slightly longer than the anal fin spine; scales with strongly convex bases and flat crowns bearing six or seven weak longitudinal ridges.

Remarks.
Absence of admedian spines is assumed based on their absence in all known specimens, but this could result from disarticulation and/or loss of the pectoral spines, as discussed below.

Genus *Culmacanthus* Long, 1983

Diagnosis.
As for the family.

Type species.
Culmacanthus stewarti Long, 1983.

Culmacanthus sp.

Description.
ANU V3376a, b (Fig. 2a, 2b) comprises an articulated fish, poorly preserved in part and counterpart. Most fine detail and nearly all of the hard parts are weathered away, and the fish is mainly preserved as impressions of each side, but with the head dorsoventrally compressed. No details of the squamation are preserved, except its extent. The 25 mm-long anterior and posterior dorsal fin spines and the 17 mm-long anal fin spine are in situ; two shorter, displaced fin spines preserved between the anal and anterior dorsal spines are interpreted as the pelvic fin spines. The insertion on the anterior dorsal fin spine (Fig. 2e) is one-third of total spine length, and is ornamented with fine parallel ridges. The exserted two-thirds has about seven parallel longitudinal dentine ridges per side. These ridges are very narrow near the trailing edge and wider towards the leading edge. No other spines are distinguishable. One scapulocoracoid lies horizontally behind the head region and the other is preserved as a worn impression, vertically oriented above the head. These elements are c. 10 mm high, with tall straight slender shafts, and a short flared base. On the counterpart, two plates overlie the base of the scapulocoracoid preserved above the head (Fig. 2c, 2d). As this scapulocoracoid has been displaced, it is not clear if it is preserved under or on top of the head. No ornament is visible on the two plates, but their shape is comparable with that of the median lorical plus a pinnal plate of *Culmacanthus stewarti* (Long 1983:fig. 2A). The lack of ornament suggests that the internal surfaces are exposed, indicating that the dorsal side of the head is uppermost. At

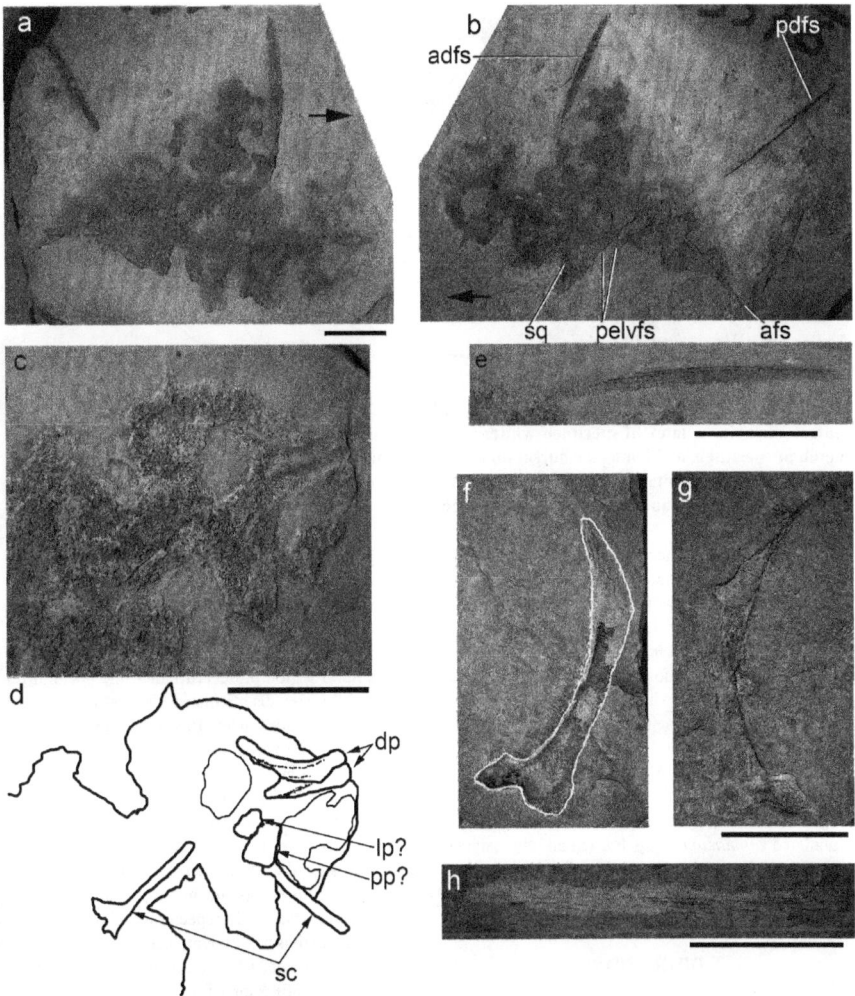

Figure 2. *Culmacanthus* sp. from the Bunga Beds, southern coast New South Wales. a-c. articulated fish ANU V3376. a, part. b, counterpart. c, closeup of head region of counterpart (specimen rotated 180° to right). d, diagrammatic sketch of c. e, anterior dorsal fin spine on counterpart. f, g, isolated scapulocoracoid ANU V3374, two sides b and a. h, isolated fin spine, ANU V3377. adfs, anterior dorsal fin spine; afs, anal fin spine; dp, dental plates; lp, lorical plate; pdfs, posterior dorsal fin spine; pelvfs, pelvic fin spine; pp, pinnal plate; sc, scapulocoracoid. Scale bar is 1 cm.

the anteriormost end of the counterpart (Fig. 2c, 2d) are impressions of two curved spathiform jaw ossifications, each about 7 mm long. A smooth oval area forming a gap in the squamation behind the jaws on the counterpart possibly represents the area where

one of the dermal cheek plates has detached. No pectoral or associated fin spines are present, nor are any details of the squamation discernible.

The isolated scapulocoracoid ANU V3374 (Fig. 2f, 2g) is 26 mm high, with a short base and high

Proc. Linn. Soc. N.S.W., 134, 2012

25

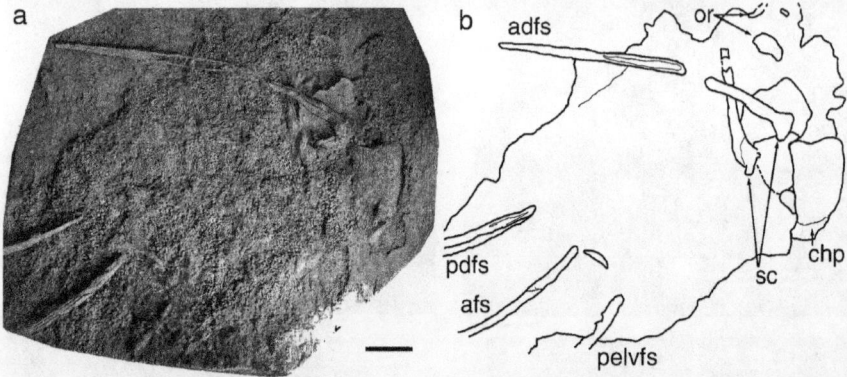

Figure 3. a, b. Cast of *Culmacanthus stewarti* NMV P230281 (part) from the Givetian of Mt Howitt, central Victoria. a, latex of specimen whitened with ammonium chloride sublimate; b, diagrammatic sketch of specimen. adfs, anterior dorsal fin spine; afs, anal fin spine; chp, ornamented cheek plate; or, sclerotic or circumorbital plates; fw, fin web; pdfs, posterior dorsal fin spine; pelvfs, pelvic fin spine; sc, scapulocoracoid; sq, squamation. Scale bar is 1 cm.

curved shaft. The element is exposed in transverse section, showing an anteroposterior oriented ventral groove for articulation with the pectoral fin spine. The element is much larger than the scapulocoracoid on the articulated *Culmacanthus* sp. from Bunga Beds, but is a similar size to those on the type specimens of *C. stewarti* from Mt Howitt, which also have a ventral groove for the pectoral spine articulation (Long 1983: fig. 6).

Isolated fin spine ANU V3377 (Fig. 2h) is a poorly preserved straight spine, 26 mm long, with longitudinal ridges comparable to those on the articulated *Culmacanthus* sp. It is tentatively assigned to this taxon. Remnants of a similar spine are preserved near the scapulocoracoid on ANU V3374.

DISCUSSION

The general dimensions, and number, size and orientation of the fin spines on ANU V3376 compare closely with *Culmacanthus stewarti* specimen NMV P230281 (Fig. 3) from Mt Howitt. In the original description of *Culmacanthus*, Long (1983:figs. 3A, 4D) labelled several fin spines as pectorals, but on reexamination we interpret these as anterior dorsal fin spines. We suggest that the specimen in his figure 3A preserves the right side with the anterior dorsal fin spine, rather than the left side with the pectoral fin spine (to view the specimen with dorsal side uppermost, the image should be rotated 180°). In

his figure 4D, the fin spine on the left is the pectoral, and the one on the right is the anterior dorsal, with the main lateral line visible running through the squamation between the two spines. In this interpretation, none of the original specimens show the pectoral region preserved intact; the pectoral fin spines have been disarticulated and lost in all of the most complete specimens. Based on reinterpretation of the spine with a long insertion as a dorsal fin spine, pectoral fin spines in *Culmacanthus*, like those in all other acanthodians, lack a deep insertion (contra Long 1983). Even on NMV P160709 (Fig. 4a), which shows the dermal pectoral plates articulated together and the disarticulated scapulocoracoids, the pectoral fin spines are missing. The possibility that *Culmacanthus* had prepectoral and/or admedian spines cannot thus be discounted, as they would likely have been dislocated when the pectoral fin spines were lost. The lack of pectoral fin spines on ANU V3376 is consistent with its assignment to *Culmacanthus*, by comparison with the loss of these spines in known specimens of *C. stewarti* (assuming the fish actually had pectoral fin spines!). Although ANU V3376 is poorly preserved, the impression on the counterpart of the insertion area on the anterior dorsal fin spine (Fig. 2e) shows the fine parallel ridges characteristic of diplacanthiform acanthodians (Burrow 2007:835). This spine also shows that the exserted ridges near the trailing edge are markedly narrower than the ridges towards the leading edge, unlike the equal-width ridges on *C. stewarti* fin spines. The isolated

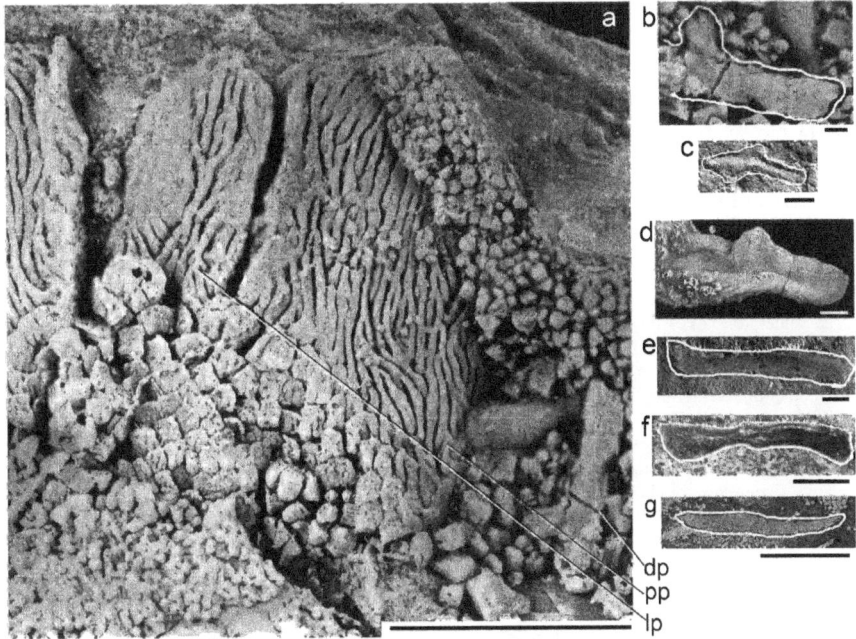

Figure 4. Lower jaw dental plates in diplacanthiform acanthodians. a, b. *Culmacanthus stewarti* NMV P160709 from the Givetian of Mt Howitt, central Victoria: a, ventral surface; b, cast of ?external surface of right dental plate. c, *Uraniacanthus curtus* NMS G.1891.92.250 from the Lochkovian of Tillywhandland Quarry, Scotland; right plate. d, *Uraniacanthus probaton* UALVP42095 from the Lochkovian MOTH locality, Northwest Territories, Canada; image flipped from Hanke & Davis 2008, figure 9D. e, *Diplacanthus longispinus* NMS G.1891.92.338 from the ?Eifelian of Gamrie, Scotland; external impression of right plate, image flipped horizontally. f, *Diplacanthus horridus* CMN 8570 from the Frasnian Escuminac Formation, Miguasha, Canada; occlusal/external surface of right plate, image flipped horizontally. g, *Milesacanthus antarctica* ANU V773, fish 1; lateral view of left plate, image flipped horizontally. cp, coronoid process; lp, lorical plate; pp, pinnal plate. Scale bar is 1 cm in a, g, 1 mm in b-f.

spine ANU V3377 (Fig. 2g) shows parallel ridges on the exserted part, but it is not possible to determine the variation in ridge width. This spine has only a short insertion, so could possibly be a pectoral fin spine; its size and type of ornament support its assignment to *Culmacanthus* rather than the unnamed ischnacanthid described by Burrow (1996), the only other acanthodian known from the Bunga Beds with spines preserved. The scapulocoracoids on ANU V3376 are of comparable dimensions to those of *C. stewarti*, with a narrow posterior flange on the scapula shaft and only a short low ventral expansion. The isolated scapulocoracoid ANU V3374 (Fig. 2h) differs from known *Culmacanthus* scapulocoracoids in having a curved rather than a straight shaft, but this could result from the structure on other specimens

being preserved in lateral or medial view, rather than anterior/posterior, with the curve of the element in the latter type of preservation matching the curve of the body.

The mouth region was not described in any of the type specimens of *C. stewarti*, however we have observed a short spathiform bone with a marked process perpendicular to the long axis, on examination of the cast of the ventral surface on NMV P160709 (Long 1983:fig. 2A; Fig. 4a, 4b). Recent work on Early Devonian diplacanthiforms from Canada and Britain has shown that *Uraniacanthus probaton* (Bernacsek & Dineley, 1977), previously *Gladiobranchus probaton*, and *Uraniacanthus curtus* (Powrie, 1870), previously *Euthacanthus curtus*, have ossified spathiform lower jaws of a comparable shape to this bone, also with a dorsally-directed process (Hanke and Davis 2008; Newman et al. in press; Fig. 4c, 4d). Hanke and Davis (2008) described the latter as a "coronoid" process; there is no evidence that this process is homologous to the structure of the same name in other gnathostome groups. Elements previously identified as mandibular bones in *Diplacanthus* spp. and *Milesacanthus antarctica* Young and Burrow, 2004 have been recharacterized as occlusal ossifications of the lower jaws, rather than bones supporting the ventral edge of the jaw cartilages (Newman et al. in press; Figure 3e-3g). Thus, all the elements previously described as mandibular bones or splints in diplacanthiforms have been reinterpreted as ossifications of the whole lower jaw, or of their occlusal surface. *Tetanopsyrus* spp. from the Lochkovian MOTH locality in Canada differ from other diplacanthiform taxa in having upper jaw ossifications as well (Hanke et al. 2001).

All determinable characters on ANU V3376 – inferred body shape and size; position, structure and relative dimensions of fin spines; scapulocoracoid shape; spathiform Meckel's cartilage ossifications; probable pectoral plate shapes – support assigning the specimen to *Culmacanthus* rather than any other acanthodian genus. Although the highly distinctive cheek plates that characterize *Culmacanthus* have not been preserved on the specimen, there is a gap in squamation on the cheek region where such a plate would be positioned, suggesting that they were lost before burial of the fish. Such a loss is consistent with *C. pambulensis* and *C. antarctica* being known only from isolated plates. Unlike acanthodian scales, which have Sharpey's fibres fixing the scale bases in the skin, the smooth inner surface of dermal plates of *Culmacanthus* lack evidence of fibrous attachment to the dermis and could thus be more easily detached from the carcass.

Because *C. pambulensis* is only known from isolated cheek plates, and the cheek plates have not been preserved on ANU V3376, it is not possible to assign this specimen to species level. The lower jaw ossifications of *Culmacanthus*, with their "coronoid" process, resemble those of the earliest Devonian (Lochkovian) genus *Uraniacanthus* from Britain and Canada rather than the simpler occlusal ossifications of the younger diplacanthiforms *Milesacanthus antarctica* from Antarctica and *Diplacanthus* spp. from Britain and Canada.

ACKNOWLEDGMENTS

CJB acknowledges the provision of basic facilities by the Queensland Museum, and support from ARC Discovery Grant DP0558499 for a visit to Canberra to examine the specimens. Fieldwork in Mimosa Rocks National Parks was conducted under a permit from the NSW National Parks & Wildlife Service, and Steve Deck and Brett Evans are thanked for facilitating access. Shirley Donaldson (Bunga Beach) allowed access through her property. We thank T. Senden, E. Papp (who found V3374, V3377), B. Young (who found V3375, 3376) for assistance with collecting the site and photography of Bunga Beds specimens, John Long (Los Angeles County Museum) for photography of Mt Howitt *Culmacanthus* latexes, and Mike Newman and Jan den Blaauwen for photography of *Diplacanthus longispinus*. The research was funded by ANU Faculties Research Fund Grant F00108, and laboratory work was funded by ARC Discovery Grant DP0558499. The research is a contribution to IGCP Project 596: Mid-Paleozoic climate and biodiversity.

REFERENCES

Berg, L.S. (1940). 'Classification of fishes, both recent and fossil [In Russian and English]'. (Edwards Brothers: Ann Arbor, Michigan).

Bernacsek, G.M. and Dineley, D.L. (1977). New acanthodians from the Delorme Formation (Lower Devonian) of N.W.T., Canada. Palaeontographica A **158**, 1-25.

Brown, I.A. (1930). The geology of the south coast of N.S.W. Part ii. Devonian and older Palaeozoic rocks. Proceedings of the Linnean Society of New South Wales **55**, 145-158.

Bucknell, W.R. (1969). The geology of the Goalen Head area (south coast, N.S.W.). 3rd year mapping project, Geology Department, Australian National University (unpublished).

Burrow, C.J. (1996). Taphonomic study of acanthodians from the Devonian Bunga Beds (Late Givetian/Early Frasnian) of New South Wales. Historical Biology **11**, 213-228.

Burrow, C.J. (2007). Early Devonian (Emsian) acanthodian faunas of the western USA. Journal of Paleontology **81**, 824–840.

Cas, R.A.F., Allen, R.L., Bull, S.W., Clifford, B.A. and Wright, J.V. (1990). Subaqueous, rhyolitic dome-top tuff cones: a model based on the Devonian Bunga Beds, southeastern Australia and a modern analogue. Bulletin of Volcanology **52**, 159-174.

Choo, B. (2009). A basal actinopterygian fish from the Middle Devonian Bunga beds of New South Wales, Australia. Proceedings of the Linnean Society of New South Wales **130**, 37-46.

Fergusson, C.L., Cas, R.A.F., Collins, W.J., Craig, G.Y., Crook, K.A.W., Powell, C.M., Scott, P.A. and Young, G.C. (1979). The Upper Devonian Boyd Volcanic Complex, Eden, New South Wales. Journal of the Geological Society of Australia **26**, 87-105.

28

Proc. Linn. Soc. N.S.W., 134, 2012

Hall, L.R. (1959). Explanatory notes on the NSW portion of the Mallacoota Geological Sheet (4-mile). *Geological Survey of New South Wales*, 16 pp.

Hall, L.R. (1960). The stratigraphy, structure and mineralisation of the Devonian strata near Eden, N.S.W. Department of Mines New South Wales Technical Report **5**, 103-116.

Hanke, G.F. and Davis, S.P. (2008). Redescription of the acanthodian *Gladiobranchus probaton* Bernacsek & Dineley, 1977, and comments on diplacanthid relationships. Geodiversitas **30**, 303-330.

Hanke, G.F., Davis, S.P. and Wilson, M.V.H. (2001). New species of the acanthodian genus *Tetanopsyrus* from northern Canada, and comments on related taxa. Journal of Vertebrate Paleontology **21**, 740-753.

Lewis, P.C., Glen, R.A., Pratt, G.W. and Clarke, I. (1994). Explanatory notes. Bega – Mallacoota 1:250 000 Geological Sheet. SJ/55-4, SJ55-8. Geological Survey of New South Wales, 1-148.

Long, J.A. (1983). A new diplacanthoid acanthodian from the Late Devonian of Victoria. Memoirs of the Association of Australasian Palaeontologists **1**, 51-65.

Long, J.A. and Young, G.C. (1995). New sharks from the Middle-Late Devonian Aztec Siltstone, southern Victoria Land, Antarctica. Records of the Western Australian Museum **17**, 287-308.

Newman, M.J., Davidson, B.G., den Blaauwen, J.L. and Burrow, C.J. (in press). The Early Devonian acanthodian *Uraniacanthus curtus* from the Midland Valley of Scotland. Geodiversitas.

Owen, R. (1846). 'Lectures on the comparative anatomy and physiology of the vertebrate animals delivered at the Royal College of surgeons, England in 1844 and 1846. Part I, Fishes'. (Longman, Brown, Green and Longmans: London).

Powell, C. McA. (1983). Geology of NSW south coast. Geological Society of Australia, Specialist Group in Tectonics and Structural Geology, Field Guide **1**, 1-118.

Powrie, J. (1870). On the earliest known vestiges of vertebrate life; being a description of the fish remains of the Old Red Sandstone rocks of Forfarshire. Transactions of the Edinburgh Geological Society **1**, 284-301.

Rickard, M.J. and Love, S. (2000). Timing of megakinks and related structures: constraints from the Devonian Bunga–Wapengo Basin, Mimosa Rocks National Park, New South Wales. Australian Journal of Earth Sciences **47**, 1009-1013.

Scott, P.A. (1972). Devonian stratigraphy and sedimentology of the Araganui area, N.S.W. Honours project, Geology Department, Australian National University (unpublished).

Young, G.C. (1982). Devonian sharks from southeastern Australia and Antarctica. Palaeontology **25**, 817-843.

Young, G.C. (1989). New occurrences of culmacanthid acanthodians (Pisces, Devonian) from Antarctica and southeastern Australia. Proceedings of the Linnean Society of New South Wales **111**, 11-24.

Young, G.C. (2005). New phyllolepids (placoderm fishes) from the Middle-Late Devonian of southeastern Australia. Journal of Vertebrate Paleontology **25**, 261-273.

Young, G.C. (2007). Devonian formations, vertebrate faunas and age control on the far south coast of New South Wales and adjacent Victoria. Australian Journal of Earth Sciences **54**, 991-1008.

Young, G.C. and Burrow, C.J. (2004). Diplacanthid acanthodians from the Aztec Siltstone (late Middle Devonian) of southern Victoria Land, Antarctica. Fossils and Strata **50**, 23-43.

Young, G.C., Burrow, C.J., Long, J.A., Turner, S. and Choo, B. (2010). Devonian macrovertebrate assemblages and biogeography of East Gondwana (Australasia, Antarctica). Palaeoworld **19**, 55-74.

30

SECTION A

Papers arising from a symposium held on 13 July 2011 at the Wildlife Conservancy's sanctuary at Scotia, far western New South Wales.

The Scotia Science Symposium 2011

Matt W. Hayward[1] and David A. Keith[2]

[1]Australian Wildlife Conservancy, Nelson Mandela Metropolitan University and Biological, Earth and Environmental Science, University of New South Wales
[2]NSW Office of Environment and Heritage and Australian Wetlands and Rivers Centre, University of New South Wales

Published on 28 August 2012 at http://escholarship.library.usyd.edu.au/journals/index.php/LIN

On the 13th of July 2011, a symposium was held at the Australian Wildlife Conservancy's Scotia Sanctuary, in far western New South Wales. This symposium focused on research in a region that is fast becoming a hub for ecological and applied conservation studies. To the east of Scotia is the University of Ballarat's Nanya Station where Martin Westbrooke and his colleagues and students have focused on vegetation and reptile community dynamics. To the south of Scotia is the NSW Office of Environment and Heritage's Tarawi Nature Reserve where David Keith, Mark Tozer and colleagues have been conducting long-term work on the fire and grazing responses of vegetation and where research on malleefowl and long-term pest animal control is occurring. To the west of Scotia is the Danggali Conservation Park in South Australia. While at Scotia itself, Australian Wildlife Conservancy staff, collaborators and students are researching threatened species ecology, threatening processes, reintroduction biology, pest animal control techniques and ecosystem services in a system that includes Australia's largest fenced conservation area (8000 ha) that is free of rabbits, goats, cats and foxes and where locally extinct native species, such as bilbies, bridled nailtail wallabies, numbats, greater stick-nest rats, boodies and woylies have been reintroduced.

The size, status and intact nature of this mallee region, as well as the proximity of so many conservation land management organisations affords unprecedented opportunities for collaborative research on ecological and conservation issues in the semi-arid zone. The wide range of studies currently underway reflect the differing management priorities of these organisations within an overarching framework of common conservation goals. Furthermore, adjacent farmland in varying states of degradation provides ideal opportunities to investigate the effects of different herbivore assemblages along a gradient from farmland, through native vegetation grazed by domestic livestock and feral hebivores to intact native vegetation where introduced species have been eradicated.

Despite the wealth of research occurring in the region, interactions amongst researchers have been limited historically. The Scotia Science Symposium was designed to bring all the researchers working in this region together with land managers, increasing our combined understanding of the ecological processes and conservation management actions that are occurring within the ecosystem, as well as providing opportunities for developing future collaborative research projects.

The 42 attendees at the Scotia Science Symposium heard 20 talks on the full gamut of research occurring in the region. A selection of seven papers are published in this special issue of the Proceedings reporting on work underway in five different institutions. Westbrooke (2012) sets the scene with a post-European ecological history of the region, concluding that the late introduction of domestic livestock was a principal reason why the region retains its conservation value as an outstanding example of mallee ecosystems.

One of the characteristic environmental features of the region is its predominantly hot and dry climate punctuated by extreme rainfall events and fires. Westbrooke et al. (2012) explore the ecological legacies of one such event, the flood of Olary Creek in February 1997. Keith & Tozer (2012) also explore the role of climatic variability on responses of dune mallee to fire and grazing in a long-term landscape experiment. This work is part of an adaptive management strategy that compares the effects of alternative fire and grazing management treatments in years with differing climatic conditions.

Another striking feature of the region, in common with most other parts of Austrlia's arid zone, is the extinction of critical weight range mammals a century ago. Gibb (2012) considers the implications of this loss on the arthropod fauna, particularly through the roles of the mammals as predators, agents of soil disturbance, parasite hosts, competitors, mutualists and nutrient cyclers. Coggan (2012) considers implications of mammal reintroductions for ecosystem services such as nutrient cycling provided by native dung beetles, which potentially suffer a dearth of food and nesting material where a guild of mammals have been eliminated. Scotia Sanctuary is renowned as site of successful mammal reintroductions and offers an important opportunity to examine these interactions in an ecosystem that has a more complete representation of biota than the landscape at large. After establishment of a sustainable population of bridled nailtail wallabies within a larger predator exclusion fence, Hayward et al. (2012) describe the outcomes of a reintroduction experiment in which a sample of male animals were released outside the fence where predators had been controlled, but not excluded. Finally, Eldridge and Huang (2012) report a study of the ecological functions of soil disturbing invertebrates along the grazing gradient described above. They found that both domestic herbivores and re-introduced extinct mammals affected a range of ecosystem processes such as pedogenesis, soil movement and water infiltration.

REFERENCES

Coggan, N. (2012) Monitoring ecosystem processes to enhance marsupial reintroduction projects: arid dung dispersal. *Proceedings of the Linnean Society of NSW* **134**, in press.

Eldridge, D. J. and Huang, N. (2012) Soil disturbance by invertebrates in a semi-arid eucalypt woodland: effects of grazing exclusion, faunal reintroductions, landscape and patch characteristics. *Proceedings of the Linnean Society of NSW* **134**, in press.

Gibb, H. (2012) How Might Terrestrial Arthropod Assemblages Have Changed After the Ecological Extinction of Critical Weight Range (CWR) Mammals in Australia? *Proceedings of the Linnean Society of NSW* **134**, in press.

Hayward, M. W. l'Hotellier, F., O'Connor, T., Ward-Fear, G., Cathcart, J., Cathcart, T., Stephens, J., Stephens, J., Herman K. and Legge S. (2012) Reintroducing bridled nailtail wallabies *Onychogalea fraenata* beyond conservation fences in New South Wales: Phase 1 of the reintroduction to Scotia Sanctuary – a male-only affair. *Proceedings of the Linnean Society of NSW* **134**, in press.

Keith, D. A. and Tozer, M. G. (2012) The roles of fire, herbivores and rainfall on vegetation dynamics in the mallee: A long-term experiment. *Proceedings of the Linnean Society of NSW* **134**, in press.

Westbrooke, M. (2012) The Pastoral History, Biological and Cultural Significance of The Scotia Country, far Western New South Wales. *Proceedings of the Linnean Society of NSW* **134**, in press.

Westbrooke, M., Florentine S. and Graz P. (2012) Impact of an Ephemeral Creek on Arid Woodland Regeneration and Weed Invasion: the Olary Creek of South Australia and New South Wales. *Proceedings of the Linnean Society of NSW* **134**, in press.

Are Native Dung Beetle Species Following Mammals in the Critical Weight Range towards Extinction?

NICOLE COGGAN

Department of Zoology, La Trobe University, Melbourne, Victoria 3086, Australia

Published on 28 August 2012 at http://escholarship.library.usyd.edu.au/journals/index.php/LIN

Coggan, N. (2012). Are native dung beetle species following mammals in the critical weight range towards extinction? *Proceedings of the Linnean Society of New South Wales* **134**, A5-A9.

Australian native mammal species within the 35 g – 5500 g critical weight range (CWR) have been declining rapidly over the last two centuries, with eighteen species becoming extinct. Inhabitants of arid and semi-arid zones are among those most at risk of extinction. Mammal declines threaten the efficiency of invertebrate-driven ecosystem processes such as nutrient recycling by artificially increasing the realised niche overlap for dung resources used by invertebrates involved with dung decomposition. Native dung beetles are one of the main taxa involved in dung decomposition, an ecosystem function necessary for nutrient recycling. Many native dung beetle species strongly prefer marsupial dung, due to their co-evolutionary history. Threatened populations of CWR species can be protected through species reintroductions. However, the long term absence of mainland CWR mammals may have compromised the effectiveness of dung decomposition as an ecosystem function by reducing dung availability. The compatibility of current coprophage assemblages with 'novel' inputs from reintroduced CWR species should therefore be questioned. Assessing the potential for persistence and/or relocation of coprophages in mainland habitats associated with CWR species will be an important part of restoring and monitoring habitats used for species recovery.

Manuscript received 18 October 2011, accepted for publication 29 February 2012.

KEYWORDS: critical weight range, conservation, decomposition, dung beetles, ecological co-extinction, ecological function, interaction, invertebrates, reintroduction.

A large proportion of Australia's mammal species have declined over the past two hundred years, a record which accounts for approximately fifty percent of mammal species extinctions worldwide (Short and Smith 1994). The largest number of mammal extinctions has occurred in semi-arid and arid habitats. The greatest risk of extinction is associated with species whose average mass falls within the 35 g – 5.5 kg critical weight range (CWR, Burbidge and McKenzie 1989). Species reintroductions into habitats within their historic range are a practical means of maintaining endangered species populations on the mainland. However, the original loss of native fauna from between 82 to more than 99 percent of their estimated ranges at European settlement (Lindenmayer 2007), is likely to have altered the effectiveness of ecosystem functions that are essential for robust species recovery (Bennett et al. 2009; Peh and Lewis in press). The scale and duration of CWR species' absences from Australian ecosystems may have significantly altered ecosystem functions

such as dung decomposition by coprophages that specialised on CWR species' dung. Dung beetles are limited by their behaviour, morphology, and life history to the types of dung they utilize (Carpaneto et al. 2005; Chown et al. 1995; Tiberg and Floate 2011). Therefore, it is very likely that dung beetles will be one of the taxa that have responded negatively to the decline of species which were central to their food supplies.

Dung beetles are coprophages that play a substantial role in the decomposition and removal of dung. They often have highly specific habitat and food requirements, as well as distinct methods used by separate species to both store and feed on dung after removing it from the parent source (Doube 1990; Hanski and Cambefort 1991; Hill 1996; Slade et al. 2007). Dung beetle activity contributes significantly to nutrient recycling (Nichols et al. 2008). As an ecosystem process, nutrient recycling maintains plant access to limiting labile nutrients, including nitrogen, potassium and phosphorus (Loreau 1995). Australia's dung beetle fauna is comprised of 23 exotic dung beetle species (Edwards 2007; Ridsdill-Smith and Edwards 2011), as well as 437 known native species, of which 355 have been formally described (Cassis et al. 2002; Ridsdill-Smith and Edwards 2011). Of these, the majority of native dung beetles exhibit a strong preference for marsupial dung (Cassis et al. 2002; Matthews 1972; 1974; 1976), whereas the exotic dung beetles generally confine themselves to ruminant livestock dung (Doube et al. 1991).

Critical weight range marsupial declines may have impacted upon services dominated by native dung beetles by disrupting local dung supplies. Without dung inputs from CWR species, dung beetle recruitment to freshly deposited dung would decrease. In extreme cases, CWR species' dung decomposition as an ecosystem function would itself become 'ecologically extinct' by becoming so inefficient that it no longer contributes to the overall ecosystem process of nutrient recycling (e.g. Estes et al. 1989). Although this may not sound particularly damaging to ecosystems hosting reintroduced CWR species, it would mean that a proportion of the energy being removed from the system by the CWR species through foraging, for example, is not being effectively returned. Similar consequences of co-decline and extinction of both species and ecosystem functions have been recorded for frugivores and seed dispersal in Tongan and Philippine forests (Hamann and Curio 1999; McConkey and Drake 2006). Complementarity between species within coprophage assemblages influences the efficiency of dung decomposition (O'Hea et al. 2010; Ridsdill-Smith and Matthiessen 1988; Slade et al. 2007). Co-declines of CWR dung-specialised coprophages alongside their preferred CWR dung suppliers would affect how efficiently the remaining dung fauna can utilize dung supplies, by shifting the balance of species with different strategies for consuming dung (Slade et al. 2007). Incompatibility between dung producers and dung consumers has been recorded in Australia, where native dung beetle assemblages were not able to make efficient use of dung pads left by cattle (Bornemissza 1960). Only the introduction of exotic dung beetle species that had co-evolved with ruminants and ungulates expedited dung decomposition in cattle pastures (Tyndale-Biscoe 1994). In itself, the lack of native dung beetles with the functional capacity to efficiently consume large dung deposits characteristic of ruminants is thought to be associated with the decline of large-bodied dung beetles associated with the mega fauna of the Pleistocene era (Cambefort 1991; Edwards 2007; Johnson 2009). If a substantial proportion of native dung fauna have been extirpated by CWR declines,

then the ability of current coprophage assemblages to effectively recognize and use dung from reintroduced CWR species may be compromised in habitats targeted for mammal reintroductions.

A high level of dung-specificity is a major assumption underpinning the suggestion that CWR species declines have negatively impacted upon dung beetle assemblages. Thus, their declines are expected to have impacted dung specialist over generalist dung beetle species. The level of specificity towards different types of marsupial dung exhibited by Australian native dung beetle species has been directly studied in tropical, but not arid and semi-arid zone habitats. Evidence from two studies which directly tested preference using a variety of native mammal dung suggests that high specificity towards dung from particular mammal species by dung beetles does exist. For example, dung beetle species in the Queensland wet sclerophyll forest partitioned limiting dung resources through selective use of dung from locally occurring CWR mammals, which included northern bettongs (*Bettongia tropica*, Potoroidae), (Vernes et al. 2005). In addition, more dung beetle species were attracted to rufous bettong (*Aepyprymnus rufescens*, Potoroidae) dung over dung from Sharman's rock wallaby (*Petrogale sharmani*, Macropodidae), (Wright 1997).

In contrast to these two studies, the majority of species-specific knowledge about native dung beetle food preferences relate to those that were attracted to cow pads prior to the introduction of exotic beetles in Queensland, south western, and south eastern Australia (Hughes 1975; Ridsdill-Smith 1993; Tyndale-Biscoe 1994). At least 73 native species are known to be attracted to cow dung pads in Queensland (Edwards 2007), and 17 native species are attracted to human dung and/or carrion in south-western Australia (Ridsdill-Smith et al. 1983). The most recent study conducted in NSW found 14 native species attracted to pig dung in riparian habitats during different stages of restoration (Gollan et al. 2011). In some cases therefore, native dung beetle species are able to recognize and utilise non-marsupial dung resources as alternative food supplies, although it is likely to be used as a marginal habitat (e.g. Morelli et al. 2002).

A targeted effort to assess the level of specificity demonstrated by arid and semi-arid zone dung beetles will be an important first-step towards assessing the status of invertebrate-driven ecosystem processes. Reintroducing CWR species into their former habitats is a practical method of preventing their extinction. Spatially isolated remnant populations of CWR marsupials on the mainland, such as the

A6

Proc. Linn. Soc. N.S.W., 134, 2012

greater bilby (*Macrotis lagotis*, Thylacomidae) and bridled nail tail wallaby (*Onychogalea fraenata*, Macropodidae) could harbour populations of dung beetle species that are still closely affiliated with CWR marsupial dung. For example, some species within the genus *Onthophagus* (Scarabaeidae: Onthophagini) possess prehensile claws that allow them to cling to fur, and were detected in a recent Queensland survey which lured them with cow dung baits. However, it was unclear whether or not these beetles were using the baits as a food and/or breeding resource (Edwards, 2007). Of particular interest is a note in Matthews (1972) revision of the Onthophagini tribe. Matthews writes that all prehensile-clawed beetles were found exclusively on small and medium sized marsupials, and never on larger macropods or rat-kangaroos (Diprotodontia: Hypsiprymnodontidae). If these specialized dung beetles were able to move with their hosts during relocation, then it is possible that at least some beetles that had evolutionary associations with CWR species may have re-established themselves in their historic habitat. This would be of significant benefit to CWR reintroduction habitats that have potentially been without a diverse dung beetle fauna since the decline of CWR species. Additionally, this information can prove beneficial to conservation programs which eradicate co-dependent fauna such as gut parasites from founder colonies prior to their reintroduction into new habitats. It may in fact be more effective in some cases to reintroduce species with their co-dependent fauna intact, as their association may increase the target species chances of survival (Burbidge et al. 2012).

There is a clear need to assess the status of Australia's native dung beetle fauna in arid and semi-arid habitats. First, we need to establish whether or not the decline of CWR species has led to a breakdown of dung beetle communities that were present in their former range. Baited pitfall trapping using fresh dung of CWR species can be used to determine whether or not dung beetle fauna caught in naturally persisting CWR species' habitats are similar to those in habitats where CWR species have been reintroduced. If the dung beetle assemblages are similar between both habitats, this indicates that none of the native beetle species were CWR species-specific. In contrast, if a subset of beetle species is found on CWR species dung in reintroduction habitats, then this may indicate some species were unable to adapt to the decline of CWR species and are likely to have become extinct, or do not occur naturally in the reintroduction habitat.

Second, we can assess the possibility of co-relocation of dung beetle species that are known to be affiliated with CWR species, such as those with prehensile claws. Co-relocation of these beetle species should complement the dung fauna in the targeted reintroduction habitat, which may help to overcome ecological barriers to effective dung decomposition triggered by the original species decline. Captured CWR marsupials in source and relocation habitats can be examined for dung beetles clinging to the fur surrounding the cloaca. If prehensile-clawed dung beetles are found on the source population for reintroduction, then we can consider the feasibility of co-relocating the dung beetles with their hosts toward the long term success of conserving our CWR mammal species.

Finally, an experimental analysis of dung decomposition with and without dung beetle exclusion in 'reintroduction' versus 'persisting' habitats can be used to gain a comparative measure of dung decomposition and dispersal efficiency in the current environment. Information gained from targeted observation and analysis of dung beetle functional diversity, community assemblage and process efficiency will be an important part of restoring and monitoring managed habitats used in species recovery projects. It is vital that we determine how readily ecosystem processes in habitats targeted for CWR species reintroductions can readjust to the 'new' inputs from reintroduced species, and whether or not it will be necessary to reintroduce entire suites of organisms involved in ecological functioning to ensure the success of threatened species conservation (Burbidge et al. 2011).

ACKNOWLEDGEMENTS

This project is supported by The Australian Wildlife Conservancy, Arid Recovery Reserve, and volunteers. Funding is provided by the ANZ trustees' Holsworth Wildlife Research Endowment and the Australia and Pacific Science Foundation. Nicole is supported through an Australian Postgraduate Award. Dr. Bernard Doube and Dr. Penny Edwards provided valuable guidance and expertise regarding dung beetle distributions and field methods. Thanks to Dr. Heloise Gibb, Dr. Matt Hayward, Assoc. Prof. David Eldridge and an anonymous reviewer for their constructive criticism of this manuscript.

REFERENCES

Bennett, A. F., Haslem, A., Cheal, D. C., Clarke, M. F., Jones, R. N., Koehn, J. D., Lake, P. S., Lumsden, L. F., Lunt, I. D., Mackey, B. G., Nally, R. M., Menkhorst, P. W., New, T. R., Newell, G. R., O'Hara, T., Quinn, G. P., Radford, J. Q., Robinson, D.,

Watson, J. E. M. and Yen, A. L. (2009). Ecological processes: A key element in strategies for nature conservation. *Ecological Management and Restoration,* **10,** 192-199.

Bornemissza, G. F. (1960). Could dung eating insects improve our pastures? *Journal of the Australian Institute of Agricultural Science,* **26,** 54-56.

Burbidge, A., Byrne, M., Coates, D., Garnett, S. T., Harris, S., Hayward, M. W., Martin, T. G., McDonald-Madden, E., Mitchell, N. J., Nally, S. and Setterfield, S. A. (2011). Is Australia ready for assisted colonization? Policy changes required to facilitate translocations under climate change. *Pacific Conservation Biology,* **17,** 259-269.

Burbidge, A. A. and McKenzie, N. L. (1989). Patterns in the modern decline of western Australia's vertebrate fauna: Causes and conservation implications. *Biological Conservation,* **50,** 143-198.

Cambefort, Y. (1991). Biogeography and Evolution. In: *Dung Beetle Ecology* (eds I. Hanski and Y. Cambefort), pp. 51-68. Princeton University Press, Princeton, NJ.

Carpaneto, G. M., Mazziotta, A. and Piattella, E. (2005). Changes in food resources and conservation of scarab beetles: from sheep to dog dung in a green urban area of Rome (Coleoptera, Scarabaeoidea). *Biological Conservation,* **123,** 547-556.

Cassis, G., Weir, T. A. and Calder, A. A. (2002). *Subfamily Scarabaeinae.* Australian Faunal Directory.

Chown, S. L., Scholtz, C. H., Klok, C. J., Joubert, F. J. and Coles, K. S. (1995). Ecophysiology, range contraction and survival of a geographically restricted African dung beetle (Coleoptera: Scarabaeidae). *Functional Ecology,* **9,** 30-39.

Doube, B. M. (1990). A functional classification for analysis of the structure of dung beetle assemblages. *Ecological Entomology,* **15,** 371-383.

Doube, B. M., Maqueen, A., Ridsdill-Smith, T. J. and Weir, T. A. (1991). Native and introduced dung beetles in Australia. In: *Dung Beetle Ecology* (eds I. Hanski and Y. Cambefort), pp. 255-278. Princeton University Press, Princeton, NJ.

Edwards, P. (2007). *Introduced dung beetles in Australia 1967-2007- current status and future directions.* Dung Beetles for Landcare Farming Committee.

Estes, J. A., Duggins, D. O. and Rathbun, G. B. (1989). The ecology of extinctions in kelp forest communities. *Conservation Biology,* **3,** 252-264.

Gollan, J. R., Reid, C. A. M., Barnes, P. B. and Wilkie, L. (2011). The ratio of exotic-to-native dung beetles can indicate habitat quality in riparian restoration. *Insect Conservation and Diversity,* **4,** 123-131.

Hamann, A. and Curio, E. (1999). Interactions among frugivores and fleshy fruit trees in a Philippine submontane rainforest. *Conservation Biology,* **13,** 766-773.

Hanski, I. and Cambefort, Y. (1991). *Dung beetle ecology.* Princeton University Press, Princeton, NJ.

Hill, C. J. (1996). Habitat specificity and food preferences of an assemblage of tropical Australian dung beetles. *Journal of Tropical Ecology,* **12,** 449-460.

Hughes, R. D. (1975). Assessment of the burial of cattle dung by Australian dung beetles. *Australian Journal of Entomology,* **14,** 129-134.

Johnson, C. N. (2009). Ecological consequences of late quaternary extinctions of megafauna. *Proceedings of the Royal Society B: Biological Sciences,* **276,** 2509 - 2519.

Lindenmayer, D. (2007). *On Borrowed Time: Australia's environmental crisis and what we must do about it.* CSIRO Publishing, Maryborough, Victoria.

Loreau, M. (1995). Consumers as maximizers of matter and energy flow in ecosystems. *The American Naturalist,* **145,** 22-42.

Matthews, E. G. (1972). A revision of the Scarabaeine dung beetles of Australia. I. Tribe Onthophagini. *Australian Journal of Zoology,* **9,** 1-330.

Matthews, E. G. (1974). A revision of the Scarabaeine dung beetles of Australia. II. Tribe Scarabaeini. *Australian Journal of Zoology,* **Supplementary Series 24,** 211.

Matthews, E. G. (1976). A revision of the Scarabaeine dung beetles of Australia. III. Tribe Coprini. *Australian Journal of Zoology,* **Supplementary Series 24,** 1-52.

McConkey, K. R. and Drake, D. R. (2006). Flying foxes cease to function as seed dispersers long before they become rare. *Ecology,* **87,** 271-276.

Morelli, E., Gonzalez-Vainer, P., and Baz, A. (2002). Coprophagous beetles (Coleoptera: Scarabaeoidea) in Uruguayan prairies: abundance, diversity and seasonal occurrence, *Studies on Neotropical Fauna and Environment,* **37,** 53-57.

Nichols, E., Spector, S., Louzada, J., Larsen, T., Amezquita, S. and Favila, M. E. (2008). Ecological functions and ecosystem services provided by Scarabaeinae dung beetles. *Biological Conservation,* **141,** 1461-1474.

O'Hea, N. M., Kirwan, L. and Finn, J. A. (2010). Experimental mixtures of dung fauna affect dung decomposition through complex effects of species interactions. *Oikos,* **119,** 1081-1088.

Peh, K. S. H. and Lewis, S. L. (*In press*). Conservation implications of recent advances in biodiversity–functioning research. *Biological Conservation.*

Ridsdill-Smith, T. J. (1993). Asymmetric competition in cattle dung between two species of *Onthophagus* dung beetle and the bush fly, *Musca vetustissima. Ecological Entomology,* **18,** 241-246.

Ridsdill-Smith, T. J. and Edwards, P. B. (2011). Biological control: Ecosystem functions provided by dung beetles. In: *Ecology and Evolution of Dung Beetles* (eds L. W. Simmons and T. J. Ridsdill-Smith), pp. 245-266. Wiley-Blackwell, Oxford, UK.

Ridsdill-Smith, T. J. and Matthiessen, J. N. (1988). Bush fly, *Musca vetustissima* Walker (Diptera: Muscidae), control in relation to seasonal abundance of scarabaeine dung beetles (Coleoptera: Scarabaeidae) in south-western Australia. *Bulletin of Entomological Research,* **78**, 633-639.

Ridsdill-Smith, T. J., Weir, T. A. and Peck, S. B. (1983). Dung beetles (Scarabaeidae: Scarabaeinae and Aphodiinae) active in forest habitats in southwestern Australia during winter. *Australian Journal of Entomology,* **22**, 307-309.

Short, J. and Smith, A. (1994). Mammal decline and recovery in Australia. *Journal of Mammalogy,* **75**, 288-297.

Slade, E. M., Mann, D. J., Villanueva, J. F. and Lewis, O. T. (2007). Experimental evidence for the effects of dung beetle functional group richness and composition on ecosystem function in a tropical forest. *Journal of Animal Ecology,* **76**, 1094-1104.

Tiberg, K. and Floate, K. D. (2011). Where went the dung-breeding insects of the American bison? *The Canadian Entomologist,* **143**, 470-478.

Tyndale-Biscoe, M. (1994). Dung burial by native and introduced dung beetles (Scarabaeidae). *Australian Journal of Agricultural Research,* **45**, 1799-1808.

Vernes, K., Pope, L. C., Hill, C. J. and Bärlocher, F. (2005). Seasonality, dung specificity and competition in dung beetle assemblages in the Australian Wet Tropics, north-eastern Australia. *Journal of Tropical Ecology,* **21**, 1-8.

Wright, K. L. (1997). An examination of the commensal interaction between the Australian native dung beetle, *Onthophagus peramelinus* and the rufous bettong, *Aepyprymnus rufescens.* B. Sc. Honours Thesis. James Cook University, Townsville.

Proc. Linn. Soc. N.S.W., 134, 2012

A9

Soil Disturbance by Invertebrates in a Semi-arid Eucalypt Woodland: Effects of Grazing Exclusion, Faunal Reintroductions, Landscape and Patch Characteristics

David J. Eldridge[1], Niki Huang[1], Jocelyn Bentley[2] and Matthew W. Hayward[2]

[1]Evolution and Ecology Research Centre, Office of Environment and Heritage, c/- School of Biological, Earth and Environmental Sciences, University of NSW, Sydney, NSW, 2052, Australia. d.eldridge@unsw.edu.au
[2]Australian Wildlife Conservancy, Scotia Sanctuary, c/- P.O. Wentworth, NSW 2648, Australia

Published on 28 August 2012 at http://escholarship.library.usyd.edu.au/journals/index.php/LIN

Eldridge, D.J., Huang, N. and Hayward, M.W. (2012). Soil disturbance by invertebrates in a semi-arid eucalypt woodland: effects of grazing exclusion, faunal reintroductions, landscape and patch characteristics. *Proceedings of the Linnean Society of New South Wales* 134, A11-A18.

Soil disturbing invertebrates are common elements of arid and semi-arid landscapes. Disturbances such as burrows, nest entrances, emergence holes and mounds of ejecta soil have large, but often poorly understood, effects on ecosystem properties and processes as broad as pedogenesis, soil movement and water infiltration. We examined disturbances created by a range of invertebrates in a semi-arid eucalypt woodland in eastern Australia in relation to three levels of disturbance varying from areas currently grazed by domestic herbivores to those where domestic herbivores have been removed, with and without the reintroduction of locally-extinct omnivorous native mammals. Overall, the tunnels and ejecta soil from ant nests comprised 80% of all invertebrate disturbances across all sites and treatments. There were significantly more invertebrate disturbances at sites where domestic herbivores had been excluded, more disturbances on dunes and in the swales than on plains, and more under shrubs than under trees. The cover of disturbances by invertebrates tended to increase with increasing cover of disturbance by native vertebrates, but only under exclosure where no locally-extinct native mammals had been reintroduced. Our results indicate that invertebrate-created disturbances are a common feature of semi-arid woodland soils, and that management activities, such as grazing and the reintroduction of locally-extinct vertebrates, will affect their density, potentially influencing a range of ecosystem processes.

Manuscript received 4 November 2011, accepted for publication 22 December 2011.

KEYWORDS: biogeomorphology, bioturbation, eucalypt, foraging, soil disturbance, invertebrates, shrubland, soil movement.

INTRODUCTION

Arid and semi-arid landscapes function most effectively when limited resources, such as water, seed, sediment and nutrients, are concentrated within patches (fertile patches; Noy-Meir 1973). This patchiness exists at a range of spatial scales, from landscapes to microsites, with smaller patches often nested within larger patches within a hierarchy (Kotliar and Weins 1990). Different organisms respond to these different scales of patchiness, consistent with their body size and behaviour (e.g. foraging and reproductive; Vanbergen et al. 2007). Thus larger animals generally respond to coarse or intermediate scales (Jackson et al. 2003) while smaller

animals, such as invertebrates, are more responsive to changes at finer scales (e.g. Martin and Major 2001; Whitehouse et al. 2002). Similarly, habitat complexity is known to affect insect diversity (Barton et al. 2010) and has been shown to alter the foraging success of ants across a range of environments (Gibb and Parr 2010).

Animals respond not only to changes in patch size and configuration but also create and maintain their own patches. For example, depressions in the soil surface created by burrowing vertebrates can trap seed, litter and animal faeces, which are often subsequently covered by eroded soil (Whitford and Kay 1999). The construction of burrows, pits and mounds by both vertebrates and invertebrates can alter soil physical and chemical properties such as texture, structure, fertility and infiltration rate (Whitford 2002) and enhance the germination and establishment of vascular plants (James et al. 2011), creating new patches or expanding existing patches (Whitford and Kay 1999). The burrows and emergence holes of soil surface-active invertebrates can act as macropores, enhancing the infiltration of water into the subsoil, and affecting landscape–level differences in soil moisture (Elkins et al. 1986, Holt et al. 1996), soil and nutrient redistribution (Nkem et al. 2000), and the development of substantial soil biomantles (Johnson 1990).

Changes in soil surface environments resulting from the activity of vertebrates can also influence the spatial distribution and abundance of other organisms such as invertebrates (Huntly & Inouye 1988; Whicker & Detling 1988; Ceballos et al. 1999; Kretzer & Cully 2001). Alteration of the physical and chemical environment of the soil surface may extend the habitat of other animals, such as occurs when, for example, prairie dog (*Cynomys* spp.) engineered soil surfaces advantage foraging by tenebrionid beetles (Bangert and Slobodchikoff 2006). Soil disturbance by vertebrates may benefit smaller animals such as ants by creating open habitat (e.g. Borchard and Eldridge 2011). Similarly, grazing-induced disturbance by livestock can affect the distribution, abundance, and diversity of soil-disturbing organisms, often in unknown directions (Nash et al. 2001).

We compared soil disturbances created by a broad suite of surface-active invertebrates at sites ungrazed by domestic livestock (with and without the reintroduction of locally–extinct soil foraging animals), with sites that are currently and heavily grazed by sheep, cattle and goats. Specifically, our objective was to determine how three different land management practices influenced soil disturbance by invertebrates, and whether this varied among different landforms (dune, swale, plain), patch types (shrub, tree) and positions within a patch type, i.e. sites ranging from close to the canopy to the open. Our three predictions were that: (1) density of disturbances created by invertebrates (mounds, depressions, emergence holes and burrows of ants, termites, scorpions, spiders, termites, ant lions, cicadas and beetles) would vary very little across the land management gradient; (2) the density of invertebrate disturbances would be most responsive to changes at small spatial scales (e.g. patch type, e.g. shrub *vs* tree) and position within the canopy than in relation to larger landscape – scale differences (e.g. dune *vs* swale). Given that native insectivorous vertebrates are known to prey on epigeal invertebrates such as

scorpions and lycosid spiders (e.g. Southgate 1990, we expected that (3) there would be relatively strong relationships between the densities of invertebrates and their vertebrate predators. We tested these predictions in a mallee eucalypt woodland across three grazing-induced treatments.

METHODS

The study site

The study was carried out at the Scotia Sanctuary and adjacent grazing properties. Scotia is a 64, 653 ha property approximately 150 km south-west of Broken Hill, Australia (33°12'S, 141°10'E). We restricted our study to three different landscapes characterised by 1) linear dunes dominated by eucalypts; 2) inter-dunal swales; 3) plains with a variable cover of trees. The dunes were predominantly west-east trending, of Quaternary alluvium, and characterized by calcareous and siliceous sands (Rudosols). They were separated by inter-dunal swales and plains, up to 500 m wide, of loamy, calcareous soils (Calcarosols). Vegetation on the dunes is dominated by open mallee (*Eucalyptus* spp.) woodland with a spinifex (*Triodia scariosa* ssp. *scariosa*) understorey and a variable cover of shrubs such as punty bush (*Senna artemisioides*) and narrow-leaved hopbush (*Dodonaea viscosa)*. The plains vegetation is dominated by scattered belah (*Casuarina pauper*) and sugarwood (*Myoporum platycarpum*), and a variable cover of punty bush, hopbush, turpentine (*Eremophila sturtii*), pinbush wattle (*Acacia burkittii*) and assorted bluebushes (*Maireana* spp.). The climate is semi-arid, with cool winters (mean ≤ 17°C) and hot summers (mean 30°C). Rainfall over the period 1996 to 2011 averaged 244 mm yr^{-1}.

Experimental design

In December 2006, we surveyed all soil surface disturbances created by animals that forage in the soil or create burrows, nests or resting sites on the surface. Our survey was carried out within two large exclosures at the Scotia Sanctuary, Stage I (termed *'Reintroduction'*) and Stage II (*'Exclosure'*), both of which are feral animal free and ungrazed by domestic livestock. A third treatment was located on adjoining pastoral properties, which are grazed by sheep and cattle and contained variable populations of rabbits (*Oryctolagus cuniculus*) and foxes (*Vulpes vulpes*; termed *'Pastoral'*). At the time of the study, locally-extinct mammals such as the greater bilby (*Macrotis lagotis*) and the burrowing bettong (*Bettongia lesueur*) had been reintroduced into Stage I but

A12

Proc. Linn. Soc. N.S.W., 134, 2012

not Stage II. All three treatment types, however, contained variable populations of the short-beaked echidna (*Tachyglossus aculeatus*) and Gould's sand goanna (*Varanus gouldii*), both of which also disturb the soil while foraging for food. European rabbits also occurred in the *Pastoral* sites. Because there is only one example of *Reintroduction* and *Exclosure* and it was not possible to replicate the treatments elsewhere, the design is therefore pseudoreplicated, and does not allow generalisation about the effects of ecosystem engineers beyond the study site. Nevertheless, this single site represents a valuable opportunity to gain information about the effects of locally extinct native animals on the structures created by invertebrates.

Field measurements

Within these three treatment areas, we assessed all animal disturbances on three landform elements (dunes, swales, plains) and within two patch types (tree, shrub) along 2–m wide transects extending from the base of each tree or shrub. Each transect was adjusted to be three times the radius of the canopy to account for different-sized trees and shrubs. Along this transect, we identified four zones: 1) trunk (0.25 x canopy radius), 2) mid-canopy (0.5 x canopy radius), 3) canopy edge (1 x canopy radius) and 4) open (1.75 x canopy radius). A total of 126 transects was measured, representing the three treatments by three landform elements (dune, swale, plain) by two macro-patch types (tree, shrub), with seven replicate transects. Measurement sites were selected so that they were evenly distributed over each of the three treatments and within 200 m of roads (for ease of access). Sites in the *Pastoral* treatment were at least 5 km from water, and other areas of excessive stock trampling were avoided e.g. near holding paddocks.

For each disturbance type, we measured the following: length and width of all pits, burrows and depressions, and the type of animal that created each disturbance (bilby/bettong, goanna, echidna, rabbit, ant, ant lion, beetle, kangaroo, scorpion, skink, spider, termite) in relation to the various nested patch types in which the disturbances occurred. Litter was carefully removed from the soil surface in order to record any animal disturbances that might have been present below the litter. These measurements were used to calculate the density of structures and their areas. While the emphasis in this paper is on invertebrate disturbances, we also report data on the density of vertebrate disturbances (Eldridge et al. 2011b) in order to examine possible relationships between vertebrate and invertebrate disturbances.

Statistical analyses

Differences in the density and cover of disturbances of the total suite of invertebrates, in relation to the three treatments, landform element, patch type and position in relation to the canopy, were analysed using a mixed-models General Linear Models ANOVA with three error terms. The first stratum considered treatment, landform element and their interaction, the second stratum patch and its two- and three-way interactions with treatment and landform, and the third stratum distance from the trunk and its two-, three- and four way interactions with the other factors. Data were transformed to a density per square metre of canopy location in order to standardise between the various sampling areas beneath the canopies of the various sized trees and shrubs. Data were checked for homogeneity of variance and normality (Minitab 2007) prior to analysis, and in most cases, $\log_{10}(X+1)$ or $\sqrt{}$–transformed to standardise the residuals prior to ANOVA. We used linear regression analyses (Minitab 2007) to determine possible relationships between the density of invertebrate and vertebrate disturbances for all factors, averaged across the four canopy locations (n=126).

RESULTS

We recorded significantly more disturbances by invertebrates in Scotia Stages I (*Reintroduction*) and II (*Exclosure*), where domestic livestock had been excluded, than where domestic grazing animals occurred (Pastoral: $F_{2,54}$=8.64, P=0.001). We also recorded more disturbances on dunes and in the swales than on plains ($F_{2,54}$=6.40, P=0.003; Figure 1A), and more disturbances around and under shrubs than trees ($F_{1,54}$=48.68, P<0.001; Figure 1B). The number of disturbances increased with increasing distance from the trunks of trees, but there were no clearly-defined trends out from the trunks of shrubs (Patch type x Distance from trunk interaction: $F_{3,324}$=10.91, P<0.001, Figure 1B). Overall, trends in relation to cover of disturbances under shrub and tree canopies were the same as for density (data held by the senior author and not shown). Further, most of the effects were due to differences in the number of disturbances by ants, which constituted about 80% of all invertebrate structures across all sites and treatments. We expected that some invertebrate burrows might occur within foraging pits or mounds of soil ejected from the pits of vertebrates, suggesting a shared habitat preference. Over all sites and quadrats,

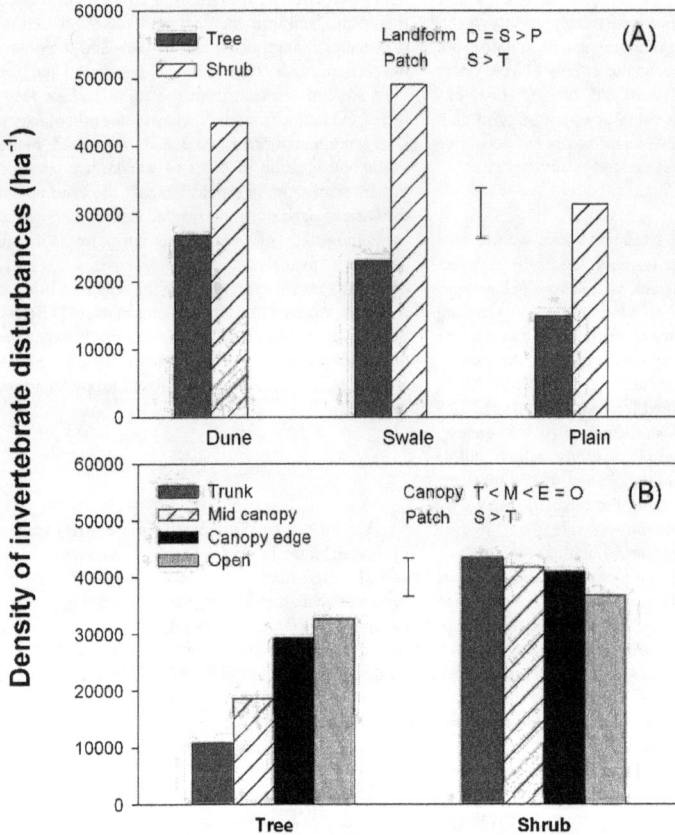

Figure 1. Mean density of disturbances (ha⁻¹) created by invertebrates in relation to (A) Landform (D = dune, S = swale, O = open) and Patch type (T = tree, S = shrub), and (B) Patch type (T = tree, S = shrub) and location within the canopy (T = trunk, M = mid-canopy, C = canopy edge, O = open). Bars indicate the 5% least significant difference (LSD) for (A) Landform x Patch type interaction and (B) the Canopy location x Patch type interaction.

A14

Proc. Linn. Soc. N.S.W., 134, 2012

however, we detected only five burrows, all from small body-sized ants, in the foraging pits of bettongs, and none from those of rabbits or echidnas. There were no significant relationships between vertebrate and invertebrate disturbances when we pooled the data for the three positions along the gradient (P=0.123), and no relationships for either *Reintroduction* or *Pastoral* when data were analysed separately. However, for the *Exclosure* sites, increasing cover of vertebrate disturbances was associated with increasing cover of invertebrate disturbances, thus:

$$I = 1.103 \times V^{0.036} \quad (1)$$

where I = cover of invertebrate disturbances, V = cover of vertebrate disturbances (R^2=0.24; P=0.001).

DISCUSSION

Many studies have demonstrated marked changes in biotic and abiotic environments in relation to grazing-induced disturbance, with sites grazed by domestic livestock characterised by a more degraded soil surface and reduced ecosystem function and stability (Nash et al. 2004; Eldridge et al. 2011b). Our gradient was characterised by a decline in the health of the soil surface from *Exclosure* to *Pastoral*, indicated by reduced plant diversity, declines in soil surface stability and increases in the cover of bare soil (Howard 2011). It is not surprising, therefore, that we recorded fewer invertebrate disturbances at sites grazed by domestic livestock, given their generally lower plant diversity and probably lower productivity (Howard 2011). Many invertebrates construct similar-shaped burrows on the surface, and often with markedly different depths and shapes below the surface. Our focus was on surface soil disturbance, and we were unable to identify the specific organism responsible for their construction other than to place structures into broad orders. We acknowledge that this is a shortcoming of our study. More information on the residents of these structures would have enabled us to make more definitive statements about the species-specific effects across the gradient.

The finding that the density of invertebrate disturbances was greatest under *Exclosure* could be related to the generally more favourable biophysical conditions within the Stage II exclosure at Scotia (e.g. greater shrub and grass cover, more litter, more extensive cryptogamic soil crust cover; Huang 2007) compared with the other treatments. Differences could also be due simply to lower rates of predation, given that only echidnas and goannas were present in Stage II at the time of the study. Bilbies are largely omnivorous, preying on a range of epigeal invertebrates and small skinks (Southgate, 1990; Navnith et al. (2009). The cover of invertebrate disturbances at the landscape scale was lower at *Pastoral* than *Reintroduction* sites even though density showed the opposite trend. This suggests a difference in the frequency distribution of disturbance sizes among the different positions along the gradient, and a substantially reduced engineering effect of small animal disturbances under grazing.

Landscape- and patch-level effects

The cover of invertebrate disturbances, which was greatest in the dunes and least in the plains, is probably a function of soil texture. However, whereas the cover of disturbances by vertebrates, such as bilbies, bettongs and echidnas, responded only to large landform–level changes (e.g. among dunes/swales and plains; Eldridge et al. 2011b), the burrowing activity of invertebrates responded to smaller localised effects. While patch type had some affect on the composition of invertebrate disturbances, this was very weak. Such a result is unexpected, as other studies have shown that invertebrates tend to be strongly influenced by changes in habitat complexity (Kaspari and Weiser 1999, Bonte et al. 2002, Whitehouse et al. 2002, Jouquet et al. 2006, Mazia et al. 2006). We did not measure litter depth nor litter composition, factors that might be expected to influence the presence of surface-active invertebrates. However, litter loads under trees, averaged over dunes and swales, ranged from 505 and 565 g m^{-2} for *Pastoral* and *Recovering* sites, respectively, to 980 g m^{-2} for *Conservation* sites (unpublished data). We did not measure litter loads under shrubs. However, litterfall from shrubs at Scotia is not inconsiderable, ranging from 14 to 30 g m^{-2} yr^{-1} for *Senna* spp. and *Acacia* spp. respectively (Samantha Travers, unpublished data). Although litter loads under shrubs would have been substantially less than under trees, the shrub canopy environment would have been more heterogeneous. The variable cover of biological soil crusts, surface cracking and microclimatic differences in shade, radiation and protection would be more aligned with the spatial differences in invertebrate distribution.

Disturbance densities were higher in association with shrubs than in association with trees, but only in the swales and plains. The soil below shrub canopies is generally more porous, with greater levels of carbon and nitrogen than the interspaces (Eldridge et al. 2011a). Shrubs also moderate surface temperatures and facilitate the growth of understorey plants that may not be present in the community in the interspaces (Soliveres et al. 2011). Greater density of disturbances under shrubs, particularly in the swales and plains, has implications for the management of shrubby woodlands where the removal of encroaching shrubs ('woody weeds') is a common pastoral practice by land managers (Eldridge et al. 2011a). Our work suggests that shrub removal will reduce the burrowing activity of invertebrates given the observation of more burrows under shrubs. Shrub removal will also likely reduce small-scale patchiness due to the close link between shrub density and the density of vertebrate-created pits and depressions, which trap water, litter and sediment and therefore become fertile, productive microsites (Eldridge et al. 2011b). The greater cover of invertebrate disturbances under trees than shrubs in the dunes (data not shown), could be a response to extensive leaf litter loads under mallee eucalypts. We observed considerable volumes of ejecta material from the emergence holes of beetles and cicadas in litter-covered mallee woodlands. Much of this loose, poorly aggregated soil is highly wind erodible and would likely be redistributed short distances by wind erosion processes, contributing to the development of soil and moisture profiles around existing plants (Sarah 2004).

Ants are one of the main taxa responsible for soil movement in arid and semi-arid ecosystems (Whitford 1996), and in our study, comprised about 80% of all invertebrate disturbances. Generally the densities of ant nests tend to be greater where soils have sandy textures (James et al. 2008; Whitford and Eldridge 2010). It is not surprising, therefore, that disturbances by ants were a substantial component of soil disturbance in sandy mallee environments. Estimates of soil movement by ants vary widely, with average global rates of soil turnover at about 5,000 kg ha^{-1} yr^{-1} (Folgarait 1998). In arid environments, the rate of soil disturbance is expected to be related to differences in soil texture and density, which both affect the energy costs of nest excavation.

Many ant taxa are thermophilic (Muser et al. 2005), so their nests would be expected to be located in exposed environments. Structures created by ants were the most dominant in our study, but previous studies have failed to find strong relationships between the presence of ant nests and the make-up of the soil surface (Huang 2007). We expected that some species of ants would have been more common under the *Pastoral* land use. For example, *Rhytidoponera* spp. readily colonise disturbed pastoral areas (Andersen 1986), and has been found as a dominant of bare, disturbed areas in degraded woodlands (Bronham et al. 1999). Our result may reflect the fact that ant species richness has been shown to be

negatively correlated with cattle grazing (Bouton et al. 2005). The most parsimonious explanation for this is that in the present study, ants building similar-sized nest structures were grouped into a single taxon. In reality, however, there were probably many functional groups of ants at our sites around Scotia, each with differing niche requirements and therefore idiosyncratic preferences for widely different habitat types at small spatial scales (Andersen 1986). The preference of invertebrates for open sites is probably related to the availability of relatively large areas of intact and compacted soils. For example, the burrows of lycosid spiders are generally found in the open, and often associated with intact soil crusts (Martin and Major 2001, Oberg et al., 2007). Scorpions, however, prefer to burrow in sandy soils (Locket 1993). This preference for open areas by invertebrates is in strong contrast to sites selected by native vertebrates, which are predominantly under the canopies of shrubs and trees (Eldridge et al. 2011b).

Invertebrate-vertebrate interactions

We detected a moderately strong correlation between the cover of vertebrate and invertebrate disturbances, but only for the *Exclosure* treatment (Scotia Stage II). It is reasonable to expect non-trophic effects of soil-disturbing native vertebrates on soil-active invertebrates given that they move a considerable mass of soil in the process of foraging and could be affecting patch conditions for the much smaller invertebrates (e.g. Schooley et al. 2000). Indeed, the decline in evidence of activity by invertebrates in areas of grazing could have been due to direct effects of animal disturbance through declines in the quality of habitat with grazing. For example, Howard (2011) showed that an index of soil stability declined from the Scotia Sanctuary to the adjoining grazing leases and this was due primarily to reductions in cryptogam cover and increases in soil compaction (Huang 2007). The effects could be due to changing the availability of resources for invertebrates i.e. making prey items more or less available, changing the abiotic environments to increase (or decrease) ease of movement by, for example, creating more bare soil surface, or conceivably, altering the competitive ability of different groups of organisms (e.g. seed harvesting vs. predatory ant species–trophic effect). It is possible that in more degraded landscapes such as those experienced at the *Pastoral* sites, all burrowing animals might avoid foraging in areas where the soil surface has been trampled by exotic grazers. Consequently, because vertebrates and invertebrates forage away from disturbed sites, their disturbances appear to be interrelated.

In summary, soil disturbance by invertebrates in our eucalypt woodland appears to be influenced by landscape- and local-scale factors. Soil movement is an important geomorphic process that is critical for the maintenance of functioning arid and semi-arid environments (Whitford 2002; Eldridge et al. 2011b). Reductions in the density, cover and composition of of invertebrate (and vertebrate) disturbances by overgrazing, for example, will lead to reductions in small-scale landscape heterogeneity, ultimately reducing stability and productivity of semi-arid systems.

ACKNOWLEDGEMENT

We thank all the staff at Scotia Sanctuary for assistance locating sites and logistical support. Terry Koen provided considerable input into the statistical analyses. We are grateful for the excellent comments provided by an anonymous reviewer.

REFERENCES

Andersen, A.N. (1986). Patterns of ant community organization in mesic southeastern Australia. *Australian Journal of Ecology* 11, 87-97.

Bangert, R.K. and Slobodchikoff, C.N. (2006). Conservation of prairie dog ecosystem engineering may support arthropod beta and gamma diversity. *Journal of Arid Environments* 67, 100-115.

Barton, P.S., Manning, A.D., Gibb, H., Lindenmayer, D.B. and Cunningham, S.A. (2010). Fine-scale heterogeneity in beetle assemblages under co-occurring *Eucalyptus* in the same subgenus. *Journal of Biogeography* 37, 1927-1937.

Bonte, D., Baert, L. and Maelfait, J.-P. (2002). Spider assemblage structure and stability in a heterogeneous coastal dune system (Belgium). *Journal of Arachnology* 30, 331–343.

Boulton, A.M., Davies, K.F. and Ward, P.S. (2005). Species richness, abundance, and composition of ground-dwelling ants in Northern California grasslands: role of plants, soil, and grazing. *Environmental Entomology* 34, 96-104.

Borchard, P. and Eldridge, D.J. (2011). The geomorphic signature of bare-nosed wombats (*Vombatus ursinus*) and cattle (*Bos taurus*) in an agriculture riparian ecosystem. *Geomorphology* 130, 365-373.

Bromham, L., Cardillo, M., Bennett, A. and Elgar, M. (1999). Effects of stock grazing on the ground invertebrate fauna of woodland remnants. *Australian Journal of Ecology* 24, 1999-2007.

Ceballos, G., Pacheco, J. and List, R. (1999). Influence of prairie dogs (*Cynomys ludovicianus*) on habitat heterogeneity and mammalian diversity in Mexico. *Journal of Arid Environments* 41, 161-172.

Eldridge, D.J., Bowker, M.A., Maestre, F.M., Roger, E., Reynolds, J.F. and Whitford, W.G. (2011a). Impacts of shrub encroachment on ecosystem structure and functioning: towards a global synthesis. *Ecology Letters* 14, 709-722.

Eldridge, D.J., Koen, T.B., Huang, N, Killgore, A. and Whitford, W.G. (2011b). Animal foraging as a mechanism for sediment movement and soil nutrient development: evidence from the semi-arid Australian woodlands and the Chihuahuan Desert. *Geomorphology* doi:10.1016/j.geomorph.2011.04.041

Elkins, N.Z., Sabol, G.V., Ward, T.J. and Whitford, W.G. (1986). The influence of subterranean termites on the hydrological characteristics of a Chihuahuan desert ecosystem. *Oecologia* 68, 521-528.

Folgarait, P.J. (1998). Ant biodiversity and its relationship to ecosystem functioning: a review. *Biodiversity and Conservation* 7, 1221-1244.

Gibb, H., and Parr, C.L. (2010). How does habitat complexity affect ant foraging success? A test using functional measures on three continents. *Oecologia* 164, 1061-1073.

Holt, J.A., Bristow, K.L. and McIvor, J.G. (1996). The effects of grazing pressure on soil animals and hydraulic properties of two soils in semi-arid tropical Queensland. *Australian Journal of Soil Research* 34, 69-79.

Howard, K. (2011). Plant-plant interactions in an arid shrubland: the role of shrubs as facilitators. Unpublished BSc (Hons.) thesis, University of NSW, Sydney. 58 pp.

Huang, N. (2007). Interrelationships between burrowing animals and arid landscapes. Unpublished BSc (Hons.) thesis, University of NSW, Sydney. 82 pp.

Huntly, N. and Inouye, R. (1988). Pocket gophers in ecosystems: patterns and mechanisms. *Bioscience* 38, 786-793.

James, A. I., Eldridge, D. J. Koen, T. B. and Moseby, K. E. 2011. Can the invasive European rabbit (*Oryctolagus cuniculus*) assume the soil engineering role of locally-extinct natives? *Biological Invasions* 13, 3027-3038.

James, A. I., Eldridge, D. J. Koen, T. B. and Whitford, W.G. (2008). Landscape position moderates how ant nests affect hydrology and soil chemistry across a Chihuahuan Desert watershed. *Landscape Ecology* 23, 961-975.

Johnson, D. L. (1990). Biomantle evolution and the redistribution of earth materials and artifacts. *Soil Science* 149, 84-102.

Jouquet, P., Dauber, J., Lagerlöf, J., Lavelle, P. and Lepage, M. (2006). Soil invertebrates as ecosystem engineers: intended and accidental effects on soil and feedback loops. *Applied Soil Ecology* 32, 153-164.

Kaspari, M. and Weiser, M.D. (1999). The size-grain hypothesis and interspecific scaling in ants. *Functional Ecology* 13, 530-538.

Kotliar, N.B. and Wiens, J.A. (1990). Multiple scales of patchiness and patch structure: a hierarchical framework for the study of heterogeneity. *Oikos* 59, 253-260.

Kretzer, J.E. and Cully, J.F. (2001). Prairie dog effects on harvester ant species diversity and density. *Journal of Rangeland Management* **54**, 11-14.

Lassau, S.A. and Hochuli, D.F. (2004). Effects of habitat complexity on ant assemblages. *Ecography* **27**, 157-164.

Martin, T.J. and Major, R.E. (2001). Changes in wolf spider (Araneae) assemblages across woodland-pasture boundaries in the central wheat-belt of New South Wales, Australia. *Austral Ecology* **26**, 264-274.

Mazía, C.N., Chaneton, E.J. and Kitzberger, T. (2006). Small-scale habitat use and assemblage structure of ground-dwelling beetles in a Patagonian shrub steppe. *Journal of Arid Environments* **67**, 177-194.

Minitab (2007). 'References Manual Release 15'. (Minitab Inc: State College Pennsylvania).

Muser, B., Sommer, S., Wolf, H. and Wehner, R. (2006). Foraging ecology of the thermophilic desert ant, *Melophorus bagoti*. *Australian Journal of Zoology* **53**, 301-311.

Nash, M.S., Bradford, D.F., Franson, S.E., Neale, A.C., Whitford, W.G. and Heggem, D.T. (2004). Livestock grazing effects on ant communities in the eastern Mojave Desert, USA. *Ecological Indicators* **4**, 199-213.

Nash, M.S., Whitford, W.G., Bradford, D.F., Franson, S.E., Neale, A.C. and Heggem, D.T. (2001). Ant communities and livestock grazing in the Great Basin, USA. *Journal of Arid Environments* **49**, 695-710.

Navnith, M., Finlayson, G.R., Crowther, M.S. and Dickman, C.R. (2009). The diet of the re-introduced greater bilby *Macrotis lagotis* in the mallee woodlands of western New South Wales. *Australian Zoologist* **35**, 90-95.

Nkem, J. N., de Bruyn, L. A. L., Grant, C. D., Hulugalle, N. R. (2000). The impact of ant bioturbation and foraging activities on surrounding soil properties. *Pedobiologia* **44**, 609-621.

Noy-Meir, I. (1973). Desert ecosystems: environment and producers. *Annual Review of Ecology and Systematics* **4**, 25-51.

Öberg, S., Ekbom, B. and Bommarco, R. (2007). Influence of habitat type and surrounding landscape on spider diversity in Swedish ecosystems. *Agriculture, Ecosystems and Environment* **122**, 211-219.

Sarah, P. (2004). Nonlinearity of ecogeomorphic processes along Mediterranean-arid transect. *Geomorphology* **60**, 303-317.

Schooley, R.L., Bestelmeyer, B.T. and Kelly, J.F. (2000). Influence of small-scale disturbances by kangaroo rats on Chihuahuan Desert ants. *Oecologia* **125**, 142-149.

Southgate, R.I. (1990). Habitat and diet of the greater bilby *Macrotis lagotis* Reid (Marsupialia: Peramelidae). In Seebeck, J.H., Brown, P.R., Wallis, R.I and Kemper C.M. (eds) 'Bandicoots and Bilbies' (Surrey Beatty & Sons: Sydney).

Vanbergen, A.J., Watt, A.D., Mitchell, R., Truscott, A.-M., Palmer, S.C.F., Ivits, E., Eggleton, P., Jones, T.H. and Sousa, J.P. (2007). Scale-specific correlations between habitat heterogeneity and soil fauna diversity along a landscape structure gradient. *Oecologia* **153**, 713-725.

Whicker, A.D. and Detling, J.K. (1988). Ecological consequences of prairie dog disturbances. *Bioscience* **38**, 778-785.

Whitehouse, M.E.A., Shochat, E., Shachak, M. and Lubin, Y. (2002). The influence of scale and patchiness on spider diversity in a semi-arid environment. *Ecography* **25**, 395-404.

Whitford, W.G. (2002). 'Ecology of Desert Systems'. (Academic Press: London).

Whitford, W.G. and Kay, F.R. (1999). Biopedturbation by mammals in deserts: a review. *Journal of Arid Environments* **41**, 203-230.

How Might Terrestrial Arthropod Assemblages Have Changed After the Dramatic Decline of Critical Weight Range (CWR) Mammals in Australia? Using Reintroductions at Scotia Sanctuary as a Model for Pre-European Ecosystems

HELOISE GIBB

Department of Zoology, La Trobe University, Melbourne, Victoria 3086, Australia
h.gibb@latrobe.edu.au

Published on 28 August at http://escholarship.library.usyd.edu.au/journals/index.php/LIN

Gibb, H. (2012). How might terrestrial arthropod assemblages have changed after the dramatic decline of Critical Weight Range (CWR) mammals in Australia? Using reintroductions at Scotia Sanctuary as a model for pre-European ecosystems. *Proceedings of the Linnean Society of New South Wales* **134**, A19-A26.

In Australia, populations of mammals within the critical weight range (CWR) of 35 to 5500 g have been severely affected by European settlement, with twenty-two species having become extinct over the past 200 years. Many highly threatened CWR mammals, such as bilbies, bandicoots and numbats, are insectivorous or omnivorous, and invertebrates comprise a significant portion of their diet. Such mammals cause significant disturbance to arthropod habitats through burrowing and engage in a range of other interactions with arthropods, including mutualisms, parasitism and competition. The loss of this trophic level is thus likely to have had considerable impacts on arthropods. Here, I consider the potential effects of the dramatic decline of native omnivores on the abundance, diversity, composition, morphology and functional roles performed by arthropods. I also discuss reintroductions such as that at Scotia Sanctuary in western NSW and other conservation sites as a model for understanding the pre-European state of arthropod-CWR mammal interactions.

Manuscript received 19 October 2011, accepted for publication 9 January 2012.

KEYWORDS: ants, arthropod assemblage, critical weight range mammal, insectivore, interactions, omnivore, predation, pre-European Australia, reintroduction, termites

INTRODUCTION

Biological invasions have been associated with extinctions world-wide, particularly on islands (Diamond 1989, Steadman 1995, Blackburn et al. 2004). On the island continent of Australia, the invasion of European humans and their associated fauna is thought to be responsible for the extinction of twenty-two mammal species within the critical weight range (CWR) of 35 to 5500 g (Burbidge and McKenzie 1989, Dickman 1996, Johnson et al. 2007, McKenzie et al. 2007). In addition, numerous previously common and widespread native mammals are now critically endangered and can be considered 'ecologically extinct' in much of Australia, i.e., they are too rare to continue to play important ecological roles (Estes et al. 1989).

CWR mammals had direct and indirect relationships with a range of other organisms. Insects and other arthropods are the key contributors to animal biodiversity worldwide (Hickman et al. 2008) and engage in a range of interactions with mammals. Although they are poorly studied, interactions between arthropods and mammals are diverse, including mutualisms, parasitism, predation, competition, necrophagy, commensalism and amensalism (Fig. 1). Some of these interactions may be species specific, whilst others are more generalised or diffuse. The ecological extinction of CWR mammals may have had significant consequences for Australian terrestrial arthropods.

Efforts to conserve CWR mammals have focused on reintroduction into large-scale predator-proof enclosures. Such sites present an opportunity

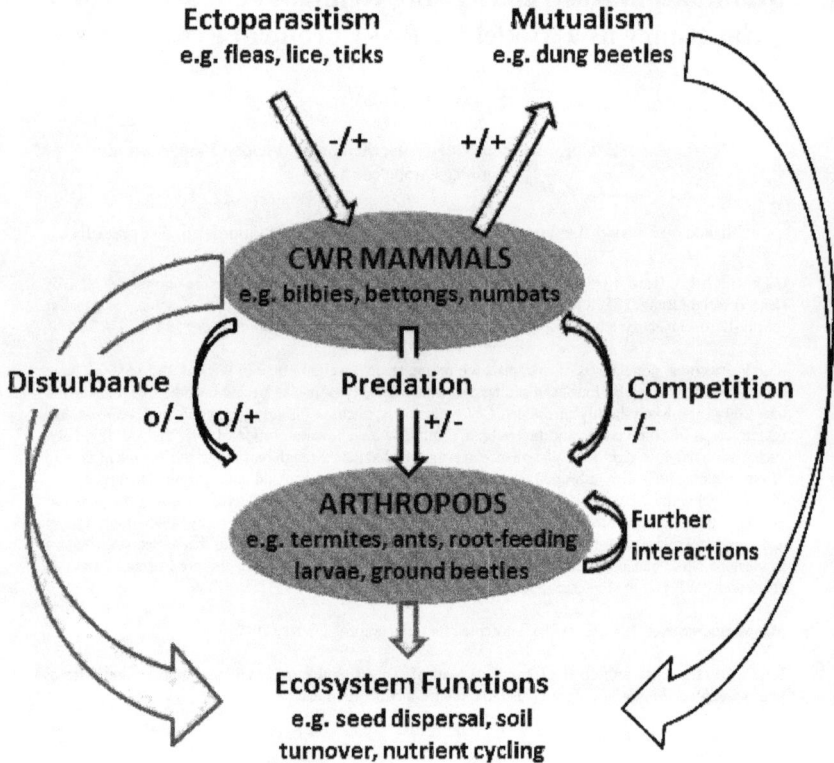

Figure 1: Interactions between critical weight range mammals and arthropods. The effects of interactions for each partner is shown the arrows (e.g. +/-). The first symbol reflects the effect of the interaction on CWR mammals, the second its effect on the arthropods involved. Arrows for biotic interactions are shown with black outlines; those for functions are shown with grey outlines. Effects on ecosystem functions are also shown. These functions may in turn benefit CWR mammals and arthropods (not shown).

to investigate the structure of Australian ecosystems in a pre-European state, where CWR mammals were common and introduced predators and herbivores rare. Scotia Sanctuary, situated in the semi-arid mallee biome in western NSW and owned by the Australian Wildlife Conservancy, presents such an opportunity. The site supports significant reintroduced populations of the bridled nail-tail wallaby (*Onychogalea fraenata*), the greater bilby (*Macrotis lagotis*), the burrowing bettong (*Bettongia lesueur*), the brush-tailed bettong (*Bettongia pencillata*), the numbat (*Myrmecobius fasciatus*) and the greater stick-nest

rat (*Leporillus conditor*) in two 4 000 ha predator-proof enclosures. Here, I consider how arthropods may have been affected by the ecological extinctions of CWR mammals and discuss Scotia Sanctuary as a model for understanding pre-European Australia. This question is not only of academic interest, but also has implications for target states for reintroduction sites.

PREDATION

Predatory impacts of some CWR mammals on arthropods may have been significant where

A20

Proc. Linn. Soc. N.S.W., 134, 2012

population densities were high. Of the six species reintroduced at Scotia Sanctuary, numbats feed only on social insects, while arthropods make up a significant proportion of the diet of the bilby (Calaby 1960, Gibson 2001, Southgate and Carthew 2006, Bice and Moseby 2008, Navnith et al. 2009). Just 5-10% of the diet of the brush-tailed and burrowing bettong is arthropods (Robley et al. 2001, Bice and Moseby 2008, Zosky et al. 2010), while the greater stick-nest rat and bridled nail-tail wallaby can be considered herbivores (Dawson et al. 1992, Ryan et al. 2003). The numbat specialises on termites (Isoptera), but may also consume ants (Hymenoptera: Formicidae), probably accidentally (Calaby 1960). The frequency of occurrence of arthropods in greater bilby scats across a range of locations is consistently >90%, with arthropods making up 30-56% of non-soil scat volume (Gibson 2001, Southgate and Carthew 2006, Bice and Moseby 2008, Navnith et al. 2009). Given the greater digestibility of arthropods relative to plant material, it is likely that their representation as a component of scat volume is an underestimate. Termites make up the greatest proportion of scat volume, followed by ants, beetles (Coleoptera), grasshoppers and crickets (Orthoptera). The remains of larvae from a range of holometabolous insects are common in scats, even though it is commonly only mouthparts that survive digestion. Cockroaches (Blattodea), flies (Diptera), moths (Lepidoptera), lace wings and ant lions (Neuroptera), spiders (Araneae), mites (Acarina), scorpions (Scorpionida) and centipedes (Chilopoda) constitute a smaller proportion of the diet (Gibson 2001, Southgate and Carthew 2006, Bice and Moseby 2008, Navnith et al. 2009, Silvey 2011). The abundance of these groups in the diet of the bilby roughly appears to reflect their relative abundances in typical arid or semi-arid zone arthropod assemblages (e.g., Kwok et al. 2010), suggesting a lack of specificity. This is also reflected by seasonal changes in arthropod composition that allow bilbies to respond to outbreaks of taxa such as locusts (Gibson 2001, Bice and Moseby 2008, Navnith et al. 2009). Arthropods in the diet of the two bettong species similarly suggest low specificity. In addition to direct predation on arthropods, bilbies have been reported to consume the seed caches of seed harvester ants (Gibson et al. 2002), which could be considered as cleptoparasitism of ants, although it is probably also associated with predation.

In the absence of ecologically equivalent species, arthropod biomass, particularly that of termites, may have increased in areas in which CWR mammals with insectivorous or omnivorous diets have become extinct or ecologically extinct. There may also have been significant turnover in species composition and trophic structure due to differing vulnerability to predation or disturbance. Previous studies suggest that invertebrates are smaller and less abundant in the presence of predatory vertebrates, even in complex systems with intra-guild predation (Spiller and Schoener 1990, Dial and Roughgarden 1995). In addition, the exclusion of vertebrate insectivores has been shown to affect above- and below-ground insect-driven ecosystem processes, such as herbivory and nutrient cycling (Spiller and Schoener 1990, Dial and Roughgarden 1995, Dunham 2008). However, the impact on arthropod diversity and abundance in Australian ecosystems depends on a number of poorly known factors. These include the pre-European population densities of CWR mammals, which are reported to have been high across much of Australia (discussed in Jones 1924, Finlayson 1958, Seebeck and Rose 1989), the metabolic rates of CWR mammals, examined in a few studies (e.g. Gibson et al. 2002, Cooper et al. 2003), and the response of arthropod populations to predation and other interactions with CWR mammals, which remains unknown.

It is likely that there is some redundancy in the generalised predatory role: predation pressure from CWR mammals may have been replaced by that from invaders such as cats and foxes. The diets of these invaders generally include at least 5% arthropod prey and sometimes up to 83% in bogong moth-rich alpine areas (Paltridge 2002, Green 2003, Claridge et al. 2010, Glen et al. 2011). Many non-threatened native species, such as lizards, consume arthropods, but the behaviour involved is often different from that of CWR mammals. Most lizards are small and diurnal and not capable of the significant foraging excavations (up to 40 cm deep, pers. obs.) created by species such as the bilby and burrowing bettong. There are exceptions to this, such as insectivorous skinks of the genus *Lerista*, and goannas (Varanidae), which burrow extensively for prey (Cogger 2000). Despite some functional redundancy, it is likely that the contemporary insectivorous assemblage targets a different component of the arthropod fauna from that consumed by pre-European insectivore assemblages. Arthropod assemblages may therefore have changed significantly since the loss of predators such as the bilby and numbat.

Effects of the loss of predation by CWR mammals on arthropod assemblages are likely to be complex and not limited to the loss of individuals through consumption. Predators have previously been shown to alter the behaviour of their arthropod prey (Venzon et al. 2000, Logan et al. 2007) and therefore the potential of prey to reproduce. In addition, predation

Proc. Linn. Soc. N.S.W., 134, 2012

A21

by CWR mammals on predatory arthropods such as scorpions may have cascading effects on arthropod assemblages (Silvey 2011).

DISTURBANCE

The burrowing activity of mammals such as the greater bilby, burrowing bettong and numbat is extensive (Eldridge and James 2009, James and Eldridge 2010) and likely to affect a range of non-prey arthropods. These interactions are either commensal or amensal, depending on whether the response of arthropods to the increased abundance of foraging pits and burrows in the presence of CWR mammals is positive or negative, respectively. Some arthropod taxa, such as opportunistic ants of the genus *Rhytidoponera* (Andersen 1990, Hoffmann and Andersen 2003), are likely to benefit directly from the increased disturbance of their habitats. Other taxa will benefit indirectly, for example improved nutrient cycling in the presence of burrowing mammals leads increased germination success of some plants (James and Eldridge 2007, 2010), which may benefit herbivorous arthropods. In addition, bilby and bettong warrens provide retreats for some arthropods that are not favoured by the warrens of introduced rabbits (Read et al. 2008).

However, the effects of changes in habitat structure due to frequent burrowing may be negative for some arthropod species. For example, gallery structures may be destroyed by foraging pits. Small-scale structural changes to habitats have previously been shown to alter the foraging success of ground-dwelling arthropod species (e.g. Sarty et al. 2006, Parr et al. 2007, Gibb and Parr 2010) and high densities of foraging pits may have a similar effect. Changes to the soil surface may alter the mobility of species (Loiterton and Magrath 1996) and foraging pits and burrows in loose soil have the additional potential to act as natural pitfall traps, ensnaring flightless foraging insects such as ants.

PARASITISM

A range of ectoparasitic arthropods, including fleas (Siphonaptera), lice (Phthiraptera), ticks and mites (Acarina) and louse and bot flies (Diptera) are associated with native Australian mammals. These taxa are commonly associated with disease transmission so may have important consequences for the health of native mammals (Ladds 2009). Several ectoparasites have been reported from the CWR mammal species present at Scotia Sanctuary. Four different native flea species are reported from the burrowing bettong and two of these, *Echnidophaga aranka* and *E. macronychia* are known only from a few examples from this host (Dunnet and Mardon 1974), so could be at risk of co-extinction. Use of marsupial hosts by the Acarina, Phthiraptera and Diptera appears less specialised, so co-extinction risk may be low (Ladds 2009).

COMPETITION

Competitive interactions between CWR mammals and arthropods may also be important, although they would likely have been diffuse, with the effect of reducing populations. Herbivorous mammals alter the success of herbivorous arthropods (e.g. Rambo and Faeth 1999, Suominen et al. 2003, Den Herder et al. 2004, Barton et al. 2011). However, herbivorous CWR mammals have commonly been replaced with introduced herbivores, such as the rabbit, *Oryctolagus cuniculus*, and a range of ungulates, so it is unclear whether effects on arthropod herbivores would differ. Competition for other plant resources, such as seeds, may have been important, evidenced by bilby usurpation of harvester ant seed caches (Gibson et al. 2002). However, the ability of more successful groups, such as the native rodents, to expand to absorb additional seed availability (Letnic et al. 2005) suggest that effects of CWR mammals on seed predation by arthropods may be limited. Many arthropods feed on invertebrate prey, presenting another avenue for competitive interactions, but little is known of the effects of this interaction on predatory arthropods.

MUTUALISMS AND NUTRIENT RECYCLING

Arthropods perform a number of functions that benefit CWR mammals, including necrophagy and coprophagy. Necrophagous arthropods such as blowflies (Muscidae), fleshflies (Sarcophagidae), hide beetles (Trogidae) and hister beetles (Histeridae) have limited specificity, consuming a range of vertebrate carcasses (Gennard 2007). Carcass availability has likely increased since European colonisation of Australia, due to large numbers of road kills (Taylor and Goldingay 2004, Kloecker et al. 2006) and culling of native and introduced species, thus boosting populations of these taxa. However, no evidence exists to indicate that changes in the availability of carcasses of CWR mammals affect necrophagous arthropods.

Mutualisms between dung beetles and mammals can be critical in reducing parasite loads, recycling nutrients, and allowing the persistence of dung beetles (Loreau 1995, Slade et al. 2007, Nichols 2008). Australian dung beetles are commonly specific to marsupial dung, but it is unclear how species-specific they might be and therefore how much they may have been affected by the ecological extinction of CWR mammals throughout much of Australia (see Coggan, next article).

BROADER IMPACTS

Interactions between CWR mammals and arthropods have the potential to influence more than just the diversity and abundance of arthropods. Arthropods play a range of important functional roles, for example, acting as seed dispersers, enhancing soil structure and recycling nutrients (Folgarait 1998, Mayer 2008, Nichols 2008). How the loss of CWR mammals affects these functions is unclear, but preliminary data suggests it may have had significant consequences for arthropod-driven functions. For example, rates of removal of seeds, mealworms and bird droppings by ants all appear slower in sites without CWR mammals (Gibb unpublished). At larger scales, CWR mammals may alter litter loads (James et al. 2009, 2010), potentially leading to impacts on nutrient cycling that would further alter biotic assemblages. The lack of baseline data for the pre-European state of Australia inhibits our ability to evaluate these changes.

SCOTIA SANCTUARY AS A MODEL FOR PRE-EUROPEAN ARTHROPOD ASSEMBLAGES

Although we lack knowledge of the pre-European state of epigaeic arthropod assemblages, reintroductions such as those behind two 4 000 ha predator-proof fences at Scotia Sanctuary, western NSW, present an opportunity to test the impact of CWR mammals on other species. Unfortunately, baseline data on arthropod assemblages does not exist for Scotia Sanctuary or any of the other Australian semi-natural reintroduction sites. While it is possible to compare inside and outside the exclusion fences, such studies are always limited by the similarity of sites. Spatial autocorrelations in the environment and biotic assemblages mean that measured differences inside and outside a single fence must be considered very cautiously, with an understanding of the limitations of pseudoreplication (Hulbert 1984). A thorough research program should work at multiple scales and experimentally eliminate the multitude of potentially confounding factors. One way in which to do this is to use replicated experimental exclosures within a reintroduction site to allow comparison of replicated sites with and without CWR mammals. Although this frees the observer from confounding factors, the scale at which such exclosures are usually constructed may limit our ability to observe changes in more mobile species. Fortunately, multiple large-scale reintroduction sites are in operation around Australia and can complement a smaller-scale approach. While few arthropod species are shared between these sites, functional approaches yield comparable results. For example, the morphologies of arthropods or the rates at which arthropod-driven functions are performed can be compared. Behavioural studies exploring the mechanisms behind observed effects are also critical in understanding how impacts are achieved.

The removal of introduced predators and the European rabbit is likely to affect populations of other vertebrates and CWR mammal-free exclosures may also be free of other arthropod predators, such as the echidna, *Tachyglossus aculeatus*. This necessitates careful interpretation of results. In addition, it is unclear whether densities of CWR mammals at Scotia Sanctuary, where mammals are protected by predator-proof fences, are similar to those in pre-European arid Australia. However, some of the limitations in terms of densities at this site can be addressed by comparing the two stages, which differ in mammal densities. Difference in depletion rates of arthropods from sites with differing CWR mammal densities could inform management by allowing us to determine sustainable carrying capacities for reintroduction sites. Key groups to investigate are the termites and ants, which constitute a large proportion of numbat and bilby prey and are functionally important (Calaby 1960, Folgarait 1998, Gibson 2001, Evans et al. 2011). Much of the burrowing activity is likely to be directed at extracting larvae, particularly the root feeding cockchafers (Coleoptera: Scarabaeidae: Melolonthinae), so this group should also be central to research efforts. In addition, an understanding of interactions with mutualists, such as dung beetles, may be critical to maximising reintroduction success (Coggan, next article).

Given the dramatic changes in CWR mammal assemblages since European colonisation of Australia, it is appalling that we know so little of the broader consequences for the Australian biota. Work on CWR mammal interactions with arthropod assemblages will fill a critical gap in our knowledge and improve our capacity to restore Australian ecosystems.

REFERENCES

Andersen, A.N. (1990) The use of ant communities to evaluate change in Australian terrestrial ecosystems: a review and a recipe. *Proceedings of the Ecological Society of Australia*, **16**, 347-357.

Barton, P.S., Manning, A.D., Gibb, H., Wood, J.T., Lindenmayer, D.B. and Cunningham, S.A. (2011) Experimental reduction of native vertebrate grazing and addition of logs benefit beetle diversity at multiple scales. *Journal of Animal Ecology* **48**, 943-951.

Bice, J. and Moseby, K.E. (2008) Diet of the re-introduced greater bilby (*Macrotis lagotis:* Peramelidae) and burrowing bettong (*Bettongia lesueur:* Potoroidae) in the Arid Recovery Reserve, northern South Australia. *Australian Mammalogy*, **30**, 1-12.

Burbidge, A.A., McKenzie, N.L. (1989) Patterns in the modern decline of western Australia's vertebrate fauna: Causes and conservation implications. *Proceedings of the Royal Society B: Biological Sciences* **270**: 1801-1808

Calaby JH (1960) Observations on the banded ant-eater *Myrmecobius f. fasciatus* Waterhouse (Marsupialia), with particular reference to its food habits. *Proceedings of the Zoological Society of London* **135**:183–207.

Claridge, A.W., Mills, D.J. and Barry, S.C. (2010) Prevalence of threatened native species in canid scats from coastal and near-coastal landscapes in south-eastern Australia. *Australian Mammalogy*, **32**, 117-126.

Cogger, H. (2000) *Reptiles and Amphibians of Australia*. Reed New Holland, Terry Hills, NSW, Australia.

Cooper, C.E., Withers, P.C. and Bradshaw, S.D. (2003) Field metabolic rate and water turnover of the numbat (*Myrmecobius fasciatus*). *Journal of Comparative Physiology B*, **173**, 687-693.

Dawson, T.J., Tierney, P.J. and Ellis, B.A. (1992) The diet of the Bridled nailtail wallaby (*Onychogalea fraenata*). I Site and seasonal influences and dietry overlap with the black striped wallaby (*Macropus dorsalis*) and domestic cattle. *Wildlife Research*, **19**, 65-77.

Den Herder, M., Virtanen, R. and Roininen, H. (2004) Effects of reindeer browsing on tundra willow and its associated insect herbivores. *Journal of Applied Ecology*, **41**, 870–879.

Dial, R. and Roughgarden, J. (1995) Experimental removal of insectivores from rain forest canopy: direct and indirect effects. *Ecology* **76**: 1821-1834

Diamond, J.M. (1989) The present, past and future of human-caused extinctions. *Philosophical Transactions - Royal Society of London, B* **325**, 469-477.

Dickman, C.R. (1996) Impact of exotic generalist predators on the native fauna of Australia. *Wildlife Biology* **2**: 185-195

Dunham, A.E. (2008) Above and below ground impacts of terrestrial mammals and birds in a tropical forest. *Oikos* **117**: 571-579

Dunnet, G.M. and Mardon, D.K. (1974) A monograph of Australian fleas. *Australian Journal of Zoology*, **30**, 1-274.

Eldridge, D.J. and James, A.I. (2009) Soil disturbance by native animals plays a critical role in maintaining healthy Australian landscapes. *Ecological Management and Restoration*, **10**, S27-S34.

Estes, J.A., Duggans, D.O. and Rathbun, G.B. (1989) The ecology of extinctions in kelp forest communities. *Conservation Biology*, **3**, 252-264.

Evans, T.A., Dawes, T.Z., Ward, P.R. and Lo, N. (2011) Ants and termites increase crop yield in a dry climate. *Nature Communications*, **2**, art. no. 262.

Finlayson, H.H. (1958). On Central Australian mammals (with notice of related species from adjacent tracts) Part III, the Potoroinae. *Records of the South Australian Museum* 3: 235-302

Folgarait, P.J. (1998) Ant biodiversity and its relationship to ecosystem functioning: a review. *Biodiversity and Conservation*, **7**, 1221-1244.

Gennard, D.E. (2007) *Forensic Entomology: An Introduction*. John Wiley and Sons, Chichester, United Kingdom.

Gibb, H. and Parr, C.L. (2010) How does habitat complexity affect ant foraging success? A test of functional responses on three continents. *Oecologia*, **164**, 1061-1073.

Gibson, L.A. (2001) Seasonal changes in the diet, food availability and food preference of the greater bilby (*Macrotis lagotis*) in south-western Queensland. *Wildlife Research* **28**: 121-134

Gibson, L.A., Hume, I.D. and McRae, P.D. (2002) Ecophysiology and nutritional niche of the bilby (*Macrotis lagotis*), an omnivorous marsupial from inland Australia: a review. *Comparative Biochemistry and Physiology*, **133**, 843-847.

Glen, A.S., Pennay, M., Dickman, C.R., Wintle, B.A. and Firestone, K.B. (2011) Diets of sympatric native and introduced carnivores in the Barrington Tops, eastern Australia. *Austral Ecology*, **36**, 290-296.

Green, K. (2003) Altitudinal and temporal differences in the food of foxes (*Vulpes vulpes*) at alpine and subalpine altitudes in the Snowy Mountains. *Wildlife Research*, **30**, 245-253.

Hickman, C.P., Roberts, L.S., Keen, S.L., Larson, A. and Eisenhour, D.J. (2008) *Animal Diversity*. McGraw Hill, USA.

Hoffmann, B.D. and Andersen, A.N. (2003) Responses of ants to disturbance in Australia, with particular reference to functional groups. *Austral Ecology* **28**, 444-464.

Hurlbert, S.H. (1984) Pseudoreplication and the design of ecological field experiments. *Ecological Monographs*, **54**, 187-211.

James, A.I. and Eldridge, D.J. (2007) Reintroduction of fossorial native mammals and potential impacts on ecosystem processes in an Australian desert landscape. *Biological Conservation*, **138**, 351-359.

James, A.I., Eldridge, D.J. and Hill, B.M. (2009) Foraging animals create fertile patches in an Australian desert shrubland. *Ecography*, **32**, 723-732.

James, A.I., Eldridge, D.J. and Moseby, K.E. (2010) Foraging pits, litter and plant germination in an arid shrubland. *Journal of Arid Environments*, **74**, 516-520.

Johnson, C.N., Isaac, J.L., Fisher, D.O. (2007) Rarity of a top predator triggers continent-wide collapse of mammal prey: dingoes and marsupials in Australia. *Proceedings of the Royal Society B*, **274**, 341-346.

Jones, F. Wood (1924). *The Mammals of South Australia*. Part II Government Printer, Adelaide pp. 133-270

Kloecker, U., Croft, D.B. and Ramp, D. (2006) Frequency and causes of kangaroo-vehicle collisions on an Australian outback highway. *Wildlife Research*, **33**, 5-15.

Kwok, A.B.C., Eldridge, D.J. and Oliver, I. (2010) Do landscape health indices reflect arthropod biodiversity status. *Austral Ecology*, **36**, 800-813.

Ladds, P.W. (2009) *Pathology of Australian Native Wildlife*. CSIRO Publishing, Collingwood, Victoria, Australia.

Letnic, M., Tamayo, B. and Dickman, C.R. (2005) The responses of mammals to La Niña (El Niño Southern Oscillation)-associated rainfall, predation, and wildfire in central Australia . *Journal of Mammalogy*, **86**, 689-703.

Logan, J.D., Wolesensky, W. and Joern, A. (2007) Insect development under predation risk, variable temperature, and variable food quality. *Mathematical Biosciences and Engineering*, **4**, 47-65.

Loiterton, S.J. and Magrath, R.D. (1996) Substrate type affects partial prey consumption by larvae of the antlion *Myrmeleon acer* (Neuroptera: Myrmeleontidae). *Australian Journal of Zoology*, **44**, 589-597.

Loreau, M. (1995) Consumers as maximizers of matter and energy flow in ecosystems. *American Naturalist*, **145**, 22-42.

Mayer, P.M. (2008) Ecosystem and decomposer effects on litter dynamics along an old field to old-growth forest successional gradient. *Acta Oecologia*, **33**, 222-230.

McKenzie, N.L., Burbidge, A.A., Baynes, A., Brereton, R.N., Dickman, C.R., Gordon, G., Gibson, L.A., Menkhorst, P.W., Robinson, A.C., Williams, M.R., Woinarski, J.C.Z. (2007) Analysis of factors implicated in the recent decline of Australia's mammal fauna. *Journal of Biogeography* **34**: 597-611

Navnith, M., Finlayson, G.R., Crowther, M.S. and Dickman, C.R. (2009) The diet of the re-introduced greater bilby (*Macrotis lagotis*) in the mallee woodlands of western New South Wales. *Australian Zoologist*, **53**, 90-95.

Nichols, E., Spector, S., Louzada, J., Larsen, T., Amezquita, S. and Favila, M.E. (2008) Ecological functions and ecosystem services provided by Scarabaeinae dung beetles. *Biological Conservation*, **141**, 1461-1474.

Paltridge, R. (2002) The diet of cats, foxes and dingoes in relation to prey availability in the Tanami Desert, Northern Territory. *Wildlife Research*, **29**, 389-403.

Parr, C.L., Andersen, A.N., Chastagnol, C. and Duffaud, C. (2007) Savanna fires increase rates and distances of seed dispersal by ants. *Oecologia*, **151**, 33-41.

Rambo, J.L. and Faeth, S.H. (1999) Effect of vertebrate grazing on plant and insect community structure. *Conservation Biology*, **13**, 1047-1054.

Read, J.L., Carter, J., Moseby, K.M. and Greenville, A. (2008) Ecological roles of rabbit, bettong and bilby warrens in arid Australia. *Journal of Arid Environments*, **72**, 2124-2130.

Robley, A.J., Short, J. and Bradley, S. (2001) Dietary overlap between the burrowing bettong (*Bettongia lesueur*) and the European rabbit (*Oryctolagus cuniculus*) in semi-arid coastal Western Australia. *Wildlife Researsch*, **28**, 341-349 .

Ryan, S.A., Moseby, K.E. and Paton, D.C. (2003) Comparative foraging preferences of the greater stick-nest rat (*Leporillus conditor*) and the European rabbit (*Oryctolagus cuniculus*): Implications for regeneration of arid lands. *Australian Mammalogy*, **25**, 135-146.

Sarty, M., Abbott, K.L. and Lester, P.J. (2006) Habitat complexity facilitates coexistence in a tropical ant community. *Oecologia*, **149**, 465-473.

Seebeck, J.H. AND Rose, R.W., (1989) Potoroidae. Pp.716-739 in *Fauna of Australia. Volume 1B. Mammalia* ed by D.W. Walton and B.J. Richardson. Australian Government Publishing Service: Canberra, Australia.

Silvey, C.J. (2011) *Threatened native omnivores affect ground dwelling arachnid assemblages: Mesopredator release and implications for intraguild predation.* Honours thesis, La Trobe University, Melbourne, Australia.

Slade, E.M., Mann, D.J., Villanueva, J.F. and Lewis, O.T. (2007) Experimental evidence for the effects of dung beetle functional group richness and composition on ecosystem function in a tropical forest. *Journal of Animal Ecology*, **76**, 1094-1104.

Southgate, R. and Carthew, S.M. (2006) Diet of the bilby (*Macrotis lagotis*) in relation to substrate, fire and rainfall characteristics in the Tanami Desert. *Wildlife Research*, **33**, 507-519.

Spiller, D.A. and Schoener, T.W. (1990) A terrestrial field experiment showing the impact of eliminating top predators on foliage damage. *Nature* **347**: 469-472.

Steadman, D.W. (1995) Prehistoric extinction of pacific island birds – biodiversity meets zooarchaeology. *Science* **267**, 1123.

Suominen, O., Niemela, J., Martikainen, P., Niemela, P. and Kojola, I. (2003) Impact of reindeer grazing on ground-dwelling Carabidae and Curculionidae assemblages in Lapland. *Ecography*, **26**, 503–513.

Proc. Linn. Soc. N.S.W., 134, 2012

A25

Taylor, B.D. and Goldingay, R.L. (2004) Wildlife road-kills on three major roads in north-eastern New South Wales. *Wildlife Research*, **31**, 83-91.

Venzon, M., Janssen, A., Pallini, A. and Sabelis, M.W. (2000) Diet of a polyphagous arthropod predator affects refuge seeking of its thrips prey. *Animal Behaviour*, **60**, 369-375.

Zosky, K., Bryant, K., Calver, M. and Wayne, A. (2010) Do preservation methods affect the identification of dietary components from faecal samples? A case study using a mycophagous marsupial. *Australian Mammalogy*, **32**, 173.

A26

Proc. Linn. Soc. N.S.W., 134, 2012

Reintroduction of Bridled Nailtail Wallabies Beyond Fences at Scotia Sanctuary – Phase 1

MATT W. HAYWARD, FELICITY L'HOTELLIER, TRUDY O'CONNOR, GEORGIA WARD-FEAR, JENNIFER CATHCART, TONY CATHCART, JOE STEPHENS, JOANNE STEPHENS, KERRYN HERMAN AND SARAH LEGGE

Australian Wildlife Conservancy, PO Box 8070, Subiaco East, Western Australia 6008
matt@australianwildlife.org

Published on 28 August 2012 at http://escholarship.library.usyd.edu.au/journals/index.php/LIN

Hayward, M.W., l'Hotellier, F., O'Connor, T., Ward-Fear, G., Cathcart, J., Cathcart, T., Stephens, Joe, Stephens, Joanne, Herman, K. and Legge, S. (2012). Reintroduction of bridled nailtail wallabies beyond fences at Scotia Sanctuary – Phase 1. *Proceedings of the Linnean Society of New South Wales* **134**, A27-A37.

Forty male bridled nailtail wallabies *Onychogalea fraenata* were translocated from an on-site captive breeding compound to two release areas beyond the 8000 ha conservation fences at Scotia Sanctuary (far western New South Wales) in late July 2010. We tested the hypothesis that site fidelity (facilitated by spreading soil laden with female bridled nailtail wallaby odour at the release site) would increase survivorship by restricting animals to Scotia where intensive pest animal control has occurred. Two groups of fifteen animals were fitted with radio collars and released at the two areas (odour-added and odour-free) and monitored intensively for three months. Seven of the bridled nailtail wallabies survived this period, 19 died and four remain unaccounted for. Of the 19 that died, three were killed by introduced red foxes *Vulpes vulpes*, two by wedge-tailed eagles *Aquila audax* and one by a dingo/dog *Canis lupus dingo*. Two bridled nailtail wallabies died from pneumonia. The causes of death for the remaining 11 individuals are unknown. Following their release, 13 bridled nailtail wallabies remained on Scotia whilst the other 13 left the sanctuary (excluding the four that were censored). Those individuals that stayed on Scotia had much higher survival (46%) than the dispersers (8%). This result demonstrates the importance of encouraging the released animals to remain within the area that is subject to intensive predator control. The bridled nailtail wallabies were released at two sites: in an attempt to encourage site-philopatry we added soil laden with bridled nailtail wallaby urine and faeces at one of these sites. Males released here tended to travel less far, and had higher survival, than the males released at the 'odour-free' site. We believe the wandering males were searching for mating opportunities. Philopatry may be encouraged and survival increased if females are released with males in future phases of the project. We note that the bridled nailtail wallaby population in Scotia's 8000 ha feral free area, and also in Scotia's captive breeding colony, continued to increase during the initial three months of the translocation.

Manuscript received 3 November 2011, accepted for publication 11 June 2012.

KEYWORDS: Australian Wildlife Conservancy, bridled nailtail wallaby, fox predation, introduced predators, *Onychogalea fraenata*, reintroduction, Scotia Sanctuary.

INTRODUCTION

Earth is amidst a conservation crisis with extinction rates thousands of times greater than the background rates (Barnosky, Matzke et al. 2011). Numerous other species are becoming threatened with extinction (Schipper, Chanson et al. 2008). Clearly our current conservation strategies are failing and new and innovative conservation strategies are required (Hayward 2011). Australia has fared no better than elsewhere, and indeed has the ignominy of leading the world in the number of mammalian extinctions over the past 250 years with 22 species considered extinct (Johnson 2006).

Introduced predators were the driver of the initial wave of mammalian extinctions in southern Australia

(Burbidge and McKenzie 1989; Kinnear, Sumner et al. 2002; Short and Smith 1994), and may be responsible for a secondary wave of declines currently affecting tropical Australia (Fitzsimons, Legge et al. 2010; Hayward 2002; Woinarski, Armstrong et al. 2010). The most effective way to protect vulnerable species from the threat of feral predators is to physically separate them. Control of feral animals via poison-baiting has traditionally been used to separate Australian fauna from introduced species (Armstrong 2004; Murray, Poore et al. 2006; Possingham, Jarman et al. 2004), however islands free from these invaders have also been used to great effect (Burbidge 2004; Burbidge, Williams et al. 1997; Dickman, Coles et al. 1992; Short 2009; Short, Bradshaw et al. 1992). Islands have limited potential to save all of Australia's threatened species largely because they provide minimal habitat diversity. Consequently, conservation managers have begun creating 'mainland islands' by fencing large mainland areas, eradicating feral animals from within, and then reintroducing native species (Dickman 2011; Hayward 2012; Hayward, Moseby et al. 2012; Short, Turner et al. 1994).

Scotia Wildlife Sanctuary is a private conservation reserve owned and managed by the Australian Wildlife Conservancy. The management of Scotia aims to improve the ecological health of the sanctuary by maintaining and restoring biodiversity and ecological function, and reducing the extent of threats. This management aim has included constructing a feral-proof fence around 8000 ha of mallee habitats, from which all feral animals except house mice *Mus musculus* have been eradicated. The site represents the largest feral-free area on the Australian mainland. Seven regionally extinct species have been successfully reintroduced into this fenced area, (Finlayson, Vieira et al. 2008; Hayward, Herman et al. 2010; Hayward, Legge et al. 2010). One of the reintroduced species was the bridled nailtail wallaby (BNTW; *Onychogalea fraenata*) and by the end of 2011 Scotia protected over 1500 BNTWs within the 8000 ha fenced area, and a further 500 in a 150 ha captive breeding compound. The Scotia animals thus represent over 70% of the world's entire BNTW population, with the remainder spread between three precarious sites in Queensland.

Following the initial, successful reintroductions, we aimed to expand the fauna restoration programme beyond the fenced areas, by implementing a large-scale intensive poison-baiting programme for introduced species, followed by translocations of selected native species that are most likely to withstand some pressure from feral predators. Of the critical weight range fauna that used to occur in the region and have

been reintroduced to the fenced area of Scotia, the BNTW was the best candidate for translocation to the unfenced areas of Scotia because:

• it is at the upper end of the critical weight range of species that have declined since European colonisation of Australia (Burbidge and McKenzie 1989; in fact, males are outside this range). Consequently, the threat to the species from a low density of predators is reduced.

• adults are somewhat vulnerable to foxes (but see point above) which are controlled in the region, but less so to cats. In other words, they are most vulnerable to the feral predator that we are best able to control by poison-baiting.

• the three small remaining populations of BNTW in Queensland all exist outside of fenced areas, although anecdotal evidence suggests that fox control benefits population persistence.

This paper describes the results of Phase 1 of the translocation of BNTW beyond Scotia's conservation fences and assesses these results in light of a set of pre-defined criteria for success (Table 1). Success for the Phase 1 release was previously set at 50% survival of the 30 collared males at the end of first three months

Study site

Scotia Wildlife Sanctuary is a 64,653 ha private conservation reserve situated in far-western New South Wales on the South Australian border between Wentworth and Broken Hill. The BNTW release area was located in the southern area of Scotia (Stage 4; Fig. 1). Release site A was situated near the Tararra homestead, while release site B was further west. Both sites had good quality grass and low shrublands for forage alongside suitable shrubby refuge areas. A water trough was also provided at each site, along with supplementary food which was provided freely for the first month and then at weekly intervals thereafter.

The release area had been subjected to an intense introduced predator control programme for almost one year prior to the BNTW release via the integrated use of M44 toxin delivery devices, standard meat and egg baits laden with 1080, and regional coordination of control activities with adjacent landowners. M44s remained in the environment continuously at 1.5 km spacing and bait heads were checked monthly, while standard baits were placed quarterly and removed after 10 days. Both release sites were within the core baiting area that was defended by M44s (Fig. 1). This was surrounded by a buffer of poison baits that extended onto Nanya (to the north-east of the core) and Belvedere Station (to the east; Fig. 1).

Table 1. Release plan, timing, sex ratio of translocated individuals and criteria for success from the original translocation plan (Herman et al. 2010).

Phase	Timing	Males (collared)	Females (collared)	Criteria for success/continuation
1		40 (30)	0	50% of collared animals survive first three months (continuation).
2	Three months post release	40 (10)	20 (20)	50% of collared animals from the subsequent supplementations survive one month.
3	Four months post release	10 (0)	30 (20)	Collared females observed with pouched young 9 months after release (medium-term success).
4	Five months	0	40 (10)	10% of animals observed will be new recruits 12 months after the initial release. Bridled nailtails persist for the life of the radio collars (3 years).
Ultimate				Self-sustaining population in Scotia and surrounds five years after this translocation. This will be evidence of long-term success.

METHODS

Forty male BNTWs were selected from animals captured in the Captive Breeding Compound at Scotia using soft-sided Bromilow cage traps (Kinnear, Bromilow et al. 1988) baited with Jack Rabbit™ pellets. These males were transported back to Scotia's Cook Laboratory in specially constructed racks on the back of 4WD vehicles that were covered with a tarpaulin to minimise temperature stress. The animals were moved into the lab and hung in bags on similar racks until processing.

Animals were sedated with inhaled isofluorothane, measured, tissue samples were taken and pit tags and radio collars were fitted. The collars were made by Sirtrack and weighed less than 3% of body mass. This process took up to 30 minutes per animal, but generally much less. After processing, the animals recovered in a quiet area of the lab under observation from an AWC staff member. Once all animals had been processed and had fully recovered, they were transported to the release area and released.

Release site A was treated weekly with soil containing odour, urine and faeces of female BNTWs in an experiment to test whether this reduced the distance moved by males from the release site and thereby improved translocation success. Release site B was not treated with odour.

All released animals were visually observed within the first week after their release to ensure the collar was appropriately fitted and that they were in good condition based on mobility, body condition, fur presence and absence of obvious injuries. Thereafter their locations were determined daily via direct observation or triangulation using Locate software (Nams 1990) with error ellipses of less than 1ha used for locations (following Hayward, de Tores et al. 2004). The range of the collars from the ground was approximately $1 - 1.5$ km, which meant that animals were undetectable beyond this distance from roads. Distance from the release site was calculated as the straight line distance from the release site to the last location of the animal using ARCGIS (ESRI USA). Aerial telemetry was used to find 'missing' or censored BNTWs. Causes of mortality were deduced from signs on the carcass and collar, and evidence at the site of death (following Augee, Smith et al. 1996; Hayward, de Tores et al. 2005) and from toxicological analyses of tissue samples conducted by Ian Japp (Mildura Veterinarian).

Fox activity was determined using the Catling-Allen index (Allen, Engeman et al. 1996) based on an array of unbaited 1.5m wide sand plots at 1.5 km spacing across tracks throughout the centre of both Stage 3 and 4 of Scotia (Fig.1). We acknowledge the substantial problems with such track based indices (Anderson 2001; MacFarland and Van Deelen 2011; MacKenzie, Nichols et al. 2006) and are moving away from them, however the long-term dataset available has used this method. The BNTW population within the captive breeding compound at Scotia was monitored via total counts during feeding before and after Phase 1 of the reintroduction.

Proc. Linn. Soc. N.S.W., 134, 2012

A29

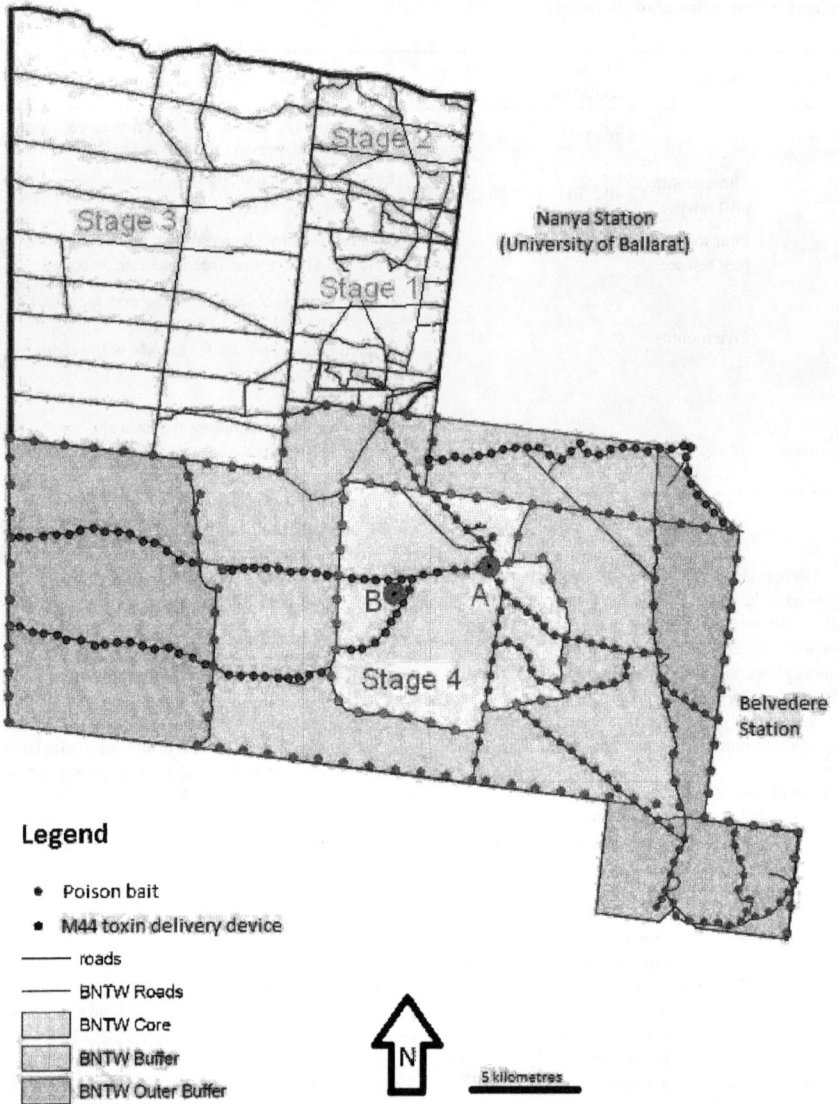

Fig. 1. Bridled nailtail wallaby release areas and fox control regions at Scotia. The release areas are shown as blue circles. BNTW refers to bridled nailtail wallaby, Std to standard meat baits and the other acronyms refer to compass directions.

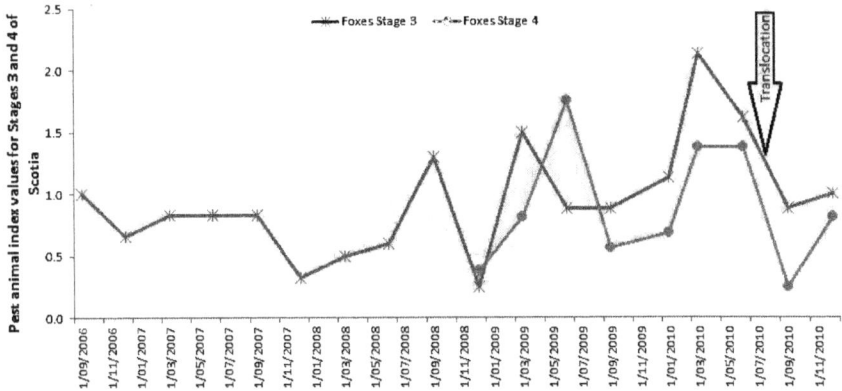

Fig. 2. Index of fox abundance and/or activity at Scotia since 2006 determined using sand plots on tracks via the Catling-Allen index. Stage 4 is the baited release site and Stage 3 is the unbaited control.

Survivorship of released BNTWs was determined by Kaplan-Meier survivorship curves with staggered entry (Pollock, Winterstein et al. 1989). We also used the known fates model in Program MARK with model selection to test the effect of the release method and heterogeneity using Akaike's information criteria and Akaike's weights (w) to represent the support for the model (White and Burnham 1999). Estimated known fate survival is presented along with 95%ile confidence intervals. Chi square tests were used to compare the number of animals surviving in the groups living on and off Scotia. Mann-Whitney tests were used to assess the period of time animals survived and t-tests were used to test for differences in the distances that surviving versus non-surviving individuals travelled. Log likelihood (G) tests were used to test whether mortality occurred uniformly throughout the release.

RESULTS

The predator control programme resulted in fox *Vulpes vulpes* index values being very low at the start of the reintroduction programme at the release site (Stage 4) before quickly increasing (Fig. 2). The regional peak in fox index value in spring of 2009 was quickly controlled in the release area (Stage 4) such that only one fox track was recorded throughout this region by early spring 2010 (Fig. 2). This contrasts with the unbaited control region (Stage 3) where the fox index remained high (Fig. 2).

Of the 30 BNTW males that were radio collared,

only seven were known to survive to three months, with four more missing and the remainder dead (Fig. 3). Three deaths were attributed to fox predation, one to dingo/dog predation and two more to wedge-tailed eagle predation. Two animals died of pneumonia (based on analysis of lung tissue samples by Ian Japp, Mildura veterinarian), which presented as pus-filled lesions on the lungs of infected animals. The cause of death of 11 individuals was unknown because they travelled into remote areas beyond Scotia's borders and the carcasses were too decomposed to determine a cause of death. Given the majority of these occurred in areas without fox control, foxes seem a likely cause.

Six of the seven surviving BNTW remained on Scotia, while all but one of those that left Scotia died (Fig. 4). There was a significant difference between the locations of the dead and surviving BNTWs with survival being much higher for animals that stayed on Scotia (χ^2 with Yate's correction factor = 6.15, d.f. = 1, $p < 0.05$). Of the set of animals that died, animals that stayed or moved off Scotia survived for similar lengths of time (Mann-Whitney $U = 1.03$, n = 26, p =0.304). Animals that died did not travel significantly further from the release site than those that survived ($t = -1.37$, $d.f. = 228$, $p = 0.169$), however surviving animals continued to travel rather than maintain a territory and their maxima were much larger (33.6 km cf 14.5 km) although this was not significant (t_{21} = -17.4, $p = 0.096$).

The majority of mortality events occurred within the first month of the reintroduction (Fig. 5); surviving animals were either warier to begin with, or lost any

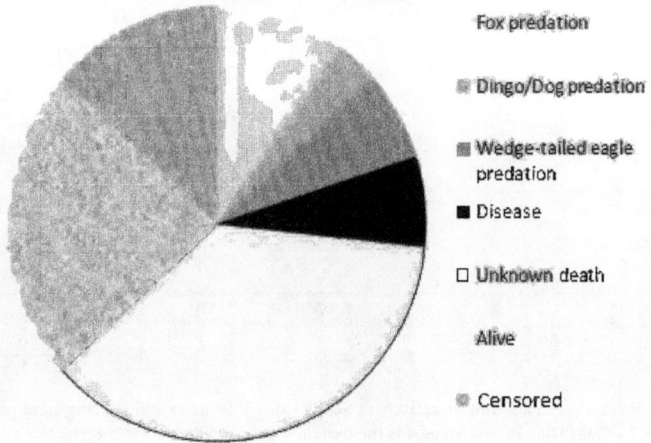

Fig. 3. Fate of the 30 collared reintroduced bridled nailtail wallaby males. 'Censored' refers to individuals that had not been detected for over two weeks.

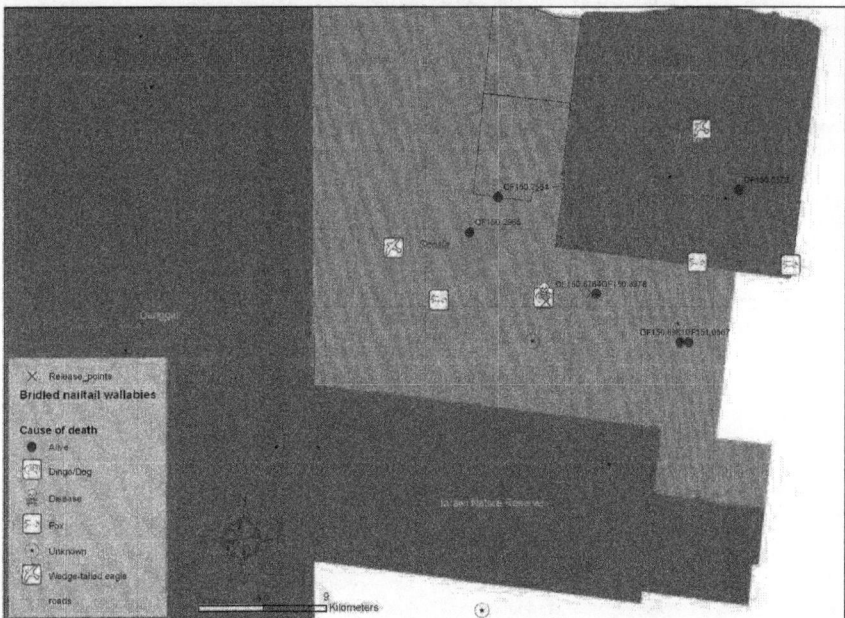

Fig. 4. Map of the locations of dead and living bridled nailtail wallabies and the cause of their death (where known). Scotia is shown in the pale green, with Nanya Station and other government conservation reserves shown in other shades of green. The conservation fences are shown as the black dashed lines to the north-east of Scotia.

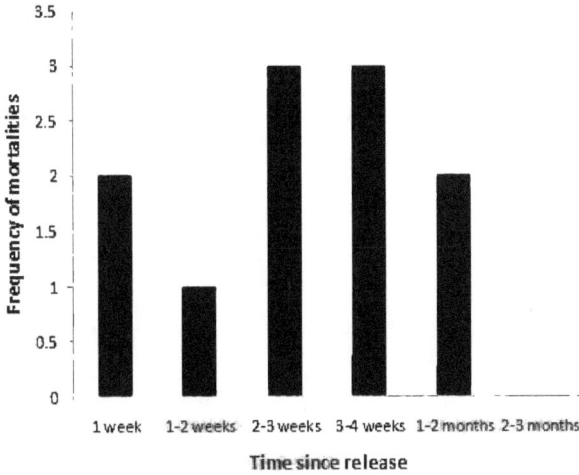

Fig. 5. Survival times of bridled nailtail wallabies after release.

MARK (S(.) model; AIC_c = 142.505, $w = 0.63$) and it yielded similar survivorship estimates of 0.21 (0.11-0.38) probability of surviving throughout the study period. A second known fates model comparing survivorship between individuals at the two release sites exhibited substantial support (ΔAIC_c = 1.400; $w = 0.31$) with animals released at the site with odour provisioned surviving better than those released without odour (Odour $S = 0.27$ (0.11-0.53) cf No Odour $S = 0.16$ (0.06-0.39)), although the overlapping 95%ile confidence intervals suggest any such differences are marginal. Although there appears to be a large dip in survivorship from late September, this is likely to be spread evenly throughout the study period as additional collars in mortality mode were collected following detection during the aerial telemetry survey. Survivorship curves of animals released at the two sites were significantly different with animals released at sites without female odour present dying at a faster rate than those released at sites where odour was provided (log-rank $G = 83.9$, d.f. = 12, $p < 0.001$).

initial naivete reasonably quickly. Animals that died survived an average of 28 days. This rapid mortality rate was significantly different from a uniform mortality rate ($G = 40.5$, d.f. = 5, $p < 0.001$; Fig. 5).

The probability of surviving the three month study period based on the Kaplain-Meier survivorship analysis was 0.29 (Fig. 6). The constant model was the most preferred of the known fates models in Program

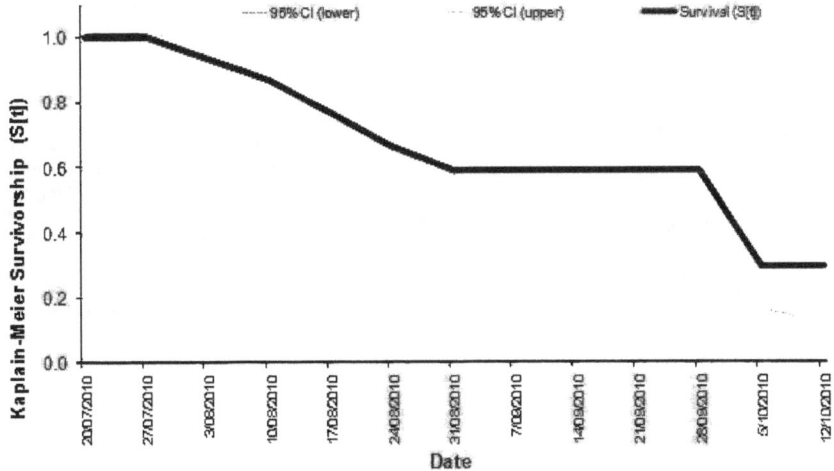

Fig. 6. Kaplain-Meier survivorship values for the 30 male bridled nailtail wallabies released outside fences at Scotia.

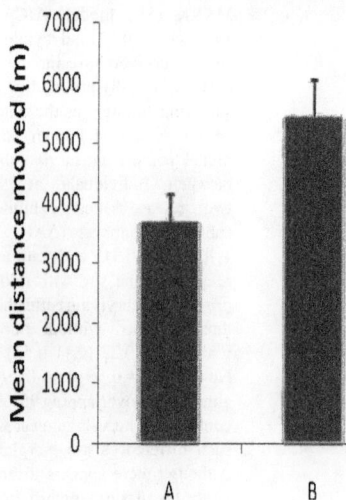

Fig. 7. Mean straight-line distance from the two release sites of released bridled nailtail wallabies at the time of their deaths.

In support of the known fates modelling that found animals from Site A survived marginally better (5 at Site A cf 2 at B), there was a significant difference between the distances moved by animals from the two release sites. Animals released at Site A (odour present) moved shorter distances from the release site (t = -5.59, $d.f.$ = 228, p < 0.001; Fig. 7). BNTWs released at Site A (odour present) also survived longer than those released at Site B (Site A mean ± 1 S.E. = 56 ± 9 days; Site B = 45 ± 10 days), although the small sample size meant this difference was not significant (Mann-Whitney U = 63.5, n = 26, p = 0.288).

At the time of the Phase 1 release, there were 660 (373-1165) BNTWs in the 8000 ha fenced area at Scotia (based on distance sampling estimates), and at least 468 BNTWs in Scotia's captive breeding compound (based on total counts during feeding). Over the three month study period, and fenced population rose to 729 (503-1066), and the captive population size rose to at least 500, despite the removal of the 40 adult males for the translocation.

DISCUSSION

Of the 30 collared male BNTWs released outside the fences at Scotia, only seven survived the first three months. The majority of deaths occurred off-site: of the 13 BNTWs that remained on Scotia throughout this period, 46% survived. Of the 13 BNTWs that moved off Scotia, only one survived. Alternatively, of seven BNTWs known to be alive at the end of three months, six had remained on Scotia, close to their release site. These results illustrate the importance of retaining the BNTW within the area of intensive predator control on Scotia and the value of intense fox control with a variety of strategies (poison baits plus M44s) over a large regional area (Danggali Conservation Park in South Australia, neighbouring leases in NSW).

Previous modelling suggested that the probability of success of BNTW reintroductions would be increased by using larger founder populations than that used here (McCallum, Timmers et al. 1995). However, we began the programme of translocating BNTWs outside Scotia's fenced area with a small group of males. The first release was partly designed to confirm that the habitats outside the conservation fences at Scotia contained sufficient food resources for BNTWs, whilst minimising impact on the breeding potential of the captive colony (hence males were translocated rather than females). All necropsied BNTWs had full stomachs, full bladders and fat stores around the kidneys, suggesting that the habitat quality outside the fenced area was adequate. Furthermore, the habitats in the release area are no different from those inside the conservation fences where populations of BNTWs have thrived since 2006 (Stage 1) and 2008 (Stage 2).

The BNTW is a strongly sexually dimorphic species with adult males almost twice the body mass of adult females (Fisher 1999). This reflects their polygynous mating system where males compete to mate with as many females as possible. The males selected for translocation were full grown and reproductively active, and this probably explains why they travelled long distances in the weeks following their release – they were most likely searching for mating opportunities. This interpretation is supported by the differences in movements and survival demonstrated between group A (released with female odours) and B (without odour). Furthermore, several animals moved back towards the feral-free fenced area, in which females occurred. Other explanations for the continued expansive movements of the adult males, such as seeking new foraging opportunities, seem unlikely given the abundance of available forage following well above average rainfall during the release.

Wedge-tailed eagles are natural predators of BNTW and they killed two during the three month monitoring period. Given the source population of

A34

Proc. Linn. Soc. N.S.W., 134, 2012

BNTWs in the Captive Breeding Compound regularly face this predation risk, it is unlikely that they are naive to eagles. Nonetheless, one of the males that was killed by a wedge-tailed eagle travelled 12 km before stopping beneath an eyrie.

At least two animals died from pneumonia. This could be prevented with prophylactic antibiotic treatment. However, discussions with the veterinarian suggested the costs of such treatment could cause as much harm (through loss of gut bacteria) as no treatment. On veterinary advice, we do not anticipate treating animals in future releases and, indeed, the translocation of associated fauna (e.g. gut parasites of Tasmanian devils *Sarcophilus harrisii*) is now recommended during reintroduction programmes (Burbidge, Byrne et al. 2011).

We used faeces and urine-soaked soil in a trial to encourage male BNTWs to remain close to the release site through thinking females in oestrus may have been present. This approach has been used for other species like black rhinoceros *Diceros bicornis* and African wild dogs *Lycaon pictus* (Borg 2010; Linklater, Flamand et al. 2006). Male BNTWs released at the site with odours tended to remain closer to their release site and survived better. In addition, refreshing the soil more frequently may have enhanced the effect.

Earlier work shows that an annual survivorship of at least 33% is necessary for BNTWs to replace themselves annually (females produce 3 young per year), but much lower is required for replacement over their 6 year lifespan (Fisher 1999). Our three month survivorship is clearly much lower than this annual value. Nonetheless, we propose retaining this threshold in future phases of the translocation programme because of the hypothesised rapid initial decline in translocated animals as they are naïve to local threats before their survivorship improves.

An important lesson from this first release has been that philopatry is critical if animals are to benefit from the protection of the extensive feral predator control programme on Scotia and neighbouring properties. Consequently, the next release of BNTWs at Scotia will include females. Scotia already protects over 70% of the entire population of BNTWs in Australia, and the population trends of the three small sub-populations in Queensland are stable to declining (AWC *unpubl. data*). Expanding the area of occupancy, and thus the population size, of BNTWs at Scotia is critical to the longer-term survival of this species.

ACKNOWLEDGEMENTS

The authors thank Mike Saxon, Damon Oliver and Brendon Neilly from the NSW Office of Environment and Heritage for their support. This translocation and the associated monitoring would not have been possible without the support of numerous supporters. This project was conducted under Ethics Approvals 10/3876 and 08/8469 from the Department of Industry and Investment and Scientific Licence number S13156 from the then NSW Department of Environment, Climate Change and Water. This manuscript was improved by reviews by Mike Augee and one anonymous referee.

REFERENCES

Allen, L., Engeman, R.M., and Krupa, H. (1996) Evaluation of three relative abundance indices for assessing dingo populations. *Wildlife Research* **23**, 197-206.

Anderson, D.R. (2001) The need to get the basics right in wildlife field studies. *Wildlife Society Bulletin* **29**, 1294-1297.

Armstrong, R. (2004) Baiting operations: Western Shield review - February 2003. *Conservation Science Western Australia* **5**, 31-50.

Augee, M.L., Smith, B. and Rose, S. (1996) Survival of wild and hand-reared ringtail possums (*Pseudocheirus peregrinus*) in bushland near Sydney. *Wildlife Research* **23**, 99-108.

Barnosky, A.D., Matzke, N., Tomiya, S., Wogan, G.O.U., Swartz, B., Quental, T.B., Marshall, C., McGuire, J.L., Lindsey, E.L., Maguire, K.C., Mersey, B. and Ferrer, E.A. (2011). Has the Earth's sixth mass extinction already arrived? Nature 471, 51-57.

Borg, E. (2010) Going to the dogs. *African Geographic* **18**, 26-31.

Burbidge, A.A. (2004) Montebello Renewal : Western Shield review - February 2003. *Conservation Science Western Australia* **5**, 194-201.

Burbidge, A.A., Byrne, M., Coates, D., Harris, S., Hayward, M.W., Nally, S. and Setterfield, S. (2011) Assisted colonisation: adapting to climate change impacts. *Pacific Conservation Biology* **In press**, Accepted 25 June 2011.

Burbidge, A.A. and McKenzie, N.L. (1989) Patterns in the modern decline of Western Australia's vertebrate fauna: causes and conservation implications. *Biological Conservation* **50**, 143-198.

Burbidge, A.A., Williams, M.R. and Abbott, I. (1997) Mammals of Australian islands: factors influencing species richness. *Journal of Biogeography* **24**, 703-715.

Dickman, C.R. (2011) Fences or ferals? Benefits and costs of conservation fencing in Australia. In 'Fencing for

Conservation'. (Eds MJ Somers and MW Hayward) pp. 43-64. (Springer: New York, U.S.A.)

Dickman, C.R., Coles, J.N. and Drew, J.M. (1992) Conservation of mammals in the Australasian region: the importance of islands. In 'Australia and the Global Environmental Crisis' pp. 175-214. (Academic Press: Canberra)

Finlayson, G.R., Vieira, E.M., Priddel, D., Wheeler, R., Bentley, J.M. and Dickman, C.R. (2008) Multi-scale patterns of habitat use by re-introduced mammals: a case study using medium-sized marsupials. *Biological Conservation* **141**, 320-331.

Fisher, D.O. (1999) Behavioural Ecology and Demography of the Bridled Nailtail Wallaby *Onychogalea fraenata.*, University of Queensland.

Fitzsimons, J., Legge, S., Traill, B.J. and Woinarski, J.C.Z. (2010) 'Into Oblivion? The Disappearing Native Mammals of Northern Australia.' The Nature Conservancy, Melbourne.

Hayward, M.W. (2002) The ecology of the quokka (*Setonix brachyurus*) (Macropodidae: Marsupialia) in the northern jarrah forest of Australia. PhD thesis thesis, University of New South Wales.

Hayward, M.W. (2011) Using the IUCN Red List to determine effective conservation strategies. *Biodiversity and Conservation* **20**, 2563-2573 doi: 10.1007/s10531-011-0091-3.

Hayward, M.W. (2012) Perspectives on fencing for conservation based on four case studies: marsupial conservation in Australian forests; bushmeat hunting in South Africa; large predator reintroduction in South Africa; and large mammal conservation in Poland. In 'Fencing for Conservation'. (Eds MJ Somers and MW Hayward) pp. 7-21. (Springer-US: New York)

Hayward, M.W., de Tores, P.J., Augee, M.L. and Banks, P.B. (2005) Mortality and survivorship of the quokka (*Setonix brachyurus*) (Macropodidae: Marsupialia) in the northern jarrah forest of Western Australia. *Wildlife Research* **32**, 715-722.

Hayward, M.W., de Tores, P.J., Augee, M.L., Fox, B.J. and Banks, P.B. (2004) Home range and movements of the quokka *Setonix brachyurus* (Macropodidae: Marsupialia), and its impact on the viability of the metapopulation on the Australian mainland. *Journal of Zoology* **263**, 219-228.

Hayward, M.W., Herman, K. and Mulder, E. (2010) Update of Australian Wildlife Conservancy Re-introductions. *Reintroduction Specialist Group e-Newsletter* **1**, 11-12.

Hayward, M.W., Legge, S., Parsons, B.C., Page, M.J., Herman, K. and Mulder, E. (2010) Woylie *Bettongia penicillata* (Potoroidae: Marsupialia) reintroduction as part of the Australian WIldlife Conservancy's Endangered Species Recovery Programme at Scotia Sanctuary, far western New South Wales, Australia. In 'Global Re-introduction Perspectives: 2010: Additional Case Studies from Around the Globe.'. (Ed. PS Soorae) pp. 202-207. (IUCN Species Survival Commission's Reintroduction Specialist Group: Abu Dhabi, UAE)

Hayward, M.W., Moseby, K.E. and Read, J.L. (2012) The role of predator exclosures in the conservation of Australian fauna. In 'Carnivores of Australia: Past, Present and Future.'. (Eds AS Glen and CR Dickman) pp. In press. (CSIRO Publishing: Heidelberg, Melbourne, Australia)

Johnson, C.N. (2006) 'Australia's Mammal Extinctions: a 50,000 Year History.' (CSIRO Publishing: Canberra, Australia)

Kinnear, J.E., Bromilow, R.N., Onus, M.L. and Sokolowski, R.E.S. (1988) The Bromilow trap: a new risk-free soft trap suitable for small to medium-sized macropodids. *Australian Wildlife Research* **15**, 235-237.

Kinnear, J.E., Sumner, N.R. and Onus, M.L. (2002) The red fox in Australia - an exotic predator turned biocontrol agent. *Biological Conservation* **108**, 335-359.

Linklater, W.L., Flamand, J., Rochat, Q., Zekela, N., Macdonald, E.A., Swaisgood, R.R., Airton, D.F., Kelly, C.P., Bond, K., Schmidt, I. and Morgan, S. (2006) Preliminary analyses of the free-release and scent-broadcasting strategies for black rhinoceros reintroduction. Ecological Journal 7, 26-35.

MacFarland, D.M. and Van Deelen, T.R. (2011) Using simulation to explore the functional relationships of terrestrial carnivore population indices. *Ecological Modelling* **222**, 2761-2769.

MacKenzie, D.I., Nichols, J.D., Royle, J.A., Pollock, K.H. and Bailey, L.L. (2006) 'Occupancy Estimation and Modelling: Inferring Patterns and Dynamics of Species Occurrence.' (Elsevier: London, U.K.)

McCallum, H.I., Timmers, P. and Hoyle, S. (1995) Modelling the impact of predation on reintroductions of bridled nailtail wallabies. *Wildlife Research* **22**, 163-171.

Murray, A., Poore, R.N. and Dexter, N. (2006) 'Project Deliverance - The Response of 'Critical Weight Range' Mammals to Effective Fox Control in Mesic Forest Habitats in Far East Gippsland, Victoria.' Department of Sustainability and Environment, Melbourne, Victoria.

Nams, V.O. (1990) 'Locate II User's Guide.' (Pacer Computer Software: Truro, Nova Scotia)

Pollock, K.H., Winterstein, S.R., Bunck, C.M. and Curtis, P.D. (1989) Survival analysis in telemetry studies: the staggered entry design. *Journal of Wildlife Management* **53**, 7-15.

Possingham, H.P., Jarman, P. and Kearns, A. (2004) Independent review of Western Shield - February 2003. *Conservation Science Western Australia* **5**, 2-11.

Schipper, J., Chanson, J.S., Chiozza, F., Hoffmann, M., Katariya, V., Lamoreux, J., Rodrigues, A.S.L., Stuart, S.N., Temple, H.J., Boitani, L., Lacher, T.E., Mittermeier, R.A., Smith, A.T., Absolon, D., Aguiar, J.M., Amori, G., Bakkour, N., Baldi, R., Berridge,

A36

Proc. Linn. Soc. N.S.W., 134, 2012

R.J., Black, P.A., Blanc, J.J., Brooks, T.M., Burton, J.A., Butynski, T.M., Catullo, G., Chapman, R., Cokeliss, Z., Collen, B., Conroy, J., Cooke, J.G., Fonseca, G.A.B.d., Derocher, A.E., Dublin, H.T., Duckworth, J.W., Emmons, L., Emslie, R.H., Festa-Bianchet, M., Foster, M., Foster, S., Garshelis, D.L., Gates, C., Gimenez-Dixon, M., Gonzalez, S., Gonzalez-Maya, J.F., Good, T.C., Hammerson, G., Hammond, P.S., Happold, D., Happold, M., Hare, J., Harris, R.B., Hawkins, C.E., Haywood, M., Heaney, L.R., Hedges, S., Helgen, K.M., Hilton-Taylor, C., Hussain, S.A., Ishii, N., Jefferson, T.A., Jenkins, R.K.B., Johnston, C.H., Kingdon, J., Knox, D.H., Kovacs, K.M., Langhammer, P., Leus, K., Lewison, R., Lichtenstein, G., Lowry, L.F., Macavoy, Z., Mace, G.M., Mallon, D.P., Masi, M., McKnight, M.W., Medellan, R.A., Medici, P., Mills, M.G.L., Moehlman, P.D., Molur, S., Mora, A., Nowell, K., Oates, J.F., Olech, W., Oliver, W.R.L., Oprea, M., Patterson, B.D., Perrin, W.F., Polidoro, B.A., Pollock, C., Powel, A., Protas, Y., Racey, P., Ragle, J., Ramani, P., Rathbun, G., Reeves, R.R., Reilly, S.B., Reynolds, J.E., Rondinini, C., Rosell-Ambal, R.G., Rulli, M., Rylands, A.B., Savini, S., Schank, C.J., Sechrest, W., Self-Sullivan, C., Shoemaker, A., Sillero-Zubiri, C., Silva, N.D., Smith, D.E., Srinivasulu, C., Stephenson, P.J., Strien, N.v., Talukdar, B.K., Taylor, B.L., Timmins, R., Tirira, D.G., Tognelli, M.F., Tsytsulina, K., Veiga, L.M., Via, J.-C., Williamson, E.A., Wyatt, S.A., Xie, Y. and Young, B.E., (2008). The status of the world's land and marine mammals: diversity, threat and knowledge. Science 322, 225-231.

Short, J. (2009) 'The characteristics and success of vertebrate translocations within Australia.' Department of Agriculture, Fisheries and Forestry, Canberra, Australia.

Short, J., Bradshaw, S.D., Giles, J., Prince, R.I.T. and Wilson, G.R. (1992) Reintroduction of macropods (Marsupialia: Macropodoidea) in Australia - a review. *Biological Conservation* **62**, 189-204.

Short, J. and Smith, A.P. (1994) Mammal decline and recovery in Australia. *Journal of Mammalogy* **75**, 288-297.

Short, J., Turner, B., Parker, S. and Twiss, J. (1994) Reintroduction of endangered mammals to mainland Shark Bay: a progress report. In 'Reintroduction Biology of Australian and New Zealand Fauna'. (Ed. M Serena) pp. 183-188. (Surrey Beatty & Sons: Chipping Norton, Australia)

White, G.C. and Burnham, K.P. (1999) Program MARK: survival estimation from populations of marked animals. *Bird Study* **46 (supplement)**, S120-139.

Woinarski, J.C.Z., Armstrong, M., Brennan, K.E.C., Fisher, A., Griffiths, A.D., Hill, B.M., Milne, D.J., Palmer, C.L., Ward, S., Watson, M., Winderlich, S. and Young, S.S. (2010). Monitoring indicates rapid and severe decline of native small mammals in Kakadu National Park, northern Australia. Wildlife Research 37, 116-126.

Proc. Linn. Soc. N.S.W., 134, 2012

A37

The Influence of Fire, Herbivores and Rainfall on Vegetation Dynamics in the Mallee: a Long-term Experiment

DAVID A. KEITH[1,2] AND MARK. G. TOZER[2]

[1]Australian Wetlands and Rivers Centre, University of New South Wales, Sydney 2052, Australia.
[2]NSW Office of Environment and Heritage, PO Box 1967, Hurstville 2220, Australia.

Published on 28 August 2012 at http://escholarship.library.usyd.edu.au/journals/index.php/LIN

Keith, D.A. and Tozer, M.G. (2012), The influence of fire, herbivores and rainfall on vegetation dynamics in the mallee: a long-term experiment. *Proceedings of the Linnean Society of New South Wales* **134**, A39-A54.

Fire regimes, grazing regimes and climatic variation potentially influence the distribution and abundance of plant species in the mallee over long time scales. For example, the timing of fires and rainfall events influences the establishment of many plant species, while herbivory and drought have selective effects on plant survival. Rainfall events influence short-term bushfire fuel dynamics and, with herbivores, determine landscape flammability. The frequency and spatial pattern of fire regimes have been identified as important management tools that may influence the persistence of mallee biota. A long term ecological experiment has been established in the Tarawi-Scotia-Danggali reserves to improve understanding of the mechanisms that influence vegetation change and the ability of the ecosystem to sustain its characteristic biota. Herbivore-specific grazing exclosures were established in tandem with planned management burning and some unplanned fires over a 12-year period. In this paper we outline the management issues and research questions that the study seeks to address, describe the design of the experiment and the data collected from the treated sites. We discuss the strengths and weaknesses of the experiment and the valuable insights that long term ecological studies of this type can produce.

Manuscript received 11 October 2011, accepted for publication 1 June 2012.

KEYWORDS: adaptive management, desert, experimental design, fire regimes, grazing, long term ecological research, management experiment, monitoring, rainfall variability, Scotia.

INTRODUCTION

Ecosystems change over time scales that vary from days to centuries. The pathways and rates of change are influenced by environmental conditions, biotic interactions, disturbance events and anthropogenic processes (Pickett and White 1985; Likens 1992; Hooper et al. 2005). Understanding how these processes operate is fundamental to informed management of ecosystems to conserve their biodiversity and maintain the services they provide to human industry and well being (Millenium Assessment 2005).

Arid and semi-arid ecosystems are notable for their relative stability punctuated by episodic boom/bust events that may leave long-lasting legacies (Bestelmeyer et al. 2009; Morton et al. 2011). Understanding the cause-effect relationships of dynamics in these systems is challenging because

many changes play out over long time scales that extend beyond the span of human lives and practicable ecological observational studies. Furthermore, these systems exhibit highly stochastic dynamics, with high levels of variability making it difficult to draw generalisations about how ecosystems may respond to particular scenarios of environmental events and human activity.

Productive insights into the mechanisms that drive ecosystem dynamics require thoughtful design of ecological investigations that permit systematic probing of causal agents, preferably under a range of conditions and over appropriate time scales (Likens 1989; Walters and Holling 1990; Lindenmayer and Likens 2010a). A systematic comparison of ecosystem responses to experimental probing is central to adaptive management approaches that seek to learn by doing (Walters and Holling 1990; Keith et al. 2011). Long-term ecological studies with their experimental design focussed on processes relevant to ecosystem management are well suited to adaptive management approaches (Walters and Holling 1990; Lindenmayer and Likens 2010b) and there is renewed interest in the benefits that these studies can bring to environmental management in Australia (Likens and Lindenmayer 2011; Lindenmayer et al. in press).

In this paper, we describe a landscape scale experiment that seeks to produce insights into the dynamics of semi-arid mallee vegetation. The study is located on the extensive red sand dune landscapes in the Scotia district of far south-western New South Wales and adjacent areas of South Australia. We first briefly review the roles of fire regimes, herbivory and rainfall in mallee vegetation dynamics. We use this as context to outline some salient questions about mechanisms of change that led to the establishment of the experiment. We then describe the study area and the experimental design, with an appraisal of its strengths and weaknesses. We conclude by considering how this type of long term ecological research can contribute to informed management of mallee ecosystems, and to a broader research infrastructure that can help to discover fundamental principles about the behaviour of ecosystems.

AGENTS OF ECOSYSTEM CHANGE

Fire regimes

Mallee woodlands are fire prone (Noble et al. 1980; Bradstock and Cohn 2002). Fires vary in size up to several thousand hectares and may return at intervals that vary from decadal to centennial scales. They may consume most or all of the standing biomass, although spatial patterns may be complex, partly because flammable mallee vegetation is juxtaposed with non-flammable belah woodland (*Casuarina pauper*) and partly because mallee vegetation is less flammable in swales than on dunes (Bradstock and Cohn 2002).

Four main components of the vegetation produce biomass that varies in its flammability and its distribution in space and time. Throughout the landscape, the dominant eucalypts contribute aerial fuels and well-aerated ground fuels comprising leaves, twigs and branches. Hummock grasses, which are most abundant on dune slopes and crests, are highly flammable surface fuels. They are typically absent from the dune swales, which are generally dominated by less flammable shrubs at varying densities. Ephemeral grasses emerge periodically in abundance after substantial rains and, when cured,

may contribute a substantial additional surface fuel throughout the system (Noble and Vines 1993).

A wide range of mallee shrubs and forbs are killed outright by fire, regenerating only from seed stored on site or dispersed from other areas (seeders), while others are equipped with vegetative recovery organs from which they may resprout new shoot biomass during the months after fire (sprouters). Many mallee plant species have seed banks that remain dormant and viable in the soil for varying lengths of time (Auld 1995a). A few species have serotinous seedbanks in which seed are retained in woody fruits for two or more years and released gradually thereafter or *en masse* when the stems are killed by fire (Wellington and Noble 1985; Bradstock and Cohn 2002b). Fires provide an important stimulus for seedling recruitment in many mallee plants, although the germination response varies greatly between different fire events. The timing of fires in relation to seed bank development is a crucial determinant of recruitment and population persistence (Keith 2011). The timing of fires also influences the suitability of habitat for a range of mallee animals. While interval and event characteristics of the fire regime affect the abundance of plants that provide particular resources such as nectar and shelter, time since fire also influences habitat suitability through the structural development of features such as loose bark and hollows associated with mallee stems and the development and degeneration of spinifex hummocks that provide shelter for various mammals, reptiles and macroinvertebrates (Haslem et al. 2011).

Herbivory

Native, feral and domestic herbivores inhabit mallee landscapes. The primary native species are large macropods including *Macropus fuliginosus* (Western Grey Kangaroo), *M. robustus* (Euro) and *M. rufus* (Red Kangaroo). In addition, the regionally extinct *Onychogalea fraenata* (Bridled Nail-tail Wallaby) has been re-introduced within large enclosures in Scotia Sanctuary. Feral herbivores include *Oryctolagus cuniculus* (Rabbit) and *Capra hircus* (Goat), while *Ovus aries* (Sheep), *Bos primigenius* (Cattle) and *C. hircus* are the main domestic livestock in the Scotia region. While the diets of these herbivores differ, consumption of plant biomass by herbivores can limit rates of survival, growth, reproduction and recruitment in palatable species (Crisp and Lange 1976, Auld 1995b) and shift the composition of communities towards dominance by unpalatable species (Landsberg et al. 2003). Herbivore activity may also involve substantial soil disturbance which, combined with the effects of reduced vegetation cover, may expose unconsolidated soils to erosion by wind (Beadle 1948). Severe episodes and symptoms of erosion associated with overgrazing are well documented in western New South Wales. The Scotia district may have been less affected than most areas due to the relatively late arrival of domestic livestock and relatively low stocking rates (Westbrooke this issue).

Important interactions are postulated between herbivory and fire (Noble et al. 2007; Keith 2011). Young post-fire plant growth may be more palatable to herbivores than older biomass due to reduced chemical and physical defences and higher nutritional content (Keith 2011). Plants exposed to elevated rates of herbivory in the post-fire environment are more prone to mortality (Walker et al. 1981; Hodgkinson and Cook 1995). Herbivores may move into recently burnt areas, increasing the impact on prey populations (e.g. Isaac et al. 2008). Consequently, vegetation within small burnt areas or around the margins of large burnt areas may suffer greater impacts than vegetation within the interior of large burnt areas (Keith 2011).

Rainfall variability

Arid climates are noted not only for low average rainfall, but high variability in rainfall between years (van Etten 2009). Extended drought periods punctuated by rainfall events of varying magnitude regulate cyclic transitions of a large ephemeral flora from dormant seedbanks to standing plant phases (Morton et al. 2011). Large infrequent rainfall events also provide cues for the recruitment of long-lived perennial plants (Watson et al. 1997; Lopez et al. 2008). Rainfall events of varying sizes also produce flushes of biomass, fruits and seeds which, together with enhanced supply of moisture, support population growth in higher trophic levels (Morton et al. 2011).

Three-way interactions are likely to exist between rainfall variability, herbivore populations and fire activity (Noble and Vines 1993; Morton et al. 2011). Large rainfall events may be antecedent to extensive fires, as growth of ephemeral vegetation enhances fuel connectivity permitting fire spread over a wider range of fire weather conditions than is normally possible (Noble and Vines 1993; Bradstock and Cohn 2002a). Increased availability of forage promotes higher densities of herbivores either through opportunistic breeding to generate population growth or nomadism that enables immigration into transient resource-rich patches (Caughley et al. 1987; Morton et al. 2011). As water availability declines, herbivores exploit plant

forage more heavily and their populations decline as the resource becomes scarce.

Research questions

The synopsis above poses a number of questions about mallee ecosystem dynamics, for which answers are needed to inform management strategies that seek to conserve mallee biodiversity. Ecological experiments provide a powerful means of developing such a knowledge base to support biodiversity management. In Table 1 we summarise some of the salient management issues and research questions about mallee vegetation dynamics as a prelude to describing the experimental design of our study.

Management concern about the effects of long fire intervals was an early motivation for our study. Parts of the district have gone without fire for almost a century (see below) and plant species richness of the standing vegetation in those areas is conspicuously lower than that of vegetation that had been burnt during the past 30 years. It seems likely that many of the plant species present in more recently burnt areas had disappeared above ground from long-unburnt areas as their standing plants senesced. These species may persist in the soil seed bank, but how long would the seed remain viable and able to re-establish standing plant populations? If soil seed banks were decaying appreciably over these long intervals and seed dispersal is limited, management fires may be required to avoid local extinctions of the affected plant species. To provide advice on this management problem, we compared the species composition of early post-fire vegetation after a number of prescribed fires carried out for protection purposes in areas that had last been burnt 20-30 years ago and >80 years ago. While preliminary results suggested that regeneration capacity was similar across this range of fire histories, the investigation illuminated a complex suite of management issues that require long-term ecological research to resolve (Table 1).

EXPERIMENTAL DESIGN

Study area and landscape

The study is located in the red aeolian sand dunefield landscape of the Scotia district within Tarawi Nature Reserve (33.44°S 141.16°E), Scotia Wildlife Sanctuary (33°17'S 141°05'E) and Danggali Nature Reserve (33° 22' S 140° 45' E) in south-western New South Wales and adjacent area of South Australia (Fig. 1). The study area sits on the south-eastern edge of the Australian arid zone. This location is close to

Proc. Linn. Soc. N.S.W., 134, 2012

A41

Table 1. Management issues and research questions related to mallee vegetation dynamics.

	Management issue	Research question
1	Long fire intervals	Does plant diversity decline with long intervals between successive fires?
2	Short fire intervals	How long does it take mallee trees and shrub species to build up seed banks after fire?
3	Diversity relationships between standing vegetation and soil seed banks	How closely does species composition of soil seedbanks resemble that of standing vegetation? Do sites with similar standing vegetation also have compositionally similar seedbanks?
4	Plant persistence	How does survivorship and fecundity of different plant species vary with time since fire?
5	Generalising plant responses to fire	How are differential responses to fire between plant species related to their life history traits?
6	Differential effects of herbivore species	Do different herbivore species have contrasting effects on standing vegetation?
7	Interaction between fire and hebivores	How does herbivore activity vary with time since fire?
8	Spatial pattern of fires	How does fire size affect post-fire herbivory by vertebrates?
9	Interactive effects of fire and rainfall on vegetation	Can varied vegetation responses to different fires be explained by inter-annual variation in rainfall?
10	Recruitment of woody plants	How does variability in fire events and climate affect seedling recruitment?
11	Drought	How does soil moisture vary with temperature and antecedent rainfall?

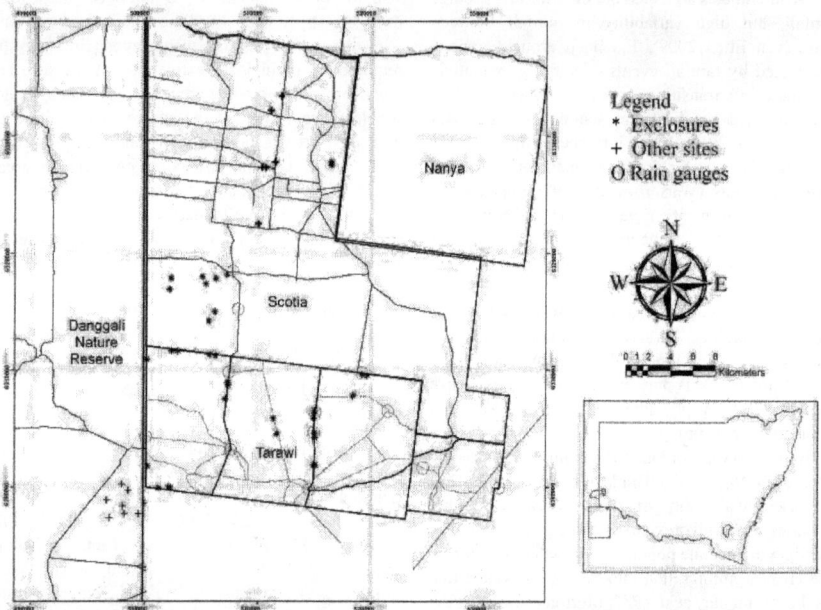

Figure 1. Location of experimental sites within Tarawi Nature Reserve, Scotia Wildlife Sanctuary and Danggali Nature Reserve study area

A42

Proc. Linn. Soc. N.S.W., 134, 2012

the arid limits of distribution of the mallee woodland biome, which stretches across the temperate semi-arid belt of southern Australia (Noble 1984). Mallee woodlands typically occur within regions receiving 200-500 mm rainfall per year. During 1940-2010, mean annual rainfall at Tarawi Homestead was approximately 240 mm, with an average of 209 mm in the last decade (data summary courtesy of John Warren, Tarawi NR).

In the Scotia district and its surrounding region, mallee woodlands occur within a landscape mosaic that includes patches of woodland dominated by *Casuarina pauper* (Belah) and shrublands dominated by *Maireana sedifolia* and *M. pyramidata* (bluebush) (Westbrooke et al. 1998). These latter vegetation types occur on gently undulating sandplains with a calcareous crust not far below the soil surface. In contrast, mallee woodlands dominate transverse east-west oriented dunefields. The dunes are characterised by deep red sandy loams dominated by *Eucalyptus socialis* (Pointed mallee), *E. dumosa* and *E. costata*, occasionally with *Callitris verrucosa*, with a mixed understorey of hummock grasses and shrubs and a largely ephemeral ground layer of tussock grasses and forbs. The intervening swales have finer textured red loams and generally support a wider range of eucalypts including *E. oleosa* and *E. gracilis*, but *C. verrucosa* is absent. Their understoreys typically include a higher density and diversity of shrubs but lack hummock grasses and the ground layer is typically sparse. Detailed descriptions of vegetation and landscapes are included in Westbrooke et al. (1998).

This study focussed on vegetation dynamics on dune crests and upper slopes, primarily because resources were insufficient to sample across the full catenary sequence of dunes and swales. Study of swale landforms was problematic because these are rarely flammable under prescribed fire conditions due to the absence of hummock grasses, which augment lateral fuel connectivity and thus promote fire spread on the dune crests and slopes.

Experimental sites and treatments

Fifty-three experimental sites were established on dune crests and upper slopes during 1996 - 2011 (Appendix 1), of which 29 are located within Tarawi NR, with 16 in Scotia and eight in Danggali NR (Figure 1). In Tarawi NR, each is marked with a steel sign on an adjacent access track. These include four pilot sites established during 1996-1998, during which the design of herbivore exclosures were developed. All but one of the 53 sites (1998/CON1) were

burnt, either in prescribed fires (33 sites) or wildfires (19 sites). Prescribed fires varied in area from 1 - 70 ha, whereas wildfires varied in area from 70 ha to 3000 ha (Appendix 1). Prescribed fires were implemented in 2000, 2001, 2003, 2005, 2006, 2009, 2010 and 2011. The 33 sites were stratified across this chronosequence, with 4 sites sampled in each burn year except 2005 (5 sites), 2009 and 2010 (2 sites each) and 2011 (8 sites). For each burn year, the sites were stratified between locations with different prior fire histories; half had previously been long unburnt (1917 or earlier) and half had been unburnt for 20-30 years (1979-1984). However, the four sites sampling prescribed burns in Scotia in 2010 only sampled a single fire history (Appendix 1).

Three surveys were undertaken in successive years at the time of treatment for all sites burnt in prescribed fires except the four sites burnt in 2010 within Scotia Sanctuary. These sites to be burnt in prescribed fires were initially marked out and surveyed one to three months prior to burning treatment (pre-fire survey). Within one to three months of burning treatment, they were fenced to exclude all vertebrate herbivores. A second survey (post-fire survey) was carried out approximately one year after the first survey. Within one to two months of the second survey, fences were modified to allow access to selected hebivores into compartments of the exclosures (see details below). During the second survey, additional plots were recorded outside the exclosures where herbivores had continual access to the vegetation prior to and after burning. A third survey (post-grazing survey) was carried out within and outside the exclosures approximately one year after the second survey. Pre-fire surveys could not be carried out at any sites burnt in wildfires. The eight sites in Danggali NR were not fenced to exclude herbivores and consequently only one post-fire post-grazing survey was carried out, equivalent to the external plots carried out on the third annual visit to the other sites.

Grazing exclosures were constructed at all sites except those in Dangalli NP and the Scotia Sanctuary sites burnt in 2009 and 2010. The latter site was within the Scotia Stage 1 fenced area from which goats and rabbits had been eliminated, kangaroos were at low densities and in which Bilbies, Numbats and Burrowing Bettongs had been introduced (Tony Cathcart, Australian Wildlife Conservancy, pers. comm.). The design of all exclosures constructed since year 2000 (inclusive) followed the layout in Fig. 2. Each comprised five contiguous fenced cells 15 m square. Initially all five cells were closed to all vertebrate herbivores for approximately a year after their construction. The basic fence design

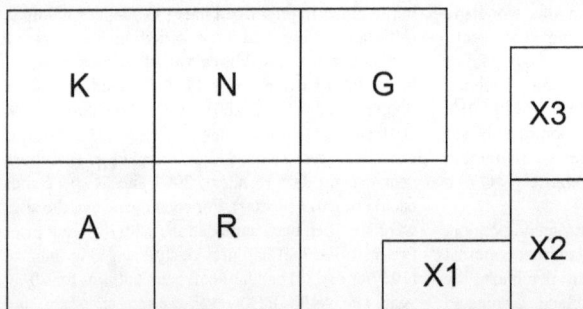

Figure 2. Standard layout of grazing exclosures at each site (K: Kangaroo entry only, A: All in, unrestricted access, N: None in, total exclusion, R: Rabbit entry only, G: Goat entry, X1 – X3: unrestricted access). Goat entry was facilitated using wooden ramps but this has proven ineffective and no goats entered these cells, which therefore replicate the total exclusion treatment. Each of the cells K, A, N, R, G, were closed to all herbivores for one year after fire, and then opened to all entry to respective herbivores. Plots X1-X3 remained unfenced throughout, allowing continuous access to all herbivores.

comprised treated pine posts at each corner, four star pickets along each side with two droppers per panel between pickets supporting a 1.8 m tall sheep mesh wire fencing with chicken mesh covering the lower 0.6 m of vertical fall and turned outward at ground level to a further 0.6 m lateral apron. After being surveyed at the end of this period total, the fences of respective cells were modified to allow selective access to different combinations of vertebrate herbivores as shown in Fig. 3. One cell was retained in an unmodified state as a total exclusion treatment (None plot). In a second cell, the chicken wire mesh was removed from two sides, leaving a gap of 0.6 m beneath the sheep wire mesh and allowing access to macropods, goats and rabbits (All plot). In a third cell, the sheep mesh was removed from two sides leaving a 0.6 m tall chicken mesh fence, allowing access to macropods but not goats or rabbits (Kangaroo plot). In a fourth cell, the mesh apron was lifted and pinned to the fence, leaving a 10 cm gap at the base of the 1.8 m tall fence, allowing access to rabbits, but not macropods or goats (Rabbit plot). The fifth cell was designed to allow access to goats, but not macropods or rabbits (Goat plot). A wooden ramp 30cm wide was constructed on the outside of the exclosure leading to a gap in the upper part of the fence 1.2 m above ground level in one corner of the plot. A similar ramp was constructed on the opposite corner of the cell, but with the ramp installed on the inside allowing exit from the cell. Subsequent scat counts indicated that

neither goats, macropods or rabbits gained access to this cell, so that in practice Goat plots functioned as a second total exclusion treatment (cf. None plot). In addition, three external plots 13 m x 7.5 m were established outside and 7.5 m from the exclosure fence, where all vertebrate herbivores had continual access to the vegetation before and after burning treatment.

The standard exclosure layout was not followed at the four pilot sites established prior to year 2000 (Appendix 1). T1996/1 had a single-celled exclosure comprising a 1.8 m fence with 0.6 m ground apron to exclude all vertebrate herbivores (None plot). T1997/1, T1997/2 and T1998/CON1 comprised four cells as described above for the None, All, Kangaroo and Rabbit plots, except that all vertebrates were initially excluded using an electric fence constructed 2 m outside the perimeter of the exclosure fence and powered by 12-Volt batteries. The electric perimeter fences were dismantled 1.5 - 2.5 years after construction to allow access to respective herbivores.

Collectively, the experiment established a set of sites that sampled a chronosequence of fire ages crossed with different grazing treatments and sampled sequentially before and after implementation of the treatments (Table 2). In addition to the sequence of three surveys carried out during establishment of the plots, an additional contemporaneous survey was carried out in spring 2011 at a random selection of 15 sites stratified by year of establishment and burn history.

Response variables and sampling protocol

The density (number of individuals per unit area) of each vascular plant species was recorded in every plot. Counts of each species were partitioned into: live reproductive plants; live non-reproductive established plants; fire-killed established plants; plants that had emerged as seedlings or resprouted after fire and subsequently died; live seedlings less than 2 years of age; and dead seedlings.

The density of macropod, goat and rabbit scats

Figure 3. Example of cellular exclosure fencing allowing selective access to different mammalian herbivores. Site T2005/5 at third census, two years after burn treatment and one year after exclosures opened to allow selective herbivore access. Note A plot (foreground right) with negligible cover of tussock grasses and soil disturbance from numerous footprints of goats and kangaroos; K plot (foreground left) with open cover of tussock grasses; R plot (background right) with very sparse cover of tussock grasses; and N plot (background left) with abundant tussock grasses and other ground layer plants. G plot is obscured from view (far background left).

was recorded in all plots as an approximate measure of herbivore activity.

In the contemporaneous survey carried out in spring 2011, several parameters estimating vegetation structure were visually estimated in each exclosure cell and external plot. These included: tree cover and height range (single estimate per plot); shrub height (single estimate of median and range per plot); shrub cover (5 5×3 m subplots per plot); hummock grass cover (5 subplots per plot); hummock grass height (10 randomly selected individuals per plot); ephemeral grass cover (5 subplots per plot); leaf and twig litter cover (5 subplots per plot); and bare ground cover (5 subplots per plot).

Seedling cohorts of *Eucalyptus* and *Callitris* that emerged after fires in 1996, 1997, 2005 and 2006 were marked with uniquely numbered metal tags and monitored for survival, growth and reproduction in subsequent years.

Environmental monitoring

Automatic weather stations were established at Tarawi Homestead and Scotia Sanctuary homestead in 1994. They record precipitation, temperature, relative humidity and wind speed and direction. Prior to that time, rainfall records had been maintained since 1941 by visually monitored rain gauge (Fig. 4). Four additional visually monitored rain gauges were established in Tarawi NR in January 1997, a further five were established in May 2001, and two were established in Scotia Sanctuary in September 2007.

In May 2011, monitoring tubes for soil moisture probes were installed at intervals along two transects extending across the catenary sequence from swale to swale across a dune crest. Tubes were installed in each swale, on the dune crest and on the upper and lower flanks on each side of the dune. Soil moisture is currently monitored at monthly intervals at depths

Proc. Linn. Soc. N.S.W., 134, 2012

A45

Site	Grazing treatments	98	99	00	01	02	03	04	05	06	07	08	09	10	11
T1998/CON1	N														
T1996/1	A,N							4							4
T1997/1	K,A,R,N				3										4
T1997/2	K,A,R,N				3										
T2000/1	K,A,R,N,G				2	3									
T2000/2	K,A,R,N,G				2	3									
T2000/3	K,A,R,N,G				2	3									
T2000/4	K,A,R,N,G				2	3									
T2001/1	K,A,R,N,G				1	2		3							4
T2001/2	K,A,R,N,G				1	2		3							
T2001/3	K,A,R,N,G				1	2		3							
T2001/4	K,A,R,N,G				1	2		3							
T2003/1	K,A,R,N,G						1	2	3						4
T2003/2	K,A,R,N,G						1	2	3						
T2003/3	K,A,R,N,G						1	2	3						
T2003/4	K,A,R,N,G						1	2	3						
T2005/1	K,A,R,N,G								1	2	3				4
T2005/2	K,A,R,N,G								1	2	3				
T2005/3	K,A,R,N,G								1	2	3				4
T2005/4	K,A,R,N,G								1	2	3				
T2005/5	K,A,R,N,G								1	2	3				
T2006/1	K,A,R,N,G									1	2	3			4
T2006/2	K,A,R,N,G									1	2	3			
T2006/3	K,A,R,N,G									1	2	3			
T2006/4	K,A,R,N,G									1	2	3			
S2007/1	K,A,R,N,G											2	3		
S2007/2	K,A,R,N,G											2	3		
S2007/3	K,A,R,N,G											2	3		
S2007/4	K,A,R,N,G											2	3		
S2007/5	K,A,R,N,G											2	3		4
S2007/6	K,A,R,N,G											2	3		
S2007/7	K,A,R,N,G											2	3		
S2007/8	K,A,R,N,G											2	3		
D2010/1	A													3	
D2010/2	A													3	
D2010/3	A													3	
D2010/4	A													3	
D2010/5	A													3	
D2010/6	A													3	
D2010/7	A													3	
D2010/8	A													3	
S2010/1	N														2
S2010/2	N														2
S2010/3	A														2
S2010/4	A														2
T2011/1	K,A,R,N,G														1
T2011/2	K,A,R,N,G														1
T2011/3	K,A,R,N,G														1
T2011/4	K,A,R,N,G														1
S2011/1	A														1
S2011/2	A														1
S2011/3	A														1
S2011/4	A														1

A46

Proc. Linn. Soc. N.S.W., 134, 2012

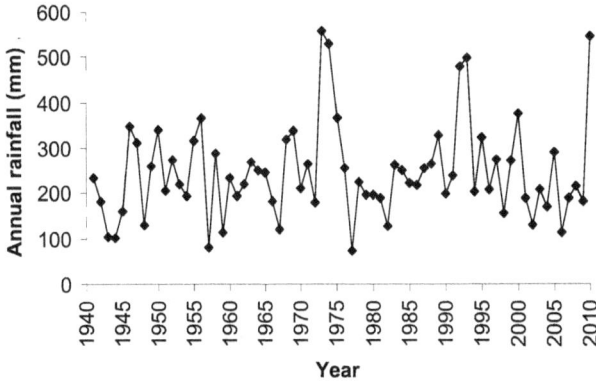

Figure 4. Annual rainfall statistics for Tarawi homestead.

of 100, 200, 300, 400, 600 and 1000 cm below the soil surface at monthly intervals using a PR2/6 Profile Probe manufactured by Delta-T Devices Ltd.

DISCUSSION

Long-term ecological studies are critical for providing insights into ecology, environmental change, natural resource management and biodiversity conservation (Lindenmayer et al. in press). The primary goal of this study is to improve understanding of how mallee vegetation responds to interacting fire regimes, herbivore activity and climatic variability. Its factorial design should enable the relative influence multiple ecosystem drivers to be evaluated under a range of environmental scenarios. In addition, the research infrastructure can contribute understanding to processes beyond the initial experimental treatments. For example, ecological baselines established in the experiment can be useful for surveillance monitoring and detection of surprise responses to rare events or 'unknown unknowns' - unforeseen phenomena that can have profound and long-lasting effects on the ecosystem, but are yet to emerge as management issues (Krebs et al. 2001; Keith 2002; Wintle et al. 2010). Important collateral benefits of long term research also emerge through contributions to ecological theory, which ultimately improve research and management efforts across a broad domain of ecosystems (Lindenmayer et al. in press). These important value-added benefits make long-term ecological research an extremely cost-effective means of developing cause-effect understanding of ecosystem change (Likens and Lindemayer 2011), provided the experiment is designed and maintained to avoid risks of failure (Lindenmayer and Likens 2010a).

The modular design of the mallee experiment enables it to be extended to examine additional permutations of the core factors (fire, grazing, climate) as opportunities arise and as understanding of salient processes develops. For example, the design of herbivore exclosures evolved from an early prototype established in 1997 that excluded all vertebrate mammalian herbivores to a cellular design that enables comparison of combined and individual effects of the major herbivore species. The original treatment was incorporated into the new design, allowing comparison of total exclusion with controls throughout the full chronosequence of sites. Other extensions to the sampling protocol include the addition of external plots in 2001 to assess the effects of immediate vs delayed post-fire access of herbivores, and addition of further sites in 2007 and 2008 to sample large unplanned fires for comparison of vegetation and herbivore responses to smaller planned cool-season fires that had been sampled in earlier treatments. Further sites were added in 2010 and 2011 to sample responses in rare high-rainfall years. Future elaborations could examine the influence of a regionally extinct assemblage of ground mammals and responses of other groups of biota such as various functional groups of invertebrates, lower plants and reptiles. These adjustments illustrate how the design of long-term ecological studies can be adapted to developing knowledge and evolving management needs without compromising the ability to address questions that were originally posed (Lindenmayer and Likens 2010b).

The current weaknesses of the mallee experiment stem primarily from logistic constraints and limitations

Table 2 (preceding page). Schedule of sampling of sites. 1- pre-fire census; 2- 1st year post-fire census; 3- 2nd year post-fire census; 4- census at multiple years post fire. Grazing treatments as per Figure 2.

on scope. The unpredictability of wildlife occurrence make it difficult or impossible to obtain pre-fire census data except by fortuitous means. Yet these data could be important to intrepetation of outcomes and strauctured comparisons with the effects of planned fires carried out under milder fire weather conditions and in smaller areas. The current scope of the mallee experiment is limited to dune crests and upper slopes. The intervening dune swales that support florstically different mallee woodlands and large tracts of sand plains that support non-flammable belah (*Casuarina pauper*) woodlands remain largely uninvestigated, but are potentially important in understanding landscape-wide processes of change, as well as contextual understanding for more localised changes on the dunes.

Experimental probing of ecosystem dynamics is a crucial element of adaptive management for biodiversity conservation (Keith et al. 2011). Current management of the mallee reserves involves i) manipulating fire regimes by controlling unplanned fires and burning to strategically manage bushfire fuels along accessible lineaments bounding landscape blocks; and ii) actively controlling and excluding feral herbivores to limit their impacts on vegetation composition and structure. These activities are carried out in a highly stochastic and unpredictable climate and in the face of highly uncertain, albeit the best available, knowledge about cause-effect relationships within the ecosystem. The experiment described above is integrated with these management activities to achieve structured learning by doing that progressively improves the knowledge base for future management (Walters and Holling 1990, Duncan and Wintle 2008). A key feature of the experiment is that it establishes a rigorous comparative experimental framework to assess the outcomes of real management actions while addressing the major ecosystem drivers: fire regimes, mammalian herbivores and climate variability. A second key feature is that it incorporates multiple alternative management options in the frequency, season, severity and size of fires, and the control or exclusion of different herbivore species across a number of years that span a range of environmental conditions. This enables risks to biodiversity associated with alternative management strategies to be evaluated under different environmental scenarios, informing the choice of management options to achieve conservation objectives with minimum risks of failure.

Detailed prior observations from precisely located points with a well-documented fine-scale environmental history provide valuable contextual evidence for distinguishing alternative causal mechanisms of ecosystem dynamics. Well maintained field research infrastructure and accessible data management systems can be attractive hubs for multi-disciplinary collaborations (Brown et al. 2001; http://www.warra.com/warra/about.html) that are capable of producing insights that are unlikely to be realised from a collection of smaller independent studies. Incorporation of the mallee ecosystem dynamics project into Australia's Terrestrial Ecosystem Research Network (http://www.tern.org.au/) will help develop collective knowledge of the processes that drive and sustain this important ecosystem.

ACKNOWLEDGEMENTS

John Warren, Andrew Willson and Ray Dayman helped to initiate and maintain this study, implement the management treatments and maintain the infrastructure. We are especially grateful to John for his tireless and scrupulous efforts to construct and maintain the exclosures and gather the rainfall and soil moisture data. Daniel Basham, Nick Corkish, Ray Dayman, Rita Enke, Else Foster, Louise Gilfedder, Meredith Henderson, Lisa Holman, Mirandra Kerr, Berin Mackenzie, Indrie Miller, Suzette Rodoreda, Chris Simpson, Dan Tindall, Andrew Willson and Renee Woodward assisted with collection of field data. This study is supported by the Long Term Ecological Research subfacility of the Terrestrial Ecosystem Rseearch Network (http://www.tern.org.au/).

REFERENCES

Auld, T.D. (1995a). Soil seedbank patterns of 4 trees and shrubs from arid Australia. *Journal of Arid Environments* 29, 33-45.

Auld, T.D. (1995b). Seedling survival under grazing in the arid perennial *Acacia oswaldii*. *Biological Conservation* 72, 27-32.

Beadle, N.C.W. (1948). 'The vegetation and pastures of western New South Wales: with special reference to soil erosion'. (Department of Soil Conservation of New South Wales: Sydney).

Bestelmeyer B.T., Havstad K.M., Damindsuren, B., Han, G., Brown, J.R., Herrick J.E., Steele, C.M. and Peters, D.P.C. (2009). Resilience theory in models of rangeland ecology and restoration: the evolution and application of a paradigm. In 'New models for ecosystem dynamics and restoration' (Eds R.J. Hobbs, K.N. Suding) pp 78- 95. (Island Press: Washington DC).

Bradstock, R.A. and Cohn, J.S. (2002a). Fire regimes and biodiversity in semi-arid mallee ecosystems. In: 'Flammable Australia: The fire regimes and biodiversity of a continent' (Eds. R. A. Bradstock, J. E. Williams and A. M. Gill) pp 238-258. (Cambridge University Press: Cambridge).

Bradstock, R.A. and Cohn, J.S. (2002b). Demographic characteristics of mallee pine (*Callitris verrucosa*) in fire-prone mallee communities of central New South Wales. *Australian Journal of Botany.* 50, 653-665.

Brown, M.J., Elliott, H.J. and Hickey, J.E. (2001). An overview of the Warra Long-Term Ecological Research Site. *Tasforests 13, 1-8.*

Caughley, G., Shepherd, N. and Short, J. (1987). Kangaroos: Their Ecology and Management in the Sheep Rangelands of Australia. (Cambridge University Press: Cambridge).

Crisp, M.D. and Lange, R.T. (1976). Age structure, distribution and survival under grazing of arid-zone shrub *Acacia burkittii. Oikos* 27, 86-92

Duncan, D.H. and Wintle, B.A. (2008). Towards adaptive management of native vegetation in regional landscapes. In 'Landscape Analysis and Visualisation. Spatial Models for Natural Resource Management and Planning' (Eds. C. Pettit, I. Bishop, W. Cartwright, D. Duncan, K. Lowell, and D. Pullar) pp. 159–182. (Springer- Verlag GmbH: Berlin).

Haslem, A., Kelly, L.T., Nimmo, D.G., Watson, S.J. Kenny, S.A. Taylor, R.S. Avitabile, S.C. Callister, K.E. Spence-Bailey, L.M., Clarke, M.F. and Bennett, A.F. (2011). Habitat or fuel? Implications of long-term, post-fire dynamics for the development of key resources for fauna and fire. *Journal of Applied Ecology* 48, 247–256.

Hodgkinson, K.C. and Cook, J.D. (1995). The ecology of perennial grass collapse under grazing. In 'Ecological research and management in the mulgalands' (Eds M.J. Page and T.S. Beutel.) pp 203–207. (University of Queensland: Gatton).

Hooper, D.U., Chapin, F.S., Ewel, J.J., Hector, A., Inchausti, P., Lavorel S., Lawton J.H., Lodge D.M., Loreau M., Naeem S., Schmid B., Setälä H., Symstad A.J., Vandermeer J., Wardle D.A. (2005). Effects of biodiversity on ecosystem functioning: A consensus of current knowledge. *Ecological Monographs* 75, 3–35.

Isaac, J.L., Valentine, L.E. and Goodman, B.A. (2008). Demographic responses of an arboreal marsupial, the common brushtail possum (*Trichosurus vulpecula*), to a prescribed fire. *Population Ecology* 50, 101-109.

Keith, D.A. (2002). Population dynamics of an endangered heathland shrub, *Epacris stuartii* (Epacridaceae): recruitment, establishment and survival. *Austral Ecology* 27, 67-76.

Keith, D.A. (2011). Functional traits: their roles in understanding and predicting biotic responses to fire regimes from individuals to landscapes. In 'Flammable Australia: Fire regimes, biodiversity and ecosystems in a changing world' (Eds. R.A. Bradstock, A.M. Gill and R.J. Williams) pp 97-125. Second edition. (CSIRO: Melbourne).

Keith, D.A., Martin, T.G., McDonald-Madden, E. and Walters, C. (2011). Uncertainty and adaptive management for biodiversity conservation, *Biological Conservation* 144, 1175–1178.

Krebs C. J., Boutin S. and Boonstra R. (2001). 'Ecosystem Dynamics of the Boreal Forest: The Kluane Project'. (Oxford University Press: New York).

Landsberg, J., James, C.D., Morton, S.R., Müller, W.J. and Stol, J. (2003). Abundance and composition of plant species along grazing gradients in Australian rangelands. *Journal of Applied Ecology* 40, 1008 -1024.

Likens G.E. (1989). 'Long-term studies in ecology. Approaches and alternatives'. (Springer-Verlag: New York).

Likens, G.E. (1992). 'The ecosystem approach: its use and abuse'. (Oldendorf/Luhe: Ecology Institute).

Likens G.E. and Lindenmayer D.B. (2011) A strategic plan for an Australian Long-Term Environmental Monitoring (LTEM) network. *Austral Ecology* 36, 1-8.

Lindenmayer D.B. and Likens G.E. (2010a). 'Effective Ecological Monitoring'. (CSIRO Publishing and Earthscan: Melbourne and London).

Lindenmayer D.B. and Likens G.E. (2010b). Adaptive monitoring: a new paradigm for long-term research and monitoring. *Trends in Ecology and Evolution* 24, 482-486.

Lindenmayer D.B., Likens G.E., Andersen, A., Bowman, D., Bull, M., Dickman, C.R., Hoffmann, A.A., Keith D.A., Liddell, M.J., Lowe, A.J., Metcalfe, D.J., Phinn S.R., Russell-Smith, J., Thurgate, N. and Wardle, G.M.. (in press). The importance of long-term studies in ecology. *Austral Ecology* DOI:10.1111/j.1442-9993.2011.02351.x.

Lopez J.C., Holmgren M., Sabate S. and Gracia, C.A. (2008). Estimating annual rainfall threshold for establishment of tree species in water-limited ecosystems using tree-ring data. *Journal of Arid Environments* 72, 602-611.

Millennium Ecosystem Assessment. (2005). 'Ecosystems and human well-being: synthesis'. (Washington DC: Island Press).

Morton, S.R. , Stafford Smith D.M., Dickman, C.R., Dunkerley, D.L., Friedel, M.H., McAllister, R.R.J., Reid, J.R.W., Roshier, D.A., Smith, M.A., Walsh, F.J., Wardle, G.M., Watson, I.W. and Westoby, M. (2011). A fresh framework for the ecology of arid Australia. *Journal of Arid Environments* 75, 313-329.

Noble, J.C. 1982. The significance of fire in the biology and evolutionary ecology of mallee *Eucalyptus* populations. In 'Evolution of the flora and fauna of arid Australia'. (Eds Barker, WR. and Greenslade, PJM.) pp. 153-159. (Peacock: Frewville).

Noble, J.C. (1984). Mallee. In: 'Management of Australia's rangelands', (Eds G.N. Harrington, A.D. Wilson and M.D. Young), pp. 223-40. (CSIRO: Melbourne).

Noble, J.C. and Vines, R.G. (1993). Fire studies in mallee (*Eucalyptus* spp.) communities of western New South Wales: grass fuel dynamics and associated weather patterns. *Rangeland Journal* 15, 270-297.

Noble, J.C., Hik, D.S. and Sinclair, A.R.E. (2007).
Landscape ecology of the burrowing bettong: fire and
marsupial biocontrol of shrubs in semi-arid Australia.
Rangeland Journal **29**, 107-119.

Noble, J.C., Smith, A.W. and Leslie, H.W. (1980). Fire in
the mallee shrublands of western New South Wales.
Australian Rangeland Journal **29**, 104-114.

Pickett, S.T.A. and White, P.S. (1985). 'The ecology of
natural disturbance and patch dynamics'. (Academic
Press: Orlando).

van Etten, E.J.B. (2009). Inter-annual rainfall variability
of arid Australia: greater than elsewhere? *Australian
Geographer* **40**, 109-120.

Walker, J., Condon, R.W., Hodgkinson, K.C. and
Harrington, G.N. (1981). Fire in pastoral areas of
poplar box (*Eucalyptus populnea*) lands. *Australian
Rangeland Journal* **3**, 12–23. doi: 10.1071/
RJ9810012

Walters C.J. and Holling C.S. (1990). Large-scale
management experiments and learning by doing.
Ecology **71**, 2060-2068.

Watson, I.W., Westoby, M. and Holm, A.McR. (1997).
Continuous and episodic components of demographic
change in arid zone shrubs: models of two
Eremophila
species from Western Australia compared with published
data on other species. *Journal of Ecology* **85**, 833-
846.

Wellington, A.B. and Noble, I.R. (1985). Seed dynamics
and factors limiting recruitment of the mallee
Eucalyptus incrassata in semi-arid, south-eastern
Australia. *Journal of Ecology* **73**, 657-666.

Westbrooke, M.E., Miller, J.D. and Kerr, M.K.C. (1998).
The vegetation of the Scotia 1:100 000 map sheet,
western New South Wales. *Cunninghamia* **5**, 665-684

Wintle, B.A., Runge M.C. and Bekessy S.A. (2010).
Allocating monitoring effort in the face of unknown
unknowns. *Ecology Letters* **13**, 1325-1337.

Appendix 1. Location and treatment of sample sites. [Co-ordinates are in Australian Geodetic Datum 66, Zone 54]

Site Label	Easting	Northing	Location	Date Burnt	Burn Type	Previous fire	Area burnt (ha)	Date Fenced	Notes
T1996/1	506741	6309952	W of west firetrail	Jan 1996	wildfire	1918	70	May 1996	permanent total exclusion (single exclosure only)
T1997/1	511943	6308381	E of spring Track	Nov 1997	wildfire	1918	436	Jul 1998	perimeter electric fence erected Nov-98 / added foot netting Feb-01 / electric fence dismantled Jul-01 and access allowed
T1997/2	512358	6308764	E of spring Track	Nov 1997	wildfire	1918	436	Jul 1998	perimeter electric fence erected Nov-98 / added foot netting Feb-01 / electric fence dismantled Jul-01 and access allowed
T1998/CON1	511466	6306052	E of spring Track control site	not burnt	not burnt	1918	-	Aug 1998	Perimeter electric fence erected Nov-99 / added foot netting Feb-01 / electric fence dismantled Jul-01 and access allowed
T2000/4	514985	6306528	W of centre firetrail	Apr 2000	prescribed	1918	40	Jul 2000	access allowed April-01 / wings on goat ramps Jul-02
T2000/3	514944	6306359	W of centre firetrail	Apr 2000	prescribed	1979	40	Jul 2000	access allowed April-01 / wings on goat ramps Jul-02
T2000/2	514898	6305897	W of centre firetrail	Apr 2000	prescribed	1979	40	Jul 2000	access allowed April-01 / wings on goat ramps Jul-02
T2000/1	514889	6301865	W of centre firetrail	Apr 2000	prescribed	1918	40	Jul 2000	access allowed April-01 / wings on goat ramps Jul-02
T2001/1	519608	6309485	S of north boundary firetrail	Apr 2001	prescribed	1918	74	May 2001	access allowed March-02 / goat ramps installed Jul-02
T2001/2	519173	6309618	S of north boundary firetrail	Apr 2001	prescribed	1984	74	May 2001	access allowed March-02 / goat ramps installed Jul-02
T2001/3	514940	6304626	E of centre firetrail	Apr 2001	prescribed	1918	74	May 2001	access allowed March-02 / goat ramps installed Jul-02
T2001/4	514981	6304238	E of centre firetrail	Apr 2001	prescribed	1984	74	May 2001	access allowed March-02 / goat ramps installed Jul-02
T2003/1	511348	6305853	W of spring track	May	prescribed	1979	4	June	access allowed May-04 / goat ramps installed

Site Label	Easting	Northing	Location	Date Burnt	Burn Type	Previous fire	Area burnt (ha)	Date Fenced	Notes
T2003/2	511664	6304552	W of spring track	2003				2003	Feb-05
T2003/3	507352	6308660	E of west firetrail	May 2003	prescribed	1918	3	June 2003	access allowed May-04 / goat ramps installed Feb-05
T2003/4	507361	6308830	E of west firetrail	May 2003	prescribed	1979	39	June 2003	access allowed May-04 / goat ramps installed Feb-05
T2005/1	506211	6311210	S of north boundary firetrail	May 2003	prescribed	1918	39	June 2003	access allowed May-04 / goat ramps installed Feb-05
T2005/2	505664	6311286	S of north boundary firetrail	Apr 2005	prescribed	1918	20	May 2005	access allowed May-06
T2005/3	502088	6299969	N of south boundary firetrail	Apr 2005	prescribed	1918	20	May 2005	access allowed May-06
T2005/4	501215	6299904	N of south boundary firetrail	Apr 2005	prescribed	1983	59	May 2005	access allowed May-06
T2005/5	502239	6299934	N of south boundary firetrail	Apr 2005	prescribed	1983	59	May 2005	access allowed May-06
T2006/1	502325	6311648	S of north boundary firetrail	Apr 2005	prescribed	1918	59	May 2005	access allowed May-06
T2006/2	502846	6311634	S of north boundary firetrail	Apr 2006	prescribed	1918	26	Jul 2006	access allowed April-07
T2006/3	507241	6308859	W of west firetrail	Apr 2006	prescribed	1918	26	Jul 2006	access allowed April-07
T2006/4	507089	6307510	W of west firetrail	Apr 2006	prescribed	1918	2.5	Jul 2006	access allowed April-07
S2007/1	505352	6317356	West of Elliots Bore	Apr 2006	prescribed	1918	2.5	Jul 2006	access allowed April-07
S2007/2	505047	6317966	West of Elliots Bore	Nov 2006	wildfire	1918	2455	June 2007	access allowed March-08
S2007/3	502124	6316984	West of Elliots Bore	Nov 2006	wildfire	1918	2455	June 2007	access allowed March-08
				Nov	wildfire	1918	2455	June	access allowed March-08

A52

Proc. Linn. Soc. N.S.W., 134, 2012

Site Label	Easting	Northing	Location	Date Burnt	Burn Type	Previous fire	Area burnt (ha)	Date Fenced	Notes
S2007/4	502260	6317844	West of Elliots Bore	Nov 2006	wildfire	1918	2455	June 2007	access allowed March-08
S2007/5	505611	6314199	South of Robinsons Dam firetrail	Nov 2006	wildfire	1918	2455	June 2007	access allowed March-08
S2007/6	506129	6314956	South of Robinsons Dam firetrail	Nov 2006	wildfire	1918	2455	June 2007	access allowed March-08
S2007/7	506196	6317912	West of Elliots Bore	Nov 2006	wildfire	1918	2455	June 2007	access allowed March-08
S2007/8	507176	6318110	West of Elliots Bore	Nov 2006	wildfire	1918	2455	June 2007	access allowed March-08
D2008/1	497965	6300213	South-east corner	Dec 2008	wildfire	1986	1297	Not fenced	Near fire boundary
D2008/2	498056	6298354	South-east corner	Dec 2008	wildfire	1918	1297	Not fenced	Remote from fire boundary
D2008/3	498546	6299680	South-east corner	Dec 2008	wildfire	1918	1297	Not fenced	Near fire boundary
D2008/4	496643	6298859	South-east corner	Dec 2008	wildfire	1986	1297	Not fenced	Remote from fire boundary
D2008/5	498203	6297708	South-east corner	Dec 2008	wildfire	1918	1297	Not fenced	Remote from fire boundary
D2008/6	496892	6297337	South-east corner	Dec 2008	wildfire	1986	1297	Not fenced	Near fire boundary
D2008/7	499463	6297689	South-east corner	Dec 2008	wildfire	1986	1297	Not fenced	Remote from fire boundary
D2008/8	500012	6298590	South-east corner	Dec 2008	wildfire	1918	1297	Not fenced	Near fire boundary

Site Label	Easting	Northing	Location	Date Burnt	Burn Type	Previous fire	Area burnt (ha)	Date Fenced	Notes
S2010/1	516401	6327780	Stage 1 Scotia Sanctuary, outside NW corner of Mala enclosure	Apr 2010	prescribed	pre-1980	5	1995	Within Stage 1 fence constructed pre-fire to exclude goats, rabbits, foxes and cats. Low density of kangaroos maintained
S2010/2	516400	6327522	Stage 1 Scotia Sanctuary, outside west boundary of Mala enclosure	Apr 2010	prescribed	pre-1980	5	1995	Within Stage 1 fence constructed pre-fire to exclude goats, rabbits, foxes and cats. Low density of kangaroos maintained
S2010/3	510298	6327321	Stage 3 Scotia Sanctuary, Sunset Boulevard	Apr 2010	prescribed	c.1980	5	Not fenced	Patchy strip burn along north side of track
S2010/4	510616	6327286	Stage 3 Scotia Sanctuary, Sunset Boulevard	Apr 2010	prescribed	c.1980	5	Not fenced	Patchy strip burn along north side of track
T2011/1	518362	6307774	North Elephant firetrail	Sep 2011	prescribed	1984	2	Dec 2011	
T2011/2	500180	6310892	Western boundary firetrail (north)	Sep 2011	prescribed	1918	1.5	Dec 2011	
T2011/3	500246	6301778	Western boundary firetrail (south)	Sep 2011	prescribed	1918	1.5	Dec 2011	
T2011/4	515025	6301859	Centre firetrail (south)	Sep 2011	prescribed	1984	1.5	Dec 2011	
S2011/1	511447	6327790	Stage 3 Scotia Sanctuary, outside Stage 1 fence line	Sep 2011	prescribed				
S2011/2	512003	6333384	Stage 3 Scotia Sanctuary, outside Stage 1 fence line	Sep 2011	prescribed				
S2011/3	511098	6332160	Stage 3 Scotia Sanctuary, outside Stage 1 fence line	Sep 2011	prescribed	1918			
S2011/4	509968	6322457	Stage 3 Scotia Sanctuary, outside Stage 1 fence line	Sep 2011	prescribed				

A54

Proc. Linn. Soc. N.S.W., 134, 2012

The Pastoral History, Biological and Cultural Significance of the Scotia Country, far Western New South Wales

MARTIN WESTBROOKE

Centre for Environmental Management, University of Ballarat, Mt Helen, Victoria 3353
(mew@ballarat.edu.au)

Published on 28 August 2012 at http://escholarship.library.usyd.edu.au/journals/index.php/LIN

Westbrooke, M. (2012). The pastoral history, biological and cultural significance of the Scotia Country, far western New South Wales. *Proceedings of the Linnean Society of New South Wales* **134**, A55-A68.

The Scotia country of far western New South Wales, once part of the vast Lake Victoria lease and subsequently split into six smaller properties after WW1, has one of the shortest grazing histories in the state. The low stocking rates due to unsuitable feed provided by the mallee vegetation and limited water supplies have left native vegetation communities relatively intact and close to original condition. A natural salt lake system with rare plants and plant communities adds to the values of the area. This paper reviews the pastoral history of the area and the features which make the Scotia of outstanding conservation and cultural significance.

Manuscript received 19 October 2011, accepted for publication 11 January 2012.

KEYWORDS: conservation, cultural, mallee, pastoral lease, plant communities, Scotia.

INTRODUCTION

The Scotia country of approximately 200,000ha is located in far western New South Wales midway between Wentworth and Broken Hill, latitude 33°43'S, longitude 143°02'E (Fig. 1).

The significance of the area relates not only to its natural characteristics but that the six homestead leases which comprise most of the geographic area were settled late in Australia's pastoral history. European land settlement in Australia commenced in 1788 when Governor Phillip claimed possession of the land for a penal colony on behalf of the British Government. All lands were vested in the name of the Crown, thus the name Crown lands. From 1791 to 1831 successive Governors issued free grants of land on behalf of the Crown to encourage and advance settlement of the State. Originally land in the far west of New South Wales (NSW) was divided into vast pastoral holdings but later the NSW Government pursued a policy of closer settlement (Heathcote 1965). This entailed resumption of large properties, subdividing them into units or home maintenance areas capable of supporting a family and allocating these by ballot (Young et al. 1984). These family leases in western NSW varied with carrying capacity from 4,000 to 40,000 ha.

BACKGROUND TO THE ESTABLISHMENT OF THE SCOTIA BLOCKS

The Scotia blocks (see Table 1) are located in far south western New South Wales to the west of the Darling Ana-Branch. The Scotia country is a region of thick mallee scrub (predominantly *Eucalyptus dumosa, E. socialis, E. oleosa and E. gracilis*), interspersed with bluebush flats and Belah, *Casuarina pauper*, woodland which begins about 40km. west of the Darling Anabranch, land traditionally owned by the Barkindji people of the Mallee country (NPWS 2001). The first European settlement on the land was by George Melrose in 1845, following exploration of the area by Sturt and Eyre (Withers 1989). Despite Melrose developing the property over the next few years, after surveys of the area were completed by the NSW Government and land offered for tender in Government Gazettes in 1854, the Lake Victoria lease which encompassed the Scotia country was granted to John McInlay who had no previous link to the area (Withers 1989).

In 1859 the Lake Victoria lease was transferred to Charles Brown and shortly after to John Hay. At this time the lease consisted of the East Rufus, West Rufus, Tara, Yantarella, Westbrook and Scrub Blocks 1, 2, 3, 4, 5, 6, 8, 9 and 10 (Jervis 1947), see figure 2.

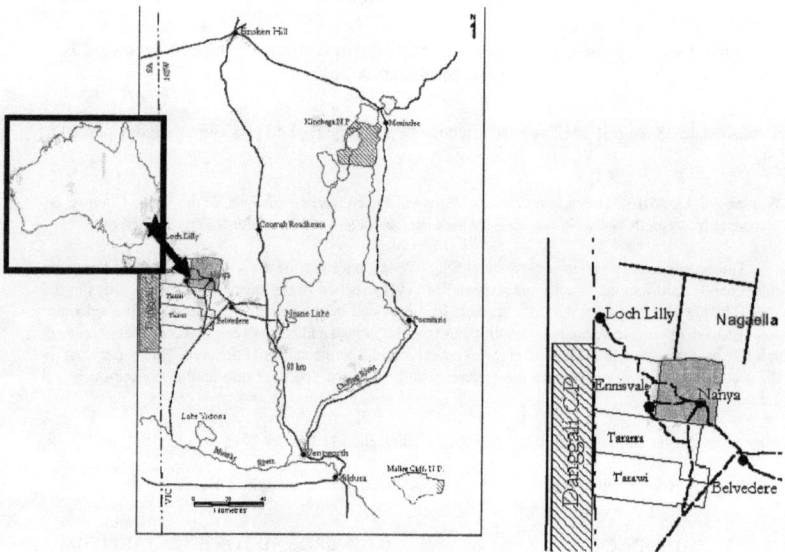

Figure 1. Location of the Scotia Country of western New South Wales

Property	Old name	1st Owner	Amalgamation phase	Current ownership and use
Nanya	Winnebaga	Gordon Cumming	Belvedere	University of Ballarat Conservation 2004 -
Nagaella	Badham	H C Cullen	Wemba	Private Goats – c1996 -
Loch Lily	Barry	Frederick Hucks	Mazar	Private Goats – c1995 -
Tarawi	Grose	Harry O'Flynn	Hyperna	National Parks and Wildlife Conservation 1996 -
Ennisvale	Scotia	Aubrey Bowerman	Tarrara	Australian Wildlife Conservancy Conservation 1994 -
Tarrara	Phillip	Toby Bornholm	Ennisvale	Australian Wildlife Conservancy Conservation 1994 -

Table 1. Summary history of the Scotia leases with current use.

Proc. Linn. Soc. N.S.W., 134, 2012

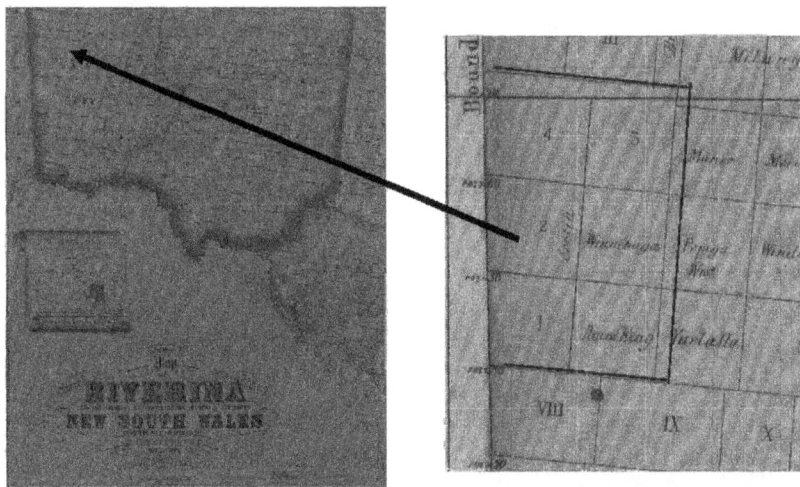

Figure 2. Runs of the Lake Victoria lease in the late 19thC (MacDonald 1879). Scotia 1, 2, 3, 4, Winnebaga and Amoskeag comprise the Scotia.

The lease consisting of 457,000 ha was sold in 1862 to Phillip Gell however he was ruined by drought and left the lease in 1869. The Argus (Melbourne) 12 February 1876 records the lease being owned by McPherson and the Wentworth Telegraph and Murray Darling News of 18 November 1882 reports its sale to Robert Tully.

The Sydney Morning Herald of 15 July 1885 reports the Lake Victoria Pastoral Holding (Leasehold No. 170) included the following runs: East and West Rufus, Pellwalka, Yantaralla, Tara, Wannawanna, Westbrook, Amoskeag, Scrub run blocks 2, 3, 4, 5, 6, 8, 9 and 10, Scotia blocks 1, 2, 3 and 4 and Winnebaga. It is assumed that at some time during the 1870s Scotia blocks 1, 2, 3 and 4, Amoskeag and Winnebaga, which along with the Scrub run blocks formed the back blocks of the Lake Victoria lease were formed by the NSW Lands Department in the hope that they could be leased as separate runs as a revenue raising exercise. On an 1879 pastoral map (MacDonald 1879) the six blocks (the subject of this paper) are encompassed by Winnebaga, Amoskeag, Scrub 8 and 9, Scotia 1, 2, 3 and 4 (Fig. 2). The name Scotia is thought to have been named by Henry Ricketson after his homeland, Nova Scotia, as Winnebaga and Amoskeag, the names of the waterholes on his neighbouring runs are similar to the Canadian words for a lake over the United States border, or a swamp, a muskeg. (Withers 1989).

In 1883, the Legislative Council of New South Wales held an inquiry into the state of the public lands following the failure of the Selection Acts to satisfy the land hunger of the new settlers. The subsequent Land Act of 1884 created the Western Division of the colony and led to the sub-division of the large pastoral holdings into two areas, leasehold to be held under a pastoral lease with tenure of fifteen years, and the resumed area which could be held by an annual occupation licence until it was claimed by Homestead lessees. Homestead leases not exceeding 4,200 ha and not less than 2,362 ha were granted within the resumed areas and on application a lessee had to pay a deposit of 1d. per acre and the cost of a boundary survey, as well as paying for any existing improvements. The lessee had to fence the boundaries within two years if possible and live on the land for at least six months of every year during the first five years of the lease. Otherwise the conditions and length of tenure were the same as those of pastoral leases (Withers 1989).

It is likely that, following this Act, the back blocks of the Lake Victoria lease which became part of the Resumed Area, were subject to boundary changes, in some cases renamed and offered as Homestead Leases. Scotia blocks 1 to 4, were initially leased by the London-based Australian Mortgage Land and finance Company which paid 70 pounds a year in rent, but there is no record of the country being stocked, and in 1897 the Scotia blocks were offered for sale by

Proc. Linn. Soc. N.S.W., 134, 2012

A57

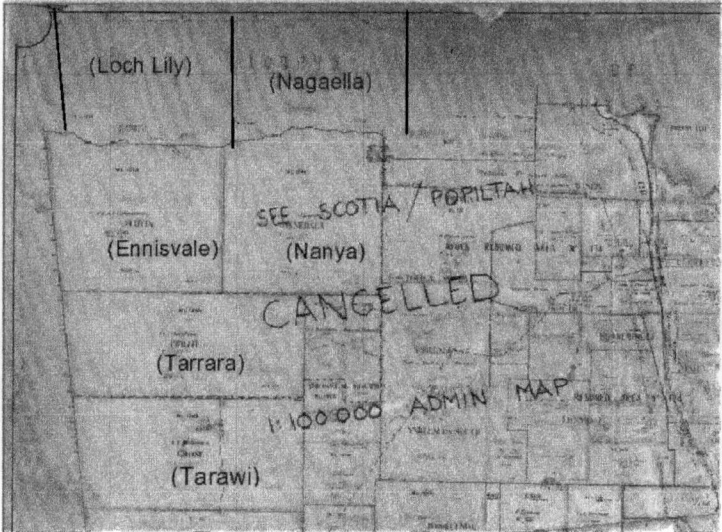

Figure 3. Section of Tara Parish map of 1926 (Land and Property Information NSW 2001) with current names overlaid

the State as Improvement Leases (Withers 1989). The name Improvement Lease indicates the requirement of potential lessees to make improvements on the leasehold area (clearing of scrub, provision of water and fencing) they would therefore have been offered for a cheaper rent than the formerly offered Homestead Leases. However without access to water all blocks except for part of Block 3 remained untenanted but sometimes the adjacent properties of Belmore and Nulla used the land to run wethers during the winter months (Withers 1989).

This situation continued through the early years the 20th century but, following George Anderson's success in finding artesian water on Belmore in 1925, the dry Scotia country comprising 432,000 acres (sic) was surveyed and divided into six Homestead leasehold blocks allocated by ballot (Withers 1989). On the Tara and Windemeyer Parish maps of 1926 (Land and Property Information NSW 2001) they were named Winnebaga, Grose [Scrub 8], Phillip [Scotia No.1], Scotia [Scotia No. 2], Badham [Scotia No.3] and Barry [Scotia No. 4] (Fig. 3).

The Sydney Morning Herald of 27 September 1928 refers to the 'leasing of the hitherto despised and neglected stretch of country known as the Scotia Country for sheep raising'. The nature of the land demonstrates the need to offer the land by ballot rather than by leasehold. All properties were approximately 30,000ha. with a rating of 3,000 sheep. Subsequently

the lease areas were again renamed most likely by the new owners.

The ballot system ensured that all the leases were taken up this time, although Mark Williams who drew a northern lease, took one look at the timber and thick scrub and forfeited it. Subsequently the forfeited lease was transferred to H. C and H. A. Cullen in 1929. Barry (Loch Lily) was drawn by Frederick Hucks and Phillip (Tararra) by Thorvald Ludwick Christian (Toby) Bornholm. Scotia (Ennisvale) was occupied by Aubrey Bowerman, whose father was an overseer at Lake Victoria, Harry O'Flynn settled at Grose (Tarawi), and Winnebaga (Nanya) was taken up by Gordon Cumming initially with his brother Lorie. (Sydney Morning Herald 1928).

LIFE ON THE SCOTIA BLOCKS (1930 – 2000)

Life on the Scotia blocks was very different to that experienced on the large pastoral holdings of the 19th century. The new leaseholders initially camped on the land and set about drilling bores, digging ground tanks and establishing fencing largely using materials off the land. At Nanya, Gordon Cumming initially camped on chaff bags before constructing a makeshift hut with bush poles and rudimentary concrete using local calcrete as a low quality aggregate and at

A58

Proc. Linn. Soc. N.S.W., 134, 2012

Nagaella, the Cullen brothers' first hut was made of flattened petrol tins. (Withers, 1989) These anecdotes indicate that the new lessees were not wealthy and the later infrastructure suggests that they did not make their wealth on the land. From establishment until their closure as pastoral leases developments were restricted to essential infrastructure with only a brief period of wealth demonstrated during the 1950s wool boom.

The properties were family run with few employees. All of the blocks would have contained relatively small largely corrugated iron clad houses dating from the 1930s however prosperity in the 1950s allowed some improvement to infrastructure. In most cases ancillary buildings were of rudimentary construction with chicken sheds and enclosures built from bush poles and wire and laundries and meat houses constructed from recycled timber and iron. The shearing sheds and quarters were also simple buildings constructed from local materials where possible and, unlike earlier large pastoral holdings, were located close to the homestead.

At Nanya the wool boom period of the 1950s is reflected in the improvements made on the property at that time. These improvements included a more substantial Red Gum framed homestead constructed adjacent to the earlier cottage and new steel machinery shed. At this time all of the Scotia blocks had a resident family and there was an active social life including weekend tennis tournaments and community Christmas functions (Norma Scadding, Belvedere Station pers comm.).

When the homestead leases of the Scotia were established in the late 1920s they were intended to have a sheep carrying capacity of approx 3,000 sheep, which was seen to be adequate for a family income. This may initially have been the case and was certainly the case during the early 1950s when wool prices were at an all-time high of $1 per 1lb. However from the early 1970s, increasing costs and declining wool values made incomes inadequate to support families. Gordon Cumming of Nanya however lived at and worked his property until he died in 1983 at the age of 97. Similarly the Bornholm brothers managed Tararra and Ennisvale until the 1990s. Stocking rates in the Scotia have always been low due to the difficulty of providing water and the unpalatable nature of the dominant mallee vegetation (Stanley and Lawrie 1980). The official grazing rating was one sheep to 10ha. but on Nanya for example during the 1970s overall stocking rates were closer to one sheep to fifteen ha. due to large areas without reliable water supply (Norm Scadding, Belvedere Station pers. comm.). These low stocking rates along

with the short grazing history (80 years compared to 160 years in much of western NSW) led to retention of relatively intact vegetation.

During the 1980s most leases were sold and amalgamated with adjacent larger properties. From 1988 staff from the University of Ballarat undertook intensive vegetation and fauna surveys in the Scotia which highlighted the high conservation significance of the area (Westbrooke et al. 1998). As wool prices further declined in the 1990s, the amalgamation trend was reversed and many leases were purchased for alternative land uses including 'farming' of feral goats and conservation. Of the six "Scotia' blocks which in the 1950s supported six families depending on income from wool four are now managed for conservation and two for feral goats (Table 1.).

BIOLOGICAL SIGNIFICANCE OF THE SCOTIA COUNTRY

Vegetation and flora

The relatively short grazing history and, due to unreliability of waterpoints and unpalatable vegetation, low grazing pressure during that time have resulted in native vegetation communities remaining in good condition. Mean percentage weediness of quadrats recorded in 1992 in mallee communities on Nanya Station were 3% compared to 4.7% for equivalent communities at Mallee Cliffs National Park (Westbrooke 1990). This may reflect the longer grazing history of the latter site prior to reservation. The short grazing history of the Scotia contrasts with most of the remainder of western NSW which was settled between the early 1850s and 1876 (Hardy 1969). Other factors which have contributed to the intactness of vegetation communities are the unsuitability of the deep sands of the mallee for rabbits and the poor water holding of the earth tanks which are the predominant water source. This latter factor has meant that high stock numbers could only be maintained during wet periods. Whilst the predominant vegetation of the Scotia is dune and swale mallee 25 communities are represented, several of which, such as *Halosarcia lylei* low shrubland (Fig. 4), are of limited distribution or restricted to the area (Westbrooke et al. 1998). Two factors contributing to this natural diversity are the presence of complex salt lake systems and proximity to the boundary of the Murray Darling Depression and Broken Hill Complex IBRA regions (Thackway and Cresswell 1995). Communities present in the Scotia with code and conservation status (Benson 2006) are given in Table 2.

Figure 4. *Halosarcia lylei* low shrubland, for NSW only recorded from Scotia

Code	Community	Conservation status
16	*Eucalyptus largiflorens* open woodland	Near threatened
190	*Eucalyptus porosa* open woodland	Near threatened
58	*Casuarina pauper* woodland/open-woodland, mixed shrub understorey	Near threatened
221	*Casuarina pauper* woodland/open-woodland, *Maireana sedifolia* understorey	Near threatened
57	*Casuarina pauper/Geijera parviflora* open-woodland	Near threatened
28	*Callitris glaucophylla* open-woodland	Vulnerable
252	*Myoporum platycarpum* open woodland	Vulnerable
199	*Hakea tephrosperma/ Hakea leucoptera* low open woodland	Near threatened
119	*Acacia aneura* open-shrubland	Near threatened
128	*Acacia loderi* tall open-shrubland	Endangered
170	*Eucalyptus* spp. open-shrubland - shrub understorey	Least concern
171	*Eucalyptus* spp. open-shrubland - *Triodia* understorey	Least concern
	Eucalyptus gracilis open shrubland – *Mesembranthemum* understorey	
191	*Eucalyptus gracilis/Melaleuca lanceolata,* open-shrubland	Least concern
143	*Dodonaea/Eremophila/Senna* shrubland	Least concern
152	*Nitraria billardieri* shrubland	Least concern
196	*Lycium australe* shrubland	Least concern
18	*Atriplex vesicaria* low open-shrubland	Vulnerable
154	*Maireana sedifolia* low open shrubland	Near threatened
64	*Halosarcia pergranulata* low shrubland	Least concern
65	*Halosarcia lylei* low open-shrubland	Vulnerable
253	Gypseous shrubland	Vulnerable
24	*Eragrostis australasicus* swamp	Least concern
165	*Stipa* spp./*Eragrostis* spp. tussock grassland	Least concern

Table 2. Vegetation communities of the Scotia Country, occurrence and conservation status (Benson 2006).

The more widespread communities are also of significance as, due to the short grazing history, they are amongst the most intact examples in NSW.

Over 400 vascular plant species have been recorded including several listed under the Threatened Species Conservation Act (Westbrooke et al 1998). Significant species include new records for New South Wales: *Hemichroa diandra* (Amaranthaceae) (Fig. 5), *Dodonaea stenozyga* (Sapindaceae), *Halosarcia lylei* (Chenopodiaceae), *Elechanthus glaber* (Asteraceae) and significant extensions to species of limited known distribution: *Acacia acanthoclada* (Mimosaceae), *Swainsona colutoides* Fabaceae), *Cratystylis conocephala* and *Kippistia suaedifolia* (Asteraceae).

Fauna

A diverse fauna has been recorded including 20 native mammals, over 50 species of reptile and over 110 species of birds (Westbrooke 2010, NPWS 2001). Of particular significance are three species listed under the Environmental Protection and Biodiversity Conservation Act which are associated with old-growth mallee: Malleefowl, Black-eared Miner and Lesser Long-eared Bat. A further twenty species are listed as endangered or vulnerable under the NSW TSC Act:

Saltlakes

Many of the significant plant communities and species are associated with the salt lakes on Nanya, Loch Lily and Tarrara (Fig.. 6). Apart from a hydrological study (Ferguson et al. 1995) there has been little investigation of these highly significant salt lake systems which have been subject to minimal disturbance.

Fire history

The Scotia has a wide range of fire histories. Significant wildfires occurred in 1917/18, 1975/6, 1985, 1997/1998 and 2005. The extent of the 1917/18 fires is not accurately known but newspaper reports at the time suggest it was extensive. The Mildura Telegraph (January 1918) reported:

...Three huge fires are raging in various parts of the lower Darling district and there

Figure 5. Tussocks of *Hemichroa diandra* (Amaranthaceae), a new record for New South Wales

Proc. Linn. Soc. N.S.W., 134, 2012

A61

Figure 6. Part of the Nanya Discharge Complex

is practically no hope of stopping them by ordinary human methods, even if water for fire-fighting carts were considerably handier than it is. The prolific growth of grass during the past two seasons has been responsible for the outbreak of fire in several places. Tremendous efforts have been made to keep it within safe limits and head it off in the unsettled Scotia country ...

In 1975 a fire burnt about 30,000ha. of Ennisvale, Loch Lily and Nagaella. Other fires have generally burnt patches of less than 5,000ha. Smaller areas have been subject to management burns for 'pasture improvement' or asset protection and areas of Tarawi and Nagaella were burnt in a CSIRO fire research program in the 1980s which aimed to demonstrate improved grazing capacity resulting from frequent fire (Noble 1989). The extensive fires tend to follow two or more years of well above average rainfall such as occurred prior to the 1917/18 and 1975/6 fires. In these circumstances extensive growth of Spear Grass in the more open swales, which normally have sparsely distributed ground fuel loads, assist the spread of fire as is noted by the Western Lands Commission:

"Speargrass to one metre in height covered the southern two-thirds of the Western Division, producing a fuel load of the order of 5-6 tons per acre (12-15 tonnes per

hectare), linking fuel types which would otherwise be very different in fire behaviour." *(Western Lands Commission, 1975)*

As a result of its fire history there is a mosaic of age classes across the Scotia, including significantly areas of mallee which have not burnt since 1917 or earlier. Preliminary studies based on a regression of stem size measurements at sites of known fire history indicate that some of these areas are approximately 135 years post fire (M. Westbrooke and S. Florentine unpublished data). This suggests that fires followed the high rainfall years of the early 1870s (Clewett et al. 1994). Further evidence of very long periods since fire is the presence of stands of single stemmed *Callitris verrucosa* forming woodland which is reported as a characteristic of long unburnt mallee (Bradstock 1990). It should be noted that 'old-growth mallee' has been defined as an area not burnt for 50+ years (NPWS 2003). The relative non flammability of bands of *Casuarina pauper/ Alectryon oleifolius* woodland occurring in wider swales has meant that even larger fires result in a mosaic of burnt and unburnt patches. This diversity of fire regimes, recognised as contributing to maintaining diversity and resilience of plant and animal communities (Bradstock et al. 1995) adds greatly to the biological significance of the Scotia.

A62

Proc. Linn. Soc. N.S.W., 134, 2012

Flooding

Areas of the Scotia have been impacted by flooding of the Olary Creek. This ephemeral creek floods in response to high rainfall events in the Olary Ranges of South Australia. The impact of a 1998 flood event and its interaction with fire and grazing has been monitored (Westbrooke and Florentine 2005, Westbrooke et al 2005) as well as its influence on invasion by the exotic shrub *Nicotiana glauca* (Florentine and Westbrooke 2005).

CULTURAL SIGNIFICANCE OF THE SCOTIA COUNTRY

The history and significance of the large pastoral leases taken up in western NSW in the 19th century are generally well understood. For example the grand homesteads and shearing sheds of the vast early pastoral leases such as Kinchega, Yanga and Willandra in NSW are well recognised and protected. Recognition of important examples from later phases, following the break-up of these large holdings into small family blocks however is often neglected. The development of the Scotia leases show another side to Australia's pastoral history and illustrate the rich pastoral history that exists in relation to small homestead leases. Although rudimentary, the remaining infrastructure tells stories of the struggle for a dependable water supply and the simple life led by those who tried to make a living off these blocks. They may not include grand structures or early colonial relics but their remoteness, starkness and demonstration of mid 20th century pastoral technologies and way of life deserve to be recognised and preserved (Westbrooke and Westbrooke 2010). Additionally relics such as yards and bores often help to explain features of current vegetation and a number of issues relating to cultural elements link with conservation management

Homestead complex buildings

Scotia buildings are generally confined to functional requirements and typically consist of one or more homesteads, shearing and machinery sheds and shearers quarters consisting of four-room accommodation block, kitchen, messroom and amenities. Since they are generally built of local materials they may provide insights into the original vegetation. The main support posts of the shearing and engine room sheds at Nanya are crudely trimmed bush poles of Native Pine, *Callitris glaucophylla*, now rare in the area.

Cultural plantings

A policy in many conservation reserves is to eliminate all exotic species both animal and plant. However cultural exotic plantings may be an important heritage element in some locations generally associated with occupation sites. In remote areas of Australia Tamarisk, *Tamarix aphylla*, Pepper Trees, *Schinus molle*, and Agave, *Agave Americana*, may be the only remaining elements of previous European occupation (Figure 7), though concentrations of exotic agricultural weeds may indicate sites of stock usage.

Fortunately most of these cultural plantings do not pose a threat to the environment and can be left as part of a heritage overlay in the limited areas of intensive past disturbance. The issue is more complex where the plantings are Australian natives 'out of place' such as Kurrajong which does not naturally occur in the western province of NSW (Harden 1990-93) and not obviously an introduced species. In some cases original plantings can be retained but any self seeding juveniles removed.

Yards and fences

Yards are associated with mustering of sheep both around shearing sheds and at remote locations. These yards often illustrate early fencing techniques such as Double Post-and-Rail or Paling fences (Pickard 2009) (Figure 8). These yards are of additional interest from an ecological point of view as the species and number of trees felled to create these fences may explain the occurrence of extensive treeless areas. These open areas remain due to the failure of many arid woodland trees to regenerate under conditions of elevated grazing pressure (Westbrooke 1998). Based on data from Pickard (1994), fencing a 30,000ha. property such as Nanya is likely to have led to the felling of 15 – 20,000 trees! This example, as well as the species of timber used for the shearing shed, demonstrates insights into ecological history can be derived from the observation of cultural artefacts.

Water supplies

Despite optimistic statements regarding water quality in the 1920s, water from bores was of high salinity and reticulation was expensive due to the short life of steel pipe. As a result of the poor quality of bore water and maintenance costs of equipment much of the stock and domestic water supply on these properties is from ground tanks. Of more than ten bores sunk in the Scotia only two are still functional but at disused bores significant mechanical artefacts remain such as the remains of a pump at the disused

Figure 7. Cultural plantings: Kurrajong and cactus – Nanya

Figure 8. Belah Paling fence and Double Post-and-Rail fence on Nanya Station

A64

Proc. Linn. Soc. N.S.W., 134, 2012

Figure 9. Remains of Southern Cross bore pump on Ennisvale Station

Crystal Bore on Ennisvale Station (Figure 9). It is important that artefacts such as this are retained in situ since they provide evidence of past disturbance.

On properties managed for conservation a high priority is reduction in total grazing pressure from exotic animals including rabbits and feral goats, and elevated populations of native kangaroos. A key strategy for this is closure of ground tanks, preferably by filling and returning the land to the original landscape profile (Figure 10). In most cases however the high cost precludes total landscaping and they are closed by blocking the inlets.

Proc. Linn. Soc. N.S.W., 134, 2012

A65

Figure 10. Functional and landscaped ground tanks

A66

Proc. Linn. Soc. N.S.W., 134, 2012

CONCLUSION

The Scotia country is a biologically diverse region through being on the boundary of two biogeographic regions and having a suite of plant communities associated with a saltlake system. The pastoral history of the Scotia has led to the survival of intact plant communities with low levels of disturbance compared to most of western NSW. This is linked to the history of grazing leases in NSW, the limited water supply and the generally unpalatable vegetation which together have led to a short and light grazing history. The result is a nationally significant refuge for biological diversity. The biological diversity and intactness provide significant research opportunities. The low pastoral value has in recent years led to land use changes which fortuitously include four of the six key constituent properties now being managed for conservation. This change to conservation management has been opportune as a combination of technological change – cheap reticulation of water with black PVC pipe – and a change from Merinos to goats or Dorper sheep – would have led to heavier grazing pressure. The properties of the Scotia are also of cultural significance as examples of small 20th century homestead leases of contrasting character and infrastructure to the better known large pastoral holdings such as Kinchega, Yanga and Toorale.

ACKNOWLEDGEMENTS

I wish to acknowledge the generous assistance given by many people in providing information on the history of the Scotia. In particular I thank Rusheen Craig, Jeanette Hope, Geoff Rhodda (dec.), Norm and Norma Scadding and Maxine Withers. I also thank many colleagues for their assistance in fieldwork in the Scotia and Peter Bevan who inspired my interest in pastoralism.

REFERENCES

Benson, J. S., Allen, C. B., Togher, C. and Lemmon, J. (2006). New South Wales Vegetation Classification and Assessment: Part 1 Plant communities of the NSW Western Plains. *Cunninghamia* 9(3): 383- 450.

Bradstock, R.A. (1990). Relationship between fire regimes, plant species and fuel in mallee communities. In: *The Mallee lands: a conservation perspective*. Proceedings of the National Mallee Conference, Adelaide, April 1989. Eds, J. C. Noble, P. J. Joss and G. K. Jones. CSIRO, Melbourne.

Bradstock, R.A., Keith, D. and Auld, T.D. (1995). *Fire and conservation: imperatives and constraints on managing for diversity*. In: Conserving Biodiversity - Threats and Solutions (eds. Bradstock et al.). Surrey Beatty and Sons, NSW.

Clewett, J.F., Clarkson, N.M., Owens, D.T. and Abrecht, D.G. (1994). 'Australian Rainman: Rainfall Information for Better Management'. Department of Primary Industries, Brisbane.

Ferguson, J, Radke, B.M., Jacobson, G.J., Evans, W.R., White, I.A., Wooding, R.A., Whitford, D. and Allan, G.L. (1995). The Scotia groundwater discharge complex, Murray

Florentine S. K. and M. E. Westbrooke. (2005) Invasion of the noxious weed *Nicotiana glauca* R. Graham after an episodic flooding event in the arid zone of Australia. *Journal of Arid Environments* 60: 531-545

Harden, G.J. (ed.) (1990-93). *Flora of New South Wales*, Vols. 1-4. New South Wales University Press, Sydney.

Hardy, B. (1969). *West of the Darling*. Jacaranda, Brisbane.

Heathcote, R.L. (1965). *Back of Bourke*. Melbourne University Press, Carlton.

Jeans, D. N. (1972). *An Historical Geography of New South Wales*. Reed, Sydney.

Jervis. J. (1947). *The West Darling Country: Its Exploration and Development*. Read before the Royal Australian Historical Society September 1947.

Land and Property Information NSW (2001). *Parish Maps, Western Lands Division Set*. Land and Property Information, Bathurst.

Lennon, J. (2007). Beyond the Pale - the plight of remote area heritage. In *Extreme Heritage : ICOMOS conference held at James Cook University*, Cairns, 19-21 July 2007.

MacDonald, A.C. (1879). *Map of the Riverina and the Northern and Northwestern Pastoral Districts, New South Wales*. A.C. MacDonald, Melbourne.

Noble, J. C. (1989). Fire studies in mallee (Eucalyptus spp.) communities of western New South Wales: the effect of fires applied in different seasons on herbage productivity and their implications for management. *Australian Journal of Ecology* 14(2) 169-187.

NPWS (2001). *Tarawi Nature Reserve, Plan of Management*. NSW National Parks and Wildlife Service, Sydney.

NPWS (2003). *Black-eared Miner (Manorina melanotis) Recovery Plan*. NSW National Parks and Wildlife Service, Sydney.

Pickard (1994) Do old survey plans help us discover what happened to western New South Wales when Europeans arrived. In: Future of the Fauna of Western New South Wales, eds. D. Lunney, S. Hand, P. Reed, and D. Butcher. *Transactions of the Royal Society of New South Wales*.

Pickard, J. (2009) *Illustrated glossary of Australian rural fence terms*. Heritage Branch, News South Wales Department of Planning, Sydney. Heritage Branch Report HB 09/01.

Stanley, R.J. and Lawrie, J.W. (1980). Pastoral use of mallee in the Western Division of New South Wales. In 'Aeolian Landscapes in the Semi-arid Zone of South Eastern Australia'. Proceedings of a Conference held at Mildura, Victoria, in October 1979. (Eds R.R. Stannier and M.E. Stannard.) pp. 231-242. Australian Society of Soil Science Inc., Riverina Branch.

Sydney Morning Herald, 27 September 1928

Thackway, R. and Cresswell, E. D. (1995) *An Interim Biogeographic Regionalisation for Australia: A Framework for Setting Priorities in the National Reserves System Cooperative Program,* Version 4.0 Australian Nature Conservation Agency, Canberra.

The Argus, 12 February 1876

Wentworth Telegraph and Murray Darling News, 18 November 1882

Westbrooke, M. E. (1990). Effects of Grazing Pressure on Weediness in Mallee Communities – Studies at Mallee Cliffs National Park and Nanya Station, Southwestern New South Wales. In: *The Mallee lands: a conservation perspective.* Proceedings of the National Mallee Conference, Adelaide, April 1989. Eds, J. C. Noble, P. J. Joss and G. K. Jones. CSIRO, Melbourne.

Westbrooke, M. E. (2010). *Nanya Station Western New South Wales: Conservation Research Education.* University of Ballarat, Mt Helen.

Westbrooke, M. E., Miller, J. and Kerr, M. (1998). Vegetation of the Scotia 1:100,000 map sheet. *Cunninghamia* 5(3): 665-684

Westbrooke, M.E. (1998). *The Ecology and Conservation Status of Belah Woodlands in South Eastern Australia.* PhD Thesis La Trobe University, Bundoora.

Westbrooke, M.E. and Florentine, S.K. (2005) Rainfall-driven episodic flood events: Are they a major factor in moulding Australian arid land vegetation patterns? *Australian Geographer* 36: 171-181.

Westbrooke, M.E., Florentine, S.K. and Milberg, P. (2005) Arid land vegetation dynamics after a rare flooding event: influence of fire and grazing. *Journal of Arid Environments* 61: 249-260.

Westbrooke, S. and Westbrooke, M. (2010) Balancing heritage and environmental conservation Management of small homestead leases in a remote pastoral landscape. Outback and Beyond, Australian ICOMOS Conference, Broken Hill April 2010.

Western Lands Commission, (1975). *Annual Report.* Western Lands Commission, Sydney.

Withers. M. (1989). *The Bushmen of the Great Anabranch.* Withers, Woodlands.

Young, M.D., Gibbs, M., Holmes, W.E. and Mills, D.M.D. (1984). Socio-economic influences on pastoral management. In: Harrington, G.M., Wilson, A.D. and Young, M.D. eds. *Management of Australia's Rangelands.* CSIRO, Melbourne.

A68

Proc. Linn. Soc. N.S.W., 134, 2012

SECTION B

Papers from the 2011 Linnean Society of NSW Symposium on "Natural History of Royal National Park"

Natural History in the Royal National Park and the Need to Better Integrate Research into Park Management

Michael B. Treanor

NSW National Parks and Wildlife Service, Royal National Park, Audley NSW 2232

This paper is part of Volume 134 of the *Proceedings of the Linnean Society of New South Wales* and was published on 3 September 2012 at http://escholarship.library.usyd.edu.au/journals/index.php/LIN

The study of national history in all its forms has been at the core of Royal National Park, one of the first national parks in the world, since its very beginnings in 1879. Along with the neighbouring Heathcote National Park, it has played an important part in the foundation of the conservation movement in Australia and the basis for national park management throughout the country. On 29-30 September 2011, the Linnean Society of NSW convened a symposium on the natural history of Royal National Park and its surrounds, bringing together a wealth of research on a broad spectrum of topics that reflect the diverse values and management issues of the area. As a prelude to the proceedings of the Symposium, I outline the challenges and opportunities facing managers and researchers alike. These include the need to clearly identify and prioritise issues and topics most in need of attention, constraints imposed by limited resources and utilisation of expertise and skills locally and willingly available. Also, I discuss some unique tools and techniques managers use to understand, utilise and implement recommendations from research undertaken in the Park every year. Finally, I look at where we can go from our current situation, to make better and more targeted use of research and experts to help shape the future of all parks. This includes how NSW National Parks and Wildlife Service (NPWS) can better connect, communicate and work with research organisations and individual experts and volunteers alike for the mutual betterment of the unique environment and heritage in Royal National Park, and make it a centre for nature history research.

INTRODUCTION

The 'National Park', or as it was to become known in 1955 the Royal National Park, has a long history as a place of research and education for both the natural science community and the general public. It also has played a pivotal role in the early development of the conservation movement in Australia since its proclamation in 1879.

For its size, the Royal National Park is one of the most biologically diverse parks in Australia. It adjoins the equally important reserves of Heathcote National Park and Garawarra State Conservation Area. It is linked by corridors of bushland to the Illawarra escarpment and west to the Blue Mountains and Dividing Range. Royal is also one of the most visited parks in NSW with more than three million visitors per year. It is also home to important indigenous and European heritage. Therefore, this presents a significant challenge for managers who have to balance the needs of visitors and recreation with the conservation of biological diversity and maintaining historical and indigenous heritage.

As the second gazetted 'national park' in the world, Royal and the neighbouring Heathcote National Park are not only significant in being amongst the first of their type in the world (Heathcote was originally a protected 'Primitive Area' – a precursor to Wilderness Areas), but they also laid the foundations for the early conservation movement. The development of the conservation movement was fuelled by early attempts to log areas in the southern end of the Park by the very Trust set up to protect it. This resulted in one of the first community- and media-driven campaigns in the early 1900's, a fore-runner to today's community and scientific involvement in the management and future development of national parks and reserves across the country.

When people consider why national parks exist and their importance, the perception is often only of recreation and conservation, they rarely link protected areas with research and other scientific endeavours. Yet, the everyday management of these parks is only possible if there is comprehensive research and monitoring of the park environment and a thorough knowledge of its diversity, heritage, surroundings and linkages.

Nearly every division of the natural sciences and history has been studied and researched in Royal, by the amateur and the professional, including students, volunteers and rangers. Yet, there is still so much more to investigate and monitor in the future. The study of all facets of natural history and science continues to be a core focus within NPWS. Particularly, as we face increased population levels, encroachment and resource pressures, impact of species loss and pests, climate change, and maintaining and enhancing the future relevance of national parks for the community and government.

However, we must ask what knowledge and information is needed to complete the picture for both scientists and managers? How do national parks work with researchers and other agencies to target and prioritise study in the areas that desperately need it?

THE CHALLENGE

So, how can natural history and related research, including the often sidelined areas of systematic monitoring and surveying, assist in supporting the future of the Royal National Park and other reserves? To some, the answer is clear; however, to many outside of the environmental sphere, it is either taken for granted that we are at the pinnacle of knowledge for most subjects or, worse, that it is a luxury in an economic sense or simply not necessary. Additionally, some sciences not traditionally associated with national parks, such as the social and behavioural sciences, are emerging as critical in our understanding of visitor use, the resulting impacts on the environment and heritage, how these can be modified, and how educational and interpretative resources (e.g. signage) can be improved upon.

This type of research is especially important, given the changing demographics of Australia and the range of cultures and belief systems that make up our modern society. Questions such as who uses the park and how different cultures use and view 'national parks' are vital to our management. Equally, the question of how to engage and integrate these cultural diversities with conservation objectives presents a challenge to managers and researchers.

Identifying and pursuing research needs, supporting long-term monitoring and studies, and engaging with researchers, volunteers, retired scientists and other parts of the community is just the beginning. Equally important is identifying who to engage with and what subject or level of technicality or complexity is best suited to their abilities and interest.

To help facilitate research and other studies in Royal and elsewhere, the general aim of a manager, from my perspective at least, is to support and facilitate research that meets identified needs. Projects likely are to be a priority if they fully or partially meet the needs of management and policy, fill data gaps, and support new and promising techniques for controlling and mitigating impacts, such as pest species control and fire management. Other research that is primarily 'pure science' in its objectives, such as studying the variation of a species across a large geographical area, will always be supported, even though it may have indirect or limited outcomes for management or conservation of a specific element of the park. However, priority will tend to be given to the 'applied sciences' with direct links and implications for the Park and management. This approach or requirement also applies to the majority of research grant criteria and funding from government agencies and non-government organisations.

When one considers the multitude of issues and challenges in managing protected areas such as Royal National Park, the potential research subjects are many and varied. Some of the management imperatives include understanding the impact of neighbours, visitors and recreational activities, the distribution of pests and weeds and their interactions with threatened species, and protecting indigenous and early European heritage sites. This means that rangers and managers must work together with scientists to access, understand and then utilise and integrate scientific information into departmental policies and local management plans. Additionally, knowledge and observations of staff and the local community should be included to implement reasoned and realistic (and hopefully successful) actions on the ground.

The current Plan of Management (2000) for the Royal, Heathcote and Garawarra reserves states that "the purpose of scientific study in the park is to improve the understanding of its natural and cultural heritage and the processes which affect them. Research will also inform the requirements for the management of particular species. Data and findings from research studies and surveys will be utilised in Park management." These broad objectives, as well as many others in the plan and other management strategies, make it challenging to identify, prioritise and implement activities without considerable expert and technical guidance. Managers have been fortunate to gain guidance from both internal and external researchers and policy makers, but many areas may never get the attention or be prioritised by managers or universities.

Many of the challenges discussed can be addressed by improving links, communications and sharing knowledge with experts, and assessing and prioritising research topics. An updatable 'Research Prospectus' or similar document can articulate these shared needs and aspirations, utilising a variety of information types and sources. The big question then becomes - how can park and other land managers deal with a lack of resources, including funding, time and staff, to assist and facilitate researchers and make the most of their skills in benefiting the reserve in question?

TOOLS OF THE TRADE

To understand the challenges that park managers face in accessing and applying science 'on the run', it is important to consider the range of tools they utilise or access on a regular basis. Consideration also should be given to overcoming the challenge of deficient resources.

The 'Calibrated Eyeball' is generally overlooked and undervalued as a skill, being traditionally passed down the line from experienced rangers and other land managers to give a 'first-pass' assessment of a range of environmental and other values and their condition. While not a replacement for expert guidance and research, it is invaluable to the manager and scientist alike. It is the combination of experience, gained knowledge and judgement. This ability began in an era where you learnt on the job and stayed in a role for life, thus enabling you to observe the passing of time and observe the environment and its dynamic nature over decades of change, e.g. peaks and troughs, boom and bust. Sadly, due to the dynamic nature of the current workforce this skill is becoming a rare commodity.

The use of existing internal policies and plans, such as the current Plan of Management for the Royal reserves, and NPWS's Parks Management and Policy Manuals, are invaluable. Their strength lies in being able to distil and combine science and legislation - including social, economic and management considerations - into a policy direction or recommendation for strategic and general park planning.

Other tools utilised to varying degrees across parks include the various ways of accessing past scientific reports and data, such as databases and information systems (i.e. the Wildlife Atlas and the two heritage information systems), and a broad range of 'grey' or internally-developed or unpublished literature and published reports, maps and reference texts. To ensure that actions are clearly identified and implemented, various land managers utilise multi-theme risk assessment and prioritisation tools such as Environmental Management Systems (EMS) and Asset Management Systems.

Gatherings of experts, interested individuals and park managers, such as the Linnean Society's Symposium on Natural History in Royal, are priceless and immensely valuable in both career and knowledge development for parks staff, but also as a networking and knowledge sharing experience for all involved. Additionally, working groups and workshops for specific issues (i.e. feral deer management) pull together the various experts, policy makers and local land managers and stakeholders to solve sometimes complex and sensitive issues. Volunteers, local environmental consultants and historic community links and knowledge also aid park managers in finding the right information and exploring what has been tried in the past for many issues.

Many of the authors in these proceedings fit into that all important category of regular long-term and environmentally concerned researchers. Some have been a key part of the Park for many decades, whereas others are retired scientists or self-taught experts whose long-term observed knowledge is of incalculable value.

WHERE TO FROM HERE

Clearly from this discussion, the need to support and improve existing relationships and ties among park managers and researchers of all disciplines, and to seek and form new links, is of highest priority. Forming closer relationships with a range of experts, improving and facilitating ties with universities and research organisations can greatly benefit all partners involved by promoting the common ethic of "what can we do for each other?" Current experts that freely provide advice and their time to the Park are of immense value to the park managers. Often we can only hope that the decisions and actions taken by park managers reflect the energy expended by the experts.

Acknowledging the diverse range of knowledge and how it was gained is also important. Valuing and working better with volunteers, 'twitchers', and never-fully-retired academics is something that rangers and managers always attempt to achieve.

The current development of the 'Royal Research and Project Prospectus' has been a valuable outcome of the Symposium. It draws from all the speakers and topics raised, with the intention that the prospectus will go to all universities and other research institutes as well as to independent experts and internal scientists to promote research activity that will help resolve the most pressing knowledge gaps.

Another idea raised and discussed at the Symposium was re-invigorating the Park as a centre for interaction between researchers, topic experts and volunteers. Having a 'Residency' for active researchers in the park for various periods of time harks back to the days of the National Park 'scientist's cabins' in the late 1800's. The opportunities to make Royal a centre for research and outdoor learning with a dedicated facility is an attractive one. Core to achieving this and the other essential objectives detailed in these proceedings is to have a comprehensive and clear Plan of Management for the reserve that pulls together and reviews previous management strategies, community input, current research, departmental policies and local management practices and tools to achieve the overall environmental and heritage conservation goals. One of the key areas that a plan must address is what and how to best monitor the myriad of human and non-human impacts, environmental variables, and the success and effectiveness, of the plan of management itself.

Finally, the success or failure of the ideas and aims expressed in this paper relies on the NPWS and researchers having an open door and an open mind. This means thinking outside the box when looking for unique and integrated solutions to management issues, working in multi-disciplinary groups to gain and share both knowledge and skills, and to create opportunities and efficiencies necessary in present social and economic times. We need to continue to work and communicate with each other for the mutual benefit of managers, researchers, visitors and most importantly the environment. Royal National Park has the potential be a future centre for demonstrating the integration and application of research and science with on-ground management and practices to government, other land managers and the broader community.

ACKNOWLEDGEMENTS

This paper is based on my presentation to the Linnean Society's 'The Nature Science of the First National Park' in September 2011, and contains my personal views only. I thank David Keith and the members of the Linnean Society for their vision and energy in organising this successful symposium, and for the speakers and participants for informing, inspiring and helping guide myself and park management into the future. Thanks also to my team in Royal National Park, and my wife and family for their support.

Royal National Park – Lessons for the Future from the Past

P. ADAM

School of Biological, Earth and Environmental Sciences, University of New South Wales, Kensington NSW
2052 (p.adam@unsw.edu.au)

Published on 3 September 2012 at http://escholarship.library.usyd.edu.au/journals/index.php/LIN

Adam, P. (2012). Royal National Park – Lessons for the Future from the Past. *Proceedings of the Linnean Society of New South Wales* **134**, B7-B24.

The area now known as Royal National Park was one of the first sites in the world designated as a national park. In 1879 the concept of a national park was very different from that held today, and in the decades following establishment of the Park substantial alterations to large areas were carried out by the Trustees. Despite these disturbances the Park retains many of its biodiversity values and still meets current criteria for designation as a national park. What the history of Royal National Park tells us about reserve selection processes is explored.

One of the outstanding features of Royal National Park is the floristic diversity of its sclerophyll communities. In Australia such diversity is characteristic of areas with low soil fertility, and is a function of geological history. The consequences of the relationship between soils and flora for conservation in a changing world are discussed.

Manuscript received 17 January 2012, accepted for publication 28 March 2012.

KEYWORDS: floristic diversty, Royal National Park, soils.

The early years.

What we now know as the Royal National Park was established, as the National Park, in 1879. The appellation 'Royal' was conferred in 1954 in commemoration of the visit to Australian by Queen Elizabeth II. It was the first area designated as a national park in Australia, and one of the first in the world, although the early history of national parks is a matter of some debate.

In 1879 Australia was not yet a nation; New South Wales was still a colony, destined, after Federation, to be a state within a nation. Designating an area 'National' was slightly presumptuous, but this does not detract from the importance of the declaration, both within Australia and more widely. Indeed the terminology 'national park' was, and continues to be, used for a particular concept of land use and management rather than necessarily reflecting the geopolitical context of an area.

The process, from floating the concept of the National Park to its formal establishment, was remarkably quick, taking only weeks (Anon 1902, Pettigrew and Lyons 1979, Hutton and Connors 1999). In contrast some more recent park declarations have been years in gestation. While called National Park,

the original objects for the declaration would not be compatible with current usage of the term. The term national park today is employed in different ways in different countries, but most widely in the sense of a category II reserve in the International Union for the Conservation of Nature (IUCN) classification of conservation reserves. While national park in IUCN terminology specifically allows for human access and use for recreational purposes, the prime objective is the conservation of nature (today nature would generally be regarded as synonymous with biodiversity).

In 1879 the intent of the Premier of New South Wales, Sir John Robertson, was to establish 'a national domain for rest and recreation' (Anon 1902). In particular there was seen to be a need to provide 'breathing spaces favoured by Nature' for the most densely populated of the inner suburbs of Sydney (such as Paddington and Surry Hills). The establishment of the National Park preceded by nearly a decade the founding of Centennial Park, situated much closer to the inner city.

There was also strong lobbying from the newly formed Zoological Society of NSW (now the Royal Zoological Society) for provision of an area which could be used for the acclimatisation of various exotic species. Walter Bradley, a leading light in the Zoological Society, was one of the first trustees of the National Park.

The National Park was established as a separate entity, rather than being part of a department of government and was administered by a Trust Board established under the Public Parks Act, and as later parks were gazetted each in turn was established with an independent trust.

The by-laws for the National Park (the 1901 version of which are reproduced in Anon 1902) suggest some limited attention to what would now be regarded as nature conservation. For example – by-law '11. No person shall, without the permission of the Trustees, remove, cut or deface any rocks, trees, shrubs, plants, seats, gates, posts, or fences, or write thereon, or shall affix any bill or stencil-mark to any rock, tree, seat, gate, post, fence, wall, pillar, railing, or to any building or other erection within the Park, or interfere with, capture, or destroy any of the birds or animals therein, except with permission of the Trustees in writing.' The by-laws illustrate the limited grasp of taxonomy held by legal draftspersons, whereby trees, shrubs and plants are different categories, and birds are distinct from animals.

Other by-laws prohibited the presence of persons 'in a state of intoxication, or of reputed bad character' and skinny dipping in the Hacking River.

Notwithstanding passing nods to what would now be regarded as nature conservation, the second edition of the Official Guide to the Park (Anon 1902) documents with pride twenty years of 'improvements' carried out by the Trustees.

What would now be regarded as among the glories of the Park, the species rich heathlands and open dry sclerophyll woodland, were of little consequence. The Park 'consists mostly of high tableland, thousands of acres being barren stony moor, with high and dry patches of soil, superior in quality, suitable for military manoeuvres, recreation and camping grounds, or for plantations of ornamental trees and shrubs' (Anon 1902). The reference to the heathland as 'moor' continues a tradition going back to Captain Cook during his first visit to Australia, and reflects the paucity of the English language for the description of vegetation outside the scope of Britain. If Australia had been, as it almost was, colonised by the French we might have referred to the same vegetation as maquis or garigue which would perhaps have given a better impression of its species richness and ecological characteristics.

There was greater appreciation for the beauty of the tall wet sclerophyll forest and rainforest patches, although that appreciation involved the writing out of history the indigenous inhabitants of the land - the tall forests consisting of 'majestic trees, which for centuries have grown in solemn silences unbroken by man's footfall' (Anon 1902). The Trustees did, however, acknowledge the Park's first human inhabitants in the adoption of many Aboriginal names for geographical locations within the Park and the Official Guide describes a number of Aboriginal carvings, although from a twenty first century perspective reference to them as 'traces of a dead race' displays both inaccuracy and a lack of sensitivity.

Amongst the attractions of the area in terms of its suitability for being a National Park were its accessibility from Sydney by road and rail and the lack of other uses for the land. Low soil fertility and topography ruled out agricultural development. In order to make the Park suitable for the recreational opportunities the Trustees were intent on providing, they embarked on a substantial works program. One of the first constructions was the damming of the Hacking River at Audley, with dredging below the dam and desnagging above it. A considerable number of roads were built, the Official Guide (Anon 1902) stating that 'the road-making history of the Trust is emphatically the history of progress'. A large number of facilities were built at Audley.

The acclimatisation ambitions of the Zoological Society were also progressed. The Deer Park was established, white swans were introduced and an aviary was constructed for the acclimatisation of other bird species. A variety of northern hemisphere temperate freshwater fish were released into the Hacking River above the dam. Australia's first marine fisheries hatchery was established in Cabbage Tree Creek (Anon 1902).

Despite the protection of (some) fauna provided for by the by-laws the Trustees were obviously selective in applying the rules to themselves. The Official Guide (Anon 1902) saw no problem in reporting 'Sometimes, but very infrequently – for it is not the policy of the Trustees to nurture or foster the growth of pests, - on a still night the eerie howl of the dingo can be heard on the lonely mountain sides, and the handsomely – marked native cat has been known to leave evidences of nocturnal depredations'. Snakes were not in favour either; the Guide takes pleasure in reporting that they were 'so rapidly disappearing that no danger need be apprehended from their presence. During the last half-dozen years the presence or killing of only about the same number of snakes has been officially reported throughout the extensive reserve'.

B8

Proc. Linn. Soc. N.S.W., 134, 2012

In particular parts of the Park flora was also modified. 'Thousands of ornamental and shade trees have been planted in avenues, groups and border lines, acre upon acres of the best land have been under-scrubbed and thoroughly cleared, and the useless under-scrub has given place to nutritious and ornamental grasses' (Anon 1902).

Plans for further modifications continued until at least the 1930s. Carter (1933) discusses a 'fine scheme' to establish a native garden on two hundred acres of the Park at Waterfall, although the Depression prevented progress.

The construction and maintenance of the Park's facilities were expensive. The Trust received an annual allocation from Treasury augmented on occasion by donations from citizens (Anon 1902), as well as income from activities. Some material for the works program was won within the park – laterite caps were quarried for road gravel and trees were felled for timber. Extant laterite cappings further west, around Lucas Heights and in the Holesworthy Range, support a distinctive assemblage of species, of which the vulnerable shrub *Melaleuca deanei* is a characteristic member. The absence of this assemblage in the modern Royal National Park may be a consequence of disturbance and clearing of habitat in the late nineteenth century. For a time in the early 1920s the Trustees permitted a private sawmill to operate within the park boundaries (Pettigrew and Lyons 1979). There was extensive use of the Park for military training prior to the First World War, including the firing of artillery, while the main visitor complex at Audley provided opportunities for a range of activities including boating, tennis and picnicking. Concern over the approach of the Trustees, and the establishment of a lobby for what we would today regard as nature conservation surfaced prior to the First World War but did not really develop until the interwar period (Pettigrew and Lyons 1979, Hutton and Connor 1999)

The Park thus functioned as a pleasure ground along the lines of Hampstead Heath and Richmond Park in London, for which a semi natural setting was important but where ideas of conservation as it is now understood were not paramount. While the choice of the name National Park might have been influenced by the use of the term in the United States, the concept was very different from that which had emerged in America (Pettigrew and Lyons 1979).

Public discussion about conservation had commenced in several of the Australian colonies before 1879, but the major focus of concern was saving forests (Hutton and Connors 1999, Mulligan and Hill 2001). In terms of national (and

international) eminence the best known figure associated with calls for forest protection was the botanist Ferdinand Mueller in Melbourne, but papers advocating conservation were presented at meetings of several of the colonial Royal Societies (including in NSW), and newly formed natural history societies also added their voice (Hutton and Connors 1999, Mulligan and Hill 2001). The Zoological Society of NSW was active in lobbying the NSW government for the establishment of the National Park, albeit that the motivation was acclimatization of exotic fauna rather than conservation in its modern sense. Despite the fact that many of the leading members of the Royal Society of NSW were also members of the Linnean Society there does not seem to have been any great advocacy for conservation from the Linnean Society in the late nineteenth century. In the early twentieth century (1908) the then President of the Linnean Society of NSW, A. H. S. Lucas used his office to advocate greater measures for conservation of birds (Hutton and Connors 1999), and in the 1940s the Society was one of the bodies advocating for conservation of the NSW Alps (Mosley 1999). More recently the Society has been a member society of the Nature Conservation Council (NCC) of NSW and through the NCC has supported a range of conservation initiatives. In the early years of the National Park perhaps the most important role of both the Linnean Society and the Royal Society of NSW was to provide forums for the publication of descriptive papers on the biota of the state. Even if relatively few were based on studies in the Park they provide the context from which we can now assess the extent of change in the landscape and the importance of the Park in containing representation of landscapes and ecosystems once more widespread.

If conservation of what we now call biodiversity was not a major goal in the late nineteenth century, there was developing another conservation ethos which valued 'nature' in itself and as a source of inspiration and solace to humans. The landscape conservation movement which developed in Europe in the nineteenth century, associated with figures such as Wordsworth, focused on the protecting of areas of 'natural beauty' (the term used in the objects of the National Trust of England and Wales), but virtually all that was proclaimed 'natural' had been modified by many centuries of human use. This is not to say that, from a current perspective, many such areas of concern are not of continuing importance for biodiversity conservation, but rather that farming and forestry have created the observed landscape and thus continuing management intervention is required to maintain the landscape in its desired state. In an analysis of sites proposed as nature reserves in Britain in 1915, Rothschild and Marren (1997) found that the most common cause of loss of conservation values in the following 75 years was 'neglect' – the failure to maintain management regimes.

In northern America, the writings of Thoreau and Emerson highlighted the importance of wilderness for humans, ideas converted into active lobbying for conservation by John Muir, who can be regarded as the progenitor of the modern concept of wilderness and promoter of National Parks (MacFarlane 2006). This early movement underestimated and undervalued the role of indigenous people in shaping the landscape and was not driven by any detailed understanding of ecology and biodiversity, although Muir was an experienced and enthusiastic field naturalist with especial interests in both botany and geology.

Muir visited Australasia briefly in 1903-1904 (Hall 1987, 1993), but, despite his contacts with a number of Australian activists, did not have a much influence on early conservation in Australia, although later he was an inspiration for the wilderness movement which blossomed from the late 1970s onwards.

The first expression in Australia of Muir's philosophical approach to conservation was seen in the successful advocacy by RM Collins and Romeo Lahey for the establishment of Lamington National Park in Queensland, gazetted in 1915 (Hutton and Connors 1999).

In NSW in the first half of the twentieth century the major advocate for national parks was Myles Dunphy (Thompson 1986, 2006) working through the Mountain Trails Club and other bushwalking groups. Dunphy was a leader in the establishment of parks in the sandstone country around Sydney, many of which are now incorporated in the Greater Blue Mountains World Heritage listing.

A prime objective was recreation, but recreation that was determined by, and sympathetic to, the landscape, rather than activities that required the modification of the environment and construction of facilities. The National Park was definitely not the model for these new parks. What is now Heathcote National Park, but was originally the Heathcote Primitive Area, with minimal facilities other than access tracks was an exemplar of a bushwalker's park (Dunphy 2006). The beauty of the bush in these areas was part of the attraction, but conservation of natural history was a secondary consideration in the establishment of parks. Even today, with suburbia abutting both Royal National Park and Heathcote National Park, it is the Royal which is the focus for mass visitation while Heathcote is comparatively

unknown.

In 1939 ANZAAS (the Australian and New Zealand Association for the Advancement of Science – at that time the peak gathering of scientists in Australasia) passed the following resolution -

"(ii) That the Commonwealth and State Governments should be warned of the immediate necessity for more adequate National Reserves for the preservation of the indigenous flora and fauna of Australia; that it is not enough to institute National Parks near the great cities, which become primarily popular resorts; that areas should be reserved in more secluded or more suitable situations with the definite aim of the preservation of wildlife; and that these reserves should be controlled by trustees chosen on account of their expert knowledge, and should be cared for by full-time and properly qualified rangers (ANZAAS 1939)."

This resolution was clearly critical of the 'National park as pleasure ground' model epitomized by the National Park and sought the establishment of reserves whose principal purpose was nature conservation. These reserves would not be promoted for visitation and could be remote from centres of human inhabitation. However, the resolution refers to trustees so that the concept of a system of reserves, administered in an integrated way had yet to dawn.

In NSW the idea of a systematic network of nature reserves became reality in the late 1940s with the creation of the position of Chief Guardian of the Fauna. The Chief Guardian had responsibility statewide for the protection and management of native fauna (or at least that small proportion of the total fauna which was recognized by legislation) throughout the State, but was also charged with the selection of sites to be designated as Nature Reserves. Given the title of the office it was clearly the intent of the legislature that the focus for creating reserves was habitat for specific fauna, but in practice the scope of Nature Reserves was much broader. Although the designation of sites could be justified on faunal grounds, there were also sites which were important exemplars of major plant communities and habitats of rare plants. Although there had been controls on the collection and sale of some native plants since the early 20th century, in general plant conservation did not enjoy a high profile, so that to an extent creating reserves of high value for flora conservation was ahead of public opinion. Importantly expectations of open public access and provision of visitor and recreational facilities were not a major part of the nature reserve model.

In 1967 there was a major change in approaches to nature conservation when the NSW National Parks and Wildlife Service was created, the first such service in Australia. This new Service was based on American models, although as it had both reserve and off reserve functions it embodied elements of both the US National Parks and the Fish and Wildlife Service. The new Service subsumed the roles of the Chief Guardian of the Fauna and management of Nature Reserves. The then existing National Park trusts were disestablished and management of parks was taken over. When I first had involvement with the NPWS in the late 1970s and early 1980s there was still a residual resentment in some parts of the State over the loss of local Trusts and imposition of a central bureaucracy. In some rural areas today there are still pockets of opposition to National Parks, but these are more generally based rather than being a hankering for a return to pre-1967 arrangements.

The establishment of NPWS allowed for the adoption of state-wide policies and procedures and heralded the expansion of the reserve network, both National Parks and Nature Reserves; an extension still continuing today. In this expansion nature conservation objectives are to the fore, but management of National Parks still had to allow for recreational visits, so that in the few parks with very high visitation rates there have continued to be conflicts between nature conservation and satisfying the demands of the general public. In some cases particular recreational demands are inevitably in conflict with conservation requirements, leading to compromises which are never fully accepted by either side.

The extension of the reserve network post 1967 was achieved through a mixture of idealism, science, pragmatism and political reality. Over the years there have been a number of reviews that have created 'shopping lists' for potential reserves. Some of these lists were based on long standing proposals from non-government organisations such as bush-walking groups, the National Parks Association and local lobby groups. Others were in response to emerging public concerns (for example rainforests in the early 1980s), while some were the result of detailed targeted surveys.

NSW has been amongst the world leaders in developing increasingly sophisticated algorithms for evaluating options for nature conservation, particularly as more data about the distribution of components of biodiversity has become available (Margules and Pressey 2000). There is no reason why application of such methodologies should necessarily be restricted to biodiversity and at least some other attributes could be incorporated, for example geodiversity and archaeology. However, while we may be able to design the ideal (at least at one moment in time) conservation reserve system, converting it to reality is a much less objective task. If the key components are privately owned, and the owners are not willing sellers, then progress is unlikely. Increasingly it is being realised that the achievement of the effective conservation outcome does not necessarily imply public ownership, despite this having been the prevailing paradigm in Australia. Progress also requires political will, which is not a given and varies over time.

On what basis do we decide that in the area should be part of the reserve system? For the last two decades the dominant paradigm has been the maximising the conservation of biodiversity. The national reserve system is seen as the means through which conservation of biodiversity is to be achieved. Biodiversity conservation is clearly an important, indeed essential, goal but it is not the only reason that can be advanced to justify reserving an area. Other reasons could include geodiversity, a broad term encompassing a range of features (Gray 2004, 2008). There is a long history of recognising significant geological and geomorphologic features within conservation reserves. In the USA reserves to conserve striking geomorphologic features and landforms are sometimes identified as Natural Monuments. Amongst the nature reserves proposed at the end of the Second World War in England and Wales were a number of geological reserves and both in the reserve system and in statutorily protected lands designated in the UK as Sites of Special Scientific Interest (SSSI), geological interests have been given a great deal of attention (see May and Hansom 2003).

The concept of geodiversity as a geological equivalent of biodiversity was developed in the 1990s in Tasmania, but while it is now well established internationally (Gray 2008) the concept has had relatively little impact in mainland Australia, although it is surprising that concern to protect major caves in NSW predated the development of conservation of surface features by more than a century (Horne 2005). Nevertheless Royal National Park has a number of features which collectively would result in recognition of high geodiversity value.

From the 19th century onwards there has been a keen interest in conserving landscapes - 'places of outstanding natural beauty'. Landscape is determined primarily by geology and geological processes, but it is the living skin of vegetation over the geological skeleton which contributes much to our appreciation of landscape. Human perceptions of beauty in the landscape vary between individuals, and fashions in landscape appreciation have changed over time.

Conserving vegetated landscapes necessarily involve collateral conservation of biodiversity.

'Heritage' has also been a major justification for conserving places and sites, although the definition of heritage is extremely elastic, and, can encompass both physical items and intangible elements. Indigenous heritage is of great significance and Royal National Park is acknowledged as being of continuing relevance to the indigenous community. In European (and European derived) cultures there is little questioning of the importance of preserving major elements of history, including Civil War battle sites in both England and the USA, sites where turning points in history occurred (such as Runnymede or Captain Cook's landing place), or grand buildings (the cathedrals and castles of Europe). Perhaps more controversial is whether or not the less grand, such as industrial buildings or vernacular housing, is also worthy of protection. To retain the history of European Australia and the National Park, should elements of the past in the form of the facilities at Audley or the shacks at Garie be conserved? Are the Rusa deer pests to be destroyed or are they part of the Park's heritage (or are they both)?

The original justification for the National Park was as green lungs for urban Sydney, and for the past 130 years the Park has provided the needs of large numbers of human visitors, many of whom have little knowledge or understanding of biodiversity or heritage. A publicly funded conservation reserve system will necessarily, and properly, be sensitive to the needs of its paymaster while giving prime attention to sustainable management of nature. There will inevitably be tension between the needs of nature conservation and the provision of recreational opportunities and facilities. There will also be the potential for questioning public spending on conserving nature reserves which most members of the public will be unable to visit. Curiously, nature reserves, although being part of the NSW government response to the need for conservation since the 1940s, have largely escaped widespread recognition. However, filling in the gaps in the biodiversity conservation network is likely to involve more new nature reserves than national parks. One of the recent shifts in conservation practice in Australia has been the increasing involvement of private organisations and individuals as conservation landholders, but the State is likely to remain the major player, and expenditure on public conservation will continue to be exposed to questioning and audit.

In the northern hemisphere the interest in nature (biodiversity) conservation developed much earlier than in Australia. In the early 20th century there was,

across Europe, strong pressure to establish nature reserves, based on concerns about the increasing rate of loss of natural (or semi-natural) areas. In 1913 the first meeting of the International Committee for the Protection of Nature was held in Berne. The Society for the Promotion of Nature Reserves (SPNR) was formed in Britain in 1912. The leading light in the SPNR was Charles Rothschild, who as well as being a prominent businessman was also an active entomologist (describing 500 species of fleas) and maintained a keen interest in many areas of natural history (Rothschild and Marren 1997). The first objective of the SPNR was to prepare a list of potential nature reserves in the UK, and in 1915 a provisional list of 282 sites was presented to the British government. The remit of the SPNR encompassed not just Britain but the Empire, and Rothschild also compiled data for reserves in Australia and New Zealand and suggested that the SPNR ask governments throughout the Colonies and Dominions to consider making reserves (Rothschild and Marren 1997). At the International Conference for the Protection of Nature in 1913, Rothschild stressed the importance of measures for conservation of nature outside the jurisdiction of individual countries as a global communal responsibility, in particular in the oceans and in the polar regions.

For the British list, information and recommendations were sought from natural history clubs and societies, and from experts in particular taxonomic groups. Rothschild stressed that the aim was to identify important areas of habitat (although a small number of the sites listed were identified for their geological significance). The list deliberately excluded sites where it was considered conservation was already guaranteed, and Rothschild and Marren (1997) demonstrate that the sites on the list were not an unbiased sample of the habitats in Britain, being weighted in favour of habitats for which Britain had excellent representation compared to mainland Europe (for example, shingle beaches), and the data assembled were taxonomically biased reflecting the interests and expertise of the informants. Nevertheless, the SPNR list represents one of, if not the, first attempts to 'design' a reserve system. The early death of Charles Rothschild took away the driving force behind the SPNR, and although the Society continued to exist there was little progress in reserve declaration. The next major initiative in Britain arose towards the end of the Second World War, with proposals that the national government assume a major role, both in the establishment of a national ecological organisation to be responsible for the conservation of nature reserves and through National Parks (the UK model of national parks is essentially

B12

Proc. Linn. Soc. N.S.W., 134, 2012

a planning scheme which aims to protect landscapes). In terms of nature reserves a committee chaired by Julian Huxley argued the case for conservation and presented a 'shopping list' of desired sites (Cmd 7122 1947). This list included many of the sites proposed thirty years earlier by the SPNR but added new areas. In terms of the broad case for conservation the report reflected the manifesto addressed to the wider public by Tansley (1945), but when it came to promoting the establishment of a government agency and reserve system the importance of reserves for education and research was emphasised. The sites proposed as reserves were to be representative of the major habitats, rather than being rare or special, and this representative characteristic was particularly relevant to their use as research and teaching sites. Looked at more than 50 years later, the list includes many sites now recognised for the occurrence of rare and threatened species. This may reflect unconscious bias by the members of the committee applying their own specialist knowledge in making recommendations, or the importance of the research and teaching function. By virtue of being centres for research they have been more intensely studied, leading to new discoveries. A further factor may be that there is now a greater contrast between reserves and the agricultural matrix; the Huxley committee certainly did not foresee the changes in agricultural practice which were about to change the British landscape, and extend the impacts of intensive agriculture even beyond the then new boundaries created during the war time emergency food production effort.

This focus on representativeness is also reflected in the current proclaimed objective for the national reserve system in Australia – that it be 'comprehensive, adequate and representative' although all three pillars of this approach are capable of accommodating a wide range of meanings. Robin (in comment at the symposium) referred to the approach as philatelic. The approach can be criticised for not considering ecosystem functions and services at the landscape scale but in terms of designing a systematic reserve system an element of stamp collecting is inevitable.

Many of the sites on the Cmd 7122 list did become nature reserves, but many did not and some remain on the wish list.

In the 1970s a broad national review of conservation in the United Kingdom was carried out (Ratcliffe 1977), which identified many more sites as being of national (and in some cases international) significance. None of these listing processes (The SPNR list of 1915, Cmd 7122 in 1947, Ratcliffe 1977) involved formal analysis of the type advocated by Margules and Pressey (2000). The methodology

they adopted is perhaps best summarised as Delphic. The important point is that they utilised the best data available, and recognised that they were not the last word. Today, systematic approaches are increasingly being used in many parts of the world. This is an important advance, as long as we keep in mind the inevitable deficiencies and patchiness in available data, that changes in the environment (including changing human perceptions of, and demands on, the environment) are inevitable and the need to temper idealism with pragmatism.

Despite many of the professional biologists and ecologists in Australia in the early twentieth century having trained in Britain, with in some cases direct connection to Tansley and his colleagues, and the general support for conservation from academics and others, there seems to have been little attempt to follow in the footsteps of the SPNR. Neither did there appear to have been much interest in establishing National Parks with the primary intent of conserving wildlife, even though the colonial powers in Africa were promoting the concept from the early 20th century. Today Australia is a global leader in developing conservation practice, but prior to the Second World War, it was somewhat of a backwater. Marshall (1966) writing just before the establishment of the NPWS in NSW, compared conservation practice in Australia unfavourably with that in both the United States and Britain, but praised the Victorian Department of Fisheries and Wildlife as a potential model for a national conservation authority.

A world without Royal?

The choice of the National Park site was doubtlessly influenced by many factors, but two at least were its accessibility by a variety of modes of transport, and its unsuitability for agriculture because of low soil fertility; if nothing else the first decades of European settlement had taught the colonists that species richness of native vegetation did not signify potential for agricultural development. The enthusiastic expectation of a fertile future shown in the naming of Botany Bay was very soon dashed. If the Park have not been declared it was extremely unlikely that it would have been developed for agriculture, while its potential for forestry was limited to a few small pockets.

In the absence of the Park perhaps there would have been greater development of recreational facilities, and maybe more extensive and permanent use by the army. Real estate development may have linked the settlements on the southern side of the Hacking estuary, and there could have been greater expansion of the suburbs along the western side of the park. Parts of the plateau not subsumed by urban development could, by the early 21st century, have been industrialised with wind turbines or coal seam gas wells. If nothing else the Park can be seen as inspired farsighted piece of town planning, putting a gap between Sydney and Wollongong.

Would we declare a national park today?

If the area had remained Crown land until now, would it be a candidate for declaration as a National Park? I would argue that there would still be an exceptionally strong case for national park status.

The values of the area in terms of landscape and natural beauty, geodiversity, heritage (Indigenous and European cultural), accessibility and for recreational activities are still relevant considerations for making decisions about reservation as a National Park, and on these grounds alone a park declaration would be eminently justifiable. For the past two decades the dominant factor in declaring reserves has been biodiversity values, but this should not make other considerations irrelevant. On biodiversity grounds alone the area would still be ranked highly for conservation reservation.

Despite its long history as a conservation reserve there are many components of its diversity about which we know little. In this respect the situation would be similar for most areas in Australia and overseas. We have lists of the vascular flora, vertebrate fauna and at least some insect groups which are close to comprehensive (although even in these groups surprises still occur – I would not have predicted that the endangered *Wilsonia rotundifolia* (Convolvulaceae) would occur in the park until it was discovered a few years ago). For groups such as fungi and bryophytes we have some information, but investigation has been far from intensive or extensive, and for microorganisms and many invertebrate phyla almost nothing is known.

Nevertheless, what we know of the richness of the vascular flora, and of the community diversity of the park is sufficient to identify the area as outstanding amongst sandstone lands of the NSW central coast.

Marsupial ghost-town?

Flannery (2003) ignited debate by suggesting that 'If we look around our national parks today, what we see in the great majority of cases are marsupial ghost-towns, which preserve only a tiny fraction of the fauna that was there in abundance two centuries ago'. He supported his thesis by reference to Royal National Park.

Does this, if true, destroy my argument that, from several perspectives, Royal National Park amply justifies its status?

Flannery's case, it seems to me, is weak. For a mammalogist to stir the possum is not inappropriate, but mammals are only part of the vertebrate fauna, which, in itself, is only a small fraction of the total fauna. Even amongst the mammals, recent surveys and studies indicate the continuing survival of a considerable number of species. We have no idea of the total fauna of the area two hundred years ago, nor the abundance of individual species. Even today, data are limited for most taxa, so that a fundamental plank of the argument is the based on assumption rather than evidence. Certainly there been severe declines and local population extinctions amongst the mammals and this is regrettable, but for many faunal groups there is no evidence of decline in either total abundance or of individual species, although it may seem reasonable to suggest that changes have occurred. There may have been decline and losses amongst the plants, although evidence is lacking, but the ecosystems of the park appear still to be functioning and to be in generally good condition.

Royal National Park was discussed by Flannery (2003) to support a more general argument against 'small' near-urban national parks. In this he was, perhaps unwittingly, expressing sentiments similar to those voiced by ANZAAS in 1939. Such parks were seen by Flannery as too small to maintain viable populations, and to be isolated from other areas so that movement of biota between reserves was impaired or prevented.

I would not wish to argue against the importance of large reserves (although pointing out that if global comparisons were made Royal National Park would, in many countries, be a large reserve) nor deny the importance of connectivity. However, the empirical evidence is clear that small areas can still retain significant values, if not indefinitely then certainly for extended periods (for example many of the most valued ancient woodland reserves in Europe have been in their present configuration for centuries).

Considerations of the maintenance of populations and diversity in reserves of different sizes are often based (frequently in very general terms) on the application to terrestrial situations of the theory of island biogeography. While this is not inappropriate, for every site there are likely to be unique factors over and above general theoretical considerations. In the case of Royal National Park an important factor is the early management history. The 'improving' activities promoted by the Trustees, including selective clearing, planting and introducing exotic fauna, will have had long term consequences, and separating out these from the effects of size and isolation will be difficult.

B14

Proc. Linn. Soc. N.S.W., 134, 2012

Royal National Park is not pristine wilderness, but in the context of the early twenty first century this is neither surprising nor particularly relevant to an assessment of its conservation value. The evidence from various papers in these proceedings is that the conservation values remain high. Even if the focus of assessment is solely on biodiversity values this is so. Even if attention is concentrated upon one small part of biodiversity, such as mammal species, without any consideration of broader biodiversity values and ecosystem services, Royal is important and worth saving. If other matters which are valued by society are considered, then the case for retention of Royal National Park is even stronger.

This is not to deny the undoubted strength of arguments in other components of Flannery's (2003) essay, but the attack on many national parks unnecessarily diminishes the overall message. Conservation must retain the support of a sufficiently large proportion of the human population for it to be sustainable politically. Providing, even if unintentionally, ammunition to those who, for a variety of reasons, are opposed to the concept of conservation, is potentially counter productive. Certainly there are many conservation dogmas which need to be rigorously examined and tested, and unanimity of views is unlikely ever to be achieved. Flannery (2003) provoked a variety of responses (Seddon 2003, Foran 2003, Brown 2003, Christoff 2003, Debus 2003 – with an even wider range of views to be found on the Web), but the argument has since retreated into the background, though it may re-emerge in the future.

Lessons from the past?

The history of the Park since its declaration offers several important lessons.

First it reminds us that conservation policy and management practice are not science, even though they can be, and must be, informed by science. Conservation conducted by government needs to be responsive to the views of the electorate, and the public understanding of the meaning of conservation is complex and changing, and only partly reflects an appreciation of scientific argument.

Policy aims and objectives are likely to change over time (something clearly illustrated at Royal National Park). Scientific knowledge and understanding will increase over time, but we must be mindful that science similarly goes through phases; what is fashionable and, importantly, what types of science attract funding change, sometimes for reasons which are unrelated to need. Biodiversity currently underpins the prevailing conservation paradigms, and it is difficult to think of it as ever not doing so in the future. However, it would be hubris to imagine that we have all the right answers. We need to plan for flexibility. Part of this will require greater commitment to the concept of adaptive management; under such a regime approaches to technical issues and details will inevitably change, but a willingness to embrace change must also extend to the possibility of fundamental changes in paradigms.

The second lesson is that some ecosystems and habitats are more resilient than we might have expected them to be. Despite the various assaults to which the Park has been subjected many of its conservation values have been retained. We cannot extrapolate from Royal to all ecosystems; since the response to disturbance will depend on the ecosystem concerned and the types of disturbance. If, for example, the early management of the nutrient poor sclerophyll vegetation of the Royal had included extensive application of fertiliser as well as selective clearing, the impacts could have been much greater and more long lasting. In assessing the conservation value of areas we should not leap to the conclusion that a history of disturbance since European colonisation will necessarily mean that an area is not worth conserving. Each case will need to be judged on its merits, but while Royal gives cause for optimism this does not give a licence to continue disturbance. Some of the past disturbances at Royal have had continuing impacts. One of the most obvious examples of actions, which seemed like a good idea at the time, but which is now regretted, was the introduction, and the subsequent naturalisation, of deer. Despite the long history of adverse consequences of introductions, there have recently been suggestions for further introductions species regarded as 'game' in NSW.

The third lesson is that despite Royal National Park having a very high visitation rate the conservation values have been retained. In part that can be put down more to good luck then judgement given that the sites of facilities and roads were established by the first Trustees without any appreciation of what would now be termed biodiversity values. However, subsequent management has aimed, with considerable success, at limiting the impact of human activities. As Sydney's population continues to grow, the pressure on recreational resources will intensify and the potential for conflict between conservation and other uses will increase. A balance between uses has been achieved for over a century; there are no grounds for a counsel of despair or for abandoning conservation as the primary objective, but maintaining the conservation values will require continuing community education and probably greater resources.

A centre for research and education.

When the Park was established, Sydney University was already two decades old and a focus for scholarly activity. The Royal Society of New South Wales had been providing a forum for discussion and publication of new findings across a range of disciplines for a comparable period, and the forerunner of ANZAAS, the Australasian Society for the Advancement of Science, was soon to provide a national stage for scientists to report and debate their endeavours. The Linnean Society of New South Wales was to provide for a narrower range of disciplines, not as a rival, but more as a sibling to the Royal Society. A glance at the journals of the time shows the wide range of investigations being pursued. The structure and organisation of science differed from that of today; there were no PhD students (the PhD was not awarded by Australian Universities until after the Second World War), there were no competitive grant schemes, and enthusiastic and skilful amateurs were still able to make significant contributions to the literature. Travel to remote areas was difficult and conditions for fieldwork onerous. In these circumstances it might have been expected that the National Park with ease of access would have become a centre for research activity. It is not clear that it did. The early official guidebook and by-laws do not make explicit mention of research, although archaeological digs were conducted (Attenbrow, these proceedings), the Zoological Society maintained a cottage as a field laboratory in the Park, and the Park was a regular venue for collecting expeditions by groups interested in particular taxa (Carter 1933). Given that collecting without permission of the Trustees would, under the by-laws, have been forbidden, there was presumably a mechanism for obtaining approval to collect or conduct research. The by-laws do not make mention of the criteria for obtaining permission, or whether there was a requirement for reporting findings. It would be an interesting research project to explore the Trust archives for information about early research activity.

With the advent of NPWS there was a formal process for applying for research licenses, although the relationship between potential researchers and the Service was not always a smooth one. Royal National Park is accessible relatively easily from all the Sydney universities and from the University of Wollongong. The number of research projects, on research grants, by the NPWS staff itself and for honours and postgraduate theses probably increased, although tracking data on approved projects is not easy and much information has possibly been lost. There is no register, of which that I am aware, of publications referring to research in the Park; not all relevant papers have Royal National Park in the title, and many are not available in digital format and so escape electronic searches. Most of the research was conducted on an independent basis, and while Park Superintendents may have had wish lists there was no co-ordinated long-term research programme.

Around the world there are many sites which are associated with long-term research by particular institutions, in a number of cases research finding have been synthesised in major publications - for examples see Savill et al. (2010) for Wytham Wood in Oxfordshire UK, possibly the most studied ecological site with the most research theses per hectare of any location; Friday (1997) for Wicken Fen, one of the oldest nature reserves in Britain, and Pomeroy and Weigert (1981) for Sapelo Island Georgia USA, a major centre for research on saltmarshes. We are not yet in such a position that a work on Royal National Park could be prepared, but these Proceedings are an important step along the way.

Research provides the necessary underpinning for education, but the nature, and strength and specificity/generalisation of the research – education nexus varies with context. At one extreme, teaching and learning about global environmental issues does not require detailed knowledge or understanding of individual sites nor of natural history. Nevertheless, thinking on such matters can be enhanced in the context of a particular location. The National Park throughout its existence has provided for the raising of 'environmental consciousness' (albeit that if that expression had been used in 1879 it would probably have been met with a blank look). Even if, for many of the vast number of visitors to the Park, it is primarily at place of recreation, simply by it being a national park conveys a message. Throughout its existence as a park, messages about the importance of natural areas have been given to visitors, although the messages have changed and developed over the years. Community education has always been a function of the park, even if not always explicitly, and over many years a range of guide books have been available, as well as interpretive programmes. Some of this material has been prepared by government agencies, some by volunteer groups (Daniels, these proceedings) and some by commercial publishers (for example, Fairley 1976).

When it comes to formal education there is again a long and diverse history. Organised field excursions from schools were not a feature of the early years of the Park, but at that time opportunities for nature rambles were available to many suburban schools, without the need for organising transport. For a long period, however, there have been school groups engaged in field trips to study ecology, environmental studies, geography and geology. In periods immediately before, and for a long time after the Second World War, natural history studies were given a degree of prominence in the New South Wales curriculum. To an extent that continues, although prohibition, or strict regulation, of collecting (necessary as the constraints are), decline in natural history skills, and occupational health and safety concerns over the conduct of excursions limit the scope of activities.

At senior high school and tertiary level the potential scope for using the Royal National Park is vast. However, for project-based studies, research permits would normally be required, and this might be a constraint. The diversity of habitats within the park (from rocky shore to rainforest) is a great attraction, although most excursions tend to be limited (through time constraints) to only a few at any one time, and some are frequently ignored (for example the saltmarshes of Cabbage Tree Creek, although historically subject of two detailed studies (Collins 1921, Kratochvil et al. 1973) are rarely investigated).

The Royal National Park Environmental Education Centre is heavily used by schools, from kindergarten to Year 12. It is a facility within the Park of the New South Wales Department of Education and Training. Its website proclaims that it is 'enabling environmental citizenship' and its mission statement is 'to foster in students an appreciation of the environment, their responsibility for its future', important goals but not immediately linked to the study of natural history. The use made of Royal by tertiary institutions is harder to assess, but there is a long tradition of excursions and use by honours and research students.

I suspect that use for excursions is less than it used to be. From my own institution, the University of New South Wales, large botany classes were held in the 1960s and 70s, organised and directed with almost military precision by Dr. Nola Hannon – indeed these excursions remain, for alumni, notable events in their undergraduate careers. Difficulties of logistics, costs and timetabling led to the demise of these excursions. When I joined the university in the late 1970s there were still a number of half day excursions, but these were rapidly becoming impractical. Increasing traffic and congestion has bitten into the time available in the field, indeed the risk of spending most of the timetabled slot stuck in a traffic jam on General Holmes Drive or The Grand Parade is high.

Lessons from the more distant past

Royal National Park is botanically extremely species rich. A long-standing interest of Australian plant ecologists has been to explain why so many species can coexist on what are, for the most part, very infertile soils. Beadle, in a series of papers (1953, 1954, 1962, and 1966) demonstrated a relationship between species richness and community distribution with soil phosphorus. Adam et al. (1989a) confirmed the very high species richness of heathland on soils with very low phosphorus – many of the data for this paper were from quadrats within Royal National Park. This association between low nutrient availability and high species richness conforms to the general model advanced by Grime (1979, 2001) which explains that under conditions of high resource availability species richness declines as a result of the vigorous growth of highly competitive species. While Adam et al. (1989a) concentrated on phosphorus, and there is little doubt that phosphorus status in itself is a major determinant of species richness, concentrations of other soil constituents are likely to be correlated with phosphorus, so that the relationship might be more generally expressed as a relationship between soil fertility and species richness. However, the availability of particular ions is likely to vary with stage of soil development – young soils being more likely to be deficient in nitrogen, while older soils have low phosphorus (Lambers et al. 2008).

Plants are only one component of biodiversity. Are other taxonomic groups likely to show similar patterns? Each species of plant provides a range of potential habitats, flowers, stems, leaves, roots, for other species, particularly invertebrates. High plant species richness is thus likely to be associated with high levels of diversity of insects, and the activities of collectors such as Carter (1933), suggest that this is so for Royal National Park. Plants growing on low nutrient soils are nevertheless able to produce (relatively) large amounts of carbon rich, nutrient poor nectar so that pollination by birds is common, with a diversity of species adapted to different flowers. The low nutrient status of the vegetation is, however, likely to limit its use by 'bulk' feeders. To obtain sufficient nutrients, mammalian herbivores would need to consume large amount of foliage. This will affect population size of large herbivores which will be present at low densities, hence maintenance of viable populations will require large areas of habitat. Similarly, large top carnivores require extensive areas of habitat (Colinvaux 1978). Designing reserves large enough to support viable populations of such a species within park boundaries is difficult, but while an overall conservation strategy may require at least some large reserves, smaller areas, lacking large – area – requiring species, may nevertheless sustain functioning ecosystems.

Proc. Linn. Soc. N.S.W., 134, 2012

B17

Demonstration of the inverse correlation between species richness and phosphorus does not prove a causal relationship. Nevertheless it does suggest that we should be cautious about increasing nutrient status. Nutrient status, at least close to roads and tracks, is likely to increase, as a result of runoff of dust from road metal, and material from vehicles and tyres, and because of the accidental or deliberate depositing of rubbish (in which biodegradable rubbish, generally thought by the general public to be benign, may be more harmful than visually offensive, but inert, material). Park managers will need to be careful in managing both existing and new tracks, to minimise potential for runoff penetrating the bush through appropriate choice of road materials and the design of the drainage system to capture and remove as much runoff as possible.

While low nutrient status of the soil is correlated with the floristic species richness of communities such as heathland and sclerophyll woodland it does not immediately explain the diversity within communities. Adam et al. (1989b) analysed quadrat data from cliff top and headland sites along the New South Wales coast. A number of the quadrats were from Royal National Park, within the Coastal Heathland recognised by Connolly et al. (these proceedings). There was sufficient commonality for some geographically widespread, floristically-defined communities to be recognised. However, within the broad communities, particular stretches of cliff, or individual headlands, could be identified as having their own characteristic suite of species, while at individual sites, within large areas of structurally and physiognomically uniform contiguous vegetation individual quadrats, while sharing many species in common, nevertheless had their own unique combination of species.

Cliff and headland vegetation is not continuous along the whole New South Wales coast. Occurrences are separated by extensive area of dunes, or by estuaries. These features have been present for a considerable period of time, and while the position of the coastline has moved with changes in sealevel, cliff habitat will always have been discontinuous, essentially existing as habitat islands (and at certain stages of sea level and coastal evolution – 'real' islands). Differences between sites may reflect stochastic processes of local extinction and uncertain success of recolonisation. For example, the coastal heathlands of the northern headland of Botany Bay, the Kurnell Peninsula and Royal National Park, although obviously similar in appearance have their own species assemblages, with the biggest difference being across the entrance to Botany Bay. Hamilton

(1917) described the vegetation on coastal headlands and sand dunes between the northern beaches and Port Hacking, documenting many local occurrences of species.

What, however, might explain the differences within localities? At the community level, the patterns of distribution shown by vegetation mapping (Connolly et al., these proceedings) can be correlated with ecological factors which have been recognized for decades – underlying geology, soil type, topography, aspect, drainage etc. It is striking for example that the inland boundary of the coastal heath at Royal National Park is roughly coincident with the distance from the cliff edge where annual input of sodium in aerosolic salt drops below 10,000 mg m^{-2} (Adam , unpublished data). Aerosolic salt, minute crystals of salt produced by the rapid evaporation of droplets of spray, is blown inland. Although it can be detected kilometres inland, particularly during storms. Deposition drops very rapidly at Royal National Park from in excess of 40,000 mg m^{-2} yr^{-1} Na$^+$ close to the cliff edge to 10,000 mg between 150 – 200m inland and then declines slowly further inland. Deposition of aerosolic salt is not uniform throughout the year, but is highest during periods of north easterly winds in summer. The high acquisition during summer could mean that if coastal heath were to burn, and burning right to the cliff edge is rare, immediate regeneration, either from seedlings or resprouting would be particularly affected by salt.

The impact of aerosolic salt is primarily on the foliage of plants. Species in Coastal Heathland generally possess either very thick cuticles or are invested with trichomes, both adaptations which will limit abrasion and consequent cell damage from salt ingress. Soils are generally well drained so that salt entering the soil is rapidly leached and roots are not exposed to high salinity. Where pockets of poor drainage occur saline soils develop and patches of vegetation floristically identical to intertidal saltmarsh occur on seacliffs.

Aerosolic salt is not just sodium, it also contains chloride and sulphate, and amongst the cations, high levels of magnesium. Does it also provide a source of nitrogen, and more particularly phosphorus, that would otherwise be nutrient deficient soil? In some parts of the world's oceans upwelling creates nutrient rich surface waters, so that aerosolic salt would contain relatively high nutrient levels. In addition, the fertility of the seawater, and the consequent abundance of plankton and fish could support large numbers of seabirds, providing an even more effective means of providing nutrient input into coastal vegetation. To a visitor from the northern hemisphere it is striking that the cliffs in Royal are not the seabird cities common

B18

Proc. Linn. Soc. N.S.W., 134, 2012

on high latitude northern hemisphere shores, but are largely barren of nesting birds.

The distribution of upwelling zones is determined by global patterns of oceanic currents and the location of continents. Over very long geological time scales tectonic movement of the continent will have changed the patterns of currents and upwelling, but the nutrient status of the waters off what is now Royal National Park is likely to have prevailed for tens of millions of years. Despite the efforts of humans discharging increasing amounts of nutrients into the sea at a global scale, changes in nutrient inputs would not be anticipated in the remotely foreseeable future.

How are we to explain the small scale (10s -100s metres) variation in floristics within communities? Not all species in any community are equally common; in most patches of vegetation there will be more species which are uncommon (or locally rare) than common, but nevertheless there are sufficient common species to define communities. Therefore one quadrat may have a very different species composition than that of another nearby quadrat (perhaps only metres away) within the same contiguous stand of vegetation. In such examples, is the composition of each quadrat essentially a random selection of the locally available pool of species (so that species are effectively sprinkled like confetti across the area), or is there a mechanistic explanation?

Local variation of this type is more frequent within species rich communities in areas which, at the regional scale, are characterised by both high species richness and high levels of endemism. Hopper (2009) has recently focussed attention on highly species rich regions by developing the OCBIL theory (very Old Climatically Buffered Infertile Landscapes, which are to be contrasted with YODFELs – Young, Often Disturbed, Fertile Landscapes).

OCBILs as recognized by Hopper (2009) are rare, and he concentrates discussion on just three areas – the Southwest Australian Floristic Region, the Greater Cape in South Africa and the Pantepui (the 'Lost World' of Conan Doyle, the summits of the tepui, in a region mainly in Venezuela but extending into Guyana and Brazil). All of these are Gondwanan, two are well studied floristically, but the Pantepui is very difficult to access and is relatively unexplored, although sufficient is known to indicate that it has a rich and distinctive flora, but in an environment differing from the other two regions in experiencing exceptionally high rainfall.

YODFELs on the other hand are extensive across the vast areas of the northern hemisphere subject to recent glaciations, but even within areas recognised as OCBILs, YODFEL landscape components occur immediately adjacent to ancient land surfaces. YODFELs are not always clothed with vegetation made up of widespread species. Within YODFELs can be localities with high species richness and significant numbers of endemics. Lord Howe Island and Hawaii provide examples of this.

OCBILs are not restricted to the three regions identified above, and Hopper (2009) acknowledges that there are more to be identified. He indicates that there are OCBIL features in the Blue Mountains, but does not include the coastal lowlands around Sydney within the OCBIL compass. The proximity to the sea and the changes which were consequent on recent sea level fluctuations would rule out classification of Royal National Park as being a very old landscape, for all that it is clearly infertile.

Mucina and Wardell-Johnson (2011) have provided a critique of Hopper (2009), in which they recognize the value of adopting aspects of the theory but suggest that many features regarded by Hopper (2009) as hallmarks of OCBILs (as he defined them) are, in fact, characteristic of a much wider range of locations which they refer to as OSLs – old stable landscapes. They also recast Hooper's (2009) predictions in forms which potentially provide testable hypotheses. Mucina and Wardell-Johnson (2011) also place much greater emphasis than Hooper (2009) on the role of fire in the development of the flora and vegetation of OSLs. Hopper (2009), while recognizing the importance of fire in contemporary landscapes suggested that many features regarded as fire adaptations were exaptations, features which while conferring abilities to survive fire had originally evolved under different selection pressures. Exaptation is a term coined by Gould and Vrba (1982) which has not been widely adopted by other biologists. Fire has been recognized as an important feature in the management and conservation of Australian ecosystems; Orians and Milewski (2007) developed a Nutrient-Poverty/Intensive-Fire theory which integrates many aspects of Australian ecology; intense fire may exacerbate the low availability of nutrients in the landscape, but Orians and Milewski (2007) extend this beyond the availability of nutrients for plants, which botanists had long identified, and point out how much of the fauna will also be influenced by nutrient availability. Similar ideas had been advanced earlier by Wisheu et al. (2000).

The issue of whether biota exhibit fire adaptations, or whether the features claimed to be adaptation are really exaptations, has provoked vigorous debate (Bradshaw et al. 2011a,b, Keeley et al. 2011), a debate which is partly semantic, and which involves suggestions which will be difficult

Proc. Linn. Soc. N.S.W., 134, 2012

B19

to test unambiguously. However, both sides of the argument agree on the importance of considering fire regime, and that imposing 'artificial' fire regimes to manage fuel load could have adverse consequences from a conservation perspective. This is obviously an important issue to be addressed in the context of Royal National Park, where decision making for fuel management has to take into account both the sensitivity of the ecosystems and the close proximity of suburban development.

In the last few decades Royal National Park has experienced several major fires. It is interesting that fire does not feature as an issue in the early guides of the Park (Anon 1902). Was the late nineteenth century a period of low fire incidence, or did fires occur but were regarded as so unremarkable as not to be recorded? The use of extensive areas of the Park for military training might have been expected to increase the likelihood of ignition, while on the other hand the extensive clearing of understory in parts of the Park by the Trustees in the name of improvement would have reduced fuel load in those areas. The fire history in the early years of the Park would be an interesting topic for archival research.

Low nutrient status of old soils is associated with plant strategies to increase nutrient uptake and retention. These include the occurrence of a large number of species with symbioses to permit nitrogen fixation (not just the well known *Rhizobium* – legume system but also other relationships involving actinomycetes or cyanobacteria), although there are few studies which have measured fixation in the field; a diversity of carnivorous plants; large numbers of mycorrhizal species, and the presence of species with various forms of cluster roots (Lambers et al. 2008, Hopper 2009, Mucina and Wardell-Johnson 2011). These features are apparent in the flora of Royal National Park (and in the Sydney sandstone more generally), although quantification of their occurrence in different communities in the Park is lacking. In extremely phosphorus deficient soils, ectomycorrhizal roots are less common than on more fertile soils, while various forms of cluster roots are more common (Shane and Lambers 2005, Denton et al. 2007, Lambers and Shane 2007, Lambers et al. 2008). Soil samples from Royal National Park had the lowest levels of phosphorus recorded by Adam et al (1989a) in their survey; on the basis of studies elsewhere in Australia it would be predicted that there would be a high incidence of cluster roots in Coastal Heathland in Royal and it would be of interest to test this hypothesis.

One of the consequences of the low fertility and low incidence of disturbance which affects the soil of OCBILs, and probably more broadly OSLs, is that restoration following damage may be difficult, and for practical purposes impossible. Hopper (2009) was cautiously optimistic that restoration following, for example, mining, would be possible. Standish and Hobbs (2010) presented a contrary view, which they characterised as realistic rather than pessimistic. They suggested the need for further research in the hope that better methods could be found. In YODFELs (particularly in the areas where much restoration has occurred, the recently glaciated landscapes of North America and Europe), regeneration on fertile soils with a relatively species poor flora, while not a trivial undertaking, has produced acceptable results reasonably quickly. This success can be attributed to the flora displaying the traits that made colonisation of deglaciated landscapes possible.

Royal National Park, by virtue of being a conservation reserve, is unlikely to suffer broadscale disturbance, but on a smaller scale there will be areas of closed tracks, road batters and the like where restoration of vegetation is required. This will not necessarily always be easy to achieve.

In terms of the consequences for management of conservation reserves arising from OCBIL (and/or OSL) theory, there are several which relate to the β diversity within communities (the high total species richness and level of endemism within OCBIL and OSL sites is justification for these being a priority for establishing reserves).

Sander and Wardell-Johnson (2011) have suggested that much of the turnover of β diversity in south- western Australia reflected the fine scale occurrence of edaphic microhabitats. If the assemblages of species are favoured by, or adapted to, these locally restricted habitats then there should be selection pressure for reduced dispersability – if propagules are spread beyond the immediate neighbourhood of their parents they are likely to encounter less favourable conditions. Hopper (2009) shows that in south-western Australia the majority of native plant species have no obvious means of seed dispersal. There are exceptional circumstances (fierce winds, extensive flooding) which could result in occasional long distance dispersal, and this could permit colonisation events (for an example in *Banksia*, see He et al. 2004) but, in general, species will stay put. Myrmecochory, which is a common feature in Australian sclerophyll communities (and also in the Greater Cape – Bond et al. 1991), is a mechanism for achieving very local dispersal, but is unlikely to facilitate medium and long distance dispersal.

If limited dispersability of most of the flora in low nutrient stable landscapes where there is fine scale habitat differentiation is indeed the rule, then it has both positive and negative consequences for conservation planning. On the positive side it may mean that small areas of habitat can be viable in the long term (Hopper 2009). This is not an argument against seeking to establish large reserves, but rather an argument against writing off small areas as lost causes without careful consideration on a site by site basis. Small areas obviously cannot support large populations of large mammals, for which other conservation strategies are required, but maintenance of flora and associated pollinator systems in small areas could be possible (see Cowling and Bond 1991).

On the negative side, if the high β diversity shown by the Park's flora reflects underlying fine scale patterning of the environment then there may be implications for the possible response of the biota to climate change, and also the way we view the landscape.

If we look at the landscape in terms of a fairly coarse delineation of 'communities' we might conclude that, for example, there is a series of patches of heathland along the coast, and that these are, in general terms, the same or very similar. Given the likelihood of future environmental change, then our long term conservation strategy might be couched in terms of facilitating exchange between the separate areas, through, for example, provision of corridors. (In the case of Royal National Park, given the proximity to Sydney this strategy would be problematic in a north-south direction, but more feasible east-west). However, if we need to define communities at a much finer scale, then the utility of linkages may be questionable (Hopper 2009). If, as suggested by Sander and Wardell-Johnston (2011) in Western Australia, there is fine scale patterning in the soil environment, and individual plant species require particular soil conditions, then the niche for individual species may be defined both in terms of a climatic envelope and soil conditions, and both sets of conditions would need to be present for the species to survive. Even if species could move in response to climate change (and the low dispersability of many species suggests that this would be unlikely) they would still require the same or similar soil conditions, which are unlikely to be present in the newly climatically suitable sites.

Hopper (2009) has suggested that provisions of links between patches of habitat within OCBILs is unlikely to promote successful natural relocation of species, and may even be undesirable in permitting the spread of generalist species. This view of linkages is from a botanist's perspective, but for some elements of the fauna, corridors might provide advantages. It is clear that provision of linkages will not be the universal panacea for addressing climate change. This could justify re-prioritisation of management aims and objectives, but equally it means that some species and communities maybe doomed to local or even total extinction. However, even what Hopper (2009) regards as stable and climatically buffered sites would have been exposed to some elements of past climate change and yet today support diverse floras, so that may be the chance rare dispersal event, such as postulated by He et al. 2004, will be sufficient to allow the survival of many species.

OCBIL or OSL theory, although still preliminary, suggests that planning for climate change will need to be even more complex than it currently is, and that we will need sophisticated approaches to determining what can be done in individual circumstances. Gaining acceptance of the need for a landscape approach for addressing conservation issues has been a major advance, but now there is a need to incorporate within that big picture a much finer grained view of what the landscape means for individual species.

The Park as a place of visitation into the future

Royal National Park is one of the most visited parks in New South Wales. We can take comfort from the survival of so many of the biodiversity values in the face of such pressures, but in the future visitor pressure may increase as the population in the greater Sydney region continues to grow.

As new parks have been created in the more distant parts of the State, a frequent justification invoked to sell the concept to the local population is that they will become tourist attractions and be the saviour of the local economy. Undoubtedly these parks do attract some visitors, but rarely sufficient to meet the promises. As Sydney gets larger, and, in all probability, fuel and travel becomes increasingly expensive, I doubt that visitation to parks in the western parts of the State will increase. Indeed, I expect that on a decadal time scale it will decline. To satisfy the demands of the population there will be greater use of parks (including Royal National Park) in and near, Sydney (Adam 2007). It is possible that visitation to Royal National Park will return to its original 1879 pattern, with much greater use of a revived public transport system. For many of the visitors their needs will be for 'green lungs' and they will have little appreciation of, or need for, the ecological values. The challenge for the future will be to manage increased human visitation to provide maximum enjoyment while at the same time effectively conserving biodiversity and the landscape.

Proc. Linn. Soc. N.S.W., 134, 2012

B21

The lesson from the past is that this is not an impossible dream; it has been achieved for over 130 years, even if for much of the time there was not direct attention given to biodiversity. With increased population pressure and with different climatic conditions the task will not be easy, and there will inevitably be changes to components of biodiversity. Nevertheless ecological processes which permit retention of a substantial part of the biodiversity of the Park can be maintained with appropriate management and resources. The Park as we see it today is the legacy of its geological history as influenced by human activity. If, to quote Mrs. Thatcher, our tenure of Royal National Park is on the basis of a full repairing lease our obligation is to ensure that it is handed on to future generations as a fully functioning assemblage of ecosystems.

ACKNOWLEDGEMENTS

I thank Jacinta Green for her assistance in preparing the manuscript. David Keith, Robert King and participants in the symposium have offered useful comments and criticisms.

REFERENCES

Adam, P., Stricker, P., Wiecek, B.M., and Anderson, D.J. (1989a). Species-richness and soil-phosphorus in plant-communities in coastal New-South-Wales. *Australian Journal of Ecology* 14, 189-198.

Adam, P., Stricker, P., Wiecek, B.M., and Anderson, D.J. (1989b). The vegetation of seacliffs and headlands in New South Wales, Australia. *Australian Journal of Ecology* 14, 515-547.

Adam, P. (2007) 'So little time'. 2007 Bushfire Conference, (Nature Conservation Council of NSW). Last accessed at http://www.nccnsw.org.au/images/stories/bushfire/adam_paper.pdf on 28 December 2011

Anon (1902). 'Official guide to the National Park of New South Wales; with map denoting roads, Port Hacking River and Port Hacking, creeks, brooks and interesting localities. Specially prepared views of picturesque scenery and a general index'. Published by authority of the Trustees. (Government Printer: Sydney). Facsimile published in 2011 (Sydney University Press: Sydney).

ANZAAS (1939). Summary of resolutions passed by the General Council. In 'Report of the twenty-fourth meeting of the Australian and New Zealand Association of the Advancement of Science. Canberra Meeting, January 1939'. pp. xxx-xxxii (Australasian Medical Publishing Company Limited: Glebe).

Beadle, N.C.W. (1953). The edaphic factor in ecology with a special note on soil phosphates. *Ecology* 34, 426-428.

Beadle, N.C.W. (1954). Soil phosphate and the delimination of plant communities in eastern Australia. *Ecology* 35, 370-374.

Beadle, N.C.W. (1962). Soil phosphate and the delimination of plant communities in eastern Australia II. *Ecology* 43, 281-288.

Beadle, N.C.W. (1966). Soil phosphate and its role in molding segments of the Australian flora and vegetation with special reference to xeromorphy and sclerophlly. *Ecology* 47, 991-1007.

Bond, W.J., Yeaton, R. and Stock, W.D. (1991). Myrmecochory in the Cape Fynbos. In 'Ant-plant interactions' (Eds C.R. Huxley and D.J. Cutler) pp. 448-462. (Oxford University Press: Oxford).

Bradshaw, S.D., Dixon, K.W., Hopper, S.D., Lambers, H. and Turner, S.R. (2011a). Little evidence for fire-adapted plant traits in Mediterranean climate regions. *Trends in Plant Science* 16, 69-76.

Bradshaw, S.D., Dixon, K.W., Hopper, S.D., Lambers, H. and Turner, S.R. (2011b). Response to Keeley *et al.*: Fire as an evolutionary pressure shaping plant traits. *Trends in Plant Science* 16, 405.

Brown, A.D. (2003). Beautiful lies. Correspondence in *Quarterly Essay* 10, 112-115. (Black Inc).

Carter, H.J. (1933). 'Gulliver in the bush. Wanderings of an Australian entomologist'. (Angus & Robertson: Sydney).

Christoff, P. (2003). Beautiful lies. Correspondence in *Quarterly Essay* 10, 116-121. (Black Inc).

Cmd 7122 (1947). Conservation of nature in England and Wales. Report of the wildlife conservation special committee (England and Wales) presented by the Minister of Town and Country Planning to Parliament by Command of His Majesty July 1947 (His Majesty's Stationery Office: London).

Colinvaux, P.A. (1978). 'Why big fierce animals are rare: an ecologists perspective'. (Princeton University Press: Princeton).

Collins, M.J. (1921). On the mangrove and salt marsh vegetation near Sydney, N.S.W, with special reference to Cabbage Tree Creek, Port Hacking. *Proceedings of the Linnean Society of NSW* 46, 376-392.

Cowling, R.M. and Bond, W.J. (1991). How small can reserves be? An empirical approach in Cape Fynbos, South Africa. *Biological Conservation* 58, 243-256.

Debus, B. (2003). Beautiful lies. Correspondence in *Quarterly Essay* 11, 112-116. (Black Inc).

Denton, M.D., Veneklaas, E.J., Freimoser, F.M. and Lambers, H. (2007). *Banksia* species (Proteaceae) from severely phosphorus-impoverished soils exhibit extreme efficiency in the use and re-mobilization of phosphorus. *Plant, Cell and Environment* 30, 1557-1565.

Dunphy, M. (2006). Morella Korong, November 1992. In 'Celebrating wilderness' (Ed I. Brown) pp. 12-15. (Envirobook: Sydney).

Flannery, T. (2003). Beautiful lies: population and the environment in Australia. *Quarterly Essay* **9**, 1-73.

Fairley, A. (1976). 'A field guide to the Sydney bushland'. (Rigby: Adelaide).

Foran, B. (2003). Beautiful lies. Correspondence in *Quarterly Essay* **10**, 108-112. (Black Inc).

Friday, L. (1997). Editor 'Wicken Fen. The making of a wetland nature reserve'. (Harley Books: Colchester).

Gould, S.J. and Vrba, E.S. (1982). Exaptation – a missing term in the science of form. *Paleobiology* **8**, 4-15.

Gray, M. (2004). 'Geodiversity: valuing and conserving abiotic nature'. (Wiley: Chichester).

Gray, M. (2008). Geodiversity: developing the paradigm. *Proceedings of the Geologists' Association*. **119**, 287-298.

Grime, J.P. (1979). 'Plant strategies & vegetation processes'. (Wiley: Chichester).

Grime, J.P. (2001). 'Plant strategies, vegetation processes, and ecosystem properties'. (Wiley: Chichester).

Hall, C.M. (1987). John Muir in New Zealand. *New Zealand Geographer* **43**, 99-103.

Hall, C.M. (1993). John Muir's travels in Australasia 1903-1904: their significance for environmental and conservation thought. In 'John Muir: life and work' (Ed S. Miller) pp. pp.286-308. (University of New Mexico Press: Alburqueque).

Hamilton, A.A. (1917). Topographical, ecological, and taxonomic notes on the ocean shoreline vegetation of the Port Jackson district. *Proceedings of the Royal Society of New South Wales* **51**, 287-355.

He, T., Krauss, S.L., Lamont, B.B., Miller, B.D. and Enright, N.J. (2004). Long –distance seed dispersal in a metapopulation of *Banksia hookeriana* inferred from a population allocation analysis of amplified fragment length polymorphism data. *Molecular Ecology* **13**, 1099-1109.

Hopper, S.D. (2009). OCBIL theory: towards an integrated understanding of the evolution, ecology and conservation of biodiversity on old, climatically buffered, infertile landscapes. *Plant Soil* **322**, 49-86.

Horne, J. (2005). 'The pursuit of wonder. How Australia's landscape was explored, nature discovered and tourism unleashed.' (The Miegunyah Press: Melbourne).

Hutton, D. and Connors, L. (1999). 'A history of the Australian environment movement'. (Cambridge University Press: Melbourne).

Keeley, J.E., Pausas, J.G., Rundel, P.W., Bond, W.J. and Bradstock, R.A. (2011). Fire as an evolutionary pressure shaping plant traits. *Trends in Plant Science* **16**, 406-411.

Kratochvil, M. Clarke, L.D. and Hannon, N.J. (1973). Mangrove swamp and salt marsh communities in southern Australia. *Proceedings of the Linnean Society of NSW* **97**, 262-274.

Lambers, H., Raven, J.A., Shaver, G.R. and Smith, S.E. (2008). Plant nutrient-acquisition strategies change with soil age. *Trends in Ecology and Evolution* **23**, 95-103.

Lambers, H. and Shane, M.W. (2007). Role of root clusters in phosphorus acquisition and increasing biological diversity in agriculture. In 'Scale and complexity in plant systems research: Gene-Plant-Crop Relations' (Eds J.H.J Spiertz, P.C. Struik and H.H. van Laar) Chapter 19 pp. 237-250. (Wageningen: The Netherlands)

MacFarlane, R. (2006). John Muir and the geography of hope. In 'Celebrating wilderness'(Ed I. Brown) pp. 16-26. (Envirobook: Sydney).

Margules, C.R. and Pressey, R.L. (2000). Systematic conservation planning. *Nature* **405**, 243-253.

Marshall, A.J. (1966). The way ahead. In 'The great extermination. A guide to anglo-Australian cupidity, wickedness & waste' (Ed A.J. Marshall) pp. 206-216. (Heinemann: Melbourne).

May, V. J. and Hansom, J. D. (2003). Coastal geomorphology of Great Britain. *Geological Conservation Review Series 28* (Joint Nature Conservation Committee: Peterborough).

Mosley, G. (1999). 'Battle for the bush. The Blue Mountains, the Australian Alps and the origins of the wilderness movement'. (Colony Foundation/ Envirobook: Sydney).

Mucina, L. and Wardell-Johnson, G.W. (2011). Landscape age and soil fertility, climatic stability, and fire regime predictability: beyond the OCBIL framework. *Plant Soil* **341**, 1-23.

Mulligan, M. and Hill, S. (2001). 'Ecological pioneers. A social history of Australian ecological thought and action'. (Cambridge University Press: Melbourne).

Orians, G.H. and Milewski, A. V (2007). Ecology of Australia: the effects of nutrient-poor soils and intense fires. *Biological Reviews* **82**, 393-423.

Pettigrew, C. and Lyons, M. (1979). Royal National Park – a history. In 'Australia's 100 years of National Parks'. pp. 15-30. (NPWS: Sydney).

Pomeroy, L. R. and Wiegert, R.G. (1981). 'The ecology of a salt marsh'. (Springer Verlag: New York).

Ratcliffe, D.A. (1977). Editor 'A nature conservation review.' 2 vol. (Cambridge University Press: Cambridge).

Rothschild, M. and Marren, P. (1997). 'Rothschild's reserves. Time and fragile nature.' (Balaban Publishers: Rehovot).

Sander, J. and Wardell-Johnson, G. (2011). Fine-scale patterns of species and phylogenetic turnover in a global biodiversity hotspot: Implications for climate change vulnerability. *Journal of Vegetation Science* **22**, 766-780.

Savill, P.S., Perrins, C.M., Kirkby, K.J. and Fisher N. (2010). 'Wytham Woods. Oxford's ecological laboratory' (Oxford University Press: Oxford).

Seddon, G. (2003). Beautiful lies. Correspondence in *Quarterly Essay* **10**, 99-107. (Black Inc).

Shane, M.W. and Lambers, H. (2005). Cluster roots: a curiosity in context. *Plant and Soil* **274**, 101-125

Standish, R.J. and Hobbs, R.J. (2010). Restoration of OCBILs in south-western Australia: Response to Hopper. *Plant Soil* **330**, 15-18.

Proc. Linn. Soc. N.S.W., 134, 2012

B23

Tansley, A.G. (1945). 'Our heritage of wild nature. A plea for organised nature conservation'. (Cambridge University Press: Cambridge).

Thomson, P. (1986). 'Myles Dunphy. Selected writings compiled and annotated by Patrick Thompson'. (Ballagrin: Sydney).

Thomson, P. (2006). Myles Dunphy. In 'Celebrating wilderness' (Ed I. Brown) pp. 27-31. (Envirobook: Sydney).

Wisheu, I.C., Rosenzweig, M.L., Olsvig-Whittaker, L. and Shmida, A. (2000). What makes nutrient-poor Mediterranean heathlands so rich in plant diversity? *Evolutionary Ecology Research* **2**, 935-955.

Soil Erosion Following Wildfire in Royal National Park, NSW

GLENN ATKINSON

Office of Environment and Heritage, PO Box 195 Kempsey NSW 2440
Glenn.Atkinson@environment.nsw.gov.au

Published on 3 September 2012 at http://escholarship.library.usyd.edu.au/journals/index.php/LIN

Atkinson, G. (2012). Soil erosion following wildfire in Royal National Park, NSW. Proceedings of the Linnean Society of New South Wales 134, B25-B38.

Soil losses from a sandstone catchment in the Royal National Park, south of Sydney Australia, were recorded regularly for 12 months following a wildfire on 9th January 1983, then irregularly for 6 years. High intensity, drought-breaking rains in mid March 1983 resulted in significant overland flow that eroded both ash and sand from the hillslopes as well as from fire trails and walking tracks. Large volumes of sand and debris were carried from the slopes into the streams and deposited in Port Hacking. Serious downstream flooding damaged houses and bridges.

Soil losses by the end of March (day72) ranged from 28.4 to 45.9 t ha^{-1} and by the end of the first year they ranged from 39.6 to 64.2 t ha^{-1}. This compares with 2.5 to 8 t ha^{-1} reported from similar terrain north of Sydney during a relatively dry year. Soil flux rates remained at 9.7 kg m^{-1}y^{-1} by the end of the first year. Litter cover did not change markedly in the first year after the initial leaf drop and most cover recovery was in the 0-0.5 m stratum. Similar high rainfall events 3.5 years after the fire produced minimal erosion of 0.25 to 2.19 t ha^{-1}. Monitoring continued until another fire in 1994.

The results of this study highlight the importance of the more extreme rainfall events as erosive agents. The high rates of soil erosion have implications for management of sandstone catchments around Sydney.

Manuscript received 14 December 2011, accepted for publication 20 April 2012.

KEYWORDS: bushfire, sandstone catchment, soil erosion, soil loss, Sydney, wildfire

INTRODUCTION

Research into post wildfire soil erosion has mainly come from the western United States, the Mediterranean (Shakesby and Doerr 2006; Shakesby 2011) and south eastern Australia (Wallbrink et al. 2004; Shakesby et al. 2007). In recent years researchers have described field observations after fires (Shakesby et al. 1996; Zierholz et al. 1995) and reported on catchment scale hydrologic changes (Collings and Ball 2003; Mayor et al. 2007; Smith et al. 2011a), some using fallout radionuclides to trace sediment sources (Wilkinson et al. 2007, 2009; Blake et al. 2009; Smith et al. 2011b) and mineral magnetic analysis to trace sediment provenance (Blake et al. 2006). They have investigated the impacts of fire on soil properties such as hydrophobicity (Doerr et al. 2006; Woods et al. 2007; Malkinson and Wittenberg 2011) and applied remote sensing techniques (Chafer 2008; Fox et al. 2008) and the revised universal soil loss equation to model anticipated soil losses (Yang et al. 2011). There have also been a number of literature reviews both in Australia (Wallbrink et al. 2004; Shakesby and Doerr 2006; Shakesby et al. 2007) and in the Mediterranean context (Shakesby 2011).

Few plot scale studies have measured the rates of soil erosion following wildfires on the ground, and few have been long term studies. There have been a limited number of studies in sandstone catchments around Sydney, despite these bushlands constituting large tracts of land around important water supply catchments, peri-urban recreational areas and national parks. In the catchment of Narrabeen Lagoon during a relatively dry year, Blong et al. (1982) measured from 2.5 to 8.2 t ha^{-1} of soil loss over 12 months with a high proportion of this moving in a single storm 47 days after the fire. They measured charcoal contents falling from 25% to about 10% after a few months and estimated that the soil loss in an average rainfall year would be about 20 t ha^{-1}. Dragovich and Morris (2002) used both closed plots and open plots for six months following a fire at Faulconbridge in 1994.

This was also a drought year with only 258 mm of rain falling in the 6 month study period. Consequently they recorded average soil losses from slope wash of only 1.02 t ha[-1] and a maximum of 2.2 t ha [-1]. At these low levels, bio-transferred sediment represented 36% of total sediment recorded. Prosser and Williams (1998) measured sediment flux in open troughs at Sandy Point also during a relatively dry year with only 363 mm of rain in the first 10 months after the fire. In this time they recorded sediment flux ranging from 0.07 to 1.44 kg m[-1]. In Victoria, after an Ash Wednesday fire, Leitch el al. (1983) reported the equivalent of 22 t ha[-1] of ash and loose soil washed from a 35 ha catchment in an intense thunderstorm but didn't isolate the soil component. The post fire erosion results from the Sydney area during dry years are similar to those observed generally in the Mediterranean where plot scale studies record first year soil losses ranging from < 1 to 10 t ha[-1] (Mayor et al. 2007; Shakesby 2011).

A wildfire in the northern part of Royal National Park on 9th January 1983 burnt out an area of 377 ha of bushland and, although relatively minor compared to the fires that swept through the park in 1994 and 2001 (McGhee 2003; Zierholz et al. 1995; Shakesby et al. 2007), it provided an opportunity to measure, in the field, the initial rate of soil loss following a wildfire in a sandstone catchment, the relationship between rainfall, soil loss and vegetation cover and, by continuing the study over an extended period, the time for these soil loss rates to return to pre fire conditions. The study benefited from the fact that there were high intensity drought breaking rains 10 weeks after the fire and that there were a series of similar magnitude rainfall events during the following years, after background groundcover conditions had re-established.

LOCATION AND METHODS

The study was undertaken in the 40 ha catchment of Campbells Creek, immediately to the west of Grays Point, a southern suburb of Sydney (Fig 1). The centre of this catchment is located in the Royal National Park at 34°03'11"S, 151°04'17"E. The terrain is typical of the Hawkesbury soil landscape described by Chapman and Murphy (1989) and Hazelton and Tille (1990) consisting of benched slopes of horizontally bedded Hawkesbury Sandstone. As the elevation of this part of the park is less than 100 m, valley incision is not pronounced. Therefore slopes are more gently inclined than the gorges that are characteristic of the sandstones at higher elevations around the perimeter of the Sydney Basin.

On the crests and ridges, soils consist of up to 20 cm of loose, coarse quartz sand overlying either bedrock or <30 cm of earthy, yellowish-brown sandy-clay-loam subsoil. Where directly over rock, it forms Lithosols (Rudisols) and where over subsoils it forms Earthy Sands or Yellow Earths (Yellow-Orthic Tenosols). Total soil depth is <50 cm. The boundary between soil materials is usually gradational and texture often increases slowly with depth. On sideslopes and benches the soils are discontinuous, with sandstone outcrop and boulders common. Usually 10-30 cm of loose, coarse quartz sand overlies bedrock forming Lithosols and Siliceous Sands (Rudisols) on the outsides of benches, whilst 5-15 cm of earthy, yellowish-brown sandy-clay-loam subsoil occurs on upper sides of benches. Boundaries between soil materials are either gradual or clear and total soil depth, although variable, is usually <70 cm. In some instances, especially along joint lines, soil depth may exceed 2 m producing Yellow Earths and Yellow Podzolic Soils (Yellow Chromosols) (Atkinson 1992). In all cases, soils are of low fertility. A description of the micro- geomorphic features on benched Hawkesbury Sandstone and soils typical of this site is found in Gould (1998).

A series of sediment traps were installed in the catchment four days after the fire. Five sampling sites were chosen as representative of the landscape elements within the catchment. These consisted of a crest, an upper sandstone bench, a sideslope, a footslope and a small valley swamp (Fig 1). For each site, the landform element, slope, soils and dominant vegetation are listed in Table 1. Soils at each site were described according to Milford et al. (2001), classified according to Stace et al. (1968) and Isbell (1996) and data recorded in the NSW SALIS database.

A runoff plot similar to that described by Riley et al. (1981) was installed at each of the crest, upper bench and footslope sites. These plots had an area of 9 m² and were designed to measure soil loss from a known area (Figs 2a and 3). An additional 17 modified Gerlach sediment traps, constructed with a one metre wide V-shaped inlet facing upslope, were installed at the five sites, to measure the amount of sediment passing a given point on the slope (sediment flux) (Figs 2b and 4). Sediment samples were collected from the plots and traps after each runoff event until day 72, then at monthly intervals for the first year, then irregularly until 1989, by which time only 14 remained intact and able to provide useful data. Samples were oven-dried. Leaves and sticks were separated from the fine sediment and the two parts weighed. A sub-sample of the fine sediment was then fired at 650°C to remove all organic matter present and the percent weight loss

B26

Proc. Linn. Soc. N.S.W., 134, 2012

Fig 1. Campbells Creek study area

on ignition (LOI%) calculated. From this figure the mineral soil loss was calculated.

In addition to the sediment sampling, two years after the fire in February 1985, a series of measurements were made of the depth of erosion, or sediment accretion, compared with the still visible burned ground surface. Depth measurements were taken every 0.5 m on a grid 2.5 m wide x 4.5 m long. This was done at nine locations immediately upslope of existing traps and was done to compare results from the two different techniques. Soil loss results using this method assume a soil bulk density of 1.0 (Hazelton and Tille (1990).

The amount of groundcover provided by litter and by vegetation in each of four height strata were recorded at each site on four occasions during the first year using a gridded point count method. This was done to assess the impact of litter and regrowth on erosion rates. Groundcover and regrowth were also recorded photographically on a monthly basis for the first two years then in January 1985, May 1986, February 1987 and finally following another fire in the area in January 1994.

Daily rainfall was measured at Audley visitors centre (BOM station 066001), 1.7 km to the southwest. More frequent readings of high intensity rainfall were taken at Grays Point.

RESULTS

Daily rainfall for 1983 is presented in Figure 5. Soil losses were recorded for each runoff producing event in the first 72 days after the fire. Results for this period are summarized in Table 2. The first runoff event was on 26th January. The bulk of sediment collected after this event was low density organic debris consisting of ash, charcoal and seed. In places, the transported ash debris formed miniature dams several centimetres high (Mitchell and Humphreys 1987) as water washed it down slope before infiltrating. Elsewhere, in depressions, ash debris accumulated to depths of 20 cm. Some sand was also transported, mainly by water concentrated along walking tracks and pre-existing channels and gully lines. Average organic matter content of the first runoff event was 35.2% reflecting the high concentration of ash and fine charcoal. By 21st March this had dropped to 6.3% and it remained at about this figure for the rest of the year (Fig 6). Blong et al. (1982) report a similar fall in charcoal from an initial 25% to < 10% after a few months. Leaf fall from the scorched canopy commenced in the last weeks of January, the resulting litter reaching a maximum cover by the end of February. This was most pronounced on the sideslope where there was a tall canopy. However, by mid-March there was no significant groundcover afforded by live vegetation.

Proc. Linn. Soc. N.S.W., 134, 2012

B27

Table 1.Terrain and vegetation at each sampling area

Landform Element	Closed Plot	No. Open Traps	Av. Slope %	Soil Type	Vegetation Structure	Dominant Species
Crest	Plot 1	3	8	Yellow Earth	Woodland	*Angophora costata*
				(Yellow-Orthic Tenosol)		*E. gummifera*
Upper	Plot 2	2	7	Earthy Eand	Low-open	*E. haemastoma*
Bench				(Leptic Rudisol)	woodland	*E. gummifera*
						Banksia serrata
Sideslope		4	18	Earthy Eand	Open	*Angophora costata*
				(Yellow-Orthic Tenosol)	forest	*E. piperita*
						E. gummifera
Footslope	Plot 3	7	12	Earthy Sand	Low-open	*Angophora hispida*
				(Yellow-Orthic Tenosol)	woodland	*E. gummifera*
						E. haemastoma
Swamp		3	2	Siliceous Sand	Closed	*Cyperaceae*
				(Stratic Rudisol)	sedgeland	

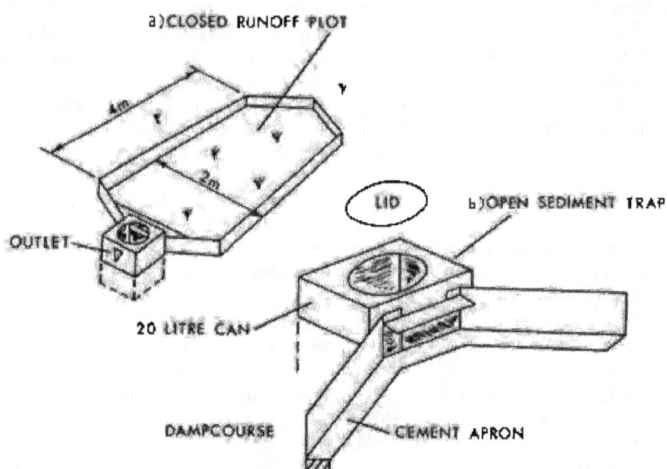

Fig 2. Design of closed plots and open sediment traps

Fig 3. Plot 1, a 9 m² closed plot installed on a crest to measure soil loss in t ha-1

Fig 4. An open sediment trap 1.0 m wide to measure sediment flux

The weather throughout February and early March was hot and dry with no rainfalls exceeding 3.5 mm and no runoff observed. Between 17th-21st March a quarter of Sydney's annual rainfall fell on the catchment, bringing to an end a four year drought. Storm rains on the 17th March the afternoon of 21st March had return frequencies of 10 years (Table 2) (BoM 2011). During the night of 16th-17th March, 120 mm of rain fell in a six hour period. A significant amount of overland flow occurred, with sand as well as ash debris transported by sheet flow. The runoff water was clear, however, indicating that little dispersed clay was being carried. Runoff durations were longer in this event than in the January rains, with greater runoff volumes. Consequently, both ash and sand were eroded from the hillslopes but only the lighter organic debris flowed through the creeks and out of the catchment. On the other hand, sand was generally trapped on the slopes by small debris dams formed by fallen leaves and sticks. Some open traps located in areas of concentrated runoff were filled beyond their 20 litre capacity.

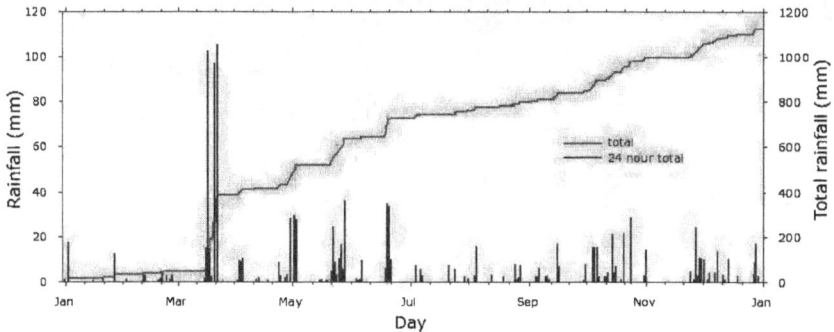

Fig 5. Cumulative daily rainfall at Royal National Park, January 1983 to January 1984

Proc. Linn. Soc. N.S.W., 134, 2012

B29

Table 2. Soil loss in the first four runoff events

Date 1983	Days since fire	Rainfall mm	Duration hours	Soil loss range t ha⁻¹	Soil flux range kg m⁻¹	% Carbon LOI%
26/1	17	16.5	0.75	0.2 – 1.4	0.01 – 0.63	35.2
17/3	67	120	6.00	2.2 – 7.2	0.2 > 21	22.5
20/3	70	100	27.0	3.8 – 10.3	>20	3.8
21/3	71	100	4.00	13.8 – 32.5	12.5 > 45	6.3

Follow-up rains fell three days later. Over 100 mm of rain was recorded in the 27 hours before noon on 21st March, with a further 100 mm falling during the next four hours. The 150 mm recorded in the 9 hours to 6pm on the 21st was also a 10-20 year return period event. This event resulted in substantial local flooding and infrastructure damage that is described in Atkinson (1984). With the soils already saturated, runoff rates were high and were accompanied by very high levels of soil erosion. Sand clogged all the open traps, not only those located in areas of concentrated flow. Many of the small debris dams formed only days earlier, were breached and large volumes of sand were carried from the slopes into the streams and out of the catchment. By comparison, the closed plots were not filled beyond their capacity. This was because the upslope plot borders prevented normal overland flow from eroding the plot surface as it did on either side. After the rain, the areas surrounding the plots were noticeably more eroded than the protected area within the plot borders. The results presented

for the closed plots can therefore be considered underestimates of the true soil loss. Similarly, annual flux figures including this date are minimum figures and cannot be used to compare sites during this event. Consequently comparative sediment flux results in Figure 7 are only for the period 22nd March, 1983 to 10th January, 1984.

Soil loss and sediment flux results for the rest of the year generally reflect the rainfall during each month, with relatively constant flux rates between March and July, dropping during a low rainfall period in August and September and returning to the higher levels from October to January 1984. There is little evidence of diminishing flux rates with increasing groundcover over time (Fig 7). Rather they continued at the a similar rate through to the end of the first year. The average flux rate of the hillslope plots was the equivalent of 9.7 kg m⁻¹ year⁻¹ for the more typical conditions that existed after March 1983.

Cumulative soil loss for the first 12 months after the fire measured in the three closed plots ranged

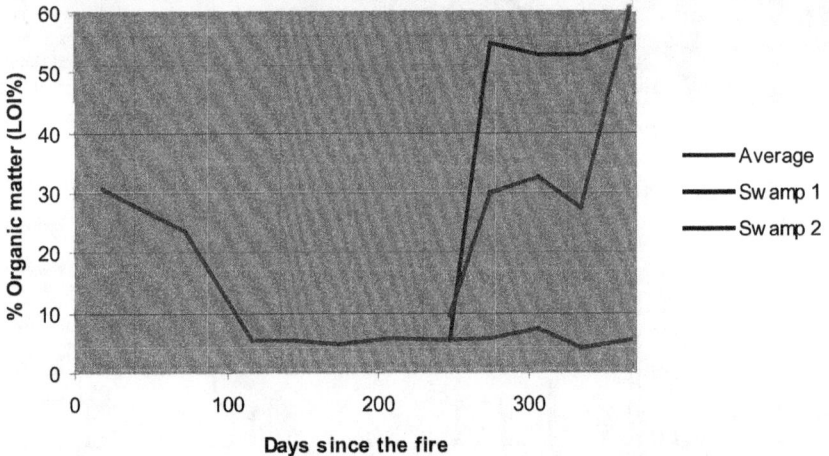

Fig 6. Organic carbon content (LOI%) of sediment vs days since the fire

B30

Proc. Linn. Soc. N.S.W., 134, 2012

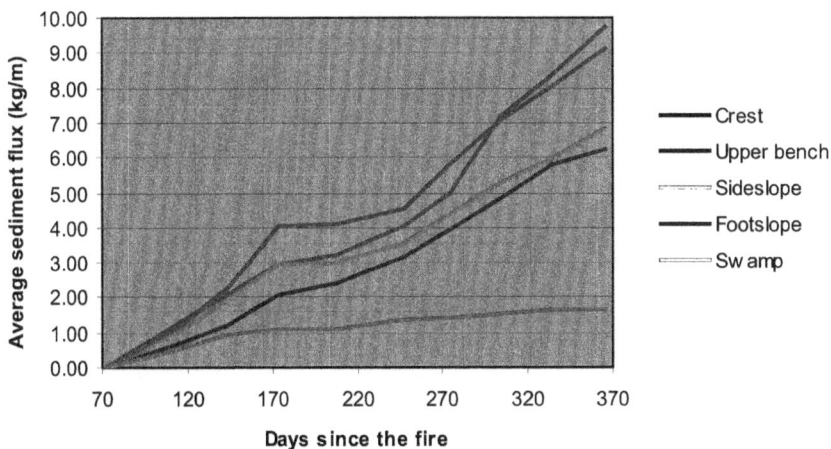

Fig 7. Cumulative sediment flux vs days since the fire, zeroed at day 72, 22nd March 1983

from of 39.6 to 64.2 t ha^{-1}, the bulk of which occurred over the four days in March (Fig 8).

Recovery of native vegetation proceeded at a steady rate during the first year (Figs 9-13). The first plants to recover were those which were able to survive the fire alive and kept on growing by resprouting (Keith 1995). They either resprouted quickly from epicormic buds on stems (e.g. *Eucalyptus, Angophora costata* and *Persoonia levis*) or ground level lignotubers (e.g. *Eucalyptus, Isopogon, Lomatia* and *Angophora hispida*) or were protected by crowded leaf bases (e.g.

Xanthorrhoea and *Doryanthes*) or resprouted from rhizomes (e.g. Cyperaceae, *Lomandra, Patersonia, Pteridium* and, Restionaceae). Seedlings began to emerge during autumn and winter and rapid growth of small plants took place through the spring as consistent rains and cooler temperatures maintained high soil moisture levels. This growth continued throughout summer with most small plants surviving the hot summer because of the regular rains. Many plants flowered during spring and summer. Larger trees such as eucalypts and *Angophora costata* shed

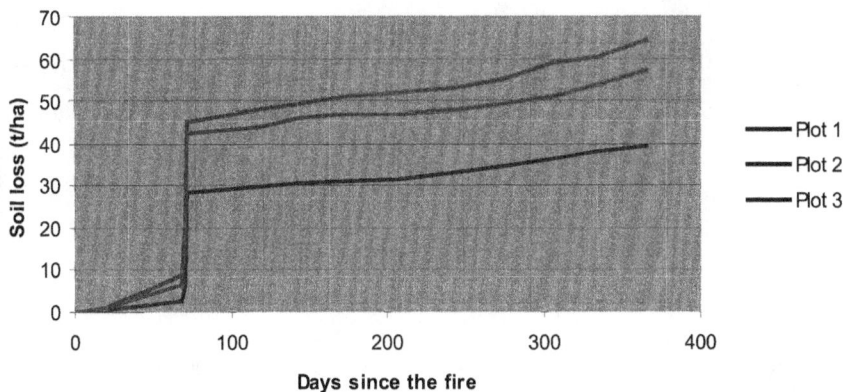

Fig 8. Cumulative soil loss measured in three 9 m2 closed plots vs days since the fire

Proc. Linn. Soc. N.S.W., 134, 2012

B31

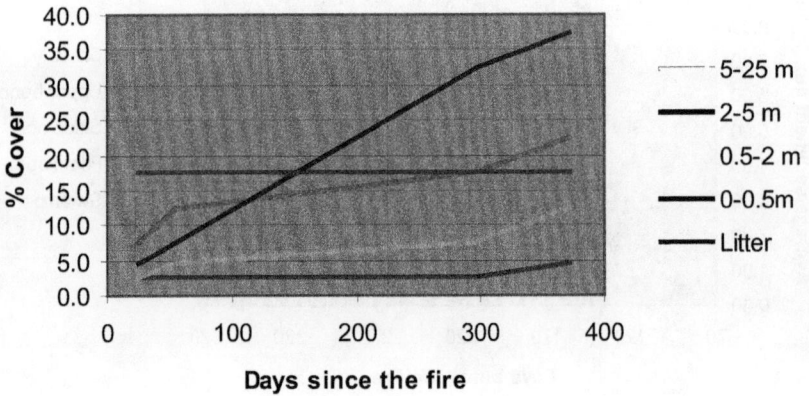

Fig. 9. Recovery of groundcover in 4 height strata and litter for 4 dates following the fire - Crest

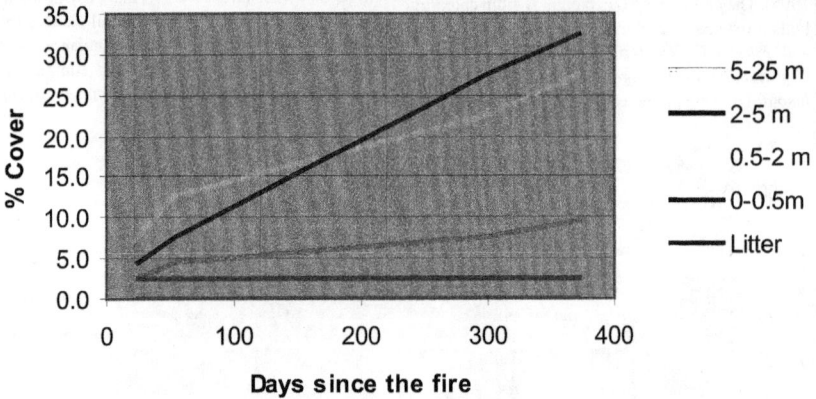

Fig. 10. Recovery of groundcover in 4 height strata and litter for 4 dates following the fire- Bench

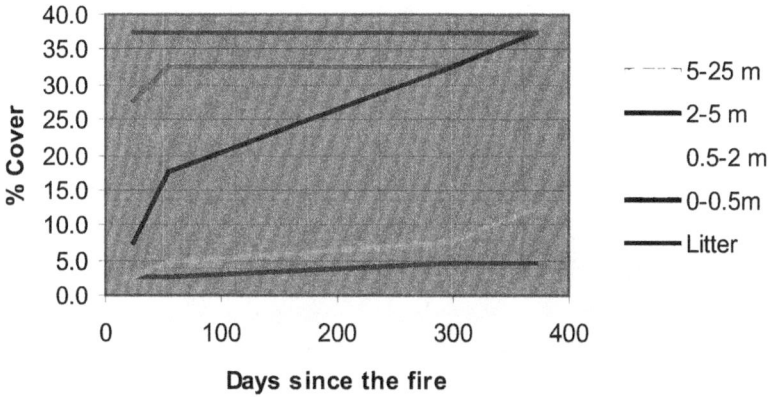

Fig. 11. Recovery of groundcover in 4 height strata and litter for 4 dates following the fire - Sideslope

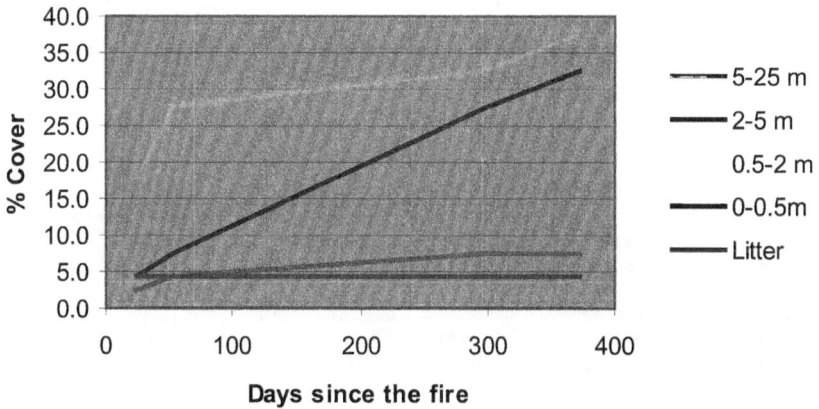

Fig. 12. Recovery of groundcover in 4 height strata and litter for 4 dates following the fire - Footslope

Proc. Linn. Soc. N.S.W., 134, 2012

B33

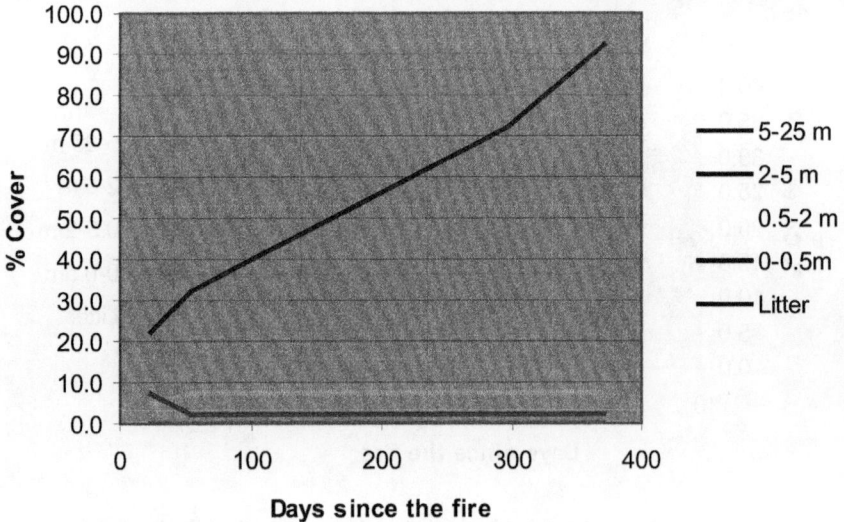

Figs 13. Recovery of groundcover in 4 height strata and litter for 4 dates following the fire - Swamp

bark and sticks in November, substantially increasing litter cover around them. However, since the initial drop of dead leaves in February, very few trees had old leaves, so the leaf litter generally did not increase since that time. Most noticeable growth was in the 0 - 0.5 m stratum, as would be expected, where most sites recorded over 30% cover by the end of the year. The only area where regrowth of vegetation could be seen to influence erosion and sedimentation rates was in the sedge swamp (Fig 7). Here flux rates tapered off to low levels after June, by which time regrowth of the sedges had been sufficient to prevent the sediment which entered the swamp from being transported through it. The corresponding change in sediment composition between sand and organic material is reflected in Figure 6 as the light organic material continued to be transported. Groundcover of sedges had reached 92% by the end of the year. These swamp results would suggest that sediment had ceased discharging from the catchment by June.

On the 9th November 1984, 22 months after the fire, 279 mm of rain was recorded at Audley. This represents a 20-50 year return period event, effectively much larger than that of March 1983. Significantly, during this event there was no flooding or infrastructure damage downstream. This can be accounted for by higher infiltration rates, improved

groundcover and increased surface roughness due to vegetation regrowth. Although localised soil loss may have still been significant there was an effective filter in place with thick vegetation in the swamp. There was however, noticeably more erosion observed along walking trails.

Measured changes in the height of the post fire ground surface upslope of nine traps in January 1985 revealed soil loss figures in the same range as was obtained in the closed plots over the first year (Table 3). Individual values near the three closed plots were 14.9 t ha[-1] for plot 1, 44.4 t ha[-1] for plot 2 and 52.7 t ha[-1] for plot 3. This method demonstrated that there was both erosion and sedimentation over short distances with 48% of points eroded, 30% with sediment accumulation and 22% with no change to the net surface height. Discrepancies between the plot results and these ground surface measurements can be partly attributed to the greater exhaustion of sediment supply in the closed plots whereas outside the plots sediment also accumulated in micro-terraces. These measurements also had greater variability demonstrating the effects of local variations in overland flow paths. As an example, measurements near two adjacent traps on the crest that had similar results in the first year had the equivalent of 14.9 t ha[-1] of soil loss and 15.8 t ha[-1] of accretion respectively

Table 3. Net soil loss measured by change in ground height at nine locations after two years

Landform element	Location above	Slope %	Soil loss t ha⁻¹
crest	Plot 1	8%	14.9
crest	Trap 4	5%	-15.8
sideslope	Trap 21	12%	36.4
footslope	Plot 3	13%	52.7
footslope	Trap 28	10%	4.9
footslope	Trap 33	13%	11.1
upper bench	Plot 2	6%	44.4
Upper bench	Trap 8	8%	32.7
Average			22.6

by the end of the second year indicating local redistribution of hillslope sediments.

Rainfall records for the 11 year period from January 1983 to January 1994 from Audley reveal that a number of high return period rainfall events occurred during this period, at least eight of which exceeded a 1:10 year return period (Table 4) (BoM 2011). Between 1986 and 1989 there were two high return period rainfall events for which soil losses were recorded (Table 5). Whilst the 20-50 year return period event of 9ᵗʰ November 1984 produced noticeable soil erosion, the events of August 1986, April 1988, February 1990, June 1991 and February 1992 passed without visible impact. Rainstorms on 5ᵗʰ and 6ᵗʰ August 1986, 3.5 years after the fire, were a 10 year return period event of similar magnitude to that of March 1983, yet this event yielded soil losses of only 0.25 to 2.19 t ha⁻¹ and flux rates which averaged 0.2 kg m⁻¹. The plots were monitored 6 months and 12 months after this storm event by which time soil losses had dropped appreciably (Table 5). Over the following 15 months to January 1989 there was only 0.07 to 1.15 t ha⁻¹ recorded despite a 20 year return rainfall event on 30ᵗʰ April 1988. Similarly, there was either no fresh sediment or up to 0.1 kg m⁻¹ sediment flux in the open traps. Again the even bigger event of June 1991 passed without impact indicating clearly that the bushland had returned sufficient groundcover to protect the soil from erosion.

DISCUSSION

The soil losses in the year following a bushfire measured in the closed plots in this study of 39.6 to 64.2 t ha⁻¹ are higher than the 2.5 to 8 t ha⁻¹ recorded in similar terrain by Blong et al. (1982). However, like Dragovich and Morris (2002), their results were obtained during a relatively dry year (60% of average rainfall) and their suggestion of soil losses in excess of 20 t ha⁻¹ in an average rainfall year is a realistic estimate for Hawkesbury Sandstone terrain. Even if the more extreme events of March 1983 are removed from the figures presented here, soil losses for the period April 1983 to January 1984 still range from 11.1 to 20.4 t ha⁻¹ which is consistent with their prediction.

However sediment flux rates measured in the open plots suggest that the closed plots significantly underestimated the actual erosion taking place on the slope during the high rainfall events in March 1983 because the plot borders were deflecting overland flow. This suggests that the open traps measuring sediment flux, despite the obvious problems in this study of undersized containers and unknown contributing areas, may well provide a more realistic measure of erosion rates than the closed plots. Soil

Table 4. High rainfall events for the period January 1983 to January 1994

Year	Date	Daily rainfall mm#	Return frequency	
1983	17ᵗʰ March	120/6 hours	10yr	
	21ˢᵗ March	150/9 hours	10-20yr	
1984	9ᵗʰ November	279*	20-50yr	
1985	5ᵗʰ December	117*	1-2yr	
1986	5ᵗʰ August	116	1-2yr	10yr
	6ᵗʰ August	142*	2-5yr	
1987	11ᵗʰ August	111	1-2yr	
	25ᵗʰ October	98*	1yr	
1988	30ᵗʰ April	173	20yr	
1990	3ʳᵈ February	175*	20yr	20yr
	4ᵗʰ February	132	2yr	
1991	11ᵗʰ June	300*	50yr	100yr
	12ᵗʰ June	108	1-2yr	
1992	9ᵗʰ February	107	1-2yr	
	10ᵗʰ February	170	20yr	
#(BoM, 2011)		* monthly record rainfall		

SOIL EROSION FOLLOWING WILDFIRE

Table 5. Soil loss during the bushland recovery phase

Date	Plot 1 t ha⁻¹	Plot 2 t ha⁻¹	Plot 3 t ha⁻¹	Average flux kg m⁻¹
8/08/1986	0.54	2.19	0.25	0.20
23/02/1987	0.21	0.94	1.29	0.15
24/09/1987	0.07	1.12	0.16	0.12
1/01/1989	0.07	1.57	0.18	0.19

loss rates remained relatively high 12 months after the fire, notwithstanding good regeneration of native vegetation, but by two years, and again 3.5 years after the fire even major rainfall events of similar magnitude to that of March 1983, produced minimal sheet erosion. However, erosion along bare walking trails was observed to continue throughout the study period.

Erosion rates measured by comparing actual soil surface deflation or accretion with the burned surface after two years indicated similar rates of soil loss to those predicted by Blong et al. (1982) but somewhat less than those recorded in the closed plots in this study, averaging 22.9 t ha⁻¹ in two years. This is attributed to small scale erosion and sedimentation on the hillslopes and the possible exhaustion of loose soil within the closed plots.

Between four and five years after the fire the soil loss rate had fallen to an average of 0.62 t ha⁻¹ and sediment flux to 0.15 kg m⁻¹ approximating 1% of the peak soil loss and 0.3% of the peak sediment flux observed in the first year.

The results of this study highlight the importance of the more intense rainfall events as erosive agents, particularly in the period immediately after the fire and that significant erosion should be expected in such circumstances. This is consistent with observations of numerous authors including Good (1973), Booker et al. (1993), Leitch et al. (1983), Prosser and Williams (1998) and Wallbrink et al. (2004). The frequency of these high rainfall events during the 11 year study period was certainly much higher than their predicted return frequency, there being eight such events in excess of 100 mm per day. This is a much higher threshold than the greater-than-one-year recurrence interval that Prosser and Williams (1998) suggest is required to generate substantial runoff and sediment yield. The observed frequency of these high magnitude events would suggest that the chances of a significant erosive rainfall event occurring before groundcover

is well established after a fire in this terrain is quite high, contrary to the predictions of Prosser and Williams (1998) that the convergence of high intensity fire and an intense storm event would be rare.

ACKNOWLEDGEMENTS

Field assistance was provided by Peter Tille, Greg Chapman, Owen Graham and David Merrican, Soil Conservation Service of NSW Sydney. Laboratory analyses were performed by Glenda Holman, Soil Conservation Service of NSW Scone.

REFERENCES

Atkinson, G. (1984) Erosion damage following bushfires. *Journal of Soil Conservation NSW* **40**, 4-9.
Atkinson, G. (1992) Soil materials – a layer based approach to soil description and classification. *Catena* **20**, 411-418.
Blake, W.H., Wallbrink, P.J., Doerr, S.H., Shakesby, R.A. and Humphreys, G.S. (2006) Magnetic enhancement in wildfire-affected soil and its potential for sediment-source ascription. *Earth Surface Processes and Landforms* **31**, 249-264.
Blake, W.H., Wallbrink, P.J., Wilkinson, S.N., Humphreys, G.S., Doerr, S.H., Shakesby, R.A. and Tomkins K.M. (2009) Deriving hillslope sediment budgets in wildfire-affected forests using fallout radionuclide tracers. *Geomorphology* **104** (3-4), 105-116.
Blong, R.J.M., Riley, S.J. and Crozier, P. (1982) Sediment yield from runoff plots following bushfire near Narrabeen Lagoon, NSW. *Search* **13** (1-2), 36-39.
Booker, F.A., Dietrich, W.E. and Collins, L.M. (1993) Runoff and erosion after the Oakland firestorm: expectations and observations. California Geology **46**, 159-173.
BOM (2011) http://www.bom.gov.au/hydro/has/cdirswcbx/cdirswebx.shtml Retrieved 10-11-11
Chapman, G.C. and Murphy, C. (1989) 'Soil landscapes of the Sydney 1:100,000 sheet'. Soil Conservation Service of NSW, Sydney.
Chafer, C.J. (2008) A comparison of fire severity measures: An Australian example and implications for predicting major areas of soil erosion. *Catena* **74** (3), 235-245.
Collings, G. and Ball, J. (2003) The hydrological effects of the 1994 wild fire on the Royal National Park. 'International Hydrology and Water Resources Symposium', Wollongong, NSW, 10-14ᵗʰ November. pp. 2.161-2.168. Institution of Engineers, Australia, Barton, ACT.

Doerr, S.H., Shakesby, R.A., Blake, W.H., Chafer, C.J., Humphreys, G.S., Wallbrink, P.J. (2006) Effects of differing wildfire severities on soil wettability and implications for hydrological response. *Journal of Hydrology* 319(1-4), 295-311.

Dragovich, D. and Morris, R. (2002) Fire intensity, slopewash and bio-transfer of sediment in eucalypt forest, Australia. *Earth Surface Processes and Landforms* 27 (12), 1309-1319.

Fox, D.M., Maselli, F. and Carrega, P. (2008) Using SPOT images and field sampling to map burn severity and vegetation factors affecting post forest fire erosion risk. *Catena* 75 (3), 326-335.

Good, R.B. (1973) A preliminary assessment of erosion following wildfires in Kosciusko National Park, N.S.W. in 1973. *Journal of Soil Conservation NSW*, 29, 191-199

Gould, S.F. (1998) Proteoid root mats stabilize Hawkesbury Sandstone biomantles following fire. *Australian Journal of Soil Research* 36 (6), 1033-1043.

Hazelton, P.A. and Tille, P.J. (1990) 'Soil landscapes of the Wollongong – Port Hacking 1:100,000 sheet'. Soil Conservation Service of NSW, Sydney.

Isbell, R.F. (1996)) 'The Australian soil classification'. CSIRO Australia, Collingwood.

Keith, D. (1995) Fire-driven extinction of plant populations: a synthesis of theory and review of evidence from Australian vegetation. *Proceedings of the Linnean Society of NSW* 116, 37-78.

Leitch, C., Flinn, D.W. and van de Graaff, R.H.M. (1983) Erosion and nutrient loss resulting from Ash Wednesday (February 1983) wildfires: a case study. *Australian Forestry* 46 (3), 173-180.

Malkinson, D. and Wittenberg, L. (2011) Post fire induced soil water repellency - modeling short and long-term processes. *Geomorphology* 125(1), 186-192.

Mayor, A.G., Bautista, S., Llovet, J, and Bellot, J. (2007) Post-fire hydrological and erosional responses of a Mediterranean landscape: Seven years of catchment-scale dynamics. *Catena* 71 (1), 68-75.

McGhee, K. (2003) A royal recovery: has fire ripped through Australia's oldest national park one too many times. *Australian Geographic* 69, 78-93.

Milford, H.B., McGaw, A.J.E. and Nixon, K.J. (eds.) (2001) 'Soil data entry handbook' (3rd Edition), NSW Department of Land and Water Conservation, Sydney.

Mitchell, P.B. and Humphreys, G.S. (1987) Litter dams and microterraces formed on hillslopes subject to rainwash in the Sydney Basin, Australia. *Geoderma* 39 (4), 331-357.

Prosser, I. P. and Williams, L. (1998) The effect of wildfire on runoff and erosion in native Eucalyptus forest. *Hydrological Processes* 12, 251-265.

Riley, S.J., Crozier, P. and Blong, R.J. (1981) An inexpensive and easily installed runoff plot. *Journal of Soil Conservation NSW* 37, 144-148.

Shakesby, R.A. and Doerr, S.H. (2006) Wildfire as a hydrological and geomorphological agent. *Earth-Science Reviews* 74 (3-4), 269-307.

Shakesby, R.A., Wallbrink, P.J., Doerr, S.H., English, P.M., Chafer, C.J., Humphreys, G.S., Blake W.H. and Tomkins, K.M. (2007) Distinctiveness of wildfire effects on soil erosion in south-east Australian eucalypt forests assessed in a global context. *Forest Ecology and Management* 238, 347-364.

Shakesby, R.A., Blake, W.H., Doerr, S.H., Humphreys, G.S., Wallbrink, P.J. and Chafer, C.J. (2006) Hillslope soil erosion and bioturbation after the Christmas 2001 forest fires near Sydney, Australia. P51-61 in Owens, P.N., and Collins, A.J. (eds) Soil erosion and sediment redistribution in river catchments. CABA Publishing, Cambridge, MA.

Shakesby, R.A. (2011) Post-wildfire soil erosion in the Mediterranean: Review and future research directions. *Earth-Science Reviews* 105 (3-4), 71-100.

Smith, H.G., Sheridan, G.J., Lane, P.N.J. and Bren, L.J. (2011a) Wildfire and salvage harvesting effects on runoff generation and sediment exports from radiata pine and eucalypt forest catchments, south-eastern Australia. *Forest Ecology and Management* 261 (3), 570-581.

Smith, H.G., Sheridan, G.J., Lane, P.N.J., Noske, P.J., Heijnis, H. (2011b). Changes to sediment sources following wildfire in a forested upland catchment, southeastern Australia. *Hydrological Processes* 25 (18), 2878-2889.

Stace, H.C.T., Hubble, G.D., Brewer, R., Northcote, K.H., Sleeman, J.R., Mulcahy, M.J. and Hallsworth, E.G. (1968) `A handbook of Australian soils'. Rellim Technical Publications, Glenside S.A.

Wallbrink, P.J., English, P., Chafer, C.J., Humphreys, G.S., Shakesby, R.A., Blake, W. and Doerr, S.H. (2004) Impacts on water quality by sediments and nutrients released during extreme bushfires: Report 1: A review of the literature pertaining to the effect of fire on erosion and erosion rates, with emphasis on the Nattai catchment, NSW, following the 2001 fires. CSIRO Land and Water Client Report.

Wilkinson, S., Wallbrink, P.J, Hancock, G., Blake, W., Shakesby, R. and Farwig, V. (2007) Impacts on water quality by sediments and nutrients released during extreme bushfires: Report 4: Impacts on Lake Burragorang. CSIRO Land and Water Science Report 6/07.

Wilkinson, S.N., Wallbrink, P.J., Hancock, G.J., Blake,W. H., Shakesby, R.A., and Doerr, S.H. (2009) Fallout radionuclide tracers identify a switch in sediment sources and transport-limited sediment yield following wildfire in a eucalypt forest. *Geomorphology* 110(3-4), 140-151.

Woods, S.W., Birkas, A. and Ahl, R. (2007) Spatial variability of soil hydrophobicity after wildfires in Montana and Colorado. *Geomorphology* 86 (3-4), 465-479.

Yang, X., Chapman, G.C. and Yeomans, R. (2011) Assessing soil erosion risk after severe bushfires in New South Wales, Australia using RUSLE and MODIS. 7th International Symposium on Digital Earth, Perth Australia, 23-25 August.

Zierholz, C., Hairsine, P.B. and Booker, F.A. (1995) Runoff and soil erosion in bushland following the Sydney bushfires. *Australian Journal of Soil and Water Conservation* **8**, 28-36.

The Aboriginal Prehistory and Archaeology of Royal National Park and Environs: A Review

VAL ATTENBROW

Australian Museum, 6 College Street, Sydney, NSW 2010, Australia (Val.Attenbrow@austmus.gov.au)

Published on 3 September 2012 at http://escholarship.library.usyd.edu.au/journals/index.php/LIN

Attenbrow, V. (2012). The Aboriginal prehistory and archaeology of Royal National Park and environs: a review. *Proceedings of the Linnean Society of New South Wales* **134**, B39-B64.

Royal National Park and its environs has a rich suite of Aboriginal sites that provide much information about the life and activities of the Aboriginal people who lived in coastal Sydney prior to British colonisation. These archaeological sites include rock engravings, shell middens in rockshelters and open locations, rockshelters with drawings and stencils, as well as grinding grooves. Archaeological excavations in Royal National Park in the 1960s were amongst the earliest in southeastern Australia to provide evidence that the tools and equipment used by Aboriginal people and their way of life had changed over time. The excavations in Royal National Park and southern Sydney, which continue today, provide evidence of the tools and equipment people used in their daily lives, the raw materials they used in manufacturing these items, as well as the animals they hunted, fished and gathered. This article presents a brief review of the contribution that past and recent archaeological excavations have made to our knowledge about the life and activities of Aboriginal people who lived in what is now Royal National Park and southern Sydney prior to British colonisation.

Manuscript received 6 January 2012, accepted for publication 3 July 2012.

KEYWORDS: archaeological sites, Australian prehistory, excavation, faunal remains, fishing, radiocarbon dates, Royal National Park, southern Sydney.

INTRODUCTION

Royal National Park is in southeastern New South Wales, Australia, with its northern boundary ~25 km south of the Sydney CBD (Fig. 1). The ~15,100 ha area known today as Royal National Park is the north-eastern section of the country of the Dharawal Aboriginal language group. Dharawal country encompasses ocean and estuarine shorelines from Botany Bay to the Shoalhaven River and forested lands as far west as the Georges River and Appin and possibly Camden. Historical accounts and images provide details about the Dharawal way of life in the late 18th–early 19th century, the earliest being the observations of Lieutenant (later Captain) James Cook and Sir Joseph Banks when they explored Kurnell Peninsula during their eight days in Botany Bay in 1770 (Beaglehole 1955, 1963).

The area of interest for this paper – Royal National Park (Royal NP) and southern Sydney (Fig. 1) – is part of the Woronora Plateau, which is rugged dissected sandstone country with freshwater, estuarine and ocean environments. The eastern boundary, fronting the Pacific Ocean, has high sandstone cliffs interspersed with small sandy beaches and rocky inlets, except where Port Hacking, Botany Bay and the Hacking and Georges Rivers extend inland. Estuarine conditions extend about 28–29 km inland along the Georges and Hacking Rivers to Liverpool and Audley respectively. The area has a highly diverse vegetation including coastal heaths, temperate rainforests, eucalypt forests and woodlands, mangrove forests, and freshwater swamps. These habitats are home to a range of mammals, birds, reptiles and frogs, whilst the ocean and estuarine shorelines provide access to a wide range of fish, marine mammals (e.g., seals, whales) and shellfish. The area thus provided a rich and varied supply of foods for its inhabitants as well as resources for manufacturing their tools and weapons.

During the ~50,000 years of recorded Aboriginal occupation of Australia the coastline has altered with variations in sea-level accompanying long-term climatic changes. Current sea-level was attained about 7,000 years ago. Around 20,000 years ago the sea-level was 120–130 m below its present level with the coastline some 6–15 km east of the current Royal NP–southern Sydney coastline (Attenbrow 2010b:38;

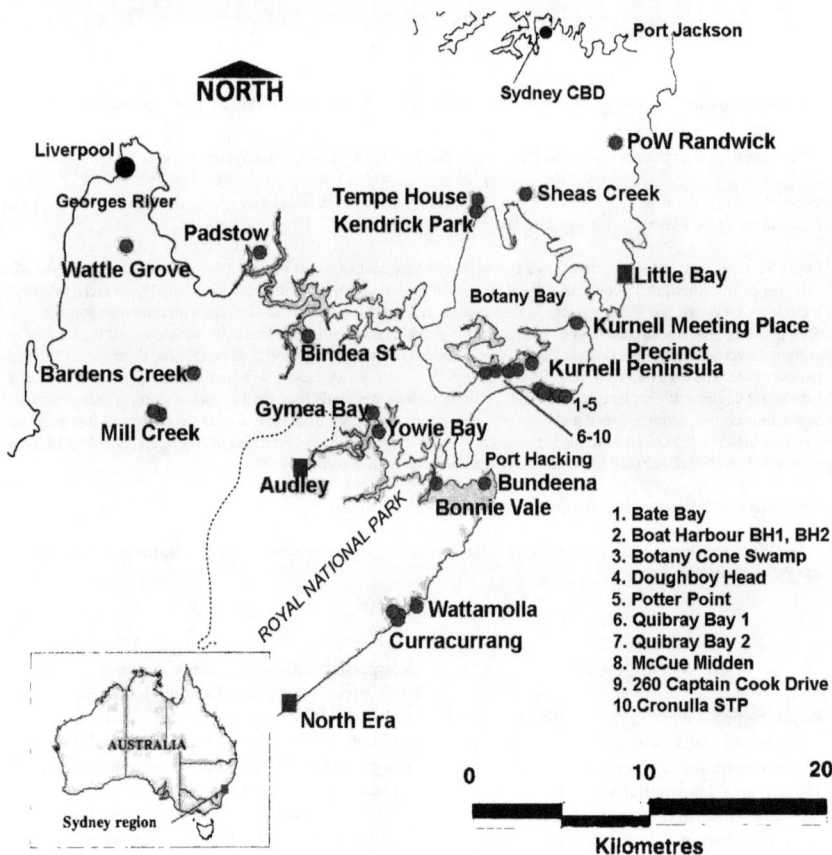

Figure 1. Royal National Park and southern Sydney: Locations of radiometrically dated sites (red circles) and other excavated Aboriginal sites mentioned in text (blue squares).

Haworth et al. 2004). At that time Port Hacking and Botany Bay, and the Hacking and Georges Rivers would have been freshwater valleys. As the sea-level gradually (though not constantly) rose land was inundated and by ~10,000 years ago the ocean waters were entering the freshwater river valleys creating the estuarine habitats of today. The estuarine resources available to the inhabitants of the region thus increased substantially from ~10,000 to ~7,000 years ago.

In examining the archaeology of Royal NP and southern Sydney, my paper focuses on the millennia before the British arrived. I focus particularly on the Aboriginal sites that have been archaeologically

excavated and radiometrically dated (Fig. 1), and the information that these provide about the way of life of the Dharawal and their ancestors. The paper highlights the contribution that these archaeological sites have made to Australian archaeology and prehistory.

ABORIGINAL SITES AND ARCHAEOLOGICAL INVESTIGATIONS IN ROYAL NATIONAL PARK AND SOUTHERN SYDNEY

More than 5,000 Aboriginal sites have been recorded in the Sydney region (Attenbrow 2010b: Plate 12), with more than 650 sites recorded in Royal NP.

B40

Proc. Linn. Soc. N.S.W., 134, 2012

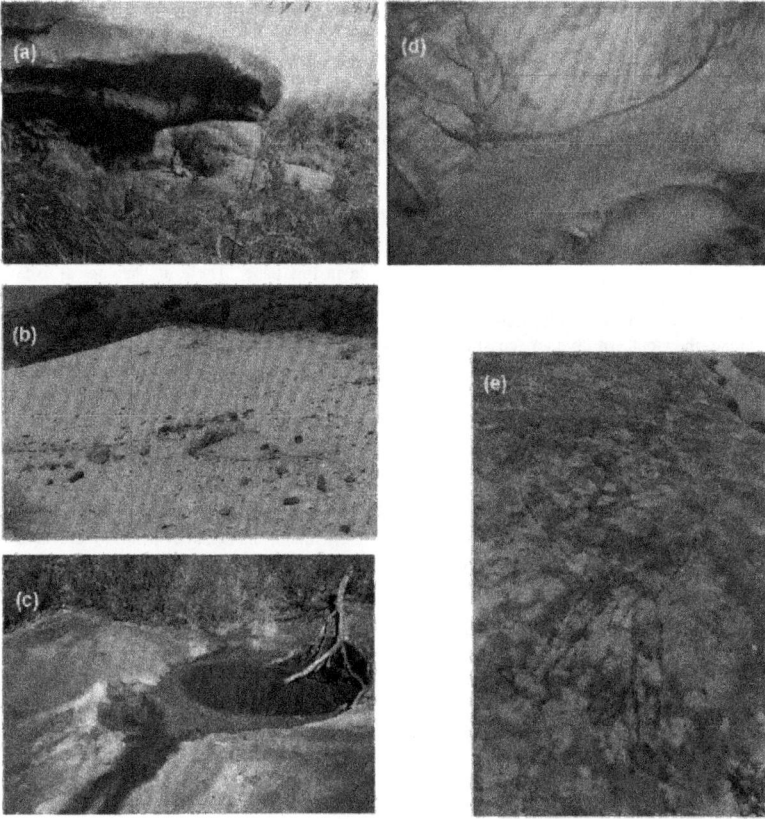

Figure 2. Archaeological sites in Royal National Park. (4a). Curracurrang 1 Rock-shelter with shell midden; (4b) North Era shell midden showing shells and clusters of hearth stones; (4c) Grinding grooves beside rock pool on South-west Arm; (4d) Red pigment fish in rockshelter on South-west Arm; (4e) Engraved anthropomorph at Jibbon, near Bundeena. (Photographs (a), (b) and (e) by Val Attenbrow; (c) and (d) by Illawarra Prehistory Group).

The rich suite of Aboriginal sites in Royal NP and southern Sydney include rock engravings on open rock platforms, shell middens in rockshelters and open locations, drawings, paintings and stencils in rockshelters, as well as grinding grooves along creek lines, beside rock pools and sometimes in shelters (Figs 2a-e). There is a long history of interest in the Aboriginal sites in Royal NP and its environs with the recording and describing of sites, collection of artefacts, and excavations dating back at least to the late 1800s. For example, Bundeena excavations (Harper 1899); north Cronulla stone artefact collections (Etheridge and Whitelegge 1907:234–

36); and rock engravings at Jibbon (*World News*, 7 November 1903 in Attenbrow 2010b:183), Bumborah Point and Frenchmans Bay on Botany Bay (Campbell 1899:6, Plate 3[Fig2]; Mathews and Enright 1895:637, Plate 99[fig 30]). (Note: in following discussions sites in Bundeena and Bonnie Vale have been included as Royal NP.)

Site Recording Fieldwork

While there has been a long history of site recording in Royal NP and southern Sydney, in recent years, the most intense site recording programme has been that of the Illawarra Prehistory Group (IPG) (Sefton 1995, 1996, 2002, 2004, 2005, 2007, 2008, 2010, 2011). Their site recording fieldwork in Royal NP over the last 15 years illustrates how the distribution of Aboriginal sites along with their differing sets of archaeological evidence provides much information about people's life and relationships to land, e.g., where they camped and what land and marine resources were used, as well as information from which we can infer social and economic organisation.

Surface Collections

Many surface artefact collections have been made along the southern Sydney coastline (e.g., Etheridge and Whitelegge 1907; Cridland 1924; Doak and Doyle 1927; Rolf 1931a, 1931b; Thorpe 1932; Dickson 1968, 1974a). The Australian Museum houses relatively large collections of stone artefacts from North Era and Garie.

"Some of the earliest and largest surface stone artefact collections come from the sandhills of North Cronulla—Kurnell Peninsula. They were made after a series of heavy storms exposed vast numbers of stone artefacts in the sandhills. The collectors, Etheridge and Whitelegge, described the scene as follows: A few stone implements were found at Botany Bay and at Kurnell, but there does not appear to be any extensive accumulations at these places. The northern end of Cronulla Beach is extremely rich in stone weapons, chips and flakes. It is covered with many mounds of oyster and other shells, some of which are nearly a hundred feet or so in height. The whole surface in addition to the shells is sprinkled with chips, flakes and weapons, and many of the best found were obtained on or near the base of these oyster mounds. Some distance to the south of the latter there exists a series of extensive flats and hummocks more or less covered with pumice stone. On this ground a large number of implements were found, all of which had evidently been used, but there was an absence of chips or flakes, such as are usually present on the "workshop" grounds." (Etheridge and Whitelegge 1907:235–36)

Dickson's 1960s (1968, 1974a) enormous collection, now held in the Australian Museum, came from a large area of the sand-hills between Kurnell and Cronulla where artefact scatters/concentrations, including knapping floors (workshops), shell concentrations and hearths, became continually exposed over time. Dickson's Kurnell collections include some 8,000 backed artefacts (principally Bondi points) (Dickson 1977:61). There is still much to learn from Dickson's Kurnell surface collections,

only some details, e.g., about the backed artefacts and stone tool technology have been published (e.g., Dickson 1968, 1974a, 1977).

Excavations

While surface collections and site recordings contribute much to answering questions about stone tool distribution patterns and technology, and resource and land use patterns, it is the excavated shell middens and deposits that can tell us about past activities in a chronological framework, and it is these that I focus on in this paper. These archaeological excavations provide evidence for the tools, weapons and equipment that people used in their daily lives, the raw materials they used in manufacturing these items, as well as the animals they hunted and gathered, and how these aspects of people's lives changed over time. Shell and bone tend not to survive in depositional contexts older than ~3,000 years in the Sydney region, and plant remains rarely survive in archaeological sites. This means evidence for plant foods, and tools and equipment made of wood and other plant materials are rarely found, and faunal evidence for diet is restricted to the last ~3,000 years.

One of the earliest documented (and earliest published) excavations in Royal NP/southern Sydney was of a shell midden in a rockshelter in a small cove between Bundeena and Jibbon Beach (Harper 1899). Harper described the shelter floor as containing 'all the edible shell-fish of Port Hacking' and 'an immense number of bones of fish, birds and small marsupials scattered amongst the shell'. The deposit had been disturbed by previous diggers and Harper focussed on describing the skeletal remains of an adult and several children as well as several unusual items that he recovered. Amongst these items were six modified black nerita shells (*Nerita atramentosa*) which are discussed further below.

It was not until the 1960s that most archaeological activity took place in Royal NP, Port Hacking and nearby Kurnell Peninsula and the Georges River. There appears to have been a gap in excavations – or at least in published or reported excavations – in the first half of the 1900s, except for Thorpe's unpublished 1912 excavations in Skeleton Cave (also called Inscription Point; Megaw 1968b) in the Kurnell Meeting Place Precinct. The 1960s excavations were directed by Vincent Megaw with Richard Wright and Peter White of the University of Sydney, and Frank Dickson, and included sites at Curracurrang Cove and Wattamolla (Megaw 1965, 1966, 1967, 1968a, 1974; Megaw and Roberts 1974); Audley (Cox et al. 1968); Boat Harbour BH1 and BH2 (Dickson 1971, 1974a,1974b); Captain Cooks Landing Place (now called The

B42

Proc. Linn. Soc. N.S.W., 134, 2012

Kurnell Meeting Place Precinct) and Inscription Point (Skeleton Cave) (Megaw 1968b, 1974, 1993); Gymea Bay (Megaw and Wright 1966); and Henry Lawson Drive Padstow (White and Wieneke undated ca 1975; Wieneke and White 1973).

The 1960s excavations were principally part of a regional research project funded by the Australian Institute of Aboriginal Studies (Megaw 1965:202; 1966:4, 9) though some (such as Gymea Bay and Henry Lawson Drive) were undertaken to record/salvage sites that had been disturbed by urban activities (Megaw and Wright 1966:23; White and Wieneke undated ca 1975). All of these sites in Royal National Park and its environs are along the ocean and estuarine shorelines.

Megaw's excavations at Curracurrang 1 and Captain Cooks Landing Place (The Kurnell Meeting Place Precinct) were not written up or published in any detailed form. However, Megaw's publications (e.g., 1965, 1966, 1968a, 1968b, 1974) indicate the richness of these sites in terms of their stone and shell artefacts and faunal assemblages.

Since the 1990s, several sites have been excavated along the coast in Royal NP and southern Sydney, mainly in the context of consulting projects prior to developments that threaten heritage sites, especially sand mining, housing and government infrastructure projects; for example at: Bate Bay (Brayshaw et al. 1992); Bonnie Vale, RNP (AMBS 2007); Bundeena Loftus Street (Mary Dallas Consulting 2008); Bundeena UC (Irish 2007; Mary Dallas Consulting 2004); Cronulla STP (Dallas et al. 2001); Gymea GYB/1 (Koettig 1998); Kurnell Meeting Place Precinct (Irish 2010); Little Bay (Godden Mackay Logan 2009); McCue Midden (Mary Dallas Consulting 2005); 260 Captain Cook Drive (Jo McDonald CHM 2008); Prince of Wales Hospital, Randwick (Godden Mackay Logan and Austral Archaeology 1997); Tempe House, Discovery Point (Jo McDonald CHM Pty Ltd 2005).

In addition, previously excavated materials have been re-analysed, e.g., the flaked stone assemblage from Henry Lawson Drive, Padstow (Hiscock 2003) and faunal remains from The Kurnell Meeting Place Precinct (Tsoulos 2007; Godfree 1995 in Tsoulos 2007:107-109). Further analyses are continuing on the excavated materials from the Meeting Place Precinct and Inscription Point, and additional samples are being radiocarbon-dated by Diana Tsoulos with a 2011 AIATSIS grant (Tsoulos pers.comm.).

RESEARCH ISSUES ADDRESSED BY ARCHAEOLOGICAL INVESTIGATIONS

The archaeological work undertaken over the past 100 years has contributed much information about the way of life of the people who lived in Royal NP and southern Sydney in the recent and distant past. These contributions, some of which are outlined below, provide evidence for the diet of these coastal communities, the tool-kits and technology they used to procure food and to make tools and weapons, as well as the procurement of stone materials and exchange networks, and the identification of other small items that were part of the material culture of the coastal communities of the Sydney region. The excavations provide evidence for the sequence of changes that took place, particularly during the Holocene (the last 11,000-10,000 years), in stone tools, and for introduction of shell fishhooks. In addition, excavations along Captain Cooks Drive (Mary Dallas Consulting 2005) reveal, albeit over a relatively small area, the probable original structure of deflated sites in other parts of the sandhills and their stratigraphic relationship to each other, as well as the location of the late 18th century shoreline inside Botany Bay which varies greatly from that of today.

Radiocarbon ages

Aboriginal occupation has been radiometrically dated back to at least 50,000 years ago in other parts of New South Wales and Australia. Along the NSW coast the earliest Aboriginal sites excavated to date are much younger with dates of 23,000–26,000 cal BP and 19,000–22,000 cal BP at Burrill Lake and Bass Point respectively (Lampert 1971; Bowdler 1976).

Within Royal NP and southern Sydney 29 excavated sites have radiometric dates (Figs 1 and 3, see Appendix). Curracurrang 1 is the earliest radiocarbon-dated site in Royal NP with the base of the cultural deposits dated to 8,000–9,000 years old when calibrated to calendar years. Other dated sites in Royal NP are less than 3,000 years old.

Including the southern Sydney area, there is a greater spread of dates with earlier sites at Tempe House (10,000–11,000 years old) and Prince of Wales Hospital (7,000–9,000 years old); but overall most ages are still less than 3,000 years old (Fig. 3a). The stratigraphic provenance of the radiocarbon date for Doughboy Head is problematic (Mary Dallas Consulting 2002; Smith et al. 1990:5, 118–119, Table 13) and is thus excluded from Figure 3. Figure 3a includes all the radiometric dates that I am aware of at the time of writing (71); many sites have more than one date, with Curracurrang 1 having 14 dates. Figure 3b indicates how many sites are estimated to have been occupied in each millennium.

Many people interpret graphs such at these in terms of population change, especially population increase. However, interpreting such graphs is difficult as sites are excavated and radiocarbon dates obtained for a variety of reasons. In addition, many dates represent short-term events (e.g., the hearths at the Prince of Wales Hospital, the butchered dugong bones Sheas Creek and others noted as ST in the

Appendix). For large area open sites it is often not known whether the dates obtained reflect all periods of the site's occupation and include its earliest occupation. It is also probable that dates obtained for sites excavated in the future may well change the configuration of the graphs substantially.

Thus, the dates that are included in these graphs cannot be taken as a representative sample reflecting regional trends in such aspects as land use and demography. In particular, neither of these graphs can be said to reflect demographic changes. They do, however, along with site distribution maps such as Figure 1, provide impressions of what parts of the country are currently known to be occupied in different periods of time. As such they indicate gaps in our knowledge and provide the basis for future research questions about Aboriginal occupation of the region. For example, it is unlikely, given the radiocarbon age of other sites in Australia and other parts of New South Wales, that the earliest sites have been found in Royal NP and southern Sydney. Most excavated sites in Royal NP and its environs are along the ocean and estuarine shorelines. Radiocarbon ages are known for only four non-coastal/hinterland sites (see Appendix). Only three open campsites (i.e., non-midden sites comprising stone artefacts only) have been excavated; two coastal and one hinterland – Gymea GYB/1, Loftus Street, and Mill Creek 14 respectively), and only the last two of these have been radiocarbon-dated. Before valid scenarios of changes over time in land and resource use patterns can be produced, more sites in non-coastal/hinterland areas need to be excavated and radiocarbon-dated.

(a)

(b)

Figure 3. Radiometric dates from Aboriginal sites in Royal National Park and southern Sydney. (4a) Number of radiometric dates (cal BP) in each millennium (N=61, excluding 4 'modern' and 1 problematic). (4b) Number of habitation sites estimated to have been occupied in each millennium (N=29 sites). This is a cumulative graph assuming that once a stratified site was first occupied it continued to be occupied at least some time in each millennium, unless sterile layers are present to indicate otherwise; short-term sites are counted only in the known millennium of occupation.

Stone tools – change over time in tool-kits

Curracurrang 1 was one of the earliest sites in New South Wales to reveal a stratified sequence of stone artefact assemblages which showed changes occurred over time in the stone tools people made and used. Prior to the excavations

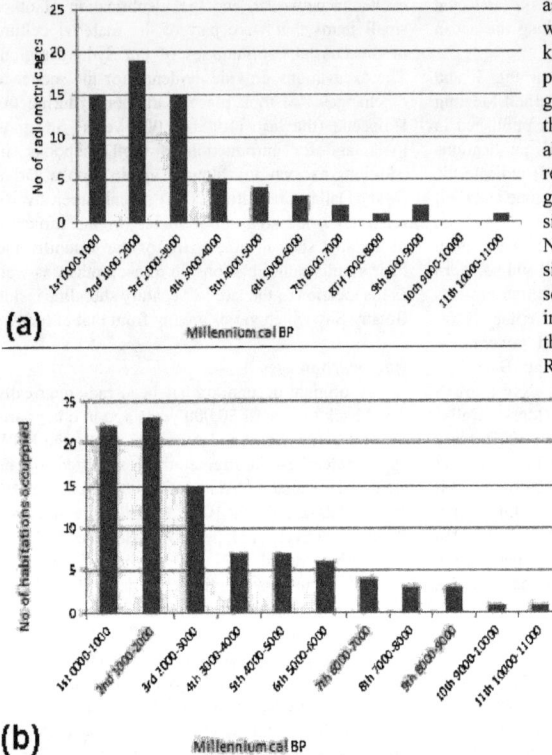

at Curracurrang, stratified stone artefact assemblages were found during excavations at Lapstone Creek just west of the Nepean River and at Capertee on the western side of the Blue Mountains. On the basis of the stratified assemblages at these two sites, F.D. McCarthy (1963) proposed a three-phase sequence of stone tool assemblages which he called the Eastern Regional Sequence.

The excavations by Megaw and his colleagues in Royal National Park and Port Hacking confirmed that a three-phase sequence extended to coastal contexts, though there were regional variations (Megaw 1965:204; 1974:35–37). Archaeological work on the NSW south coast (Bowdler 1976; Lampert 1971), Blue Mountains (Stockton and Holland 1974), and north coast (McBryde 1974) also showed such sequences existed over a wide area of southeastern Australia but again with regional variations. The sequence of changes included: the mid-Holocene appearance of backed artefacts and their demise in most regions 1,500–1,000 years ago; the appearance of ground-edged implements 4,000–3,500 years ago and their increase in number ca 1,500 years ago; and changes in raw materials including an increased use of quartz and a decrease in fine grained materials such as silcrete and tuff in the last one or two millennia. However, more detailed analyses are required of the Curracurrang 1 stone assemblages to clarify the nature and chronology of the foregoing changes at this important site.

These changes over time in the introduction and abundance of various stone tools and the use of stone materials may have been associated with shifts in long-term environmental/climate conditions (Attenbrow et al. 2009) and/or were likely accompanied by changes in social behaviour – e.g., changes in social networks and exchange systems between neighbouring and distant communities of other language groups (Grave et al. 2012), and religious belief systems.

Fishing and fishhooks

Fishing was one of the most common activities described in the historical accounts, paintings and drawings. There was a division of labour in fishing activities along the NSW central and south coasts; women used hook and line with shell fish-hooks from canoes, whereas the men used multi-pronged spears from canoes and rock platforms (Fig. 4, note woman carrying hook and line and man holding a multi-pronged fishing spear).

Many shell fishhooks have been recovered from excavated sites in Royal NP and southern Sydney, e.g., Wattamolla, and particularly The Kurnell Meeting Place Precinct where some 200 completed

and partially complete hooks were found (Megaw 1993:44). Most of the shell fishhooks at the Kurnell Meeting Place Precinct were found in one area (Square BB4), and, as it was the women who made and used the shell fishhooks, this suggests this may have been a women's work area. All identified fishhooks in the Sydney region are made of shell. After microscopic examination, use-wear specialist Richard Fullagar considered the 'stone fishhook' from Curracurrang 7 (Tracey 1974:23, 18) to be a natural piece of stone (Attenbrow 2010b:87).

In addition to the shell fishhooks, small stone files are found at many sites, e.g., Curracurrang 2, Quibray Bay, and Boat Harbour. They are considered to have been used in making shell fishhooks, as they have the same geographical and chronological distribution as the shell fishhooks which appear in southeastern NSW archaeological sites ca 1,000 years ago (Attenbrow 2010a). However, use-wear and residue studies indicate they were also used for other purposes, such as bone-working (Attenbrow et al. 1998; Kononenko 2009). Two stone files at Curracurrang 2 were initially reported as being in levels dating to 1930±80

Figure 4. A Family of New South Wales, by William Blake (engraver) from a sketch by Governor King, in Hunter 1793, opposite page 414. (Reproduced courtesy Australian Museum Research Library).

Proc. Linn. Soc. N.S.W., 134, 2012

B45

BP (Glover 1974:14, 17, Table 2, Figure 12, 14), but subsequent reassessment of the location of the stone files and the dated charcoal sample, throws doubt on there being any association between the files and charcoal sample and it is not possible to establish their age (Attenbrow et al. 1998:136).

Evidence for movement of objects, raw materials, shells and/or people

Even at the time Etheridge and Whitelegge (1907) were describing the amazing stone artefact assemblages revealed by the storms along the Sydney coastline, they reported 'It is quite clear that the siliceous material was derived in a great measure from the surrounding Hawkesbury Sandstone, but the others were probably obtained from distant sources'.

In addition to being an indicator of chronological change in technology, ground-edged hatchets also provide evidence for the movement of goods and/or people, especially hatchets made of volcanic rocks that can be traced as coming from sources that are geographically limited in availability. Amongst the artefacts excavated from Curracurrang 1 was a hatchet made of a rock called tinguaite, an unusual rock known to crop-out along the south coast only in the Minnamurra area – some 60 km away (Branagan and Megaw 1969:14–15). Another ground-edged implement found at Botany Bay (AM Reg. No E.57826) was shown during a recent pilot study using non-destructive pXRF technology (Grave et al. 2012) to be made of basalt probably from a source near Mangrove Mountain in the NSW Central Coast (~80 km distant). Results such these indicate the distances that raw materials or objects were moved and over which exchange systems and social networks extended. The pilot study by Grave et al. is being expanded to include a substantially larger sample of hatchets from a wider region of southeast Australia, including southern Sydney, in a study now supported by the Australian Research Council.

During their fieldwork, the IPG listed the shellfish species observed at the sites they recorded. From their site recordings, they (Sefton 2002:46, 2004:42, Fig.16, 2011:48–49, Fig. 15) identified variations in the distribution of estuarine shells (Sydney cockle *Anadara trapezia*) and shells from exposed open coast environments (small turban *Subninella undulata*, triton *Cabestana spengleri*, cartrut *Thais orbita*, limpet *Cellana tramoserica* and chiton [unidentified]) which were on the surface of shelter floor deposits in unexcavated sites in the western half of the Park (Fig. 5). In the south of the Park, people carried coastal shellfish (e.g., small turbans) from the ocean shoreline up to 6 km inland to the upper non-estuarine reaches of the Hacking River above Audley. In the north, people focussed their shellfishing along the estuaries, but they transported estuarine shells up to 11 km away from the estuarine shorelines. This patterning shows that people moved between the coast, estuaries and forested lands. Interestingly, the species of shell that was carried furthest was the estuarine Sydney cockle, a shell which historically was described as being used as a tool (Attenbrow 2010b:119), suggesting it may have been carried for practical purposes as much as for food.

Faunal remains – subsistence/diet

The 1960s Royal NP and Kurnell excavation reports provide only brief lists of identified marine and land fauna (Glover 1974:Table 7; Megaw 1965:203, 1967:283-84, 1968a:326, 1968b:17-18; Megaw and Roberts 1974:Table 4), but even so they indicate that the statements made by some First Fleet journalists that the local inhabitants 'lived by fish alone' were mistaken. Marine mammal bones, e.g., Fur seal *Arctocephalus* sp. and whale bone, were also reported, as well as unidentified crustacea.

Subsequent lists of marine and land fauna, which come from recently excavated Kurnell sites (e.g., Brayshaw et al. 1992:Table 4.1.1; Dallas et al. 2001:21-26, Tables 4.3-4.6; Mary Dallas Consulting 2005:134-40, Tables 5.14-5.17; Irish 2010:48-56) and re-analysis of the 1960s excavated Kurnell assemblages (Tsoulos 2007; Godfree 1995 in Tsoulos 2007) provide much fuller and more comprehensive lists.

These lists indicate that the local inhabitants of this area ate of a wide variety of fish and land animals (Tables 1 and 2). The dominant shellfish species included rock oyster *Saccostrea glomerata*, mud oyster *Ostrea angasi*, large turban *Turbo torquata*, small turban *Subninella undulata*, hairy mussel *Trichomya hirsuta*, edible mussel *Mytilus edulis planulatus*, Sydney cockle, black nerita *Nerita atramentosa*, colourful limpets *Cellana tramoserica*, Cartrut *Thais orbita*, Spenglers triton *Cabestana spengleri,* and Hercules whelk *Pyrazus ebeninus*, depending on the shell midden's environmental context (i.e., whether ocean or estuarine). Fish bone assemblages were dominated by snapper *Pagrus auratus* and bream *Acanthopagrus australis* (Sparidae), with blue groper/ wrasse (Labridae) leatherjackets (Monacanthidae), flatheads (Platycephalidae) and catfishes (Plotosidae) common. Garfish (Hemiramphidae) were tentatively identified at Inscription Point by Megaw (1968b:17), but subsequent re-analysis by Diana Tsoulos (pers. com.) has not identified them at this site and they have not been identified at any other coastal Sydney

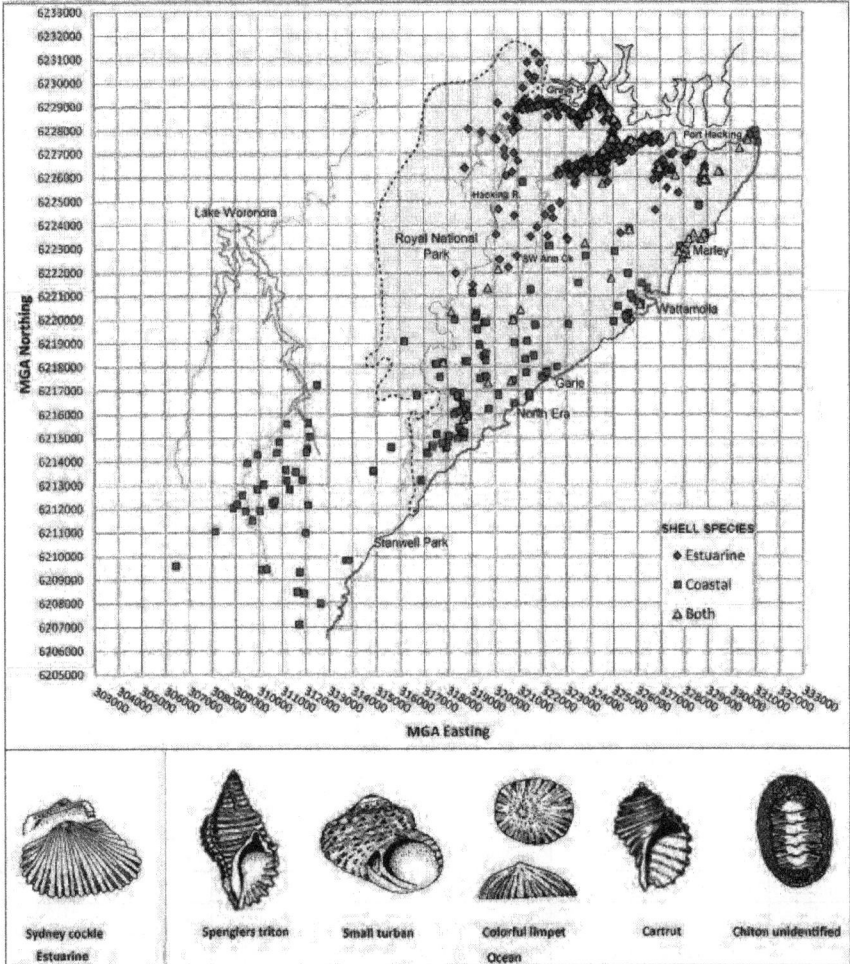

Figure 5. Distribution of Royal National Park sites that have coastal and estuarine shell, recorded by Illawarra Prehistory Group to 2011. Map provided by and reproduced with permission of Bruce Scurr of the Illawarra Prehistory Group. Line drawings of shells from Child 1969.

site (Colley and Attenbrow 2012). Land animals included kangaroo *Macropus* sp, wallaby *Wallabia bicolor*, possum, potoroo *Potorous tridactylus* and bandicoots *Isoodon macrourus*. Current analyses being undertaken during Tsoulos' current AIATSIS-funded project will enable more complete descriptions of the animals caught.

Body ornaments, rattles, musical instruments or fishing lures?

Amongst the items of interest that William Harper found during his 1890s excavation of the Bundeena rockshelter were six black nerita shells (*Nerita atramentosa*), each with a small square hole cut into their back (Fig. 6(a[i and ii]); a kangaroo fibula 9¾ inches (24 cm) long, well-polished with

			Royal Nat'l Park			Kurnell Peninsula				
Family	Taxa	Common name	Curracurang 2	Wattamolla WL and WB	Bundeena UC Midden	The Meeting Place Precinct	McCue Midden	Cronulla STP	260 Captain Cook Drive	Bates Bay
Anguillidae	Unidentified	Eel unidentified					♦			
Arripididae	*Arripus trutta*	Eastern Australian Salmon				♦				
Arripididae	*Arripus* sp.	Australian Salmon				♦				
Balistidae	Unidentified	Triggerfishes [1]								
Carangidae	*Pseudocaranx dentex*	Silver or White Trevally				♦				
Carangidae	Unidentified	Travelly				♦				
Cheilodactylidae	*Nemadactylus* spp.	Morwong/Jackass			♦					
Cheilodactylidae	Unidentified	Morwongs								
Diodontidae	Unidentified	Porcupinefishes				♦			♦	
Elasmobranch	*Carcharias taurus*	Greynurse Shark				♦	♦			
Elasmobranch	*Heterodontus portusjacksoni*	Port Jackson Shark				♦				
Elasmobranch	Unidentified	Shark/Ray/Skate				♦	♦			
Elasmobranch	Unidentified	Shark				♦	♦			
Kyphosidae [2]	*Girella* sp.	Luderick/Blackfish				♦	♦	♦		♦
Kyphosidae	*Girella, Kyphosus* or *Scorpis*	Drummers				♦			♦	
Labridae	*Achoerodus viridis*	Eastern Blue Groper	♦[3]	♦[3]			♦			
Labridae	Unidentified	Wrasse, Blue Groper				♦			♦	
Labridae	Labrid unident	Parrotfish/Wrasse				♦				
Labridae	*Pseudolabrus gymnogenis*	Crimson-banded Wrasse	♦							
Labridae	*Pseudolabrus* sp.	Wrasse		♦	♦		♦	♦		
Monacanthidae	Monacanthid unidentified	Leatherjacket	♦[4]	♦[4]		♦	♦	♦	♦	
Moridae	Unidentified	Morid cods				♦				
Platycephalidae	Platycephalid unidentified	Flathead				♦	♦	♦	♦	
Plotosidae	Unidentified	Catfishes				♦			♦	
Pomatomidae	*Pomatomus saltatrix*	Tailor				♦				
Rajiformes	Unidentified	Stingrays				♦				
Sciaenidae	*Argyrosomus japonicus*	Mulloway/Jewfish				♦	♦[5]			
Scorpaenidae	Unidentified	Scorpionfishes				♦				
Serranidae	*Acanthistius* sp.	Wirrah				♦				
Serranidae	*Epinephelus* sp.	Rock Cod				♦			♦	
Serranidae	Unidentified	Rockcods, Seaperches				♦				
Sillaginidae	*Sillago ciliata*	Sand Whiting				♦			♦	
Sillaginidae	*Sillago* sp.	Whiting				♦			♦	
Sparidae	*Acanthopagrus australis*	Yellowfin Bream				♦		♦	♦	
Sparidae	*Acanthopagrus* sp.	Bream	♦[6]		♦		♦			♦
Sparidae	*Pagrus auratus*	Snapper		♦		♦	♦	♦	♦	♦
Sparidae	*Rhabdosargus sarba*	Tarwhine				♦	♦	♦	♦	
Sparidae	Unidentified	Unidentified			♦		♦	♦	♦	

B48

Proc. Linn. Soc. N.S.W., 134, 2012

some modifications, which he considered to be a 'nose bone', but acknowledged it may have been a 'netting needle' or a 'death bone or pointer', concluding with the option that such objects may have been at times put to several different uses and this object 'may have once been useful as well as ornamental' (Harper 1899:329-32).

However, it is the black nerita shells that have been the focus of recent discussions. Some 100 years after William Harper interpreted the modified black nerita shells in the Bundeena rockshelter as parts of a necklace, Paul Irish recovered several black nerita shells similarly modified from another midden at Bundeena (Fig. 6a[iii]; Irish 2007) and again at the Kurnell Meeting Place Precinct during salvage excavations in re-opening Cooks Stream (Fig. A[iv]; Irish 2010:83). Microscopic examination of these shells and experimental work by Nina Kononenko (2009) confirmed that the shells were definitely humanly modified (probably cut with a stone knife) and that the modification was highly unlikely to have been for food extraction purposes. Thus Irish (2007) proposed they were some form of personal adornment.

In 2009 three black nerita shells and a *Bembicium* sp. shell, found in auger samples from a shell midden at Little Bay, showed signs of possible modification and it was proposed that they may have had a similar function to those from Bundeena (Godden Mackay Logan 2009:60–61). Subsequently Farquharson and Brown (2010) hypothesised that rather than being from a necklace the modified black nerita could have been part of a musical instrument called a systrum. As support for their suggestion, Farquharson and Brown referred to an engraving at Allambie Heights (Fig. 6b) which was interpreted by W.D. Campbell (1899:Plate 12) as a systrum, 'a shell-jingling musical instrument that was used as an accompaniment to the beating together of sticks'. Another engraving at Wheeler Heights (Fig. 6b) comprising 18 small circles forming a loop was also interpreted as a systrum by Campbell (1899:22–23, Plate 10) though Stanbury

and Clegg (1996:39, Fig.23) refer to it as 'an underwater rattle used to attract marine animals'. Another interpretation of the shells is that they may be from a children's rattle (pers.com. Oliver Brown 2011), perhaps similar to those collected by Walter Roth in Northern Queensland in 1899 (Kahn 2003:58–59).

Whatever their use, these small items provide valuable insights and stimulate our thoughts about the range of objects people used and the activities they participated in.

SUMMARY AND CONCLUSIONS

Many hundreds of Aboriginal sites have been recorded in Royal NP but artefact collections and archaeological excavations have been undertaken at relatively few sites within the Park. The earliest published excavations were undertaken in the 1890s at Bundeena. Much later in the 1960s a major archaeological programme excavated several sites within the Park at Curracurrang and Wattamolla, and also in the Kurnell Meeting Place Precinct in Kamay-Botany Bay NP. Recent archaeological work, which has been focussed to the north and northwest of the Park, has been undertaken on sites being impacted by a variety of developments, in contrast to the earlier fieldwork which was undertaken for academic research. However, the archaeological work undertaken, from earliest to most recent, provides much information about the Dharawal inhabitants of this area prior to British colonisation.

The earliest occupation of an Aboriginal site excavated in Royal NP dates to around 8,000–9,000 years ago and in southern Sydney the site at Tempe House dates back to 10,000–11,000 years before present. These radiocarbon ages are much more recent that the earliest dates for occupation of Australia ca 50,000 years ago, or even the NSW south coast where occupation levels dating back to 23,000–26,000 cal BP and 19,000–22,000 cal BP were revealed at Burrill Lake and Bass Point respectively (Lampert

Table 1 (preceding page). Identified fishes from selected excavated Aboriginal archaeological sites in Royal National Park and southern Sydney. Scientific names according to Hutchins and Swainston 1986 and The Australian Museum Ichthyology Fish database. ♦ present at site. Sources: Brayshaw et al. 1992: Table 4.1.1; Dallas et al. 2001:21-26, Tables 4.3-4.6; Glover 1974: Table 7; Irish 2010:48-56; Table 4.6; Jo McDonald CHM 2008: Table 50; Megaw and Roberts 1974:Table 4; Mary Dallas Consulting 2004:Tables 6.6 to 6.10; Mary Dallas Consulting 2005:134-40, Table 5.13; Tsoulos 2007:Table 5.4. ([1] common name for Balistidae listed as leatherjacket in Brayshaw et al.1992); ; [2] Girellidae now renamed Kyphosidae; [3] Listed as *A. gouldii* blue groper in Megaw and Roberts 1974 and Glover 1974; [4] listed as Aluteridae leatherjackets in Megaw and Roberts 1974, Glover 1974; [5] listed as *S. antarctica* in Mary Dallas Consulting 2005; [6] listed as *Mylio* sp. in Glover 1974 and Brayshaw et al 1992; [7] listed as *Chrysophrys auratus*.

Table 2. Identified land and marine mammals, reptiles and birds from selected excavated Aboriginal sites in Royal National Park and southern Sydney. Sources: Brayshaw et al. 1992:Table 4.1.1; Dallas et al. 2001:21-26, Tables 4.3-4.6; Glover 1974:Table 7; Irish 2010:48-56; Table 4.6; Jo McDonald CHM 2008:Table 50; Megaw and Roberts 1974:Table 4; Mary Dallas Consulting 2004:Table 6.6 to 6.10; Mary Dallas Consulting 2005:134-40, Tables 5.14-5.17; Tsoulos 2007:Tables 5.8 and 5.9.

Family	Taxa	Common name	Royal NP			Kurnell Peninsula				Bates Bay BHW
			Currarurrang 2	Wattamolla WL and WB	Bundeena UC Midden	The Meeting Place Precinct [CCLP]	McCue Midden	Cronulla STP	260 Captain Cook Drive	
LAND MAMMALS										
Canidae	*Canis lupus dingo*	Dingo	◆			◆	◆			◆? dog, poss dingo
Dasyuridae	*Antechinus flavipes*	Yellow-footed Antechinus					◆			
Dasyuridae	*Antechinus stuartii*	Brown Antechinus				◆				
Dasyuridae	*Antechinus sp*	Antechinus				◆				
Dasyuridae	*Dasyurus maculatus*	Spotted-tailed Quoll				◆	◆			
Dasyuridae	Dasyuridae sp.	Marsupial mouse			◆					
Dasyuridae	Dasyurid unidentified	Marsupial mouse					◆			
Dasyuridae	*Phascogale tapoatafa*	Brush-tailed Phascogale				◆				
Macropodidae	*Macropus giganteus*	Eastern Grey Kanagaroo				◆				◆ or *E.robustus*
Macropodidae	*Macropus robustus*	Euro/Wallaroo				◆				◆ or *E.giganteus*
Macropodidae	*Macropus rufogriseus*	Red-necked Wallaby				◆				
Macropodidae	*Macropus sp.*	Kangaroos				◆				
Macropodidae	*Petrogale penicillata*	Brush-tailed Rock Wallaby						◆		
Macropodidae	*Thylogale thetis*	Red-necked Pademelon			◆		◆			
Macropodidae	*Wallabia bicolor*	Swamp Wallaby				◆				
Macropodidae	Macropodid unidentified	e.g., kangaroo, wallaby	◆		◆	◆	◆	◆	◆	

Family	Species	Common name
Muridae	*Pseudomys sp.*	New Holland Mouse
Muridae	*Rattus fuscipes*	Bush rat
Muridae	*Rattus fuscipes assimilis*	Bush rat
Muridae	*Rattis lutreolus*	Swamp rat
Muridae	*Hydromys chrysogaster*	Water rat
Muridae	*Rattus sp.*	unidentified rat
Muridae	Murid	unidentified rat or mouse
Peramelidae	*Isoodon macrourus*	Northern Brown Bandicoot
Peramelidae	*Perameles nasuta*	Long-nosed Bandicoot
Peramelidae	Peramelid unidentified	unidentified bandicoot
Petauridae	*Petauridae sp.*	unidentified glider, possum
Phalangeridae	*Trichosurus vulpecula*	Brushtail Possum
Phalangeridae	*Cercartetus nanus*	Eastern Pygmy Possum
Phalangeridae	Phalangerid	unidentified possum
Potoroidae	*Potorous tridactylus*	Long-nosed Potoroo
Pseudocheiridae	*Pseudocheirus peregrinus*	Common ring-tail Possum
Monotremata	*Tachyglossus aculeatus*	Short-beaked Echidna
MARINE MAMMALS		
Delphinidae	*Delphinus delphis*	Common Dolphin
Delphinidae	*Tursiops truncatus*	Bottlenose Dolphin
Delphinidae	Unidentified	Unidentified dolphin
O.Cetacea	*Cetacea sp.*	Whale (attributed)
Otariidae	*Arctocephalus pusillus*	Fur seal
Otariidae	*Arctocephalus sp.*	Fur seal
Otariidae	Unidentified	Fur seal
Phocidae	Unidentified	Seal
O.Pinnipedia	*Pinnipedia sp.*	Seal

Table 2 continued

Family	Taxa	Common name	Royal NP					Kurnell Peninsula		
			Curracurrang 2	Wattamolla WL and WB	Bundeena UC Midden	The Meeting Place Precinct [CCLP]	McCue Midden	Cronulla STP	260 Captain Cook Drive	Bates Bay BHW
INTRODUCED SPECIES										
	Bos taurus	Cow				♦				
	Mus sp.	House mouse				♦				♦
	Oryctolagus cuniculus	Rabbit				♦				
	Ovis aries	Sheep				♦				
REPTILES: LIZARDS AND SNAKES										
Agamidae		Dragon lizard				♦			♦	
Ophidia		Snake				♦				
Pygopodidae		Snake			♦					
Scincidae		Large skink				♦				
Varanidae	*Varanus* sp.	Goanna			♦	♦			♦	
		Lizard unidentified					♦			
		Reptile unidentified snake					♦			
		Reptile unidentified								
BIRDS										
	Puffinus tenuirostris	Short-tailed shearwater, Muttonbird		♦						
	Puffinus sp.	Shearwater, Muttonbird	♦							
	Bird, probably *Pterodromamacroptera*	Petrel ?		♦						
		Muttonbirds								
		Birds unidentified		♦		♦	♦	♦		♦
FROGS										

B52

Proc. Linn. Soc. N.S.W., 134, 2012

V. ATTENBROW

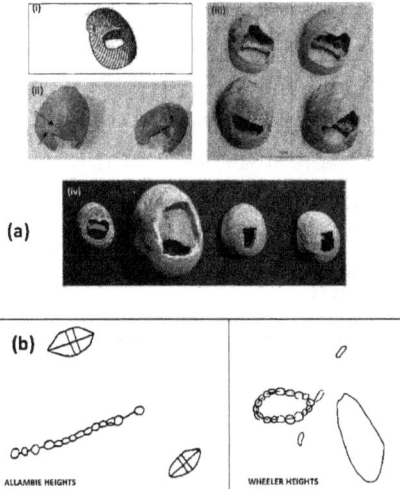

(a)

(b)

ALLAMBIE HEIGHTS

WHEELER HEIGHTS

Figure 6: (a) Modified Nerita atramentosa shell from: (i) and (ii) Bundeena Beach excavations (WR Harper 1899; Australian Museum Registration No E.08582); (iii) Bundeena UC Midden (Paul Irish 2007:Fig. 2); (iv) Cooks Stream, Kurnell (Irish 2010:Fig. 4.30). (b) Engraved figures interpreted by W.D. Campbell as a systrum at Allambie Heights with two shields; and at Wheeler Heights with footprints and unknown figure (reproduced from Campbell 1899: Plates 10 and 12; no scales provided).

1971; Bowdler 1976). No doubt in those earlier times people were occupying the country that is now Royal NP and southern Sydney, and so sites older than 10,000–11,000 year old may one day be found when further sites are excavated in these areas.

This brief review has been able to report only some of the results of archaeological work in Royal NP and southern Sydney. However, it shows how archaeological data gathered from this area provides evidence about many aspects of Aboriginal life in the past: the foods eaten – the species of fish, shellfish and land animals; the tools and weapons used and the way the tool-kit changed over time with the introduction of backed artefacts, ground-edges hatchets and shell fishhooks at different times during the Holocene, and the recent decline in production of backed artefacts; and the raw materials used in manufacturing their tools and the sources from which such materials were gained.

Thus, the results of archaeological investigations

in Royal NP and southern Sydney have contributed and will continue to make valuable contributions to our knowledge about the way of life and the changes that took place in the lives and behaviour of Aboriginal people in southeastern Australia in the near recent and distant past. To date, however, most archaeological work has concentrated along the coast and estuaries and a programme of excavations in stratified datable sites in the western non-coastal areas of Royal NP and southern Sydney would shed much light on how Dharawal people lived and behaved when in the northern hinterland parts of their country.

ACKNOWLEDGEMENTS

Many thanks to Bruce Scurr of the Illawarra Prehistory Group for providing the map reproduced as Figure 5; to Caryll Sefton of the Illawarra Prehistory Group for sharing her knowledge and giving permission to reproduce images in Figures 2c and 2d; to Diana Tsoulos for discussions and information about faunal remains from Megaw's Kurnell excavations; Paul Irish and Oliver Brown for discussions on the modified Nerita atramentosa shells; to Sarah Colley and Paul Irish for discussions and comments on a draft version of this paper. I also thank the two referees for their comments and suggestions, and Kimberlee Newman for finalising Figures 1 and 5.

REFERENCES

AINSE. (2009). Refining marine radiocarbon ages in Australia. *Annual Report,* Section 1. Lucas Heights: ANSTO.

AMBS Consulting (2003). Report on the Salvage Excavation of a Portion of the Kendrick Park Midden, Tempe, NSW. Report to Marrickville Council.

AMBS Consulting. (2007). Bonnie Vale Day Use and Camping Area, Royal National Park. Test Excavation Report for Department of Environment and Conservation, NSW.

Attenbrow, V. (2010a). Aboriginal fishing on Port Jackson, and the introduction of shell fishhooks to coastal NSW, Australia. In Hutching, P., Lunney, D. and Hochuli, D. (eds), *The Natural History of Sydney,* pp.16–34. Mosman: Royal Zoological Society of NSW.

Attenbrow, V. (2010b). *Sydney's Aboriginal Past.* (2nd ed). Sydney: UNSW Press.

Attenbrow, V. and Conyers, B. (1983). Off Bindea Street, Bonnet Bay. Proposed Residential Subdivision: Archaeological Investigations. Report to Stocks and Holdings Pty Ltd.

Attenbrow, V., Fullagar, R. and Szpak, C. (1998). Stone files and shell fish-hooks in southeastern Australia. In

Proc. Linn. Soc. N.S.W., 134, 2012

B53

ABORIGINAL PREHISTORY AND ARCHAEOLOGY

Fullagar, R. (ed.), *A Closer Look: Recent Australian Studies of Stone Tools,* pp. 127–148. Archaeological Computing Laboratory, School of Archaeology, University of Sydney.

Attenbrow, V.J. and Negerevich, T. (1984). The assessment of sites. Lucas Heights Waste Disposal Depot: A case study. In: Sullivan, S. and Bowdler, S. (eds), *Site Surveys and Significance Assessment in Australian Archaeology,* pp. 136–51. Canberra: Department of Prehistory, RSPacS, ANU.

Attenbrow, V., G. Robertson and P. Hiscock. (2009). The changing abundance of backed artefacts in south-eastern Australia: a response to Holocene climate change? *Journal of Archaeological Science* 36:2765-2770. doi:10.1016/j.jas.2009.08.018.

Beaglehole, J.C. (ed.) (1955). The Voyage of the Endeavour 1768–1771. The Journals of Captain James Cook on his Voyages of Discovery. Cambridge: Hakluyt Society at the University Press.

Beaglehole, J.C. (ed.) (1963). *The 'Endeavour' Journal of Joseph Banks 1768–1771.* Vol. 2. 2nd edn. Sydney: Trustees of the Public Library of NSW in assoc. with Angus and Robertson.

Bowdler, S. (1976). Hook, line and dilly bag: An interpretation of an Australian coastal shell midden. *Mankind* 10(4): 248–258.

Branagan, D.F. and Megaw, J.V.S. (1969). The lithology of a coastal Aboriginal settlement at Curracurrang, NSW. *Archaeology and Physical Anthropology in Oceania* 4(1):1–17.

Brayshaw, H., Dallas, M., Byrne, D., Baker, N., Donlon, D. and Ross, A. (1992). Sydney Destination Resort. Excavation of Site BHW [52-3-724], Bate Bay, Kurnell Peninsula, NSW. Report to Besmaw Pty Limited through Planning Workshop, Sydney.

Campbell, W.D. (1899). *Aboriginal Carvings of Port Jackson and Broken Bay. Memoirs of the Geological Survey of NSW.* Sydney: NSW Geological Survey.

Child, J. (1969). *Australian Sea Shells.* Melbourne: Cheshire-Lansdowne

Colley, S. and Attenbrow, V. (2012). Does technology make a difference? Aboriginal and colonial fishing in Port Jackson, New South Wales. *Archaeology in Oceania* 47, 69-77.

Cox, J., Maynard, L. and Megaw, J.V.S. (1968). The excavation of a rock shelter at Audley, Royal National Park, NSW. *Archaeology and Physical Anthropology in Oceania* 3(2):94–104.

Cridland, F. (1924). The Story of Port Hacking, Cronulla and Sutherland Shires. Sydney: Angus and Robertson.

Dallas, M., Irish, P., Steele, D. and Czastka, J. (2001). Archaeological Excavations of an Aboriginal Shell Midden Cronulla STP 1 on Captain Cook Drive, Cronulla, NSW. Report to Bovis Lend Lease Pty Limited on behalf of Sydney Water.

Dickson, F.P. (1968). *Aboriginal Technology – Some evidence from Kurnell Peninsula, Botany Bay.* Department of Industrial Arts Monograph. Sydney: University of New South Wales.

Dickson, F.P. (1971). Preliminary Report. Excavation of a Midden at Boat Harbour, Kurnell during August 1971, under Permit No A/1846. Report to NSW National Parks and Wildlife Service

Dickson, F.P. (1974a). Aboriginal prehistory of Botany Bay. Part 2: Historical Background. In Anderson, D.J. (ed.), *The Botany Bay Project. A Handbook of the Botany Bay Region – Some Preliminary Background Papers,* pp. 44–50. Sydney: Botany Bay Project Committee.

Dickson, F.P. (1974b). Report. Excavation of an Aboriginal Midden at Boat Harbour. 12 August 1974. Report to NSW National Parks and Wildlife Service.

Dickson, F.P. (1977). Multiple Bondi points. *Mankind* 11(1):61.

Doak, J.K. and Doyle, C.M. (1927). The white heart of Cronulla: an ethnological study of the Aboriginal middens at Cronulla. *Journal of The Science Society, University of Sydney* 11:30–40.

Etheridge, R.J. Jr and Whitelegge, T. (1907). Aboriginal workshops on the coast of New South Wales, and their contents. *Records of the Australian Museum* 6(4):233–250.

Farquharson, L. and Brown, O. (2010). From Little Things: Management and Archaeological Investigation at the Little Bay Midden, NSW. Paper presented at the Australian Archaeological Association Annual Conference, Batemans Bay.

Glover, E. (1974). Report on the excavation of a second rock shelter at Curracurrang Cove, New South Wales. In Megaw J.V.S (ed.), *The Recent Archaeology of the Sydney District – Excavations 1964–1967,* pp. 13–18. Canberra: Australian Institute of Aboriginal Studies.

Godden Mackay Logan Heritage Consultants. (2009). Little Bay Shell Midden. Test Excavation Report. Report prepared for Landcom.

Godden Mackay Pty Ltd and Austral Archaeology Pty Ltd. (1997). Prince of Wales Project 1995. Randwick Destitute Children's Asylum Cemetery. Archaeological Investigation. Vol. 2 – Archaeology Part 3 - Aboriginal Archaeology. Report for South Eastern Sydney Area Health Service, Heritage Council of NSW and NSW Department of Health, Sydney.

Godfree, R. (1995). Analysis of Vertebrate Bone Remains from an Aboriginal Shell Midden Located at Kurnell, N.S.W. BA(Hons) thesis, Macquarie University.

Grave. P., Attenbrow, V., Sutherland, L., Pogson, R. and Forster, N. (2012). Non-destructive pXRF of mafic stone tools. *Journal of Archaeological Science* 39:1674-1686 (doi:10.1016/j.jas.2011.11.011).

Harper, W.R. (1899). Results of an exploration of Aboriginal rock-shelters at Port Hacking. *Proceedings of the Linnean Society of NSW* 24(2):322–332.

Haworth, R.J., Baker, R.G.V. and Flood, P.J. (2004). A 6000 year-old fossil dugong from Botany Bay: inferences about changes in Sydney's climate, sea levels and waterways. *Australian Geographical Studies* 42(1):46–59.

Hiscock, P. (2003). Quantitative exploration of size variation and the extent of reduction in Sydney Basin assemblages: A tale from the Henry Lawson Drive Rockshelter, *Australian Archaeology* 57: 64–74.

Hughen, K.A., Baillie, M.G.L., Bard, E. et al. (2004). MARINE04 marine radiocarbon age calibration, 0-26 cal kyr BP. Radiocarbon 46(3): 1059–1086.

Hunter, J (1793[1968]). *An Historical Journal of the Transactions at Port Jackson and Norfolk Island,* .... Printed for John Stockdale, Piccadilly, London. [Australiana Facsimile Editions No. 148, Libraries Board of South Australia, Adelaide].

Hutchins, B. and Swainston, R. (1986). *Sea Fishes of Southern Australia.* Perth: Swainston Publishing.

Irish, P. (2007). Bundeena bling? Possible Aboriginal shell adornments from southern Sydney. *Australian Archaeology* 64:46–49.

Irish, P. (2010). *Final Report on Aboriginal Archaeological Monitoring and Salvage Excavations. Meeting Place Precinct, Botany Bay National Park, Kurnell, NSW.* Report to Design Landscapes Pty Ltd and Department of Environment and Climate Change. Australian Archaeologists Consulting Association Monograph No 3.

Jo McDonald CHM Pty Ltd. (2005). Archaeological Testing and Salvage Excavation at Discovery Point, Site No 45-6-2737 in the former grounds of Tempe House, NSW. Report to Australand Holdings Pty Ltd.

Jo McDonald CHM Pty Ltd. (2008). Final Aboriginal Archaeological Test Excavations at 260 Captain Cook Drive, Kurnell. Report to Parist Holdings Limited.

Khan, K. (2003). *Catalogue of the Roth Collection of Aboriginal Artefacts from North Queensland,* Volume 3. Sydney: Australian Museum.

Koettig, M. (1990). Salvage Excavations at M14, Upper Mill Creek, near Lucas Heights, Sydney. Report for NSW Metropolitan Waste Management Authority, Sydney.

Koettig, M. (1998). Salvage Excavation at GYB/1, Gymea Bay, Sydney. Report to Stirling Estates.

Kononenko, N. (2009). Use-Wear/Residue Analysis of Collection of Stone, Bone and Shell Artefacts from Kurnell Test Pits and Salvage Excavations at Botany Bay National Park, Kurnell, NSW. In Irish, P. 2010. Final Report on Aboriginal Archaeological Monitoring and Salvage Excavations. Meeting Place Precinct, Botany Bay National Park, Kurnell, NSW. Report to Design Landscapes Pty Ltd and Department of Environment and Climate Change. AACA Inc Monograph 3.

Lampert, R.J. (1971). *Burrill Lake and Currarong.* Canberra: Department of Prehistory, Research School of Pacific Studies, The Australian National University.

Mary Dallas Consulting Archaeologists (2002). Sutherland Shire Council Aboriginal Cultural Heritage study. Report to Sutherland Shire Council.

Mary Dallas Consulting Archaeologists (2004). Aboriginal Archaeological Test Excavations. United Church

Conference Centre, Bundeena, NSW. Report to the Uniting Church in Australia.

Mary Dallas Consulting Archaeologists. (2005). Aboriginal Archaeological Test Excavation Report. McCue Midden Site, Lot 8 Captain Cook Drive, Kurnell, NSW. Report to Rocla Pty Ltd.

Mary Dallas Consulting Archaeologists. (2008). Aboriginal Archaeological Test and Salvage Excavation Report. 96-98 Loftus Street, Bundeena, NSW. Report to Mars Developments Pty Ltd.

Mathews, R.H. and Enright, W.J. (1895). Rock paintings and carvings of the Aborigines of New South Wales. In Shirley, J. (ed.), Report of the Sixth Meeting of the Australasian Association for the Advancement of Science held at Brisbane, Queensland, January 1895, pp. 624–637, Australasian Association for the Advancement of Science, Sydney.

McBryde, I. (1974). *Aboriginal Prehistory in New England.* Sydney: Sydney University Press.

McCarthy, F.D. (1963). The prehistory of the Australian Aborigines. *Australian Natural History* 14(8):233–241.

McCormac, F.G., Hogg, A.G., Blackwell, et al. (2004). SHCAL04 southern hemisphere calibration, 0-11.0 cal kyr BP. Radiocarbon 46(3): 1087-192.

Megaw, J.V.S. (1965). Excavations in the Royal National Park, New South Wales: A first series of radiocarbon dates from the Sydney district. *Oceania* 35(3): 202–07.

Megaw, J.V.S. (1966). Report on excavations in the south Sydney district 1964–65. *Australian Institute of Aboriginal Studies Newsletter* 2(3):4–15.

Megaw, J.V.S. (1967). Archaeology, art and Aborigines. A survey of historical sources and later Australian prehistory. *Journal of the Royal Australian Historical Society* 53(4):277–94.

Megaw, J.V.S. (1968a). A dated culture sequence for the south Sydney region of New South Wales. *Current Anthropology* 9(4):325–329.

Megaw, J.V.S. (1968b). Trial excavations in Captain Cook's Landing Place Reserve, Kurnell, N.S.W. *Australian Institute of Aboriginal Studies Newsletter* 2(9): 17-20.

Megaw, J.V.S. (1974). The recent archaeology of the south Sydney district–a summary. In Megaw, J.V.S. (ed.), *The Recent Archaeology of the Sydney District. Excavations 1964-1967,* pp. 35–38. Canberra: Australian Institute of Aboriginal Studies.

Megaw, J.V.S. (1993). Something old, something new: further notes on the Aborigines of the Sydney district as represented by their surviving artefacts, and as depicted in some early European representations. In Specht, J.R. (ed.), *FD McCarthy, Commemorative Papers (Archaeology, Anthropology, Rock Art),* pp 25–44. *Records of the Australian Museum,* Supplement 17. Sydney: The Australian Museum.

Megaw, J.V.S. and Roberts, A. (1974). The 1967 excavations at Wattamolla Cove - Royal National Park, New South Wales. In Megaw, J.V.S. (ed.),

The Recent Archaeology of the Sydney District. Excavations 1964-1967, pp. 1–12. Canberra: Australian Institute of Aboriginal Studies

Megaw, J.V.S. and Wright, R.V.S. (1966). The excavation of an Aboriginal rock-shelter on Gymea Bay, Port Hacking, NSW *Archaeology and Physical Anthropology in Oceania* **1**(1):23–50.

Poiner, G. (1974). The trial excavation of an estuarine rock shelter at Yowie Bay. In: Megaw, JVS (ed.), *The Recent Archaeology of the Sydney District, Excavations 1964–1967*, pp. 28–34. Canberra: Australian Institute of Aboriginal Studies.

Rolfe, J.S. (1931a). An Aboriginal midden at Quibray Bay. *Mankind* **1**(2):36–37.

Rolfe, J.S. (1931b). An Aboriginal midden at Quibray Bay–Part II. *Mankind* **1**(3): 61-63.

Roy, P.S. and Crawford, E.A. (1981). Holocene geological evolution of the southern Botany Bay – Kurnell region, central NSW coast. *Records of the Geological Survey of NSW* **20**(2):159–250.

Sefton, C. (1995). 1994–1995 Archaeological Survey of Kangaroo Creek, Royal National Park by the Illawarra Prehistory Group. Report for AIATSIS, Canberra.

Sefton, C. (1996). 1995–1996 Archaeological Survey of the North and Western Side of the Hacking River including Royal National Park and Garrawarra State Recreation Area by the Illawarra Prehistory Group. Report for AIATSIS, Canberra.

Sefton, C. (2002). Archaeological Survey of the Eastern Drainage of the Hacking River to Upper Peach Trees by the Illawarra Prehistory Group. Unpublished report.

Sefton, C. (2004). Archaeological Survey of the Eastern Drainage of the Hacking River from Upper Peach Trees to Leg of Mutton Bay by the Illawarra Prehistory Group. Unpublished report.

Sefton, C. (2005). Archaeological Survey of the Hacking Estuary from Leg of Mutton Bay to Grahams Point. Unpublished report.

Sefton, C. (2007). Archaeological Survey of the Western Catchment of Southwest Arm to Grahams Point, Royal National Park by the Illawarra Prehistory Group. Unpublished report.

Sefton, C. (2008). Archaeological Survey of the Eastern Catchment of Southwest Arm to Coast Heights Spur, Royal National Park by the Illawarra Prehistory Group. Unpublished report.

Sefton, C. (2010). Archaeological Survey of Port Hacking from Costens Point to Cabbage Tree Point, Royal National Park by the Illawarra Prehistory Group. Unpublished report.

Sefton, C. (2011). Archaeological Survey from Cabbage Tree Point Port Hacking to Bulgo Beach, Royal National Park by the Illawarra Prehistory Group. (Unpublished report).

Smith, L.J., Rich, E. and Hesp, P. (1990). Aboriginal sites on Kurnell Peninsula: A Management Study. Vol. 1. Report for NSW NPWS, Sydney, and the Australian Heritage Commission, Canberra.

Stanbury, P. and Clegg, J. (1996). *A Field Guide to Aboriginal Rock Engravings*. Reprint. Oxford University Press.

Stockton, E.D. and Holland, W.N. (1974). Cultural sites and their environment in the Blue Mountains. *Archaeology and Physical Anthropology in Oceania* **9**(1):36–65.

Thorpe, W.W. (1932). Aboriginal relics of the Sydney district. In *Handbook for New South Wales*, pp 21–23. Prepared for the members of the Australian and New Zealand Association for the Advancement of Science on the occasion of its Meeting in Sydney, August, 1932. Sydney: Government Printer.

Tracey, R. (1974). Three minor sites near Curracurrang Cove with a preliminary note on a rock shelter at Newport. In Megaw, J.V.S. (ed.), *The Recent Archaeology of the Sydney District. Excavations 1964–1967*, pp. 19–27. Canberra: Australian Institute of Aboriginal Studies.

Tsoulos, D. (2007). The Kurnell Excavations (1968–1971) Revisited (amended version). BA(Hons) Thesis, Macquarie University, Sydney.

Ulm, S. (2006). Australian marine reservoir effects: A guide to ΔR values. *Australian Archaeology* **63**:57–60.

White, E. (1997[1998]). Archaeological Salvage of Site WGO3-2 (NPWS No 45-5-971) at Wattle Grove, NSW. Report for Jo McDonald Cultural Heritage Management for Delfin Management Services Pty Ltd.

White, J.P. and Wieneke, C. (undated, ca 1975). Henry Lawson Drive Rockshelter Excavation Report. Report for the NSW National Parks and Wildlife Service.

Wieneke, C. and White, J.P. (1973). Backed blades: another view. *Mankind* **9**(1):35–38.

APPENDIX

Radiometric ages listed according to sub-regions within Royal National Park and southern Sydney (ST=short-term event). Except where noted, radiocarbon age estimates are based on 2 sigma radiocarbon age calibrations using Calib 5.0.1; for charcoal samples [ch] the Southern Hemisphere atmospheric option; and shell samples [sh] the marine option at $\Delta R = -39\pm11$ 14C years (AINSE 2009:7; Ulm 2006); and calibration datasets: Hughen et al. 2004; McCormac et al. 2004.

Site name	Sample provenance	Material	Dating method	Conventional age	Standard Deviation	Lab No	Cal BP age 2sigma[greatest relative area]	Cal BP Median Probability	Publication, Report and Comments
						ROYAL NATIONAL PARK			
Bonnie Vale	Square 206E 845N, Spit 6	sh	C14	887	30	Wk-19344	481-607[1.00]	528	AMBS Consulting 2007:42.
Bundeena, Loftus St	C15/1/4 (Sample 1)	ch	C14	3,643	32	Wk-22761	3,869-4,011[0.80]	3,958	Mary Dallas Consulting 2008:44-46, Table 4.3, Appendix 5
	C15/1/4 (Sample 2)	ch	C14	3,662	53	Wk-22762	3,848-4,099 [0.95]	3,991	
	H15/1/3	ch	C14	4,563	33	Wk-22763	5,054-5,188 [0.53] 5259-5322 [0.40]	5,181	
	H15/1/4	ch	C14	4,151	32	Wk-22764	4,574-4,773 [0.80]	4,695	
Bundeena UCCC	Square 1, spit 7; lowest midden in shelter	sh	C14	1,034	35	Wk-15437	552-699[1.00]	640	Mary Dallas Consulting 2004: Addendum 2004; Irish 2007:46
	Square 2, spit 6; basal midden on talus below shelter	sh	C14	2,024	36	Wk-15436	1,524-1,741 [1.00]	1,635	
Curracurrang 1	Cutting 15, layer Ma	ch	C14	Modern <200		GaK-462	n/a		Megaw 1965:203, 1968a:Table 2, 1974: Table 1
	Cutting 15, layer Mb	sh	C14	Modern <230		GaK-483	n/a		Megaw 1965:203, 1968a:Table 2

ROYAL NATIONAL PARK

Site name	Sample provenance	Material	Dating method	Conventional age	Standard Deviation	Lab No	Cal BP age 2sigma [greatest relative area]	Cal BP Median Probability	Publication, Report and Comments
	Cutting 7E, level 2, upper midden	ch	C14	Modern <250		GaK-897	n/a		Megaw 1968a:Table 2
	Cutting 7, level 4	ch	C14	840	90	Gak-689	630-912 [0.94]	729	Megaw 1968a:Table 2, 1974:Table 1
	Baulk 4-7a/b (11-15)	ch	C14	1,430	90	GaK-894	1,068-1,418 [0.97]	1,289	Megaw 1968a:Table 2
	Cutting 10-15B	ch	C14	1,580	130	GaK-481	1,177-1,717 [1.00]	1,438	Megaw 1965:203, 1968a:Table 2
	Cutting 16, level 4, hearth	ch	C14	2,110	90	GaK-896	1,823-2,208 [0.94]	2,030	Meg
	Level 10 B/L	ch	C14	2,150	180	I-1135	1,613-2,494 [0.99]	2,079	Megaw 1965:203, 1968a:Table 2
	Cutting 7S, level 6	ch	C14	2,230	80	GaK-895	1,988-2,345 [0.99]	2,177	Megaw 1968a:Table 2
	Cutting 4, level 6	ch	C14	2,360	90	GaK-688	2,111-2,547 [0.89]	2,324	Megaw 1968a:Table 2, 1974:Table 1
	Cutting 10, level L	ch	C14	2,500	400	GaK-393b	1,560-3,443 [1.00]	2,506	Megaw 1965:203, 1968a:Table 2
	Cutting 5, level La	ch	C14	3,880	150	GaK-394a	3,827-4,629 [0.98]	4,224	Megaw 1965:203, 1968a:Table 2

B58

Proc. Linn. Soc. N.S.W., 134, 2012

Site	Description					Lab code	Calibrated range		Reference
	Cutting 5, level Lb	ch	C14	3,000	120	GaK-394b	2,841-3,380 [0.98]	3,109	Megaw 1965:203, 1968a:Table 2, 1974:35
	Cutting 15L, basal occupation	ch	C14	7,450	180	GaK-482	7,916-8,550 [0.98]	8,207	Megaw 1965:203, 1968a:Table 2, 1974:35
Curracurrang 2	Layer 3, middle of black sand	ch	c14	1,930	80	GaK-898	1,606-1,995 [1.00]	1,808	Glover 1974:14,17, Fig. 11
Curracurrang 7	Basal date	ch	C14	1,050	100	ANU-0179	724-1,096 [0.97]	907	Tracey 1974:25, Megaw 1974:36, Table 1,
	Pit A1, shelly midden, strata 1	ch	C14	560	130	ANU-0176	303-691 [0.99]	531	Megaw and Roberts 1974:4; Megaw 1974:Table 1
Wattamolla WL	Cutting G1 (shell less) strata 2	ch	C14	840	160	ANU-0177	509-990 [0.99]	744	
	Cutting D4 bottom/ex. strata 3	ch	C14	1,900	115	ANU-0178	1,518-2,061 [0.99]	1,773	
KURNELL PENINSULA									
Bate Bay Site BHW	Square B1, spit 4	ch	C14	2010	150	SUA-3009	1,561-2,208 [0.95]	1,910	C14 ages reported to author by Brayshaw (pers.comm.) after Brayshaw et al. 1992 was written.
	Square B1, spit 7	ch	C14	830	210	SUA-3010	447-1,173 [0.99]	746	
	Square B2, spit 5	ch	AMS	2402	88	NZA-2323	2,287-2,620 [0.69]	2,407	
	Square C2, spit 1	ch	C14	Modern		SUA-3011	n/a	n/a	
	Square C2, spit 6	ch	C14	1,400	110	SUA-3012	1,049-1,420 [0.94]	1,250	
Boat Harbour BH1	Spit 1, top of midden layer	ch	C14	470	60	ANU-0896	429-547 [0.73]	477	Dickson 1974b:17-18; 1974a:47 reports st.dev. as ±80.

Proc. Linn. Soc. N.S.W., 134, 2012

B59

Site name	Sample provenance	Material	Dating method	Conventional age	Standard Deviation	Lab No	Cal BP age 2sigma[greatest relative area]	Cal BP Median Probability	Publication, Report and Comments
Botany Cone Swamps BCS5, Boat Harbour	Base of midden/earliest occupation [poss spit 10]	ch	C14	1,930	70	ANU-0895	1,687-1,953 [0.92]	1,809	Dickson 1974b:17-18; 1974a:47 reports date as 1950±100
	Charcoal from insitu hearth exposed in dune blow out (ST)	ch	C14	1,520	90	SUA-2857	1,233-1,551 [0.98]	1,374	Smith et al. 1990:121, 123, Table 13; sparse scatter of fragmented shell and stone artefacts
The Meeting Place Precinct (Captain Cooks Landing Place BB4/-, Kurnell, Botany Bay	BB4/F, 85-90cm, base of upper midden, layer 7	ch	C14	360	110	ANU-0722	239-540 [0.82]	366	Megaw 1974:36, Table 1
	Site location B, BB4/F, lower midden (above bedrock)	ch	C14	1,330	100	ANU-0721	972-1,345 [1.00]	1,187	
Cronulla STP1, Captain Cook Drive, Kurnell Peninsula	Midden D, trench SB3/1, from a dark circular feature with charcoal	ch	C14	3,240	70	Wk-8845	3,241-3,577 [0.99]	3,411	Dallas et al. 2001, Appendix 2
	Trench SB2/4	sh	C14	2,880	60	Wk-8844	2,489-2,827 [1.00]	2,693	
260 Captain Cook Drive, Kurnell Peninsula	Square A3/2/C3/Bulk	sh	C14	2,262	38	Wk-23797	1,811-2,027 [1.00]	1,913	Jo McDonald CHM 2008:37-38, Appendix 3
	Square A3/2/C4/1	sh	C14	2,216	37	Wk-23798	1,751-1,971 [1.00]	1,861	
	Square A3/2/C2/2	sh	C14	2,165	37	Wk-23796	1,694-1,901 [1.00]	1,802	

B60

Proc. Linn. Soc. N.S.W., 134, 2012

Site	Sample description	Material	Method	Age	±	Lab number	Calibrated range [rel. area]	Cal. age	Reference
Doughboy Head 1, DH1, Kurnell Peninsula	Adjacent to a 'creek' line	ch	C14	12,190	110	Beta-36920	13,786-14,526 [0.99]	14,066	Smith et al. 1990:5, 118-119, Table 13. Mary Dallas Consulting (2002: Table 2.2) says 'problematic date due to inadequate collection procedure'
McCue Midden, Kurnell Peninsula, Botany Bay	Transect A, Square 110, Unit 02, Bulk; top of midden	ch	C14	760	40	Beta-165769	631-726 [0.80]	664	
	Transect A, Square 110, Unit 05, Bulk	ch	C14	770	40	Beta-165770	634-729 [0.87]	671	Mary Dallas Consulting 2005: Table 5.2
	A101/2/2; Transect A, Square 101, Unit 2, Spit 2	ch	C14	1,670	40	Beta-165768	1,402-1,609 [1]	1,495	
	Transect A, Square 110, Unit 8, bulk, base of midden	ch	C14	1,840	40	Beta-165771	1,595-1,822 [0.98]	1,708	
	Transect A, Square 22A, Unit 5, bulk	ch	C14	200	50	Beta-165767	131-301 [0.67]	174	
	Transect B, Square TT2, Unit 2, Spit 2	ch	C14	930	40	Beta-165772	727-909 [1.00]	793	
Potter Point, Kurnell Peninsula	Peat overlaying a pebble tool (ST)	peat	C14	5,620	70	ANU-0402	6,262-6,498 [0.96]	6,360	Dickson 1974a:46. The only information Dickson provided is 'from material collected during my own investigations at Potter Point, Kurnell ..... on the high ground'; but see Mary Dallas Consulting 2002: Table 2.2

Site name	Sample provenance	Material	Dating method	Conventional age	Standard Deviation	Lab No	Cal BP age 2sigma [greatest relative area]	Cal BP Median Probability	Publication, Report and Comments
Quibray Bay QB1, Botany Bay	Skeletal remains in shell midden (ST)	human bone	C14	2,210	360	ANU-0261	1,327-2,970 [0.99]	2,164	Dickson 1974a:47
Quibray Bay QB2, Botany Bay	Shell from top of shell midden buried beneath sand (ST)	sh	C14	4,130	111	SUA-0518	3,917-4,535 [1.00]	4,243	Roy and Crawford 1981:204, Table 1 (cited as 3680±111 BP)
PORT HACKING and SOUTHERN SYDNEY COAST									
Bindea Street, Bonnet Bay	Ph4/Tb/spit 14, unit D	ch	C14	2,340	100	Beta-005787	2,038-2,543 [0.92]	2,292	Attenbrow and Conyers 1983:23
Gymea Bay, Port Hacking GY	Earliest occupation	ch	C14	1,220	55	NSW-06	961-1,185 [0.94]	1,086	Megaw 1965:206; Megaw and Wright 1966:26-28, 43
Henry Lawson Drive, Padstow	Level III at base of midden inside shelter	ch	C14	870	95	SUA-0059	635-927 [0.97]	756	White and Wieneke c.1975, 7,17
	Level III-sub 55 cm deep outside shelter	ch	C14	5,240	100	SUA-0060	5,710-6,208 [0.99]	5,951	
Kendrick Park Midden, Marrickville	Midden 'top' at present	sh	C14	3,901	53	Wk-11291	3,767-4,090 [1.00]	3,930	AMBS 2003:18; Upper part of midden probably removed post-contact, so early date at top does not represent abandonment
	Midden base	shell	C14	4,328	50	Wk-11004	4,374-4,696 [1.00]	4,510	

B62

Proc. Linn. Soc. N.S.W., 134, 2012

Site	Sample	Material	Method	Age	±	Lab code	Calibrated range [probability]	calBP	Reference
Prince of Wales Hospital, Randwick	Charcoal adhering to hearthstone, Feature 203	ch	C14	7,860	50	Beta-87211	8,428-8,727[0.99]	8,582	Godden Mackay and Austral Archaeology 1997:25-26
	Hearthstone, Feature 203 (ST)	hearth-stone	TL	5,200	400	not provided	not necessary		
		hearth stone	TL	8,400	800	not provided	not necessary		
Sheas Creek, Alexandria	Dugong bone in estuarine creek sediments (ST)	bone marine	C14	5,520	70	Wk-8616	6,145-6,541 [see comment]	6,300	Haworth et al. 2004:46, 50-51, Table 1; calBP age adjusted for marine residence time
Discovery Point, Tempe	Charcoal pit feature Locus 2	ch	C14	9,376	61	Wk-16167	10,366-10,694[0.93]	10,522	Jo McDonald CHM 2005:56
Yowie Bay WA/-	WA/18M	ch	C14	2,230	70	ANU-0308	2,001-2,336 [1.00]	2,181	Poiner 1974:29; Poiner states site abandoned and not occupied in first millennium BP
	WA/18B	ch	C14	2,500	85	ANU-0307	2,345-2,735 [1.00]	2,575	
	WA/6B (basal)	ch	C14	2,670	85	ANU-0175	2,451-2,884 [0.96]	2,717	
HINTERLAND TO ROYAL NP and SOUTHERN SYDNEY									
Bardens Creek 9	Square A3, spit 2	ch	C14	1,630	90	SUA-1746	1,303-1,630 [0.96]	1,471	Attenbrow and Negerevich 1984:143. Occupation evidence extends belowC14 dated level

HINTERLAND TO ROYAL NP and SOUTHERN SYDNEY

Site name	Sample provenance	Material	Dating method	Conventional age	Standard Deviation	Lab No	Cal BP age 2sigma|greatest relative area|	Cal BP Median Probability	Publication, Report and Comments
Mill Creek M11, Menai	Shelter A, square 1, spit 3	ch	C14	520	50	SUA-2255	451-560 [0.97]	518	Revised dates in Koettig 1990:24
	Shelter A, square 1, spit 5	ch	C14	1,450	50	SUA-2256	1,239-1,396 [0.97]	1,311	
	Shelter A, square 1, spit 9	ch	C14	2,110	50	SUA-2257	1,891-2,148 [1.00]	2,022	
	Shelter A, square 2, spit 3	ch	C14	980	50	SUA-2258	742-929 [1.00]	847	Koettig 1990:24
	Shelter A, square 2, spit 9,	ch	C14	2,690	50	SUA-2259	2,698-2,867 [0.92]	2,759	
Mill Creek M14, Menai	Square E9/ spit 3 (hearth)	ch	C14	2,160	80	Beta-27197	1,918-2,313 [0.98]	2,088	Koettig 1990:16, 27
Wattle Grove 3-2	Trench 5 (hearth; ST)	ch	C14	1,580	60	Beta-120747	1,307-1,532 [1.00]	1,418	White 1997[1998] Lab Report

The Holocene History of the Vegetation and the Environment of Jibbon Swamp, Royal National Park, New South Wales

Jane M. Chalson[1] and Helene A. Martin[2]

[1]46 Kilmarnock St. Engadine N.S.W. 2233
[2] School of Biological, Environmental and Earth Sciences, University of New South Wales, Sydney Australia
2052 (h.martin@unsw,edu.au)

Published on 3 September 2012 at http://escholarship.library.usyd.edu.au/journals/index.php/LIN

Chalson, J.M. and Martin, H.A. (2012). The Holocene history of the vegetation and the environment of Jibbon Swamp, Royal National Park, New South Wales. *Proceedings of the Linnean Society of New South Wales* **134**, B65-B91.

Jibbon Swamp, in the north eastern part of Royal National Park, yielded a sedimentary history of 8,000 years. The present vegetation was mapped and the modern pollen deposition studied in order to assist interpretation. The palynology infers little change in the vegetation, other than a shifting mosaic of sclerophyllous communities similar to those seen in the area today.

The nature of the accumulating sediments and their algal and fungal spore content can be interpreted to reflect the hydrological history of the swamp. An initial establishment period of 8,000 to 5,500 year ago was followed by a permanent pool of water too deep for the sedgeland swamp vegetation, from 5,500 to 2,400 years ago and then a vegetated swamp that dried out periodically, from 2,400 years ago to present, as it does today.

Changes in the sediments and algae/fungi record suggest a wetter early Holocene and a drier mid-late Holocene climate, with an intensification of the dry periods about 2,500 years ago. This pattern of change seems to reflect regional climatic change. There is very little change in the less sensitive sclerophyllous vegetation. The likely impact of rising Holocene sea levels on this near-coastal environment is discussed.

Manuscript received 6 February 2012, accepted for publication 18 June 2012.

KEYWORDS: Holocene palynology, Holocene sea levels, Jibbon Swamp, Royal National Park, Vegetation history.

INTRODUCTION

Jibbon Swamp (Fig. 1) is located in the northeastern part of Royal National Park, behind Jibbon Beach and Port Hacking Point (Fig. 2). Its position is within a mosaic of sclerophyllous plant communities on nutrient poor sandstone soils. Currently, human interference in the area is minimal, considering its proximity to urban areas and disturbance is restricted to walking tracks and fire trails, but before European settlement, the Aborigines used the area. There are extensive rock engravings at Jibbon Head and small shell middens at Jibbon Beach (Attenbrow, 2002). The Aborigines were rapidly displaced after European settlement (Radford, 1999).

A large property was subdivided and the township of Bundeena was founded in 1898. During the 1930's Depression and World War II, there was an influx of people into the township and in shacks in the Park. The increased human influence probably caused greater disturbance and more fires (Radford, 1999).

The open areas around the swamp are grazed by native animals and introduced deer, the latter causing considerable damage. The fire frequency over most of the area is high, with the western border of the study area being burnt every year (in the early 1980's) for protection of the township of Bundeena (Chalson, 1983).

The fire history of Jibbon Lagoon has been studied in an attempt to determine if charcoal content could be correlated with known historic fire events (Radford, 1999; Mooney et al., 2001). The Holocene vegetation and environment has been reconstructed for sites on the nearby Kurnell Peninsula (Johnson, 1994; Martin, 1994).

This study examines the palynology of the swamp sediments and reconstructs the history of the vegetation, which in turn may indicate some change in climate. The close proximity of the swamp to the coastline means that changes in sea levels could have had an impact on the environment (Smith et al., 2011; Fleming et al., 1998).

Fig. 1. Jibbon Swamp in 1983

THE ENVIRONMENT

The area is situated on Hawkesbury Sandstone that has been covered, in part, by sheets of dune sand. Jibbon Swamp lies in a swale of the dunes. The bedrock of Hawkesbury Sandstone produces soils that are mainly lithosols and yellow podsols in the study area. All the soils are sandy throughout their profile and are acidic and poor in nutrients (Beadle, 1981).

The Hawkesbury Sandstone is impermeable but a system of vertical joints throughout facilitate the percolation of surface water and the result is very water stressed conditions for plants over large areas, especially on exposed sites such as ridge tops. Clay derived from the weathering of the sandstone collects in the dune swales forming a relatively impermeable layer that locally raises the watertable and may form a swamp, such as Jibbon Swamp (Branagan, 1979).

The climate is influenced by the proximity of Jibbon Lagoon to the coast and its low altitude of about 10 m above sea level. The temperature and humidity contrasts are reduced when compared with more inland sites (Bureau of Meteorology, 1991). The mean annual rainfall is about 1,220 mm (for the Cronulla South Bowling Club, elevation 31 m: BoM, 2011), some 2 km to the northwest. Rainfall is fairly evenly distributed throughout the year, with the wettest months February to June, recording an average of over 120 mm per month, and the driest months September to December with a mean of 62 to 87 mm per month. The mean maximum temperatures range from 26.4 °C in January to 17 °C in July while the mean minimum temperatures range from 18.8 °C in January to 7.1 °C in July (for Sydney Airport AMO: BoM, 2011).

METHODS

Fieldwork was carried out in 1983 when the vegetation was surveyed, using a combination of aerial photos and random transects. As many species as possible were collected and identified. The plant communities were defined on structure of the vegetation and the dominant species, following the classification of Specht (1970). Surface pollen samples for the definition of the pollen signature of the communities were collected from the surface of the soil. A number of samples from each plant community were mixed and sub sampled to prevent over-representation by the close proximity of one particular species.

The stratigraphy of Jibbon Swamp was explored using a Russian or D-section core sampler (Birks and Birks, 1980) for the clay sediments in the swamp and for samples used in pollen analysis. It was necessary to use a soil auger in the sandy soils around the swamp. The swamp was surveyed with one N-S transect the length of the swamp and four E-W transects across the swamp.

Samples for palynology were collected from a core in the deepest part of the swamp. The samples

B66

Proc. Linn. Soc. N.S.W., 134, 2012

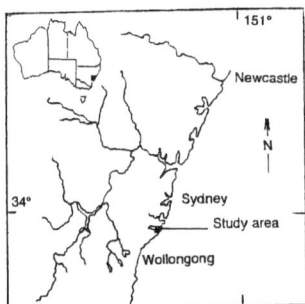

Fig. 2. Location of Jibbon Swamp in Royal National Park.

were taken at 10 cm intervals, or closer if the stratigraphy was complex. Samples chosen for radiocarbon dating were taken from the base of the major stratigraphic units and were dated by Mr. V. Djohadze of the then School of Nuclear and Radiation Chemistry at the University of New South Wales. These samples were dated just before the laboratory was closed, and laboratory numbers for the samples have not been located.

Samples for pollen analysis were spiked with an exotic pollen (*Alnus*) suspension of known concentration and processed with a procedure

adapted from Brown (1960). Reference pollen collected from species growing in the area was treated by the standard acetolysis method (Birks and Birks, 1980). Sediment and reference pollen residues were mounted in glycerine jelly.

Identification of the pollen from the swamp sediments was done by comparison with the reference pollen. The similarity of the myrtaceous pollen required a careful analysis of the finer morphological features (Chalson and Martin, 1995) to achieve identification. Algal spores were identified by consulting the literature as a reference collection was not available. Total concentration of fungal spores was estimated and further identification was not attempted. For a quantitative analysis, pollen on transects across the slide were counted. Tests showed that a minimum of 140 grains was sufficient to give a representative sample.

Both percentages and pollen concentrations for individual pollen types were calculated from the counts. As these two different methods gave very similar results (Chalson, 1983), percentages have been used to construct the pollen spectra diagrams presented here.

STRATIGRAPHY OF THE SWAMP SEDIMENTS

Fig. 3 shows the location of two cross-sections of the swamp and Fig. 4 presents the profiles of the swamp sediments. The core for palynology was taken close to test hole A7, in the deepest part of the swamp and Fig. 5 shows the stratigraphy for this hole. Table 1 presents the radiocarbon dates: the base of the swamp is 7,250±120 radiocarbon years, or 8,224-7,786 calibrated years before the present (8.2-7.7 cal ka BP).

At the base of the swamp, there is a continuous, irregular layer, 5 to 10 cm thick of a fine-grained black material with a thin, reddish brown clay layer, and a mottled grey clay layer above it. Above the mottled layer, a thick layer of olive clay merges horizontally with grey and brown clays to the north. A black clay layer caps the olive clay and humic clay and peat form the uppermost layer. In the north, there are some intrusive sand wedges.

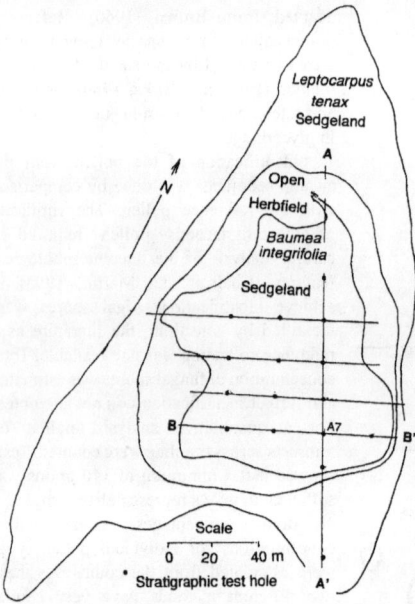

Fig. 3 (left). Location of transects and stratigraphic test holes across swamp.

THE VEGETATION

The *Eucalyptus/Corymbia/Angophora* woodlands and forests on soils of low fertility have a richly diverse sclerophyllous understorey (Beadle, 1981). In this near coastal location, wind and salt spray has a considerable effect, especially on moisture relationships. The areas fully exposed to the wind usually only support heaths or shrublands where the tree species remain stunted to about 2 m high. The soils are well drained and water stress is probably common. In recent historic times, frequent fires are also a feature of the environment of these communities (Mooney et al., 2001). Appendix 1 presents the species found in each of the plant communities described below and the distribution of these communities is shown in Fig. 6.

Cupaniopsis/Eucalyptus botryoides Open Forest occupies the barrier dune along the rear of Jibbon beach in areas with least exposure to winds, salt spray and fire. Compared with the rest of the

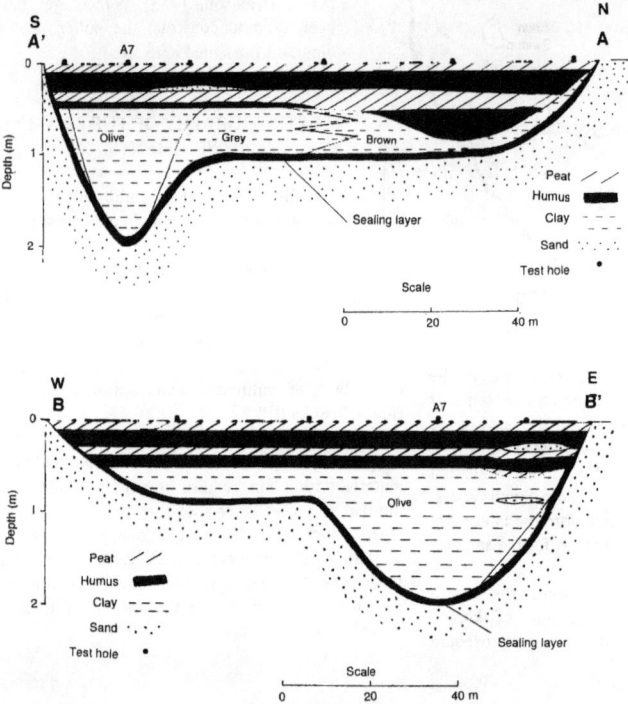

Figure 4 (left). North-south and east-west stratigraphic profiles of the swamp sediments. The location of the transects on the swamp is shown in Fig. 3.

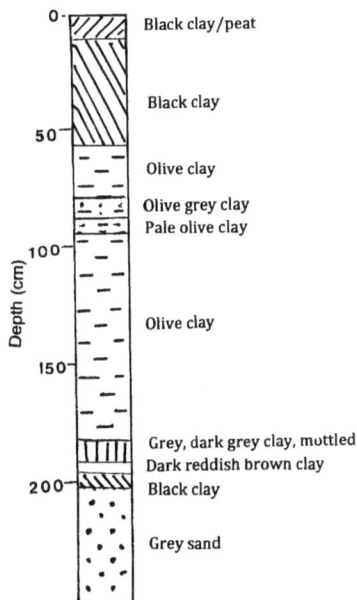

Black clay/peat

Black clay

Olive clay

Olive grey clay
Pale olive clay

Olive clay

Grey, dark grey clay, mottled
Dark reddish brown clay
Black clay

Grey sand

Fig. 5. Stratigraphy of hole A7 from the deep-st part of the swamp. For location, see Fig. 2.

area, the soil is relatively well developed. The canopy is 10 to 12 m high with *Cupaniopsis anacardioides* dominant at the eastern end and both this species and *Eucalyptus botryoides* dominant at the western end

of the community. The dense understorey is 1 to 3 m high and dominated by *Acmena smithii* and the introduced *Cestrum parqui. Asparagus plumosus* and *A. aethiopicus* dominate the ground layer to a height of half a metre. This community has largely escaped burning.

Angophora costata/Eucalyptus botryoides Low Open Forest is found in a narrow strip at the northeastern end of Jibbon Beach and in a small area to the southeast. It grows on shallow but well developed soil over the Hawkesbury Sandstone that is more retentive of moisture than most soils in the region. It is well protected from winds, salt spray and fire by the sand dunes to the north and east. The open canopy, 3 to 6 m high, is dominated by *A. costata, E. botryoides* and *Corymbia gummifera.* The understorey ranges from 0 to 2 m in height and is dominated by *Leptospermum laevigatum* and *Banksia serrata.*

Angophora costata/ Corymbia gummifera Low Open Forest occupies a large area to the west of Jibbon Swamp and grows exclusively on dune sand with a moderate soil development and poor water retaining capacity. Dune crests form the eastern boundary of this community and it appears that they protect it from salt damage (P. Stricker, pers. comm.). The open canopy is 3 to 6 m high and is dominated by *A. costata* and *C. gummifera.* An understorey up to 1 m high is dominated by *Lomandra longifolia* and *Pteridium esculentum.* The latter two species are often indicative of disturbance to the native vegetation. This community has been frequently burnt as a firebreak for the township of Bundeena.

Banksia ericifolia/Persoonia lanceolata Closed Scrub is found in a small area adjacent to the *A. costata/E. botryoides* Forest to the northeast. Here,

Table 1. Radiocarbon dates of the sediments

Sample depth (cm)	Nature of material	Radiocarbon years	Calibrated Age[a] (relative area under probability distribution)	Years Before Present (BP[b])
20-30	Black clay	NSW 1400±80	cal AD 560- 881 (100%)	1390-1069 BP
40-50	Black clay	NSW 2600±100	cal BC 846- 402 (98.9%)	2796-2352 BP
60-70	Olive clay	NSW 3100±100	cal BC 1510- 1004 (100%)	3460-2954 BP
180-190	Olive clay	NSW 4980±100	cal BC 3961- 3518 (99.7%)	5911-5468 BP
190-200	Black clay	NSW 6740±120	cal BC 5838- 5463 (96.2%)	7788-7413 BP
210-220	Sand	NSW 7250±120	cal BC 6274- 5836 (94.9%)	8224-7786 BP

The radiocarbon dates were calibrated using the Southern Hemisphere atmosphere data set (SHCal04.14C H terrestrial dataset) in CALIB version 6.0html, available at http://calib.qub.ac.uk/calib/ accessed October 2011. The calibrated ages represent the 2-sigma (95.4 %) calendar age ranges with the highest relative area under the probability distribution (with the relative area indicated in brackets) (Reimer et al., 2004)
BP=before 1950

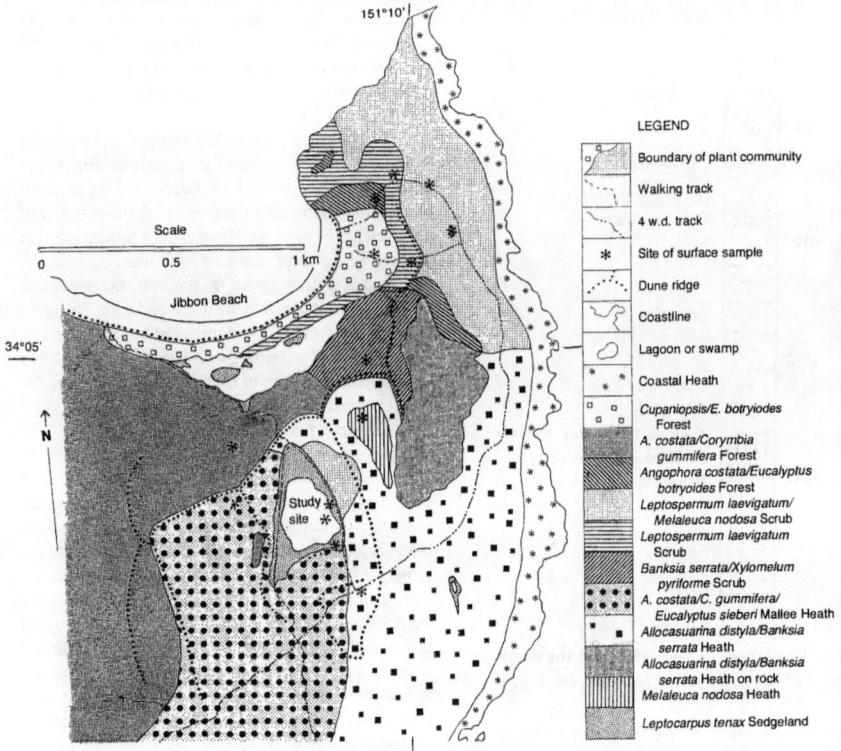

Fig. 6. Vegetation communities in the area around Jibbon Swamp, in the early 1980's

the soils are shallow and moderately developed on Hawkesbury Sandstone. The scrub is drier than the forest and more exposed to wind and fire. The over storey is extremely dense extending from 0.5 to 2 m high. Floristically, it is very diverse and the following species are the most common: *B. ericifolia*, *P. lanceolata*, *Callistemon rigidus*, *Kunzea ambigua* and *Melaleuca nodosa*. The understorey is up to 0.3 m high and dominated by Cyperaceae, mosses and *Drosera* species.

Leptospermum laevigatum/Melaleuca nodosa Closed Scrub occupies a large area to the northeast of the region and this community is bounded to the east by a narrow band of highly pruned, salt tolerant plants of the Coastal Heath, and to the west by *L. laevigatum* Scrub. The underlying soils are moderately developed on dune sand. The drainage varies considerably and the community often contains small shallow swamps

3 to 4 m across, adjacent to very dry, well drained areas. This community is highly exposed to wind, salt spray and fire although it has not been burnt since a wildfire in 1955 (up to the early 1980's P. Stricker, pers. comm.). The over storey is extremely dense, extending from 0.5 to 2 m high. The dominant species are *L. laevigatum* and *M. nodosa*, but it is floristically very diverse. The understorey is 0 to 0.3 m high and is dominated by Cyperaceae and Poaceae. Clearing for picnic and camping areas have altered parts of this community considerably.

Banksia serrata/ Xylomelum pyriforme Open Scrub is found east of Jibbon Lagoon, on poorly developed but well-drained soils on deep dune sands. It is highly exposed to fire, although less so to wind and salt spray. Since the wildfire in 1955 and up to the early 1980's, it has undergone regular hazard reduction burning (P. Stricker, pers. comm.). The over storey is irregular, occurring in thickets and extending from about 0.5 to 2 m in height. The dominants are *Banksia serrata, Xylomelum pyriforme, Allocasuarina distyla, Leptospermum laevigatum* and *Melaleuca nodosa.* Cyperaceae and Poaceae dominate the understorey.

Leptospermum laevigatum Closed Scrub forms a narrow band around the southern, eastern and northeastern boundaries of the *Cupaniopsis/ Eucalyptus botryoides* Forest. To the north, it is found on shallow sandy soils of the Hawkesbury Sandstone, but to the east and south, it grows more luxuriantly on poor soils of the sand dunes. The scrub is protected from wind and salt spray by dune crests along its boundary and has not been burnt since 1955 and up to 1983, forming a buffer zone for the *Cupaniosis/E. botryoides* Forest. The dense canopy, 5 to 7 m high, is exclusively *Leptospermum laevigatum.* There are a few scattered *Banksia serrata* shrubs, 2 m high and a more extensive ground cover, to 0.3 m high, dominated by *Phebalium squamulosum* and *Lepidosperma concavum.*

Melaleuca nodosa Closed Heath is found in the dune swale immediately to the east of the swamp and receives runoff from a Hawkesbury Sandstone ledge to the east, but the moderately developed soils are well drained. The community is sheltered from wind and salt spray by a sand dune ridge that runs over the ledge. The community has been subjected to hazard reduction burning prior to 1983. *M. nodosa* is the dominant species with a few scattered *Banksia serrata* shrubs about 30 m apart. The only understorey species is the fungus *Cantharellus cibarius* var. *australiensis* (A.E. Wood, pers. comm.).

Angophora costata/Corymbia gummifera/ Eucalyptus sieberi Mallee Heath (Low Shrubland) occupies a large area to the south west of the region. In the north, the mallee heath grows on dune sand with poor soil development and in the far south, beyond Bundeena, it is found on shallow soils of the Hawkesbury Sandstone. This community is very exposed to wind, salt spray and fire, being regularly burnt for hazard reduction purposes in the early 1980's. The over storey, 0.5 to 2 m high, is a diverse heathland with patches of short, multistemmed mallees of *A. costata, C. gummifera* and *E. sieberi.* The dominants are *Banksia serrata, Hakea dactyloides, Allocasuarina distyla, Styphelia viridus* and *Melaleuca nodosa.* The understorey, up to 0.5 m is a sparse mix of Cyperaceae and Poaceae.

Allocasuarina distyla/Banksia serrata Closed Heath occupies a large area to the south east of the study site and is found on the poor soils of the dune sand and occasional patches of very thin soils of the Hawkesbury Sandstone. The community is floristically very diverse and the dominants, *B. serrata* and *A. distyla* are only slightly more frequent than many other species. There is no layering, the tallest plants being 1 m high. The community has the richest diversity in the dune sands and is floristically poorer, more open and lower in height on the sandstone soils. The heathland is highly exposed to wind, salt spray and fire, being regularly burnt for hazard reduction purposes in the early 1980's.

Leptocarpus tenax Closed Sedgeland is found on the extensive flat area around Jibbon Swamp. The area has poor soil but good moisture relationships as runoff from the dune ridges on three sides collect here, and at times of high rainfall, may be waterlogged. The community is well protected from wind and salt spray but it has been regularly burnt in the 1980's for fire hazard reduction. The dominant sedges are *L. tenax* and *Schoenus brevifolius*, forming a layer about 0.8 m high. There is a low, 2 cm understorey of *Goodenia paniculata* and *Gonocarpus micranthus.*

Open Herbfield is found in a 1 to 5 m wide zone between the *Leptocarpus tenax* Sedgeland and the *Baumea teretifolia* Sedgeland of the swamp proper. There is no visible soil development although there are faint broad colour bands down the profile. Protection, drainage and water relations are approximately the same as for the *L. tenax* Sedgeland. There is only about a 10% plant cover and a few pioneer heathland species become established in drier conditions. There are several species of Asteraceae (not native) and several large patches of *Viola sieberana.*

Baumea teretifolia Sedgeland is found in the swamp that usually contains standing water, except in extended dry periods when most of it dries out. The soils are usually waterlogged. *B. teretifolia* is the dominant sedge, with *Baumea juncacea* and *Chorizandra sphaerocephala* found along the fringes of the swamp. *Triglochin procera* grows in disturbed sites.

MODERN POLLEN DEPOSITION

The most abundant pollen types in the pollen spectra produced by the communities are shown in Fig. 7A, 7B, and the low frequency and rare types found in each community are recorded in Table 2. Knowledge of the pollen spectra produced by the plant communities should assist in the interpretation of the spectra found in the swamp sediments.

The pollen spectra show that only a few pollen types contribute substantial percentages, e.g. *Allocasuarina/Casuarina.* Other types contribute less pollen that may still vary between communities e.g.

Proc. Linn. Soc. N.S.W., 134, 2012

B71

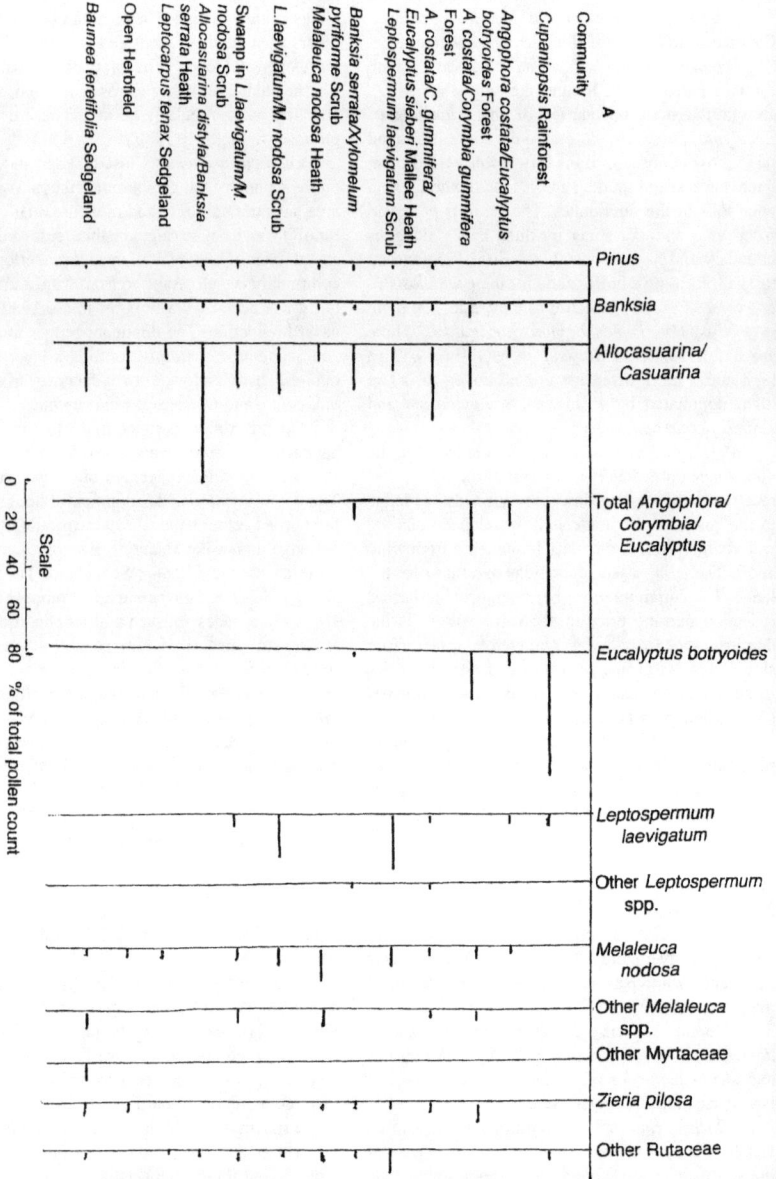

Fig. 7. Modern pollen deposition by the communities.

B72

Proc. Linn. Soc. N.S.W., 134, 2012

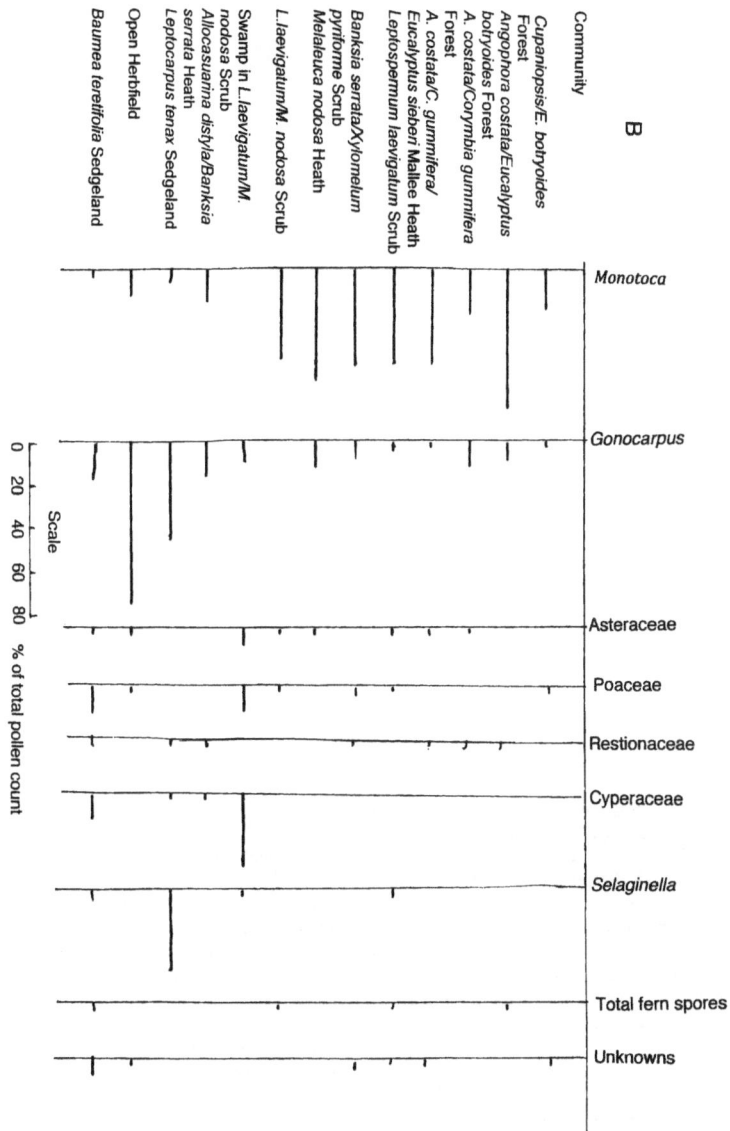

Proc. Linn. Soc. N.S.W., 134, 2012

B73

Table 2. Modern pollen deposition: low frequency and rare species

Key to species numbers

1. *Angophora cordifolia*	7. *Persoonia* sp
2. *Eucalyptus haemastoma*	8. *Achronychia* sp
3. *E. sieberi*	9. *Geijera salicifolia*
4. *Leptospermum trinervum*	10. *Zieria* sp.
5. *Melaleuca armillaris*	11. *Correa reflexa*
6. *M. quinquinerva*	12. *C. alba*

Pollen percentages of total count given.

Community	1	2	3	4	5	6	7	8	9	10	11	12
Cupaniopsis/E. botryoides Forest									2		3	
Angophora costata/ Eucalyptus botryoides Forest	2	1									1	
A. costata/Corymbia gummifera Forest	1					2					2	
A. costata/C. gummifera/ E. sieberi Mallee Heath					2	2						
Leptospermum laevigatum Scrub								1				
Banksia serrata/Xylomelum pyriforme Scrub	1		1				2					
Melaleuca nodosa Heath					3							
L. laevigatum/M. nodosa Scrub									1	2		2
Swamp in *L.laevigatum/M. nodosa* Scrub				1		1						5
Allocasuarina distyla/Banksia serrata Heath									1			1
Leptocarpus tenax Sedgeland											1	
Open Herbfield						3						1

Leptospermum laevigatum, but some are only ever found in low frequencies e.g. *Banksia, Zieria pilosa* (Fig. 7, Table 2). Many factors influence the pollen representation and whether a taxon is wind or animal pollinated is perhaps the most important. Wind pollinated species usually produce copious quantities of relatively small grains that may be widely distributed, e.g. *Allocasuarina/Casuarina*, whereas animal pollinated plants usually produce fewer, larger and stickier grains that are less likely to be distributed widely, e.g. *Banksia*.

An examination of the pollen spectra shows that some distinctive features may be used to deduce the nature of the community. Pollen of *Allocasuarina/ Casuarina* may be found almost everywhere, but Table 3 shows that where it is dominant, there is over 40%: where present but not dominant, from 20 to 40%,

and where it is not present, less than about 20% of the pollen spectrum. *Eucalyptus botryoides* contributes a substantial percentage to the *Cupaniopsis/E. botryoides* Forest, where it is a co-dominant, but the other co-dominant, *Cupaniopsis* does not contribute any pollen to the spectrum. It seems puzzling that *E. botryoides* contributes relatively little pollen to the spectrum of the *Angophora costata/E. botryoides* Forest, but this latter spectrum has relatively high percentages of *Monotoca* pollen. *Monotoca* is common in this community, but not in the *Cupaniopsis/E. botryoides* Forest. *Angophora* and *Corymbia* have larger grains than *Eucalyptus* and are usually not well distributed.

Variable preservation of the grains may sometimes be a factor influencing representation in the spectrum.. There are both dryland and swamp

B74

Proc. Linn. Soc. N.S.W., 134, 2012

Table 3. **Distinctive Pollen Features of the Communities**
Key to pollen type numbers.

1. *Angophora*	6. *Gonocarpus*
2. *Eucalyptus/Corymbia*	7. Restionaceae
3. *Melaleuca*	8. Cyperaceae
4. *Leptospermum*	9. *Selaginella*
5. *Allocasuarina/Casuarina*	10. Total fern spores

Pollen percentages of total count given

Community	Pollen type									
	1	2	3	4	5	6	7	8	9	10
Cupaniopsis/E. botryoides Forest	2	67	5	3	<20	-	-	-	-	-
Angophora costata/Eucalyptus botryoides Forest	-	7	-	5	<20	8	-	-	-	-
A. costata/Corymbia gummifera Forest	3	13	-	-	<20	11	-	-	-	-
A. costata/C. gummifera/ Eucalyptus sieberi Mallee Heath	-	-	7	-	20-40	-	-	-	-	-
Leptospermum laevigatum Scrub	-	-	6	22	<20	-	-	-	-	-
Banksia serrata/Xylomelum pyriforme Scrub	-	-	-	-	20-40	-	-	-	-	-
Melaleuca nodosa Heath	-	-	21	_	<20	9	-	-	-	-
L. laevigatum/M. nodosa Scrub	-	-	-	22	20-40	-	-	-	-	-
Allocasuarina distyla/Banksia serrata Heath	-	-	-	-	>40	12	-	-	-	-
Leptocarpus tenax Sedgeland	-	-	-	-	<22	40	5	-	35	-
Open Herbfield	-	-	-	-	<20	70	-	-	-	-
Baumea teretifolia Sedgeland	-	-	7	-	-	13	-	12	5	5

species of Cyperaceae. The pollen of Cyperaceae is particularly thin-walled and subject to crumpling that makes identification difficult. The *Leptospermum laevigatum/Melaleuca nodosa* Scrub was sampled twice, one in the same manner as all the other surface samples and the other from a small swamp in the community. The swamp sample has appreciable pollen of Cyperaceae whereas the dryland sample has none. Nearly all of the surface samples were taken from dryland situations, a necessity in this environment, hence they are not exactly equivalent to the core samples taken from the swamp. Still, the surface pollen spectra should give some guidance for the interpretation of the core samples.

Algal and fungal spores found in the surface samples are presented in Fig 8. The Unknown algal type 1 (see Fig. 9) is common in all the communities, but relatively less is found in the *Baumea teretifolia* Sedgeland swamp community. *Zygnema*-type is found occasionally in low frequencies. Zygnemataceae are found in fresh-water ponds, ditches and streams, and are characteristic of oxygen-rich, shallow, stagnant water (Head, 1992). Its presence in these dryland communities may be ephemeral following particularly wet weather.

Botyococcus braunii is common in the *Baumea teretifolia* Sedgeland, but it is absent from, or there is very little in most of the other dryland communities. *B. braunii* is a widespread planktonic species that is found in fresh/brackish waters (Pentacost, 1984). Algal type 2 (See Fig. 9) is rarely seen.

The fungal spore concentration in most communities is high, but one of the lowest is found in the *B. teritifolia* Sedgeland. A high concentration of fungal spores is usually regarded as a sign of a relatively dry environment, at least seasonally (Van Geel and Van der Hammen, 1978).

Proc. Linn. Soc. N.S.W., 134, 2012

B75

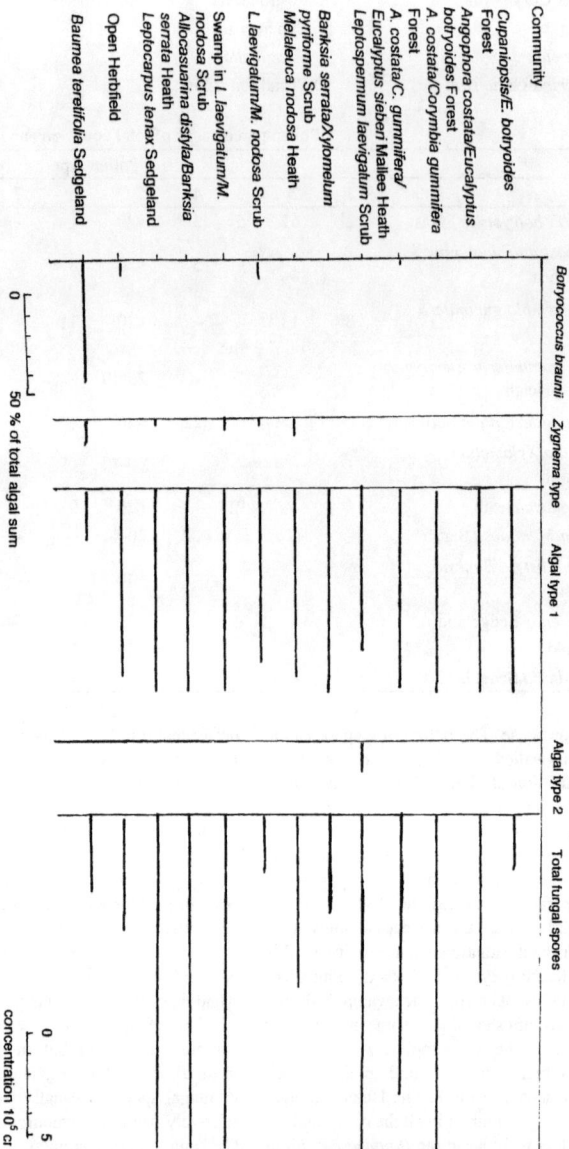

Fig. 8. Modern algal and fungal spore found in the communities.

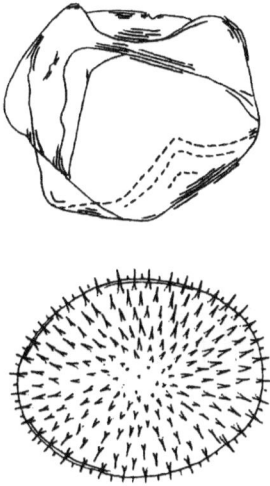

Fig. 9. Unknown algal spores. Top, Algal type 1, possibly a Zygnemataceae (see Head, 1992). Bottom, Algal type 2. For named algal spore types, see Pentecost (1984).

PALYNOLOGY OF THE SWAMP SEDIMENTS

The most abundant pollen types in the swamp sediment pollen spectra are shown on Figs 10A and 10B and the low frequency and rare pollen types are presented in Table 4. A comparison with the distinctive pollen features of the communities (Table 3) shows that the spectra are a combination of some dryland community and the on-site swamp community.

In general, the whole of the dryland part of the spectra best fits the modern *Angophora costata/ Corymbia gummifera/Eucalyptus sieberi* mallee heath community, with the exception that the *Monotoca* content is far lower than in the modern community. The surface pollen samples (Figs 7A, 7B) show that *Monotoca* pollen is more abundant in the dryland communities and less so in the sedgelands and herbfield around the swamp and the lesser quantities in the swamp sediments many simply reflect this.

Some spectra, however, suggest other communities. The 195 cm level (peak C of Chalson, 1983) is comparable with the *Angophora costata/Corymbia gummifera* Forest community and has the highest peak for *Angophora/ Corymbia/Eucalyptus* and an unusually low *Allocasuarina/Casuarina* content of <20%. This level is within the black humus layer sealing the swamp.

The representation of Cyperaceae, Restionaceae and *Sellaginella* are comparable to the *Baumea teretifolia* Sedgeland, the community on the swamp itself.

The 140-150 cm and 70-80 cm levels have percentages for *Allocasuarina/Casuarina* exceeding 40%, suggesting that it was dominant, at times. *Angophora/Corymbia/Eucalyptus* is not represented at these levels. Again, the representation of Cyperaceae and Restionaceae are comparable to the *Baumea teretifolia* Sedgeland.

The vegetation in the whole of the profile, representing about 8 cal ka BP, is thus very similar to that of today, with a suggestion that there may have been a forest in the oldest part of the profile. The variations in the pollen spectra probably represent shifting patterns, perhaps with a slightly different assortment of species within the sclerophyllous vegetation that was essentially similar to today.

The algal and fungal components (Fig. 11) show some patterns of change and they indicate hydrological conditions in the swamp. The algae and fungi, with their short life cycles, can respond quickly to environmental changes. The swamp sediments are zoned on the hydrological changes thus:

Zone 3: 220-180 cm, ~ 8.0-5.5 cal ka BP. *Botryococcus braunii* is mostly low, the *Zygnema* type is well represented, *Spirogyra* is usually present, Algal type 1 (see Fig. 9) is usually abundant and the fungal spores are well represented. *B. braunii* is a planktonic species and indicates standing fresh to brackish water (Pentacost, 1984). The Zygnemataceae (*Zygnema* and *Spirogyra*) are found in freshwater lakes and pools. Many forms prefer temporary standing water and the increased temperatures experienced as the pool dries out would encourage spore formation, a necessity for preservation in the swamp sediments. The surface pollen spectra show that Algal type 1 is associated with dryland conditions and fungal spores indicate dry conditions (van Geel and van der Hammen, 1978). Thus Zone 3 suggests a swamp that had standing water at times, but it dried out regularly. After periods of wet weather, there were temporary pools of water that soon dried out.

Zone 2: 170-40 cm, ~ 5.5-2.4 cal ka BP. The *B. braunii* content is greater and the *Zygnema* type and Algal type 1 are lower than in the zone below. Standing water, too deep for sedgelands that would have been confined to the edge of the swamp, was consistently present in this zone. Fungal spores are generally low, indicating moist conditions, except for the 100-70 cm level, where they are higher. There is no change in the algal abundance in this level, suggesting that any seasonal dry periods were insufficient to influence the maintenance of the permanent pool of water.

Proc. Linn. Soc. N.S.W., 134, 2012

B77

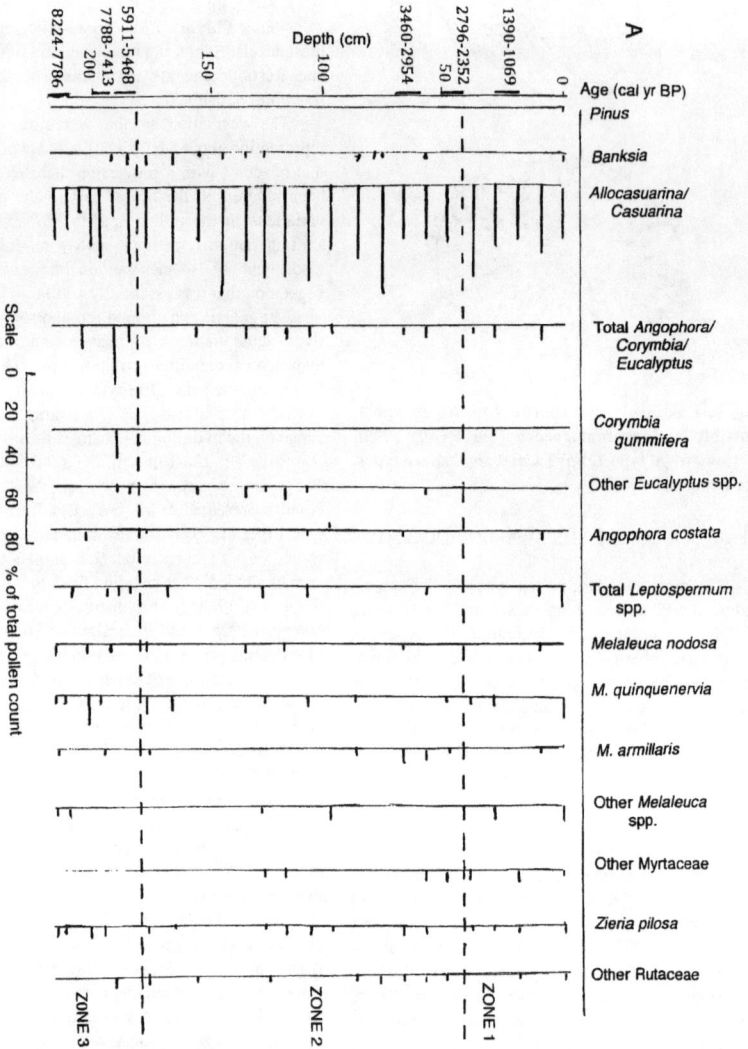

Fig. 10. Pollen spectra from the swamp sediments.

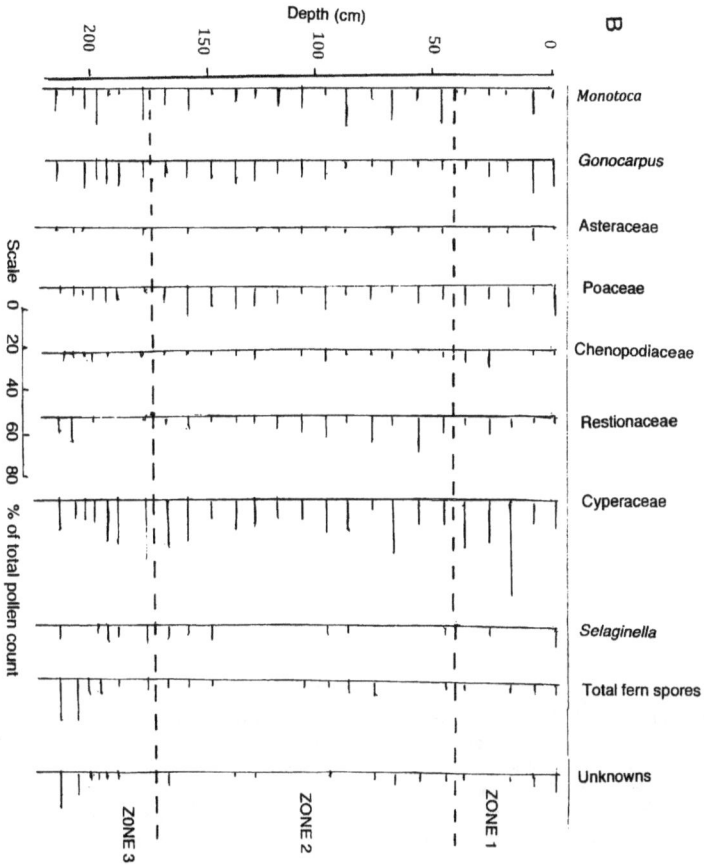

Proc. Linn. Soc. N.S.W., 134, 2012

B79

Table 4. Low frequency and rare species in the pollen profile
Key to species numbers

1. *Eucalyptus sieberi*	8. *Persoonia*
2. *E. leuhmaniana*	9. *Tasmannia*
3. *E. haemastoma*	10. *Acronychia*
4. *Angophora cordifolia*	11. *Euodia*
5. *Leptospermum trinervium*	12. *Geijera salicifolia*
6. *L. polygalifolium*	13. *Correa* spp.
7. *L. laevigatum*	14. Ericaceae

Pollen recorded as % of total pollen count.

Depth (cm)	Species													
	1	2	3	4	5	6	7	8	9	10	11	12	13	14
0				1									1	
10					3					1				
20													2	1
30														
40	1									3				
50	1										3		1	
60			3										1	
70														
80														
90														
100								1		1	1		1	
110		2												
120	2	4				2						2		
130									1					1
140	2				2							3		
150											2			
160				1							3		2	
170														
180				2	2									
190		3		3						1	2		2	1
200								1						1
210				2	2								1	
220				2				1			1		2	

Zone 1: 30-0 cm, ~ 2.4-0 cal ka BP. Here, the *B. braunii* content is reduced and the *Zygnema*, Algal type 1 and fungal spores are increased, thus conditions would have been drier, with the swamp drying out more often, at least for short periods. Sedgelands were able to colonise the whole of the swamp surface under these conditions.

A summary of the age, stratigraphy and zones is shown on Fig. 12.

DISCUSSION

Jibbon Swamp was initiated ~8 cal ka years ago when the dune swale was stabilised by vegetation that acted as a trap for the fine-grained particles derived from the Hawkesbury Sandstone. Decomposition of organic material occurred in a waterlogged environment where sulphur bacteria were active, judging from the odour of the sediment. The reddish brown layer indicates exposure to air and oxidising conditions and the mottled layer was formed under a fluctuating water table. This complex of layers acted as a sealant over the basal sand substrate and enabled water to accumulate in the swamp (Fig. 4).

The thick olive green clay layer suggests reducing conditions of an anaerobic environment (Reeves, 1968) with a water depth of more than a few centimetres. The water was too deep for sedgelands that would have been restricted to the edges of the

B80

Proc. Linn. Soc. N.S.W., 134, 2012

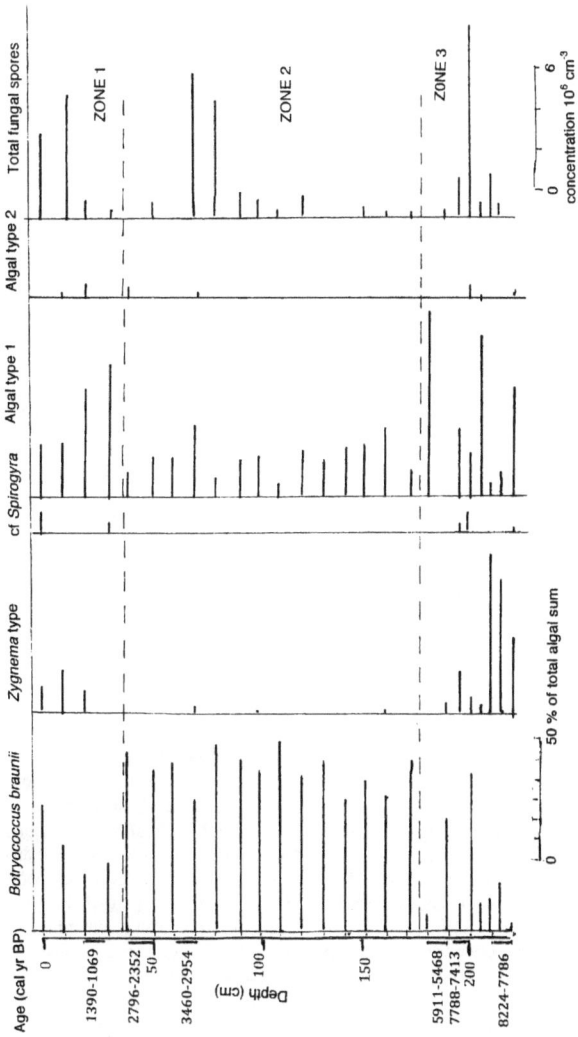

Fig. 11. Algal and fungal spores from swamp sediments

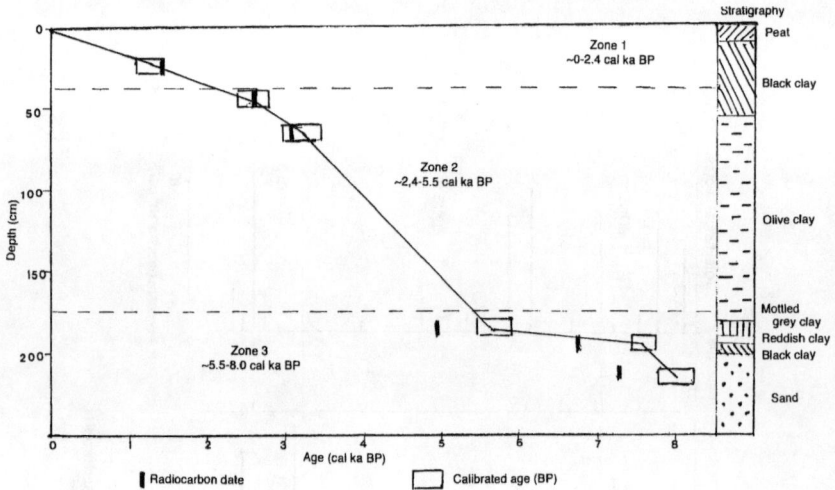

Fig. 12. Summary diagram of stratigraphy, zones and age of the sediments in Jibbon Swamp.

swamp. The grey clays were probably anaerobic but not reducing, and the brown clays were at times exposed to oxidising conditions. The north-south section (A - A', Fig. 4) suggests that the deepest southern part of the swamp was permanently wet with an appreciable depth of water and the extent of standing water fluctuated to the north.

Peat accumulated in layers above the clay when the water depth was shallow enough to allow sedgelands to colonise the swamp surface. When decomposition was more active, probably due to microbial activity in intermittent anaerobic conditions, the structure of the plant material was destroyed, producing humus. The alternating peat/humus layers near the surface reflect wetter/drier conditions when the swamp may have dried out for relatively short periods, as it does today.

Two wedges of sand in the northern part of the swamp probably were the result of dune instability

Throughout the ~8 cal ka that the swamp sediments represent, the vegetation would have been essentially similar to that of today. The same species as today were present the whole time, with the exception of *Melaleuca quinquenervia* that occurs throughout the sedimentary profile but it is not recorded from the vegetation of the area. Today, *M. quinquenervia* is found north of Botany Bay (N.S.W. Flora Online 2011), some 6-8 km to the north. The pollen types recorded at any one level suggest that at any one time, the community may have been somewhat different

from those described in the area today. This is not surprising: these nutrient-poor soils are only suitable for sclerophyllous formations, and even with climate change, some form of sclerophyllous vegetation would persist.

The algal and fungal spore content, however, does show changes. Their short life cycles allow them to respond quickly to environmental changes, unlike the higher plants that have long life cycles that may allow the plants to persist for some time after favourable environmental conditions for regeneration have deteriorated. The algae chart the establishment of the swamp, a period when the swamp had a permanent pool of water, then a drier period when the swamp dried out, at least for short periods, similar to today.

In such a coastal location as this, rising sea levels have most likely had an influence on the history of the swamp. Global sea levels rose slowly after the last glacial maximum (~20-18 ka BP) as temperatures rose and ice melted (Fleming et al., 1998). The late Pleistocene experienced colder temperatures: the "Antarctic cold reversal" (starting ~14.5 cal ka BP) in the southern hemisphere (Blunier et al., 1997) and the "Younger Dryas" (~12.8-11.5 cal ka BP) in the northern hemisphere (Alley, 2000). These cold periods slowed ice melt and the rise in global sea levels. In the early Holocene, temperatures were warmer and deglaciation proceeded, resulting in a rapid rise of sea levels during the period 11.6-7.0 cal ka BP. It is estimated that there was a rise of ~60 m over most of the globe during this period (Smith et al. 2011). After 7 cal ka BP, only about 3-5 m has been added to sea levels, bringing them to about their present position ~6 cal ka BP (Fleming et al., 1998).

Evidence from the east coast of Australia indicates that sea levels followed these general global trends, but after 7 ka, they were about 1-1.5 m higher than those of today. Sea levels gradually lowered to their present position after 2-2.5 ka. There were fluctuations within the high stand (Sloss et al, 2007; Lewis et al, 2008; Woodroffe, 2009; Switzeret al., 2010).

The probable coastline offshore of Jibbon Swamp may be inferred from these studies of sea level changes. About 10 ka BP, before the formation of Jibbon Swamp, the sea level was some 60-65 m lower than its present level (Smith et al., 2011), and the coastline would have been over 5 km away from the site (Fig. 13). Port Hacking and Bate Bay were dry land, and the Jibbon Swamp site would have been at an elevation of over 70 m. The early Holocene rapid rise in sea level brought the coastline close to its present position about 8-7 cal ka BP, flooded Port Hacking and Bate Bay, and brought the elevation of the site down to about 10 m. The shallow seas in Bate Bay and Port Hacking are likely to have been a significant source of evaporation and local rainfall. At this lower elevation, drainage would have been sluggish. Concurrently, Jibbon Swamp was established. The sea level gradually lowered 1-1.5 m after 2.5 cal ka BP (Sloss et al., 2007), probably improving drainage. About this time, the water level in the swamp became lower, allowing the sedgelands to colonise the whole surface of the swamp. The swamp would have dried out on occasions, as it does today.

Sites on the Kurnell Peninsula, some 8 km to the NNE also have an 8 ka vegetation history (Martin, 1994), but unlike Jibbon Swamp, they are in an estuarine environment. The oldest sediments indicate woodland and a slowly accumulating swamp. About 5 ka, a protobarrier was destabilised, the tree pollen types declined and the swamp became a rapidly

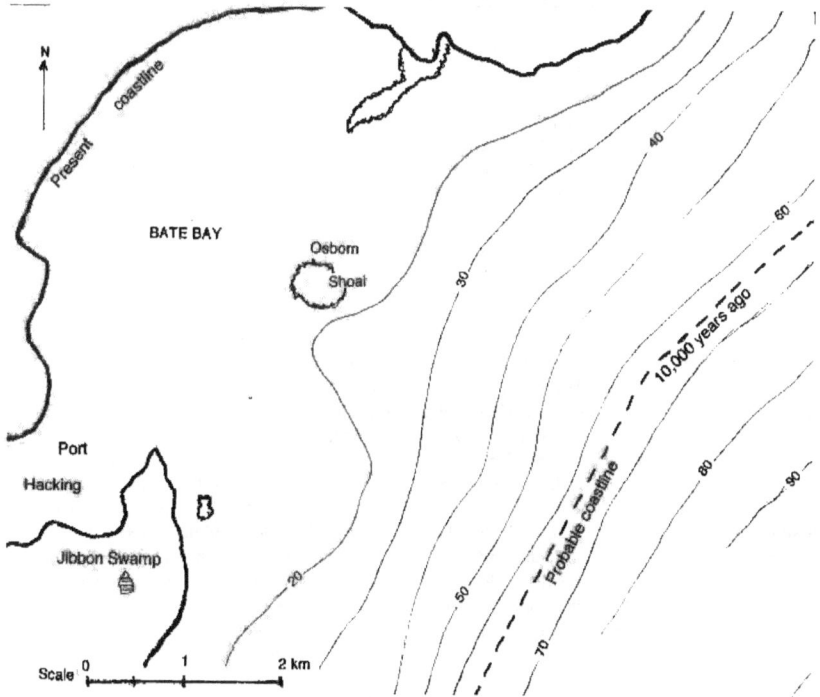

13. Location showing probable coastline before the formation of Jibbon swamp about 8 cal ka BP. From Smith et al (2011) and the Port Hacking Topographic Map, 1:25 000, second edition (1985)

accumulating fen peat. After 2.5 ka, the shrubby element became more prominent in the dryland vegetation and the swamp became more acid, with species typically found in wet heaths and bogs. *Sphagnum* was sometime present: it is not found in the region today (Martin, 1994). Thus the Kurnell site experienced substantial changes in the vegetation about the same time as those at Jibbon swamp.

The late Holocene history of a coastal plain site near Kiama (Jones, 1990), ~70 km to the SSW of Jibbon Swamp, indicates wet sclerophyll/rainforest vegetation, similar to that in the region today. There was a change in the swamp environment, about 2.5 ka: most likely from intertidal to fresh water, probably associated with a lower sea level or the development of a more effective barrier. Casuarinaceae decreases about this time (Jones, 1990). This change at Kiama occurred about the same time as a change in the hydrology at Jibbon Swamp.

Palynological studies in more inland sites in the Sydney Basin indicate the early Holocene was warmer and wetter and the late Holocene was drier, Otherwise, suggestions of climatic change after the mid Holocene are relatively slight, and do not show consistent patterns. Small changes in the late Holocene vegetation seem to be site specific and may have more to do with the dynamics of the swamp development (Chalson and Martin, 2009; Robbie and Martin, 2007; Rose and Martin, 2007; Black et al., 2006; Black and Mooney, 2006; 2007). The resilient nature of the sclerophyllous vegetation on these poor sandstone soils may mean that it is relatively insensitive to minor climatic changes (Black and Mooney, 2007). The three coastal sites, however, suggest that changes in sea level had some influence on changes in the hydrology and vegetation.

A review of Holocene pollen evidence in eastern Australia (Donders et al., 2007) indicates an early Holocene moisture optimum ~8 cal ka BP, an initial drying period ~5.5 cal ka BP followed by a further intensification of the dry periods after ~3 cal ka BP, although there is considerable variation in the dates and the intensity of the event due to local conditions. These trends are seen further afield in the Southern Hemisphere, and it is thought that they reflect the intensification of the El Nino-Southern Oscillation cycles (ENSO) towards frequencies and intensities similar to modern times (Donders et al., 2008).

CONCLUSIONS

Jibbon Swamp has a sedimentary record of about 8,000 years and exhibits three zones: an initial

establishment zone of a fine-grained sealant layer and several other thin layers that indicate the swamp occasionally dried out, then a middle zone when the swamp was permanently wet with a pool of water too deep for vegetation to grow there, followed by a shallower top zone that was vegetated and occasionally dried out.

A survey of the vegetation in the study area shows a complex mosaic of sclerophyllous forest, mallee, scrub and heath communities on nutrient poor soils. The modern pollen deposition under these communities provides guidelines for the interpretation of the palynology of the swamp sediments.

A study of the palynology shows that the vegetation would have been similar to the sclerophyll communities occupying the area today. It is difficult to match the pollen spectra from the swamp precisely with a surface pollen sample from a particular community, suggesting that there was a shifting mosaic of communities. The swamp pollen profile shows almost no zonation, with only a suggestion that the vegetation was probably a sclerophyllous forest in the oldest part of the profile and mallee heath in younger parts.

The algal and fungal spore content indicates three hydrological zones: a lower drier zone (~8.0 to 5.5 cal ka BP), a middle wetter zone (~ 5.5 to 2.4 cal ka BP) and a drier top zone (2.4 cal ka BP to present). These algal/fungal zones correspond to the sedimentary zones.

An examination of global sea levels shows that there was a rapid rise of about 60 m in the early Holocene. Before this sea level rise, Jibbon Swamp would have been at an elevation of over 70 m and the coastline about 5 km away. After this rise, the elevation was about 10 m, the coastline was near to its present position and drainage would have been more sluggish. The altered hydrologic environment probably initiated the establishment of Jibbon Swamp.

The hydrologic regime suggests that the early Holocene climate was wetter and the mid-late Holocene drier, but this trend is slight and hardly registers in the less sensitive sclerophyllous vegetation.

These results are in general accord with other sites in the Sydney Basin: a wetter early Holocene and a drier late Holocene, but with no consistent trends in the latter. However, Jibbon and two other coastal sites suggest that changing sea levels may have had some influence on hydrology and hence the observed palynology, particularly of the swamp environment.

B84

Proc. Linn. Soc. N.S.W., 134, 2012

ACKNOWLEDGEMENTS

We wish to thank the National Parks and Wildlife Service for permission to work in Royal National Park. Mr. Bob Crombie suggested working on Jibbon Lagoon and assisted with background information. Colleagues in the then School of Botany assisted in many ways. Special thanks go to Mr. Peter Stricker for many days assisting in fieldwork. Thanks go to family and friends who assisted and gave continual encouragement. Mrs. Susan Sweller proof-read the manuscript.

REFERENCES

Alley, R.B. (2000). The Younger Dryas cold interval as viewed from central Greenland. *Quaternary Science Reviews* 19, 213-226.

Attenbrow, V. (2002). "Sydney's Aboriginal Past: investigating the archaeological and historical records". (University of New South Wales Press, Sydney) 225 pp.

Beadle, N.C.W. (1981). 'The Vegetation of Australia". (Cambridge University Press, London) 690 pp.

Birks, H.J.B. and Birks, H.H. (1980). "Quaternary Palaeoecology" (Edward Arnold, London) 289 pp.

Black, M.P. and Mooney, S.D. (2006). Holocene fire history from the Greater Blue Mountains World Heritage Area, New South Wales, Australia: the climate, humans and fire nexus. *Regional Environmental Change* 6, 41-51.

Black, M.P. and Mooney, S.D. (2007). The response of Aboriginal burning practices to population levels and El Nino-Southern Oscillation Events during the mid- to late-Holocene: a case study from the Sydney Basin using charcoal and pollen analysis. *Australian Geographer* 38, 37-52.

Black, M.P., Mooney, S.D. and Martin, H.A. (2006). A >43,000-year vegetation and fire history from Lake Baraba New South Wales, Australia. *Quaternary Science Reviews* 25, 3003-3016.

Blunier, T., Schwander, J., Stauffer, B. et al. (1997). Timing of the Antarctic Cold Reversal and the atmospheric CO_2 increase with respect to the Younger Dryas. *Geophysical Research Letters* 24 (21), 2683-2686.

BoM (2011). Commonwealth Bureau of Meteorology Website (http://www.bom.gov.au). Accessed November 2011.

Branagan, D. (Ed.) (1979). "An outline of the Geology and Geomorphology of the Sydney Basin". (Science Press, Marrickville NSW) 61 pp.

Brown, C.A. (1960). "Palynological Techniques". (C.A. Brown, Baton Rouge) 188 pp.

Bureau of Meteorology (1991). 'Climatic Survey 1991 Sydney NSW' (Commonwealth of Australia, Canberra ACT) 105 pp.

Chalson, JM. (1983). Palynology and paleoecology of Jibbon Swamp, Royal National Park, N.S.W. Hons. BSc, University of New South Wales (unpubl.)

Chalson, J.M. and Martin, H.A. (1995). The pollen morphology of some co-occurring species of the family Myrtaceae from the Sydney region. *Proceedings of the Linnean Society of New South Wales* 115, 163-191.

Chalson, J.M. and Martin, H.A. (2009). A Holocene history of the vegetation of the Blue Mountains, New South Wales. *Proceedings of the Linnean Society of New South Wales* 130, 77-109.

Donders, T.H., Haberle, S.G., Hope, G. et al., (2007). Pollen evidence for the transition of the Eastern Australian climate system from the post-glacial to the present-day ENSO mode. *Quaternary Science Reviews* 26, 1621-1637.

Donders, T.H., Wagner-Cremer, F. and Visscher, H. (2008). Integration of proxy data and model scenarios for the mid-Holocene onset of modern ENSO variation. *Quaternary Science Reviews* 27, 571-579.

Fleming, K., Johnston, P., Zwartz, D. et al. (1998). Refining the eustatic sea-level curve since the Last Glacial Maximum using far- and intermediate-field sites. *Earth and Planetary Science Letters* 163, 327-342.

Head, M.J. (1992). Zygospores of the Zygnematales (Division Chlorophyta) and other fresh water algal spores from the uppermost Pliocene, St. Erth Beds of Cornwall, southwestern England. *Micropaleontology* 38, 237-269.

Johnson, A.G. (1994). Late Holocene environmental changes on Kurnell Peninsula, NSW. *Proceedings of the Linnaen Society of New South Wales* 114: 119-132.

Jones, R.L. (1990). Late Holocene vegetational changes on the Illawarra Coastal Plain, New South Wales. *Review of Palaeobotany and Palynology* 65, 37-46

Lewis, S.E., Wust, R.A.J., Webster, J.M. and Shields, G.A. (2008). Mid-late Holocene sea-level variability in eastern Australia. *Terra Nova* 20, 74-81.

Martin, A.R.H. (1994). Kurnell Fen: an eastern Australian coastal wetland, its Holocene vegetation, relevant to sea-level change and Aboriginal land use. *Review of Palaeobotany and Palynology* 80: 311-332.

Mooney, S.D., Radford, K.L. and Hancock, G. (2001). Clues to the "burning question": Pre-European fire in Sydney coastal region from sedimentary charcoal and palynology. *Ecological Managementand & Restoration* 2(3): 203-212.

N.S.W. Flora Online (2011). Website http://plantnet. rbgsyd.nsw.gov.au/ (accessed April 2011)

Pentacost, A. (1984). "Introduction to Freshwater Algae" (Richmond Publishing Company, Richmond, England) 147 pp.

Radford, K.L. (1999). A fine resolution reconstruction of the fire history of Jibbon Lagoon, Royal National Park, New South Wales. University NSW BSc (Hons) Thesis (unpubl).

Proc. Linn. Soc. N.S.W., 134, 2012

B85

Reeves Jr., C.C. (1968). "Introduction to Paleolimnology".
Elsevier Publishing Co., Amsterdam) 228 pp.

Reimer, P.J., Baillie, M.G.L., Bard, E. et al. (2004).
IntCal04 Terrestrial radiocarbon age calibration, 26
- 0 ka BP. *Radiocarbon* 46, 1029-1058.

Robbie, A. and Martin, H.A. (2007). The history of
the vegetation from the Last Glacial Maximum at
Mountain Lagoon, Blue Mountains, New South
Wales. *Proceedings of the Linnean Society of New
South Wales* 128, 57-80.

Rose, S and Martin, H.A. (2007). The vegetation history
of the Holocene at Dry Lake, Thirlmere, New South
Wales. *Proceedings of the Linnean Society of New
South Wales* 128, 15-55.

Sloss, C.R., Murray-Wallace, C.V. and Jones, B.G. (2007).
Holocene sea-level change on the southeast coast of
Australia: a review. *The Holocene* 17.7, 999-1014.

Smith, D.E., Harrison, S., Firth, C.R. and Jordan, J.T.
(2011). The early Holocene sea level rise. *Quaternary
Science Reviews* 30, 1846-1860.

Specht, R.L. (1970). Vegetation. In 'The Australian
Environment" (Ed. G.W. Leeper) pp 44-68.
(Melbourne University Press, Carlton Vic.)

Switzer, A . D., Sloss, B.G., Jones, B.G. and Bristow, C.S.
(2010). Geomorphic evidence for mid-late Holocene
higher sea level from southeastern Australia.
Quaternary International 221, 13-22.

Van Geel, B. and Van der Hammen, T. (1978).
Zygnemataceae in Quaternary Columbian sediments.
Review of Palynology and Palaeobotany 25, 377-392.

Woodroffe, S.A. (2009). Testing models of mid to late
Holocene sea-level change, North Queensland,
Australia. *Quaternary Science Reviews* 2474-2488

Appendix

Jibbon Lagoon check list of species found in 1983. For location of plant communities, see Fig. 5. D, dominant, +, present in the community, * introduced species. For authority of species, see NSW Flora Online (2011).

Plant communities:

1. *Cupaniopsis* Forest
2. *Angophora costata/Corymbia gummifera* Forest
3. *Angophora costata/Eucalyptus botryoides* Forest
4. *Banksia ericifolia/Persoonia lanceolata* Scrub
5. *Leptospermum laevigatum/Melaleuca nodosa* Scrub
6. *Banksia serrata/Xylomelum pyriforme* Scrub
7. *Leptospermum laevigatum* Heath
8. *Melaleuca nodosa* Heath
9. *Angophora costata/Corymbia gummifera/Eucalyptus sieberi* Mallee Heath
10. *Allocasuarina distyla/Banksia serrata* Heath
11. *Leptocarpus tenax* Sedgeland
12. Open Herbfield
13. *Baumea teretifolia* Sedgeland.

Plant formation		Forest			Scrub			Heath			Sedge/herb		
Plant community	1	2	3	4	5	6	7	8	9	10	11	12	13
Species													
Pteridophytes													
Adiantaceae													
Pellaea fastigata var. *fastigata*	+												
Dicksoniaceae													
Calochlaena dubia			+										
Gleicheniaceae													
Gleichenia microphylla												+	
Sellaginaceae													
Sellaginella uliginosa											+		
Angiosperms: Dicotyledons													
Asclepiadaceae													
Marsdenia flavescens	+												
Asteraceae													
Arrhenechthites mixta	+												
Erigeron karvinskianus	+												
Senecio bipinnatisectus	+												
Caryophyllaceae													
Stellaria media													
Casuarinaceae													
Allocasuarina distyla					+	D			D	D			
Casuarina glauca													+
Chenopodiaceae													
Rhagodia candolleana subsp. *candolleana*	+												

Plant formation	Forest				Scrub			Heath			Sedge/herb		
Plant community	1	2	3	4	5	6	7	8	9	10	11	12	13
Dilleniaceae													
Hibbertia monogyna					+								
H. scandens	+		+										
H. serpyllifolia										+			
Droseraceae													
Drosera peltata					+								
D. spathulata											+	+	
Elaeocarpaceae													
Elaeocarpus reticulatus	+												
Ericaceae													
Astroloma pinifolium										+			
Brachyloma daphnoides										+			
Epacris longiflora				+									
E. microphylla				+									
Leucopogon ericoides		+				+				+			
Lissanthes strigosa										+			
Monotoca elliptica			+	+	+								
Styphelia viridis													
Euphorbiaceae													
Amperea xiphoclada		+											
Breynia oblongifolia	+		+										
Ricinocarpos pinifolius						+				+			
Poranthers corymbosa										+			
Fabaceae: Faboideae													
Aotus ericoides						+				+			
Bossiaea heterophylla		+											
B. scolopendria		+								+			
Dilwynia retorta var. *retorta*					+								
Gompholobium glabratum									+	+			
Hardenbergia violaceae		+											
Oxylobium cordifolia										+			
Sphaerolobium vimineum													+
Fabaceae: Mimosoideae													
Acacia decurrens		+								+			
A. longifolia		+							+				
A. suaeveolens		+											
A. terminalis										+			
A. ulicifolia		+											
Goodeniaceae													
Goodenia paniculata											+		

B88

Proc. Linn. Soc. N.S.W., 134, 2012

Plant formation	Forest				Scrub			Heath			Sedge/herb		
Plant community	1	2	3	4	5	6	7	8	9	10	11	12	13
Haloragaceae													
Gonocarpus micranthus ssp. *micranthus*										+			
G. teucriodies									+				
Menispermaceae													
Stephania japonica var. discolor	+												
Moraceae													
Ficus oblique	+												
F. rubiginosa	+												
Myrtaceae													
Acmena smithii	D												
Angophora costata		D	D						D				
Callistemon rigidus				D									
Corymbia gummifera		D	D						D				
Darwinia fascicularis ssp. *fascicularis*				+	+								
Eucalyptus botryoides	D		D										
E. sieberi									D				
Kunzea ambigua				D									
Leptospermum laevigatum			D		D	+	D		+	+			
L. juniperinum										+			
L. polygalifolium ssp. *polygalifolium*		+											
L. trinervium									+				
Melaleuca armillaris		+											
M. nodosa				D	D	+		D	D	+			
M. thymelifolia													+
Oleaceae													
Notelaea longifolia	+		+										
Proteaceae													
Banksia ericifolia				D	+								
B. integrifolia	+	+	+							+			
B. marginata						+			+	+			
B. serrata		+	D			D	+	D	D	D			
Conospermum ellipticum						+							
Grevillea sphacelata		+			+					+			
Hakea dactyloides						+			D	+			
H. sericea						+							
Isopogon anemonifolius					+	+			+	+			
Lambertia Formosa									D	+			
Persoonia lanceolata		+		D		+			+	+			
Petrophile pulchella					+	+			+	+			
Xylomelum pyriforme		+				D			+	+			

Plant formation	Forest				Scrub			Heath			Sedge/herb		
Plant community	1	2	3	4	5	6	7	8	9	10	11	12	13
Rhamnaceae													
Cryptandra amara									+	+			
Rutaceae													
Acronychia oblongifolia	+												
Boronia ledifolia					+	+			+	+			
B. parviflora					+				+	+		+	
Phebalium squamosum ssp. *argentum*													
Philotheca buxifolia										+			
Santalaceae													
Leptomeria acida			+										
Sapindaceae													
Cupaniopsis anacardiodes	D												
Solanaceae													
Cestrum parqui	D												
Solanum linnaeanum	+												
S. stelligerum	+												
Sterculiaceae													
Lasiopetalum ferrugineum						+				+			
Thymeliaceae													
Pimelea linifolia										+			
Apiaceae													
Actinotus helianthi										+			
Xanthosia pilosa													
Hydrocotyle acutiloba	+												
Violaceae													
Viola sieberiana												+	
Angiosperm: Monocotyledons													
Anthericaceae													
Thysanotus tuberosus											+		
Asparagaceae													
Asparagus aethiopicus	D												
A. plumosus	D												
Cyperaceae													
Baumea juncea													+
B. teretifolia													D
Chorizandra sphaerocephala													D
Caustis pentandra						+				+			+
Eleocharis sphacelata													+
Lepidosperma concavum			+				D			+			
Leptocarpus tenax											D		
Schoenus brevifolius											+		
Scirpus nodosus											+		

Plant formation	Forest				Scrub			Heath			Sedge/herb		
Plant community	1	2	3	4	5	6	7	8	9	10	11	12	13
Haemodorum sp										+			
Iridaceae													
Patersonia glabrata									+				
P. sericea									+				
Juncaginaceae													
Triglochin procera													+
Luzuriagaceae													
Eustrphus latifolius	+												
Geitonoplesium cymosum	+												
Phormiacaeae													
Dianella caerulea		+	+										
Poaceae													
Anisopogon avenaceus											+		
Cynodon dactylon												+	
Eragrostis brownii												+	
Imperata cylindrica	+												
Poa sp.	+												
Tetrarrhena juncea											+		
Themeda australis												+	
Restionaceae													
Hypolaena fastigata									+	+			
Leptocarpus tenax											D		
Lepyrodia scariosa				+									
Smilacaceae													
Smilax glyciphylla		+	+										
Xanthorrhoeaceae													
Lomandra glauca								+					
L. longifolia	+	D							+				
Xanthorrhoea resinosa ssp. *resinosa*		+								+			

Developing an Interactive Plant Identification Tool for the Royal National Park

RHONDA DANIELS

Australian Plants Society (Sutherland Group), 2a Glenelg St, Sutherland NSW 2232
(rhdaniels@bigpond.com)

Published on 3 September 2012 at http://escholarship.library.usyd.edu.au/journals/index.php/LIN

Daniels, R. (2012). Developing an interactive plant identification tool for the Royal National Park.
Proceedings of the Linnean Society of New South Wales 134, B93-B100.

This paper describes the development of an educational resource to help the community identify and understand the native flora of the Royal National Park. The resource, titled 'Coastal Plants of the Royal National Park', is an electronic identification tool available on CD-Rom. The resource features an interactive identification tool with multi-entry keys, a look-up glossary and over 1,200 photographs to support identification of 300 plant species, representing about one-quarter of the Royal National Park's total native flora. It was initiated and developed as a volunteer project by the Australian Plants Society, Sutherland Group to produce a user-friendly resource specially designed for non-botanists. It demonstrates community engagement in environmental education. Over 1,400 CDs have been distributed since the launch in 2006, indicating considerable success in achieving the project aims.

Manuscript received 14 December 2011, accepted for publication 19 June 2012.

KEYWORDS: Community engagement, education, plant identification, Royal National Park.

INTRODUCTION

Plant identification is a specialist task, typically requiring tertiary education and/or years of experience for individuals to achieve proficiency and expertise. This, together with the richness of plant species in many Australian landscapes including the Sydney region, can make it difficult for interested non-professionals to identify native flora and develop their understanding. Resources for professional botanists refer to complex technical details of plants (e.g. Pellow et al. 2009). While there are well-used guides with keys (Robinson 2003) and photographs for plants in the Sydney region (Fairley and Moore 2010), there is still a need for identification resources for the community that minimise complexity while providing reasonably certain outcomes for species identification.

Identifying and responding to these needs, the Australian Plants Society (Sutherland Group), a community group, developed an educational resource to help the community to identify and understand native flora in the Royal National Park. The coastal portion of the park was identified as a focus for the project because of high visitor numbers and because its flora is diverse yet manageable for a comprehensive treatment. Many of the plants are also typical of those found in Sydney sandstone in other areas of Sydney. This paper describes the development and features of the identification resource, 'Coastal Plants of the Royal National Park CD-Rom', and its dissemination to the community, highlighting community engagement in both identifying the need for the resource and completing the project on a volunteer basis.

DEVELOPMENT OF THE EDUCATION RESOURCE

Project concept

The project concept was originally developed by a member of the Australian Plants Society (Sutherland Group), Doug Irving, with the aim of creating a product which would help non-specialists such as himself to identify native plants. Doug Irving used books and printed keys for identification, but wanted to improve on the printed tools available in the early 2000s. The central tenet of his concept was to promote community education and engagement by producing an informative, comprehensive and diagnostic, identification guide to plant identification that is more accessible and user friendly to non-botanists than existing books and plant keys.

Sutherland Group of the Australian Plants Society (formerly the Society for Growing Australian Plants) assembled a project team to develop the concept as a voluntary project. The Society is an active community organisation, established in 1958, which aims to increase and disseminate general knowledge of Australian native plants. The Sutherland Group was established in 1963 and has an active program of activities including monthly meetings with guest speakers, walks, garden visits, and working bees at Joseph Banks Native Plants Reserve at Kareela. The principal project team comprised Doug Irving, Margaret Bradhurst, Gwen Caddy, Rhonda Daniels, Connie McPherson, Aileen Phipps, Doug Rickard and Ruchir Sodhani, with additional support from many other people as required. The team had skills in project management, plant identification, computer programming and information technology, education, photography and marketing.

Project specification

The project team engaged fellow members of the Australian Plants Society to help frame the scope and structure of the identification resource specially designed for non-botanists. A range of options for the design and specifications of the resource were discussed at a series of meetings to obtain input from a sample of potential users. Draft features of the software were demonstrated, with participants testing modules of the software as versions were developed. Meetings were also held with professional botanists with experience in development of keys and teaching plant identification. This input ensured technical accuracy from the design phase and provided valuable feedback through demonstrations of draft software at various stages of development.

Several key specifications for the identification resource emerged from this iterative consultation and trial process:
• the resource should have an explicit geographic scope and include the most common plant species found in that area
• descriptions of plant species should be both pictorial and written, with the latter highlighting diagnostic plant features that are essential to distinguish each species from others
• the identification process should be flexible, allowing users multiple points of entry based on

features that their skills and season of visit permit them to observe
• the identification process should allow users to view a list of species that match the features that they observe, and progressively reduce this list as more features are observed
• technical botanical terms should be avoided but, where essential, should be explained in an accessible, plain-language glossary.

The geographic scope of the project focussed on the flora seen along the Coast Track in the Royal National Park. The Coast Track covers a wide range of habitats, from coastal dunes in the north, through sandstone landscapes and the shale escarpment in the south, traversing through heathlands, wetlands, woodlands, eucalypt forests and rainforests. Although a broader geographic scope encompassing the entire Park was not feasible, many plants in these coastal habitats are also found in other parts of the Royal National Park and elsewhere in the Sydney Basin.

Project development

An initial set of plant species in the area was compiled from lists of species prepared for various locations in Royal National Park and Sutherland Shire by the late Pat Akkersdyk, also a member of the Australian Plants Society (Sutherland Group). This initial list was subsequently checked and refined through field reconnaissance of the Coast Track by members of the project team. A total of 300 plant species were ultimately included in the identification resource.

The field trips also provided opportunities to take photographs of each species and document features such as habitats and flowering times. Multiple trips were undertaken at different times of year to take photographs of the plant, leaves, flowers, fruits and, where relevant, bark, with an average of four photographs for each plant species and 1,200 in total included in the resource.

A set of diagnostic features for each species was compiled in a table from published sources (Harden 1992, 1993, 2000, 2002), field observations and consultation with experts. The features were grouped into six types: flowers, fruit, leaves, bark, plant type and habitat. The focus was on descriptions that would be useful to and identifiable by community users. Characteristics were intended to be observed in situ without the need to collect specimens or disturb habitat. Flowers were described in terms of colour, flower shape, flower form, petal/sepal number, or flowering month. Fruits were described in terms of type, colour and other features (fleshy, hairy, hard, ribbed or woody). Leaves were described in terms

B94

Proc. Linn. Soc. N.S.W., 134, 2012

of arrangement, type, shape, length, margins and attachment. Plant type was described as tree, shrub, herb/orchid, climber/scrambler, or sedge/rush. For non-flowering plants, the different set of features for ferns includes trunk, frond form, frond length, sori arrangement and rhizome type.

Computer software was programmed to implement identification, search and query functions, drawing on the attribute table and the photographs (described in detail below). The software was designed to run on Windows operating systems. Functionality was extensively tested by members of the project team and external experts.

The project received financial support from the federal government's Natural Heritage Trust Envirofund with a $5,060 grant in 2002, and from the Australian Plants Society NSW through the Lisle Pearce Bequest Fund ($900) and from Sutherland Group. These grants funded travel and photography costs, a GPS device to record locations, and the production costs of the CD-Rom.

FEATURES OF THE IDENTIFICATION TOOL

The main screen of the identification resource 'Coastal Plants of the Royal National Park' features seven menu tabs across the top of the screen providing access to introductory information about Royal National Park and its environment, the main search tool, the photograph gallery, glossary, habitat descriptions, supporting information and help functions. The key features of the search tool and the species gallery are described below.

Search tool

The Search tool (Fig. 1) is the main feature of the interactive identification software. On the left hand side of the main screen (Fig. 1), the software allows the user to select (by ticking a box) the observed characteristics of a plant to be identified. For flowering plants, the characteristics are arranged in collapsible hierarchical menus for flowers, fruit, leaves, bark, plant type and habitat. There are several options for each of these features. For instance, the flowers can be described in terms of colour, flower shape, flower form, petal/sepal number, or flowering month. Within flower form, the three options are single, cluster, and spike, and within flower shape the six options are regular, irregular, globular, cylindrical, pea, and tubular/bell-shaped. Fruit can be described in terms of type, colour and other features (fleshy, hairy, hard, ribbed or woody). Leaves can be described in terms of arrangement, type, shape,

length, margins and attachment. Ferns have their own sets of features including trunk, frond form, frond length, sori arrangement and rhizome type (creeping, erect, underground).

The list of possible characteristics is very long when all the options are displayed, but not all features have to be selected and described for each plant to be identified. The software works best when only the five or six most distinctive characteristics of the plant are chosen. The characteristics and written descriptions use common terms to make identification accessible to non-specialists, and the software also includes a glossary describing the terms such as simple and compound leaves, and regular and irregular flower shape, sometimes illustrated by line drawings.

The user's selections of characteristics are summarised in the top right window (Fig. 1). The software then matches those selections across the database of characteristics for each of the 300 plants and produces a list of plants which share those characteristics, shown in the bottom right window of the main screen (Fig. 1). The list also includes a score indicating the number of selected features that match each species. By selecting each of the most likely species on the list and clicking the 'view' button, users can visit the gallery to visually match photographs and examine written descriptions of each feature to confirm the identity of the species (see below).

The interactive identification software is specially designed to support users who are not botanists. Traditional plant identification keys require users to make many sequential "yes" or "no" decisions. If users make the wrong decision early on, they may finish on the wrong branch of a hierarchical tree. The software is based on the weight of evidence from multiple characteristics. Each characteristic selected, such as flower colour=yellow or fruit type=berry, scores a "1" if it matches the feature as recorded in the tool's database. The subset of species in the database with the highest number of matches are listed in descending order, and the user can look at the photographs in the gallery (described below) to confirm the identification.

Although the main identification pathway is by selecting the characteristics of a plant as described above, users can also search a plant name – either the botanical name, common name or family name. This allows the user to query how many species with a given name (such as Acacias or Banksias) are amongst the 300 coastal plants included in the guide or to go directly to the gallery to examine written and photographic descriptions (see below).

Use of the software is illustrated by reference to the plant featured on the CD-Rom disk and case,

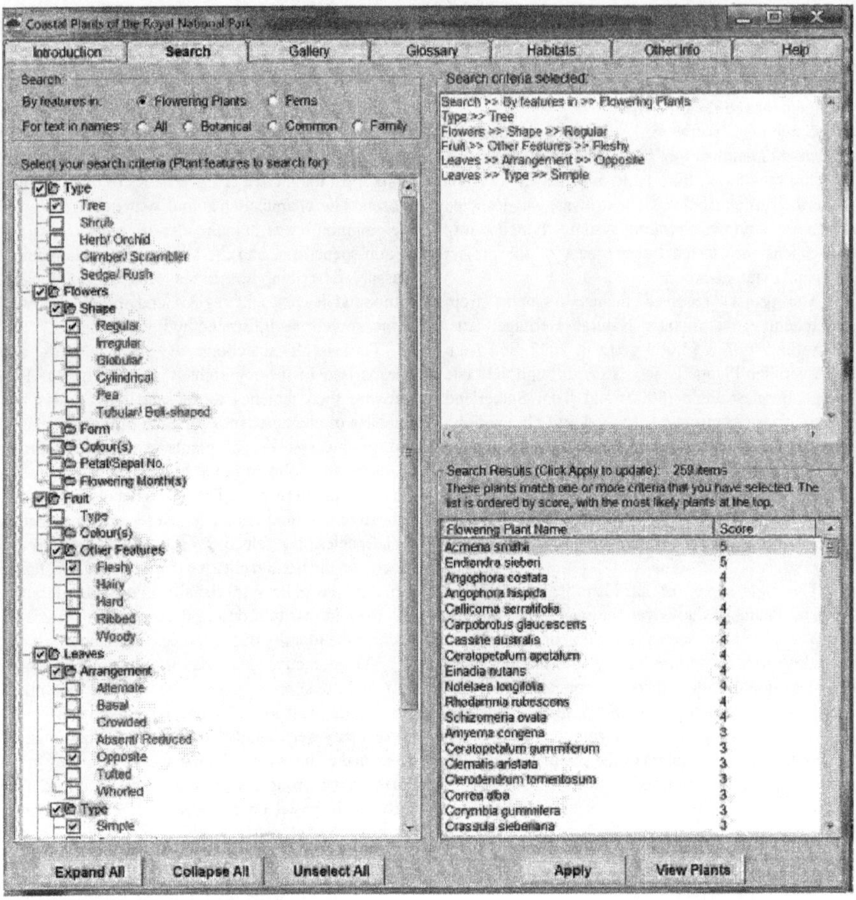

Figure 1. Identification search tool showing character menus with selections and candidate plant species scored by the number of character matches.

Epacris longiflora. This species can be described by up to 14 characteristics of the flowers and leaves, but the species could be identified correctly with fewer characteristics such as flower shape=tubular, flower colour=red, leaf length=tiny leaves, leaf other feature=sharp tips, and habitat=heath. Other plants, including other *Epacris* species, also share some of those characteristics, but these alternatives may be evaluated using the scoring matches and the photograph gallery (see below). The matching approach allows non-specialists to make mistakes in describing a plant, but still generate a list of the most likely plants. The database accommodates natural variation in plants in different conditions, and for user uncertainty in describing plants. For instance, six characteristics may be selected including flowering month=May. No plant in the database may have those six characteristics. But a plant with five of those characteristics, but with flowering month=April, may be the correct plant based on scores and verification against the photographs and written descriptions.

B96

Proc. Linn. Soc. N.S.W., 134, 2012

Photograph gallery

The gallery (Fig. 2) is designed to be used in conjunction with the identification tool to confirm identification by visual matching. The gallery contains over 1,200 photographs of the 300 plant species. The available photos for each species are listed across the top right of the gallery screen. Each photograph may be selected and enlarged to full screen size. For each plant, there are usually four photographs showing the growth form of the plant, the leaves, flowers and fruit or bark. The gallery also contains a text description of each plant, on the left hand side of the screen. The text gives the family, genus, species and common name and is arranged in a standard format for each species with descriptions of the plant type, flowers (including flowering time), fruit, leaves, bark (where appropriate) and habitat. The description also gives the origin of the botanical name and includes a table summarising the full set of characters in the database. This information allows users to browse through the plausible identification alternatives and select the species that best matches their observations in the field.

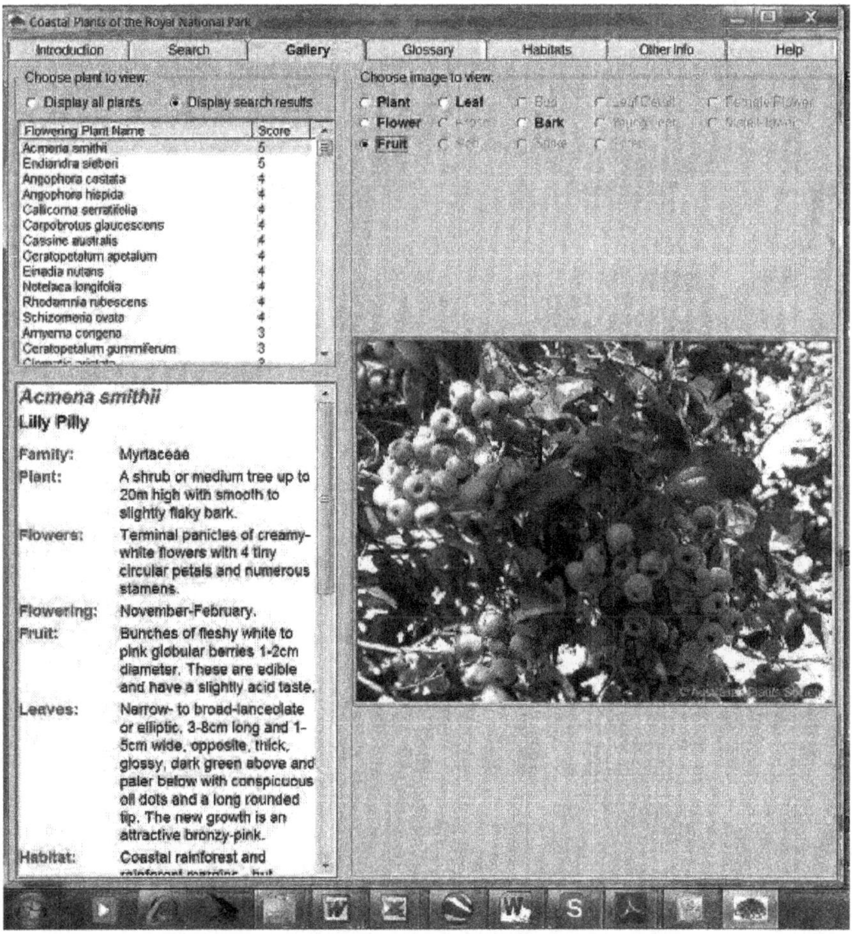

Figure 2a. Gallery showing the text description and photographic images of fruit for one of the the top two candidate species in Figure 1, *Acmena smithii*.

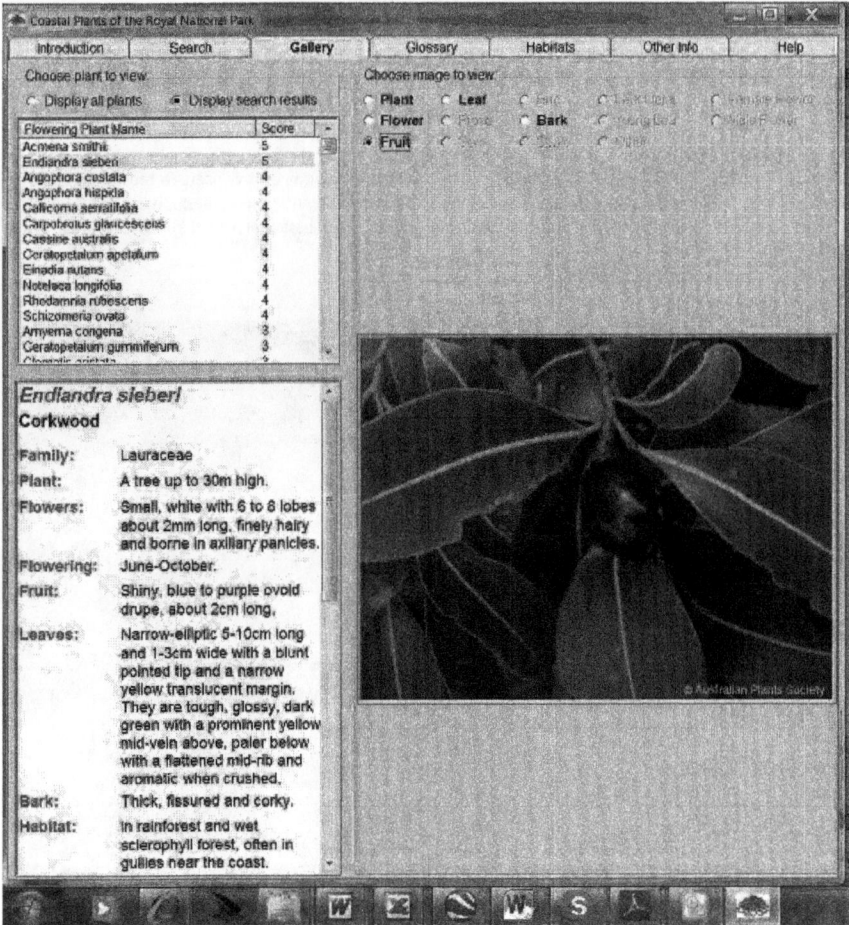

Figure 2b. Gallery showing the text description and photographic images of fruit for one of the top two candidate species in Figure 1, *Endiandra sieberi*.

Other features

The identification resource has several other features to assist identification including a Glossary, with a plain English description of common botanical terms, and often with a line drawing. It also includes descriptions of the main habitat types in the Royal National Park including rainforest, wet sclerophyll forest, dry sclerophyll forest, heathland and beach strand. Other features designed to enhance utility to users include printable sheets containing identification guidelines, a data collection form and an identification guide. It also features lists of plants in the database, and relevant references. The Help function is structured by Frequently Asked Questions.

DISSEMINATION OF THE EDUCATION RESOURCE

Launch

An important aspect of the project was the dissemination of the CD-Rom to the community.

B98

Proc. Linn. Soc. N.S.W., 134, 2012

The project was officially launched on 25 November 2006 at Audley in the Royal National Park by environmentalist Bob Walshe OAM, Patron of the Sutherland Shire Environment Centre. The launch was attended by local politicians and Sutherland Shire Councillors, staff of the National Parks and Wildlife Service, members of the Australian Plants Society including the project team, and members of the local community.

The launch was featured in the local newspaper, *The St George and Sutherland Shire Leader* (Field 2006). Other publicity for the resource included an article on Doug Irving in *The Sydney Morning Herald* (Galvin 2006), an article in *Burke's Backyard* magazine (Burke 2007), and articles in Australian Plants Society publications such as *Native Plants for New South Wales* quarterly journal.

Dissemination to the community

Copies of the CD-Rom were deposited with the National Library of Australia, the State Library of NSW and Sutherland Council Library. The CD was disseminated in several ways including direct sales from the Australian Plants Society and through commercial outlets. During the five years since the launch in November 2006, over 1,400 copies of the resource have been sold with a recommended retail price of $20. The price was chosen to convey a value for the product but make it affordable to the community. A marketing strategy was developed to identify likely markets and promotion approaches.

Direct sales were made from the Society's website (http://sutherland.austplants.com.au) and through presentations by Sutherland Group members to other community and environment groups such as Australian Plants Society groups, Probus, Rotary, National Parks Association, Friends of the Botanic Gardens, gardening clubs, bushwalking clubs, Sutherland Shire Bushcare and environmental education groups. A powerpoint presentation was developed so different members could present the CD, share the story of its development and demonstrate the interactive identification features.

About half the CDs have been sold through commercial outlets such as the Royal National Park Visitor Centre, the Botanic Gardens shops, Sydney Wildflower Nursery at Heathcote, Florilegium bookshop, Sutherland Council Nursery, and other local outlets. The CD has been very well-received, shown by the repeat orders by the retail stockists. The CD has been purchased by people in Sutherland Shire, Sydney and beyond, including schools, botanists, people living outside Sydney and tourists.

In hindsight, the title of Coastal Plants of the Royal National Park may have limited the market. Although focusing on the plants seen along the Coast Track in the Royal National Park, the collection of plants on the resource represents plants which are found throughout Sydney on Sydney sandstone and a broader title may have conveyed this to potential buyers. It was also difficult to convey to some potential buyers the nature of the tool – that it was a piece of software for the computer, not a CD or video to watch on television. The best way to convey the tool and the identification features was a live demonstration.

FEEDBACK AND FUTURE DEVELOPMENT

Community feedback

The total sales since the launch show that the resource is meeting a need in the community for an educational resource on identifying Australian native plants. The CD is being used in various ways in the community. Two examples of feedback illustrate the different uses of the resource.

Scout Group leaders from Hurstville wrote: "Thank you for the good work with putting the CD together. Hubby and I love walking in the Royal and this CD will certainly help us to identify some of the beautiful plants we see but have little idea about their names. I can also help our Cub Scouts to learn more."

Wakehurst Public School in the north of Sydney produced a brochure on Duffys Forest plants. The School wrote: "I would like to thank you so much for allowing us to use the marvellous photos on the CD-Rom. Being able to use these greatly enhanced the quality of the booklet we produced. This booklet is a K-6 environmental education program where each child will learn at least one tree, shrub and groundcover per year."

Future developments

Sutherland Group is working on further developments to the resource including an online version, an extension to include more plants, and information on Aboriginal uses of plants. A simplified demonstration version of the tool was made available on the Sutherland Group website (http://sutherland. austplants.com.au) in February 2012. It offers some limited features of the many searches available on the CD-Rom, but does not have the full search capability of the CD-Rom, particularly as it only lists plants which match all the selected criteria. There has been interest from other groups in developing the tool for their own uses such as a database on local plants in their area or for other aspects of the environment such as birds. Sutherland Group is willing to make the software available with step-by-step guidance to assist other groups that aim to produce similar products for other areas. As the database is programmed in an expandable format, new applications can start small, with more plants added over time. Size is limited more by the resources required to compile information and photographs, rather than software limits.

CONCLUSION

The electronic interactive identification resource, *Coastal Plants of the Royal National Park*, was initiated by an enthusiastic community member who wanted to learn more about Australian native plants and improve identification, and was completed as a volunteer project involving many members of the Sutherland Group of the Australian Plants Society. The project is a demonstration of community engagement in environmental education, with the community, through Australian Plants Society members, identifying the need for the project, developing the project and then disseminating the resource to other community users where it has been well-received. Two key strengths of the project underpinned its success. Firstly, dedicated project team members contributed over 4,000 volunteer hours over several years to ensure the ambitious project was completed. Secondly, early and continuing collaboration and consultation with professional botanists and community members who would use the product ensured the scientific accuracy of the product and its relevance to end users.

Sutherland Group of the Australian Plants Society is proud to have used the Royal National Park as an education resource and produced an electronic interactive identification tool to help the community learn more about native plants in the Park and beyond. It is likely the resource is being used in educational ways Sutherland Group had not imagined.

ACKNOWLEDGEMENTS

This paper is written on behalf of Sutherland Group of the Australian Plants Society. Member Ralph Cartwright presented the paper at the Symposium on the Royal National Park in September 2011.

The concept of a plant identification tool for the general community was developed by Doug Irving, who joined Sutherland Group in the late 1990s towards the end of his academic career in a non-botanical field. He was very enthusiastic about Australian native plants, and keen to learn more using available tools including books and printed keys. Doug Irving and Margaret Bradhurst took the photographs and Doug designed and programmed several developmental versions of the software. Doug Irving, Margaret Bradhurst, Gwen Caddy, Connie McPherson and Aileen Phipps walked the Coast Track in the Royal National Park many times in different seasons to identify all the plants seen, record their features and photograph each of them at different stages.

When Doug Irving died in December 2003 before the project was completed, Sutherland Group completed the project as a team effort, with Doug Rickard co-ordinating the project. Ruchir Sodhani was responsible for refining and completing the software, with involvement from Doug Irving's son Frazer. Project team members checked information, tested many iterations of the software, prepared the glossary of terms (Aileen Phipps) and produced line drawings to illustrate the glossary (Ken Smith). External experts including Belinda Pellow and David Keith provided advice on design of the resource and other scientific issues and also tested the resource.

REFERENCES

Australian Plants Society (2006). Coastal Plants of the Royal National Park: an interactive identification guide. Sutherland Group, Australian Plants Society, Sutherland. http://sutherland.austplants.com.au

Burke, D. (2007) Walk in the park, *Burke's Backyard*, July 2007, p. 130.

Fairley, A. and Moore, P. (2010). *Native Plants of the Sydney Region: from Newcastle to Nowra and west to the Dividing Range*. Allen and Unwin, Sydney.

Field, D. (2006) Stuff you need to know but were too afraid to ask about, *The St George and Sutherland Shire Leader*, 23 November 2006, p. 6.

Galvin, N. (2006) A royal floral tribute, *The Sydney Morning Herald*, 30 November 2006. http://www.smh.com.au/news/house--home/a-royal-floral-tribute/2006/11/28/1164476208951.html

Harden, G. J. (ed.) (1992) *Flora of New South Wales Volume 3*, New South Wales University Press, Sydney.

Harden, G. J. (ed.) (1993) *Flora of New South Wales Volume 4*, New South Wales University Press, Sydney.

Harden, G. J. (ed.) (2000) *Flora of New South Wales Volume 1 - Revised Edition*, New South Wales University Press, Sydney.

Harden, G. J. (ed.) (2002) *Flora of New South Wales Volume 2 - Revised Edition*, New South Wales University Press, Sydney.

Pellow, B., Henwood, M. and Carolin, R. (2009) *Flora of the Sydney Region*. Fifth edition. Sydney University Press, Sydney.

Robinson, L. (2003) *Field Guide to the Native Plants of Sydney*, Third Edition, Kangaroo Press.

Population Ecology of Waratahs, *Telopea speciosissima* (Proteaceae): Implications for Management of Fire-prone Habitats

ANDREW J. DENHAM AND TONY D. AULD

Office of Environment and Heritage, NSW Department of Premier and Cabinet
PO Box 1967 Hurstville NSW 1481 (andrew.denham@environment.nsw.gov.au)

Published on 3 September 2012 at http://escholarship.library.usyd.edu.au/journals/index.php/LIN

Denham, A.J. and Auld, T.D. (2012). Population ecology of waratahs, *Telopea speciosissima* (Proteaceae): implications for management of fire-prone habitats. *Proceedings of the Linnean Society of New South Wales* **134**, B101-B111.

Waratah (*Telopea speciosissima*) post-fire floral displays are a prominent feature of the landscape in Royal National Park and elsewhere in southeastern Australia, but factors governing the persistence of the species are poorly known. We examined long term patterns of fecundity, recruitment and survival of waratahs in Royal NP in relation to two major wildfires. Flowering occurred mainly over 3 years following both the 1994 and 2001 fires, but fewer plants flowered, fewer seeds were produced and fewer seedlings established after the 2001 fire. After the 1994 fire, limited seed dispersal resulted in most seedlings establishing near fruiting individuals. Only 14% of the plants that established as seedlings after the 1994 fire survived the 2001 fire. At the time of the 2001 fire, these plants were 4-6 years old and post-fire survival was highest in older plants. A logistic model predicts that it would take 5.9 (95% CI 5.4-7.5) years of growth after germination for plants to have greater than 25% survival probability if burnt (equivalent to a fire return period of about 9 years). Waratahs are long lived, have long primary juvenile periods and occasional opportunities for recruitment. Each fire may not lead to successful recruitment. While recruitment failure after one or more fires may not be significant, understanding the proximate factors that limit recruitment is important to predict the impact of long term changes such as altered fire regimes under a changing climate.

Manuscript received 14 December 2011, accepted for publication 14 April 2012.

KEYWORDS: fecundity, fire frequency, pyrogenic flowering, resprout, seedling establishment, spatial patterns

INTRODUCTION

The waratah (*Telopea speciosissima* Sm.) is a member of the Gondwanan family Proteaceae. As the New South Wales floral emblem, waratahs are an important conservation icon. Their post-fire floral displays are a prominent feature of the landscape in Royal National Park and elsewhere in the Sydney region, but our understanding of the requirements necessary to manage the species in the wild in perpetuity is still limited.

In contrast, our ability to cultivate waratahs for their bold red flowering spikes or conflorescences is more advanced (Harden et al. 2000). Development of cultivars for the cut-flower market and for domestic gardens has driven a considerable research agenda, leading to important knowledge of plant pathology, micro-propagation techniques and pollination biology

(e.g., Summerell et al. 1990, Offord et al. 1992, Offord and Campbell 1992, Offord 2004, Peterson et al. 2004). Patterns of fruit set and pollinator interactions have also been investigated by Whelan and co-workers, leading to improved understanding of flowering patterns, pollination syndromes and identifying the species as an obligate outcrosser (Whelan and Goldingay 1989, Goldingay and Whelan 1993, Goldingay 2000, Whelan and Denham 2009).

Given their occurrence in fire prone environments, it is clear that fires are likely to be a major influence on waratah demography and, hence, on their persistence in the landscape. Above ground parts of waratahs are killed and often consumed by fire, but individual plants survive fire by having dormant buds in underground lignotubers, from which new stems can resprout (Bradstock 1995). Waratahs do not have persistent long-lived seed banks, either on the plant or in the soil, and they rely on post-fire flowering for the establishment of new individuals (Denham and Auld 2002, Denham 2008). This establishment of new individuals is critical to the long-term survival of the species as these individuals can replace those mature plants that may die between or during fires. Thus waratahs are a part of the obligate pyrogenic flowering group of species. While such species occur in fire-prone habitats, they are less common, and their ecology is less well understood, than species with either a serotinous (canopy stored seed bank) or persistent soil seed bank (Auld and Ooi 2008). In the Sydney region, the functional group that the waratah belongs to also includes a number of monocotyledons (e.g. *Xanthorrhoea* spp Keith 1996, Tozer and Keith 2012; *Doryanthes excelsa* – Denham and Auld 2002), but only a few woody plants (e.g. *Angophora hispida* - Auld 1986; *Lomatia silaifolia* - Denham and Whelan 2000) including significant structural or functional members of several vegetation types.

To manage for biodiversity conservation (Bradstock and Kenny 2003) and to improve our ability to predict plant community responses (Pausas et al. 2004) a greater understanding of pyrogenic flowering species is critical. A key conservation issue for such species is what fire frequencies can be tolerated? Currently, for waratahs, the spatial and temporal patterns of recruitment, the time required for these recruits to become fire resistant and the time required for juveniles to become adults have not been well documented. To inform the management of fire in landscapes occupied by *T. speciosissima*, we quantified post-fire flowering, seed production, seedling recruitment and juvenile survival after two wildfires (January 1994 and December 2001) in Royal National Park, south of Sydney.

MATERIALS AND METHODS

Study sites

Three sites were selected within a 10 km radius in Royal National Park, approximately 35 km south of Sydney (34°03'151°03'). All sites had identical recent fire histories (all burnt in January 1994 and December 2001). Royal NP includes substantial habitat suitable for waratahs, on soils derived from Triassic Hawkesbury Sandstone Formation. Our Sites 1 and 2 occurred in Sydney Coastal Dry Sclerophyll Forest (Keith 2004) and Site 3 occurred in Sydney Coastal Heath vegetation (Keith 2004). For detailed descriptions see Denham and Auld (2002) for Sites 1 and 3, and Denham (2007) for Site 2.

Experimental methods

After the 1994 fire, a 30 m by 30 m plot was marked out within Sites 1 and 3. The area of the marked plot and a buffer zone of approximately 5 m beyond was surveyed and all *Telopea speciosissima* individuals were tagged and mapped. The reproductive effort of individuals was monitored annually until 2011 by scoring the number of flowering stems, the number of inflorescences and the subsequent infructescences and follicles. Seedling recruitment was monitored after flowering events by surveys from 1996 to 2001 and then subsequently after the 2001 fire. Seedlings were tagged and mapped and their survival monitored intermittently until the fire in December 2001. Post-fire survival of these juveniles was initially scored from February 2002. After the 2001 fire, an additional site (Site 2) was marked out and monitored for reproductive effort, seedling recruitment and survival until 2011.

Analysis

The effects of juvenile age, site and distance from an adult on juvenile survival through the 2001 fire were assessed using logistic regression. The model with the best fit was obtained using backward stepwise regression. For calculation of survival quantiles with juvenile age, the distance from adults was fixed at 1.5m (the approximate median value for all seedlings). The distance from adults of surviving juveniles and those killed during the 2001 fire were compared with a t-test. These analyses were done with Systat 11 for Windows (SPSS 2004). Spatial patterns were assessed for departure from a random distribution by calculation of Moran's I and its z-normal derivative using Rookcase (Sawada 1999). Where |z-normal I| > 1.96, individuals were considered likely to be autocorrelated, either evenly distributed (z-normal I <-1.96) or clumped (z-normal I >1.96).

RESULTS

Reproductive effort

Initial flowering after the 1994 fire occurred in spring 1995. Flowering effort at both study sites was concentrated in the first three flowering seasons (greatest in 1995 and 1996, reduced in 1997) and declined thereafter (Fig. 1). Fruiting success followed a similar pattern, with most flowering individuals maturing fruit in the first three flowering years, and no seed was produced after this period (Table 1). Total seed production was estimated to be 2.0 and 2.9 seeds per m^2 at Sites 1 and 3 respectively (Fig. 2). A similar pattern was found after the 2001 fire with

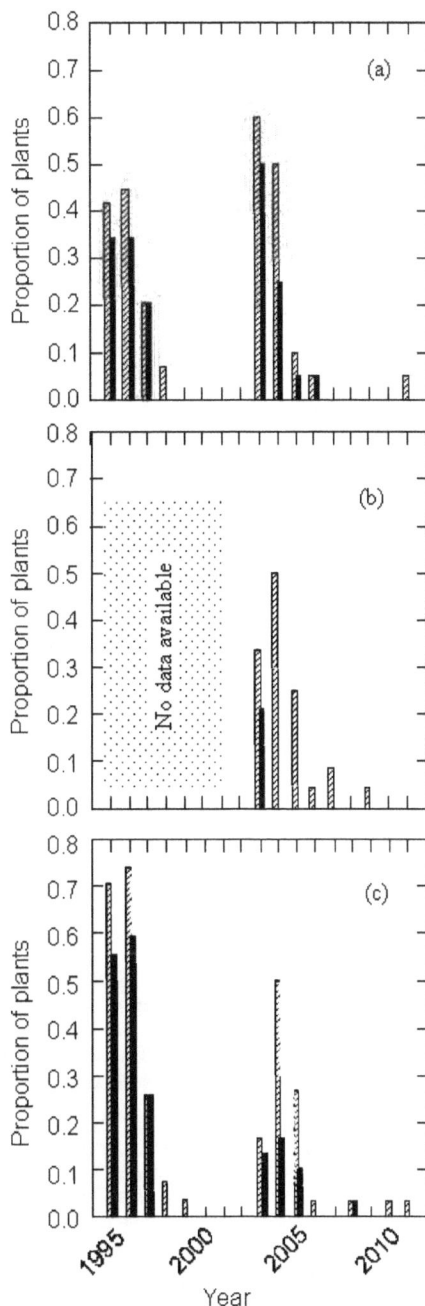

flowering effort also peaking soon after fire. The greatest proportion of plants flowered in the first 2-3 flowering seasons after the fire (2003, 2004 and 2005) and declined in subsequent years, with only sporadic flowering to the end of the study. At Site 1, the proportion of plants that matured fruit was similar after the 1994 and 2001 fires, but at Site 3 considerably fewer plants matured fruit after the 2001 fire compared to after the 1994 fire. There was little successful fruit production at Site 2, for which we have no pre-2001 data (Fig. 1). At all sites there were fewer infructescences and fewer follicles per fruiting plant after the 2001 fire than after the 1994 fire (Table 1), with total seed production post-2001 a third or less of the post-1994 production (0.74 and 0.67 seeds per m^2 at Sites 1 and 3 respectively and 0.44 seeds per m^2 at Site 2, see Fig. 2).

Seedling recruitment

Seedling recruitment was essentially confined to the first few years after a fire. The magnitude of recruitment varied across both sites and post-fire years (Fig. 2) but some patterns of recruitment were apparent. Recruitment was much greater at Site 1 compared to Site 3 after the 1994 fire with a density 0.29 seedlings/m^2 representing 14.5% of seeds establishing as seedlings at Site 1, but only 0.03 seedlings/m^2 (1.0%) at Site 3. Seedling recruitment after the 2001 fire was low at all sites, with 0.04 (5.3%), 0.01 (2.0%) and 0.03 seedlings/m^2 (4.6% of seeds produced) at Sites 1, 2 and 3 respectively (Fig. 2). Notably, at Site 3, a single adult plant produced fruit and subsequent seedlings in 2008, some 7 years after fire.

Young juvenile survival through the 2001 fire

Relatively few young juveniles that established as seedlings after the 1994 fire survived the 2001 fire. At Site 1, some 91 young juveniles were alive in the year prior to the fire, but only 18 (19.8%) resprouted subsequently. Survival was greatest in the oldest juveniles, such that none of the juveniles from the 1997 flowering survived (of 14 observed); 11% (3/28) of the juveniles from the 1996 flowering survived; and 31% (15/49) of the juveniles from the 1995 flowering survived. At Site 3, 71 seedlings were alive in the year prior to the fire, but only four (5.3%) survived and subsequently resprouted.

Figure 1. Proportion of adult *T. speciosissima* individuals flowering (hatched bars) and fruiting (solid bars) for the years 1994 to 2011 within the plot at (a) Site 1, (b) Site 2 and (c) Site 3. No data are available for pre-2001 flowering for Site 2.

Proc. Linn. Soc. N.S.W., 134, 2012

B103

Table 1. Estimates of fruit production in *T. speciosissima* at sites in Royal National Park for the period 1994-2010. Data for infructescences and follicles are means per fruiting adult ± SE.

Site	Year	Fruiting plants	Infructescences per fruiting plant	Follicles per fruiting plant
1	1995	10	2 (0.5)	8.6 (3.0)
1	1996	10	2 (0.4)	5.6 (2.8)
1	1997	6	1.8 (0.3)	2.3 (0.8)
1	1998-2002	0		
1	2003	10	1.1 (0.6)	3.8 (1.9)
1	2004	5	1 (0)	2.9 (1.1)
1	2005	1	1	1
1	2006	1	1	2
1	2007-10	0		
2	2002	0		
2	2003	5	1.6 (1.2)	4.4 (1.3)
2	2004-10	0		
3	1995	15	1.7 (0.2)	5.9 (1.0)
3	1996	16	2.4 (0.6)	8.4 (3.3)
3	1997	7	1.1 (0.1)	2.6 (0.6)
3	1998 – 2002	0		
3	2003	4	1 (0)	5 (1.9)
3	2004	6	1.2 (0.7)	2.5 (1.5)
3	2005	3	1 (0)	4 (2.1)
3	2006-7	0		
3	2008	1	1	7
3	2009-10	0		

Again, there was a pattern of greater survival in older juveniles, such that: none of the juveniles from the 1997 flowering survived (of 9 observed); 3% (1/40) of the juveniles from the 1996 flowering survived; and 14% (3/22) of the juveniles from the 1995 flowering survived. In the logistic model, survival probability was significantly affected by juvenile age and the interaction of age and distance from an adult, but Site and distance from an adult alone were not significant (Table 2, Fig. 3). The logistic model was considered to be a reasonably good predictor of outcomes with 2 and 14 % improvement over a random model for response and reference variables respectively (Table 3, Steinberg and Colla 2004). However, the absence of data in older age classes limits confidence in the model, as expressed by the widening confidence intervals beyond 6 years (Fig. 3).

Spatial patterns of flowering and seedling recruitment

Adult distribution was clumped at Sites 1 and 3, although not at Site 2 (Table 4, Fig. 4). Most adults flowered after one or both fires, with only a few failing to flower after either fire (Fig.4). With some exceptions, seedlings established in close proximity to fecund adults after the 1994 fire, reflecting a leptokurtic seed rain (Figs 4 and 5). Although there was also evidence of a clumped distribution of seedlings at the site scale (Moran's I>0), it was only significant at Site 3 (Table 4). Similar patterns of seedling establishment in relation to adults were apparent after the 2001 fire (Figs 4 and 6), but there was no significant clumping (Table 4). Differential survival through the 2001 fire at Site 1 resulted in a more even pattern of seedlings but again, it did not

B104

Proc. Linn. Soc. N.S.W., 134, 2012

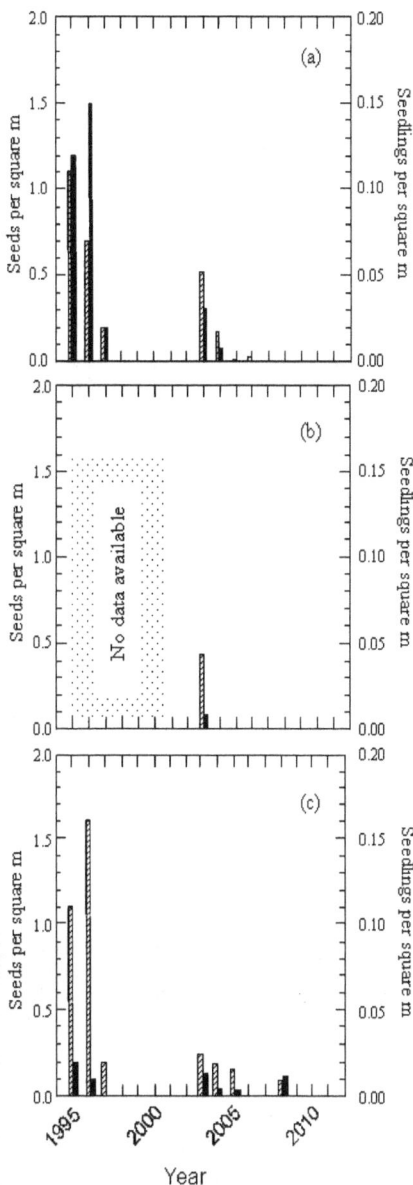

Figure 2. Estimated density of *T. speciosissima* seeds (hatched bars) and seedlings (solid bars) for the years 1994 to 2010 within the plot at (a) Site 1, (b) Site 2 and (c) Site 3. No data are available for pre-2001 flowering for Site 2. Note the different scales for seeds and seedlings.

differ from a random distribution. There were too few survivors at Site 3 to allow a statistical assessment. The proximity of surviving seedlings (post-fire resprouters) to adults at Site 1 was less pronounced after the 2001 fire (Fig. 5a). Although there was only weak support for proximity to adults to affect survival in the logistic model (Table 2), at Site 1 there was a significant difference in the mean distance between survivors and adults compared to mortalities and adults (3.69m cf. 2.21 m, $t=-2.08$, $P=0.034$). There was no evidence of this effect at Site 3, possibly due simply to the low number of survivors (Fig. 5b).

DISCUSSION

Pyrogenic flowering species such as *T. speciosissima* present difficulties for management because of their long life history stages, along with episodic recruitment linked to fire. Here we show how a long term study spanning consecutive fires can highlight key demographic parameters and provide insights into predictions about the likely tolerance of pyrogenic species to critical components of the fire regime, particularly fire frequency.

Recruitment linked to fire

Flowering and seed production in *T. speciosissima* is strongly linked to fire, with a pattern of increased flowering and fruiting in the years soon after fire and a subsequent decline (Pyke 1983). However, at the same time-since-fire, flowering effort, fruiting success and seedling recruitment all varied after different fires and at different locations. While a low level of flowering activity can be maintained up to a decade after fire, as previously observed by Goldingay (2000), recruitment of new plants was largely driven by fire, as observed previously (Bradstock 1995, Denham and Auld 2002). A similar proportion of plants flowered after the 1994 and 2001 fires. However, fewer fruits were matured after the 2001 fire, leading to a greatly reduced pool of seeds available for seedling recruitment. This was borne out by a much lower number of seedlings becoming established after the 2001 fire compared to the 1994 fire, although an increase in the relative intensity of seed predation may also have contributed to this difference (Denham 2008). Interestingly, many of the new recruits at Site 3 after the 2001 fire were established in 2009 from seeds released some 7 years after fire. This suggests that *T. speciosissima* has the capacity to establish seedlings long after the conventional post-fire recruitment period (of about 3 years – Denham et al. 2009), but the probability of these seedlings surviving the next fire is greatly

Proc. Linn. Soc. N.S.W., 134, 2012

B105

Table 2. Results of logistic regression model for juvenile survival through fire. Only significant model parameters are shown, factors with odd ratios whose 95% CI do not include 1 make a meaningful contribution to the model.

Model parameter	Parameter estimate	SE	t-ratio	P
Constant	11.06	2.95	3.74	<0.001
Juvenile age	-1.66	0.56	-2.97	0.003
Juvenile age X distance from adult	-0.07	0.03	-2.55	0.011
	Odds ratio	Upper 95%	Lower 95%	
Juvenile age	0.19	0.57	0.06	
Juvenile age X distance from adult	0.93	0.98	0.88	

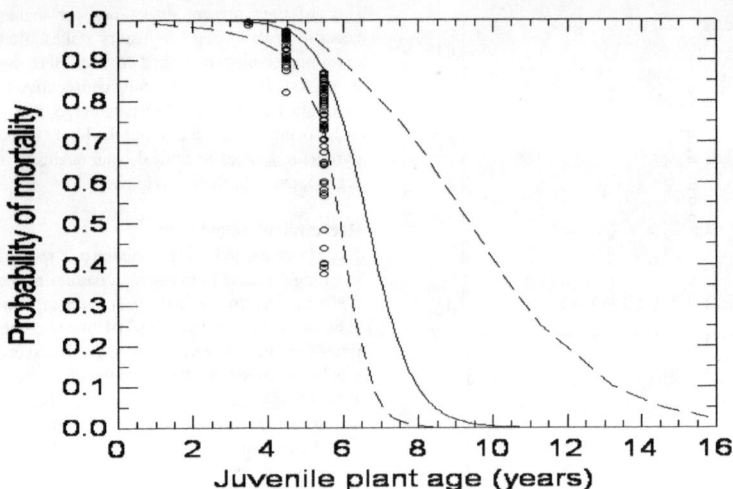

Figure 3. Logistic regression curve showing the predicted relationship between juvenile age and probability of mortality during fire (solid line) with 95% CI (dashed lines). Distance from an adult was fixed at 1.5m to generate these curves. Data points (open circles) are the predicted probability of mortality for each observed combination of age and distance from an adult. Regression equation is y = (exp(-1.66*age+11.1))/(1+exp(-1.66*age+11.1)), log likelihood ratio = -52.3, p<0.001.

reduced, unless there is a fire free period long enough for them to become fire resistant (see below).

The 2001 fire caused no mortality of plants that had survived the 1994 fire, in contrast to Bradstock (1995) who described 2-17% fire mortality in juvenile and adult plants. However, Bradstock's data were after a severe wildfire in Brisbane Waters NP and fire intensity at our sites during the 2001 fire was moderate by comparison (A. Denham unpub. data). Young juvenile mortality in the 2001 fire was high, but comparable to rates found by Bradstock (1995) and there was a pattern of greater chance of survival with increased age of the juveniles (Fig. 3). Examination of quartiles derived from the logistic model suggest 25% survival at 5.9 years (95% CI 5.4-7.5), 50% at 6.6 (5.9-9.4) years and 75% at 7.3 (6.4-11.3) years. Given that seedling recruitment generally occurs 2-3 years after fire, the model indicates that a 9 year fire frequency (January 1994 to December 2001 being almost 8 years) should allow a quarter of new juveniles

Table 3. Prediction success table for the logistic model of juvenile survival through fire. The success indicator shows the improvement in prediction that the model makes over a random model for both response and reference.

Actual Choice	Response	Reference	Actual total
Response	124	16.0	140
Reference	16	6.0	22
Predicted total	140	22	162
Correct	0.89	0.27	
Success indicator	0.02	0.14	
Total correct	0.80		

to be recruited into the adult population. The absence of data for older juveniles and the widening 95% confidence intervals when estimating larger quartiles, indicate that caution is required when predicting how long after fire the majority of new juveniles would be fire resistant (9-14 years for 75% survival). Similar requirements for fire free periods have been have previously been suggested for *T. speciosissima* (Bradstock 1995) and for other pyrogenic flowering species (e.g. *Angophora hispida* – Auld 1986, *Lomatia silaifolia* – Watson and Wardell-Johnson 2004), while for others such as *Xanthorrhoea resinosa* (Tozer and Keith 2012) shorter fire free periods may be more acceptable or even desirable.

Spatial patterns

There was evidence of clumped patterns in the arrangement of adult plants at Sites 1 and 3, while at Site 2 the arrangement of adults was not significantly different from a random distribution. Seedlings were also clumped at Site 3, as well as being clustered around adult plants at all sites. It seems likely that these spatial patterns are largely driven by the patterns of seed dispersal that follow a classic leptokurtic shape (Denham and Auld 2002). However, the alteration of this pattern by differential fire survival of seedlings suggests that although establishment opportunities may be widespread within the sites (i.e., there is no microsite limitation), not all of these sites are suitable for fire survival. Indeed, we found some evidence that the adults may actually reduce fire survival of their offspring, possibly through altering the patterns of litter accumulation or reducing the capacity of seedlings to develop underground lignotubers. Experimentally establishing seedlings at a variety of locations within these sites prior to the next fire may provide insights into these mechanisms (see also Whelan et al. 2002; Denham 2008; Denham et al. 2011).

Conclusions

Telopea speciosissima is one of only a few woody pyrogenic flowering species (Keith 1996; Auld and Ooi 2008). This group has been considered to be highly resilient to frequent fire because adults usually survive fire and population declines may be difficult to detect. However, persistence of populations is also dependent upon recruitment and if frequent fire eliminates recruits (Bradstock 1995) then such species should be considered sensitive to frequent fire, rather than resilient (Watson and Wardell-Johnson 2004). The current fire return interval in the habitat of *T. speciosissima* is around 7-17 years (Bradstock and Kenny 2003), although fire

Table 4. Spatial statistics for adult and seedling distributions. For Sites 2 and 3 there were insufficient data for analysis of all variables. Moran's I values can be transformed to z-scores in which values greater than 1.96 or less than −1.96 indicate spatial autocorrelation that is significant at the 5% level.

Site	Variable	N	Moran's I	z-Normal I (variance)	Mean distance m (SD)
1	Adults	46	0.178	2.23 (0.008)	11.3 (8.9)
	Post-1994 seedlings	246	0.042	1.15 (0.002)	12.5 (7.0)
	Pre-2001 seedlings	182	0.076	1.75 (0.002)	12.5 (6.8)
	Post-2001 resprouters	36	-0.11	-0.79 (0.010)	12.3 (6.9)
	Post-2001 seedlings	58	-0.054	-0.45 (0.006)	12.0 (8.4)
2	Adults	50	-0.061	-0.47 (0.007)	19.1 (9.5)
3	Adults	74	0.220	3.26 (0.005)	16.4 (10.4)
	Post-1994 seedlings	150	0.229	4.61 (0.003)	17.5 (5.9)
	Pre-2001 seedlings	142	0.196	3.88 (0.003)	17.5 (5.6)
	Post-2001 seedlings	50	-0.043	-0.26 (0.007)	16.8 (6.2)

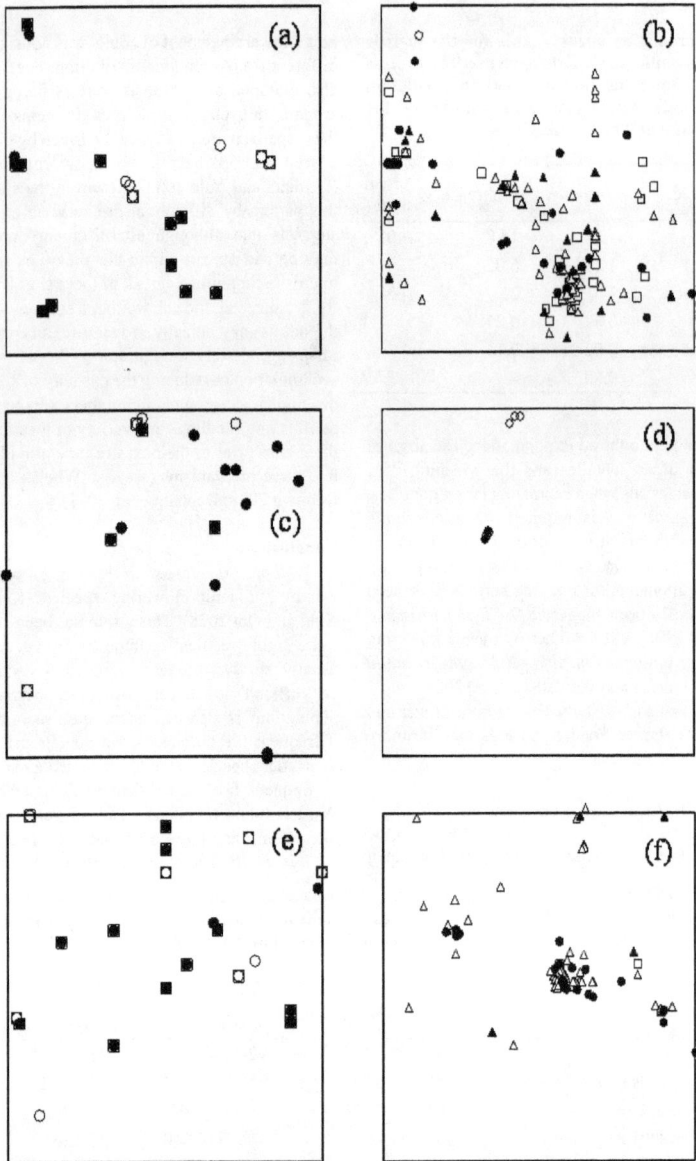

Figure 4. Maps of *T. speciosissima* adults (a,c,e) and seedlings (b,d,f) within the same 900 m2 plots at Sites 1 (a and b), 2 (c and d) and 3 (e and f) in Royal National Park. For adults (a,c,e), filled circles represent plants that flowered after the 1994 fire, while open circles represent those that did not. Open squares represent those plants that flowered in the period 2002 to 2011 (after the 2001 fire). At Site 2, post-1994 flowering effort was estimated from old infructescences that remained after the 2001 fire. For seedlings (b,d,f), triangles and squares represent those that established after the 1994 fire. Open squares are those that died prior to the 2001 fire, open triangles those killed by the 2001 fire and filled triangles those that survived the 2001 fire. Circles represent seedlings that established after the 2001 fire, filled circles are those that were alive in September 2011.

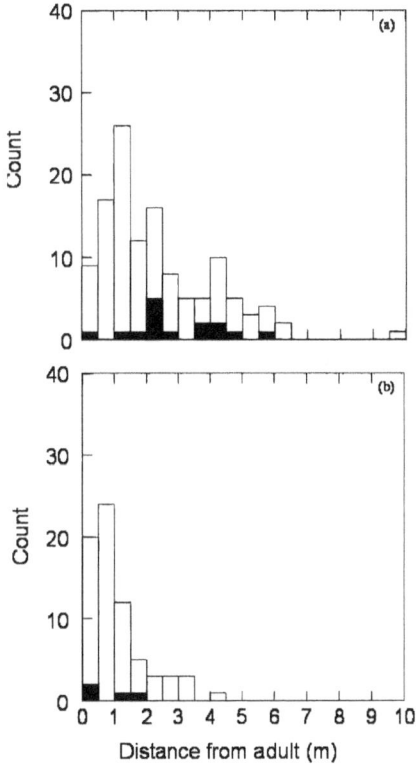

Figure 5. Frequency histogram of the distance between adult plants and seedlings established after 1994 at (a) Site 1 and (b) Site 3. Open bars represent plants that were present before the 2001 fire, filled bars represent those that survived the 2001 fire.

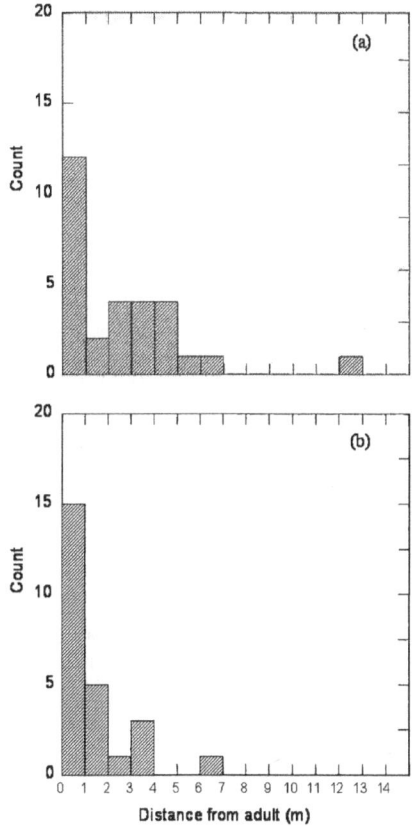

Figure 6. Frequency histogram of the distance between adult plants and seedlings established after the 2001 fire at (a) Site 1 and (b) Site 3.

frequencies are likely to have increased greatly since European settlement (Mooney et al. 2011). Thus juveniles of *T. speciosissima* would need to become fire resistant within 7 years after fire to avoid the risk of fire frequency impacts. Bradstock (1995) also found that young juvenile survival through fire was a critical factor in the life history of *T. speciosissima*, and suggested that variable fire frequencies with occasional fire free periods of more than 10 years were likely to allow persistence. Our results of a long term study that allowed comparisons across two successive fires, and found a similar fire free period (in the order of 8-10 years) is needed to ensure that at least 25%

of young juvenile plants can survive a fire. While recruitment failure after one or two fires is unlikely to significantly affect population persistence, on-going recruitment failure under a high fire frequency would lead to declines and possibly local extinction. Our study provides important insights into how fire drives both the factors controlling seedling recruitment and the mechanisms that may limit juvenile survival. Further changes to fire regimes, including expected increases in fire frequency with increases in extreme weather under a changing climate (Hennessy et al 2006; Bradstock et al. 2009; Clarke et al. 2011)

Proc. Linn. Soc. N.S.W., 134, 2012

B109

will reduce the recruitment capacity of pyrogenic flowering species like *T. speciosissima*. This in turn will impact on the long-term persistence of this iconic species.

ACKNOWLEDGMENTS

Thanks to Paul Mooney, Mark Ooi, Mark Tozer and Berin Mackenzie for their help in the field and to the referees for helpful suggestions.

REFERENCES

Auld, T.D. (1986). Post-fire demography in the resprouting shrub *Angophora hispida* (Sm.) Blaxell: Flowering, seed production, dispersal, seedling establishment and survival. *Proceedings of the Linnean Society of New South Wales* **109**, 259-269.

Auld, T.D. and Ooi, M.K.J. (2008). Applying seed germination studies in fire management for biodiversity conservation in south-eastern Australia. *Web Ecology* **8**, 47–54.

Bradstock, R.A., Cohn, J.S., Gill, A.M., Bedward, M. and Lucas, C. (2009). Prediction of the probability of large fires in the Sydney region of south-eastern Australia using fire weather. *International Journal of Wildland Fire* **18**, 932-943.

Bradstock, R.A. (1995). Demography of woody plants in relation to fire: *Telopea speciosissima*. *Proceedings of the Linnean Society of New South Wales* **115**, 25-33.

Bradstock, R.A. and Kenny, B.J. (2003). An application of plant functional types to fire management in a conservation reserve in southeastern Australia. *Journal of Vegetation Science* **14**, 345-354.

Clarke, H.G., Smith, P.L. and Pitman, A.J. (2011). Regional signatures of future fire weather over eastern Australia from global climate models. *International Journal of Wildland Fire* **20**, 550-562.

Denham, A.J. (2007). Seedling establishment in a pyrogenic flowering species: the role of time-since-fire, litter and post-dispersal seed predation. MSc thesis, University of Wollongong.

Denham, A.J. (2008). Seed predation limits post-fire recruitment in the waratah (*Telopea speciosissima*). *Plant Ecology* **199**, 9-19.

Denham, A.J. and Auld, T.D. (2002). Flowering, seed dispersal, seed predation and seedling recruitment in two pyrogenic flowering resprouters. *Australian Journal of Botany* **50**, 545-557.

Denham, A.J. and Whelan, R.J. (2000). Reproductive ecology and breeding system of *Lomatia silaifolia* (Proteaceae) following a fire. *Australian Journal of Botany* **48**, 261-269.

Denham, A.J., Whelan, R.J. and Auld, T.D. (2009). Characterising the litter in post-fire environments:

implications for seedling recruitment. *International Journal of Plant Sciences* **170**, 53-60.

Denham, A.J., Whelan, R.J., Auld, T.D. and Denham, R.J. (2011). The coupling of recruitment and disturbance by fire in two resprouting Proteaceae species. *Plant Ecology* **212**, 471-481.

Goldingay, R.L. (2000). Further assessment of pollen limitation in waratah (*Telopea speciosissima*). *Australian Journal of Botany* **48**, 209-214.

Goldingay, R.L. and Whelan, R.J. (1993). The influence of pollinators on fruit positioning in the Australian shrub *Telopea speciosissima* (Proteaceae). *Oikos* **58**, 501-509.

Harden, G.J., Hardin, D.W. and Godden, D.C. (2000). 'Proteaceae of New South Wales'. (UNSW Press: Sydney).

Hennessy K., Lucas C., Nicholls N., Bathols J., Suppiah R. and Ricketts J. (2006) 'Climate change impacts on fire-weather in south-east Australia'. (CSIRO, Australia.)

Keith, D.A. (1996). Fire-driven extinction of plant populations: a synthesis of theory and review of evidence from Australian vegetation. *Proceedings of the Linnean Society of New South Wales* **116**, 37-78.

Keith, D.A. (2004). 'Ocean shores to desert dunes: The native vegetation of New South Wales'. (Department of Environment and Conservation (NSW): Hurstville, Australia).

Mooney, S.D., Harrison, S.P., Bartlein, P.J., Daniau, A.-L., Stevenson, J., Brownlie, K.C., Buckman, S., Cupper, M., Luly, J., Black, M., Colhoun, E., D'Costa, D., Dodson, J., Haberle, S., Hope, G.S., Kershaw, P., Kenyon, C., McKenzie, M. and Williams, N. (2011). Late Quaternary fire regimes of Australasia. *Quaternary Science Reviews* **30**, 28-46.

Offord, C.A. (2004). An examination of the reproductive biology of *Telopea speciosissima* (Proteaceae) with emphasis on the nature of protandry and the role of self-pollination in fruit set. *International Journal of Plant Sciences* **165**, 73-83.

Offord, C.A. and Campbell, L.C. (1992). Micropropagation of *Telopea speciosissima* R. Br. Proteaceae 2. Rhizogenesis and acclimatisation to ex-vitro conditions. *Plant Cell Tissue and Organ Culture* **29**, 223-230.

Offord, C.A., Campbell, L.C. and Mullins, M.G. (1992). Micropropagation of *Telopea speciosissima* R. Br. Proteaceae 1. Explant establishment and proliferation. *Plant Cell Tissue and Organ Culture* **29**, 215-221.

Pausas, J.G., Bradstock, R.A., Keith, D.A., Keeley, J.E. and GCTE (Global Change of Terrestrial Ecosystems) Fire Network (2004). Plant functional traits in relation to fire in crown-fire ecosystems. *Ecology* **85**, 1085-1100.

Peterson, S.A., Summerell, B.A. and Burgess, L. (2004). Population structure of *Phyllosticta telopeae*, a foliar pathogen of Waratah (*Telopea speciosissima*) in production and natural ecosystems in NSW. *Phytopathology* **94**, S84.

B110

Proc. Linn. Soc. N.S.W., 134, 2012

Pyke, G.H. (1983). Relationship between time since the last fire and flowering in *Telopea speciosissima* R.Br. and *Lambertia formosa* Sm. *Australian Journal of Botany* **31**, 293-296.

Sawada, M. (1999). Rookcase: an Excel 97/2000 Visual Basic (VB) add-in for exploring global and local spatial autocorrelation. *Bulletin of the Ecological Society of America* **80**, 231-234.

SPSS. (2005). Systat 11 for Windows. (Systat Software Inc.: Point Richmond, CA. USA).

Steinberg, D. and Colla, P. (2005). Logistic Regression. In 'Systat 11: Statistics II'. pp. 207-278. (Systat Software Inc.: Point Richmond, CA. USA)

Summerell, B.A., Nixon, P.G. and Burgess, L.W. (1990). Crown and stem canker of waratah caused by *Cylindrocarpon destructans*. *Australasian Plant Pathology* **19**, 13-15.

Tozer, M.G. and Keith D.A. (2012) Population dynamics of *Xanthorrhoea resinosa* over two decades: implications for fire management. *Proceedings of the Linnean Society of New South Wales*, this volume.

Watson, P. and Wardell-Johnson, G. (2004). Fire frequency and time-since-fire effects on the open-forest and woodland flora of Girraween National Park, south-east Queensland, Australia. *Austral Ecology* **29**, 225-236.

Whelan, R.J. and Denham, A.J. (2009). Causes of spatial patterns of fruit set in waratah: Temporal vs. spatial interactions between flowers on an inflorescence. *Austral Ecology* **34**, 24-34.

Whelan, R.J. and Goldingay, R.L. (1989). Factors affecting fruit-set in *Telopea speciosissima* (Proteaceae): the importance of pollen limitation. *Journal of Ecology* **77**, 1123-1134.

Whelan, R.J., Rodgerson, L., Dickman, C.R. and Sutherland, E.F. (2002). Critical life cycles of plants and animals: developing a process-based understanding of population changes in fire-prone landscapes. In 'Flammable Australia: The fire regimes and biodiversity of a continent'. (Eds R.A. Bradstock, J.E. Williams and A.M. Gill) pp. 94-124. (Cambridge University Press: Cambridge, UK).

Proc. Linn. Soc. N.S.W., 134, 2012

B111

Visitor Attitudes and Erosional Impacts on the Coast Walk, Royal National Park

DEIRDRE DRAGOVICH AND SUNIL BAJPAI

School of Geosciences F09, University of Sydney, NSW 2006
deirdre.dragovich@sydney.edu.au; sunil.bajpai@sydney.edu.au

Published on 3 September 2012 at http://escholarship.library.usyd.edu.au/journals/index.php/LIN

Dragovich, D. and Bajpai, S. (2012). Visitor attitudes and erosional impacts on the Coast Walk, Royal National Park. *Proceedings of the Linnean Society of New South Wales* **134**, B113-B118.

National Parks preserve native fauna and flora and provide recreational opportunities for visitors. However, eroded and degraded trails threaten the ecological integrity of Parks and diminish their recreational, aesthetic, cultural and educational value. Pathway erosion has the potential to divert visitors' attention from the enjoyment of nature and to make travel uncomfortable, difficult or unsafe. Problems of recreational use in protected areas are known to be a function of user numbers and visitor attitudes and behaviour. This research surveyed 100 users of the 26 km long Coast Walk. Most Park visitors were from Sydney and nearby regions (88%), many were young adults (37%), and a high proportion of visitors had tertiary qualifications (66%). Visitors were mainly attracted to the Park for the beauty of nature (77%) and the desire to exercise (49%). Most visitors noticed erosion on the trails: 91% of 'Frequent' visitors were aware of erosion and 75% of 'First time' visitors. Almost half of the users (43%) indicated that they have sometimes trampled vegetation in their attempt to avoid uneven walking surfaces. A well-maintained, well-indicated and even-surfaced walking track will be perceived as safe and comfortable to walk on, thereby reducing erosion-related degradation of pathways and damage to surrounding vegetation.

Manuscript received 22 November 2011, accepted for publication 10 May 2012.

KEYWORDS: erosion impacts, recreation management, resource protection, Royal National Park, soil erosion, trails, trampling

INTRODUCTION

Recent years have seen worldwide concern, growing public awareness of and a positive political will for nature conservation. In 1962, protected areas covered 3% of the Earth's land surface: by the early 2000s they encompassed 12% or 18.8 million km^2 (Bushell et al. 2007). However, the reality is that mere designation of an area as protected does not ensure its preservation. The conservation objective in protected areas can become seriously undermined due to adverse resource impacts resulting from overuse and/or inappropriate management (Hohl and Tisdell 1995; Wanhill and Buhalis 1999). In recent years, nature-based tourism, recreation and ecotourism have experienced significant growth (Coccossis, 2004; Worboys et al. 2005). This trend is expected to continue due to increasing environmental/nature awareness in people (Papayannis 2004) and the anticipated increase in leisure time for most working persons. Thus, visitations to protected areas can be expected to grow significantly. Although an increase in tourism tends to reflect improvements in economic conditions and the generation of lifestyles with greater leisure time, protected areas are required to justify a dual mandate: they are legislated to balance both conservation and recreational objectives. An example of such legislation in Australia is the *Wilderness Act 1987 (NSW)*, Section 6(1). The Act states:

An area of land shall not be identified as wilderness by the Director unless the Director is of the opinion that –

(a) the area is, together with its plant and animal communities, in a state that has not been substantially modified by humans and their works or is capable of being restored to such a state,

(b) the area is of a sufficient size to make its maintenance in such a state feasible, and

(c) the area is capable of providing opportunities for solitude and appropriate self-reliant recreation.

Management plays a critical role in facilitating attainment of the dual mandate (Cole and McCool 1997; Bruner et al. 2001; Gager and Conacher 2001; Worboys et al. 2005). Therefore, it is imperative that protected areas be strategically and scientifically managed so that the challenges faced by these areas, such as adverse impacts arising from significantly increased visitations, are adequately addressed. This will allow the benefits from conservation to be maximized, and at the same time degradation and conflicts arising from recreational use minimised.

One of the serious management concerns connected with recreational use of protected areas is erosion on access trails (Fig. 1). Development of informal or unauthorised trails and deterioration of existing formal trails in such areas have damaging environmental effects through erosion and consequent degradation of soils, vegetation and water quality. Erosion rates on Park trails are accelerated by human

activities that amplify naturally-occurring erosion. In addition, eroded and degraded trails have the potential to diminish visitors' perception of nature and are uncomfortable, dangerous or unsafe for walking (Cole 1981; Grieve et al. 1995; Leung and Marion 1996; Gager and Conacher 2001).

Trails represent access networks in a Park. They are used by Park employees for management activities, and by Park visitors for recreational purposes. From a management perspective, trails are a means of presenting recreational opportunities to visitors along aesthetically pleasing routes in a Park. Moreover, trails play a vital role in resource protection. They keep visitors on a particular pathway and direct them to certain areas thereby shielding other valued and sensitive ecosystems (Leung and Marion 1996; Gager and Conacher 2001). However, trails start to erode and degrade under continuous use (Bayfield 1985; Lance et al. 1989; Legg 2000). A prime cause of accelerated rates of erosion on Park access trails is trampling. Trampling removes or significantly reduces the vegetation cover and exposes the underlying soil. Exposed soil surfaces are

Fig. 1 **An eroded and degraded sandy section of the Coast Walk, Royal National Park**

considerably more vulnerable to agents of erosion – wind and water – than are vegetated surfaces. Moreover, trampling on clayey and silty soils causes compaction, the most common and prominent form of damage resulting from human activity. Trampling also leads to structural degradation by churning in saturated soils and sands. A compacted or saturated soil surface increases local runoff and leads to accelerated rates of erosion on access tracks (Quinn et al. 1980; Calais and Kirkpatrick 1986; Garland 1987; Bhuju and Ohsawa 1998; Toy et al. 2002), whereas loosened sandy surfaces become prone to both water and wind erosion.

Pioneering work relating to the impacts of recreational activities on natural ecosystems began with Bayfield (1971, 1973). His studies dealt specifically with the effects of trampling-generated erosion on vegetation and soil, and identified positive correlations between trampling and destruction of vegetation. The formation of unauthorised trails and degradation of existing trails was attributed to increased recreational use by walkers. Furthermore, most visitors exhibited a consistent track use pattern which added to the erosion impetus, including trampling of vegetation to avoid uncomfortable sections of a trail, and stepping laterally to avoiding wet surfaces on a trail thereby causing widening and/ or creating additional "nested" paths. Hence, eroded and degrading trails seriously undermine both of the prime protected area management objectives of conservation and recreation.

The popular 26 km Coast Walk in the Royal National Park (RNP) has sandy, clayey and stony sections. On the basis of field observations, this study assessed erosion patterns on track sections (sites) on the Coast Walk by classifying sites as having low, moderate or high erosion levels. A visitor survey was conducted to investigate if visitor activities (attitude and behaviour) were related to the extent of pathway erosion.

RESULTS AND DISCUSSION

One hundred visitors were surveyed with a questionnaire. The survey was conducted by the second author at various locations along the Coast Walk. Apart from visitors who were less than 18 years of age, everybody who was in the vicinity of the researcher was approached and requested to take the survey. Most visitors agreed to participate in the survey, only three people who were returning late to catch the ferry declined. The questionnaire had 22 questions designed to seek information about visitor demographics, motivations for visiting RNP, activities in the Park, walking experience on the Coast Walk and desirable walking conditions on the Coast Walk.

Gender composition of the visitor mix was found to be approximately equal, with the 47% (n=47) of females closely matched by males (53%, n=53). A total of 39% of female and 34% of male visitors were in the age group 18-30 years, making this age category the principal one, with a total of 37% of all surveyed visitors. However, if the age group categories of 31-40 (male 23%, female 22%) and 41-60 (male 30%, female 22%) were aggregated into one category for the "middle aged", this amalgamated group would have the single largest proportion of visitors, namely 48% or nearly half of all the visitors. These results suggest that recreation in natural areas is popular among young adults and middle aged visitors of both genders.

Most visitors (88%) were from Sydney and nearby areas, with only 12% of visitors from elsewhere (1% from other states in Australia and 11% from overseas). At 11% the number of international tourists was of interest because, although the number of their park visits throughout NSW is much lower than for domestic visitors, the proportion of international tourists visiting a national park (75%) is relatively high (NSW Department of Environment and Climate Change 2008).

Most visitors (60%) had used a car as their mode of transport to reach RNP. However, nearly one-third of visitors (30%) had made use of public transport. Such details are useful when planning resources such as parking places and/or public transport facilities. The majority of visitors (66%) had tertiary qualifications (degree holders) and were professionals by occupation; 12% of visitors had vocational qualifications (TAFE) and were tradesmen; and 5% of the visitors were retirees. Most visitors (73%) were in the company of friends when in the Park, and their group sizes ranged from 2 to 4 persons. Family groups (13%, usually a group size of 4), were found to be the next most popular formation in which visitors were found in RNP. However, there were also visitors who accessed the Park independently i.e. alone (10%).

The questionnaire provided various possible reasons for visiting RNP and respondents were asked to indicate how important each reason was to them. The beauty of nature was deemed to be the most important motivation of those listed: 77% of the visitors indicated that they were mainly attracted to RNP for this reason. The desire to exercise was given by 49%. Also, "to get away from the pressures of life" (48%) and "to relax with family and friends" (47%) were important considerations for visitors (Table 1).

Proc. Linn. Soc. N.S.W., 134, 2012

B115

Table 1   Motivations for visiting Royal National Park

Reasons	Very Important	Quite Important	Not Very Important	Not Important
To observe the beauty of nature	77	18	1	4
To exercise	49	29	14	8
It's a peaceful and spiritual experience	43	34	11	12
To relax with family and friends	47	32	6	15
To picnic with friends or relatives	18	26	23	33
To observe aboriginal art forms	9	20	35	36
To observe native plants and animals	51	33	9	7
To get away from the pressures of life	48	29	8	15

Many visitors (27%) went to the Park four or five times a year and were classified here as 'Frequent' visitors. Another 11% visited weekly, fortnightly or monthly. Thirty-eight percent of the surveyed visitors were visiting RNP for the first time and are here referred to as 'First timers'. Although it is not known what proportion of these 'First timers' will become frequent visitors, their numbers suggest that RNP visitation is likely to continue increasing and that the Park's managers need to monitor resource use in preparation for this eventuality.

Visitor perceptions relating to erosion and degradation on the Coast Walk also were investigated. A large majority of visitors (84%) confirmed they noticed erosion on the Coast Walk: 91% of 'Frequent' visitors were aware of erosion and 75% of the 'First time' visitors. As responses were anonymous it was not possible to conduct a follow-up investigation to determine whether the same 'First time' visitors became more aware of erosion after repeat visits to RNP. A subsequent question related to visitors' understanding about this erosion and was assessed by a description of the Coast Walk surface. A majority of visitors (77%) described the Coast Walk surface as 'Occasionally rough and with boulders, but more or less safe to walk on' and 6% considered the surface as 'Even and safe to walk on'. Of the remaining visitors, 16% described the Coast Walk as having 'Some sections quite rough and unsafe to walk on' and 1% as 'very damp and slippery'. However, no visitors indicated 'The track is not safe to walk on'.

Visitors were then asked about their walking experience on the Coast Walk, and specifically whether they sometimes had to trample vegetation in order to avoid unsafe or uncomfortable surfaces. Nearly half of the respondents (43%) agreed to having done this and most of these (86%) went on to say that erosion makes some track sections difficult or unsafe

to walk on. Such a pattern of walking behaviour allows existing erosion to continue on the main pathway and adds further opportunity for erosion on the widened devegetated areas. Where erosion is in the form of rills or gullies, these may enlarge laterally as a result of adjacent new pathways also becoming loci of erosion.

In order to further understand visitor attitudes and behaviour, visitors were asked if they would like the track to be more direct, or wider. The majority of visitors (94%) did not want the track to be shorter or more direct and most of the visitors (74%) indicated that they do not wish the track to be wider. Of those who would prefer a wider track, 11 of the 26 were 'First time' visitors. Lack of familiarity with RNP therefore did not appear to influence attitudes about this aspect of track provision.

Visitors were then asked to give their opinion about information systems and signage in RNP. Signage was found to be particularly important and informative. A large number of visitors endorsed the importance of 'Signs on the track' (85%), 'Information boards' (75%) and 'Pathway direction indicators' (82%). Such a response from visitors seems to indicate that they would like to remain on the track and find signage in this regard very useful.

Based on responses visitors provided in this survey it would appear that: (a) a majority of walkers or track users do not wish the track to be wider or shorter, and would remain on the main pathway so long as they continued to meet favourable walking conditions in the form of comfortable and even walking surfaces; and that (b) signage and information systems in RNP help visitors to remain on the main track. Conversely, visitors stray from the track or step laterally when uncomfortable or unsafe conditions are present on the track, when they do not know which of the tracks is the main track, or where a poorly signposted track is

B116

Proc. Linn. Soc. N.S.W., 134, 2012

not obvious. These situations lead visitors to trample vegetation adjacent to the track, thereby contributing to trail widening, formation of nested trails and/or informal trails.

The key implication for management is that a well-maintained, well-indicated and even-surfaced walking track will most probably keep walkers on a track, hence mitigating erosion-related degradation. It is most likely that an even track surface would be perceived by walkers as safe and comfortable to walk on.

CONCLUSION

National parks are required to meet both conservation and recreation objectives. People visit parks primarily in order to enjoy the beauty of nature but also to exercise, get away from the pressures of life, and to relax with family and friends. Although they provide visitors with access to parks, walking trails often contribute to accelerated erosion and vegetation loss through trampling. Also, the majority of 'Frequent' and 'First time' visitors noticed erosion on trails but they did not favour wider trails or more direct routes. Visitors' appreciation of signage suggests that well-indicated and well-maintained tracks improve visitor experience and safety. By limiting informal trail widening and formation of new or parallel paths, clearly indicated and smooth-surfaced trails also will assist in minimising damage to sensitive ecosystems in the RNP.

REFERENCES

Bayfield, N.G. (1971). A simple method for detecting variations in walker pressure laterally across paths. *Journal of Applied Ecology,* **8**, 533-536.

Bayfield, N.G. (1973). Use and deterioration of some Scottish hill paths. *Journal of Applied Ecology,* **10**, 633-644.

Bayfield, N.G. (1985). Effects of extended use on footpaths in mountain areas of Britain. In 'The Ecological impacts of outdoor recreation on mountain areas in Europe and North America' (Eds N.G. Bayfield and G.C. Barlow) pp. 100-110. (Nature Conservancy Council: Peterborough, UK).

Bhuju, D.R. and Ohsawa, M. (1998). Effects of nature trails on ground vegetation and understory colonization of a patchy remnant forest in an urban domain. *Biological Conservation,* **85**, 123–135.

Bushell, R., Staiff, R. and Eagles, P.F.J. (2007). Tourism and protected areas: benefits beyond boundaries. In

'Benefits Beyond Boundaries: Proceedings of the 5th IUCN World Parks Congress' (Eds R. Bushell and P.F.J. Eagles) pp. 1-11. (CAB International: Wallingford, UK).

Bruner, A.G., Gullison, R.E., Rice, R.E. and Da Fonseca, G.A.B. (2001). Effectiveness of Parks in protecting tropical biodiversity. *Science,* **291**,125-128.

Calais, S.S. and Kirkpatrick, J.B. (1986). Impact of trampling on natural ecosystems in the Cradle Mountain-Lake St Clair National Park. *Australian Geographer,* **17**, 6-15.

Cole, D.N. (1981). Vegetation changes associated with recreational use and fire suppression in the Eagle Cap Wilderness, Oregon: some management implications. *Biological Conservation,* **20**, 247–270.

Cole, D.N. and McCool, S.F. (1997) Limits of acceptable change and related planning processes: a workshop. In 'Proceedings – Limits of acceptable change and related planning processes: progress and future directions' (Eds P. McCool, F. Stephen and D.N. Cole) pp.1-2. (U.S. Department of Agriculture, Forest Service: Rocky Mountain Research Station, USA).

Coccossis, H. (2004). Sustainable tourism and carrying capacity: a new context. In 'The Challenge of Tourism Carrying Capacity Assessment: Theory and Practice' (Eds H. Coccossis and A. Mexa) pp. 2-14. (Ashgate: UK).

Gager, P. and Conacher, A. (2001). Erosion of access tracks in Kalamunda National Park, Western Australia: cause and management implication. *Australian Geographer,* **32**, 343-357.

Garland, G. (1987). Rates of soil loss from mountain footpaths: an experimental study in the Drakensberg Mountains, South Africa. *Applied Geography,* **7**, 41-54.

Grieve, I.C., Davidson, D.A. and Gordon, J.E. (1995). Nature, extent and severity of soil erosion in upland Scotland. *Land Degradation and Rehabilitation,* **6**, 41-55.

Hohl, A.E. and Tisdell, C.A. (1995). Peripheral tourism: development and management. *Annals of Tourism Research,* **22**, 517-534.

Lance, A.N., Bough, I.D. and Love, J.A. (1989). Continued footpath widening in the Cairngorm Mountains, Scotland. *Biological Conservation,* **49**, 201-214.

Legg, C. (2000). Review of published work in relation to monitoring of trampling impacts and change in montane vegetation. *Scottish Natural Heritage Review,* No. 131.

Leung, Y-F. and Marion, J. L. (1996). Trail degradation as influenced by environmental factors: a state-of-the-knowledge review. *Journal of Soil and Water Conservation,* **51**,130-136.

NSW Department of Environment and Climate Change (2008) 'New South Wales Taskforce on Tourism and National Parks: Final Report'. (New South Wales Department of Environment and Climate Change: Sydney).

Proc. Linn. Soc. N.S.W., 134, 2012

B117

Papayannis, T. (2004). Tourism carrying capacity in areas of ecological importance. In 'The Challenge of Tourism Carrying Capacity Assessment: Theory and Practice' (Eds H. Coccossis and A. Mexa) pp. 151-161. (Ashgate: UK).

Quinn, N.W., Morgan, R.P.C. and Smith, A.J. (1980). Simulation of soil erosion induced by human trampling. *Journal of Environmental Management*, **10**, 155-165.

Toy, T.J., Foster, G.R. and Renard, K.G. (2002). 'Soil erosion: processes, prediction, measurement, and control.' (John Wiley & Sons Inc.: New York).

Wanhill, S.T. and Buhalis, D. (1999). Introduction: challenges for tourism in peripheral areas. *International Journal of Tourism Research*, **1**, 295-297.

Worboys, G., Lockwood, M. and De Lacy, T. (2005). 'Protected Area Management: Principles and Practice', second ed. (Oxford University Press: Oxford, UK).

What Role Does Ecological Research Play in Managing Biodiversity in Protected Areas? Australia's Oldest National Park as a Case Study

Ross L. Goldingay

School of Environmental Science & Management, Southern Cross University, Lismore, NSW 2480

Published on 3 September 2012 at http://escholarship.library.usyd.edu.au/journals/index.php/LIN

Goldingay, R.L. (2012). What role does ecological research play in managing biodiversity in protected areas? Australia's oldest National Park as a case study. *Proceedings of the Linnean Society of New South Wales* **134**, B119-B134.

How we manage National Parks (protected areas or reserves) for their biodiversity is an issue of current debate. At the centre of this issue is the role of ecological research and its ability to guide reserve management. One may assume that ecological science has sufficient theory and empirical evidence to offer a prescription of how reserves should be managed. I use Royal National Park (Royal NP) as a case study to examine how ecological science should be used to inform biodiversity conservation. Ecological research relating to reserve management can be: i) of generic application to reserve management, ii) specific to the reserve in which it is conducted, and iii) conducted elsewhere but be of relevance due to the circumstances (e.g. species) of another reserve. I outline how such research can be used to inform management actions within Royal NP. I also highlight three big challenges for biodiversity management in Royal NP: i) habitat connectivity, ii) habitat degradation and iii) fire management. A key issue for local managers is finding a mechanism to enable their management to be informed by ecological research in their Park in an ongoing way and to be able to encourage further research. If resolved, Royal NP could provide a model to be used by other protected areas.

Manuscript received 6 January 2012, accepted for publication 18 June 2012.

KEYWORDS: Ecological effectiveness, ecological performance, *Hoplocephalus bungaroides, Petauroides volans,* Royal National Park

INTRODUCTION

National Parks and Nature Reserves (protected areas) may be established for a variety of reasons such as to protect areas of visual beauty, to protect individual species, to protect geological values, or to protect cultural sites. However, the primary role that many now have is to protect and conserve biodiversity. Indeed, biodiversity values have been the driving force in new designations of protected areas in the last 15 years, and there has been much debate about whether the areas designated have been appropriately located with respect to sampling biodiversity (e.g. Pressey et al. 2002; Grantham et al. 2010). This has led to a focus on what is contained within the boundaries of protected areas (e.g. Pressey 1994; Kharouba and Kerr 2010) but little focus on how those areas are managed to retain their biodiversity once established.

The issue of how reserves are managed is a vexed one (Chapple et al. 2011). All reserves have competing interests for their management resources, and in many cases managing people in a reserve becomes the primary focus of reserve management. Fire management can also become an issue of immense importance that consumes a lot of time of reserve managers. But this leaves the question of how is biodiversity managed? Is management actively informed by ecological science or take place by benign neglect (*sensu* Soule et al. 1979), relying simply on protection within a reserve where human access or impacts may be controlled. One may assume that ecological science can offer a prescription for how to manage reserves, but this needs to be tested by examination of current reserve management.

One fundamental insight provided by ecological science is that reserve area is a primary determinant of the persistence of species within reserves (e.g. Newmark 1995; Gurd et al. 2001). Furthermore, that the persistence of species will be greatly influenced by the combined area of habitats within and surrounding reserves (Wiersma et al. 2004). This highlights two key points. Firstly, that many reserves may not be fully isolated but may become so over time. Consequently, they can expect to lose species (Kitchener et al. 1980a; Newmark 1987). Secondly, every effort should be made to expand reserves or to provide connectivity with other reserves (e.g. Gurd et al. 2001). Thus, the equilibrium theory of island biogeography (MacArthur and Wilson 1967) can be used to guide reserve management at the largest spatial scale. But reserve management should be informed by other findings of ecological science.

Over the last decade there has been a focus on assessing the effectiveness of how protected areas are being managed (e.g. Hockings 2003; Hockings et al. 2009). However, these assessments are largely confined to the management processes themselves. Indeed, Hockings et al. (2004) stated that an assessment of the effectiveness of management should consider "design/planning issues, adequacy and appropriateness of management resources, systems and processes, and delivery of protected area objectives". Whilst this approach has obvious merit and is well suited to evaluation across large protected area networks and where large numbers of reserves are included (e.g. Hockings et al. 2009), it may fail to produce better outcomes in biodiversity conservation. Consequently, there is growing recognition that there must be a focus on measuring the ecological effectiveness or performance of reserves and a need for case studies that address the issue (Gaston et al. 2006, 2008). A key element to achieve ecological effectiveness is the extent to which ecological research is being used and encouraged to improve reserve management.

Within Australia there has been limited attention in the published literature given to the ecological effectiveness of reserves and the use of research findings to achieve ecological effectiveness. In this paper I use Royal National Park, Australia's oldest National Park, as a case study. My reasoning for this choice is that a reserve that has been established for a long period of time should have an established approach to managing biodiversity and there should be a record of the adequacy of that management. I ask two questions: how is biodiversity being managed within Royal National Park and what role does ecological research play? I focus on native vertebrate wildlife because this element of biodiversity should be well described and readily targeted by management.

BRIEF OVERVIEW OF ROYAL NATIONAL PARK

Royal National Park (hereafter Royal NP) is located 24 km south-west of the Sydney CBD. It is approximately 15,000 ha in area and defines the southern boundary of the Sydney metropolitan area. Its eastern boundary is the coastline, while its western boundary is the Princess Hwy, the F6 Freeway and associated urban development (Figs 1, 2). It is bounded to the north by urban development and Port Hacking. Its southern boundary is Garawarra State Conservation Area (SCA) (formerly a State Recreation Area) (900 ha) and south of that is the town of Helensburg. Immediately adjacent to Royal NP on the western side of the Princes Hwy is Heathcote NP (2250 ha). Royal NP was declared by legislation in 1879, while Heathcote NP was reserved in 1943 and Garawarra SCA in 1987 (NPWS 2000).

There are 347 species of vertebrate wildlife known to occur in or visit Royal NP, Heathcote NP and Garawarra SCA (DECCW 2011). Of these, 38 species are listed by the New South Wales *Threatened Species Conservation Act* 1995 and six are listed by the Australian *Environmental Protection & Assessment Act* 1999. Thus, these reserves and Royal NP in particular, have an important role to play in the conservation of vertebrate wildlife in New South Wales (NSW).

HOW ARE RESERVES FORMALLY MANAGED IN NEW SOUTH WALES?

To examine the management of biodiversity in Royal NP requires an understanding of the statutory requirements for management. National Parks and State Conservation Areas are managed in accordance with a Plan of Management as required by the *National Parks and Wildlife Act* 1974. This is a legal document that describes how these areas are to be managed and which prevents operations taking place that are not specified by the Plan (NPWS 2000).

The Plan of Management relating to Royal NP also includes Heathcote NP and Garawarra SCA (NPWS 2000). It describes the following general objectives for managing National Parks in NSW:

- "the protection and preservation of scenic and natural features;
- the conservation of wildlife and natural biodiversity;
- the maintenance of natural processes as far as is possible;

B120

Proc. Linn. Soc. N.S.W., 134, 2012

Figure 1. Urban development around Heathcote and Engadine separate Royal National Park from Heathcote National Park in the north-west.

Figure 2. Royal National Park is divided from Heathcote National Park for much of its western boundary by the Southern Freeway. The bridge over the freeway for Cawley Creek Rd (a management road) could be partially converted to a wildlife land-bridge.

Proc. Linn. Soc. N.S.W., 134, 2012

B121

- the preservation of Aboriginal sites and historic features;
- the provision of appropriate recreation opportunities; and
- the encouragement of scientific and educational enquiry into environmental features and processes, prehistoric and historic features and park use patterns".

The Plan of Management (NPWS 2000) also lists the following specific management objectives for Royal NP, Heathcote NP and Garawarra SCA, in relation to conserving biodiversity:

- "Royal National Park will be used as a primary venue within the southern Sydney Metropolitan area for the promotion of natural and cultural heritage conservation in NSW generally and for promoting the work of the Service.
- The protection and where necessary restoration of nature conservation values within Royal National Park, Heathcote National Park and Garawarra State Recreation Area as part of the system of parks and other protected lands of the Woronora Ramp within the Sydney Basin, with emphasis on the protection of biodiversity and maintenance of the ecological relationships between the reserves and adjacent natural lands.
- Garawarra State Recreation Area will be managed as an extension of Royal National Park for the protection of its nature conservation values."

Both the general and specific objectives make it clear that natural heritage conservation is fundamental to Royal NP while the specific objectives introduce the idea of the restoration of nature conservation values. The Plan of Management (NPWS 2000) describes the following policies in relation to the conservation of native animals:

- "Habitats will be protected to maintain the diversity of animal species.
- Research into the life history and habitat requirements of key species will continue to be encouraged.
- Habitats of species subject to international treaty agreements will be protected from disturbance."

A single action relating to native animals is described to satisfy these policies, namely: "fauna surveys will be carried out in the three areas, with priority on threatened or restricted species, including bats and herpetofauna."

The Plan of Management also describes the kind of use of the Park that is deemed appropriate. Research is one form of use and it is recognised that "The purpose of scientific study in the park is to improve the understanding of its natural and cultural heritage and the processes which affect them. Research will also establish the requirements for the management of particular species. Data and findings from research studies and surveys will be utilised in Park management." Examination of the Plans of Management for several other Parks in NSW (e.g. NPWS 1997, 2002a, 2003) reveals that, broadly speaking, these plans are generic with some local details. All of these plans place a strong reliance on encouraging research, particularly that relating to Park management, but the Royal plan is the only one that makes an explicit statement of an intention to use research findings to inform the management of the Park. It is also the only one that refers to the "restoration of nature conservation values".

TYPES OF ECOLOGICAL RESEARCH RELEVANT TO RESERVE MANAGEMENT

Ecological research relating to reserve management can fall into one of three categories: i) that of generic application to reserve management, ii) that which is specific to the reserve in which it is conducted, and iii) that conducted elsewhere but which is of relevance to another reserve due to the circumstances (e.g. species) of that reserve. I will review each of these categories.

Ecological research of generic application to reserve management

Ecological research can be very broad and cover a diversity of topics. I briefly review three topics here to make the point that reserve management can be guided by many areas of ecological research and can benefit from the many generalisations that arise from such research. That research does not need to be in the context of reserve management. The key point here is that the management of a specific reserve does not depend on only the research conducted within that reserve.

The Theory of Island Biogeography – The Theory of Island Biogeography postulates that the number of species on islands is in equilibrium between the rate of colonisation and extinction of species (MacArthur and Wilson 1967). For any given island these rates will be influenced by island area and distance to a mainland. Extinction rates will be higher on small compared to large islands, while colonisation by new species will be more rapid on islands near as opposed to far from a mainland. Diamond (1975) subsequently recognised that the theory could be used to account for the number of species found in nature reserves and postulated some reserve design principles, including the notion of using corridors to connect reserves, which may enhance rates of colonisation and therefore minimise the loss of species. Although some authors highlight the limitations of the theory of island biogeography when applied to habitat fragmentation, there is agreement that the theory provides some important guiding principles such as the influence of fragment area and isolation on species richness (e.g. Laurance 2008). Thus, reserve managers should aim to limit habitat fragmentation within their reserves, as well as attempt to expand the area of their reserves and to connect their reserves to other reserves where feasible. A key realisation from the theory is that the reserve is unlikely to be in equilibrium and will lose species over time (e.g. Kitchener et al. 1980a,b; Soule et al. 1988). Combining reserves into larger assemblages by connecting corridors may be the most efficient means of preventing this loss (e.g. Gurd et al. 2001).

Fire ecology – fire management will be a key issue in most reserves. For Royal NP, 95% of the reserve was burnt by wildfire in January 1994 (Whelan et al. 1996; Andrew 2001) and ca. 60% of the reserve burnt again in 2001. The initial impact of such wildfires can be devastating for some wildlife (Whelan et al. 1996; Baker et al. 2010) but the actual longer term impact on populations is less well understood (e.g. Banks et al. 2011). Despite several decades of research on this topic in Australia there remain many gaps in knowledge (Driscoll et al. 2010). These gaps relate to the response of many species to fire, the influence of the spatio-temporal sequence of fire on species and how other biological factors (e.g. predation) interact with fire to determine ultimate population response. The greater glider (*Petauroides volans*) provides an example of this within Royal NP. Prior to the 1994 fire it was reasonably common in the tall forests at the southern end of the Park (Keast 1995; Andrew 2001). It was detected once immediately after the 1994 fire but was not seen again until March 2012 (Andrew 2001; Maloney 2007; DECCW 2011). It is possible it suffered a local extinction event following the 1994 fire. This provokes the question whether wildfire within Royal NP may trigger population collapses of other species.

Prescribed burning of the landscape may reduce the extent of wildfires but the ecological benefits that may be associated with fire mosaics are yet to be demonstrated, requiring more research to guide biodiversity management (Bradstock et al. 2005; Baker et al. 2010; Penman et al. 2011). However, a precautionary approach should be adopted to minimise population loss so a more active approach to fire management in Royal NP is required to prevent a repeat of the 1994 fire event (see below).

Road ecology – this topic is of particular relevance to reserve management because roads are often extensive within Parks. Roads may create partial or complete barriers to the movement of wildlife and produce high numbers of road-kill. Taylor and Goldingay (2010) recently reviewed this topic, highlighting gaps in knowledge as well as the current understanding about how road impacts may be mitigated. Several studies have been conducted on this topic in Royal NP (see below), which suggest that road-kill is a key management issue requiring attention. For other reserves, individual studies are not required to highlight road mortality as a management issue. Sufficient studies have been done at many locations to be able to conclude that roads through native habitats will produce road mortalities.

Ecological research of specific relevance to the reserve in which it is conducted

I conducted a literature search to identify papers published since 1995 that describe research in Royal NP on vertebrate wildlife. I searched *Scopus* and the *Web of Science* databases using keywords such as Royal National Park and the name of some of the key species found in the Park. I also checked the reference lists of any papers obtained. Although there are many unpublished theses that describe research conducted in Royal NP, these are more difficult to reliably search for and may have less influence on management because they are unpublished.

This search revealed 10 papers and two published agency reports. The reports described wildlife surveys conducted throughout Royal NP while the papers described studies on a small number of species; the broad-headed snake (*Hoplocephalus bungaroides*), eastern pygmy-possum (*Cercartetus nanus*), sooty owl (*Tyto tenebricosa*), swamp wallaby (*Wallabia bicolor*) and brown antechinus (*Antechinus stuartii*) (Table 1). These species-based studies can be organised into various broad management issues. Those on the endangered broad-headed snake deal with threatened species management as well as habitat degradation. Those that provide direct management recommendations include those that document road fatalities in Royal NP and those that describe impacts to the habitat of the broad-headed snake. To reduce

Proc. Linn. Soc. N.S.W., 134, 2012

B123

Table 1. Studies published since 1995 on vertebrate wildlife in Royal NP.

Management issue	Topic	Reference
Threatened species	Broad-headed snake genetics	Sumner et al. (2010)
management	Eastern pygmy-possum response to food availability	Tulloch and Dickman (2007)
	Sooty owl diet	Bilney et al. (2007)
	Sooty owl movements	Kavanagh and Jackson (1997)
	Broad-headed snake regional surveys	Shine et al. (1998)
Fire response	Eastern pygmy-possum habitat use	Tulloch and Dickman (2006)
	Fire ecology of small mammals	Whelan et al. (1996)
Road impacts	Swamp wallaby road kills	Ramp and Ben-Ami (2006)
	Wildlife road kills	Ramp et al. (2006)
Habitat degradation	Broad-headed snake regional habitat	Newell and Goldingay (2005)
	Broad-headed snake habitat degradation	Goldingay and Newell (2000)
	Broad-headed snake	Goldingay (1998)
Various issues	Vertebrate survey	DECCW (2011)
	Vertebrate survey	Andrew (2001)

road fatalities, it was suggested that speed reduction should occur at fatality hotspots, that exclusion fencing and underpasses should be trialed and there was a need to educate Park users (Ramp and Ben-Ami 2006; Ramp et al. 2006). None of these suggestions has been adopted and the recent wildlife survey of the Park (DECCW 2011) has highlighted that several threatened species, including the eastern pygmy-possum and the heath monitor (*Varanus rosenbergi*), may be severely impacted by road-kill. Studies on the loose rock habitat of the broad-headed snake have highlighted on-going degradation of this habitat by Park users, the need for habitat restoration, as well as the education of Park users and closure of walking tracks (Goldingay 1998; Goldingay and Newell 2000; Newell and Goldingay 2005). Minimal adoption of these recommendations has occurred; research into the education of Park users has been initiated (Hayes and Goldingay 2012) and some further research into habitat restoration has occurred (Goldingay and Hayes, unpublished). Exclusion fencing has been installed behind Heathcote Oval to restrict access by mountain bikes and to the habitat of the broad-headed snake.

Ecological research of specific relevance but conducted elsewhere

Research conducted in other reserves may be of direct relevance to management because it involves key species found in Royal NP or a specific issue of relevance to management in Royal NP. The key species may be threatened species or other species that have been identified as significant within Royal NP. This could include studies conducted at almost any location where these species occur but I illustrate this point by referring to a select number of studies. It is beyond the scope of this review to cover more than a few species.

Of the threatened species occurring in Royal NP, the broad-headed snake is one whose conservation has important implications for Park management. The studies conducted in Royal NP have established that rock habitat degradation is continuing and must be addressed (Goldingay 1998; Goldingay and Newell 2000). This species has been studied in detail in Morton NP, establishing many aspects of its ecology (Table 2). These studies are of direct relevance to understanding aspects of how the broad-headed snake should be managed in Royal NP. Regional surveys of the broad-headed snake and its rock habitat (Shine et al. 1998; Newell and Goldingay 2005) have demonstrated that rock habitat degradation is not restricted to Royal NP but occurs in all Parks examined. Indeed, a study conducted in Gibraltar Range NP in northern NSW (Goldingay and Newell 2006) found that rock habitat disturbance also occurs where the underlying geology is granite. The apparent ubiquity of this management issue for rock habitats suggests that Royal NP could provide an exemplar for other Parks of how it is addressed.

A number of studies have been conducted on three threatened species that are believed to be extinct

Table 2. Studies published since 1995 on selected vertebrate wildlife species and topics relevant to Royal NP

Management issue	Topic	Reference
Threatened species	Eastern bristlebird genetics	Roberts et al. (2011)
management	Population ecology of long-nosed potoroo	Norton et al. (2010a)
	Habitat of long-nosed potoroo	Norton et al. (2010b)
	Eastern pygmy-possum detection	Harris and Goldingay (2005)
	Broad-headed snake ecology	Webb and Shine (1997a,b, 1998)
	Broad-headed snake habitat restoration	Webb and Shine (2000)
	Broad-headed snake poaching	Webb et al. (2002)
	Broad-headed snake and climate change	Penman et al. (2010)
	Bristlebird translocations	Baker (2009)
	Bristlebird translocations	Bain and French (2009)
Road impacts	Mitigating road impacts on ground-dwelling wildlife	Taylor and Goldingay (2003)
	Mitigating road impacts on gliding mammals	Goldingay et al. (2011)
	Mitigating road impacts on arboreal mammals	Weston et al. (2011)
Fire response	Ground parrots and fire	Baker et al. (2010)
	Eastern bristlebird and fire	Baker (2000)
	Eastern bristlebird and fire	Baker (1997)
Habitat degradation	Rock habitat in Gibraltar Range NP	Goldingay and Newell 2006

within Royal NP: the eastern bristlebird (*Dasyornis brachypterus*); eastern ground parrot (*Pezoporus wallicus*); long-nosed potoroo (*Potorous tridactylus*) (Table 2). These studies have relevance if management decides to reintroduce these species (see below) because they were conducted at Barren Grounds Nature Reserve, the nearest location to Royal NP (ca. 60 km south-west) where established populations of these species still occur. These studies may also help to understand why these species were lost from Royal NP and may provide insight to prevent the loss of some other species. The studies of the eastern bristlebird and eastern ground parrot have addressed fire management which also has direct relevance to management in Royal NP.

Another key threatened species is the eastern pygmy-possum. Studies in Royal NP (Andrew 2001; Tulloch and Dickman 2006; Harris 2010; DECCW 2011) have revealed that this species is relatively abundant and that it should feature in deliberations of how biodiversity in Royal NP is managed. Insights from studies at Barren Grounds Nature Reserve (Harris and Goldingay 2005; Harris 2010) have relevance to this.

Road impacts on wildlife are now a major issue for wildlife management (Taylor and Goldingay 2010). The key elements of this topic, such as the

likely impacts on species and how impacts should be mitigated, are relatively well known. Several studies have investigated the potential effectiveness of various kinds of impact mitigation (Table 2). The mitigation measures adopted in Royal NP will depend on their cost. Strategic road closures (e.g. seasonal night-time closure between McKell Ave and Bundeena Dr) may be one measure that has not been considered previously. Road impacts and how they are addressed are also of relevance to maintaining movement of wildlife between Heathcote and Royal NP across major roads (see below).

THREE BIG MANAGEMENT CHALLENGES
FOR ROYAL NP

There are of course many management issues to be addressed to manage biodiversity in Royal NP. The three biggest issues that must be confronted without delay because they will take several years to resolve are: i) habitat connectivity, ii) habitat degradation and iii) fire management.

Royal NP exists as something of an island surrounded by boundaries that operate as filters to the movement of wildlife in and out. Although Heathcote NP extends along the western side of

Royal NP, the western boundary is the 4-lane wide Princes Hwy, which divides into the F6 Freeway (Fig. 2) about two-thirds of the way south along the western boundary. The Princes Hwy creates a break in habitat of at least 30 m width whilst the F6 Freeway (Southern Freeway) creates a break of at least 40 m. The Illawarra railway line follows the Princes Hwy and creates a break in habitat of at least 25 m. Where the highway splits from the freeway, the railway moves east of the highway but still creates a break in habitat of ca. 20 m along its length. These breaks in habitat will create barriers to the movement of some but not all species. Thus, it is likely that Royal NP is isolated for many small ground-dwelling species and arboreal mammal species.

The challenge here is to devise an effective management response. A recent approach to help breach road barriers is the installation of wildlife land-bridges (Bond and Jones 2008; Hayes and Goldingay 2009). These are very expensive structures (~$2 million), which is likely to prevent their installation when needed. However, there is an existing road-bridge linking between Royal NP and Heathcote NP that was built over the Southern Freeway to carry Cawley Creek Rd when the freeway was constructed (Fig. 2). This is a gated maintenance road that appears to receive little use and could be modified to make it more attractive for use by wildlife. Glide poles

(Goldingay et al. 2011) and rope bridges (Weston et al. 2011) could be installed on the bridge to enable arboreal mammals to cross, or these could be installed elsewhere along the freeway. Some tree-dependent arboreal mammals can become genetically isolated when tree cover is lost (see Taylor et al. 2011). Approximately 3 km south of the Cawley Creek Rd bridge, the Princess Hwy passes under the Southern Freeway (Fig. 3). Although the highway forms something of a barrier (8-12-m wide at this point) the road underpass may provide some opportunity for species to cross under the 40-m wide freeway. This crossing point could be modified to be more attractive for wildlife to cross.

Royal NP contains a population of the broad-headed snake, Australia's most endangered snake. During the cooler months of the year this snake shelters under loose rocks in rocky habitat (Webb and Shine 1997a,b, 1998). This specialisation makes this species vulnerable to the loss in availability or quality of these shelter sites. Within Royal NP, damage to rock outcrops is on-going and is caused by hikers as well as reptile poachers (Goldingay and Newell 2000; Newell and Goldingay 2005). The impacts of this disturbance are not confined to the broad-headed snake because many species are associated with rocks in rock outcrops (Newell and Goldingay 2005; Goldingay and Newell 2006). This form of

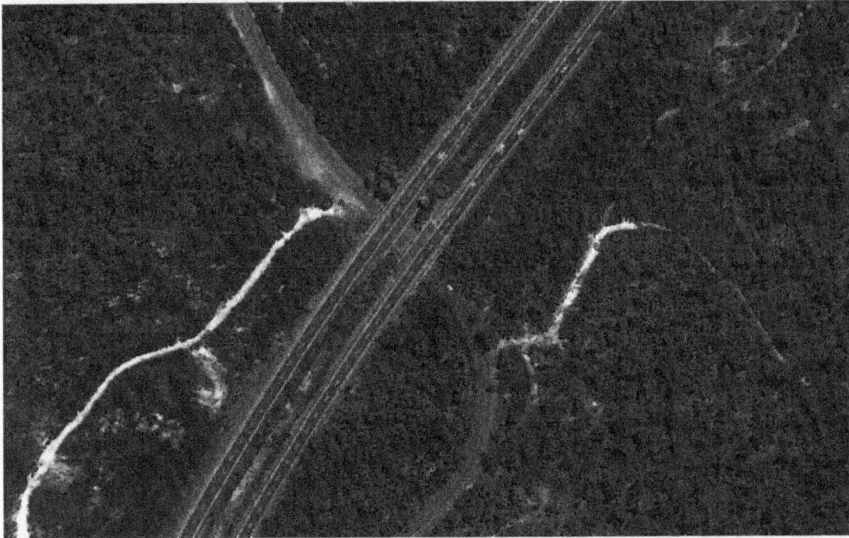

Figure 3. The location where the Princess Hwy passes under the Southern Freeway could be enhanced to facilitate occasional movement by wildlife.

habitat degradation needs to be addressed by Park management to reduce its impact.

Wildfires burnt >50% of Royal NP in each of 1968/69, 1988/89, 1994 and 2001 (NPWS 2002b). The 1994 fire in particular, burnt 95% of the Park and was of high intensity (Whelan et al. 1996). In most cases wildfire is not likely to lead to the loss of species. However, the ability for wildlife populations to persist following a wildfire will depend on their ability to survive the passage of the fire, the availability of unburnt habitat, the ability of the post-fire environment to sustain the population and the availability of a source of recruits to the burnt landscape (Whelan et al. 1996; Bain et al. 2008; Bradstock 2008; Lindenmayer et al. 2008; Taylor and Goldingay 2009; Baker et al. 2010; Banks et al. 2010). Because Royal NP is something of a habitat island for some species (see above), a wildfire that burns a majority of the Park may have a severe impact on the populations of some species. For example, the 1994 fire appears to have triggered a collapse of the population of the greater glider in Royal NP (see Andrew 2001; Maloney 2007). Thus, a precautionary approach to managing biodiversity in the context of fire is to manage the Park to minimise the probability of extensive wildfires. Although the notion of a mosaic of fire ages being favourable to wildlife has been questioned (Bradstock et al. 2005), the goal for Royal NP should be to prevent extensive wildfire and to ensure the availability of unburnt refuges to enable recolonisation when fires occur.

The fire management plan for Royal NP (NPWS 2002b) includes among its strategies "determining and implementing appropriate fire regimes to maintain biodiversity to prevent species or communities becoming extinct and to protect specific natural assets; assessing environmental impacts prior to undertaking fire management works; and monitoring vegetation regeneration following fire events". The main performance indicator that relates to this is: "There is no significant decline of species' populations (common or endangered) due to inappropriate fire regimes, suppression activities or other fire management works, during the planning period". A fire management strategy was produced in 2009 (DECC 2009). This identifies fire management zones and fire thresholds of the vegetation (whether mapped areas should be protected from or allowed to burn) and provides operational guidelines. It also documents the locations of records of threatened species and lists actions to be avoided for these locations (e.g. avoid burning around nest trees).

Research within Royal NP is needed to address the above strategies and the specified performance indicator in the fire management plan. A focus must be placed on vertebrate wildlife to understand how they respond to wildfire. A small number of species should be selected and research commenced before another wildfire occurs. The species I see as most relevant here are three threatened species, the eastern pygmy-possum, broad-headed snake and red-crowned toadlet (*Pseudophryne australis*), and the non-listed rockwarbler (*Origma solitaria*). This covers all vertebrate classes and focuses on Sydney basin endemics. The eastern pygmy-possum is not restricted to the Sydney basin but its population in Royal NP is one of the most significant in NSW (Bowen and Goldingay 2000; Harris 2010). Comprehensive surveys in Royal NP that target this species, with an emphasis on methods of detection, have already occurred (Tulloch and Dickman 2006; Harris 2010; Rueegger 2011), enabling future studies of fire response. Likewise the broad-headed snake has been studied over many years in Royal NP (Goldingay 1998; Goldingay and Newell 2000, unpubl. data; Hayes 2010), with a large number of survey sites established that could be resurveyed in the context of a fire. The red-crowned toadlet and the rockwarbler have not been the subject of specific studies in Royal NP but are widespread (DECCW 2011) and surveys could be readily established.

THE LOCAL EXTINCTION OF SPECIES WITHIN ROYAL NP

Although not considered a management challenge requiring immediate attention, the loss of species from Royal NP does require consideration. Indeed, a specific management objective for Royal NP, Heathcote NP and Garawarra SCA is the "protection and where necessary restoration of nature conservation values" (NPWS 2000). This could be taken to mean that management must consider restoring species that suffer local extinction.

So what consideration should be given to a documented local extinction in a reserve such as Royal NP? Should these losses be accepted and conservation efforts focussed only on remaining species? Or should there be an attempt to reverse these losses, as a part of "necessary restoration". One perspective is that restoration may provide new insight that can guide future management of other vulnerable species in NSW. Trying to understand why those species have become locally extinct in itself may provide fundamental insight for future management of biodiversity within Royal NP and other reserves.

Table 3. Species recorded in Royal NP and which are now extinct and presumed extinct. This list is taken from DECCW (2011) and using information in Baker (1997) and Andrew (2001).

Status	Species	Last record
Extinct on mainland	Eastern quoll (*Dasyurus viverrinus*)	Date not available
Locally extinct	Eastern bristlebird (*Dasyornis brachypterus*)	1880
	Eastern ground parrot (*Pezoporus wallicus*)	1923
	Bushstone curlew (*Burhinus grallarius*)	1938
	Regent bowerbird (*Sericulus chrysocephalus*)	1920s
	Parma wallaby (Macropus parma)	1920s
	Long-nosed potoroo (*Potorous tridactylus*)	1970s
Presumed extinct	Green and golden bell frog (*Litoria aurea*)	1980
	Stuttering frog (*Mixophyes balbus*)	1994
	Dusky antechinus (*Antechinus swainsonii*)	1974
	Red-necked pademelon (*Thylogale thetis*)	1980s
	Spotted-tailed quoll (*Dasyurus maculata*)	1970s
	Platypus (*Ornithorhynchus anatinus*)	1970s
	Water rat (*Hydromys chrysogaster*)	1964

A comprehensive inventory and survey of vertebrate wildlife in Royal NP (and adjoining reserves) is described by DECCW (2011). This study has sifted through the various species records and produced a list of species that have become or are presumed to be locally extinct (Table 3). I will focus on two species: the green and golden bell frog (*Litoria aurea*) and the ground parrot. Each is still present within the region and extensive areas of suitable habitat remain in Royal NP. I believe there is value in attempting reintroductions of some species and treating these as part of an adaptive management process in which such intervention is used as a learning exercise that provides management insight that can benefit future management of those species (see Goldingay 2008).

Green and golden bell frog

This species was known from Jibbon and Marley Lagoons in Royal NP but has not been detected since 1980 (White and Pyke 1996; DECCW 2011). It is still present on the Kurnell Peninsula (White and Pyke 2008), approximately 6 km away. It has undergone a major contraction in geographic range since the 1970s and is still in decline (White and Pyke 2008a; Goldingay and Lewis 1999). The primary causes implicated in its decline are habitat loss, introduced fish (gambusia) and chytrid fungus (Goldingay 2008). Jibbon (Fig. 4) and Marley Lagoons still offer largely undisturbed breeding habitats that appear to be unaffected by gambusia (Goldingay pers. obs.). The continuing loss of populations suggests that re-

introduction to locations such as Royal NP should be included in any long-term recovery plan for the green and golden bell frog. Re-establishment within a National Park has merit because few populations of this species occur within such protected areas (White and Pyke 2008a). Furthermore, bell frog populations immediately south in the Illawarra are far from secure (Goldingay and Lewis 1999; Goldingay 2008). The green and golden bell frog has been the subject of four attempted translocations but all have failed (Daly et al. 2008; Pyke et al. 2008; Stockwell et al. 2008; White and Pyke 2008b). Many lessons were learnt from the failure of these earlier translocations. The population at Kurnell could provide a source of tadpoles for translocation. The persistence of the Kurnell population may suggest that either the waterbodies are sufficiently saline to reduce the virulence of the chytrid fungus or that individuals within this population show some natural immunity.

Eastern ground parrot

The last confirmed record within Royal NP was in 1923, though an unconfirmed record exists from 1996 (DECCW 2011). Heathland, the habitat of this species, occupies >20% of Royal NP (DECCW 2011) so there are extensive areas of apparently suitable habitat. The nearest population of the ground parrot occurs at Barren Grounds Nature Reserve and the adjacent Budderoo NP (Baker et al. 2010), approximately 60 km away, though there are single recent records from the nearby Woronora Special Area and at Malabar (DECCW 2011). The next

Figure 4. Jibbon Lagoon offers undisturbed habitat for various species. This is a former location of the green and golden bell frog.

population north occurs on the NSW central coast. This species is of regional conservation significance and due to the extensive heathland areas within Royal NP, should feature in deliberations of managing vertebrate wildlife within the Park. This will require extensive surveys to determine whether the ground parrot does occur within Royal NP. If these are unable to detect the species from a concerted survey effort then a program of reintroduction should be devised.

THE NEAR EXTINCTION OF THE GREATER GLIDER

The greater glider is a large (900-1700 g), gliding folivorous marsupial, which is widely distributed in eastern Australia, from north Queensland to western Victoria. Its presence in Royal was well documented prior to the wildfire in 1994 (Andrew 2001; Malony 2007). A single observation of this species was made approximately one month after the fire but until 20 March 2012 none were seen, including 12 surveys of 1.5 h duration along 1 km sections of Lady Wakehurst and Lady Carrington Drives during 2003-2006 (Andrew 2001; Maloney 2007). I conducted a 2-h spotlight survey on 20 December 2011 along sections of Lady Carrington Drive and McKell Ave but detected no greater gliders. However, on 20 and 30 March 2012, a single greater glider was observed near the southern end of Lady Carrington Drive (Andrew et al. 2012).

Whether this represents a rare long-distance dispersal event (see Taylor et al. 2007) or dispersal from a previously unsurveyed location within Royal is unknown. There are locations within 15 km of Royal NP where the greater glider still occurs (Maloney 2007) but recolonisation from such locations requires dispersal across major roads, which is predicted to be difficult for this species (see Taylor and Goldingay 2009). The isolation of Royal NP makes recolonisation extremely difficult once it has disappeared. This may be why 18 years elapsed between observations at Lady Carrington Drive.

Ongoing surveys will be required to determine whether the greater glider becomes re-established within the forest surrounding Lady Carrington Drive, rather than this representing an unsuccessful dispersal event. Its reappearance should not be taken for granted. The presence of the powerful owl within Royal may hamper recolonisation. This owl can prey heavily on greater gliders and even cause a local decline when the greater glider is a primary prey item (Kavanagh 1988). It is now recognised that the greater glider is susceptible to decline, though the causes are not always clear (Kavanagh 1988; Lindenmayer et al. 2011). Its decline after wildfire has been observed (Lindenmayer et al. 2011). Population viability analysis predicts the vulnerability of isolated populations of this species to wildfire (Taylor and Goldingay 2009). Ongoing study of the greater glider can provide some valuable lessons about the management and conservation of other species within Royal.

Proc. Linn. Soc. N.S.W., 134, 2012

B129

DISCUSSION

The management of protected areas is a complex undertaking (Chapple et al. 2011). Within Australia this management is likely to be primarily focussed on Park visitors, fire, exotic species and native biodiversity. My focus here is on how biodiversity can be maintained and conserved. It is fundamental that ecological research must inform how biodiversity is managed within any protected area. Although local research will be central to this there is now a large body of research findings that can inform biodiversity management within any protected area. This information needs to be synthesised, periodically updated and integrated into local management. The challenge to local managers is finding a mechanism that can achieve this (e.g. Burbidge et al. 2011). The current plans of management for National Parks and Nature Reserves in NSW are too generic, which consequently requires local managers to perhaps independently, identify more specific priorities and actions. One solution may be the establishment of a biodiversity management committee that includes research ecologists among its members, and that this committee formulate the specific plan for the local reserve. Royal NP could serve as a model for how this would work and how it might be applied in other reserves.

Undertaking local ecological research will be needed to manage local biodiversity. How can this be financed or encouraged? This may be done by identifying projects and allocating small research grants to attract students. Plans of management already state that a prospectus of preferred research projects will be prepared (e.g. NPWS 2000, 2002a). These should be made available on the web site for each reserve. Providing facilities such as local accommodation can also help to offset research costs. This has been helpful within Royal NP where accommodation within the Park has often been provided to researchers. Other forms of assistance will facilitate research projects and make them attractive to researchers. Royal NP has benefited in attracting researchers by being located close to universities in Sydney and Wollongong. Other Parks more distant from universities may struggle to attract researchers. However, providing research grants and establishing links with research ecologists may allow some progress to be made. It may also be feasible to involve volunteers (e.g. Andrew 2001), such as recent graduates or community members experienced in ecological studies to assist with or in some cases to independently conduct projects.

The findings of local ecological research need to be linked back to the biodiversity management committee. Students often move onto other activities once a research project is completed. Reports or theses need to be provided and stored by the local managers. The biodiversity management committee needs to decide how that new knowledge may be used. Royal NP has occasionally hosted seminar days for the presentation of local research. This should continue with a commitment that it would be a regular event (e.g. annual) as a forum for the communication of local research findings, and with summaries available through the Park web site.

Management within protected areas should be adaptive (e.g. Burbidge et al. 2011; Chappell et al. 2011) but one aspect of this that is often overlooked is that it should be informed by small-scale field experiments. Management actions are often applied over large spatial scales (e.g. pest species control) without full appreciation of the cost implications if an action is unsuccessful or if it has adverse unintended consequences (e.g. decline of non-target species). Small-scale field experiments should be employed to understand and refine particular management actions (e.g. Goldingay and Newell 2000). Such experiments should cover a sufficient period of time to be adequately evaluated before being scaled up.

Much of the wildlife research in Royal NP (and elsewhere) is focused on threatened species (e.g. Tulloch and Dickman 2006; Bilney et al. 2007; Baker et al. 2010; Norton et al. 2010a). This is appropriate because the knowledge gaps associated with these species are often the most pressing and some funding is made available for recovery actions for these species. Royal NP can make a significant contribution to the conservation of many listed threatened species, so it is appropriate that ecological research and management in the Park continue to have a focus on them. What also needs to be recognised is that Royal NP could be developed as a model of how ecological research can be used to inform the effective management of biodiversity within a protected area.

ACKNOWLEDGEMENTS

This paper is based on conducting research within Royal NP over a 15-year period. I thank the many rangers, including Tony Dowd, Jessica Herder and Josh Madden, and area managers Peter Hay and Michael Treanor for their support and assistance.

REFERENCES

Andrew, D. (2001). 'Post fire vertebrate fauna survey – Royal and Heathcote National Parks and Garawarra State Recreation Area'. (Report to NSW National Parks & Wildlife Service: Sydney).

Andrew, D., Koffel, D., Harvey, G., Griffiths, K. and Fleming, M. (2012). Rediscovery of the greater glider (*Petauroides volans*) in the Royal National Park, NSW. *Proceedings of the Linnean Society of New South Wales* (in press).

Bain, D. and French, K. (2009). Impacts on a threatened bird population of removals for translocation. *Wildlife Research* 36, 516–521.

Bain, D.W., Baker, J.R., French, K.O. and Whelan, R.J. (2008). Post-fire recovery of eastern bristlebirds (*Dasyornis brachypterus*) is context-dependent. *Wildlife Research* 35, 44–49.

Baker, J. (1997). The decline, response to fire, status and management of the eastern Bristlebird. *Pacific Conservation Biology* 3, 235–243.

Baker, J. (2000). The eastern bristlebird: cover-dependent and fire-sensitive. *Emu* 100, 286–298.

Baker, J. (2009). Assessment of eastern bristlebird habitat: refining understanding of appropriate habitats for reintroductions. *Ecological Management & Restoration* 10, S136-139.

Baker, J., Whelan, R.J., Evans, L., Moore, S. and Norton, M. (2010). Managing the ground parrot in its fiery habitat in south-eastern Australia. *Emu* 110, 279–284.

Banks, S.C., Knight, E.J., McBurney, L., Blair, D., and Lindenmayer, D.B. (2011). The effects of wildfire on mortality and resources for an arboreal marsupial: resilience to fire events but susceptibility to fire regime change. *PLoS One* 6, e22952

Bilney, R.J., Kavanagh, R.P., and Harris, J.M. (2007). Further observations on the diet of the sooty Owl *Tyto tenebricosa* in the Royal National Park, Sydney. *Australian Field Ornithology* 24, 64-69.

Bond, A.R. and Jones, D.N. (2008). Temporal trends in use of fauna friendly underpasses and overpasses. *Wildlife Research* 35, 103–112.

Bowen, M. and Goldingay, R. (2000). Distribution and status of the eastern pygmy possum (*Cercartetus nanus*) in New South Wales. *Australian Mammalogy* 21, 153-64.

Bradstock, R.A. (2008). Effects of large fires on biodiversity in south-eastern Australia: disaster or template for diversity? *International Journal of Wildland Fire* 17, 809–822.

Bradstock, R.A., Bedward, M., Gill, A.M., and Cohn, J.S. (2005). Which mosaic? A landscape ecological approach for evaluating interactions between fire regimes, habitats and animals. *Wildlife Research* 32, 409–423.

Burbidge, A.H., Maron, M., Clarke, M.F., Baker, J., Oliver, D.L., and Ford, G. (2011). Linking science and practice in ecological research and management: How can we do it better? *Ecological Management & Restoration* 12, 54 -60.

Chapple, R.S., Ramp, D., Bradstock, R.A., Kingsford, R.T., Merson, J.A., Auld, T.D., Fleming, P.J.S., and Mulley, R.C. (2011). Integrating Science into Management of Ecosystems in the Greater Blue Mountains. *Environmental Management* 48, 659–674.

DECC (2009). 'Royal and Heathcote National Parks and Garawarra SCA, Fire Management Strategy'. (NSW Department of Environment and Climate Change: Sydney).

DECCW (2011). 'The vertebrate fauna of Royal and Heathcote National Parks and Garawarra State Conservation Area'. (NSW Department of Environment, Climate Change and Water: Sydney).

Daly, G., Johnson, P., Malolakis, G., Hyatt, A. and Pietsch, R. (2008). Reintroduction of the green and golden bell frog *Litoria aurea* to Pambula on the south coast of New South Wales. *Australian Zoologist* 34, 261-270.

Diamond, J.M. (1975). The island dilemma: lessons of modern biogeographic studies for the design of natural reserves. *Biological Conservation* 7, 129–146.

Driscoll, D.A., Lindenmayer, D.B., Bennett, A.F., Bode, M., Bradstock, R.A., Cary, G.J., Clarke, M.F., Dexter, N., Fensham, R., Friend, G., Gill, M., James, S., Kay, G., Keith, D.A., MacGregor, C., Russell-Smith, J., Salt, D., Watson, J.E.M., Williams, R.J. and York, A. (2010). Fire management for biodiversity conservation: Key research questions and our capacity to answer them. *Biological Conservation* 143, 1928–1939.

Gaston, K.J., Charman, K., Jackson, S.F., Armsworth, P.R., Bonn, A., Briers, R.A., Callaghan, C.S.Q., Catchpole, R., Hopkins, J., Kunin, W.E., Latham, J., Opdam, P., Stoneman, R., Stroud, D.A. and Tratt, R. (2006). The ecological effectiveness of protected areas: the United Kingdom. *Biological Conservation* 132, 76–87.

Gaston, K.J., Jackson, S.F., Cantú-Salazar, L. and Cruz-Piñón, G. (2008). The ecological performance of protected areas. *Annual Review of Ecology Evolution and Systematics* 39, 93–113.

Goldingay, R. (1998). Between a rock and a hard place: conserving the broad-headed snake in Australia's oldest National Park. *Proceedings of the Linnean Society of New South Wales* 120, 1-10.

Goldingay, R.L. (2008). Conservation of the green and golden bell frog: what contribution has ecological research made since 1996? *Australian Zoologist* 34, 334-349.

Goldingay, R. and Lewis, B. (1999). Development of a conservation strategy for the green and golden bell frog in the Illawarra Region of NSW. *Australian Zoologist* 31, 376-87.

Goldingay, R.L. and Newell, D.A. (2000). Experimental rock outcrops reveal continuing habitat degradation for an endangered Australian snake. *Conservation Biology* 14, 1908-1912.

Goldingay, R.L. and Newell, D.A. (2006). A preliminary assessment of disturbance to rock outcrops in

Gibraltar Range National Park. *Proceedings of the Linnean Society of New South Wales* 127, 75-81.

Goldingay, R.L., Taylor, B.D. and Ball, T. (2011). Wooden poles can provide habitat connectivity for a gliding mammal. *Australian Mammalogy* 33, 36-43.

Grantham, H.S., Pressey, R.L., Wells, J.A., and Beattie, A.J. (2010). Effectiveness of biodiversity surrogates for conservation planning: different measures of effectiveness generate a kaleidoscope of variation. *PLoS ONE* 5, e11430.

Gurd, D.B., Nudds, T.D., and Rivard, D.H. (2001). Conservation of mammals in eastern North American wildlife reserves: How small is too small? *Conservation Biology* 15, 1355-1363.

Harris, J.M. (2010). The natural history, conservation status and ecology of the eastern pygmy-possum (*Cercartetus nanus*). PhD thesis, Southern Cross University, Lismore.

Harris, J.M. and Goldingay, R.L. (2005). Detection of the eastern pygmy-possum *Cercartetus nanus* (Marsupialia: Burramyidae) at Barren Grounds Nature Reserve, New South Wales. *Australian Mammalogy* 27, 85-88.

Harris, J.M. and Goldingay, R.L. (2009). Museum holdings of the broad-headed snake *Hoplocephalus bungaroides* (Squamata: Elapidae). *Proceedings of the Linnean Society of New South Wales* 130, 1-19.

Hayes, I.F. (2010). Different approaches to conserving the broad-headed snake in Royal National Park: habitat restoration and visitor education. Honours Thesis, Southern Cross University, Lismore.

Hayes, I. and Goldingay, R.L. (2009). Use of fauna road-crossing structures in north-eastern New South Wales. *Australian Mammalogy* 31, 89-95.

Hayes, I. and Goldingay, R.L. (2012). Visitors' knowledge of the broad-headed snake in Royal National Park. *Proceedings of the Linnean Society of New South Wales* (this volume).

Hockings, M. (2003). Systems for assessing the effectiveness of management in protected areas. *BioScience* 53, 823-832.

Hockings, M., Stolton, S., and Dudley, N. (2004). Management effectiveness— assessing management of protected areas? *Journal of Environmental Policy and Planning* 6, 157-174.

Hockings, M., Cook, C.N., Carter, R.W. and James, R. (2009). Accountability, reporting, or management improvement? Development of a State of the Parks assessment system in New South Wales, Australia. *Environmental Management* 43, 1013-1025.

Kavanagh, R.P. (1988). The impact of predation by the powerful owl, *Ninox strenua*, on a population of the greater glider *Petauroides volans*. *Australian Journal of Ecology* 13, 445-450.

Kavanagh, R.P. and Jackson, R. (1997). Home-range, movements, habitat and diet of the sooty owl *Tyto tenebricosa* near Royal National Park. In 'Australian Raptor Studies' (Eds G.V. Czechura and S.J.S. Debus). pp. 2-13. (Birds Australia Monographs No.3, RAOU: Melbourne).

Keast, A. (1995). The Sydney ornithological fraternity, 1930s-1950: anecdotes of an admirer. *Australian Zoologist* 30, 26-32.

Kharouba, H.M. and Kerr, J.M. (2010). Just passing through: Global change and the conservation of biodiversity in protected areas. *Biological Conservation* 143, 1094-1101.

Kitchener, D.J., Chapman, A., Dell, J., Muir, B.G. and Palmer, M. (1980a). Lizard assemblage and reserve size and structure in the Western Australian wheatbelt – some implications for conservation. *Biological Conservation* 17, 25-62.

Kitchener, D.J., Chapman, A., Muir, B.G. and Palmer, M. (1980b). The conservation value for mammals of reserves in the Western Australian wheatbelt. *Biological Conservation* 18, 179-207.

Laurance, W.F. (2008). Theory meets reality: How habitat fragmentation research has transcended island biogeographic theory. *Biological Conservation* 141, 1731-1744.

Lindenmayer, D.B., Macgregor, C., Welsh, A.W., Donnelly, C.F., Crane, M., Michael, D., Montague-Drake, R., Cunningham, R.B., Brown, D., Fortescue, M., Dexter, N., Hudson, M., and Gill, A.M. (2008). Contrasting mammal responses to vegetation type and fire. *Wildlife Research* 35, 395-408.

Lindenmayer, D.B., Wood, J.T., McBurney, L., MacGregor, C., Youngentob, K. and Banks, S.C. (2011). How to make a common species rare: A case against conservation complacency. *Biological Conservation* 144, 1663-1672.

MacArthur, R.H. and Wilson, E.O. (1967). 'The theory of island biogeography'. (Princeton University Press: Princeton, New Jersey).

Maloney, K.S. (2007). The status of the greater glider *Petauroides volans* in the Illawarra region. MSc thesis, University of Wollongong, Wollongong.

Newell, D.A. and Goldingay, R.L. (2005). Distribution and habitat assessment of the broad-headed snake (*Hoplocephalus bungaroides*). *Australian Zoologist* 33, 168-179.

Newmark, W.D. (1987). A land-bridge island perspective on mammalian extinctions in western North American parks. *Nature* 325, 430-32.

Newmark, W.D. (1995) Extinction of mammal populations in western North American national parks. *Conservation Biology* 9, 512-526.

Norton, M.A., Claridge, A.W., French, K. and Prentice, A. (2010). Population biology of the long-nosed potoroo (*Potorous tridactylus*) in the Southern Highlands of New South Wales. *Australian Journal of Zoology* 58, 362-368.

Norton, M.A., French, K. and Claridge, A.W. (2010b). Habitat associations of the long-nosed potoroo (*Potorous tridactylus*) at multiple spatial scales. *Australian Journal of Zoology* 58, 303-316.

NPWS (1997). 'Broadwater National Park, Bundjalung National Park and Iluka Nature Reserve, Plan of Management'. (NSW National Parks & Wildlife Service: Sydney).

B132

Proc. Linn. Soc. N.S.W., 134, 2012

NPWS (2000). 'Royal National Park, Heathcote National Park and Garawarra State Recreation Area, Plan of Management'. (NSW National Parks & Wildlife Service: Sydney).

NPWS (2002a). 'Ku-ring-gai Chase National Park and Lion Island, Long Island and Spectacle Island Nature Reserves, Plan of Management'. (NSW National Parks & Wildlife Service: Sydney).

NPWS (2002b). 'Draft Fire Management Plan for Royal, Heathcote National Parks and Garawarra State Recreation Area'. (NSW National Parks & Wildlife Service: Sydney).

NPWS (2003). 'Yuraygir National Park and Yuraygir State Conservation Area, Plan of Management'. (NSW National Parks & Wildlife Service: Sydney).

Penman, T.D., David A. Pike, D.A., Webb, J.K. and Shine, R. (2010). Predicting the impact of climate change on Australia's most endangered snake, *Hoplocephalus bungaroides*. *Diversity and Distributions* 16, 109–118.

Pressey, R.L. (1994). Ad hoc reservations: forward or backward steps in developing representative reserve systems? *Conservation Biology* 8, 662–68.

Pressey, R.L., Whish, G.L., Barrett, T.W. and Watts, M.E. (2002). Effectiveness of protected areas in north-eastern New South Wales: recent trends in six measures. *Biological Conservation* 106, 57-69.

Pyke, G.H., Rowley, J., Shoulder, J. and White, A. (2008). Attempted introduction of the endangered green and golden bell frog to Long Reef Golf Course: a step towards recovery? *Australian Zoologist* 34, 361-372.

Ramp, D. and Ben-Ami, D. (2006). The effect of road-based fatalities on the viability of a peri-urban swamp wallaby population. *Journal of Wildlife Management* 70, 1615-1624.

Ramp, D., Wilson, V.K. and Croft, D.B. (2006). Assessing the impacts of roads in peri-urban reserves: Road-based fatalities and road usage by wildlife in the Royal National Park, New South Wales, Australia. *Biological Conservation* 129, 348-359.

Rueegger, N. (2011). Use of shelter sites and aspects of the ecology of the eastern pygmy-possum (*Cercartetus nanus*) in Royal National Park. Honours thesis, Southern Cross University, Lismore.

Roberts, D.G., Baker, J. and Perrin, C. (2011). Population genetic structure of the endangered eastern bristlebird, *Dasyornis brachypterus*; implications for conservation. *Conservation Genetics* 12, 1075–1085.

Shine, R., Webb, J., Fitzgerald, M. and Sumner, J. (1998). The impact of bush-rock removal on an endangered snake species, *Hoplocephalus bungaroides* (Serpentes: Elapidae). *Wildlife Research* 25, 285-295.

Soulé, M.E., Wilcox, B.A. and Holtby, C. (1979). Benign neglect: a model of faunal collapse in the game reserves of East Africa. *Biological Conservation* 15, 259–272.

Soulé, M.E., Bolger, D.T., Alberts, Wright, J., Sorice, M. and Hill, S. (1988). Reconstructed dynamics of rapid extinctions of chaparral-requiring birds in urban habitat islands. *Conservation Biology* 2, 75–92.

Stockwell, M.P., Clulow, S., Clulow, J. and Mahony, M. (2008). The impact of the amphibian chytrid fungus *Batrachochytrium dendrobatidis* on a green and golden bell frog *Litoria aurea* reintroduction program at the Hunter Wetlands Centre Australia in the Hunter Region of NSW. *Australian Zoologist* 34, 379-386.

Sumner, J., Webb, J.K., Shine, R. and Keogh, J.S. (2010). Molecular and morphological assessment of Australia's most endangered snake, *Hoplocephalus bungaroides*, reveals two evolutionarily significant units for conservation. *Conservation Genetics* 11, 747–758.

Taylor, A.C., Tyndale-Biscoe, H., and Lindenmayer, D.B. (2007). Unexpected persistence on habitat islands: genetic signatures reveal dispersal of a eucalypt-dependent marsupial through a hostile pine matrix. *Molecular Ecology* 16, 2655-2666.

Taylor, A.C., Walker, F.M., Goldingay, R.L., Ball, T., and van der Ree, R. (2011). Degree of landscape fragmentation influences genetic isolation among populations of a gliding mammal. *PLoS ONE* 6 (10), e26651.

Taylor, B.D. and Goldingay, R.L. (2003). Cutting the carnage: a study of wildlife usage of road culverts in northeast New South Wales. *Wildlife Research* 30, 529-37.

Taylor, B.D. and Goldingay, R.L. (2009). Can road-crossing structures improve population viability of an urban gliding mammal? *Ecology and Society* 14(2), 13.

Taylor, B.D. and Goldingay, R.L. (2010). Roads and wildlife: impacts, mitigation and implications for wildlife management in Australia. *Wildlife Research* 37, 320-331.

Tulloch, A. and Dickman, C. (2006). Floristic and structural components of habitat use by the eastern pygmy-possum (*Cercartetus nanus*) in burnt and unburnt habitats. *Wildlife Research* 33, 627-637.

Tulloch, A.I. and Dickman, C.R. (2007). Effects of food and fire on the demography of a nectar-feeding marsupial: a field experiment. *Journal of Zoology* 273, 382–388.

Webb, J.K. and Shine, R. (1997a). A field study of the spatial ecology and movements of a threatened snake species *Hoplocephalus bungaroides*. *Biological Conservation* 82, 203-217.

Webb, J.K. and Shine, R. (1997b). Out on a limb: conservation implications of tree-hollow use by a threatened snake species (*Hoplocephalus bungaroides*: Serpentes, Elapidae). *Biological Conservation* 81, 21-33.

Webb, J.K. and Shine, R. (1998). Using thermal ecology to predict retreat-site selection by an endangered snake species (*Hoplocephalus bungaroides*: Serpentes, Elapidae). *Biological Conservation* 86, 233-42.

Webb, J.K. and Shine, R. (2000). Paving the way for habitat restoration: can artificial rocks restore degraded habitat of endangered reptiles? *Biological Conservation* 92, 93-99.

Webb, J.K., Brook, B.W. and Shine, R. (2002). Collectors
endanger Australia's most threatened snake, the
broad-headed snake *Hoplocephalus bungaroides*.
Oryx **36**, 170-181.

Weston, N., Goosem, M., Marsh, H., Cohen, M., and
Wilson, R. (2011). Using canopy bridges to link
habitat for arboreal mammals: successful trials in the
Wet Tropics of Queensland. *Australian Mammalogy*
33, 93-105.

Whelan, R. J., Ward, S., Hogbin, P. and Wasley, J. (1996).
Responses of heathland *Antechinus stuartii* to the
Royal National Park wildfire in 1994. *Proceedings of
the Linnean Society of New South Wales* **116**, 97–108.

White, A.W. and Pyke, G. H. (1996). Distribution and
conservation status of the green and golden bell
frog *Litoria aurea* in New South Wales. *Australian
Zoologist* **30**, 177-89.

White, A.W. and Pyke, G.H. (2008a). Green and golden
bell frogs in New South Wales: current status and
future prospects. *Australian Zoologist* **34**, 319-333.

White, A.W. and Pyke, G.H. (2008b). Frogs on the hop:
translocations of green and golden bell frogs *Litoria
aurea* in Greater Sydney. *Australian Zoologist* **34**,
249-260.

Wiersma, Y.F., Nudds, T.D. and Rivard, D.H. (2004).
Models to distinguish effects of landscape patterns
and human population pressures associated with
species loss in Canadian national parks. *Landscape
Ecology* **19**, 773–786.

Visitors' Knowledge of the Broad-headed Snake in Royal National Park

IAN F. HAYES AND ROSS L. GOLDINGAY

School of Environmental Science and Management, Southern Cross University, PO Box 157, Lismore, NSW 2480.

Published on 3 September 2012 at http://escholarship.library.usyd.edu.au/journals/index.php/LIN

Hayes, I.F, and Goldingay, R.L. (2012). Visitors' knowledge of the broad-headed snake in Royal National Park. *Proceedings of the Linnean Society of New South Wales* **134**, B135-B146.

Humans continue to have a negative impact on wildlife and habitat within protected areas. Anthropogenic disturbance to rock habitat within Royal National Park in southern Sydney is reducing the availability of vital retreat sites used by the endangered broad-headed snake (*Hoplocephalus bungaroides*). One approach that may reduce this disturbance is to educate Park users about the broad-headed snake and the threats to its habitat. We conducted questionnaire surveys of Park users during 2010 to determine their level of awareness of this snake, and to assess whether educating Park users about the snake may assist in its conservation. Only 14% of 181 respondents knew this snake occurred within Royal National Park. Some respondents (6%) had observed people tampering with rock habitats, while 85% of respondents believed that people would be more likely to report such activities if aware of its impact on the broad-headed snake. A majority (53%) of respondents believed rock disturbance would not continue if people were informed of its impact. These results suggest that conservation of the broad-headed snake in Royal National Park would benefit if Park users were better informed.

Manuscript received 5 December 2011, accepted for publication 12 June 2012.

KEYWORDS: Habitat disturbance; *Hoplocephalus bungaroides*; questionnaire survey

INTRODUCTION

Humans continue to have a detrimental effect on the natural environment, including National Parks. Protected areas are threatened by the anthropogenic influences of population growth, demand for natural resources, possible introduction of non-native species and climate change (Kessler 2008). Within protected area boundaries, increasing numbers of visitors are also exerting pressure on ecosystems (Buckley and Pannell 1990; Buckley 2003; Hadwen et al. 2007). Visitor impacts include: soil erosion and compaction; damage to vegetation; disturbance to wildlife; litter; water pollution; noise; increased fire frequency; and vandalism (Buckley and Pannell 1990; Marion and Read 2007; Kerbiriou et al. 2009). Wildlife mortality due to animal-vehicle collisions (e.g. Ramp et al. 2006) or illegal hunting also occur, while the collection of endangered species is a major concern (e.g. Webb et al. 2002). These impacts can lead to the loss of species if left unmanaged (Marion and Read 2007).

Royal National Park (NP), on the southern outskirts of the Sydney metropolitan area, is under increasing pressure from visitation. Approximately three million people visit Royal NP each year (NPWS 2000). The Park was established in 1879 primarily as an area for rest and recreation, with nature conservation gradually becoming incorporated into management practice (DEWHA 2009).

One species of conservation significance occurring in Royal NP is the broad-headed snake (*Hoplocephalus bungaroides*) (Fig. 1) (Goldingay 1998), which is recognised as Australia's most endangered snake (Webb et al. 2002). Anthropogenic disturbance to rock habitat within this Park (see Goldingay 1998; Goldingay and Newell 2000; Newell and Goldingay 2005) has impacted on vital rock retreat sites used by this snake during the cooler months of the year (Shine et al. 1998; Webb and Shine 1998a, b). While some studies have implicated bush-rock removal for use in landscaping as the cause of decline in habitat value (Shine and Fitzgerald 1989; Mahony 1997; Shine et al. 1998), others suggest that

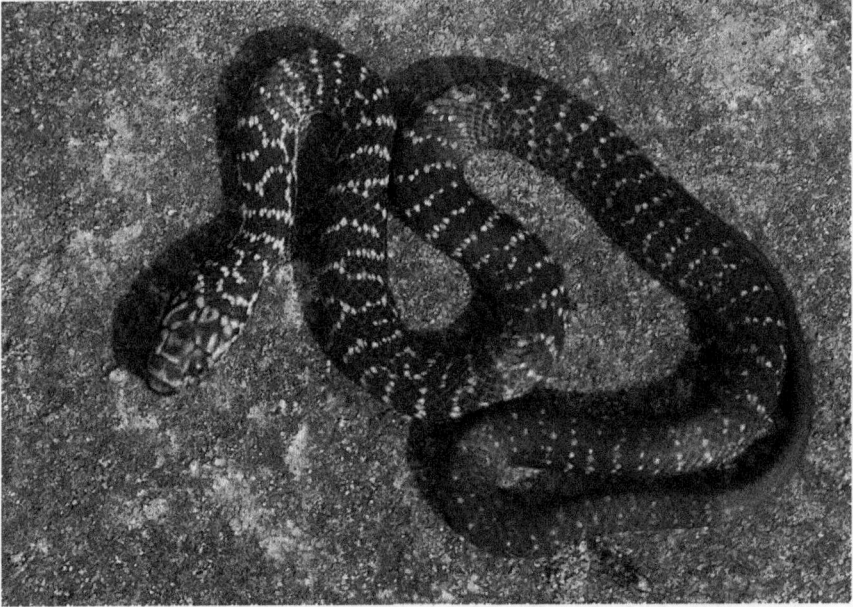

Figure 1. The broad-headed snake (photo: Hayes 2009).

much of the rock disturbance is caused by vandals, hikers and reptile poachers (Goldingay and Newell 2000; Webb and Shine 2000; Webb et al. 2002; Newell and Goldingay 2005). Habitat restoration may ameliorate rock habitat degradation, but the cause of the decline must also be addressed. This requires the monitoring and management of visitors as well as public education to minimise their impacts (Eagles et al. 2002; Hadwen et al. 2007).

Visitor surveys can provide an important insight into understanding the behaviour of visitors. Moore and Polley (2007) note that the information visitors provide can greatly assist with the management of protected areas. Although visitor impacts consume a large proportion of resources for management and maintenance (Buckley 2003), few protected areas have current and accurate records on visitor loads (Hadwen et al. 2007). Therefore, periodic data collection is required to guide management, though this may be constrained due to inadequate funding and staffing levels (Buckley and Pannell 1990; Buckley 2003; Hadwen et al. 2007).

Several authors have noted the value of using visitor education programs as a conservation tool for protected areas (see Goldingay 1998; Papageorgiou 2001; Eagles et al. 2002; Marion and Reid 2007; Littlefair and Buckley 2008; Kerbiriou et al. 2009).

Goldingay (1998) recommended that an education program be used in an attempt to reduce anthropogenic disturbance to the rock habitat of the broad-headed snake. Several methods can be employed to inform and educate Park users with a view to changing their behaviour to reduce impacts. Park information on ecology, geology, rules and regulations, and appropriate visitor behaviour may be provided to visitors via leaflets, maps, the internet, local radio, signs, visitor centres and face-to-face advice (Eagles et al. 2002). Studies indicate that interpretation can be an effective educational tool (Duncan and Martin 2002; Buckley and Littlefair 2007; Littlefair and Buckley 2008; Kim et al. 2011). Interpretation through nature trails, field guides, maps, guided walks or tours and interactive displays is seen as a way of providing a stimulated learning experience for visitors to gain an understanding and appreciation for the natural environment (Eagles et al. 2002).

Education/interpretation may not be sufficient in itself to reduce impacts. Regulatory strategies need to be enacted to control or restrict the actions or numbers of visitors (Papageorgiou 2001; Marion and Reid 2007). While law enforcement addresses illegal actions, effective communication of Park regulations and laws may prevent some of these actions from occurring in the first place (Roggenbuck 1992).

The broad-headed snake provides an excellent case study of a threatened species whose habitat is being degraded by users of protected areas and where education and visitor behavioural change may reduce this impact. However, educating the public and inducing behavioural change requires an initial understanding of the level of knowledge that visitors have of the broad-headed snake and its dependence on rock habitats. Thus, the aims of this study were to describe this knowledge for visitors to Royal NP and to evaluate the possible effectiveness of providing information designed to reduce habitat disturbance.

METHOD

Study area

This study was conducted in the Royal NP, which lies approximately 30 km south of Sydney, New South Wales. Broad-headed snakes have been recorded from the study area over a long period of time (Goldingay 1998; Newell and Goldingay 2005; Harris and Goldingay 2009). The Park is 15,068 ha in size, bounded by Port Hacking to the north, the South Pacific Ocean to the east, the Princes Highway, F6 Freeway and Illawarra Railway to the west and Garawarra State Recreation Area (900 ha) and the township of Helensburgh to the south (NPWS 2000). Visitation to Royal NP is high due to its close proximity to Sydney and accessibility by road to many areas within the Park. Due to the Park's location and visitation, it is highly susceptible to disturbance.

Questionnaire surveys

Questionnaire surveys were conducted in the Park in 2010. The Visitor Information Centre at Audley and the beginning of popular walking tracks were targeted to engage Park users. Visitors were approached and asked to complete the questionnaire in their own handwriting. It was made clear upon introduction that participation to complete the questionnaire was voluntary. No-one under the age of 18 was approached, so as to comply with the requirements of the Southern Cross University's Human Research Ethics Committee Guidelines.

The questionnaire was devised in consultation with the Parks and Wildlife Group (formerly National Parks and Wildlife) NSW, so as to be congruent with their conservation management needs. A short description of the snake, its habitat and conservation status were provided to each respondent, together with the aims of the project. The questionnaire comprised multiple-choice-answer questions (see Appendix A). The location and date of the survey were also

recorded. The questionnaire was designed to not only provide an insight into patterns of knowledge but also inform Park users of the broad-headed snake, threats to the snake's habitat and Park rules that relate to the broad-headed snake. Questions related to activities undertaken by Park users, their frequency of visits, opinions on conservation measures, knowledge of and observation of the broad-headed snake and observation of disturbance events.

RESULTS

The questionnaires were completed by 181 Royal NP users across seven locations. This comprised 63% (n=114) at the Visitor Information Centre; 9% (n=17) at Karloo Track and 8% (n=15) at Garie Beach. Thirty-one people declined to participate. Males comprised 53% (n=95) of respondents and females 40% (n=72), while 14 did not note their gender. Some questions were not answered. Respondents were relatively evenly distributed across three age groups (20-30 years: 35%; 30-40 years: 27%; 40+ years: 37%) (n=63, 48, 67, respectively). One respondent represented the 18-20 year age-group while two did not indicate their age.

The 181 respondents reported a total of 1,748 visits per annum to Royal NP. Visits to the Park were reported as weekly (10% of respondents), monthly (33%), yearly (26%) or rarely (32%). There were 17 activities listed by respondents, with hiking (n=121; 71% of male and 64% of female respondents) and picnicking (n=84; 46% of both male and female respondents) the most frequent (Fig. 2).

Almost all of the respondents (98%; n=178) indicated they observed signs within Royal NP. While 87% (n=156) of respondents indicated that they stayed on formal walking tracks, 23 wandered off tracks. Male respondents were no more likely to wander off tracks than females (χ^2 =0.2, df=1, P=0.66) (Fig. 3). The frequencies in the answer categories to other questions were also independent of gender (P>0.05) so pooled values are given.

Only 25 respondents (14%), of which 17 were male, knew that the broad-headed snake existed within Royal NP. There was only one certain sighting of the broad-headed snake by a respondent. Eight respondents may have seen the snake, while another 11 were uncertain.

There were 6% of respondents who had observed rock disturbance within Royal NP (Fig. 4). Overall, 27% of respondents did not know it was illegal to interfere with rock habitat (Fig. 4).

Proc. Linn. Soc. N.S.W., 134, 2012

B137

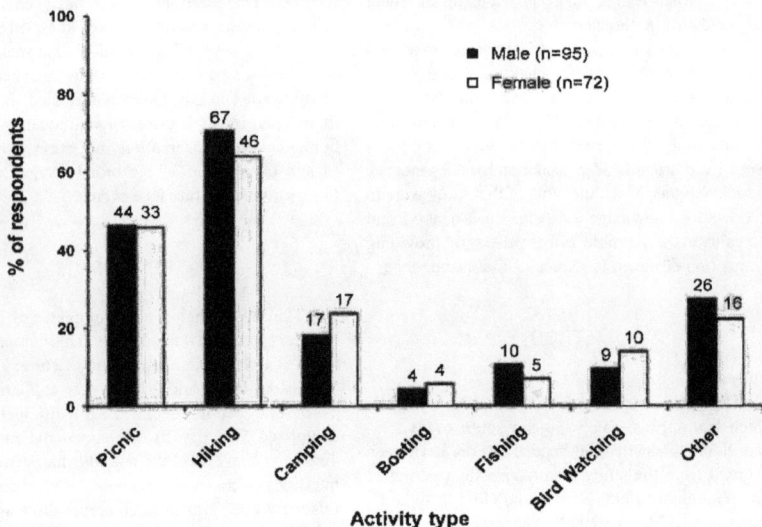

Figure 2. Activities conducted in Royal National Park by male and female respondents. The number of respondents is shown above bars. Those who did not indicate their gender (n=14) are omitted.

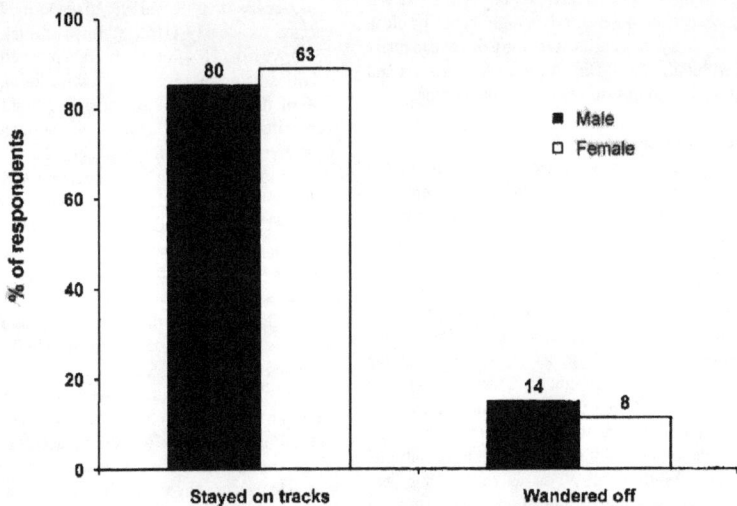

Figure 3. Percentage of male and female respondents that stayed on or wandered off walking tracks. The number of respondents is shown above bars. The gender was not given for a further 13 who stayed on tracks and one who wandered off tracks.

Proc. Linn. Soc. N.S.W., 134, 2012

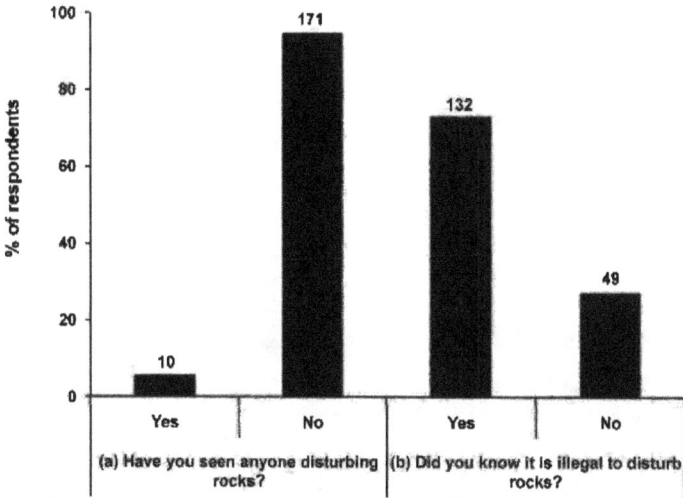

Figure 4. The percentage of respondents who stated (a) whether or not they had seen somebody disturbing loose rocks, and (b) whether they knew it was illegal to do so. The number of respondents is shown above bars.

After being informed about the dependence of the endangered broad-headed snake on sandstone habitat, 85% of respondents thought that people would be more likely to report acts of disturbance to rock habitat (Fig. 5). There were 53% of respondents who believed that rock disturbance would not continue if

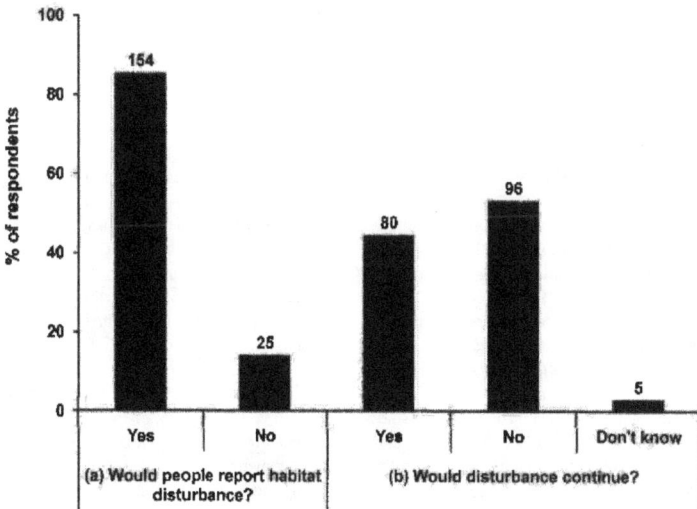

Figure 5. The percentage of respondents who stated (a) whether people would report observations of activities disturbing rock habitat, and (b) whether they thought disturbance would continue if people were better informed. The number of respondents is shown above bars.

Proc. Linn. Soc. N.S.W., 134, 2012

B139

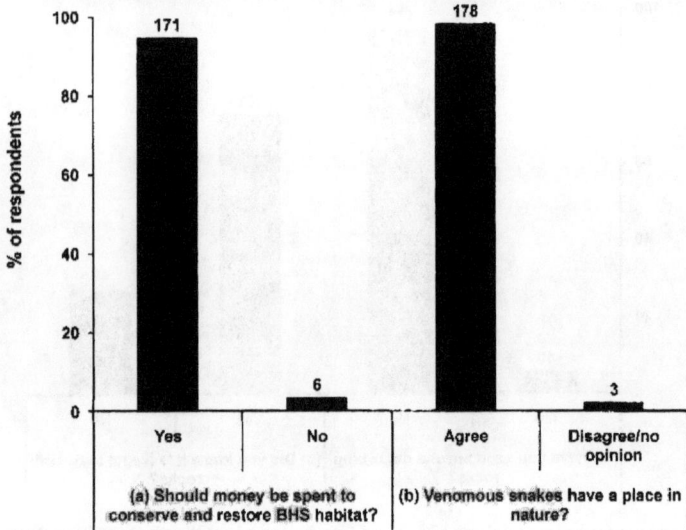

Figure 6. The percentage of respondents who stated whether or not (a) money should be spent to conserve and restore the habitat of the broad-headed snake, and (b) venomous snakes have a place in nature. The number of respondents is shown above bars.

people were better informed about its impact on the broad-headed snake (Fig 5).

A majority of respondents (95%) agreed that restoring and conserving broad-headed snake habitat should be funded (Fig. 6). A majority (98%) also indicated they 'strongly agree' or 'agree' with the statement, 'venomous snakes have a place in nature' (Fig. 6).

DISCUSSION

The endangered broad-headed snake is highly dependent on loose rocks for shelter (Fig. 7) and, as a consequence, it is vulnerable to degradation of its rock habitat (see Shine et al. 1998; Webb et al. 2002). The activities of Park users have been identified as one of the main causes of habitat degradation and this disturbance is ongoing (Goldingay 1998; Goldingay and Newell 2000; Newell and Goldingay 2005; Goldingay and Newell 2006). The present study sought to describe the level of knowledge that Park users had of the snake and its habitat, and from this identify some approaches that may reduce impacts to rock habitat.

Ignorance of the broad-headed snake and its habitat dependence may be partly responsible for the on-going incidence of disturbance to its rock habitat. Only 14% of visitors knew that this species occurred within Royal NP, while 27% did not know it was illegal to interfere with rock habitat. This suggests that there is considerable scope to educate visitors about the snake and its habitat. Indeed, 53% of respondents believed that rock disturbance would cease if people were informed about its impact on the broad-headed snake.

The walking track system attracts many visitors to Royal NP, with over 150 km of tracks (NPWS 2000; DECCW 2009). In 1988, 38% of visitors surveyed identified hiking as their main activity (NPWS 2000). In our study, hiking was the most frequent activity (67%) undertaken by respondents. Hikers are potentially one of the biggest threats to the rock habitat of the broad-headed snake because some hikers move or damage rocks and create rock cairns (Goldingay and Newell 2000; Newell and Goldingay 2005; Figs 8, 9). Many of the walking tracks in the Park extend along rocky ridges and other areas of rock habitat that are used by the snake, which brings hikers directly into contact with the snake's habitat (Fig. 10). This has been highlighted for many years (Goldingay 1998) but so far has not led to any rationalisation of the walking track network within the Park.

B140

Proc. Linn. Soc. N.S.W., 134, 2012

Figure 7. Typical loose rock habitat used by the broad-headed snake in Royal National Park (photo: Hayes 2010).

Figure 8. Rocks illegally broken by hikers in Royal National Park (photo: Hayes 2009).

Figure 9. Rock cairn created illegally by hikers in Royal National Park (photo: Hayes 2009).

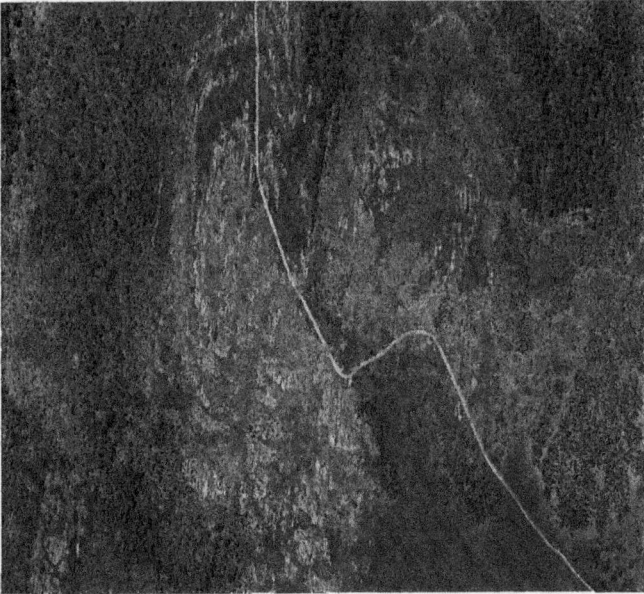

Figure 10. Aerial view of Mt Bass walking track in Royal National Park. Note that the light shaded areas indicate rock habitat (photo: Google Earth 2009).

Thirteen percent of respondents reported that they wandered off tracks. Buckley and Littlefair (2007) warn that results based on self-reported behaviour should be treated with caution as this may deviate from actual behaviour. Thus, this value should be treated as a conservative percentage of people who wandered off tracks. Such behaviour is of concern because it may lead to inadvertent disturbance to rock habitat, in addition to direct interference. There is likely to be a benefit in educating Park users about potential impacts to habitat. There is no mention of staying on tracks in the Royal NP brochure/map (DECCW 2009), though the NSW Department of Environment, Climate Change and Water (now NSW Office of Environment & Heritage) website does include this, with information on hiking behaviour under 'Visiting a Park – be a considerate park visitor' (DECCW 2008). Information could be more conspicuous within the Park, to advise that treading on or disturbing loose rocks may degrade important habitat for many species.

Signs and information boards may help to reduce disturbance by informing visitors of the sensitivity of the broad-headed snake to rock disturbance and to stay on walking tracks. This may be effective because 98% of respondents claimed they read and observed signs. Jacobi (2003) found that signs significantly decreased the addition of rocks to cairns, which are used to mark trails, though it was acknowledged that signs alone were insufficient in resolving the problem of disturbing rock habitat. Kim et al. (2011) also found that environmental interpretation can be effective in influencing visitor behaviour. It is recommended that changes be made to the signage and literature within Royal NP, with an emphasis on improving visitors' awareness in an attempt to reduce impacts on habitat, particularly rock habitat. The location of signs is critical and it is suggested that key areas, such as the beginning of walking tracks and other high use areas (e.g. lookouts) that overlap potential snake habitat be targeted.

A review by Marion and Read (2007) found that most efforts to educate visitors did improve knowledge, behaviour and resource conditions. Royal NP actively encourages education/interpretation through various programs and literature (NPWS 2000). Clearly, more can be done to raise the awareness of the broad-headed snake and its habitat, and to manage visitors' activities. Currently, the only broad-headed snake signage present in the Park is an enforcement sign, located on the western edge of the Park at Heathcote Oval, to restrict entry into that area. An information sign on protecting rock habitat and the broad-headed snake had been erected near the kiosk at Audley,

but has since been removed due to renovations. It is anticipated that a computer-based interpretive display in the Visitor Information Centre will replace this in the near future (M. Treanor, Parks and Wildlife Group, pers. comm.). Kerbiriou et al. (2009) found that disturbance from humans can have severe impacts on wildlife and possibly disrupt population viability. They recommended an education program to increase awareness of the negative consequences of human disturbance.

Goldingay (1998) suggested that a program of public education "could be used to encourage reporting of people who may interfere with the snake's habitat". In the present study, 85% of respondents thought people would report acts of disturbance to rock habitat once they knew of the dependence on this habitat by the broad-headed snake. This could be effective because 6% of respondents reported they had observed people interfering with rock habitat. It may also help to reduce the incidence of reptile poaching, which is prevalent in the Park and significantly disturbs rock habitat (Newell and Goldingay 2005).

The overwhelming support for the funding of projects to restore broad-headed snake habitat and the agreement that 'venomous snakes have a place in nature' (95% and 98% of respondents, respectively), reflect the current interest in environmental issues and conservation. However, the results may not reflect the same level of support across the broader community. The results may be biased in that all respondents were Park users, and therefore, may be more sympathetic towards conservation. Knight (2008) claims that "those who engage in outdoor naturalistic or recreational activities will have higher levels of support for protecting species than those who do not". Nevertheless, Park management needs to be aware of the strong support shown by Park users in this study for the conservation of the broad-headed snake.

Monitoring visitors and their activities is an important component of management because this information can be used to assess the state of natural resources, identify potential threats and indicate whether management actions have been successful (Buckley 2002; Buckley et al. 2008). In Australia, there is a paucity of detailed monitoring data within National Parks, particularly on visitor activities, which is probably due to a lack of resources (see Hadwen et al. 2007; Buckley et al. 2008). The effectiveness of an education program to induce behavioural change of Park visitors could be evaluated in this case by periodic monitoring of specially constructed rock outcrops (see Goldingay and Newell 2000). Additional questionnaire surveys could be conducted

Proc. Linn. Soc. N.S.W., 134, 2012

B143

to assess specific elements of the education program, such as determining whether interpretive signs lead to more visitors knowing that the broad-headed snake occurs within Royal NP. Buckley et al. (2008) highlighted the need for increased monitoring data on both visitors and endangered species populations within Australian NPs. This applies to Royal NP due to its very high number of visitors and the potential impact they can have on native species and habitat.

CONCLUSION

Protected areas are one of the primary mechanisms for conserving threatened species. Increasing use by Park visitors will increase the threat to population viability of these species (e.g. Kerbiriou et al. 2009). This will require novel approaches to how species and people within Parks are managed. The broad-headed snake within Royal NP offers something of a model system because the impacts of visitors can be readily quantified, allowing measurement of the effectiveness of programs to induce behavioural change amongst visitors. Developments within this system could be used to inform other cases where the activities of visitors disrupt the life cycle of threatened or other significant species. Adequate funding will be essential for such a project involving the broad-headed snake in Royal NP.

ACKNOWLEDGEMENTS

We are extremely grateful for the consent of this project and support provided to us from the Department of Environment, Climate Change and Water (New South Wales), in particular, Michael Treanor (Parks and Wildlife Group Area Manager). We would also like to thank Vicky Petersen, Robyn Young, Glen Harvey, Leesa Smid and Vanessa Gilbert from the Visitors Information Centre at Audley, for their assistance with conducting the questionnaire survey and for their support generally. We also thank Kurtis Lindsay for his assistance with fieldwork.

REFERENCES

Buckley, R. (2002). Managing tourism in parks: research priorities of industry associations and protected area agencies in Australia. *Journal of Ecotourism* 1, 162–172.

Buckley, R. (2003). Ecological indicators of tourist impacts in parks. *Journal of Ecotourism* 2, 2003.

Buckley, R. and Littlefair, C. (2007). Minimal-impact education can reduce actual impacts of park visitors.

Journal of Sustainable Tourism 15, 324-325.

Buckley, R. and Pannell, J. (1990). Environmental impacts of tourism and recreation in national parks and conservation reserves. *Journal of Tourism Studies* 1, 24-32.

Buckley, R., Robinson, J., Carmody, J. and King, N. (2008). Monitoring for management of conservation and recreation in Australian protected areas. *Biodiversity and Conservation* 17: 3589-3606.

(DECCW) Department of Environment, Climate Change and Water (2008). *Be a considerate park visitor.* [Online], Available: http://www.environment.nsw. gov.au/lookingafterparks/BeAConsiderateParkVisitor. htm, Last updated 22-02-2008. [Accessed 27-03-10].

DECCW (2009). *Royal National Park.* Brochure No. DECC2008/422. Department of Environment, Climate Change and Water.

(DEWHA) Department of Environment, Water, Heritage and the Arts (2009). *Australian Heritage database place details: Royal National Park and Garawarra State Conservation Area, Sir Bertram Stevens Dr, Audley, NSW, Australia.* [Online], Available: http:// www.environment.gov.au/cgi-bin/ahdb/search. pl?mode=place_detail;place_id=105893, [Accessed 28-03-09].

Duncan, G.S. and Martin, S.R. (2002). Comparing the effectiveness of interpretive and sanction messages for influencing wilderness visitors' intended behaviour. *International Journal of Wilderness* 8, 20-25.

Eagles, P.F.J., McCool, S.F. and Haynes, C.D.A. (2002). *Sustainable tourism in protected areas: guidelines for planning and management.* International Union for the Conservation of Nature (IUCN) Publications, Gland, Switzerland and Cambridge, UK.

Goldingay, R. (1998). Between a rock and a hard place: conserving the broad-headed snake in Australia's oldest National Park. *Proceedings of the Linnean Society of NSW* 120, 1-10.

Goldingay, R.L. and Newell, D.A. (2000). Experimental rock outcrops reveal continuing habitat disturbance for an endangered Australian snake. *Conservation Biology* 14, 1908-1912.

Goldingay, R.L. and Newell, D.A. (2006). A preliminary assessment of disturbance to rock outcrops in Gibraltar Range National Park. *Proceedings of the Linnaean Society of NSW* 127, 75-81.

Hadwen, W.L., Hill, W. and Pickering, C.M. (2007). Icons under threat: why monitoring visitors and their ecological impacts in protected areas matters. *Ecological Management and Restoration* 8, 177-181.

Harris, J.M. and Goldingay, R.L. (2009). Museum holdings of the broad-headed snake *Hoplocephalus bungaroides* (Squamata: Elapidae). *Proceedings of the Linnean Society of New South Wales* 130, 1-19.

Jacobi, C. (2003). *Using signs to reduce visitor-built cairns: Gorham Mountain Trail, Acadia National Park.* ANP Natural Resource Report 2003-11. US Department of the Interior, National Park Service, Acadia National Park.

B144

Proc. Linn. Soc. N.S.W., 134, 2012

Kerbiriou, C., Le Viol, I., Robert, A., Porcher, E., Gourmelon, F., and Julliard, R. (2009). Tourism in protected areas can threaten wild populations: from individual response to population viability of the chough *Pyrrhocorax pyrrhocorax*. *Journal of Applied Ecology* **46**, 657–665.

Kessler, E. (2008). Protecting protected areas. *Ambio* **37**, 329.

Kim, A.K., Airey, D. and Szivas, E. (2011). The multiple assessment of interpretation effectiveness: promoting visitors' environmental attitudes and behavior. *Journal of Travel Research* **50**, 321–334.

Knight, A.J. (2008). "Bats, snakes and spiders, Oh my!" How aesthetic and negativistic attitudes, and other concepts predict support for species protection. *Journal of Environmental Psychology* **28**, 94–103.

Littlefair, C. and Buckley, R. (2008). Interpretation reduces ecological impacts of visitors to World Heritage site. *Ambio* **37**, 338–341.

Mahony, S. (1997). Efficacy of the "threatening processes" provisions in the Threatened Species Conservation Act 1995 (NSW): bush-rock removal and the endangered broad-headed snake. *Environmental and Planning Law Journal* **14**, 3-16.

Marion, J.L. and Reid, S.E. (2007). Minimising visitor impacts to protected areas: the efficacy of low impact education programmes. *Journal of Sustainable Tourism* **15**, 5-27.

Moore, S.A. and Polley, A. (2007). Defining indicators and standards for tourism impacts in protected areas: Cape Range National Park, Australia. *Environmental Management* **39**, 291–300.

Newell, D.A. and Goldingay, R.L. (2005). Distribution and habitat assessment of the broad-headed snake *Hoplocephalus bungaroides*. *Australian Zoologist* **33**, 168-179.

(NPWS) National Parks and Wildlife Service (2000). *Royal National Park, Heathcote National Park and Garawarra State Recreation Area Plan of Management*. NSW National Parks and Wildlife Service, Sydney.

Papageorgiou, K. (2001). A combined park management framework based on regulatory and behavioral strategies: use of visitors' knowledge to assess effectiveness. *Environmental Management* **28**, 61–73.

Ramp, D., Wilson, V.K. and Croft, D.B. (2006). Assessing the impacts of roads in peri-urban reserves: road-based fatalities and road usage by wildlife in the Royal National Park, New South Wales, Australia. *Biological Conservation* **129**, 348-359.

Roggenbuck, J.W. (1992). Use of persuasion to reduce resource impacts and visitor conflicts. In *Influencing Human Behavior: Theory and Applications on Recreation, Tourism, and Natural Resources Management* (Ed. M.J. Manfredo) pp. 149–208. Sagamore Publishing: Champaign, Illinois.

Shine, R. and Fitzgerald, M. (1989). Conservation and reproduction of an endangered species: the broad-headed snake, *Hoplocephalus bungaroides* (Elapidae). *Australian Zoologist* **25**, 65-67.

Shine, R., Webb, J., Fitzgerald, M. and Sumner, J. (1998). The impact of bush-rock removal on an endangered snake species, *Hoplocephalus bungaroides* (Serpentes: Elapidae). *Wildlife Research* **25**, 285-95.

Webb, J.K., Brook, B.W. and Shine, R. (2002). Collectors endanger Australia's most threatened snake, the broad-headed snake *Hoplocephalus bungaroides*. *Oryx* **36**, 170-181.

Webb, J.K. and Shine, R. (1998a). Using thermal ecology to predict retreat-site selection by an endangered snake species. *Biological Conservation* **86**, 233–242.

Webb, J.K. and Shine, R. (1998b). Ecological characteristics of a threatened snake species, *Hoplocephalus bungaroides* (Serpentes, Elapidae). *Animal Conservation* **1**, 185-193.

Webb, J.K. and Shine, R. (2000). Paving the way for habitat restoration: can artificial rocks restore degraded habitats of endangered reptiles? *Biological Conservation* **92**, 93–99.

APPENDIX A - Questionnaire

Please circle which category you belong to:

Male   Female

Age: <20 yrs 20-30 yrs   30-40 yrs
>40 yrs

1.   Please tick the boxes that best represent the activities you undertake most often in Royal National Park?
☐ Picnicking
☐ Hiking
☐ Camping
☐ Boating
☐ Fishing
☐ Bird watching
☐ Other (please specify)
....

2.   How often do you visit this park?
☐ Weekly
☐ Monthly
☐ Yearly
☐ Rarely

3.   How often do you visit other National Parks?
☐ Weekly
☐ Monthly
☐ Yearly
☐ Rarely

4.   Do you read and observe information signs that are provided in Royal National Park?
☐ Yes
☐ No

5.   If you go on a hike would you ...
☐ Stay on formal walking tracks
☐ Wander off the track to go exploring

6.   Were you aware that a species of endangered snake known as the broad-headed snake exists within Royal National Park?
☐ Yes
☐ No

7.   Have you ever seen a broad-headed snake in Royal National Park?
☐ No
☐ Maybe
☐ Uncertain

8.   Have you ever observed anybody tampering with or removing sandstone bush-rock from Royal National Park?
☐ Yes
☐ No

9.   Did you know it's illegal to interfere with rock habitats within a National Park?
☐ Yes
☐ No

10.   After being informed about the dependence of the endangered broad-headed snake on sandstone habitat, do you think people would be more likely to report activities that disturb this habitat to the Parks and Wildlife Service?
☐ Yes
☐ No

11.   People may inadvertently disturb rock habitats. Do you think this would continue if people were better informed about its impact on an endangered species?
☐ Yes
☐ No

12.   Should money be spent to restore and conserve the habitat of the broad-headed snake?
☐ Yes
☐ No

13.   Please indicate how you feel about the following statement:
Venomous snakes have a place in nature.

Strongly agree   Agree   No opinion

Disagree   Strongly disagree

Spatial Analysis of Risks Posed by Root Rot Pathogen, *Phytophthora cinnamomi*: Implications for Disease Management

DAVID A. KEITH[1,2], KEITH L. MCDOUGALL[1,3], CHRISTOPHER C. SIMPSON[1] AND JILLIAN L. WALSH[1]

[1] NSW Office of Environment & Heritage, PO Box 1967, Hurstville NSW 2220.
[2] Australian Wetlands and Rivers Centre, University of New South Wales, Sydney NSW 2052.
[3] Department of Environmental Management & Ecology, La Trobe University, PO Box 821, Wodonga, Victoria 3689.

Published on 3 September 2012 at http://escholarship.library.usyd.edu.au/journals/index.php/LIN

Keith, D.A., McDougall, K.L., Simpson, C.C. and Walsh, J.L. (2012). Spatial analysis of risks posed by root rot pathogen, *Phytophthora cinnamomi:* implications for disease management. *Proceedings of the Linnean Society of New South Wales* 134, B147-B179.

Phytophthora cinnamomi, a soil-borne pathogen that infects the roots of plants, is listed as a Key Threatening Process under Commonwealth and NSW state biodiversity legislation due to its deleterious effects on native flora. In warm temperate eastern Australia, the disease may cause insidious declines in plant species that have slow rates of population turnover, and thereby threaten their long term persistence. *Phytophthora cinnamomi* has been known to occur in Royal National Park since the 1970s and systematic surveys for the pathogen were carried out a decade ago. Development of effective management strategies to mitigate the impacts of the disease requires information on the spatial distribution of risks posed by the disease. In this study, we use limited disease survey data to identify areas that are most at risk. We propose and apply a simple risk model in which risks of disease impact are proportional to the product of habitat suitability for the pathogen and abundance of susceptible biota. We modelled habitat suitability of the pathogen from available survey data and found that soil landscapes and topographic variables were the strongest predictors. Susceptible flora were concentrated on sandstone plateaus. Disease risks were greatest on the sandstone plateaus and lowest in the shale gullies with intermediate levels of risk on shale ridges and the coastal sand plain. The outcomes of this spatially explicit risk assessment will help inform the development of management strategies and priorities for the disease in the Park. Our approach lends itself to broader application to conservation planning in other landscapes and to other threats to biodiversity.

Manuscript received 11 January 2012, accepted for publication 2 May 2012.

KEYWORDS: disease susceptibility, conservation planning, risk assessment, risk mapping, Royal National Park, species distribution model.

INTRODUCTION

Phytophthora cinnamomi Rands is a soil-borne plant pathogen with a very broad host range. It is damaging to crops and native vegetation in many countries. Genetic evidence suggests that it is a recent introduction to Australia (Dobrowolski et al. 2003) but has been present in most States since at least the early 20th Century (Cahill et al. 2008).

Since the association between infection by *P. cinnamomi* and death in native plants in Australia was established in the late 1960s (Podger 1968), severe damage in native vegetation has been documented in all Australian States (Cahill et al. 2008). Many plants in the families Ericaceae, Fabaceae, Proteaceae and Xanthorrhoeaceae are especially susceptible (McDougall 2006; Figure 1). The threat from *P. cinnamomi* is recognised in its listing as a key threatening process nationally under the *Environment Protection and Biodiversity Act 1999* and in NSW under the *Threatened Species Conservation Act 1995*.

Phytophthora cinnamomi spreads by motile spores in moist soil over short distances or by vegetative growth between roots. Spores also enable long distance dispersal in storm run off and creeks, or in soil attached to cars and boots. For this reason, it is often found beside roads, tracks and other places of soil-disturbance, and waterways. Infection occurs when motile spores germinate on or near plant roots

Figure 1. Sporadic mortality of susceptible plant species (e.g. *Banksia marginata*) in spring is characteristic of root rot disease caused by *Phytophthora cinnamomi* in Royal National Park.

or stem bases. These produce vegetative strands (mycelia) that grow in host tissue, destroying water conducting cells. Infected plants therefore typically display drought-like symptoms. Death may occur where a host is especially susceptible to infection or where other stresses are operating on the host (e.g. drought or insect attack). The mycelia may then produce sporangia (the structure that releases motile spores) or, under unfavourable conditions, a resting spore, which is resistant to drying (Cahill et al. 2008). Importantly, *P. cinnamomi* is not dispersed in the air.

Host plants vary in their susceptibility, ranging from tolerant (where there are no visible symptoms) to highly susceptible (where plants are rapidly killed). Hosts may be tolerant in some habitats but not others, or only under some climatic conditions (Shearer & Dillon 2006). The overall impact of *P. cinnamomi* on native vegetation is determined by local environmental conditions, host availability and time since infestation (Cahill et al. 2008). For instance, *P. cinnamomi* can be present and have no visual impact if hosts are tolerant, can have an impact in one area but not another, despite similar susceptible hosts, if environmental conditions are not conducive to spread and infection, or the impact can appear minimal long after infestation if susceptible hosts disappear. At sites dominated by

highly susceptible species, the impact will commonly involve major structural change with flow-on effects to habitat-dependent plants and animals (McDougall et al. 2005). Importantly, once introduced to a site that favours its life cycle, *P. cinnamomi* is likely to persist because of the presence of tolerant hosts and the production of resting spores. Recolonisation of infested sites by susceptible hosts may occur and has been recorded (e.g. Weste et al. 1999; McDougall and Summerell 2003) but these colonists will be highly vulnerable to further infection and their likelihood of long-term survival is low. *P. cinnamomi* is putting many species at risk of extinction (Cahill et al. 2008).

The susceptibility to infection is known for very few native Australian species (McDougall 2006) but there are taxonomic patterns that can allow the susceptibility of other species to be inferred (Cahill et al. 2008). For instance, all species of *Andersonia* (family Ericaceae) in Western Australia, for which susceptibility is known, are highly susceptible (Wills and Keighery 1994), and species of *Xanthorrhoea* (family Xanthorrhoeaceae) tend to be moderately to highly susceptible (McDougall 2006). Curiously, all Western Australian species of *Banksia* are moderately to highly susceptible whereas few eastern Australian

Banksia species are highly susceptible (McCredie et al. 1985). However, almost all *Banksia* species are susceptible to infection to some extent (Figure 1). Extrapolation of susceptibility will not always be reliable within genera and families but offers a means of assessing likely vulnerability of communities or local floras to *P. cinnamomi*. Site environmental conditions can greatly influence the impact of *P. cinnamomi* (Wilson et al. 2000; Cahill et al. 2008). It is able to complete its life cycle under a great range of temperature (mean annual temperature > 7°C) and rainfall (> 400 mm / annum) conditions. Some soil types, however, have been found to be less favourable to *P. cinnamomi* activity (e.g. those with antagonistic micro-organisms (Halsall 1982), high fertility (Shearer and Crane 2003), or high pH / high calcium content (Shearer and Hill 1989)). Putative relationships have also been reported between the incidence of *P. cinnamomi* and soil texture, as well as topographic features that influence soil moisture (Wilson et al. 2000; 2003).

There is no effective, long-term treatment for *P. cinnamomi* once it enters an ecosystem. A chemical (phosphonate) increases plant resistance but can be phytotoxic and needs frequent re-application. Prevention is therefore the most important form of management for sites suspected to be free of the pathogen. Preventive measures include routine surveillance of symptoms, restriction of access when soils are wet and the likelihood of spread is greatest, hygiene stations for cleaning shoes or vehicles, construction of well-drained tracks that will not support the pathogen, or chemical control (Cahill et al. 2008).

Phytophthora cinnamomi was first located in Royal National Park in 1974 (Gerrettson-Cornell 1986). No importance was attached to its presence until recently when deaths of *Xanthorrhoea resinosa* were linked to infection by *P. cinnamomi* (McDougall and Summerell 2003). Walsh et al. (2006) found that *P. cinnamomi* is widespread in Royal National Park, concluding that hygiene measures were likely to be ineffective at containing its spread. The pathogen was, however, found not to be ubiquitous or evenly distributed. It was, for instance, not located at any sites containing *Telopea speciosissima* (Waratah), which is typically highly susceptible to *P. cinnamomi*. This suggests that some parts of the Park are still free of *P. cinnamomi* and that preventive measures are worthwhile to protect iconic species such as this and localised or threatened species that may be susceptible. Spatial patterns in occurrence of the pathogen may be investigated using models of habitat suitability that link observed occurrence to environmental variables

(Wilson et al. 2003). An understanding of the spatial pattern of risks posed to biodiversity by *P. cinnamomi* will help direct threat abatement actions to areas where they address the greatest risks.

In this paper we illustrate a method for mapping the spatial pattern of risks by combining a habitat suitability model for the pathogen with a map showing the abundance and diversity of susceptible flora. Our study area includes Royal and Heathcote National Parks, Garrawarra State Conservation Area and adjacent areas, approximately 30 km south of Sydney city (Figure 2). We first developed a habitat suitability model for the pathogen using data for *P. cinnamomi* presence obtained by Walsh et al. (2006) to relate the occurrence of infested soil samples to a set of spatially explicit environmental predictor variables. We then produced a distribution map of susceptible flora by combining vegetation survey data with susceptibility ranks for each species and weighting species association with mapped vegetation types using their frequencies of occurrence. Finally, we combined habitat suitability for the pathogen with susceptibility of flora to produce a *Phytophthora* risk map for the study area - we used this to identify areas where threat abatement efforts should be focussed.

METHODS

Phytophthora cinnamomi detection

Soil sampling of *P. cinnamomi* within Royal National Park was conducted in 2001 and 2002 for two distinct projects: a targeted survey of 14 sites, nine containing *Xanthorrhoea resinosa* and five containing *Telopea speciosissima* (Waratah); and a systematic survey of the plant communities. For the targeted survey, soil was sampled from the bases of 20 plants of the target species at each site. Sampling was repeated in the following year on two randomly selected plants at each site, giving a total of 308 samples over two years. Each sample consisted of three 100 g subsamples. For the plant community survey, walking tracks were selected such that they approximately represented the proportional distribution of the five broad vegetation types: heathland/open scrub, *Eucalyptus* forest, *Eucalyptus* woodland, wetland and rainforest. Along each track, a pair of samples was collected approximately every 150 m, one sample from directly adjacent to the track on the downslope side, and the other approximately 30 m from the track in an upslope direction. In total, 120 pairs of samples were collected. All samples were taken from the top 15 cm of the soil profile and included root fragments, as soils near the root zone yield higher populations of

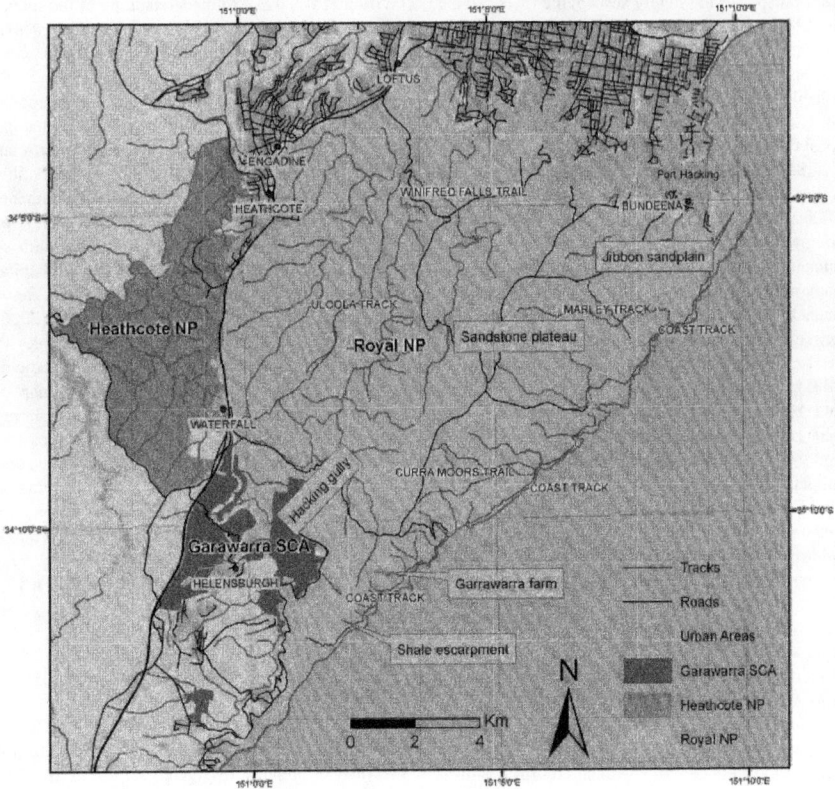

Figure 2. Study area.

P. cinnamomi (Tsao 1983). Equipment was sprayed with methylated spirits after each sample to ensure that inoculum was not transferred between samples. Samples were stored in sealed plastic bags and processed the following day. The baiting technique used to isolate *P. cinnamomi* is described in Walsh et al. (2006). The presence of *P. cinnamomi* was confirmed by examining selective media containing baits under a compound microscope. The location co-ordinates of all sample sites were recorded with a global positioning system and recorded as present or absent depending on the outcomes of baiting tests.

Model of habitat suitability

To model habitat suitability for *P. cinnamomi*, spatial data were assembled within a geographic information system (GIS) for seven environmental variables that we hypothesised may influence the

distribution of *P. cinnamomi*. The seven predictor variables were: soil landscapes (Hazelton & Tille 1990); slope, aspect (sine-tranformed); wetness index (number of grid cells in the catchment above the focal cell); local topographic position (proportional distance between local ridge and local gully); topographic position (difference between elevation of focal cell and mean of neighbouring cells within a 250 m radius); topographic roughness (sum of absolute differences in elevation between the focal cell and neighbouring cells within a 250 m radius). These represent spatial proxies for local environmental variables such as soil fertility and pH, site moisture status and temperature that have previously been implicated as having an influence on the development and life cycle of the pathogen (Wilson et al. 2000; Cahill et al. 2008). All layers were projected onto a standard 25 m grid.

To ensure spatial independence of samples, we pooled samples within pairs from the plant community survey. The presence-absence records and environmental spatial data were used to construct a Maximum Entropy model (MaxEnt) of habitat suitability for *P. cinnamomi* (Phillips et al. 2006). This approach estimates a target probability distribution of occurrence by finding a distribution that is closest to uniform, subject to constraints represented by observations of presence and absence in relation to the predictor variables. The estimated distribution maximises agreement with the set of observations, without assuming anything that is not known about their underlying distribution (Jaynes 1990). MaxEnt performed well in comparative accuracy tests of numerous alternative methods of species distribution modelling (Elith et al. 2006).

All seven predictors were included in the initial model with a hinging value set to 0.5. Predictor variables were excluded from the model if they explained less than 5% of variation in the data, given inclusion of other predictors, or if they were correlated (r>0.4) with another predictor that explained more variation in the data. After checking the range of environmental data values across the study area in relation to the coverage of the training data set, model fit was evaluated by inspecting the area under the receiver operating curve (AUC). A map of habitat suitability for *P. cinnamomi* was produced by projecting the final model onto the study area using the spatial data layers.

Ranking species and mapping susceptibility of vegetation

The susceptibility of vascular plant taxa recorded in the study area to infection by *P. cinnamomi* was scored using lists of known susceptibility (Weste 2001; McDougall 2006) and personal observations

(Table 1). Taxa were ranked as low, moderate or high susceptibility based on the severity of symptoms in the wild or glasshouse experiments. In some cases, susceptibility has been inferred from patterns of plant death observed in the field at sites that were known to be infested with *P. cinnamomi* (McDougall 2006). Those taxa that do not commonly develop symptoms regardless of whether colonisation by *P. cinnamomi* occurs were treated as field resistant. Taxa not directly known to be susceptible, but with known susceptible congeneric taxa were recorded as suspected susceptibility.

A set of 230 floristic quadrats collected in a stratified systematic survey was used to estimate the relative frequency of susceptible plant species in each vegetation type within the study area (NPWS, unpubl. data). A vegetation classification was generated from the data using a cluster analysis (see Tozer et al. 2010 for methods) and a map of the resulting units was drafted with the aid of aerial photographs and soil landscape maps. The mean frequency of each plant taxon in each vegetation type was calculated from their occurrences in quadrats assigned to respective types. An index of disease susceptibility was calculated for each vegetation type by summing the frequencies of all susceptible plant taxa and dividing by the sum frequencies of all recorded taxa. A second index was calculated from the summed frequencies of only the moderately and highly susceptible taxa. Both indices were mapped by joining vectors of the values for each vegetation type to the attribute table of the vegetation map in a GIS.

Risk mapping

Risks to biodiversity from *P. cinnamomi* at any given site were assumed to be a function of the likelihood of infection by the disease and the susceptibility of vegetation. We therefore produced

Table 1. Descriptions of susceptibility classes of vascular plant taxa to root rot disease caused by *Phytophthora cinnamomi*.

Susceptibility class
Field resistant
Of unknown susceptibility
Not known to be susceptible but other species in genus known to be of low to moderate susceptibility
Not known to be susceptible but other species in genus known to be highly susceptible
Known to be of low susceptibility or susceptible but degree of susceptibility not documented
Known to be of moderate susceptibility
Known to be of high susceptibility

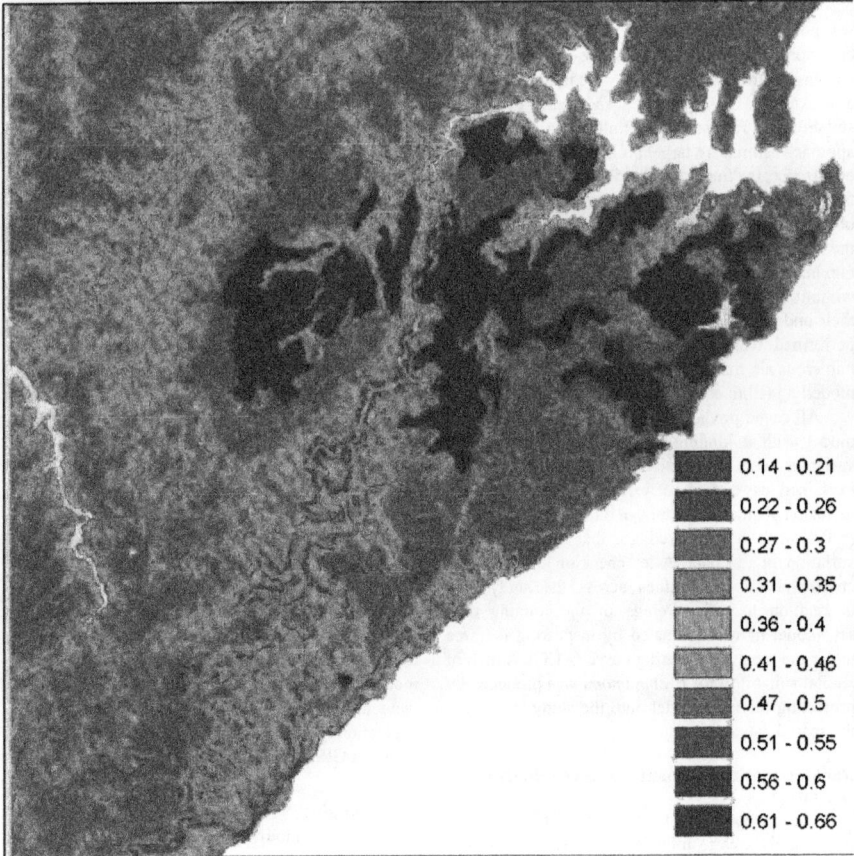

Figure 3. Predicted habitat suitability for *Phytophthora cinnamomi* in the study area.

a map of risk by multiplying spatial data layers for habitat suitability and the relative susceptibility indices.

RESULTS

Habitat suitability

The best distribution model of *P. cinnamomi* included three predictor variables. Soil landscape was the most important predictor, explaining 71% of variation, while slope explained a further 20% and topographic position explained 9%. Sites with clay loam soils derived from Narrabeen Group shales had lower probability of *P. cinnamomi* presence than other soil types. Presence was also less likely on steep slopes than flat slopes and less likely in deep gullies than shallow gullies, slopes and ridges.

More than 95% of the study area was modelled within the range of the training data. The remaining area was on steeper slopes than any of the sampled sites. The best model was a relatively poor fit to the data with an AUC of 0.69.

When projected on a map of the study area, the upper Hacking River valley and southern coastal escarpment showed a conspicuously low probability of *P. cinnamomi* presence compared to the surrounding sandstone plateau (Figure 3). Within the Hacking valley itself and also on the sandstone plateau, gullies and steep slopes had a subtly lower probability of presence than other landscape elements.

B152

Proc. Linn. Soc. N.S.W., 134, 2012

Susceptibility of vegetation

Two hundred and eighty-four vascular plant taxa recorded in a systematic vegetation survey of the study area were identified as known or suspected to be susceptible to disease caused by *P. cinnamomi*, representing approximately one-quarter of the total vascular flora of the reserves (Appendix 1). The most widespread dry sclerophyll forest communities had susceptibility scores of 40 or more, while the most widespread heathland community had a susceptibility score of 35 (Table 2). In contrast, rainforests and estuarine wetlands had the lowest susceptibility scores, generally less than 8, and wet sclerophyll forests and freshwater wetlands generally had susceptibility scores of less than 20 (Table 2). Of the 284 susceptible taxa, 128 were identified as moderately or highly susceptible. The susceptibility relationships between plant communities based on this subset of taxa were generally similar to those based on all susceptible taxa except that moderately or highly susceptible taxa were more abundantly represented in heathlands relative to dry sclerophyll forests (Table 2).

Susceptible plant taxa were most abundant across northern and central parts of the study area on the sandstone plateau, and least abundant in the southern part of the area in the upper Hacking valley and along the coastal escarpment (Figure 4). Localised saline wetlands along the shores of Port Hacking also had low abundances of susceptible taxa. Localised patches with intermediate abundance of susceptible taxa include the Jibbon sand plains in the far northeast of the study area and shale capped ridges at Loftus and Garrawarra farm, respectively, in the north and south of the study area. Spatial patterns in the relative abundance of all susceptible species were similar to those for highly and moderately susceptible species (Figure 4a cf. 4b). The main differences were on the sandstone plateau. All susceptible taxa were slightly more abundant on western parts of the plateau dominated by dry sclerophyll forests (Figure 4a). In contrast, moderately and highly susceptible taxa were more abundant on eastern parts of the plateau, reflecting the greater frequency of occurrence of these taxa in heathlands, which are more widespread in the east, and slightly lower frequencies of these taxa in dry sclerophyll forests of sandstone gullies, which are more widespread in the west (Figure 4b).

Spatial patterns of risk

Spatial patterns in risks to vegetation posed by *P. cinnamomi* are shown in Figure 5. Risks were greatest on the sandstone plateaus and lowest in the shale gullies with intermediate levels of risk on shale ridges and the coastal sand plain, reflecting patterns in habitat suitability for the pathogen and distribution of susceptible flora, described above. A focus on the most susceptible flora (Figure 5b) showed a slightly greater contrast in risks between different geological parent materials and higher risks in the eastern heathlands relative to the western sclerophyll forests.

DISCUSSION

Spatial patterns in disease risks

Phytophthora cinnamomi poses the greatest risk to native vegetation in heathlands and dry sclerophyll woodlands of the sandstone plateau, particularly on flat terrain of the plateau surface, ridges and upper slopes. Rainforests in deep gullies on shale-derived soils are at least risk, while wet sclerophyll forests and wetlands are at low levels of risk. These generalisations hold irrespective of whether the risk analysis includes all species known or suspected to be susceptible to the disease or only those that are highly or moderately susceptible. They are also consistent with previous reports that disease impacts appear to be greatest in seasonally dry oligotrophic landscapes (Cahill et al. 2008).

Comparatively low levels of risk were estimated for heathlands and sclerophyll woodlands on the Jibbon coastal sand plain relative to adjoining sandstone landscapes. This is a surprising result, given that sandplain habitats elsewhere have suffered major impacts from the disease, for example on the Swan coastal plain in southwestern Australia (Shearer & Hill 1989). Examination of the susceptibility data and soil survey data shows that modest levels of estimated risk are driven primarily by the fact that a relatively low number of vascular plant taxa recorded in plant communities of the Jibbon sand plain are currently known to be susceptible to the disease. Furthermore, soil sampling on the sand plain was extremely limited. Until more comprehensive soil testing and a more comprehensive appraisal of susceptible flora is carried out, our inferences about disease risks on the Jibbon sand plain should be treated with caution and similar management strategies and priorities should be applied to this area as applied to the high-risk heathlands of the sandstone plateau.

Limitations of risk assessment

Our risk assessment was limited primarily by the available data. Although the habitat suitability predictions for *P. cinnamomi* were largely within

Proc. Linn. Soc. N.S.W., 134, 2012

B153

Table 2. Susceptibility scores (summed frequencies of susceptible taxa) for each vegetation map unit (see DECCW 2010). Map unit codes: DSF- dry sclerophyll forests; FoW forested wetlands; FrW- freshwater wetlands; GL- grasslands; HL- heathlands; RF- rainforests; SW- saline wetlands; WSF- wet sclerophyll forests (after Keith 2004a).

Map unit code	Map unit name	Susceptibility score (all susceptible taxa)	Susceptibility score (moderately& highly susceptible taxa)
S_DSF03	Coastal Sand Apple-Bloodwood Forest	18	6
S_DSF04	Coastal Enriched Sandstone Sheltered Forest	20	6
S_DSF05	Coastal Sandstone Exposed Scribbly Gum Woodland	39	19
S_DSF06	Coastal Sandstone Foreshores Forest	16	5
S_DSF07	Coastal Sandstone Gully Moist Heath	44	20
S_DSF08	Coastal Sandstone Riparian Forest	21	8
S_DSF09	Coastal Sandstone Sheltered Peppermint-	39	17
S_DSF13	Southern Sydney Sheltered Forest	26	9
S_DSF14	Sydney Ironstone Bloodwood-Silvertop Ash Forest	37	14
S_DSF15	Woronora Sandstone Exposed Bloodwood Woodland	40	19
S_DSF16	Woronora Sandstone Mallee-Heath Woodland	45	22
S_DSF21	Coastal Sand Bangalay Forest	9	4
S_FoW01	Coastal Alluvial Bangalay Forest	8	2
S_FoW05	Hinterland Riverflat Paperbark Swamp Forest	3	1
S_FoW08	Estuarine Swamp Oak Forest	0	0
S_FrW01	Coastal Upland Damp Heath Swamp	25	9
S_FrW02	Coastal Upland Wet Heath Swamp	17	8
S_FrW04	Coastal Sand Swamp Paperbark Scrub	4	2
S_FrW05	Coastal Sand Swamp Sedgeland	5	0
S_GL02	Coastal Headland Grassland	5	3
S_HL02	Coastal Tea-tree-Banksia Scrub	8	3
S_HL04	Coastal Sandplain Heath	25	11
S_HL06	Coastal Headland Banksia Heath	20	9
S_HL08	Coastal Sandstone Heath-Mallee	35	18
S_IIL09	Coastal Sandstone Plateau Rock Plate Heath	11	7
S_HL10	Hinterland Sandstone Dwarf Apple Heath-Woodland	23	10
S_RF01	Illawarra Escarpment Subtropical Rainforest	1	0
S_RF03	Coastal Warm Temperate Rainforest	3	1
S_RF07	Coastal Escarpment Littoral Rainforest	7	3
S_RF08	Coastal Headland Littoral Thicket	2	0
S_RF09	Coastal Sandstone Riparian Scrub	16	6
S_SW01	Estuarine Mangrove Forest	0	0
S_SW02	Estuarine Saltmarsh	0	0
S_WSF02	Coastal Enriched Sandstone Moist Forest	20	7
S_WSF03	Coastal Sand Littoral Forest	6	2
S_WSF04	Illawarra Escarpment Bangalay-Banksia Forest	11	5
S_WSF05	Illawarra Escarpment Blackbutt Forest	13	4
S_WSF06	Coastal Shale-Sandstone Forest	25	9
S_WSF07	O'Hares Creek Shale Forest	9	3
S_WSF09	Sydney Turpentine-Ironbark Forest	22	5

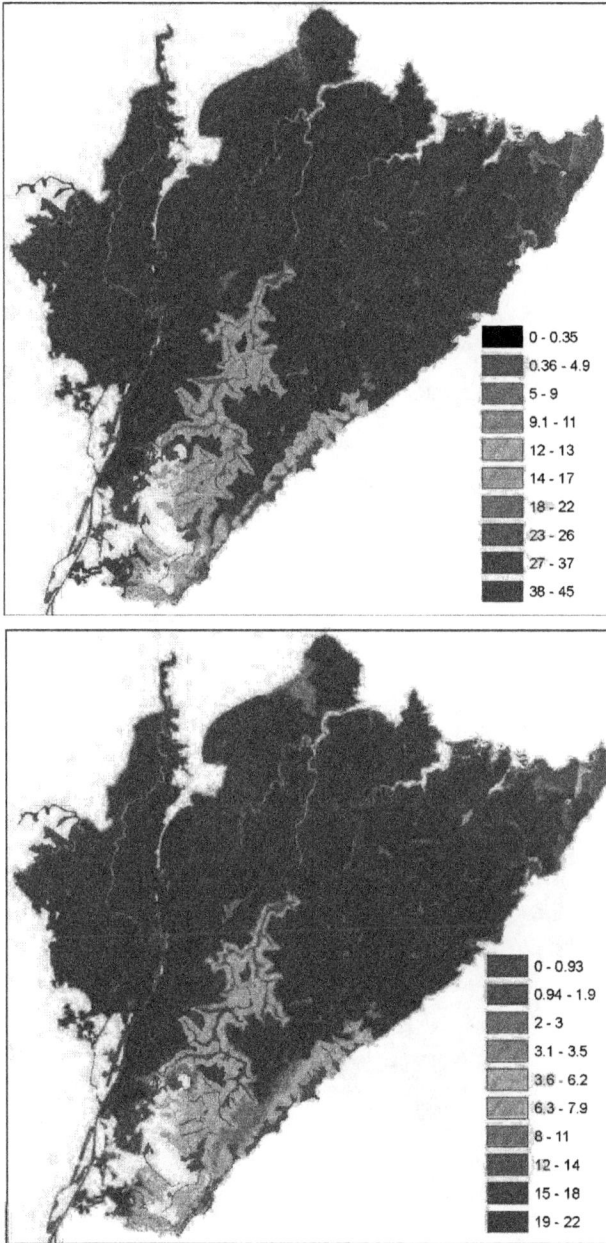

Figure 4. Spatial patterns in the relative abundance of a) all susceptible vascular plant taxa and b) highly and moderately susceptible vascular plant taxa.

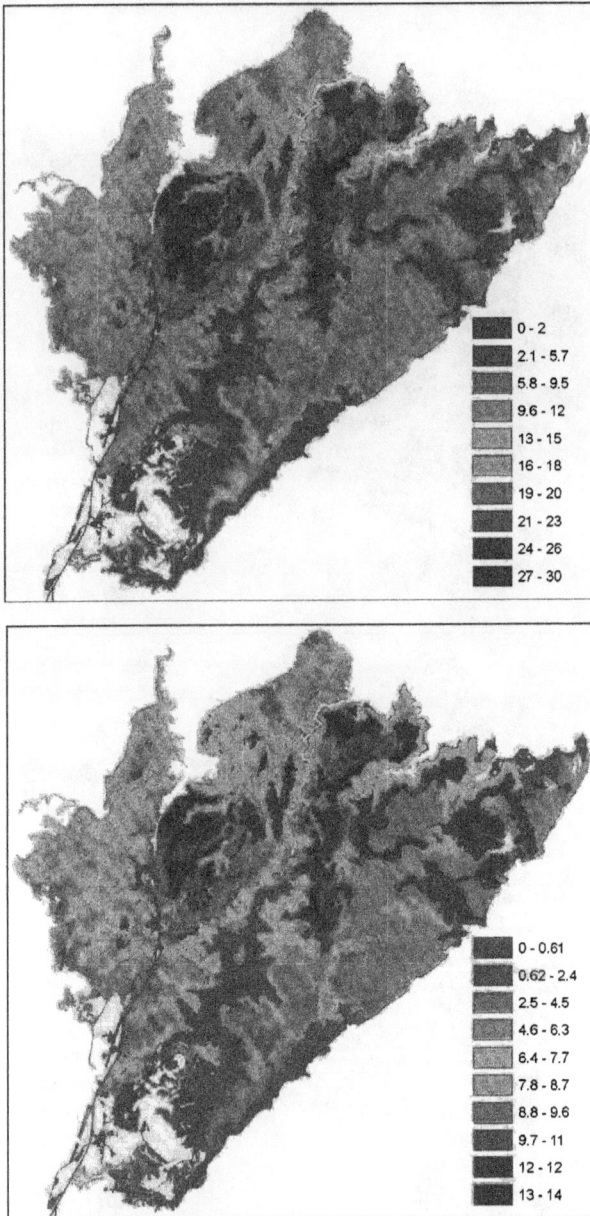

Figure 5. Spatial patterns in risks posed to native vegetation by *Phytophthora cinnamomi* based on (a) all susceptible taxa and (b) highly and moderately susceptible taxa.

the domain of the training data, some of the more restricted landscape types were not well sampled, notably the Jibbon sand plain. In addition, high levels of variability and some false negative test outcomes may be expected due to difficulties in detecting the disease, and may have been responsible for the mediocre performance of the habitat suitability model. Consequently, relatively large numbers of subsamples may be required to detect the disease (or confirm its absence) at any given site. Hierarchical Bayesian detectability models are well suited to deal with these uncertainties by modelling the probability that the disease is detected given that it is present at a site (McCarthy 2008).

An alternative approach to modelling habitat suitability for the pathogen based on occurrence in soil survey sites would be to model expression of disease symptoms in vegetation. This would be informative for risk assessment because the disease may not cause significant impacts on plant diversity in every habitat and location in which a habitat suitability model predicts it could occur. However, diagnosis of symptoms can be uncertain because there may be other causes of plant tissue death and because the symptoms can be relatively transient and hence difficult to detect in early stages of infection and several years after infection when dead remains have decayed. Thus both types of models have strengths and limitations.

Outcomes of the risk assessment may also be sensitive to incomplete data on the susceptibility of vascular flora to the disease. Precise assessments of susceptibility require experimental inoculation of test plants under a range of environmental conditions or thorough field investigations. This has not been done for a large majority of the local flora, although the susceptibility ranks for many species in Royal National Park were assigned by extrapolation from recovery of *P. cinnamomi* from symptomatic plants that were sampled elsewhere (McDougall 2006). This assumes that host susceptibility relationships are consistent within taxa across their geographic distributions. While some intraspecific genetic variation and environmentally regulated variation in susceptibility may be expected across the distribution of each host taxon, our approach was precautionary because it assumes that a species could be susceptible in the study area if symptoms have been recorded on individuals of the same or related species anywhere within their broader range. Although we believe that taxonomic patterns of host susceptibility are sufficiently strong (Cahill et al. 2008) to justify our approach, the models would benefit from improved

susceptibility data to produce a more precise spatial representation of risks posed by the pathogen.

While we caution against interpretation of fine scale spatial patterns in disease risk, and interpretation of risk levels at precise locations, we believe that the major generalisations about the landscapes and areas that are most and least susceptible to the disease (outlined above) are likely to provide a robust basis for disease management, despite the limitations in the underlying data. This is because frequencies of the disease recorded in shale gullies were extremely low (7% positive test results recorded from 114 locations in shale gullies, cf. 23% from 109 locations on sandstone plateau and gullies), and few of the known susceptible species occur within plant communities of shale landscapes. Both of these results contrast markedly with findings for heathlands and sclerophyll woodlands on the sandstone plateau. Secondly, the spatial patterns in disease habitat suitability were reinforced by similar patterns in the distribution of susceptible biota that were derived from independent data. Furthermore, the results are corroborated by more general patterns of disease impacts reported from other parts of temperate Australia (Cahill et al. 2008). The distinction between sandstone ridges, upper slopes and gullies is more subtle and together with risk assessment for the Jibbon sand plain, warrants more precautionary treatment in the design of management strategies until uncertainties can be resolved.

Our model did not address the risks of pathogen introduction. As *P. cinnamomi* can be spread through earthworks and mud on footwear and vehicle tyres, an association may be expected between infestation and roadsides, fire trails, walking tracks and associated drains into bushland. Walsh et al. (2006) failed to detect diminished infestation over distances of 30 m from walking tracks, although a relationship may exist over larger distances extending to remote areas that are more buffered from movement of humans and other dispersal agents. Modelling of risks associated with these relationships would require improved survey data on the occurrence of *P. cinnamomi* that is more evenly stratified in relation to distance and drainage from locations of past and present anthropogenic disturbance. Ideally, it would also incorporate data on the frequency and pattern of track usage, especially when soil surfaces are saturated after rain, as well as fine-scale drainage patterns.

Disease management

Impacts of *P. cinnamomi* are less conspicuous in the Sydney region than in parts of south western

Proc. Linn. Soc. N.S.W., 134, 2012

B157

Australia, Victoria and Tasmania (Cahill et al. 2008). Nonetheless, the disease may cause insidious declines in key biota that have major implications for ecosystem diversity and function, especially on the sandstone plateau where we have shown that risks of disease impacts are greatest. For example, populations of *Xanthorrhoea resinosa*, a major structural component of heathlands on the plateau, are currently undergoing insidious declines related to synergistic effects of fire and disease (Regan et al. 2011). These declines are projected to continue, but the rate of decline will depend on how both disease and fire are managed. There are essentially two groups of management actions for the disease: those that seek to minimise spread; and direct treatment of the disease or its effects. The relative merits of these options depend on context. For example, Keith (2004b) found that quarantine measures to limit the spread of *P. cinnamomi* were likely to have little effect on the viability of highly susceptible *Epacris barbata* populations, whereas direct treatment could be more effective, but only if the treatment reduced plant mortality by at least 90%.

Although the disease is widespread across the study area, there still appear to be some areas that are at considerable risk of impact that are not yet infected. For example, *P. cinnamomi* was not recorded at any of the five sites supporting susceptible populations of *Telopea speciosissima*, despite comprehensive soil sampling. For these and similar sites, hygiene measures, such as restrictions on access during wet conditions and washdown or change of footwear protocols, may help to reduce the risk of infection by limiting dispersal of infected mud.

The habitats most at risk from *P. cinnamomi* are widely distributed and are traversed by some of the most popular walking tracks, including the Coast track, Marley track, Winifred Falls track, Curra Moors track and Uloola track, each of which is used by thousands of walkers each year. High-usage unkerbed roadways also traverse the study area; maintenance of their verges may increase the likelihood of pathogen spread, especially if undertaken during wet weather. As infections are already scattered along these routes, the major management task will be to limit further spread and protect the most valuable assets at risk. These routes, because of their high visitation rates, also provide opportunities to increase public awareness about the impacts of the disease and support for research and management initiatives to minimise its impact. Educational signage, strategically located wash-down stations, adherence to formed tracks, wash-down protocols for offroad

vehicles, precautionary track closures, restrictions on wet weather use and regular dry-weather track maintenance to minimise development of muddy sinks are all appropriate measures to limit disease impacts in these circumstances.

CONCLUSIONS

By combining spatial data on habitat suitability for a disease and the distribution of susceptible biota, it is possible to carry out a spatial analysis of risks posed by disease to support the development of strategies and priorities for disease management. We were able to construct a disease risk map that is likely to be robust for this general purpose using relatively limited disease survey data, available vegetation survey data, existing data bases on plant susceptibility and simple modelling techniques. The axiom of our approach that risks should be proportional to the product of proneness to a threatening process and abundance of susceptible assets should be widely applicable to other management areas as well as other threats to biodiversity. Furthermore this risk model is readily transformed into spatial dimensions, providing a simple information resource for conservation planning.

REFERENCES

Cahill, D.M., Rookes, J.E., Wilson, B.A., Gibson, L. and McDougall, K.L. (2008). *Phytophthora cinnamomi* and Australia's biodiversity: impacts predictions and progress towards control. Turner Review No. 17. *Australian Journal of Botany* 56, 279-310.

DECCW (2009). Draft Native Vegetation of the Sydney Metropolitan Catchment Management Authority Area. NSW Department of Environment, Climate Change and Water, Sydney.

Dobrowolski, M.P., Tommerup, I.C., Shearer, B.L. and O'Brien, P.A. (2003). Three clonal lineages of *Phytophthora cinnamomi* in Australia revealed by microsatellites. *Phytopathology* 93, 695-704.

Elith, J., Graham, C.H., Anderson, R.P. *et al.* (2006). Novel methods improve prediction of species' distributions from occurrence data. *Ecography* 29, 129-151.

Gerrettson-Cornell, L. (1986). *Phytophthora cinnamomi* in New South Wales. Forestry Commission of New South Wales, Sydney.

Halsall, D. (1982). A forest soil suppressive to *Phytophthora cinnamomi* and conducive to *Phytophthora cryptogea*. II. Suppression of sporulation. *Australian Journal of Botany* 30, 27-37.

Hazelton, P.A. and Tille, P.J. (1990). Soil Landscapes of the Wollongong-Port Hacking 1:100 000 Sheet. Soil Conservation Service of NSW, Sydney.

Jaynes, E.T. (1990). Notes on present status and future prospects. In 'Maximum entropy and Bayesian methods' (Eds W.T. Grady Jnr and L.H.Schick) pp. 1-13. (Kluwer: Drordrecht).

Keith, D.A. (2004a). 'Ocean shores to desert dunes: the native vegetation of New South Wales and the ACT'. (NSW Department of Environment and Conservation: Sydney).

Keith, D.A. (2004b). Australian heath shrub (*Epacris barbata*): viability under management options for fire and disease. In 'Species Conservation and Management: case studies' (Eds. H.R. Akcakaya, M.A. Burgman, O. Kindvall, C.C. Wood, P. Sjogren-Gulve, J.S. Hatfield and M.A. McCarthy) pp. 90-103. (Oxford University Press: Oxford).

McCarthy, M.A. (2008). Bayesian methods for ecologists. Cambridge University Press, Cambridge.

McCredie, T.A., Dixon, K.W. and Sivasithamparam, K. (1985). Variability in the resistance of *Banksia* L. f. species to *Phytophthora cinnamomi* Rands. *Australian Journal of Botany* 33, 629-637.

McDougall, K.L. (2006). The responses of native Australian plant species to *Phytophthora cinnamomi*. Appendix 4. In Management of *Phytophthora cinnamomi* for biodiversity conservation in Australia: Part 2. National best practice (E. O'Gara, K. Howard, B. Wilson and G.E.StJ. Hardy) pp. 1-52. (Department of the Environment and Heritage: Canberra).

McDougall, K.L., Hobbs, R.J. and Hardy, G.E.StJ. (2005). Distribution of understorey species in forest affected by *Phytophthora cinnamomi* in south-western Western Australia. *Australian Journal of Botany* 53, 813 – 819.

McDougall, K.L. and Summerell, B.A. (2003). The impact of *Phytophthora cinnamomi* on the flora and vegetation of New South Wales – a re-appraisal. In '*Phytophthora* in Forests and Natural Ecosystems' (Eds J.A. McComb, G.E.StJ. Hardy and I.C. Tommerup) pp. 49-56. (Murdoch University Print: Murdoch, Western Australia).

Phillips, S.J., Anderson, R.J. and Schapire, R.E. (2006). Maximum entropy modelling of species geographic distributions. *Ecological modelling* 190, 231-259.

Pellow, B.J., Henwood, M.J.and Carolin, R.C. (2009). Flora of the Sydney region. Fifth edition. Sydney University Press, Sydney.

Podger, F. D. (1968). Aetiology of jarrah dieback and disease of dry sclerophyll *Eucalyptus marginata* Sm. forests in Western Australia. MSc Thesis, University of Melbourne.

Regan, H.M., Keith, D.A., Regan, T.J., Tozer, M.G. and Tootell, N. (2011). Fire management to combat disease: turning interactions between threats into conservation management. *Oecologia* 167, 873–882.

Shearer, B.L. and Crane, C.E. (2003). The influence of soil from a topographic gradient in the Fitzgerald River National Park on mortality of *Banksia baxteri*

following infection by *Phytophthora cinnamomi*. In '*Phytophthora* in Forests and Natural Ecosystems' (Eds J.A. McComb, G.E.StJ. Hardy and I.C. Tommerup) pp. 267–268. (Murdoch University Print: Murdoch, Western Australia)

Shearer, B.L. and Dillon, M. (1996). Susceptibility of plant species in Banksia woodlands on the Swan Coastal Plain, Western Australia, to infection by *Phytophthora cinnamomi*. *Australian Journal of Botany* 44, 433–445.

Shearer, B.L. and Hill, T.C. (1989). Diseases of *Banksia* woodlands on the Bassendean and Spearwood Dune systems. *Journal of the Royal Society of Western Australia* 71, 113-114.

Tozer, M.G., Turner, K., Keith, D.A., Tindall, D., Pennay, C., Simpson, C., MacKenzie, B., Beukers, P. and Cox, S. (2010). Native vegetation of southeast NSW: a revised classification and map for the coast and eastern tablelands. *Cunninghamia* 11, 359-406.

Tsao, P. H. (1983) Factors affecting isolation and quantitation of *Phytophthora* from soil. In '*Phytophthora*, Its Biology, Taxonomy, Ecology and Pathology' (Eds D.C. Erwin, S. Bartnicki-Garcia and P.H. Tsao) pp. 219-236. (The American Phytopathological Society: St. Paul, Minnesota).

Walsh, J.L., Keith, D.A., McDougall, K.L., Summerell, B.A. and Whelan, R.J. (2006). *Phytophthora* Root Rot: Assessing the potential threat to Australia's oldest national park. *Ecological Management and Restoration* 7, 55-60.

Weste, G. (2001). Interaction between *Phytophthora cinnamomi* and Victorian native plant species growing in the wild. *Australasian Mycologist* 20, 64-72.

Weste, G., Walchhuetter, T. and Walshe, T. (1999). Regeneration of *Xanthorrhoea australis* following epidemic disease due to *Phytophthora cinnamomi* in the Brisbane Ranges, Victoria. *Australasian Plant Pathology* 28, 162-169.

Wills, R.T. and Keighery, G.J. (1994). Ecological impact of plant disease on plant communities. *Journal of the Royal Society of Western Australia* 77, 127-132.a

Wilson, B.A., Aberton, J. and Cahill, D.M. (2000). Relationships between site factors and distribution of *Phytophthora cinnamomi* in the Eastern Otway Ranges, Victoria. *Australian Journal of Botany* 48, 247-260.

Wilson, B.A., Lewis, A. and Aberton, J. (2003). Spatial model for predicting the presence of cinnamon fungus (*Phytophthora cinnamomi*) in sclerophyll vegetation communities in south-eastern Australia. *Austral Ecology* 28, 108-115.

Appendix 1

Susceptibility to *Phytophthora cinnamomi* of plant taxa recorded in Royal National Park, Heathcote National Park and Garrawarra State Conservation Area. Nomenclature follows Pellow et al. (2009). 1 - known or suspected to be susceptible. 0 - not known or suspected to be susceptible (includes taxa with no data). Known susceptibility is based on isolation of the pathogen from plants exhibiting disease symptoms. Suspected susceptibility is based on evidence from a congeneric taxon.

Taxon	High, moderate or low susceptibility to Phytophthora (known or suspected)	High or moderate susceptibility to Phytophthora (known or suspected)
Abrophyllum ornans	0	0
Acacia binervata	1	0
Acacia binervia	1	0
Acacia brownii	1	0
Acacia elongata	1	0
Acacia floribunda	1	0
Acacia hispidula	1	0
Acacia implexa	1	0
Acacia irrorata subsp. *irrorata*	1	0
Acacia linearifolia	0	0
Acacia linifolia	1	0
Acacia longifolia subsp. *longifolia*	1	0
Acacia longifolia subsp. *sophorae*	1	0
Acacia longissima	1	0
Acacia maidenii	1	0
Acacia mearnsii	1	0
Acacia melanoxylon	0	0
Acacia myrtifolia	1	0
Acacia obtusifolia	1	0
Acacia stricta	1	0
Acacia suaveolens	1	0
Acacia terminalis	1	1
Acacia ulicifolia	1	0
Acmena smithii	0	0
Acronychia oblongifolia	0	0
Acrotriche divaricata	1	1
Actinotus helianthi	0	0
Actinotus minor	0	0
Adiantum aethiopicum	0	0
Adiantum formosum	0	0
Adiantum hispidulum	0	0
Adiantum silvaticum	0	0

Taxon	High, moderate or low susceptibility to Phytophthora (known or suspected)	High or moderate susceptibility to Phytophthora (known or suspected)
Aegiceras corniculatum	0	0
Alectryon subcinereus	0	0
Allocasuarina distyla	1	1
Allocasuarina littoralis	1	0
Allocasuarina nana	1	1
Allocasuarina paludosa	0	0
Allocasuarina torulosa	1	1
Allocasuarina verticillata	0	0
Almaleea paludosa	0	0
Alphitonia excelsa	1	0
Alternanthera denticulata	0	0
Amperea xiphoclada	1	0
Amphipogon strictus var. *strictus*	1	0
Angophora costata	1	0
Angophora floribunda	1	0
Angophora hispida	1	0
Anisopogon avenaceus	0	0
Aotus ericoides	1	1
Aphanopetalum resinosum	0	0
Apium prostratum	0	0
Aristida vagans	0	0
Aristida warburgii	0	0
Arthropodium milleflorum	0	0
Arthropteris tenella	0	0
Asplenium australasicum	0	0
Asplenium flabellifolium	0	0
Asplenium polyodon	0	0
Astroloma humifusum	1	1
Astroloma pinifolium	1	0
Austrodanthonia monticola	0	0
Austrodanthonia racemosa var. *racemosa*	0	0
Austromyrtus tenuifolia	0	0
Austrostipa puberula	0	0
Austrostipa pubescens	1	0
Avicennia marina subsp. *australasica*	0	0
Backhousia myrtifolia	0	0
Baeckea imbricata	1	1
Baeckea linifolia	1	1

Taxon	High, moderate or low susceptibility to Phytophthora (known or suspected)	High or moderate susceptibility to Phytophthora (known or suspected)
Baloskion gracile	0	0
Banksia ericifolia subsp. *ericifolia*	1	0
Banksia integrifolia subsp. *integrifolia*	1	1
Banksia marginata	1	0
Banksia oblongifolia	1	1
Banksia robur	1	1
Banksia serrata	1	0
Banksia spinulosa	1	0
Bauera microphylla	1	1
Bauera rubioides	1	0
Baumea acuta	0	0
Baumea articulata	0	0
Baumea juncea	0	0
Baumea rubiginosa	0	0
Baumea teretifolia	0	0
Bertya pomaderroides	0	0
Billardiera scandens	0	0
Blandfordia nobilis	1	1
Blechnum camfieldii	0	0
Blechnum cartilagineum	0	0
Blechnum indicum	0	0
Blechnum nudum	0	0
Blechnum patersonii	0	0
Blechnum wattsii	0	0
Boronia ledifolia	1	1
Boronia parviflora	0	0
Boronia serrulata	1	1
Bossiaea ensata	1	1
Bossiaea heterophylla	1	1
Bossiaea rhombifolia subsp. *rhombifolia*	1	1
Bossiaea scolopendria	1	1
Bossiaea stephensonii	1	1
Brachyloma daphnoides	1	0
Brachyscome angustifolia	1	0
Breynia oblongifolia	0	0
Brunoniella australis	0	0
Brunoniella pumilio	0	0
Burchardia umbellata	0	0

B162

Proc. Linn. Soc. N.S.W., 134, 2012

Taxon	High, moderate or low susceptibility to Phytophthora (known or suspected)	High or moderate susceptibility to Phytophthora (known or suspected)
Bursaria spinosa	0	0
Callicoma serratifolia	0	0
Callistemon citrinus	0	0
Callistemon linearis	0	0
Callistemon subulatus	0	0
Callitris muelleri	0	0
Callitris rhomboidea	0	0
Calochlaena dubia	0	0
Calystegia marginata	0	0
Calystegia sepium subsp. *roseata*	0	0
Calytrix tetragona	1	1
Carex appressa	0	0
Carex breviculmis	0	0
Carex brunnea	0	0
Carex gaudichaudiana	0	0
Carpobrotus glaucescens	0	0
Cassinia aculeata	0	0
Cassinia aureonitens	0	0
Cassinia denticulata	0	0
Cassinia trinerva	0	0
Cassytha glabella	0	0
Cassytha pubescens	0	0
Casuarina glauca	0	0
Caustis flexuosa	0	0
Caustis pentandra	0	0
Caustis recurvata	0	0
Cayratia clematidea	0	0
Cenchrus caliculatus	0	0
Centella asiatica	0	0
Centrolepis fascicularis	0	0
Centrolepis strigosa subsp. *strigosa*	0	0
Ceratopetalum apetalum	0	0
Ceratopetalum gummiferum	0	0
Cheilanthes sieberi subsp. *sieberi*	0	0
Chloanthes stoechadis	0	0
Chordifex dimorphus	0	0
Chordifex fastigiatus	0	0
Chorizandra cymbaria	0	0

Proc. Linn. Soc. N.S.W., 134, 2012

B163

Taxon	High, moderate or low susceptibility to Phytophthora (known or suspected)	High or moderate susceptibility to Phytophthora (known or suspected)
Chorizandra sphaerocephala	0	0
Christella dentata	0	0
Chrysocephalum apiculatum	0	0
Cissus antarctica	0	0
Cissus hypoglauca	0	0
Citronella moorei	0	0
Claoxylon australe	0	0
Clematis aristata	1	0
Clematis glycinoides var. *glycinoides*	1	0
Clerodendrum tomentosum	0	0
Comesperma defoliatum	0	0
Comesperma ericinum	1	0
Comesperma retusum	0	0
Comesperma sphaerocarpum	0	0
Comesperma volubile	0	0
Commelina cyanea	0	0
Conospermum ellipticum	1	0
Conospermum longifolium	1	0
Conospermum taxifolium	1	0
Conospermum tenuifolium	1	0
Convolvulus erubescens	0	0
Coprosma quadrifida	0	0
Coronidium elatum	0	0
Coronidium scorpioides	0	0
Correa alba var. *alba*	1	0
Correa reflexa	1	0
Corymbia gummifera	1	0
Crassula sieberiana	0	0
Crowea saligna	1	0
Cryptandra amara	1	0
Cryptandra ericoides	1	0
Cryptocarya glaucescens	0	0
Cryptocarya microneura	0	0
Cupaniopsis anacardioides	0	0
Cyathea australis	0	0
Cyathea leichhardtiana	0	0
Cyathochaeta diandra	0	0
Cyclophyllum longipetalum	0	0

B164

Proc. Linn. Soc. N.S.W., 134, 2012

Taxon	High, moderate or low susceptibility to Phytophthora (known or suspected)	High or moderate susceptibility to Phytophthora (known or suspected)
Cymbopogon refractus	0	0
Cyperus enervis	0	0
Cyperus gracilis	0	0
Cyperus imbecillis	0	0
Cyperus polystachyos	0	0
Cyperus sanguinolentus	0	0
Cyperus tetraphyllus	0	0
Dampiera purpurea	1	0
Dampiera stricta	1	0
Darwinia diminuta	1	1
Darwinia fascicularis	1	1
Darwinia leptantha	0	0
Davallia solida var. pyxidata	0	0
Daviesia acicularis	0	0
Daviesia alata	1	1
Daviesia corymbosa	1	1
Daviesia ulicifolia	1	0
Dennstaedtia davallioides	0	0
Desmodium brachypodum	0	0
Desmodium rhytidophyllum	0	0
Desmodium varians	0	0
Dianella caerulea	1	0
Dianella longifolia	1	0
Dianella prunina	1	0
Dianella revoluta var. revoluta	1	0
Dichelachne crinita	0	0
Dichelachne micrantha	0	0
Dichelachne rara	0	0
Dichondra repens	0	0
Dicksonia antarctica	0	0
Digitaria parviflora	0	0
Dillwynia elegans	1	1
Dillwynia floribunda	1	1
Dillwynia glaberrima	1	1
Dillwynia ramosissima	1	1
Dillwynia retorta	1	1
Dioscorea transversa	0	0
Diospyros australis	0	0

Proc. Linn. Soc. N.S.W., 134, 2012

B165

Taxon	High, moderate or low susceptibility to Phytophthora (known or suspected)	High or moderate susceptibility to Phytophthora (known or suspected)
Diploglottis cunninghamii	0	0
Dodonaea triquetra	0	0
Doodia aspera	0	0
Doodia caudata	0	0
Doryanthes excelsa	0	0
Doryphora sassafras	0	0
Drosera auriculata	1	0
Drosera binata	1	0
Drosera peltata	1	0
Drosera pygmaea	1	0
Drosera spatulata	1	0
Duboisia myoporoides	0	0
Echinopogon caespitosus var. *caespitosus*	0	0
Echinopogon ovatus	0	0
Einadia hastata	0	0
Einadia nutans	0	0
Elaeocarpus reticulatus	1	1
Elaeodendron australe	0	0
Eleocharis acuta	0	0
Eleocharis sphacelata	0	0
Empodisma minus	0	0
Endiandra sieberi	0	0
Entolasia marginata	0	0
Entolasia stricta	0	0
Epacris longiflora	1	1
Epacris microphylla	1	1
Epacris obtusifolia	1	0
Epacris pulchella	1	1
Epaltes australis	0	0
Eragrostis brownii	0	0
Eriostemon australasius	0	0
Eryngium vesiculosum	0	0
Eucalyptus agglomerata	1	0
Eucalyptus botryoides	1	0
Eucalyptus botryoides <--> *saligna*	1	0
Eucalyptus camfieldii	1	0
Eucalyptus capitellata	1	0
Eucalyptus consideniana	1	0

Taxon	High, moderate or low susceptibility to Phytophthora (known or suspected)	High or moderate susceptibility to Phytophthora (known or suspected)
Eucalyptus globoidea	1	0
Eucalyptus haemastoma	1	0
Eucalyptus luehmanniana	1	0
Eucalyptus multicaulis	1	0
Eucalyptus oblonga	1	0
Eucalyptus obstans	1	0
Eucalyptus paniculata subsp. paniculata	1	0
Eucalyptus pilularis	1	0
Eucalyptus piperita	1	0
Eucalyptus punctata	1	0
Eucalyptus racemosa	1	0
Eucalyptus resinifera	1	0
Eucalyptus saligna	1	0
Eucalyptus scias	1	0
Eucalyptus sieberi	1	0
Eucalyptus squamosa	1	0
Eucalyptus tereticornis	1	0
Euchiton gymnocephalus	0	0
Eupomatia laurina	0	0
Euroschinus falcatus var. falcatus	0	0
Eurychorda complanata	0	0
Euryomyrtus ramosissima subsp. ramosissima	1	0
Eustrephus latifolius	0	0
Exocarpos cupressiformis	0	0
Exocarpos strictus	0	0
Ficinia nodosa	0	0
Ficus coronata	0	0
Ficus obliqua var. obliqua	0	0
Ficus rubiginosa	0	0
Ficus superba var. henneana	0	0
Flagellaria indica	0	0
Gahnia aspera	0	0
Gahnia clarkei	0	0
Gahnia erythrocarpa	0	0
Gahnia melanocarpa	0	0
Gahnia microstachya	0	0
Gahnia radula	0	0
Gahnia sieberiana	0	0

Taxon	High, moderate or low susceptibility to Phytophthora (known or suspected)	High or moderate susceptibility to Phytophthora (known or suspected)
Galium propinquum	0	0
Geijera salicifolia	0	0
Geitonoplesium cymosum	0	0
Geranium homeanum	0	0
Geranium solanderi	0	0
Gleichenia dicarpa	1	0
Gleichenia microphylla	1	0
Gleichenia rupestris	1	0
Glochidion ferdinandi	0	0
Glycine clandestina	0	0
Glycine microphylla	0	0
Gompholobium glabratum	1	1
Gompholobium grandiflorum	1	1
Gompholobium latifolium	1	1
Gompholobium minus	0	0
Gonocarpus micranthus	1	0
Gonocarpus tetragynus	1	0
Gonocarpus teucrioides	1	0
Goodenia bellidifolia subsp. *bellidifolia*	1	0
Goodenia dimorpha	1	0
Goodenia hederacea subsp. *hederacea*	1	0
Goodenia heterophylla	1	0
Goodenia ovata	1	0
Goodenia paniculata	0	0
Goodenia stelligera	1	0
Grammitis billardierei	0	0
Grevillea buxifolia subsp. *buxifolia*	1	1
Grevillea diffusa	1	1
Grevillea longifolia	1	1
Grevillea mucronulata	1	1
Grevillea oleoides	1	0
Grevillea parviflora subsp. *parviflora*	1	1
Grevillea sericea subsp. *sericea*	1	1
Grevillea sphacelata	1	1
Guioa semiglauca	0	0
Gymnoschoenus sphaerocephalus	0	0
Gymnostachys anceps	0	0
Haemodorum corymbosum	0	0

B168

Proc. Linn. Soc. N.S.W., 134, 2012

Taxon	High, moderate or low susceptibility to Phytophthora (known or suspected)	High or moderate susceptibility to Phytophthora (known or suspected)
Haemodorum planifolium	0	0
Hakea dactyloides	1	0
Hakea gibbosa	1	1
Hakea propinqua	1	1
Hakea salicifolia	1	1
Hakea sericea	1	1
Hakea teretifolia	1	1
Hardenbergia violacea	0	0
Harmogia densifolia	0	0
Hedycarya angustifolia	0	0
Hemarthria uncinata var. uncinata	0	0
Hemigenia purpurea	0	0
Hibbertia acicularis	0	0
Hibbertia aspera subsp. aspera	1	1
Hibbertia bracteata	1	1
Hibbertia dentata	1	1
Hibbertia empetrifolia subsp. empetrifolia	1	1
Hibbertia fasciculata	1	1
Hibbertia linearis	1	1
Hibbertia monogyna	1	1
Hibbertia nitida	1	1
Hibbertia obtusifolia	0	0
Hibbertia riparia	1	1
Hibbertia scandens	1	1
Hibbertia serpyllifolia	1	1
Histiopteris incisa	0	0
Hovea linearis	1	1
Hovea longifolia	1	1
Hybanthus monopetalus	1	0
Hydrocotyle acutiloba	0	0
Hydrocotyle geraniifolia	0	0
Hydrocotyle laxiflora	0	0
Hydrocotyle sibthorpioides	0	0
Hydrocotyle tripartita	0	0
Hymenophyllum cupressiforme	0	0
Hypericum gramineum	0	0
Hypericum japonicum	0	0
Hypolaena fastigiata	0	0

Taxon	High, moderate or low susceptibility to Phytophthora (known or suspected)	High or moderate susceptibility to Phytophthora (known or suspected)
Hypolepis muelleri	0	0
Hypoxis hygrometrica	0	0
Imperata cylindrica	0	0
Indigofera australis	0	0
Ipomoea brasiliensis	0	0
Isachne globosa	0	0
Isolepis cernua	0	0
Isolepis inundata	0	0
Isopogon anemonifolius	1	0
Isopogon anethifolius	1	1
Isotoma fluviatilis	0	0
Joycea pallida	0	0
Juncus continuus	0	0
Juncus kraussii subsp. *australiensis*	0	0
Juncus planifolius	0	0
Juncus prismatocarpus	0	0
Juncus usitatus	0	0
Kennedia rubicunda	1	1
Korthalsella rubra	0	0
Kunzea ambigua	1	0
Kunzea capitata	1	0
Lachnagrostis filiformis	0	0
Lagenophora stipitata	0	0
Lambertia formosa	1	0
Lasiopetalum ferrugineum	1	0
Lasiopetalum parviflorum	0	0
Lasiopetalum rufum	1	0
Lastreopsis acuminata	0	0
Lastreopsis decomposita	0	0
Lastreopsis microsora subsp. *microsora*	0	0
Laxmannia gracilis	0	0
Legnephora moorei	0	0
Leionema dentatum	1	0
Lepidosperma concavum	0	0
Lepidosperma filiforme	0	0
Lepidosperma forsythii	0	0
Lepidosperma gunnii	0	0
Lepidosperma latens	0	0

Taxon	High, moderate or low susceptibility to Phytophthora (known or suspected)	High or moderate susceptibility to Phytophthora (known or suspected)
Lepidosperma laterale	0	0
Lepidosperma limicola	0	0
Lepidosperma longitudinale	0	0
Lepidosperma neesii	0	0
Lepidosperma urophorum	0	0
Lepidosperma viscidum	0	0
Leptinella longipes	0	0
Leptocarpus tenax	0	0
Leptomeria acida	1	0
Leptospermum arachnoides	1	0
Leptospermum continentale	1	0
Leptospermum grandifolium	1	0
Leptospermum juniperinum	1	0
Leptospermum laevigatum	1	0
Leptospermum morrisonii	1	0
Leptospermum parvifolium	1	0
Leptospermum polygalifolium subsp. polygalifolium	1	0
Leptospermum squarrosum	1	0
Leptospermum trinervium	1	0
Lepyrodia anarthria	0	0
Lepyrodia scariosa	0	0
Leucopogon amplexicaulis	1	1
Leucopogon ericoides	1	1
Leucopogon esquamatus	1	1
Leucopogon juniperinus	1	1
Leucopogon lanceolatus var. lanceolatus	0	0
Leucopogon microphyllus	1	1
Leucopogon parviflorus	1	0
Leucopogon setiger	1	1
Leucopogon virgatus	0	0
Lindsaea linearis	1	0
Lindsaea microphylla	1	0
Lissanthe strigosa	1	1
Livistona australis	0	0
Lobelia anceps	0	0
Lobelia andrewsii	0	0
Lobelia dentata	0	0

Taxon	High, moderate or low susceptibility to Phytophthora (known or suspected)	High or moderate susceptibility to Phytophthora (known or suspected)
Logania albiflora	1	0
Lomandra brevis	1	1
Lomandra confertifolia	0	0
Lomandra cylindrica	0	0
Lomandra filiformis	1	1
Lomandra fluviatilis	1	1
Lomandra glauca	1	1
Lomandra gracilis	1	1
Lomandra longifolia	0	0
Lomandra multiflora subsp. *multiflora*	1	1
Lomandra obliqua	0	0
Lomatia myricoides	1	0
Lomatia silaifolia	1	0
Lophostemon confertus	0	0
Ludwigia peploides subsp. *montevidensis*	0	0
Lycopodium deuterodensum	1	0
Macrozamia communis	0	0
Macrozamia spiralis	1	1
Marsdenia flavescens	0	0
Marsdenia rostrata	0	0
Marsdenia suaveolens	0	0
Melaleuca armillaris subsp. *armillaris*	1	1
Melaleuca deanei	1	1
Melaleuca ericifolia	1	1
Melaleuca hypericifolia	1	1
Melaleuca nodosa	1	1
Melaleuca styphelioides	1	1
Melaleuca thymifolia	1	1
Melodinus australis	0	0
Mentha satureioides	0	0
Micrantheum ericoides	0	0
Microlaena stipoides var. *stipoides*	0	0
Micromyrtus ciliata	0	0
Microsorum scandens	0	0
Mirbelia rubiifolia	0	0
Mirbelia speciosa	0	0
Mitrasacme paludosa	0	0
Mitrasacme polymorpha	0	0

Taxon	High, moderate or low susceptibility to Phytophthora (known or suspected)	High or moderate susceptibility to Phytophthora (known or suspected)
Monotaxis linifolia	1	0
Monotoca elliptica	1	0
Monotoca scoparia	1	1
Morinda jasminoides	0	0
Muellerina celastroides	0	0
Muellerina eucalyptoides	0	0
Myrsine howittiana	0	0
Myrsine variabilis	0	0
Nematolepis squamea subsp. *squamea*	0	0
Neolitsea dealbata	0	0
Notelaea longifolia	0	0
Notelaea ovata	0	0
Notelaea venosa	0	0
Notodanthonia longifolia	0	0
Olax stricta	1	0
Olearia microphylla	1	0
Olearia viscidula	1	0
Omalanthus nutans	0	0
Opercularia aspera	1	0
Opercularia diphylla	1	0
Opercularia hispida	1	0
Opercularia varia	1	0
Oplismenus aemulus	0	0
Oplismenus imbecillis	0	0
Oxalis chnoodes	0	0
Oxalis exilis	0	0
Oxalis perennans	0	0
Oxalis rubens	0	0
Ozothamnus diosmifolius	0	0
Palmeria scandens	0	0
Pandorea pandorana	0	0
Panicum simile	0	0
Parsonsia straminea	0	0
Paspalidium distans	0	0
Paspalum distichum	0	0
Passiflora herbertiana subsp. *herbertiana*	0	0
Patersonia fragilis	1	1
Patersonia glabrata	1	0

Taxon	High, moderate or low susceptibility to Phytophthora (known or suspected)	High or moderate susceptibility to Phytophthora (known or suspected)
Patersonia longifolia	1	1
Patersonia sericea	1	1
Pelargonium australe	0	0
Pelargonium inodorum	0	0
Pellaea falcata	0	0
Pellaea paradoxa	0	0
Peperomia blanda var. *floribunda*	0	0
Peperomia tetraphylla	0	0
Persicaria decipiens	0	0
Persicaria praetermissa	0	0
Persoonia lanceolata	1	1
Persoonia laurina	1	1
Persoonia levis	0	0
Persoonia linearis	0	0
Persoonia pinifolia	1	1
Petrophile pulchella	1	1
Petrophile sessilis	1	1
Phebalium squamulosum	1	1
Philotheca buxifolia	0	0
Philotheca salsolifolia	0	0
Philotheca scabra subsp. *scabra*	0	0
Philydrum lanuginosum	0	0
Phragmites australis	0	0
Phyllanthus gunnii	0	0
Phyllanthus hirtellus	0	0
Phyllota phylicoides	1	1
Pimelea linifolia	1	0
Pittosporum multiflorum	0	0
Pittosporum revolutum	0	0
Pittosporum undulatum	0	0
Planchonella australis	0	0
Plantago debilis	0	0
Platycerium bifurcatum	0	0
Platylobium formosum	1	1
Platysace ericoides	1	0
Platysace lanceolata	0	0
Platysace linearifolia	1	0
Platysace stephensonii	1	0

Taxon	High, moderate or low susceptibility to Phytophthora (known or suspected)	High or moderate susceptibility to Phytophthora (known or suspected)
Plectranthus parviflorus	0	0
Poa affinis	0	0
Poa labillardierei var. *labillardierei*	0	0
Poa poiformis var. *poiformis*	0	0
Podocarpus spinulosus	1	0
Polymeria calycina	0	0
Polyosma cunninghamii	0	0
Polyscias elegans	1	0
Polyscias murrayi	1	0
Polyscias sambucifolia	1	0
Polystichum australiense	0	0
Pomaderris andromedifolia	0	0
Pomaderris discolor	0	0
Pomaderris elliptica subsp. *elliptica*	0	0
Pomaderris ferruginea	0	0
Pomaderris intermedia	0	0
Pomaderris lanigera	0	0
Pomax umbellata	0	0
Poranthera corymbosa	0	0
Poranthera ericifolia	0	0
Poranthera microphylla	0	0
Potamogeton tricarinatus	0	0
Pratia purpurascens	0	0
Prostanthera densa	1	1
Prostanthera incisa	1	1
Prostanthera linearis	1	1
Pseudanthus pimeleoides	0	0
Pseuderanthemum variabile	0	0
Psilotum nudum	0	0
Psychotria loniceroides	0	0
Pteridium esculentum	1	0
Pteris tremula	0	0
Ptilothrix deusta	0	0
Pultenaea blakelyi	1	1
Pultenaea daphnoides	1	1
Pultenaea dentata	1	1
Pultenaea flexilis	1	1
Pultenaea hispidula	1	1

Taxon	High, moderate or low susceptibility to Phytophthora (known or suspected)	High or moderate susceptibility to Phytophthora (known or suspected)
Pultenaea linophylla	1	1
Pultenaea parviflora	0	0
Pultenaea retusa	1	1
Pultenaea scabra	1	0
Pultenaea stipularis	1	1
Pultenaea tuberculata	1	1
Pyrrosia rupestris	0	0
Ranunculus inundatus	0	0
Ranunculus lappaceus	0	0
Rhagodia candolleana subsp. *candolleana*	0	0
Rhodamnia rubescens	1	0
Rhytidosporum procumbens	0	0
Ricinocarpos pinifolius	0	0
Ripogonum album	0	0
Rorippa gigantea	0	0
Rubus moluccanus var. trilobus	0	0
Rubus parvifolius	0	0
Rubus rosifolius	0	0
Rulingia hermanniifolia	0	0
Rumex brownii	0	0
Samolus repens	0	0
Santalum obtusifolium	0	0
Sarcocornia quinqueflora subsp. *quinqueflora*	0	0
Sarcopetalum harveyanum	0	0
Scaevola ramosissima	1	0
Schelhammera undulata	0	0
Schizaea bifida	0	0
Schizaea fistulosa	0	0
Schizaea rupestris	0	0
Schizomeria ovata	0	0
Schoenus apogon	0	0
Schoenus brevifolius	0	0
Schoenus ericetorum	0	0
Schoenus imberbis	0	0
Schoenus lepidosperma subsp. *pachylepis*	0	0
Schoenus melanostachys	0	0
Schoenus moorei	0	0
Scolopia braunii	0	0

B176

Proc. Linn. Soc. N.S.W., 134, 2012

Taxon	High, moderate or low susceptibility to Phytophthora (known or suspected)	High or moderate susceptibility to Phytophthora (known or suspected)
Selaginella uliginosa	1	0
Senecio bipinnatisectus	0	0
Senecio hispidulus	0	0
Senecio lautus	0	0
Senecio linearifolius	0	0
Senecio minimus	0	0
Sigesbeckia orientalis subsp. *orientalis*	0	0
Sloanea australis	0	0
Smilax australis	0	0
Smilax glyciphylla	0	0
Solanum americanum	0	0
Solanum aviculare	0	0
Solanum prinophyllum	0	0
Solanum stelligerum	0	0
Sowerbaea juncea	0	0
Sphaerolobium vimineum	1	0
Spinifex sericeus	0	0
Sporadanthus gracilis	0	0
Sporobolus virginicus	0	0
Sprengelia incarnata	1	1
Stackhousia viminea	0	0
Stenocarpus salignus	0	0
Stephania japonica var. *discolor*	0	0
Stylidium graminifolium	1	1
Stylidium laricifolium	0	0
Stylidium lineare	1	1
Stylidium productum	1	1
Styphelia triflora	1	1
Styphelia tubiflora	1	1
Styphelia viridis subsp. *viridis*	1	1
Symphionema paludosum	0	0
Syncarpia glomulifera subsp. *glomulifera*	0	0
Synoum glandulosum subsp. *glandulosum*	0	0
Syzygium australe	0	0
Syzygium oleosum	1	0
Syzygium paniculatum	0	0
Tasmannia insipida	1	1
Telopea speciosissima	1	1

Proc. Linn. Soc. N.S.W., 134, 2012

B177

Taxon	High, moderate or low susceptibility to Phytophthora (known or suspected)	High or moderate susceptibility to Phytophthora (known or suspected)
Tetragonia tetragonioides	0	0
Tetraria capillaris	0	0
Tetrarrhena turfosa	0	0
Tetratheca ericifolia	1	1
Tetratheca neglecta	1	1
Tetratheca shiressii	1	1
Tetratheca thymifolia	1	1
Thelionema umbellatum	0	0
Themeda australis	1	0
Thysanotus juncifolius	1	0
Thysanotus tuberosus subsp. *tuberosus*	1	0
Todea barbara	0	0
Toona ciliata	0	0
Trachymene incisa subsp. *incisa*	0	0
Trema tomentosa var. *aspera*	0	0
Tricoryne elatior	0	0
Tricoryne simplex	0	0
Tricostularia pauciflora	0	0
Triglochin procera	0	0
Triglochin striata	0	0
Tristania neriifolia	0	0
Tristaniopsis collina	0	0
Tristaniopsis laurina	0	0
Trochocarpa laurina	1	0
Trophis scandens subsp. *scandens*	0	0
Tylophora barbata	0	0
Urtica incisa	0	0
Utricularia australis	0	0
Utricularia dichotoma	0	0
Utricularia lateriflora	0	0
Utricularia uliginosa	0	0
Vernonia cinerea var. *cinerea*	0	0
Veronica plebeia	0	0
Villarsia exaltata	0	0
Viminaria juncea	0	0
Viola betonicifolia subsp. *betonicifolia*	0	0
Viola hederacea	0	0
Viola sieberiana	0	0

Taxon	High, moderate or low susceptibility to Phytophthora (known or suspected)	High or moderate susceptibility to Phytophthora (known or suspected)
Wahlenbergia gracilis	0	0
Westringia fruticosa	0	0
Wilkiea huegeliana	0	0
Woollsia pungens	1	0
Xanthorrhoea arborea	1	1
Xanthorrhoea latifolia subsp. *latifolia*	1	1
Xanthorrhoea macronema	1	1
Xanthorrhoea media	1	1
Xanthorrhoea resinosa	1	1
Xanthosia pilosa	0	0
Xanthosia tridentata	0	0
Xerochrysum bracteatum	0	0
Xylomelum pyriforme	1	0
Xyris gracilis	0	0
Xyris operculata	0	0
Zieria compacta	0	0
Zieria laevigata	0	0
Zieria pilosa	0	0
Zieria smithii	0	0
Zornia dyctiocarpa var. *dyctiocarpa*	0	0

Proc. Linn. Soc. N.S.W., 134, 2012

B179

Vegetation Dynamics in Coastal Heathlands of the Sydney Basin

David A. Keith[1,2] and Mark G. Tozer[1]

[1]New South Wales Office of Environment and Heritage, PO Box 1967, Hurstville NSW 2220, Australia.
Email: david.keith@unsw.edu.au
[2]Australian Wetlands and Rivers Centre, University of New South Wales, Sydney NSW 2052, Australia.
Email: mark.tozer@environment.nsw.gov.au

Published on 3 September 2012 at http://escholarship.library.usyd.edu.au/journals/index.php/LIN

Keith, D.A. and Tozer, M.G. (2012). Vegetation dynamics in coastal heathlands of the Sydney Basin. *Proceedings of the Linnean Society of New South Wales* **134**, B181-B197.

Heathlands are dynamic ecosystems that change in response to fire regimes and climate variations, as well as endogenous processes such as competition between component species. An understanding of how heathlands change through time is central to the development of management strategies that aim to conserve them and maintain coexistence of their plants and animals. We briefly review the development of this understanding for Sydney's coastal heathlands from the emergence of the first published work in the 1930s. In our previous work, we focussed on fire regimes and interspecific competition between plants as important processes that drive ecosystem dynamics (succession) and mediate species coexistence and diversity. Here, we synthesise our understanding of heathland dynamics into a state and transition framework. We first develop a simple classification of heathland states based on their composition of plant functional types and developmental stage with time since fire. We then propose a qualitative model that predicts transitions between states conditional upon intervals between fires,, fire-mediated life cycle processes of component plant species and interactions between species. We applied the model to predict qualitative changes in heathland state under contrasting fire regime scenarios, and tested example predictions using a long-term study of heathland dynamics in Royal National Park. Empirical observations of overstorey and understorey change were generally consistent with model predictions, subject to variability between sites. Importantly, the model helps to identify fire scenarios that promote dynamic coexistence of multiple heathland states that each support different components of heathland biota. We conclude that simple process models can be very useful for informing management decisions by describing expected responses to alternative management strategies. These predictions lend themselves to testing in adaptive management experiments that seek to spread risks and improve understanding of ecosystem dynamics for future management.

Manuscript received 26 March 2012, accepted for publication 29 May 2012.

Keywords: adaptive management, biodiversity monitoring, competition, fire management, fire regime, long term ecological study, plant functional types, state and transition model, succession, vegetation change.

INTRODUCTION

Heathlands are a spectacular feature of Sydney's coastline, familiar to residents who venture into the city's bushland, as well as visitors who approach the city by air or sea. These heathlands are greatest in extent and diversity within Royal National Park, although the peninsula between Sydney Harbour and Botany Bay may once have supported a similar area and diversity of heathland communities. The striking transformation of bushland into urban landscapes within a few human generations makes it easy to think of the remaining bushland as unchanged. Yet these ecosystems themselves undergo remarkable cyclical and directional changes over decadal time scales and there is evidence that this dynamism is partly responsible for maintenance of biological diversity within heathland landscapes (Keith et al. 2007a). Understanding cause - effect mechanisms of vegetation dynamics is therefore fundamental to the development of management strategies for conservation of biodiversity in the remaining natural areas.

By summarising a set of beliefs about how the world works, process models can help explain the

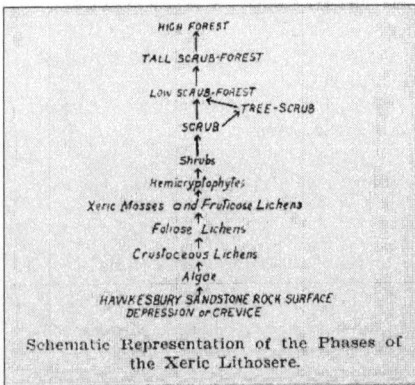

HIGH FOREST
↑
TALL SCRUB-FOREST
↑
LOW SCRUB-FOREST
↑ ↗ TREE-SCRUB
SCRUB
↑
Shrubs
↑
Hemicryptophytes
↑
Xeric Mosses and Fruticose Lichens
↑
Foliose Lichens
↑
Crustaceous Lichens
↑
Algae
HAWKESBURY SANDSTONE ROCK SURFACE
DEPRESSION or CREVICE

Schematic Representation of the Phases of
the Xeric Lithosere.

Figure 1. Pidgeon's (1938) model of plant succession on the Hawkesbury sandstone (Source: Proceedings of the Linnean Society of New South Wales Volume 63, p16). Heath is represented by the terms 'shrubs' and 'scrub'.

causes and effects of ecosystem behaviour. Models may be verbal, graphical, diagrammatic, physical or quantitative representations of ecosystem behaviour (Pickett and Cadenasso 2002). As well as serving explanatory roles, models may be used to make predictions about future ecosystem responses to particular scenarios or circumstances. The construction of a model can also have collateral benefits by enforcing logical consistency, promoting scrutiny of dependencies between ecosystem components and highlighting gaps in current knowledge that may be pivotal to predictive outcomes. Process models are therefore useful tools for translating concepts and generalisations into practical support for decision-making in ecosystem management (Hobbs and Suding 2009) and are central to adaptive management strategies where they can be used to inform setting of objectives, designing plausible alternative management strategies and measuring performance of management actions (Rumpff et al. 2011).

In this paper we present the first step in the development of a model of vegetation dynamics for coastal heathlands of the Sydney basin. We focus on heathlands in Royal National Park, but also draw from research in other Sydney coastal heathlands, so the model is generically applicable to those areas. We first describe the heathlands and briefly review the development of knowledge about salient processes that govern vegetation dynamics. We then construct a model framework to describe alternative heathland states, identify the variables that define them, and

the salient processes that govern transitions between different states over time. We apply the model to different scenarios of environmental change and compare predictions to observed outcomes by use of retrospective comparisons. Finally, we summarise some implications of model predictions for future management and research in the heathlands and comment on the potential of the model to contribute to adaptive management.

Sydney coastal heathlands

The scope of our model is defined by the Sydney Coastal Heaths vegetation class described by Keith (2004). These heaths are fire-prone plant communities restricted to very infertile soils derived from Triassic and Permian quartzose sandstones on elevated plateaus within a few kilometres of the coast between Gosford and Jervis Bay. They are characterised by a high diversity of sclerophyllous plants from families Proteaceae, Myrtaceae, Ericaceae, Fabaceae, Lomandraceae, Xanthorrhoeaceae, Cyperaceae and Restionaceae, including many taxa that are endemic to the Sydney basin. Tozer et al. (2010) provide a detailed floristic description and distribution map (see their map units p117 'Coastal sandstone plateau heath', p126 'Coastal rock plate heath' and p127 'Sandstone headland scrub'). Related vegetation classes include Coastal heath swamps, found within drainage-impeded sites on the coastal sandstone plateaus; Wallum sand heaths, found on coastal sand plains; and Sydney montane heaths of the Blue Mountains and Morton plateaus (Keith 2004).

HEATHLAND VEGETATION DYNAMICS

The purpose of our review is to highlight some key developments in understanding processes that drive heathland vegetation change, rather than a comprehensive evaluation of published literature. One of the earliest interpretations of vegetation dynamics in the region was Pidgeon's (1938) study of plant succession on the Hawkesbury sandstone. Her model of landscape evolution proposed that vegetation developed on bare rock through a sequence of stages culminating in 'high forest' (Fig. 1). The mosaic of plant communities observable on sandstone plateaus were interpreted as patches in varying stages of development, in some cases arrested by local conditions. Moisture availability was a key process driving change in Pidgeon's (1938) model, with deeper soil profiles and shelter from desiccating winds promoting greater moisture retention and thus supporting development of 'more advanced' vegetation (i.e. with greater biomass). Heathlands, described by Pidgeon (1938) as 'scrub', were an intermediate stage in this succession, with high levels of sclerophylly and low stature indicating their ability to tolerate periods of moisture deprivation without wilting. While Beadle (1966) and subsequent workers established the association between sclerophylly and soil nutrition, Pidgeon (1938) postulated that progression from scrub to forest was allogenic, and controlled by development of both soil and topographic shelter from severe wind, through their effects on moisture retention.

Pidgeon (1938) also identified fire as having an influence on the distribution of sandstone vegetation. She suggested that, as the flora was particularly rich in species capable of vegetative regeneration, there was a tendency for similar floristic composition before and after pyric denudation. Seedlings apparently were at a disadvantage to renascent individuals, even though many species regenerated from resistant seeds or fruits that were either attached to plants or lying in soil at the time of fire (Pidgeon 1938). Hence, post-pyric seedlings only matured in dense stands where competition from resprouters was less severe.

The dynamism and potential vulnerability of plant species that lack vegetative recovery organs and rely only on seed for population persistence were first reported by Siddiqi et al. (1976). They observed that stands of these obligate-seeder species were eliminated from an area exposed to a short interval (<5 years) between successive fires because there had been insufficient time for post-fire seedlings from the first fire to mature and re-establish a seedbank before the next fire. Seeder species with canopy seedbanks (serotinous) appear to be the species most vulnerable to elimination. Bradstock and O'Connell (1988) quantified the relationship between fire intervals and population persistence for *Banksia ericifolia* and *Petrophile pulchella*, showing that optimal population growth occurred when fire return intervals were longer than 15 years and that populations may be eliminated when intervals were less than 6 years.

Morrison et al. (1995) and Cary and Morrison (1995) demonstrated strong fire frequency effects at the community level within Sydney coastal heathlands. They showed that diversity of obligate seeders was reduced in heathlands exposed to short fire intervals and that these trends were essentially independent of changes that occurred in composition with time since fire.

Obligate seeding plants may be buffered from elimination by adverse fire regimes, at least in the short term, if they have a persistent soil seedbank that may be released from dormancy by fire-related cues such as heath shock or smoke (Auld and O'Connell 1991; Morris 2000; Thomas et al. 2003). A majority of heathland plant species have persistent soil seedbanks (Auld and Ooi 2008), which may remain dormant and viable for several years to several decades (Auld et al. 2000). In some of these species, a residual fraction of the soil seedbank may remain dormant and viable after a fire, providing some capacity for regeneration after a second fire even if the intervening period was too short to permit seedbank replenishment (Auld and Denham 2006; Ayre et al. 2009).

Resprouters are often considered to be resilient to a wide range of fire regimes (Morrison et al. 1995; Pausas et al. 2004), but mortality of standing plants occurs through several fire-related mechanisms (Zammit 1988; Bradstock and Myerscough 1988; Keith et al. 2007a). Depending on fire regimes, replenishment of these individuals may be insufficient to maintain population stability due to low rates of fecundity and growth (Keith et al. 2007b). Sequences of short fire intervals or severe fires may cause gradual attrition or episodic declines, respectively, of established woody resprouters (Regan et al. 2011) if losses are not compensated by equivalent levels of recruitment. The factors promoting establishment of resprouters and increases in their populations are still not well understood.

Competition is another potential mechanism of change in plant diversity. As well as strong self-regulatory effects within populations of some heathland species (Morris and Myerscough 1988), there is evidence of strong competitive hierarchies related to plant stature within Sydney coastal heathlands (Keith and Bradstock 1994; Tozer and Bradstock 2003; Keith et al. 2007a). Resprouters may have a competitive advantage over seedlings in the initial post-fire period (Pidgeon 1938), however recruits of woody obligate seeders with large canopies eventually overtop the resprouters, casting deep shade that substantially reduces rates of growth, fecundity and survival of plants beneath their canopies. The role of below-ground competition is uncertain, but could also be significant. Nevertheless, above-ground competition is mediated by periodic fires that interrupt the elimination of inferior competitors and promote co-existence. Furthermore, there is evidence that thickets of competitive dominants move around the landscape in response to spatial and temporal variations in fire regimes (Keith 1995; Keith et al. 2007a).

Functional classification of species based on plant life-history traits has proved to be valuable for interpretation of vegetation change in Sydney

Proc. Linn. Soc. N.S.W., 134, 2012

B183

heathlands. This approach provides an adaptable conceptual framework for predicting responses to contrasting scenarios, as species with shared traits tend to have similar mechanisms of response (Keith and Bradstock 1994; Morrison *et al.* 1995; Keith *et al.* 2007a; Keith 2012).

In summary, there have been substantial advances in understanding of vegetation dynamics in Sydney coastal heathlands since Pidgeon's (1938) early studies. While soil development and topography tend to structure major vegetation patterns on the sandstone plateaus and control long-term transitions between heathlands and other communities, both fire regimes and soil moisture variation have key roles in dynamics of the heathland mosaic over decadal time scales, and potentially generate long-lasting legacies. A synthesis of these processes is needed to support management for conservation of the diverse heathland biota. Below, we contribute to such a synthesis by constructing a model that incorporates the salient processes reviewed above.

MODEL STRUCTURE

We adopted a state and transition framework for our model of heathland vegetation dynamics. This structure involves classification of heathland vegetation into a number of alternative states, each of which is defined by a set of state variables. The values of these state variables may change through time or in response to particular environmental cues or events. Consequently, transitions may occur between certain states under particular conditions. State and transition models are used widely as explanatory and predictive tools in ecology, management and restoration (Westoby *et al.* 1989; Bestelmeyer *et al.* 2009; Rumpff *et al.* 2011). They involve a significant abstraction by representing vegetation as discrete classes, rather than as a continuum, but this is offset by many advantages. State and transition models are easy to grasp in their simplest diagrammatic form and therefore powerful communication tools between scientists and managers. They also have capacity for extension to mathematically explicit quantitative predictions and may be implemented in ways that accommodate uncertainties and permit updating as new knowledge emerges (Rumpff *et al.* 2011).

State variables

A set of state variables describes the floristic, structural and environmental features of alternative heathland states. We used the classification of species functional types proposed by Keith *et al.* (2007a) to define floristic state variables. This approach allows a substantial simplification of the flora by classifying more than 200 vascular plant taxa found in heathland into six broad functional types based on life history attributes. Selection of life history attributes was based on salient processes that mediate heathland vegetation dynamics (reviewed above): fire response of standing plants; propagule characteristics; timing of life life-history processes; and competitive relationships. Initial species groupings were based on factorial combinations of traits and were simplified by deleting trait combinations that did not exist in nature (due to correlations between traits), and grouping those considered likely to have similar responses to the mediating processes (Keith *et al.* 2007a; Table 1).

Structural state variables included the height and combined projective cover (foliage and branches) of tall shrub, mid shrub, ground layer and litter strata. These variables were assessed by assigning individual plants to a stratum based on their potential height at maturity. Thus, it would be possible for the tall shrub stratum to be shorter than the ground layer if the former was at an immature stage.

The environmental state variables include soil depth, drainage, topography and post-fire age. Although more realistic and elaborate characterisations would be possible, we characterised variation in these attributes using broad categories.

Heathland states

In this study we only used qualitative descriptors of the attribute states to illustrate our modelling approach, although it is possible to characterise them with quantitative estimates (Table 2). For example, each heathland state was characterised floristically as having high, medium or low relative abundance and diversity of each of the six plant functional types, rather than using metrics of diversity and abundance. Similarly, we used qualitative descriptors to characterise structural variables (e.g. cover of tall shrub stratum was described as absent, sparse or dense) and a categorical descriptor for the environmental state variable. We limited our current analysis to treeless vegetation on shallow, moderately drained soils of exposed sandstone plateaus, although we recognise that these coexist with other vegetation states including heathlands on rock plates, woodlands and upland swamps, which differ notably in environmental state variables soil depth and drainage. Consequently, several structural and environmental state variables are essentially invariant amongst the subset of states considered (Table 2).

Table 1. Summary of six major plant functional types (PFTs) in Sydney coastal heathlands and their life history traits (adapted from Table 1 in Keith et al. 2007a). For authorities, see Pellow et al. (2009).

Functional Type	Fire persistence	Propagule type	Vertical stratum	Standing plant longevity	Example
1 Serotinous obligate seeder shrubs	killed	serotinous seedbanks	upper	30-50 years	*Banksia ericifolia*
2 Non-serotinous obligate seeder shrubs	killed	persistent soil seedbanks	middle	10-30 years	*Epacris microphylla*
3 Resprouter shrubs	survives	serotinous, persistent and transient soil seedbanks	middle	>50 years	*Banksia oblongifolia*
4 Fire ephemeral herbs	killed	Persistent soil seedbanks	ground	<5 years	*Mitrasacme polymorpha*
5 Non-rhizomatous herbs and graminoids	survives	Persistent and transient soil seedbanks	ground	>10-50 years	*Burchardia umbellata*
6 Rhizomatous herbs and graminoids	survives	Persistent and transient soil seedbanks, vegetative propagation	lower	>50 years	*Leptocarpus tenax*

Transitions

The heathland states (Table 2) were organised into four main lineages according to their developmental relationships (Fig. 2): diverse thicket (DT); depauperate thicket (PT); diverse heath (DH); and depauperate heath (PH). Thus, a given stand of heathland may undergo autogenic transitions between states of increasing time since fire within the same lineage. Transitions between lineages are triggered allogenically in response to particular fire events, or may also occur autogenically late in the fire cycle (Fig. 2). The states and transitions represented diagrammatically in Fig. 2 were incorporated into a conditional matrix model, which defines the possible transitions from each state and conditions under which they may occur (Table 3). With a matrix model framework, it is possible to specify the rates and probabilities of transitions. In this paper, however, we focus on the structure of the model and only show qualitative information on the transitions. Below, we use example scenarios to demonstrate the application of the model.

MODELLING ALTERNATIVE FIRE REGIME SCENARIOS

Methods

We used the model to predict qualitative vegetation responses to example fire regime scenarios and compared the predictions with observed responses. The example scenarios were developed by examining the fire history and historical vegetation states in an area of heathland on the sandstone plateau between Jibbon Hill and the Marley track, Royal National Park (Fig. 3). Studies of heathland vegetation dynamics have been ongoing since a fire burnt the entire site in October 1988 (Keith 1991; Keith and Bradstock 1994; Keith 1995). In this paper, we use observations gathered at Transects 2 and 7 to evaluate specific model predictions. Prior to 1988, fires occurred in 1976 (both transects) and 1980 (Transect 7 only). A subsequent fire burnt the entire area in January 1994.

We determined the fire history and structural states of vegetation at the transect sites by interpreting a chronosequence of aerial photographs (Keith 1995). At Transect 2, Diverse Thicket developed after the

State variable / State	Floristic						Structural					Environmental
	1 Serotinous obligate seeder shrubs	2 Non-serotinous obligate seeder shrubs	3 Resprouter shrubs	4 Fire ephemeral herbs	5 Non-rhizomatous herbs and graminoids	6 Rhizomatous herbs and graminoids	Tall shrub height	Tall shrub cover	Mid shrub cover	Ground cover	Litter cover	Time since fire (years)
DTb Post-fire diverse thicket	high	high	high	high	high	low	low	absent	dense	dense	sparse	tsf<5
DTj Juvenile diverse thicket	high	high	high	low	medium	high	medium	sparse	medium	dense	medium	5<tsf<10
DTy Young-mature diverse thicket	high	low	high	low	medium	medium	tall	dense	sparse	dense	dense	10<tsf<20
PTb Post-fire depauperate thicket	high	high	low	high	low	low	low	absent	sparse	sparse	sparse	tsf<5
PTj Juvenile depauperate thicket	high	high	low	low	low	medium	medium	sparse	medium	medium	medium	5<tsf<10
PTy Young-mature depauperate thicket	high	low	low	low	low	low	tall	dense	sparse	medium	dense	10<tsf<20
PTo Old-mature depauperate thicket	high	low	low	low	low	low	tall	dense	sparse	sparse	dense	20<tsf<30
PTs Senescent depauperate thicket	medium	low	low	low	low	low	tall	sparse	sparse	medium	dense	tsf>30
DHb Post-fire diverse heath	low	high	high	high	high	high	low	absent	dense	dense	sparse	tsf<5
DHj Juvenile diverse heath	low	high	high	low	high	high	medium	dense	dense	dense	sparse	5<tsf<10
DHy Young-mature diverse heath	low	high	high	low	high	high	tall	sparse	dense	dense	medium	10<tsf<20
DHo Old-mature diverse heath	low	low	high	low	high	high	tall	sparse	dense	dense	medium	20<tsf<30
DHs Senescent diverse heath	low	low	high	low	high	high	tall	sparse	dense	dense	medium	tsf>30
PHb Post-fire depauperate heath	low	medium	low	high	low	low	absent	absent	medium	dense	sparse	tsf<5
PHj Juvenile depauperate heath	low	medium	low	low	medium	medium	medium	sparse	medium	dense	sparse	5<tsf<10
PHy Young-mature depauperate heath	low	medium	low	low	medium	medium	tall	sparse	sparse	dense	sparse	10<tsf<20
PHo Old-mature depauperate heath	low	low	low	low	medium	medium	tall	sparse	sparse	dense	medium	20<tsf<30
PHs Senescent depauperate heath	low	low	low	low	medium	medium	tall	sparse	sparse	dense	medium	tsf>30

B186

Proc. Linn. Soc. N.S.W., 134, 2012

Figure 2. Aerial photograph of Jibbon study area taken in 2001, seven years after previous fire, showing open heath (grey-green) in vicinity of Transect 2 and development of thicket shrub canopy (dark green) in vicinity of Transect 7. Canopies of individual serotinous obligate seeder shrubs are visible within the open heath.

1976 fire and was in a young mature state (DTy, Table 2) when it was burnt in 1988. Diverse Thicket reached a juvenile state (DTj) when it was burnt again in 1994. At Transect 7, the 1980 fire interrupted development of Diverse Thicket and the vegetation underwent a putative transition to burnt Diverse Heath (NBB fire history in Fig. 5 of Keith 1995). Transect 7 was positioned 5 m from the 1980 fire boundary, beyond which Diverse Thicket continued to develop

Table 2 (Opposite). Attribute states of alternative heathland states for six floristic state variables (relative abundance and diversity of plant functional types, Table 1), five structural state variables and one environmental state variable. Two structural variables and three environmental state variables not shown as they are essentially invariant across listed heathland states (Mid shrub height - medium, Ground layer height - low, Soil depth - 0.2 - 0.6 m, Soil moisture - periodically damp and dry with limited humus accumulation, Topographic shelter - exposed plateau surface).

until the 1988 fire. Following the 1988 fire, Transect 7 underwent a transition from Diverse Heath to Diverse Thicket due to dispersal of seed from an adjacent thicket (<5 m away). Since 1994, both Transects have remained unburnt except for a small fire in 2005 that partially scorched small areas of Transect 7. For purposes of prediction, we assumed that this last fire had no effect on the transect.

The model predictions were evaluated using data on population densities of selected plant species collected from Transects 2 and 7 in repeated surveys between 1990 and 2011 (see Keith and Bradstock 1994 for field methods).

Predictions

Based on the above history, we identified several scenarios with contrasting initial states and fire events at the two transects and used the model to predict measurable outcomes (Fig. 4). We first focussed on transitions at each transect as a consequence of the 1988 and 1994 fires (Scenarios 0 - 2, Table 4). At the

Proc. Linn. Soc. N.S.W., 134, 2012

B187

Proc. Linn. Soc. N.S.W., 134, 2012

	DTb	DTj	DTy	PTb	PTj	PTy	PTo	PTs	DHb	DHj	Dhy	DHo	DHs	PHb	PHj	PHy	PHo	PHs
DTb	FD	F	F					FD		FD	FD	FD			FD	FD		
DTj	NF																	
DTy		NF																
PTb				FD	F	F	F								FD	FD	FD	FD
PTj				NF														
PTy					NF													
PTo			NF			NF												
PTs							NF											
DHb	FN	FN							FD	F	F	F	F	F		FD	FD	
DHj										NF								
Dhy											NF							
DHo												NF						
DHs												NF	NF					
PHb				FN	FN		FN	FN	FN						F	F	F	F	F
PHj															NF			
PHy																NF		
PHo																	NF	
PHs								NF									NF	NF

NF	No fire
FN	Fire with no dispersal
FD	Fire with dispersal
F	Fire with or without dispersal

Table 3. A stand-based conditional state and transition matrix model for Sydney coastal heaths. Heathland states are arranged in four lineages: DT - diverse thicket; PT - depauperate thicket; DH - diverse heath; and PH - depauperate heath. Within each lineage are a time series of states that vary in post-fire age: b - burnt recently (0-5 years ago); j - juvenile (5-10 years since fire); young mature (10-20 years since fire); old mature (20-30 years since fire); s - senescent (>30 years since fire). Entries in cells indicate the fire and dispersal conditions required for a transition from an initial state (top row of matrix) to a new state (left column of matrix). We assume that fires consume or scorch the canopies of shrubs in the modelled stand. Dispersal denotes an influx of propagules for all plant functional types from adjacent stands of heathland.

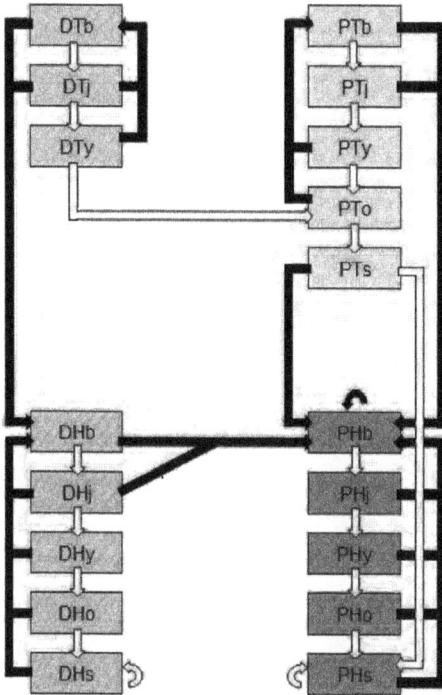

Figure 3. Simplified diagrammatic state and transition model for a stand of Sydney coastal heath. Heathland states represented in boxes are defined in Table 2. States within the same lineage are shown in the same colour. White arrows show autogenic transitions that occur with time in the absence of fire. Black arrows show allogenic transitions initiated by crown fires, assuming no dispersal of plant propagules from outside the patch. The matrix model in Table 3 incorporates additional transitions with propagule dispersal.

time of the 1988 fire, Diverse Thicket was present at Transect 2 and Diverse Heath was present at Transect 7. Transect 2 was a post-fire age of 12 years and at the young-mature diverse thicket stage (DTy) while Transect 7 was a post-fire age of 8 years and at the juvenile diverse heath stage (DHj), (Table 2). At Transect 2, the model predicts transition from DTy to DTb (Table 4 Scenario 0), and at Transect 7, the model predicts transition from DHj to DHb or DTb, depending on whether seeds of thicket dominants were dispersed from the adjacent area that was unburnt in 1980. We show only the latter transition in Fig. 4b (Table 4 Scenario 2). At the time of the

1994 fire both sites were a post-fire age of 5.3 years, on the interface between burnt and juvenile states (Table 2). At both transects the model predicts transition from DTj to either DTb or DHb (Scenario 1), depending on whether serotinous obligate seeders were at maturity (Table 3). For brevity, we show only the latter prediction in Fig. 4a.

We next focussed on transitions at each transect over the 13 years after the 1994 fire (Scenarios 3 and 4, Table 4). In the absence of subsequent fire, the model predicted transition from DHb through DHj to DHy at Transect 2 (Scenario 3, Fig. 4c), with the community maintaining an open structure and an abundance of rhizomatous sedges (PFT 6). At Transect 7, the model predicted an autogenic progression from DTb through DTj to DTy (Scenario 4, Fig. 4d), with the development of a tall dense shrub canopy, and a coincident decline in resprouters (PFTs 3, 5 and 6).

Finally, we applied the model to the interval between the 1988 and 1994 fires (Scenarios 5 and 6). Prior to 1988, Transect 7 was occupied by Diverse Heath and, there had been no suppression of rhizomatous sedges (PFT 6) by a dense shrub overstorey. Consequently, in Scenario 5 (Fig. 4e) the model predicted consistently high abundance of PFT 6 during the post-1988 transition from DTb to DTj (Table 4). In contrast, Transect 2 had been occupied by Diverse Thicket which had reached a post fire age of 12 years (DTy) by 1988, potentially reducing population densities of rhizomatous sedges (PFT6). In Scenario 6 (Fig. 4f), the 1988 fire was predicted to release these species from competitive suppression, allowing their density to increase by vegetative spread during the transition from DTb to DTj.

Observations

Transect 2 underwent transition from thicket (DTj) before the 1988 fire to heath (DHb) after the 1994 fire, and the density of serotinous obligate seeder shrubs was reduced by three orders of magnitude

Proc. Linn. Soc. N.S.W., 134, 2012

B189

Figure 4. Diagrammatic representation of predicted transitions between heathland states. Black arrows represent allogenic transitions initiated by crown fires, white arrows represent autogenic transitions in the absence of fire. See Table 1 for description of plant functional types and Table 2 for description of heathland states. Plant functional Types:

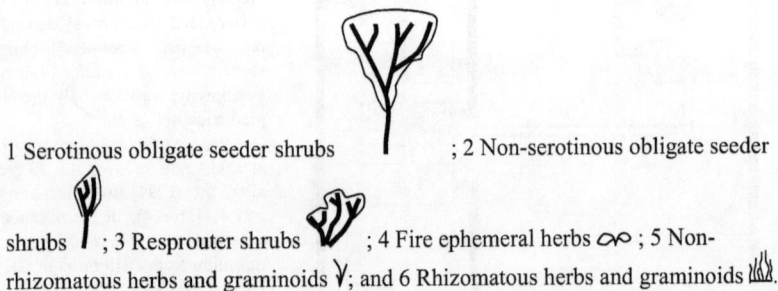

1 Serotinous obligate seeder shrubs ; 2 Non-serotinous obligate seeder shrubs ; 3 Resprouter shrubs ; 4 Fire ephemeral herbs ; 5 Non-rhizomatous herbs and graminoids ; and 6 Rhizomatous herbs and graminoids.

Juvenile diverse thicket (DTj) — 5-10 years since fire

Burnt diverse heath (DHb) — <5 years since fire

(a) Scenario 1: transition from juvenile diverse thicket (post-fire age 5.3 years) to burnt diverse heath in response to crown fire.

Juvenile diverse heath (DHj) — 5-10 years since fire

Burnt diverse thicket (DTb) — <5 years since fire

(b) Scenario 2: transition from juvenile diverse heath to burnt diverse thicket in response to crown fire.

B190

Proc. Linn. Soc. N.S.W., 134, 2012

Figure 4 Continued

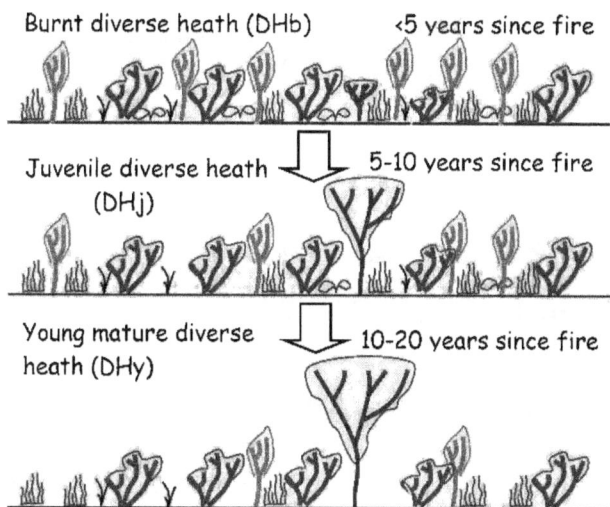

Burnt diverse heath (DHb)   <5 years since fire

Juvenile diverse heath   5-10 years since fire
(DHj)

Young mature diverse   10-20 years since fire
heath (DHy)

(c) Scenario 4: transition from burnt diverse heath to young mature diverse heath with time since fire.

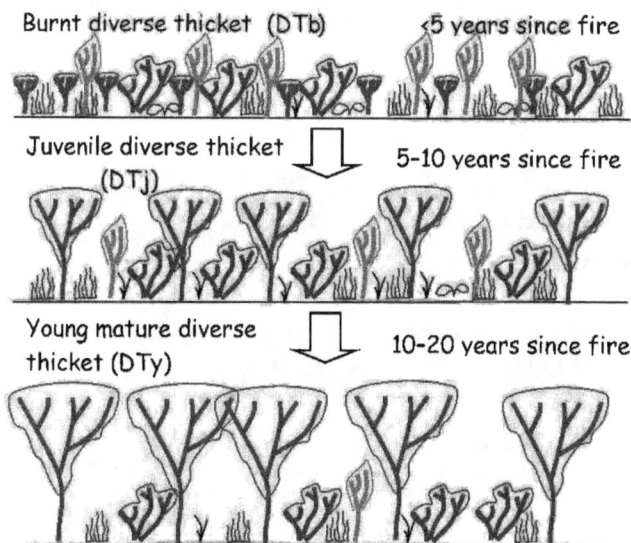

Burnt diverse thicket (DTb)   <5 years since fire

Juvenile diverse thicket   5-10 years since fire
(DTj)

Young mature diverse   10-20 years since fire
thicket (DTy)

(d) Scenario 4: transition from burnt diverse thicket to young mature diverse thicket with increasing time since fire.

Proc. Linn. Soc. N.S.W., 134, 2012

B191

Figure 4 Continued

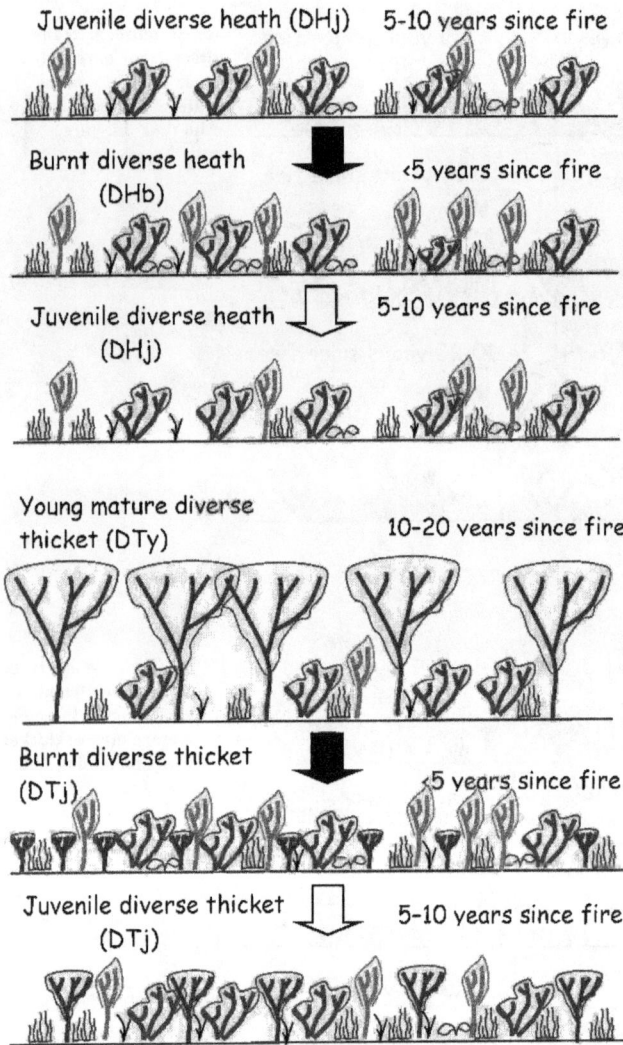

(e) Scenario 5: transition from burnt diverse heath to juvenile diverse heath with time since fire after prior occupancy by juvenile diverse heath.

Juvenile diverse heath (DHj)   5-10 years since fire

Burnt diverse heath (DHb)   <5 years since fire

Juvenile diverse heath (DHj)   5-10 years since fire

(f) Scenario 6: transition from burnt diverse thicket to juvenile diverse thicket with time since fire after prior occupancy by young mature diverse heath.

Young mature diverse thicket (DTy)   10-20 years since fire

Burnt diverse thicket (DTj)   <5 years since fire

Juvenile diverse thicket (DTj)   5-10 years since fire

(Fig. 5). Conversely, the density of these shrubs increased from zero before the 1988 fire to more than 10 per square metre after the 1994 fire at Transect 7, signalling a transition from juvenile thicket (DTj) to burnt thicket (DTb). These observations were consistent with predicted transitions if Scenario 1 occurred at Transect 2 without dispersal and at Transect 7 with some serotinous obligate seeders at maturity (Table 3). Thus, the difference between sites was due to slightly faster maturation and development of a seedbank in the vicinity of Transect 7 after the 1994 fire (pers. obs.).

The development of a tall dense shrub canopy at Transect 7 after 1994 (Scenario 4) can be tracked on

Table 4. Qualitative predictions of the process model for six scenarios at Transects 2 and 7.

Scenario	Initial state	Predicted transition	Time frame	Response variable	Predicted change	Observed change	Site
0) Fire	DTy	DTb	before/after 1988 fire	PFT1 density	stable	stable	Transect 2
1) Fire without dispersal	DTj	DHb	before/after 1994 fire	PFT1 density	elimination	near elimination	Transect 2
2) Fire with dispersal	DHj	DTb	before/after 1988 fire	PFT1 density	increase	increase, Fig. 5	Transect 7
3) No fire	DHb	DHy	13-yr interval after 1994 fire	tall shrub cover	remains low	patchy development (aerial photos)	Transect 2
			13-yr interval after 1994 fire	PFT6 density	stable or slight decline	stable for 8 years, then gradual decline	Transect 2
4) No fire	DTb	DTy	13-yr interval after 1994 fire	tall shrub cover	marked increase	marked increase (aerial photos)	Transect 7
			13-yr interval after 1994 fire	PFT6 density	decline	strong decline	Transect 7
5) No fire, no prior thicket	DHb	DHj	5-yr interval after 1988 fire	PFT6 density	stable	stable	Transect 7
6) No fire, prior occupancy by dense thicket	DTb	DTj	5-yr interval after 1988 fire	PFT6 density	increase	increase, Fig. 6	Transect 2

a chronosequence of aerial photographs (e.g Fig. 3). Canopy development was similar to that tracked after earlier fires in the same area (Keith 1995). By 2001, the developing shrub canopy at this site had exceeded the height of mid-stratum shrubs (PFTs 2 and 3) and ground layer plants (PFTs 4, 5 and 6). These PFTs underwent a prolonged decline after the 1994 fire. For example, *Leptocarpus tenax*, a rhizomatous graminoid (PFT 6, Table 1), declined in density by two orders of magnitude over the 13 years since the 1994 fire (Fig. 6). In contrast, a continuous canopy of serotinous obligate seeders did not develop under Scenario 3 at Transect 2 due to the low densities of serotinous obligate seeding shrubs (Fig. 5). Instead, only a patchy cover of tall shrubs can be seen on

aerial photographs after 2001. In the absence of a dense canopy, the density of *L. tenax* was essentially stable at Transect 2 after the 1994 fire, contrasting markedly with its decline at Transect 7 during the same time (Fig. 6). These observations are consistent with predictions of the model for transitions from DTb to DTy and DHb to DHy, respectively (Tables 2 and 3).

Transect 7 had consistently dense populations of *L. tenax* (PFT 6) during 1990-1994 (filled triangles, Fig. 6). Under Scenario 5, this site had been free of a tall shrub canopy for some years due to elimination of serotinous obligate seeder shrubs (PFT 1) by a short fire interval during 1976-1980 (reported in Keith 1995). In contrast, under Scenario 6, Transect 2 had

Proc. Linn. Soc. N.S.W., 134, 2012

B193

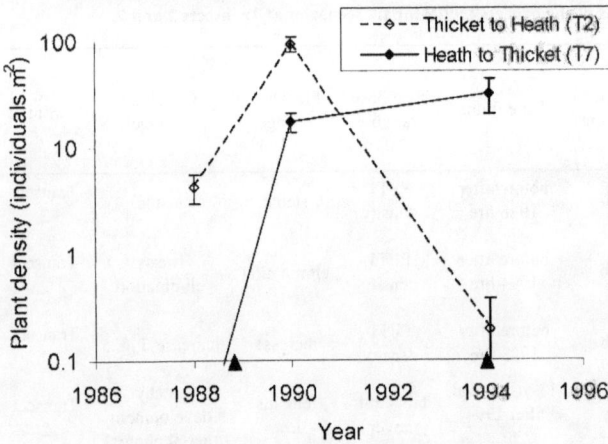

Figure 5. Change in population density of serotinous obligate seeder shrubs (PFT 1), primarily Banksia ericifolia, before and after the 1994 fire. Triangles on x-axis indicate timing of fires. Data for heath to thicket transition from Transect 7 and data for thicket to heath transition from Transect 2. Density estimates for 1988 were for mature stands (zero individuals recorded for T7), those for 1990 and 1994 were for post-fire seedlings, indicative of the capacity for future thicket development.

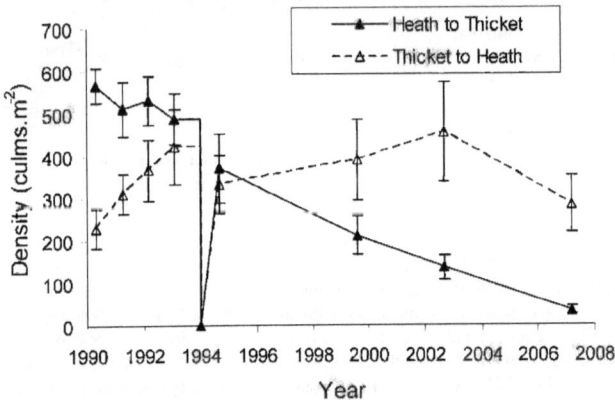

Figure 6. Trends in population density of Leptocarpus tenax (PFT 6) in relation to the 1994 fire. Data for heath to thicket transition from Transect 7 and data for thicket to heath transition from Transect 2. Note: preceding fire occurred in 1988, 5.3 years before the 1994 fire.

been occupied by young-mature thicket (DTy) prior to the 1988 fire. Just prior to 1988, serotinous obligate seeder shrubs (PFT 1) were present at a mean ($\pm$se) density of 7.0 ± 1.2 plants. m^{-2} (data from Keith 1991), forming a dense canopy 2 - 3 m tall. After removal of this canopy by the 1988 fire, *L. tenax* showed a steady increase in density until the site was burnt again in 1994 (Fig. 6). This change is consistent with model prediction for a transition from DTy to DHb in response to fire with no dispersal (Tables 2 and 3).

DISCUSSION

State and transition model

Model predictions were consistent with observed changes in heath vegetation at our Jibbon study site over recent decades. The predictions examined included species from two functional types and a range of fire scenarios. These findings agree with those of earlier studies that examined a broader range of functional types at different times and places within Sydney coastal heathlands and heath-swamps (Keith and Bradstock 1994; Keith 1995; Tozer and Bradstock 2003; Keith et al. 2007a). Collectively, these studies demonstrate the sensitivity of serotinous obligate seeder shrubs to short fire intervals (≤ 5 years), the sensitivity of woody and non-woody resprouters to competition from dense thickets of seeder shrubs, and the mobility of these thickets around sandstone landscapes over a series of fire intervals.

The most equivocal performance of the model was in Scenarios 1 and 2, which produced different observed outcomes at different sites, despite similar contemporary fire intervals. Two factors potentially explain these differences. First, the model predicted different outcomes depending on whether the sites were assigned to burnt or juvenile initial states, and the assignment of sites to one of these states was uncertain. The sites had a post-fire age of 5.3 years when burnt in 1994, which was very close to the nominal 5-year threshold age delimiting burnt and juvenile states in the model (Table 2). The observed response for Transect 2 was consistent with predictions for a burnt initial state, whereas the response for Transect 7 was consistent with predictions for a juvenile initial state. Although the age threshold delimiting states was specified precisely, and the age of the sites was accurately known, assignment of sites to states was vague (Regan et al. 2002) partly because the distinction between states is only indirectly related to age (as a proxy for reproductive capacity of serotinous obligate seeder shrubs). More broadly, vagueness is a pervasive form of uncertainty whenever two categories are delimited by thresholds or boundaries (Regan et al. 2002). A second source of uncertainty is attributable to natural variation. It seems likely that there were subtle differences in maturation and seedbank accumulation rates between the sites, which may have been responsible for establishment of serotinous obligate seeder shrubs at one site and not the other. This variability is likely to be most influential on transitions when the fire interval is close to the maturation period of obligate seeders, as it was in Scenarios 1 and 2. In summary, the model was able to accommodate these uncertainties to some degree by predicting alternative transitions from each initial state, conditional upon spatial variation in maturation times (Table 3).

State and transition models have been applied successfully in a range of ecosystems for a variety of explanatory and predictive purposes (Henderson and Wilkins 1975; Moore and Noble 1990; Hobbs and Suding 2009; Rumpff et al. 2011). Our model enables a synthesis of complex dynamics in which outcomes depend on the initial state of vegetation, its recent historical states, fire regimes, competitive interactions between species, propagule dispersal and functional traits of the species under consideration. Diagrammatic representation of the model enables effective communication with managers who need a logical framework to explore alternative future scenarios to support their management decisions for biodiversity conservation. Matrix representation of the model enables more complex scenarios to be explored by simulation over longer time frames that encompass multiple fires. In this paper we presented a qualitative matrix model. In future we will develop a numerically and spatially explicit matrix model capable of analysing uncertainties and conservation risks by simulation of alternative management options.

Management

Our model of vegetation dynamics provides a lucid framework for conservation of biodiversity in Sydney Coastal Heaths. Conservation of biodiversity requires persistence of the species within all six plant functional types. According to our model, this is only possible if management aims to: i) maintain both heath and thicket states within the landscape; and ii) promote diverse states and avoid depauperate states. In other words, a landscape configuration that includes a balanced and sustainable (albeit dynamic) representation of diverse heath and diverse thicket is more likely to meet the overall goal of biodiversity persistence than other landscape configurations. These aims can be achieved with a management strategy that is responsive to the current state of the landscape and cognisant of alternative pathways of change that may result from alternative management strategies and unplanned events. This approach should be combined with experimentation aimed at learning more about responses to alternative scenarios (Keith et al. 2011). For example, if a large proportion of the landscape is occupied by thicket (or soon will be), consideration should be given to alternative means of promoting transition from thicket to heath. Options include implementing fire intervals of less than 5 years in parts of the landscape or allowing parts of the landscape to go more than 30 years without fire (Table 3). This approach is the antithesis of management strategies based on fixed burning schedules and suppression plans that seek to avoid extremes in fire regimes. These strategies generally fail to account for the ecological state of the system, even though the schedules may be based on careful monitoring of fire history, and lack the flexibility to influence variability in fire regimes and their spatial patterns to promote specific transitions within targeted areas.

Finally, in focussing on management of plant functional types and vegetation states, our model currently risks ignoring other components of biodiversity that are important targets of conservation. Management strategies structured around the

Proc. Linn. Soc. N.S.W., 134, 2012

B195

persistence of diversity of plant functional types are implicitly relevant to other biota. For example, serotinous obligate seeder shrubs (PFT 1) provide an important winter food source and nesting substrate for a range of avian and mammalian fauna (Keith *et al.* 2002). The much greater diversity of plant genera among the non-serotinous obligate seeder shrubs (PFT 2) is likely to support the greatest diversity of dependent invertebrate fauna, including insects with narrow host plant ranges (Moir *et al.* 2011). Thus, management trade-offs in the persistence of these two plant functional types also affect persistence of biota in other trophic levels. To address the persistence of all biota more explicitly in management strategies, however, these elements and their dependencies need to be integrated into the structure of future process models.

References

Auld, T.D. and Denham, A.J. (2006). How much seed remains in the soil after a fire? *Plant Ecology* **187**: 15-24.

Auld, T.D., Keith, D.A. and Bradstock, R.A. (2000). Patterns in longevity of soil seedbanks in fire-prone communities of south-eastern Australia. *Australian Journal of Botany* **48**: 539-548,

Auld, T.D. and O'Connell, M.A. (1991). Predicting patterns of post-fire germination in 35 Eastern Australian Fabaceae. *Australian Journal of Ecology.* **16**: 53-70.

Auld, T.D. and Ooi, M.K.J. (2008). Applying seed germination studies in fire management for biodiversity conservation in south-eastern Australia. *Web Ecology* **8**: 47–54.

Ayre, D.J., Ottewell, K.M., Krauss, S.L. and Whelan, R.J. (2009). Genetic structure of seedling cohorts following repeated wildfires in the fire-sensitive shrub *Persoonia mollis* ssp *nectens*. *Journal of Ecology* **97**: 752-760.

Beadle, N.C.W. (1966). Soil phosphate and its role in molding segments of the Australian flora and vegetation with special reference to xeromorphy and sclerophylly. *Ecology* **47**: 991-1007.

Bestelmeyer, B.T., Havstad, K.M., Damindsuren, B., Han, G., Brown, J.R., Herrick. J.E., Steele, C.M. and Peters, D.P.C. (2009). Resilience theory in models of rangeland ecology and restoration: the evolution and application of a paradigm. In New models for ecosystem dynamics and restoration, R.J. Hobbs and Suding KN (eds), Island Press, Washington DC, pp 78 - 95.

Bradstock, R.A. and Myerscough, P.J. (1988). The survival and population response to frequent fires of

2 woody resprouters *Banksia serrata* and *Isopogon anemonifolius*. *Australian Journal of Botany* **36**: 415-431.

Bradstock, R.A. and O'Connell, M.A. (1988). Demography of woody-plants in relation to fire – *Banksia ericifolia* Lf. and *Petrophile pulchella* (schrad) RBr. *Australian Journal of Ecology* **13**: 505-518.

Cary, G.J. and Morrison, D.A. (1995). Effects of fire frequency on plant species composition of sandstone communities in the Sydney region: combinations of inter-fire intervals. *Australian Journal of Ecology* **20**: 418–26.

Henderson W. and Wilkins C. W. (1975). Interaction of bushfires and vegetation. *Search* **6**, 130-133.

Hobbs, R.J. and Suding, K.N. (2009). New models for ecosystem dynamics and restoration. Island Press, Washington DC.

Keith, D.A. (1991). Coexistence and species diversity in upland swamp vegetation: the roles of an environmental gradient and recurring fires. PhD thesis, University of Sydney.

Keith, D.A. (1995). Mosaics in Sydney heathland vegetation: the roles of fire, competition and soils. *CALMScience Supplement* **4**: 199-206.

Keith, D. A. (2004). Ocean shores to desert dunes: the native vegetation of New South Wales and the ACT. NSW Department of Environment and Conservation, Sydney.

Keith D.A. (2012). Functional traits: their roles in understanding and predicting biotic responses to fire regimes. In Flammable Australia: fire regimes, biodiversity and ecosystems in a changing world, second edition, R.A. Bradstock, A.M. Gill and R.J. Williams (eds), CSIRO, Melbourne.

Keith, D.A. and Bradstock, R.A. (1994). Fire and competition in Australian heath: a conceptual model and field investigations. *Journal of Vegetation Science* **5**: 347-354.

Keith, D.A., Holman, L., Rodoreda, S., Lemmon, J. and Bedward, M. (2007a). Plant Functional Types can predict decade-scale changes in fire-prone vegetation. *Journal of Ecology* **95**: 1324-1337.

Keith, D.A., Martin, T.G., McDonald-Madden, E. and Walters, C. (2011). Uncertainty and adaptive management for biodiversity conservation. *Biological Conservation* **144**: 1175–1178.

Keith, D. A., McCaw, W. L. and Whelan, R. J. (2002). Fire regimes in Australian heathlands and their effects on plants and animals. In Flammable Australia: the fire regimes and biodiversity of a continent, R.A. Bradstock, J.E. Williams and A.M. Gill (eds), Cambridge University Press, Cambridge, pp 199-237.

Keith, D.A., Tozer, M.G., Regan, T.J. and Regan, H.M. (2007b). The persistence niche: what makes it and what breaks it for two fire-prone plant species. *Australian Journal of Botany* **55**: 273-279.

Moir, M.L., Vesk, P.A., Brennan, K.E.C., Keith, D.A., McCarthy, M.A. and Hughes, L. (2011). Identifying and managing threatened invertebrates by assessing coextinction risk. *Conservation Biology* 25: 787–796.

Moore, A.D. and Noble, I.R. (1990). An individualistic model of vegetation stand dynamics. *Journal of Environmental Management* 31: 61-81.

Morris, E.C. (2000). Germination response of seven east Australian *Grevillea* species (Proteaceae) to smoke, heat exposure and scarification. *Australian Journal of Botany.* 48: 179-189.

Morris, E.C. and Myerscough, P.J. (1988). Survivorship, growth and self-thinning in *Banksia ericfolia*. *Australian Journal of Ecology* 13: 181-189.

Morrison D.A., Cary G.J., Pengelly S.M., Ross, D.G, Mullins, B.G., Thomas, C.R. and Anderson, T.S. (1995). Effects of fire frequency on plant species composition of sandstone communities in the Sydney region: inter-fire interval and time-since-fire. *Australian Journal of Ecology* 20: 239–47.

Pausas, J., Bradstock, R. A., Keith, D. A., Keeley, J. and GTCE (2004). Plant functional traits in relation to fire in crown-fire ecosystems. *Ecology* 85: 1085-1100.

Pellow, B.J., Henwood, M. and Carolin, R.C. (2009). Flora of the Sydney region, fifth edition. Sydney University Press, Sydney.

Pickett S.T.A. and Cadenasso M.L. (2002). The ecosystem as a multidimensional concept: meaning, model, and metaphor. *Ecosystems* 5: 1–10.

Pidgeon, I.M. (1938) The ecology of the central coast area of New South Wales. II. Plant succession on the Hawkesbury sandstone. *Proceedings of the Linnean Society of New South Wales* 63: 1-26.

Regan, H.M., Colyvan, M. and Burgman, M.A. (2002). A taxonomy and treatment of uncertainty for ecology and conservation biology. *Ecological Applications* 12: 618– 628.

Regan, H.M., Keith, D.A., Regan, T.J., Tozer, M.G. and Tootell, N. (2011). Fire management to combat disease: turning interactions between threats into conservation management. *Oecologia* 167: 873–882.

Rumpff, L., Duncan, D.H., Vesk, P.A., Keith, D.A. and Wintle, B.A. (2011). State-and-transition modelling for Adaptive Management of native woodlands. *Biological Conservation* 144: 1224–1236. [doi:10.1016/j.biocon.2010.10.026].

Siddiqi, M.Y., Carolin, R.C. and Myerscough, P.J. (1976). Studies in the ecology of coastal heath in New South Wales. III. Regrowth of vegetation after fire. *Proceedings of Linnean Society of New South Wales* 101: 53-63.

Thomas, P.B. Morris, E.C. and Auld, T.D. (2003). Interactive effects of heat shock and smoke on germination of nine species forming soil seed banks within the Sydney region. *Austral Ecology* 28: 674-683.

Tozer, M.G. and Bradstock, R.A. (2003) Fire-mediated effects of overstorey on plant species diversity and abundance in an eastern Australian heath. *Plant Ecology* 164: 213-223.

Tozer, M.G., Turner, K., Keith, D.A., Tindall, D., Pennay, C., Simpson, C., MacKenzie, B., Beukers, P. and Cox, S. (2010). Native vegetation of southeast NSW: a revised classification and map for the coast and eastern tablelands. *Cunninghamia* 11: 359-406.

Westoby, M., Walker, B. and Noy-Meir, I. (1989). Opportunistic management for rangelands not at equilibrium. *Journal of Range Management* 42: 266–274.

Zammit, C. (1988). Dynamics of resprouting in the lignotuberous shrub *Banksia oblongifolia*. *Australian Journal of Ecology* 13: 311–320

Proc. Linn. Soc. N.S.W., 134, 2012

B197

First Record of *Hemiboeckella searli* Sars, 1912 (Calanoida: Centropagidae) in New South Wales

Tsuyoshi Kobayashi[1*], Ian A.E. Bayly[2], Simon J. Hunter[1],
Stephen J. Jacobs[1] and Michael B. Treanor[3]

[1]Scientific Services Division, Office of Environment and Heritage NSW, Department of Premier and Cabinet,
PO Box A290 Sydney South, New South Wales 1232
[2]School of Biological Sciences, Monash University, Melbourne, Victoria 3800
[3]Royal National Park, NSW National Parks and Wildlife Service, Office of Environment and Heritage, PO
Box 144 Sutherland, New South Wales 1499
*Author for correspondence: Yoshi.Kobayashi@environment.nsw.gov.au

Published on 3 September 2012 at http://escholarship.library.usyd.edu.au/journals/index.php/LIN

Kobayashi, T., Bayly, I.A.E., Hunter, S.J., Jacobs, S.J. and Treanor, M.B. (2012). First record of
Hemiboeckella searli Sars, 1912 (Calanoida: Centropagidae) in New South Wales. *Proceedings of the
Linnean Society of New South Wales* **134**, B199-B204.

The calanoid copepod *Hemiboeckella searli* Sars is recorded for the first time from New South Wales
in Jibbon Lagoon, Royal National Park (34°05'12"S/151°09'53"E). This calanoid species is endemic to
Australia and occurs in a narrow range of southern latitudes with a wide longitudinal distribution (Tasmania,
Victoria and Western Australia). Our record of *H. searli* in Jibbon Lagoon represents a ~250 km northerly
latitudinal extension from previous records of the species in south-eastern Australia.

Manuscript received 5 December 2011, accepted for publication 29 February 2012.

KEYWORDS: centropagid calanoid, *Hemiboeckella searli*, Jibbon Lagoon, New South Wales, Royal
National Park

INTRODUCTION

Royal National Park (~15,000 ha) on the
southern border of Sydney (34°05'S/151°09'E) is
the oldest national park in Australia, dedicated by the
NSW Government as a national domain for rest and
recreation in 1879 (Thorvaldson 1978). The park has
terrestrial and aquatic habitats including heathland,
woodland, eucalypt forest, rainforest, creeks, rivers
and wetlands (lagoons and upland swamps) (New
South Wales National Parks and Wildlife Service
2000). The park is home to diverse terrestrial and
aquatic vertebrates including ~50 species of mammals,
240 species of birds, 40 species of reptiles and 30
species of amphibians. The park also provides habitat
for hundreds of species of terrestrial invertebrates
such as insects and snails, but little is known about
the aquatic invertebrates. As part of a study of aquatic
invertebrates in the park, we collected zooplankton
from Jibbon Lagoon (a deflation hollow with a sandy
bottom) in September 2011. We report the first record
of the centropagid calanoid *Hemiboeckella searli* in
NSW.

MATERIALS AND METHODS

Study area

Jibbon Lagoon (34°05'12"S/151°09'53"E)
is in the north-eastern area of sand dunes in Royal
National Park (Figs. 1 and 2). The lagoon is a
deflation hollow filled with fresh water, even though
it is below sea level (New South Wales National Parks
and Wildlife Service 2000; Mooney et al. 2001). It
has an entire basin area of ~3.2 ha and a maximum
depth of ~2 m. The water in the lagoon derives from
direct precipitation and runoff from the surrounding
small catchment, and it dries out almost completely
during dry periods. The catchment vegetation is
dominated by coastal heathland, Sydney Red Gum
(*Angophora costata*) dune forest, and a *Cupaniopsis*
littoral closed forest assemblage consisting of
Tuckeroo (*Cupaniopsis anacardioides*) and Bangalay
(*Eucalyptus botryoides*) (Chalson 1983). Parts of the
lagoon are dominated by emergent Tall Spike Rush
(*Eleocharis sphacelata*) which is surrounded by a
closed sedgeland assemblage (Goldstein 1976).

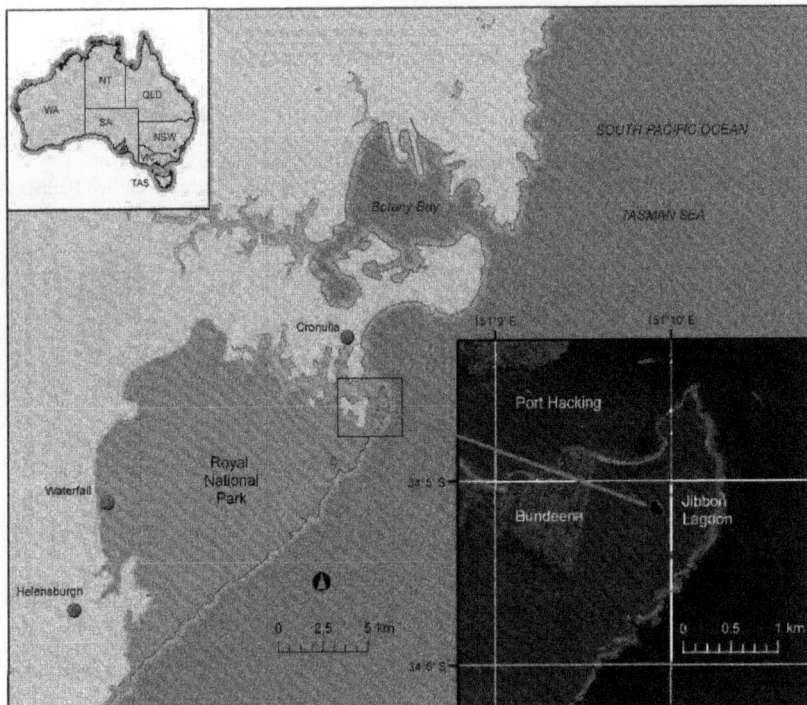

Figure 1. Location of Jibbon Lagoon in Royal National Park.

Figure 2. Jibbon Lagoon on 12 September 2011 (south-east view).

Zooplankton sampling and water quality measurements

We sampled zooplankton in Jibbon Lagoon on 1 and 12 September 2011, by towing two conical plankton nets (63 μm and 150 μm mesh sizes) around near shore areas (both open and littoral) for about 20 minutes.

Specimens were preserved in 70% ethanol. In the laboratory, zooplankton specimens were examined and sorted under a Leica M80 stereomicroscope at a magnification of × 20 to × 50. Calanoid species were identified (Bayly 1992) under a Leica Diaplan compound microscope at a magnification of ×100. In the field, water temperature and dissolved oxygen

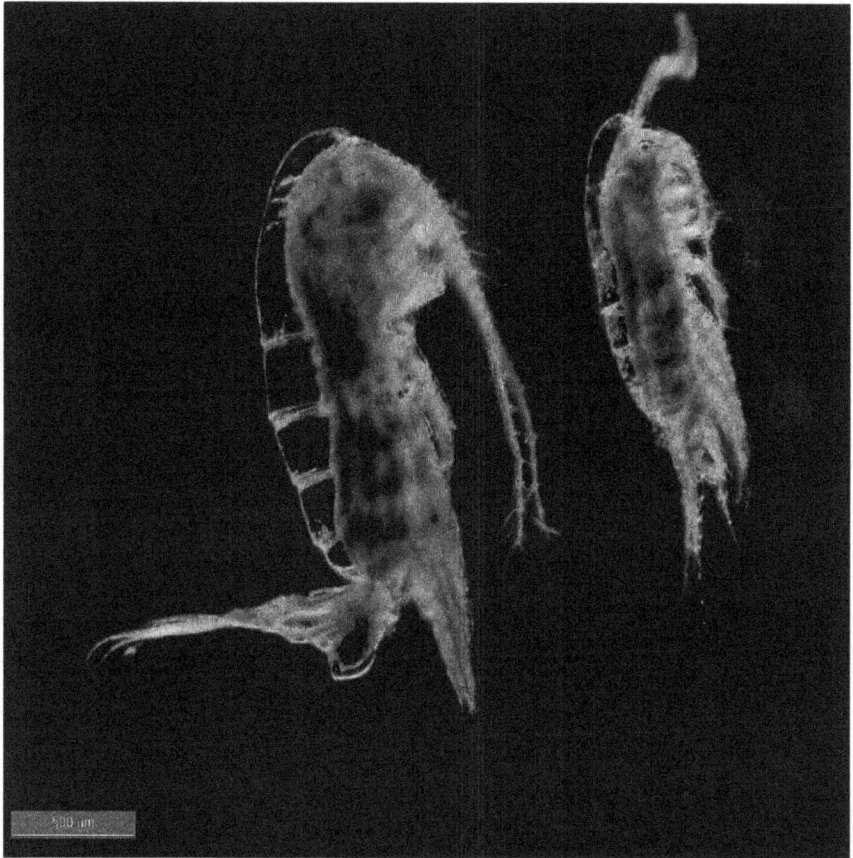

Figure 3. Microphotograph of *Hemiboeckella searli* Sars collected in Jibbon Lagoon on 12 September 2011 (left: female; right: male). Scale bar: 500 μm.

concentration were measured using a YSI Model 5100 Dissolved Oxygen/Temperature Metre (YSI Inc., Ohio). Water samples were also collected to measure conductivity (ORION Model 160 conductivity meter, Orion Research Inc., Massachusetts), turbidity (NTU) (HACH 2011AN turbidimeter, Hach Company, Colorado) and pH (ORION Thermo Model 720A pH meter, Orion Research Inc., Massachusetts), and to analyse nutrients in the laboratory. The method of nutrient analysis followed Hosomi and Sudo (1986) and Eaton et al. (2005).

RESULTS

Hemiboeckella searli was found in samples collected from Jibbon Lagoon on 1 and 12 September 2011 (Fig. 3). The prosomal length of *H. searli* was 1.00 ± 0.011 mm (mean±standard error, $n=16$) for males and 1.44 ± 0.019 for females ($n=10$). *Calamoecia tasmanica tasmanica* (Smith) was the only other centropagid calanoid found in the samples. Physico-chemical analyses indicated that Jibbon Lagoon water was fresh, acidic, with low levels of turbidity and nutrients. Water samples collected at ~1300 hrs on 1

Proc. Linn. Soc. N.S.W., 134, 2012

B201

September 2011 had the following properties: water temperature: 21.3 °C; dissolved oxygen: 9.1 mg l⁻¹; conductivity: 337 µS cm⁻¹; pH: 6.1; turbidity: 1.6 NTU; dissolved inorganic nitrogen: 185 µg l⁻¹; total nitrogen: 399 µg l⁻¹; dissolved inorganic phosphorus: 1 µg l⁻¹; and total phosphorus: 7 µg l⁻¹.

DISCUSSION

Hemiboeckella searli was first described by Sars (1912) from a collection of samples by J. Searle from Caulfield which is now an inner suburb of Melbourne city, Victoria. The species occurs mainly in temporary pools in coastal areas. It is also found in fringing littoral vegetation in inland permanent waters (Morton and Bayly 1977; Bayly 1979). Jibbon Lagoon is a particularly suitable habitat for the species because it is both a temporary water body and has well-developed littoral vegetation.

Of the three species of *Hemiboeckella* that occur in Australia, *Hemiboeckella searli* is the only species which occurs in both eastern and western Australia (Maly and Bayly 1991), with previous records from Tasmania (Bayly 1964), Victoria (Bayly 1964; Morton and Bayly 1977; Green and Shiel 1999) and Western Australia (Bayly 1992; Edward et al. 1994) (Fig. 4). All previous records of *H. searli* are in a relatively narrow latitudinal range in south-eastern Australia. Our record of *H. searli* in Jibbon Lagoon represents a significant (~250 km) northerly latitudinal extension in south-eastern Australia from the records of Green and Shiel (1999). However, it represents only a ~40 km northerly latitudinal extension from previous records in Western Australia (Edward et al. 1994).

In other locations, *Hemiboeckella searli* co-occurs with centropagid calanoids of different sizes such as *Boeckella major*, *B. pseudochelae* and *B. minuta* (Morton and Bayly 1977; Maly 1984; Green and Shiel 1999). In Jibbon Lagoon, *H. searli* co-occurs with *Calamoecia tasmanica tasmanica* whose distribution in eastern Australia is documented by Bayly (1964) and Timms (1982, 1997). These calanoid species differ in body size and feeding behaviour which most likely allow them to co-occur in the lagoon (i.e. food niche separation, Kobayashi 1995): the larger *H. searli* is carnivorous and the smaller *C. tasmanica tasmanica* is herbivorous (Maly 1984; Green and Shiel 1999; Kobayashi, personal observations). The prosomal lengths given above produce a female to male size ratio of 1.44 which is exceptionally high and comparable with the value of 1.51 given by Bayly (1978) who produced data showing that the degree of sexual dimorphism in

Hemiboeckella is exceptionally high for non-marine calanoids. It is also possible that *H. searli* occurs as a shallow water/littoral fringe inhabitant, leaving the open water/eulimnetic habitat to *C. tasmanica tasmanica* (i.e. spatial niche separation). This aspect could be explored by carefully and independently sampling the open and littoral waters in the lagoon.

There are diverse coastal freshwater bodies in eastern Australia, with different modes of origin, water chemistry and biological features (Timms 1982, 1986). The species of calanoid copepods recorded in these water bodies in NSW now include *Calamoecia tasmanica tasmanica* (the most common), *Boeckella propinqua*, *Boeckella saycei* and *Hemiboeckella searli* (Bayly 1964; Timms 1982, 1997; present study). *B. saycei* was known only from temporary ponds in southern Victoria, mainly in the Gippsland region (Morton and Bayly 1977) until Timms (1997, p. 254) reported it in a dune-contact lake in southern NSW.

ACKNOWLEDGEMENTS

We thank Daniel Lunney and David Keith for initial advice, the officers of Royal National Park, NSW NPWS for logistic support, Ed Czobik for nutrient analyses, and two anonymous reviewers for helpful comments. We are grateful to Adam McSorley for producing a panoramic-view photograph of Jibbon Lagoon (Fig. 2), and Cheryl Tang for taking a microphotograph of *H. searli* (Fig. 3).

REFERENCES

Bayly, I.A.E. (1964). A revision of the Australasian species of the freshwater genera *Boeckella* and *Hemiboeckella* (Copepoda: Calanoida). *Australian Journal of Marine and Freshwater Research* **15**, 18-238.

Bayly, I.A.E. (1978). Variation in sexual dimorphism in nonmarine calanoid copepods and its ecological significance. *Limnology and Oceanography* **23**, 1224-1228.

Bayly, I.A.E. (1979). Further contributions to a knowledge of the centropagid genera *Boeckella*, *Hemiboeckella* and *Calamoecia* (athalassic calanoid copepods). *Australian Journal of Marine and Freshwater Research* **30**, 103-127.

Bayly, I.A.E. (1992). The non-marine Centropagidae (Copepoda: Calanoida) of the world. Guides to the identification of the microinvertebrates of the continental waters of the world 2. SPB Academic Publishing bv, The Hague. 30 pp.

Chalson, J. (1983). Palynology and Palaeoecology of Jibbon Swamp, Royal National Park. Honours thesis,

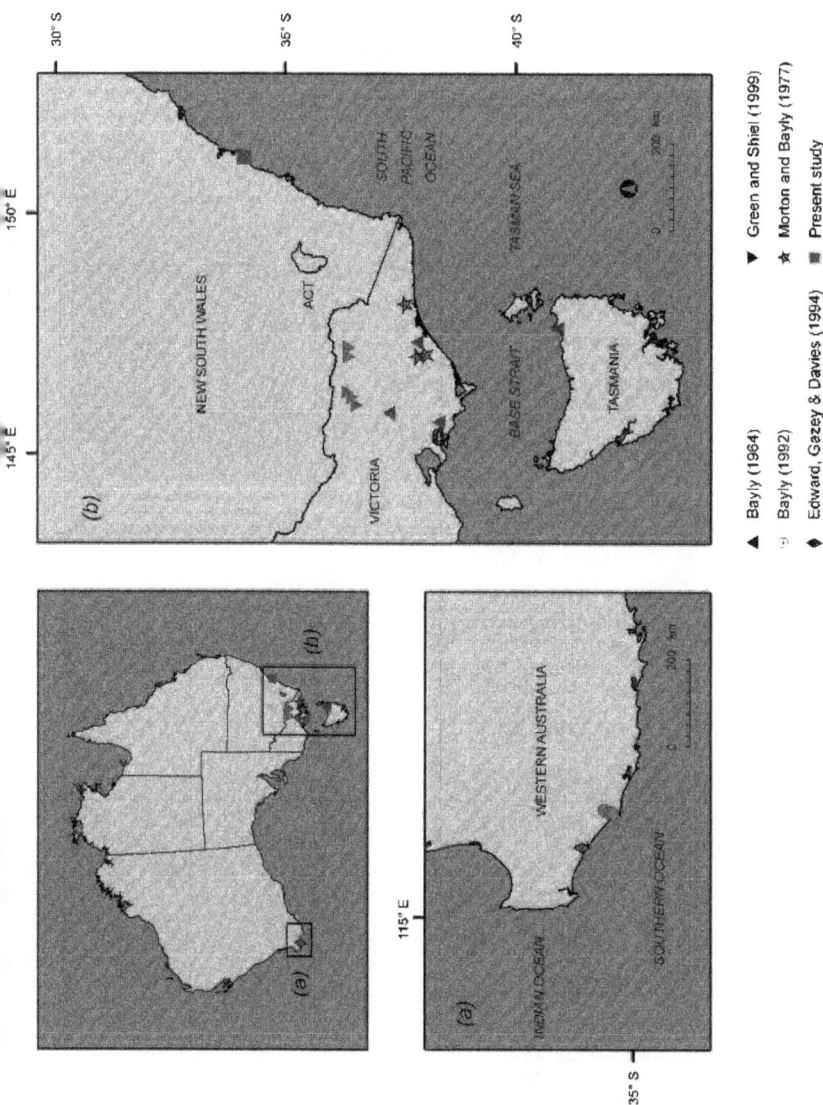

Figure 4. Geographical distribution of *Hemiboeckella searli* Sars in Australia (Bayly 1964, 1992; Edward et al. 1994; Green and Shiel 1999; Morton and Bayly 1977; present study).

University of New South Wales, Sydney.

Eaton, A.D., Clesceri, L.S., Rice, E.W. and Greenberg, A.E. (Eds) (2005). Standard methods for examination of water & wastewater. Centennial edition, 21ˢᵗ edn. (American Public Health Association: Washington, D.C., USA).

Edward, D.H.D., Gazey, P. and Davies, P.M. (1994). Invertebrate community structure related to physico-chemical parameters of permanent lakes of the south coast of Western Australia. *Journal of the Royal Society of Western Australia* **77**, 51-63.

Goldstein, W. (1976). Royal National Park. Environmental Education and Wildlife Extension Section, National Parks and Wildlife Service, Sydney.

Green, J.D. and Shiel, R.J. (1999). Mouthpart morphology of three calanoid copepods from Australian temporary pools: evidence for carnivory. *New Zealand Journal of Marine and Freshwater Research* **33**, 385-398.

Hosomi, M. and Sudo, R. (1986). Simultaneous determination of total nitrogen and total phosphorus in freshwater samples using persulfate digestion. *International Journal of Environmental Studies* **27**, 267-275.

Kobayashi, T. (1995). Different patterns of resource use between two coexisting freshwater calanoid species. *Marine and Freshwater Research* **46**, 481-484.

Maly, E.J. (1984). Dispersal ability and relative abundance of *Boeckella* and *Calamoecia* (Copepoda: Calanoida) in Australian and New Zealand waters. *Oecologia* **62**, 173-181.

Maly, E.J. and Bayly, I.A.E. (1991). Factors influencing biogeographic patterns of Australasian centropagid copepods. *Journal of Biogeography* **18**, 455-461.

Mooney, S. D., Radford, K. L. and Hancock, G. (2001). Clues to the 'burning question': pre-European fire in the Sydney coastal region from sedimentary charcoal and palynology. *Ecological Management and Restoration* **2**, 203-212.

Morton, D.W. and Bayly, I.A.E. (1977). Studies on the ecology of some temporary freshwater pools in Victoria with special reference to microcrustaceans. *Australian Journal of Marine and Freshwater Research* **28**, 439-454.

New South Wales National Parks and Wildlife Service (2000). Royal National Park, Heathcote National Park and Garawarra Recreation Area plan of management. New South Wales National Parks and Wildlife Service, Sydney.

Sars, G.O. (1912). Additional notes on freshwater Calanoida from Victoria, Southern Australia. Archiv for Mathematik og Naturvidenskab **32**, 3-20.

Thorvaldson, F. (1978). Royal National Park. An Illustrated Pocketbook. Colona Printing, Sydney.

Timms, B.V. (1982). Coastal dune waterbodies of north-eastern New South Wales. *Australian Journal of Marine and Freshwater Research* **33**, 203-222.

Timms, B.V. (1986). The coastal dune lakes of eastern Australia. In 'Limnology in Australia' (Eds P. De Deckker and W.D. Williams) pp. 421-432. (CSIRO/ Dr W. Junk Publ.: Melbourne, Australia/Dordrecht: The Netherlands).

Timms, B.V. (1997). Study of coastal freshwater lakes in southern New South Wales. *Marine and Freshwater Research* **48**, 249-256.

Is an Island Reserve Enough? The Decline and Fall of the White-fronted Chat (Aves: Meliphagidae) in Southern Sydney

R.E. Major and J. L.T. Sladek.

Terrestrial Ecology, Australian Museum, 6 College St, Sydney NSW 2010
Corresponding author, richard.major@austmus.gov.au

Published on 3 September 2012 at http://escholarship.library.usyd.edu.au/journals/index.php/LIN

Major, R.E. and Sladek, J.L.T. (2012). Is an island reserve enough? The decline and fall of the White-fronted Chat (Aves: Meliphagidae) in southern Sydney. *Proceedings of the Linnean Society of New South Wales* **134**, B205-B214.

Ecological theory predicts that local extinction and recolonisation are normal events, but the frequency of each is likely to change as the habitat matrix between local populations becomes less suitable. Despite these predictions, local extinctions are seldom documented and there is a popular belief that nature reserves conserve biodiversity. This paper traces the decline of the White-fronted Chat (*Epthianura albifrons*) in the region surrounding Royal National Park and examines preliminary data on the species' ecology and population dynamics. Although once widespread across the region White-fronted Chats are now confined to a single breeding population of approximately 20 individuals that spends much of its time as a single flock, mostly roosting, nesting and foraging within Towra Point Nature Reserve. Numbers appear to be relatively stable, but the population has lost genetic variability. In spite of a high abundance of potential nest predators, there is ongoing recruitment, with pairs nesting twice per season. The population is threatened by mangrove encroachment of salt marsh, ongoing development of the Kurnell peninsular, increased predation rates due to anthropogenically-elevated predator abundances, and demographic factors associated with small population size. The history of this species is a clear demonstration that even conservation reserves with a relatively high degree of protection from human disturbance cannot protect regional biodiversity in the absence of active management if they are isolated.

Manuscript received 28 November 2011, accepted for publication 29 February 2012.

KEY WORDS: island biogeography, *Epthianura albifrons*, genetic diversity, microsatellite, nest success, Royal National Park, salt marsh, survivorship, urbanisation, White-fronted Chat.

INTRODUCTION

National parks and nature reserves are often referred to as the "jewels in the crown", providing the backbone for government efforts directed towards the conservation of biodiversity (SEWPaC 2011). As well as providing the habitat in which populations of animals can be maintained, reserves have the potential to produce recruits that can populate sub-optimal habitat patches in the landscape, thereby contributing to off-reserve conservation. Both these benefits are ultimately dependent on the size of the reserve and the degree of similarity between the reserve and the surrounding environment. If reserves are small, thereby supporting small populations, and surrounded by a matrix of habitat that is unsuitable for a particular species, that species is more prone to

local extinction. Ecological theory predicts that local extinctions will occur periodically, but subsequent dispersal from other patches will allow recolonisation and persistence through time. If a reserve is remote from other reserves that provide similar habitat, however, the likelihood of recolonisation is low and the local extinction may be permanent. Despite their predicted occurrence, local extinctions are seldom documented and there is a popular belief that animal populations in reserves are secure. The aim of this study is to document the decline of a bird species that was once widespread across southern Sydney, including occurrences in Royal National Park and Towra Point Nature Reserve.

The White-fronted Chat (*Epthianura albifrons*) is a small (13 g) bird which belongs to the honeyeater family (Driskell and Christidis 2004), despite foraging almost exclusively on ground insects (Major 1991a). The species occupies damp, open habitats in the southern part of Australia from Carnarvon on the Western Australian coast across to South West Rocks in New South Wales (Barrett et al. 2003). In New South Wales its distribution is split by the forests and woodlands of the Great Dividing Range, with coastal birds largely confined to coastal salt marsh, and inland birds occupying wetlands bordered by chenopod shrublands or grasslands. A significant decline in reporting rate over a 20 year period has been identified in New South Wales (Barrett et al. 2007, Jenner et al. 2011) and the species is listed as vulnerable under the New South Wales Threatened Species Conservation Act (NSWSC 2010a). Coastal populations are showing the greatest decline, and the population in the Sydney Metropolitan Catchment Management Authority area has been listed as an endangered population (NSWSC 2010b). This study reviews the decline of the species in the region surrounding Royal National Park and provides preliminary data on population size, connectivity, habitat selection, adult survival and reproductive success. These data are necessary to determine the viability of the population and the extent to which it is protected by the reserve system.

METHODS

Historical distribution

Information on the historical distribution of the White-fronted Chat in the region surrounding Royal National Park (Parramatta River south to Helensburgh – Fig. 1) was compiled from three forms of data: 1) published accounts of early Australian ornithologists (Ramsay 1863, Gould 1865, North 1904); 2) the collection databases of the Australian Museum and Museum Victoria, and 3) the historical database of the New South Wales Bird Atlassers, which is compiled from published records from the ornithological literature. Location data from each record were mapped and duplicate records from the different sources were excluded.

Current population size

White-fronted Chats currently occur in the study region only at Towra Point Nature Reserve in Botany Bay and at Newington Nature Reserve on the Parramatta River (NSW Scientific Committee 2010b, Jenner et al. 2011), although the Newington population appears doomed, consisting only of four males (unpubl. data). The Towra Point population was therefore the focus of this work, and the size

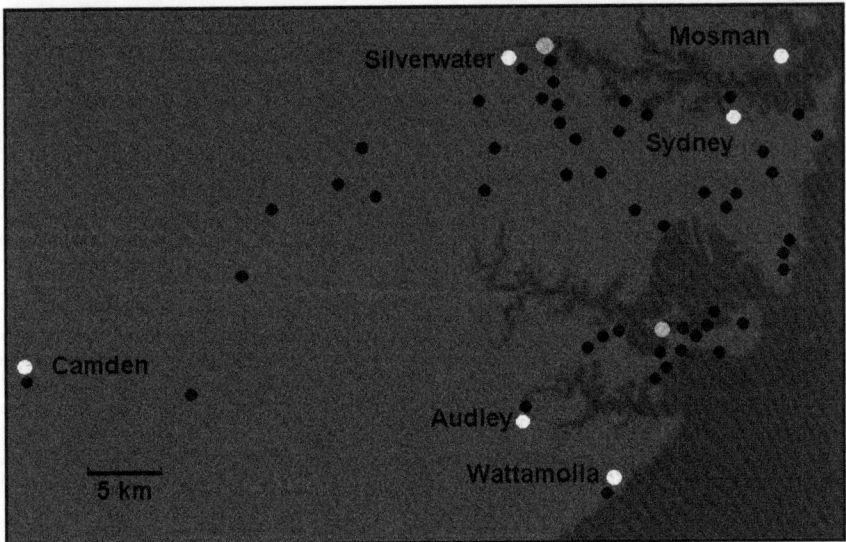

Figure 1. Historical localities of White-fronted Chats in the study region which extends from Royal National Park in the south to the Parramatta River in the north. Historical localities are shown by filled black circles. The two extant localities are shown by yellow filled circles: Newington Nature Reserve on the Parramatta River, and Towra Point Nature Reserve in Botany Bay. White filled circles mark place names.

B206

Proc. Linn. Soc. N.S.W., 134, 2012

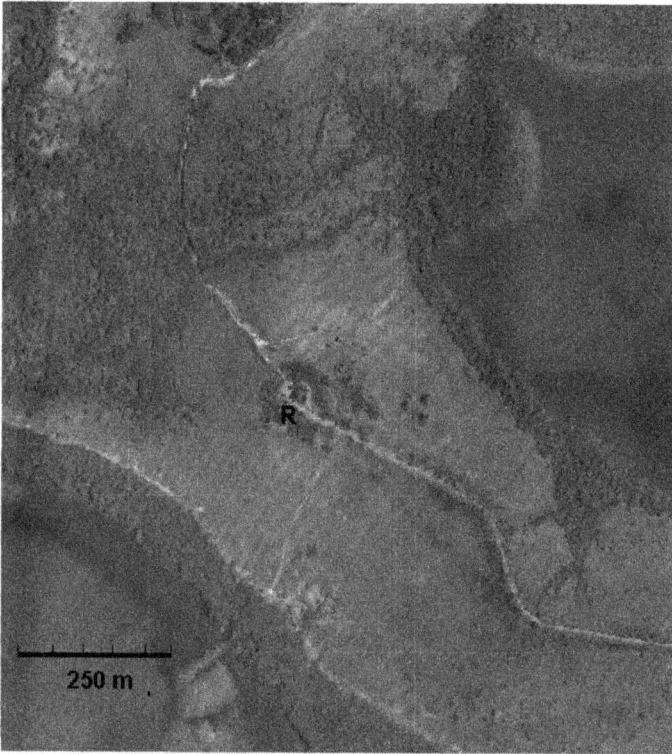

Figure 2. Air photo of the salt marsh at the "neck" of Towra Point which was the predominant area used by White-fronted Chats. Salt marsh appears as the fine texture, with mangroves appearing as the course texture. R = the location of the mangroves in which the birds roosted during June 2010.

of the population was estimated from 63 surveys conducted between September 2009 and February 2011. Each survey was a minimum of three hours duration, and traversed the 50 ha patch of salt marsh habitat in "the neck" of Towra Point (Fig. 2) (Mitchell and Adam 1989). On each survey we recorded the location of each group of birds encountered and the number of birds in each group. The population size on a particular day was estimated as the maximum number of birds known to be present at one instant. This normally corresponded to the size of the largest flock observed on the day, but on some occasions it included additional birds known to be foraging away from the main flock.

Population isolation

To determine whether the Towra Point population was closed to immigration, we compared the genetic structure of birds from Towra Point (n=10) with birds from the nearest neighbouring populations at Homebush Bay (n=6) and Shoalhaven Heads (n=8). DNA was extracted from feather samples taken from birds captured in mist nets and each bird was genotyped for 19 microsatellite markers (unpubl. data). The program STRUCTURE (Pritchard et al. 2000) was used to determine the number of genetically distinct clusters and to assign each bird to a cluster based only on its genotype (rather than including information from its sampling location). Levels of allelic diversity and heterozygosity were determined using the program GENALEX (Peakall and Smouse 2006).

Use of habitat

To identify important patches of habitat for the Towra Point population, we mapped the location

Proc. Linn. Soc. N.S.W., 134, 2012

B207

of flocks of birds during 103 hours of observations during winter, and the location of nests during 104 hours of observation during the spring of 2010. Winter observations were assisted by intensive monitoring of three birds fitted with radio transmitters. Transmitters weighing 0.5 g were glued to the backs of each bird using the technique of Sykes et al. (1990). Each bird was tracked for up to 21 days between 9th and 30th June, 2010, by which time all batteries had discharged. Important breeding habitat was identified by locating nests during the breeding season between 1st September and 20th December, 2010 (see 'Survival rates below).

Survival rates

To measure the survival rate of adults, a sample of birds was marked with unique combinations of coloured leg bands. Individual birds were identified by observing their bands with a 20 X spotting scope and annual survival was determined by calculating the percentage of birds known to be alive in the spring of 2009 (n=11) that were resighted alive in the spring of 2010.

To measure reproductive success, weekly nest searches were conducted by 1-3 observers during the 2010 breeding season between 1st September and 20th December. Each search lasted for 4-8 hrs commencing between 0 and 1 hrs after sunrise. Nests were located by observing distraction displays (Major 1991b) or watching from a hide at locations where the same banded bird was seen repeatedly. Once located, nests were checked weekly to monitor their outcome, continuing until the contents were depredated or the parents were seen attending fledglings away from the nest.

RESULTS

Historical distribution

There are historical records of White-fronted Chats from numerous localities in the region to the north of Royal National Park as well as a few records from within the Park itself (Fig. 1). There are two atlas records from Audley in 1982, one from Wattamolla in 2001 and four records from unspecified locations (not shown in Fig. 1) in Royal National Park between 1948 and 1960.

The observations of Ramsay (1863) that: "about Botany and the Parramatta River, upon the borders of the Hexham swamps etc., they are plentiful", are confirmed by numerous records throughout the early to mid-1900s that are concentrated around the Kurnell Peninsular and Homebush Bay (Fig. 1). The distribution of the species appears to have been continuous between Botany Bay and the Parramatta

River, with records indicating a western link along the Cooks River through Canterbury, Enfield, Strathfield and Homebush; and an eastern link through Mascot, Eastlakes, Centennial Park, Bondi and Rose Bay. Birds in these locations were likely to be resident, given that nesting is also recorded: e.g., "At Canterbury, New South Wales, on the 15th November, 1892, while walking among some rushes, I flushed a male from a tuft where I found it had been sitting on four fresh eggs." (North 1904). The Australian Museum's egg collection indicates that birds were also resident at, amongst other locations, Enfield, Belmore, Randwick, Centennial Park and Bondi. The historic distribution also extended in a south-westerly direction from the Parramatta River through Auburn, Cabramatta, Ingleburn, Campbelltown and Camden.

Population isolation

Analysis of the genotypes of individuals from the three White-fronted Chat populations revealed strong population structuring with the best genetic model identifying three distinct clusters (Fig. 3). There was a strong correspondence between the sampling location of individuals and their position within the clusters, indicating that birds from the three locations made up three distinct genetic populations. All ten birds from Towra Point were strongly assigned to cluster one, all eight birds from Shoalhaven Heads were strongly assigned to cluster two, and five of the six birds from Homebush Bay were strongly assigned to cluster 3, with the sixth bird (H6) in this sample showing ancestry from both clusters two and three.

A loss of genetic diversity, expressed in both heterozygosity and allelic diversity, was evident in the small populations at Towra Point and Homebush Bay, compared with the population at Shoalhaven Heads. Heterozygosity was lower at Towra Point (UHe=0.60±0.05 s.e.) and Homebush Bay (UHe= 0.64±0.05) than at Shoalhaven Heads (UHe=0.77±0.04). Mean allelic diversity per locus was lower at Towra Point (Ne=2.71±0.23 s.e.) and Homebush Bay (Ne= 2.88±0.25) than at Shoalhaven Heads (Ne=4.60±0.48).

Current population size

Apart from the four remaining males at Homebush Bay (unpubl. data) the only records of White-fronted Chats in the Sydney region since 2001 have been from Towra Point Nature Reserve. The maximum number of individuals seen on any one day ranged from 1 to 24 birds (mean 12.9±6.9 sd birds) over the 63 surveys, excluding 6 surveys when no birds were detected. The estimated population size was lowest during the two spring seasons (Fig. 4), presumably because most birds were breeding and

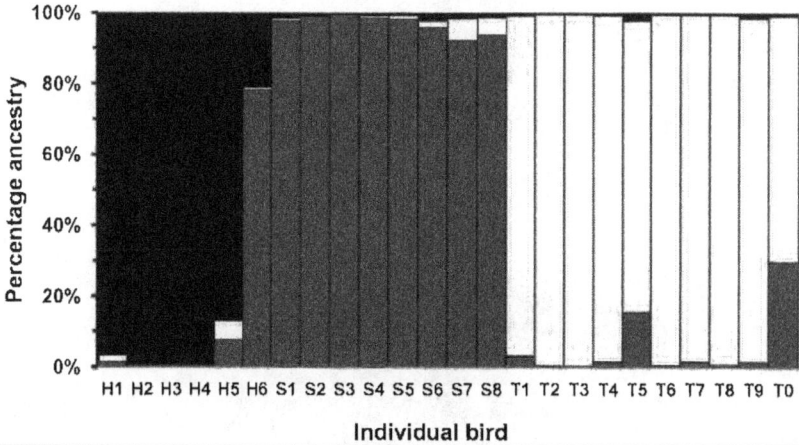

Figure 3. Inferred ancestry (expressed as a percentage) of individual birds from each of three genetic clusters (cluster 1 = black, cluster 2 = grey and cluster 3 = white). The location from which each individual was sampled is indicated by a letter: H = Homebush Bay, S= Shoalhaven Heads and T=Towra Point.

so nesting activities prevented all birds from forming the single foraging flock that was observed in late summer and winter. No birds were detected during four surveys during autumn 2010.

Use of habitat

Despite searching throughout Towra Point, birds with radio-transmitters were detected only

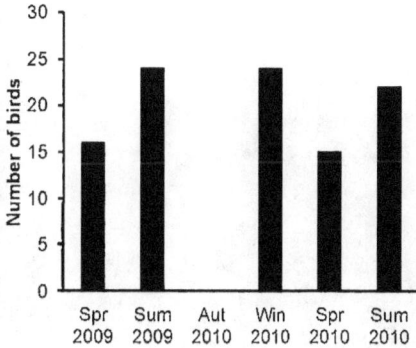

Figure 4. Estimates of the size of the Towra Point population in each season, defined as the maximum number of birds identified on any survey during the season. Each of the 63 surveys had a minimum duration of 3 hrs. No birds were detected during four surveys in autumn 2010.

within the large patch of salt marsh along the "neck" of Towra Point (Fig. 5). One radio-transmitter failed after only seven days, but each of the remaining two birds (151.382MHz, and 151.051MHz) was observed to forage in flocks of up to 24 birds in several locations across the salt marsh (Fig. 5a, b). For both of these birds, there appeared to be a shift in the area used between the winter and spring seasons.

Anecdotal observations indicate that many of the winter foraging locations were in low salt marsh vegetation comprised mostly of *Sarcocornia quinqueflora* while most of the spring observations were made near nest sites, which were in slightly higher salt marsh vegetation comprised of *Juncus krausii* and *Suaeda australis*. A similar pattern is apparent from records of the locations of all flocks of five or more birds and the location of all nests found during the spring of 2010 (Fig. 5c). Only a single nest and no flocks of birds were located outside the "neck" of Towra Point.

The radio-transmitters also allowed identification of the locations in which birds roosted at night during June 2010. The three birds roosted together with other birds in a clump of isolated mangroves for 20, 14 and 6 nights respectively (Fig. 2), apart from one night during which a single bird roosted in mangroves 200 m to the south.

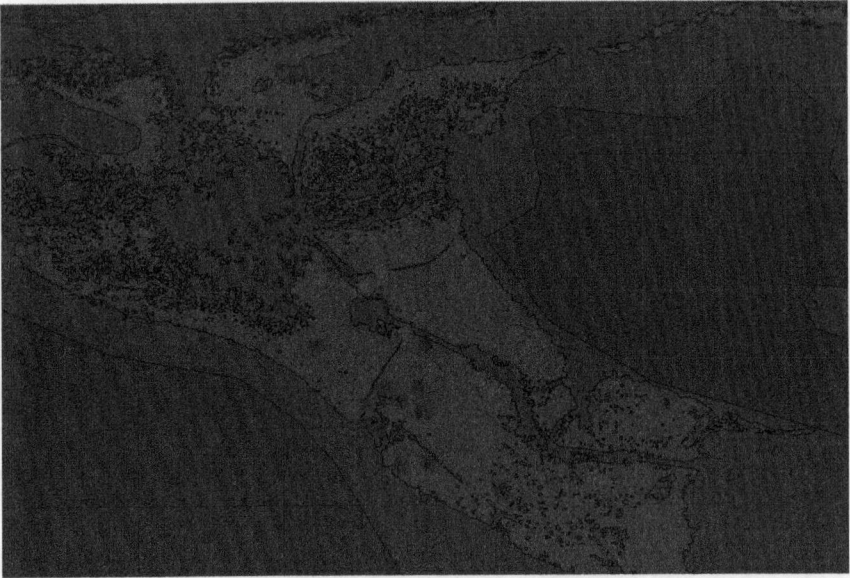

Figure 5a

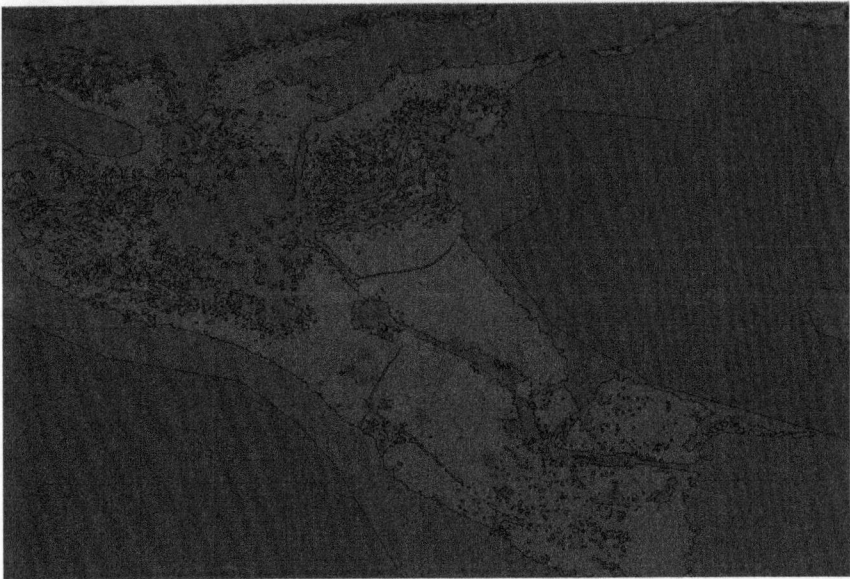

Figure 5b

Figure 5c

Figure 5. Winter (red filled circles) and spring (blue) records of White-fronted Chats at Towra Point. (a) Locations of a male fitted with a radio transmitter (151.382MHz); (b) locations of a male fitted with a radio transmitter (151.051 MHz); (c) locations of flocks of five or more birds (red) and the locations of nests (blue).

Survival rates

A total of eleven adult White-fronted Chats, comprised of seven males and four females were colour banded and, through observations, were known to be alive in the spring of 2009. All four females and five of the males were subsequently identified in the spring of 2010. This equates to an adult annual survival rate of 80%.

We were able to identify 13 nesting attempts by seven separate pairs of birds, of which six pairs made two nesting attempts during the spring of 2010. Two pairs were successful with both their nests, four pairs were successful with one of their attempts, and the pair with the single attempt was unsuccessful. Nesting behaviour was observed for another pair but we were unable to locate the nest and so it is not included in the calculations of reproductive success. Overall nest success was 60%, with three failures presumed to be the result of predation given that the entire nest contents disappeared. Two nests were deserted leaving undeveloped eggs in the nest and as one of these nests had been incubated for at least 11 days prior to desertion it appears that the eggs were infertile. Overall, we followed the fate of 33 eggs, of which 22 hatched and 13 fledged, equivalent to a fledging success rate of 40%.

DISCUSSION

Historical evidence indicates that White-fronted Chats were once widespread and relatively common inhabitants of the region between Royal National Park and the Parramatta River. Records suggest that the most favourable locations were in open habitats along the Cooks River, Georges River and the chain of swamps running through the eastern suburbs into Botany Bay. Salt marsh vegetation was particularly favoured (Ramsay 1863, Keast 1995), and the two extant populations inhabit the two largest remnant patches of salt marsh on the Parramatta River and Georges River respectively. There are few records from Royal National Park and the location

Proc. Linn. Soc. N.S.W., 134, 2012

B211

information of the early records in not specific. The only significant area of salt marsh in Royal National Park is at "The Basin" between Maianbar and Bundeena, but it is much smaller than the patches at Homebush Bay and Botany Bay.

Urban development has not only destroyed most of the suitable habitat for White-fronted Chats in the region, but it has transformed the matrix between suitable patches into a medium that restricts its passage. The species is sensitive to direct human disturbance as was noted by Gould (1865): "It is rather shy in its disposition, and when disturbed flies off with considerable rapidity to the distance of two or three hundred yards before it alights again". More recent research indicates that the species is less tolerant of people and human habitation than other species with which it co-occurs (Hoskin et al. 1991, Jenner et al. 2011). Preliminary data presented here indicate genetic isolation of the Towra Point population despite it being distant from its nearest neighbour by a distance of only 20 km. Given that the species has been recorded flying a distance of at least 18 km across the ocean from Rottnest Island to mainland Australia (Williams 1979) and that movements across Bass Strait are suspected (Schodde and Mason 1999), it appears that the urban environment represents a severe barrier to dispersal for this species.

Given that the Towra Point population is the last breeding population in Sydney, prospects for the continued survival of the species in the region surrounding Royal National Park are not promising. We estimate the population to be extremely small, with a maximum of 24 birds, comparable with previous counts of White-fronted Chats at Towra Point of 20 birds in 1995 (Keast 1995), 16 birds in 2006 (Shultz 2006) and 18 birds in 2008 (Jenner et al. 2011). White-fronted Chats were occasionally absent from the salt marsh at Towra Point, notably in the autumn of 2010, which provides some possibility that there may be patches of suitable habitat on the Kurnell peninsular that are unknown to us, and potentially supporting a larger population. Anecdotal observations from shorebird observers indicate that birds were sometimes present on Spit Island, just off the northern end of Towra Point and 1.5 km distant from the winter roost site; and we have occasionally observed banded birds flying to feed in grassland 2 km to the south west. Although we cannot confirm the absence of additional birds, information collected from the radio transmitters supports our contention that 24 birds was the maximum size of the Towra Point population during our fieldwork: whenever the flock of 24 birds was encountered, all birds with functioning transmitters were always present. Furthermore, the

loss of genetic diversity in the population provides a further indication of its small size.

Although of small size, the populations appears to have been relatively stable over the last 15 years, and neither adult survival (Robinson 1990a, Debus 2006) nor reproductive success (Robinson 1990b, Berry 2001) are low by comparison with other Australian passerines. As they nest close to the ground, White-fronted Chats are prone to predation from both mammalian and avian predators and reproductive success can be extremely low (18%), even in large stable populations (Major 1991b). An active fox-baiting program was in place at Towra Point during this study which may have contributed to the relatively high nesting success, although our sample size was unavoidably small and it is possible that our single-season sample was unrepresentative. Large numbers of ravens (up to 80 individuals originating from urban and industrial land adjoining Towra Point) were observed foraging in the salt marsh on most days of fieldwork, and such a strong presence of this confirmed nest predator (Major 1991b) represents a significant threat to the population of White-fronted Chats. With its small population size and recent isolation, demographic stochasticity could rapidly move this population below a critical level. Additionally, there is already an indication that the population is susceptible to genetic effects associated with inbreeding, further compounding this threat.

There are two other likely threats that may have resulted in the small population size at Towra Point, despite the relatively large patch of salt marsh habitat. Firstly, White-fronted Chats have frequently been reported to make medium scale (up to 3 km) foraging excursions away from their roost sites (Major 1991a), and the numerous historical locations from which birds have been reported on the Kurnell peninsular suggest that the Towra Point population may once have exploited foraging opportunities outside the reserve. With ongoing development of the peninsular, there has been a large decline in potential foraging area. Secondly, there is a well documented decline in the area of salt marsh, resulting from mangrove invasion (Mitchell and Adam 1989), and White-fronted Chats are likely to have used a much larger area of salt marsh in the past. At present we have no knowledge of the extent of habitat required to support a viable population.

Overall, this study provides an example of how intensification of land use in a region can result in the gradual extinction of local populations occupying remnant habitat. Without management intervention it seems inevitable that the population of White-fronted Chats in the region surrounding Royal

B212

Proc. Linn. Soc. N.S.W., 134, 2012

National Park will become extinct, due to the small size of suitable habitat protected in nature reserves and their isolation by an urban matrix. As well as its obvious consequences for regional biodiversity, the loss of this population, along with the recent loss of populations on the Illawarra and Central coasts, will open up a discontinuity between the Shoalhaven and Hunter Rivers. Depending on the level of connectivity between inland and coastal populations, this discontinuity may have consequences for the long term persistence of the northern end of the species distribution.

ACKNOWLEDGEMENTS

This project was funded by grants from Lake Macquarie City Council and the Herman Slade Foundation. We are grateful to the New South Wales Bird Atlassers, the National Museum of Victoria and the Australian Museum for providing their historical records, and to Rebecca Johnson, Andrew King and Georgina Cooke for assistance with DNA analysis. We thank Greg West from the Port Stephens Fisheries Institute (Industry and Investment, NSW) for providing mapping data on the distribution of salt marsh. Birds were banded under a scientific licence (S12586) issued under the NSW National Parks and Wildlife Act, and an Australian Bird and Bat Banding Scheme license A1166. Ethics approval for this project was granted by the Australian Museum Animal Care and Ethics approval number10/01.

REFERENCES

Barrett GW, Silcocks AF, Barry S, Cunningham R, Poulter R (2003) 'The new atlas of Australian birds.' (RAOU: Hawthorn East).

Barrett GW, Silcocks AF, Cunningham R, Oliver DL, Weston MA, Baker J (2007) Comparison of atlas data to determine the conservation status of bird species in New South Wales, with an emphasis on woodland-dependent species. *Australian Zoologist* 34, 37-77.

Berry L (2001) Breeding biology and nesting success of the Eastern Yellow Robin and the New Holland Honeyeater in a southern Victorian woodland. *Emu* 101, 191-197.

Debus SJS (2006) Breeding and population parameters of robins in a woodland remnant in northern New South Wales, Australia. *Emu* 106, 147-156.

Driskell AC and Christidis L (2004) Phylogeny and evolution of the Australo-Papuan honeyeaters (Passeriformes, Meliphagidae). *Molecular Phylogenetics and Evolution* 31, 943-960.

Gould J (1865) 'Handbook to the Birds of Australia.' (Reprinted by Lansdowne Press 1972: Melbourne).

Hoskin ES, Hindwood KA, McGill AR (1991) 'The Birds of Sydney, County of Cumberland.' (Surrey Beattie: Chipping Norton, NSW).

Jenner B, French K, Oxenham K, Major RE (2011) Population decline of the White-fronted Chat (*Ephthianura albifrons*) in New South Wales, Australia. *Emu* 111, 84-91.

Keast A (1995) Habitat loss and species loss: the birds of Sydney 50 years ago and now. *Australian Zoologist* 30, 3-25.

Major RE (1991a) Flocking and feeding in the white-fronted chat *Ephthianura albifrons*: The relationship between diet, food availability and patch selection. *Australian Journal of Ecology* 16, 395-407.

Major RE (1991b) Breeding biology of the white-fronted chat *Epthianura albifrons* in a saltmarsh near Melbourne. *Emu* 91, 236-249.

Mitchell ML, Adam P (1989) The decline of saltmarsh in Botany Bay. *Wetlands (Australia)* 8, 55-60.

North AJ (1904) 'Nest and eggs of birds found breeding in Australia and Tasmania. Vol. 1. Australian Museum Special Catalogue No. 1, Facsimile edition 1984. Trustees of the Australian Museum, Sydney.' (Oxford University Press: Melbourne).

NSWSC (2010a) 'Final Determination to list the White-fronted Chat Epthianura albifrons (Jardine & Selby, 1828) as a vulnerable species.' (New South Wales Scientific Committee: http://www.environment.nsw. gov.au/determinations/ whitefrontedchatvsFD.htm).

NSWSC (2010b) 'Final determination to list a population of the White-fronted Chat *Epthianura albifrons* (Jardine & Selby, 1828) in the Sydney Metropolitan Catchment Management Authority area as an endangered population. .' (New South). Wales Scientific Committee: http://www.environment.nsw. gov.au/ determinations/whitefrontedchatpopFD.htm

Peakall R, Smouse PE (2006) GENALEX 6: genetic analysis in Excel. Population genetic software for teaching and research. . *Molecular Ecology Notes* 6, 288-295

Pritchard JK, Stephens M, Donnelly P (2000) Inference of population structure using multilocus genotype data. *Genetics* 155, 945–959.

Ramsay EP (1863) Notes on the birds breeding in the neighbourhood of Sydney, New South Wales. *Ibis* 5, 177-180.

Robinson D (1990a) The social organisation of the Scarlet Robin *Petroica multicolor* and Flame Robin *P. phoenicea* in southeastern Australia: a comparison between sedentary and migratory flycatchers. *Ibis* 90, 78–94.

Robinson D (1990b) The nesting ecology of sympatric Scarlet Robin *Petroica multicolor* and Flame Robin *P. phoenicea* populations in open eucalypt forest. *Emu* 90, 40-52.

Schodde R, Mason I (1999) 'The directory of Australian birds. Passerines.' (CSIRO Publishing: Melbourne).

Shulz M (2006) 'Fauna survey, Towra Point Nature Reserve area. Report to the NSW Department of Environment and Climate Change, Mornington, Victoria.'

Proc. Linn. Soc. N.S.W., 134, 2012

B213

SEWPaC (2011) 'Australian Government Biodiversity
Policy. A healthy natural environment, now and
always. Consultation draft.' (Australian Government:
Canberra). http://environment.gov.au/epbc/
publications/pubs/consultation-draft-biodiversity-
policy.pdf (accessed 31/10/2011).

Sykes PW, Carpenter JW, Holzman S, Geissler PH (1990)
Evaluation of three miniature radio transmitter
attachment methods for small passerines. *Wildlife
Society Bulletin* **18**, 41-48.

Williams CK (1979) Ecology of Australian chats
(*Epthianura* Gould): reproduction in aridity.
Australian Journal of Zoology **27**, 213-229.

B214

Proc. Linn. Soc. N.S.W., 134, 2012

Vertebrate Fauna: a Survey of Australia's Oldest National Park and Adjoining Reserves

Martin Schulz[1] and Elizabeth Magarey[2]

[1]34 Wilford Street, Corrimal NSW 2518; [2]Office of Environment and Heritage, PO Box 1967, Hurstville NSW 1482 (Elizabeth.Magarey@environment.nsw.gov.au)

Published on 3 September 2012 at http://escholarship.library.usyd.edu.au/journals/index.php/LIN

Schulz, M. and Magarey, E. (2012). Vertebrate fauna: a survey of Australia's oldest national park and adjoining reserves. *Proceedings of the Linnean Society of New South Wales* **134**, B215-B247.

This study compiles an inventory of amphibians, reptiles, birds and mammals in Royal National Park, Garawarra State Conservation Area and Heathcote National Park. It investigates patterns of species occurrence and puts the results into a regional context. Systematic and targeted field surveys were undertaken and previously existing data were reviewed. The surveys detected 283 species. This high species richness can be attributed to the diversity of habitats present. The Rainforests and Heathlands vegetation formations each support a distinct suite of fauna, while many species only occur on the ocean and/or estuarine shoreline. Rainforests and Heathlands have a restricted distribution in the Sydney basin, and in that context the reserves support large numbers of heath-dependant fauna species. The reserves also have relatively high numbers of at least five threatened species. The field surveys detected seven species not previously documented, including Australasian bittern (*Botaurus poiciloptilus*) and eastern grass owl (*Tyto longimembris*). Also notable is the discovery of roosts of eastern horseshoe-bat (*Rhinolophus megaphyllus*) and little bent-wing-bat (*Miniopterus australis*). However, many species previously known from the reserves could not be found, such as ground parrot (*Pezoporus wallicus*), green and golden bell frog (*Litoria aurea*), parma wallaby (*Macropus parma*) and platypus (*Ornithorhynchus anatinus*).

Manuscript received 26 July 2012, accepted for publication 14 August 2012.

KEYWORDS: Garawarra State Conservation Area, Heathcote National Park, management, Royal National Park, species loss, systematic survey, targeted survey, threatened species, vegetation formation.

INTRODUCTION

Information that describes the type, distribution and status of biodiversity in NSW is required for regulation, conservation assessment and land management. In the Sydney Basin Bioregion over 60 per cent of extant native vegetation occurs in Office of Environment and Heritage (OEH) reserves. OEH is working towards generating comprehensive information on flora and vertebrate fauna across all reserves in this region, irrespective of size and location, and ensuring that biodiversity data is collected in a strategic and systematic way. The current study in Royal National Park (NP) and the adjoining Garawarra State Conservation Area (SCA) and Heathcote NP is part of this biodiversity data acquisition program.

Royal NP, proclaimed in 1879, was the first national park gazetted in Australia (NPWS 2000a). Garawarra SCA was dedicated in 1934 as a primitive wilderness and Heathcote NP was gazetted in 1943 as a primitive area; the primary objective of both reserves was the retention of natural conditions (NPWS 2000a). From the early days of Royal NP the Trustees determined to "effectively preserve the flora and fauna committed to their care" thus making it an offence to "discharge firearms or interfere in any way with the birds and animals in the Park" (Trustees 1915). Yet despite the perceived importance of the fauna the vertebrate species present at or prior to the gazettal of the reserves has been little documented, with the exception of isolated accounts of single visits (Cayley 1923) or as part of past regional assessments (Robinson 1987, 1988).

More recent accounts of bird, mammal, reptile and amphibian species exist in several forms. Current avifauna within the three reserves has been summarised by Anyon-Smith (2006). Fauna records are reported in various reports as components of larger studies (such as the nationwide Atlas of Australian

Birds (Blakers et al. 1984; Barrett et al. 2003)) and regional fauna surveys (NPWS 2000b, 2002; DECC 2008), in reports on local fauna surveys undertaken by consultants (Kevin Mills and Associates 1995; LesryK Environmental Consultants 1996, 2005, 2007, 2008, 2010), and as records gathered by various government agencies and private individuals which have been entered into statewide databases (OEH 2012) or posted on internet sites (e.g. Birding-aus and NSW Birdline). A number of single species studies have been undertaken in the reserves, such as on the sooty owl (Chafer and Anderson 1994; Kavanagh and Jackson 1997; Bilney et al. 2007), brown antechinus (Whelan et al. 1996), eastern pygmy-possum (Tulloch 2001), swamp wallaby (Evans 2000; Ramp and Ben-Ami 2006), and the rusa deer (Tuck 1971; Giles and McKenzie 1973; Hamilton 1981; Mahood 1981; Moriarty 2004; Keith and Pellow 2005). A post-fire fauna survey was undertaken following the 1994 wildfire which burnt over 90 per cent of Royal NP (Andrew 2001). This transect-based survey included cage trapping, hair tube sampling, transect spotlighting, predator scat collection, transect bird censuses, pitfall trapping, Elliott trapping, active searches for diurnal and nocturnal herpetofauna, nocturnal call playback for owls, bat trapping and bat ultrasound censuses. A subset of sites was resampled in January 2006 concentrating on heathland communities in Royal NP, and then following the 2001 wildfire that burnt over 90 per cent of Heathcote NP, a repeat survey of all Heathcote NP sites was undertaken (Nolan 2006). The aims of these post-fire surveys were to investigate the impact on vertebrate fauna of the 1994 and 2001 wildfires. The surveys concentrated on widespread vegetation types in particular parts of the reserves, with little or no survey effort in restricted habitats such as freshwater wetlands, mangroves, saltmarsh and grasslands.

This study sought to compile a current accurate and comprehensive inventory of terrestrial vertebrate fauna species on the reserves, assess species relative distributions and broad habitat associations, and put the occurrence of fauna species in a regional context. The field survey design was based upon systematic survey techniques that are currently used by OEH across the Sydney Basin Bioregion, thus contributing to a large region-wide data set that enables comparison across areas and is repeatable in the future. The study also undertook targeted survey techniques and a review of previously existing data, to enable comparison with historical records and an assessment of species that may have been lost from the reserves. The information is intended to assist land managers with conservation and management of vertebrate fauna on the reserves.

MATERIALS AND METHODS

Study area

The study area comprised Royal NP (15,315 ha), Heathcote NP (2,727 ha) and Garawarra SCA (973 ha). These reserves are situated on the southern fringe of metropolitan Sydney and the northern margins of the Wollongong Local Government Area. The area is bounded to the east by the Pacific Ocean and to the west primarily by Holsworthy Military Area and the water catchments that include Woronora Special Area. The coastline of the study area includes intertidal zones such as rock platforms, beaches and rocky cliff bases of the ocean shoreline, however subtidal and adjacent inshore waters were excluded from the study.

The study area consists of a Triassic Hawkesbury sandstone plateau rising to over 200 m above sea level. It is deeply dissected by the Hacking River system which drains northward to the Port Hacking estuary and the Woronora River system which drains into the Georges River. The landscape is characterised by steep valleys and ridges, rocky outcrops and streams, many of which are punctuated by waterfalls and pools (NPWS 2000a). In the east, the plateau is characterised by broad, gently sloping ridges and small eastward-flowing drainage lines. The coastline is dominated by variable height cliffs cut in the Hawkesbury sandstone north of Curracurrong Creek, while extending to the south the cliffs are formed from the softer Narrabeen group of rocks with small beaches at creek mouths (Young and Young 2006). There are a number of geomorphological features that vary from the typical Hawkesbury sandstone plateau environment. Such features include: the cliff-top dunes of unconsolidated sand in the Jibbon Head and Marley Beach areas of Royal NP; a system of low beach ridges on the eastern side of Cabbage Tree Basin in Royal NP; patches of laterite on the higher parts of ridges across the area; and upland swamp areas on low-relief terrain primarily in parts of Royal NP (NPWS 2000a; Young and Young 2006).

A wide range of vegetation communities are present owing to the reserves' coastal location, geological and geomorphological characteristics and variation in climate (Keith and Tozer unpublished; DECCW 2009). The reserves are dominated by Hawkesbury sandstone forests, woodlands and heaths, although smaller patches of a variety of other vegetation types occur. For example, maximum rainfall occurs in the south due to the increased elevation and coastal escarpment resulting in the formation of rainforest communities (NPWS 2000a). For the purposes of the current study vegetation was identified into formations following the statewide

B216

Proc. Linn. Soc. N.S.W., 134, 2012

Table 1. Vegetation formations (after Keith 2004) present in the three reserves in order of area covered.

Statewide vegetation formation	Area (ha)	Distribution within the reserves
Dry Sclerophyll Forests (DSF)	11,372	The most widely distributed vegetation formation occurring on Hawkesbury sandstone ridges, slopes and gullies. For this study riparian scrub, which occurs along larger watercourses, has been included in this formation.
Heathlands (HL)	4,780	Occurs widely on skeletal rock sandstone, including coastal headlands, and on coastal sand dunes at Jibbon and Marley beaches.
Wet Sclerophyll Forests (WSF)	1,690	The shrubby subformation of Wet Sclerophyll Forest (after Keith 2004) is found in the southern end of Royal NP in protected Narrabeen sandstone gullies. Small stands of the grassy subformation of Wet Sclerophyll Forests (after Keith 2004) are distributed on residual shale and ironstone caps at Garawarra, Heathcote and Otford.
Rainforests (RF)	384	Situated in the southern end of Royal NP and parts of Garawarra SCA in protected Narrabeen sandstone gullies, headlands and escarpment slopes.
Freshwater Wetlands (FrW)	217	Includes isolated patches of sedgelands and heaths on poorly drained sandstone ridgetops and gentle slopes, as well as depressions within the sand dunes behind Jibbon and Marley beaches.
Grasslands (GL)	58	Includes small patches of maritime grasslands on exposed coastal headlands and along frontal beach sand dunes.
Forested Wetlands (FoW)	39	Occurs as small patches primarily in the Bundeena-Bonnievale area.
Saline Wetlands (SW)	32	Mangrove swamps and estuarine saltmarshes restricted to the estuarine mudflats exposed to tidal inundation on the lower Hacking River to Bundeena in Port Hacking.

vegetation classification of Keith (2004). The allocation of vegetation community to statewide formation largely follows the system used in the draft mapping of vegetation across the Sydney metropolitan area (DECCW 2009). Under this classification eight vegetation formations occur within the reserves (Table 1; Fig. 1). Additional environments that are not covered by the Keith (2004) classification also occur as follows: shoreline including intertidal reef platforms and sandy beaches; open waterbodies such as larger river reaches; parkland and other modified habitats including picnic areas and mown landscapes.

Review of previous records

Previous fauna records were compiled by a review of scientific publications and published books, published regional fauna survey reports which included parts of the study area, unpublished OEH and consultancy reports, records entered into wildlife databases and on birding internet sites, relevant files held in the OEH office at Royal NP and interviews with local bird watchers, naturalists and OEH staff. All compiled information on fauna species recorded in the reserves was reviewed. To ensure the compiled species inventory was accurate, species were excluded if they met any of the following criteria: a) all of the records have poor location accuracy where the

locality description does not actually occur within the reserves, or where the methods used to identify the location of the sighting had very low spatial accuracy; b) all of the records are probable misidentifications as no suitable habitat is present, the species is outside it's known range, and/or the species has been target surveyed within the reserves by experts on the species and never confirmed to occur; c) they are non-local species that have not established wild populations in the study area or neighbouring lands, including aviary escapees; or d) they are pelagic species that do not use the reserves for resting, foraging or nesting purposes such as various cetacean, seabird and marine reptile species.

Field survey

The field survey included systematic and targeted survey techniques, supported by incidental observations. The majority of surveys were undertaken between July 2009 and June 2010 across all three reserves. An earlier survey was undertaken between February and September 2007 in the Kelly Falls area of Garawarra SCA and the Bulgo-Bald Hill area in the far south of Royal NP.

All data collected during the field survey, together with the systematic survey effort, is stored in the Atlas of NSW Wildlife (OEH 2012) which is available to the public.

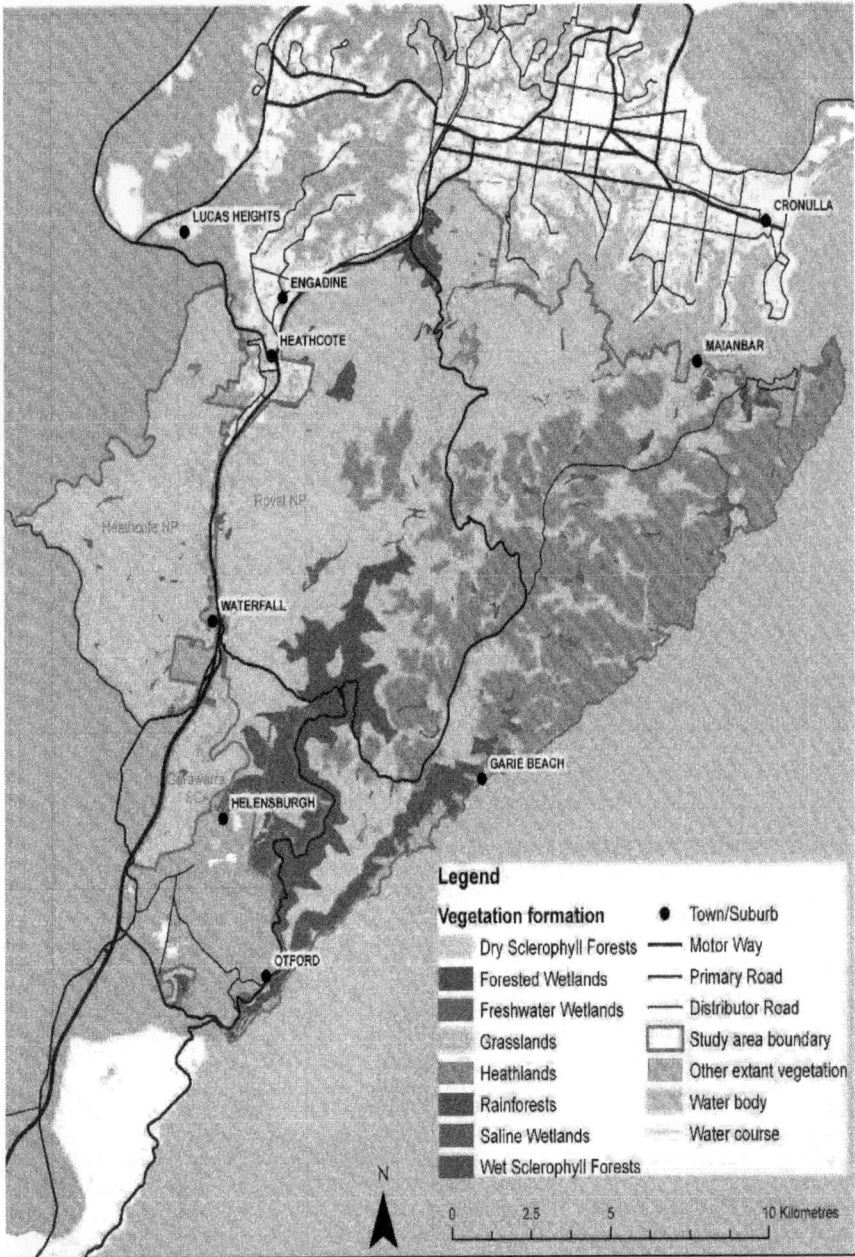

Figure 1. Vegetation formations within Garawarra SCA, Royal and Heathcote NP (adapted from Keith and Tozer unpublished; DECCW 2009).

Table 2. Systematic fauna survey techniques.

Name of technique	Fauna group	Census/equipment type	Effort	Area of search	Climatic conditions and timing
Diurnal bird census	Active diurnal birds	Visual and aural search	20 minutes	100 x 200 m	During periods of relatively high bird activity (early morning and less frequently late afternoon) and reasonable detectability (e.g. low wind and cicada activity).
Diurnal herpetofauna search	Active and sheltering reptiles and frogs	Active search of microhabitats by hand	60 minutes	100 x 50 m	Between mid-morning and late afternoon. Not during overcast, rainy or windy conditions.
Site spotlighting census	Active nocturnal mammals and birds	Active search with 50 watt hand-held spotlight	30 minutes	200 m transect. Predominantly confined to areas with trees taller than 5 m.	Not during windy conditions.
Nocturnal streamside search	Active nocturnal frogs	Active search with 50 watt hand-held spotlight	30 minutes	200 m transect along a watercourse or the edge of a still waterbody.	Primarily on warm, dark, humid and wet nights within two days of rain.
Harp trapping	Active microbats	Single harp trap	1 night	-	Traps set on tracks, over watercourses or in gaps between trees.
Bat ultrasound recording	Active microbats	SD1 Anabat detector (Titley Electronics, Ballina, NSW). Recorded signals indentified by one of the authors (MS).	30 minutes	-	Not during rainy or windy conditions.

Systematic survey techniques

This study deployed the point-based systematic fauna survey techniques that are currently widely used by OEH across the Sydney region and elsewhere in NSW (Table 2). An important component of the OEH systematic survey design is stratification, that is sampling fauna habitats in approximate proportion to the area they cover. Statewide vegetation formation (Keith 2004) was used as the a priori surrogate for fauna habitat.

A gap analysis was undertaken of OEH systematic survey techniques in the study area which had previously been entered into the Atlas of NSW Wildlife (OEH 2012). This analysis identified that limited OEH systematic surveys had been conducted for the following fauna groups: amphibians (n=4), diurnal birds (n=17), reptiles (n=19) and microchiropteran bats (n=5 using ultrasonic detectors and n=31 using harp traps). Nocturnal birds were considered adequately sampled by OEH systematic survey (n=58), as were small mammals (n=63 using Elliott and cage trapping, n=45 using pitfall trapping and n=58 using hair tubes).

This study aimed to fill identified gaps in OEH systematic survey effort. As an a priori surrogate for habitat type, the study sought to sample each vegetation formation by each systematic survey technique in approximate proportion to the area the formation covered. However, additional OEH systematic survey techniques were undertaken at additional sites where time allowed, particularly in vegetation formations that occupied a small total area. A systematic site is defined as any locality where one or more OEH systematic survey techniques were undertaken; not every technique was undertaken at each site. Multiple sites were selected and surveyed in each vegetation formation to account for variation within formations (Table 3). Systematic sites were selected using a Geographic Information System (ArcGIS 9.3) coupled with information from DECCW (2009), topographic maps and knowledge held by OEH staff and other park users. Wherever possible, sites with the same systematic survey techniques were separated by a straight-line distance of 1 km (Fig. 2). However due to the limited distribution of some vegetation formations this was not always possible. Vegetation

Proc. Linn. Soc. N.S.W., 134, 2012

B219

Table 3. Number of each systematic survey technique undertaken in each vegetation formation.

Statewide vegetation formation	Diurnal bird census	Diurnal herpetofauna search	Site spotlighting census	Nocturnal streamside search	Harp trapping	Bat ultrasound recording
Dry Sclerophyll Forests	44	33	31	7	33	17
Forested Wetlands	7	7	6	2	3	2
Freshwater Wetlands	16	8	1	5	1	6
Grasslands	5	5	0	2	0	0
Heathlands	22	22	0	0	2	1
Rainforests	20	15	12	3	16	7
Saline Wetlands	3	3	0	0	1	0
Wet Sclerophyll Forests	17	16	13	1	7	9
Total	134	109	63	20	63	42

formations occupying less than 0.5% of the reserves were sampled by a minimum of two systematic survey sites, separated by a straight-line distance of 0.5 km. Vegetation formations occupying greater than 0.5% of the reserves had a minimum of six systematic survey site replicates which were separated by a straight-line distance of more than 1 km. Sites were positioned primarily adjacent or close to access trails and walking tracks to maximise the number of sites that could be accessed. The exceptions to this were sites selected in restricted vegetation formations. The placement of harp traps to capture microbats was limited by the availability of suitable fly-ways, such as vegetation constrictions along roads and creek lines.

Targeted survey techniques

Targeted survey techniques (Table 4, Fig. 3) were applied to sample species that had uncertain status in the study area (based on review of previous records), are not adequately sampled by the OEH systematic survey techniques and had not previously been adequately surveyed. These species included cryptic and rare taxa. A list of target species was derived, with particular emphasis on regionally restricted species (following Chafer et al. 1999; DECC 2007a; DECC 2008) and threatened species listed under the NSW Threatened Species Conservation Act 1995 (TSC Act). Techniques were designed to target each species or group of species and centred on the known ecology and habitat preferences for the species (e.g. for birds: Higgins 1999; Higgins and Davies 1996; Higgins and Peter 2002; Higgins et al. 2001). Established survey techniques for particular species were used where possible. Targeted survey techniques were separated by a minimum straight-line distance of 300 m.

Incidental observations

Incidental records were collected of species that were opportunistically encountered and were not well sampled by the systematic or targeted techniques of this study, such as large ground mammals, raptors, non-vocalising birds and secretive or cryptic fauna species. Additionally, incidental records were collected of fauna species that were not recorded during systematic or targeted surveys at a given location. A number of incidental records were collected during traverses across sections of the reserves where no systematic or targeted survey sites were located, and during driving of roads at night (particularly during warm humid conditions in search of active and road killed individuals). Predator scats were collected whenever encountered during the survey and analysed for the identification of mammalian prey remains.

Data analysis

Results of the OEH systematic survey techniques were compiled to examine patterns in fauna species distribution across vegetation formations. Sites that did not conform to a single vegetation formation were considered to be heterogeneous habitats and were excluded from the analysis (n=7).

Relative occurrence of species across vegetation formations

For all species detected twice or more by any of the systematic survey techniques, the number of systematic survey techniques in which the species was detected was tallied for each vegetation formation. This total was then converted to a percentage for each vegetation formation. All systematic techniques were included in this analysis.

Differences in fauna species composition between vegetation formations

The aim of these analyses was to typify the fauna species that use different vegetation formations in the reserves and identify distinct habitats. The software

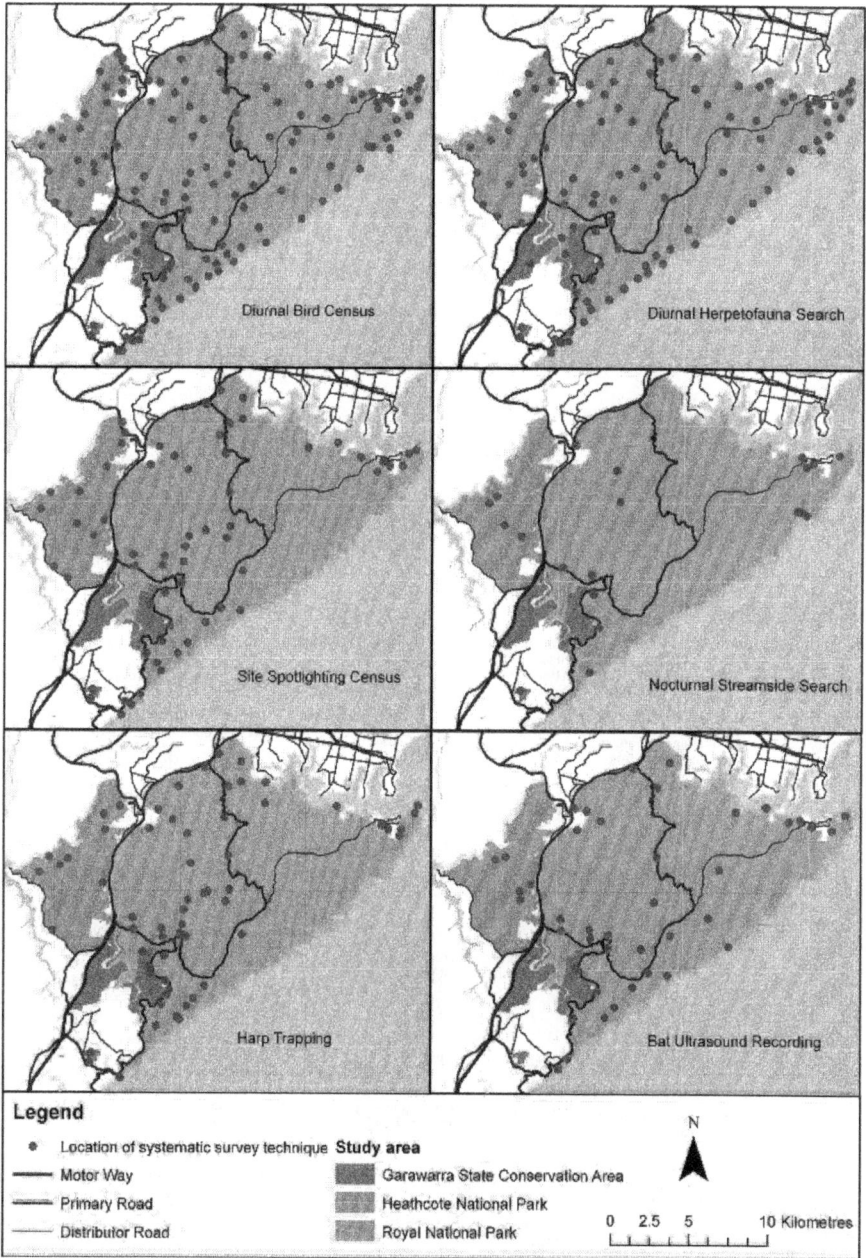

Figure 2. Location of OEH systematic survey techniques undertaken during the current study.

Table 4. Targeted fauna survey techniques.

Name of technique	Target species	Location/habitat type	Census/equipment type
Early evening call playback and passive listening in wet heaths and wetlands	Eastern grass owl, ground parrot, king quail, Australasian bittern	Areas of potential habitat identified by aerial photography (primarily wetlands and wet heaths dominated by sedgelands with little tree or shrub cover, including extensive sedgeland areas fringing mangroves).	Listening survey commenced approximately one hour prior to dusk and continued until dark. Included five minutes call playback of ground parrot and king quail before dusk, and five minutes call playback of eastern grass owl and Australasian bittern after dusk. Only undertaken during calm conditions.
Active daytime searching in wet heaths and wetlands	Above species	Areas of potential habitat identified by aerial photography (primarily wetlands and wet heaths dominated by sedgelands with little tree or shrub cover, including extensive sedgeland areas fringing mangroves).	Active searching comprising an observer undertaking criss-cross traverse of sites during the day looking for roosting or sheltering target species.
Riparian dusk watch and listening	Platypus, water rat, black bittern	Straight reaches of watercourses where there was good visibility of the water.	Survey commenced approximately one hour prior to dusk and continued until dark. An observer sat at the water's edge listening and watching for active target species (following techniques of Rohweder and Baverstock (1999) and Curtis (2001)).
Infra-red camera trapping	Dusky antechinus, spotted-tailed quoll, parma wallaby, red-necked pademelon, ground parrot, eastern bristlebird (depending on location)	Areas of potential habitat for one or more target species.	A single Moultrie Model 160 Digital Game Camera at each location, attached to a sapling or small tree, and aimed at a bait station approximately two metres from the camera and baited with peanut butter, rolled oats, honey and walnuts. Left in place for 7-12 nights. Species in the photos were identified by one of the authors (MS).
Targeted nocturnal call playback	Barking owl	Loftus Heights-Heathcote areas where there are previous records (Anyon-Smith 2006; OEH 2012; R. Jackson pers. comm.).	After dusk an observer listened for five minutes and searched the area with a 50 watt hand-held spotlight. Five minutes of call playback was then undertaken, followed by a final listening period.
Listening survey for amphibians	Brown toadlet, wallum froglet, Littlejohn's tree frog	Brown toadlet: Goarra Ridge area where there are previous records. Wallum froglet: wetlands on sand or alluvium in the Bundeena-Jibbon and Marley Lagoon areas. Littlejohn's tree frog: wet sedgelands and adjoining watercourses in Heathcote NP.	Listening surveys were undertaken during peak calling periods for each species (after Lemckert and Mahony 2008).
Tadpole survey	Stuttering frog, green and golden bell frog	Areas of potential habitat for one or more target species.	Searches for tadpoles, as well as for active adults, were undertaken between spring and autumn (after Anstis 2002).
Active searching of caves, tunnels, overhangs and culverts	Roosting microbats	All caves, overhangs and abandoned railway tunnels that were either identified during interviews with OEH staff, naturalists and park users, or were incidentally encountered during the field survey.	Active searches were undertaken with a head torch or hand-held spotlight.
Active searching of yellow-throated scrubwren nests	Roosting golden-tipped bat	All accessible yellow-throated scrub-wren nests encountered in rainforest and wet sclerophyll forest (n=44).	The golden-tipped bat primarily roosts in the suspended nests of the yellow-throated scrub-wren (Schulz 2000a, b, c), modifying the nest to provide access through a basal hole (Schulz 2000a). Surveys involved checking these nests for roosting bats or the presence of basal holes.
Active searching in mangroves	Mangrove gerygone	All larger mangrove patches.	Aural surveys were undertaken on at least two occasions at each location, by a single observer on a kayak at high tide.
Active searching in flowering swamp mahogany	Swift parrot, regent honeyeater	Flowering stands of swamp mahogany (*Eucalyptus robusta*) in the Bundeena area.	Visual and aural searches for the target species were undertaken on 20 occasions during autumn.
Shoreline observations	Australian pied oystercatcher, sooty oystercatcher, little tern, eastern osprey, water rat and other species using the shoreline.	Oceanic shoreline and Port Hacking shoreline.	Routine scanning of shoreline areas was undertaken during all seasons. The presence of water rat was assessed by searching for signs (tracks and the chewed remains of molluscs, yabbies and other food items that may have been deposited on flat rocks, stumps or logs (Triggs 2001)).

B222

Proc. Linn. Soc. N.S.W., 134, 2012

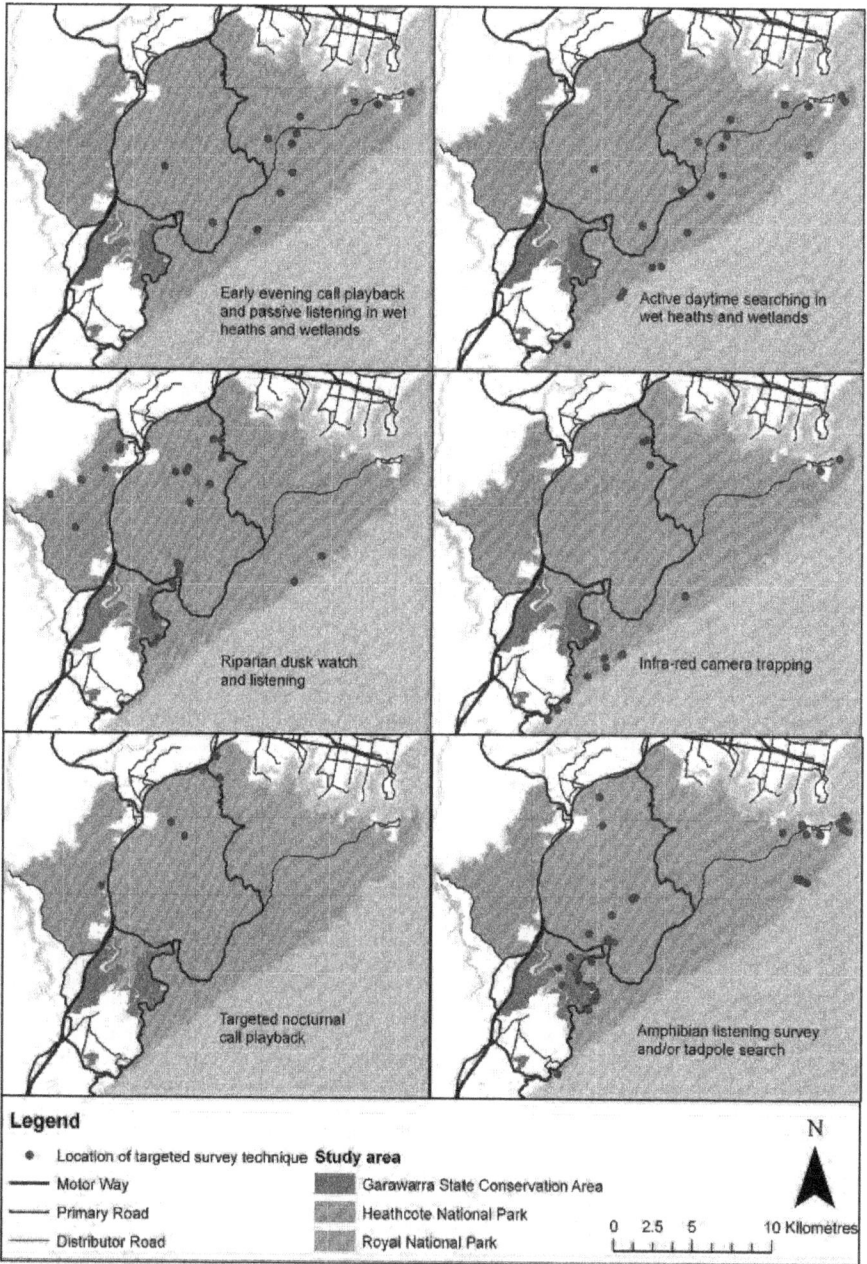

Figure 3. Location of selected targeted survey techniques undertaken during the current study.

Proc. Linn. Soc. N.S.W., 134, 2012

B223

package Primer 6 (Version 6.1.10) was used for statistical analyses. Only results from the diurnal bird and diurnal herpetofauna systematic techniques were used in these analyses as these techniques and fauna groups had the greatest number of replicates and species, giving sufficient power to statistical analyses. Bird and reptile data were analysed together, and hence only sites that had both diurnal bird and diurnal herpetofauna censuses undertaken at them were used. A site by species table was constructed, populated by presence-absence data for each species at each site. Species that were only recorded from a single site were excluded, so that single occurrences of rare species did not overly influence the data. A Bray-Curtis resemblance (similarity) matrix was then derived. An Analysis of Similarities (ANOSIM) was conducted to test for differences in the fauna species composition between the eight statewide vegetation formations. Non-parametric multi-dimensional scaling (MDS) was used to graphically present the pattern of similarity between sites, categorised by statewide vegetation formation. Several factors were considered in determining whether pairs of vegetation formations were different, following the method of Clarke and Warwick (2001), including the R statistic and significance level % for each pair-wise comparison (as generated by the ANOSIM), the number of randomly-generated R values that were above the pair-wise R value (also generated from ANOSIM) and the relative separation between pairs in the three-dimensional MDS. Finally, similarity percentages (SIMPER) was used to identify which fauna species primarily account for the observed differences between vegetation formations, and hence species that typify the formations.

RESULTS

Systematic survey results and analyses

A total of 228 species were detected by the systematic survey techniques (Appendix 1). One hundred and forty-seven bird species were recorded on site during diurnal bird censuses, the three most frequent species being the white-browed scrub-wren (66% of censuses), brown thornbill (72%) and eastern spinebill (72%). The diurnal herpetofauna searches detected 34 reptile and 8 frog species, the most frequent being the dark-flecked garden sunskink (81% of searches) and eastern water-skink (33%). The dark-flecked garden sunskink was even encountered basking on logs on the edge of saltmarsh and mangrove areas in Port Hacking. The site spotlighting censuses detected 15 nocturnal mammal, 9 nocturnal

bird, 11 frog and 5 nocturnally active reptile species, the most frequent being the sugar glider (49% of censuses) and Australian owlet-nightjar (43%). The nocturnal streamside searches detected 12 frog and 2 reptile species, with the common eastern froglet (75% of searches) and leaf-green tree frog (60%) the most frequently detected. The harp trapping resulted in capture of 12 microbat species, with the little forest bat captured in 60% of traps. Gould's wattled bat was the most frequently identified microbat from the bat ultrasound recording sites (identified from 60% of sites), followed by the little forest bat at 55% of sites; this technique detected a total of 7 microbat species.

An examination of the distribution of fauna species across vegetation formations (Appendix 1) found that many species are widespread across vegetation types, while others are restricted. The dark-flecked garden sunskink, Australian raven, brown thornbill, silvereye, superb fairy-wren and the welcome swallow were each detected in all formations, while the common eastern froglet, crimson rosella, eastern spinebill, variegated fairy-wren, white-browed scrub-wren and the little forest bat were recorded in all but one formation. In contrast, 21 species which were recorded more than once using systematic survey techniques were only detected in a single vegetation formation. Eleven of these species were restricted to Dry Sclerophyll Forests: Lesueur's frog, wood gecko, thick-tailed gecko, pale-flecked garden sunskink, eastern blue-tongue, brush cuckoo, buff-rumped thornbill, scarlet honeyeater, striated pardalote, varied sittella and greater broad-nosed bat. Four species were only located in Heathlands, comprising the Cunningham's skink, eastern brown snake, peregrine falcon and Horsfield's bronze-cuckoo. Four species were only located in Rainforests, comprising the wonga pigeon, green catbird, sooty owl and the long-nosed bandicoot. Three additional species, the large-billed scrubwren, logrunner and the eastern shrike-tit, were confined to Rainforests and adjoining Wet Sclerophyll Forests with a well developed mesic understorey. Based on records from systematic techniques only, no species were only detected in Saline Wetlands, Forested Wetlands, Grasslands or Wet Sclerophyll Forests.

The results of the ANOSIM indicated that there is a significant difference in bird and reptile species composition between statewide vegetation formations (global R=0.559, significant at the p<0.1% level). Differences were not clear between all formations, however, with some proving distinctive and others not. Table 5 displays pair-wise comparisons between each vegetation formation and whether each are considered significant. The three-dimensional MDS plot had a stress of 0.17 and the two-dimensional plot a stress of

B224

Proc. Linn. Soc. N.S.W., 134, 2012

Table 5. Degree of separation in bird and reptile species composition between statewide vegetation formations. Assessment of significance is derived from outputs of the ANOSIM analysis and visual examination of the three-dimensional MDS.

	Rainforests	Wet Sclerophyll Forests	Grasslands	Dry Sclerophyll Forests	Heathlands	Freshwater Wetlands	Forested Wetlands
Wet Sclerophyll Forests	Yes (moderate) R = 0.409						
Grasslands	Yes (strong) R = 0.969	Yes (strong) R = 0.898					
Dry Sclerophyll Forests	Yes (moderate) R = 0.481	No (weak) R = 0.177	Yes (strong) R = 0.849				
Heathlands	Yes (strong) R = 0.919	Yes (strong) R = 0.869	Yes (strong) R = 0.89	Yes (moderate) R = 0.449			
Freshwater Wetlands	Yes (strong) R = 0.812	Yes (moderate) R = 0.621	Yes (moderate) R = 0.636	No (weak) 0.336	No (moderate) R = 0.402		
Forested Wetlands	Yes (moderate) R = 0.619	No (weak) R = 0.309	No (moderate) R = 0.644	Yes (moderate) 0.409	Yes (moderate) R = 0.798	No (weak) R = 0.347	
Saline Wetlands	Yes (strong) R = 0.972	Yes (strong) R = 0.929	No (weak) R = 0.446	Yes (strong) 0.805	Yes (strong) R = 0.929	No (moderate) R = 0.573	Yes (moderate) R = 0.575

0.23. For ease of viewing, the two-dimensional plot is shown in Fig. 4, coded by vegetation formation, though the three-dimensional plot was used to examine separation of vegetation formations. The formations that were most distinct from the other groups were Rainforests (different from all other formations) and Heathlands (different from all formations except Freshwater Wetlands). The species that contributed most to the distinction of Rainforests are the brown gerygone, rufous fantail, golden whistler, black-faced monarch, yellow-throated scrubwren and green catbird. The species recorded more consistently in Heathlands than in the other formations are welcome swallow, White's skink, beautiful firetail, southern emu-wren, tawny-crowned honeyeater and pheasant coucal. Table 6 shows the bird and reptile species that are typical of Heathlands and Rainforests.

The weakest separation in vegetation formation pairs was between Dry Sclerophyll Forests and Wet Sclerophyll Forests (R=0.177). Since Dry and Wet Sclerophyll Forests were not found to be significantly different from each other, yet each had a large number of sites and together cover a large proportion of reserves, the typical species that occur in both of these formations are listed in Table 6 together. The degree of difference in species composition for the wetlands and grasslands formations, between themselves and in comparison to the above formations, is variable. These formations also tended to have a lower degree of similarity between sites within the formation, with the exception of Grasslands which have a mixed history of disturbance; for these reasons the typical species have not been presented in Table 6.

Targeted and incidental survey results

A total of 55 species were detected only by targeted survey techniques and/or incidental observations (Appendix 1).

The targeted surveys of wet heaths and wetlands (i.e. the early evening call playback and passive listening and the active daytime searching) resulted in the detection of the Australasian bittern and eastern grass owl in one location each. The Australasian bittern was detected on two occasions at Jibbon Lagoon (July and October 2009), while the eastern grass owl was flushed from a densely vegetated wetland in a drainage line south of Bundeena Drive in March 2010. The detection of the eastern grass

Proc. Linn. Soc. N.S.W., 134, 2012

B225

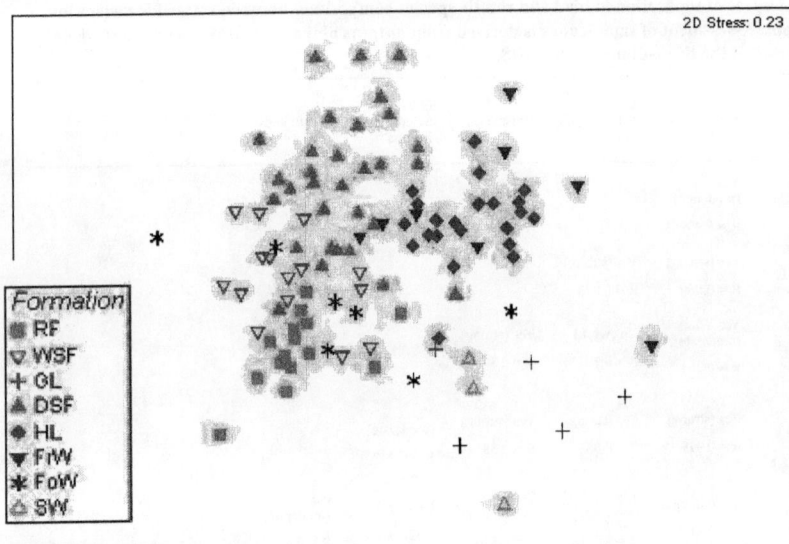

Figure 4. Two-dimensional MDS of sites coded by statewide vegetation formation.

owl is particularly noteworthy since this species is generally considered to be a rare visitor to the Sydney region, with one confirmed record from Homebush Bay in October 1982 and one from St Albans in the Hawkesbury Valley in September 1991 (Hobcroft and James 1997). However, prior to the sighting during the current study a single individual was flushed from a coastal sand swamp sedgeland inland of Cape Baily Lighthouse in Kamay Botany Bay NP some 14 km to the north east (Schulz and Magarey 2010).

The riparian dusk watch and listening surveys did not detect the target species. However, a single black bittern was flushed incidentally from the tidal limits of Cabbage Tree Creek.

The infra-red camera trapping did not detect the target species. However this technique detected 25 other species, comprising 9 mammal species and 16 bird species. Three species were only detected in the study area by the use of infra-red camera trapping, being the emerald dove, noisy pitta and buff-banded rail. The first two species were each located once in Rainforests, the emerald dove in Hell Hole north of Bulgo and the noisy pitta south of Bald Hill. Both of these species are considered rare in the Illawarra region (Chafer et al. 1999).

The active searches of caves, tunnels, overhangs and culverts resulted in the location of a number of microbat roosts. The most significant find was a maternity roost of the eastern

horseshoe-bat in the Bola Creek area, with up to 100 individuals present. This location is one of the only documented maternity roosts within the Sydney Basin Bioregion (OEH 2012). The eastern horseshoe-bat was the most frequently encountered cave-dwelling bat species, also found roosting in aggregations of less than 10 individuals in culverts and under bridges in the Hacking River valley and Garie Beach areas. Up to 20 individuals were encountered in Dingo Tunnel, while less than five individuals were encountered in a deep rock fissure adjacent to the Woronora River in Heathcote NP and various locations in Royal NP including in caves west of Yenabilli Point and adjacent to Flat Rock Creek crossing.

Another significant find was the location of at least 20 roosting little bentwing-bat individuals in March 2007 in the abandoned Stanwell Park-Otford railway tunnel which passed under the extreme southern edge of the study area. This is the southern-most documented roost for this species, with the nearest known roost being in a concrete-lined underground section of Brookvale Creek on the Northern Beaches of Sydney (DECC 2008). The roost site in the Stanwell Park-Otford railway tunnel was resurveyed in March and May 2010, and trapping undertaken near the tunnel entrance, but this species was not subsequently located. Hence the status of this species within the study area remains uncertain. Small eastern bentwing-bat roosts of less than 20

B226

Proc. Linn. Soc. N.S.W., 134, 2012

Table 6. Typical bird and reptile species of statewide vegetation formations. In brackets is the percentage of sites in the vegetation formation that contained the species (derived from the SIMPER analysis).

Statewide vegetation formation	Typical species
Rainforests (RF)	Brown thornbill (93%), brown gerygone (87%), eastern yellow robin (87%), rufous fantail (80%), golden whistler (80%), silvereye (80%), dark-flecked garden sunskink (80%), black-faced monarch (73%), Lewin's honeyeater (67%), yellow-throated scrubwren (67%), white-browed scrubwren (60%), eastern spinebill (60%), large-billed scrubwren (53%), three-toed skink (53%), eastern whipbird (53%), crimson rosella (47%), eastern water-skink (40%), bassian thrush (40%), superb lyrebird (40%).
Heathlands (HL)	White-browed scrubwren (95%), New Holland honeyeater (95%), welcome swallow (82%), little wattlebird (68%), dark-flecked garden sunskink (68%), variegated fairy-wren (64%), copper-tailed skink (64%), chestnut-rumped heathwren (59%), white's skink (59%), eastern whipbird (55%), common eastern froglet (50%), beautiful firetail (50%), jacky lizard (41%), brown thornbill (41%), southern emu-wren (41%), tawny-crowned honeyeater (36%), pheasant coucal (32%).
Dry and Wet Sclerophyll Forests combined (DSF and WSF)	Dark-flecked garden sunskink (90% DSF, 100% WSF), brown thornbill (55% DSF, 80% DSF), white-browed scrubwren (71% DSF, 67% WSF), eastern spinebill (81% DSF, 53% WSF), striated thornbill (55% DSF, 47% WSF), variegated fairy-wren (45% DSF, 47% WSF), eastern water-skink (35% DSF, 53% WSF), yellow-faced honeyeater (39% DSF, 47% WSF), crimson rosella (32% DSF, 40% WSF), grey fantail (35% DSF, 60% WSF), eastern yellow robin (23% DSF, 47% WSF), spotted pardalote (35% DSF, 47% WSF), grey shrike-thrush (23% DSF, 27% WSF), little wattlebird (29% DSF, 27% WSF).

individuals were also located in the abandoned Stanwell Park-Otford railway tunnel, as well as in deep overhangs west of Yenabilli Point. The only roost location found for the southern myotis was in the disused Otford-Stanwell Park railway tunnel, where at least 20 individuals were present in March 2007. However, similar to the little bentwing-bat no individuals were located on the revisit to the tunnel in March and May 2010. It is likely that the southern myotis roosts in additional sites in the study area. The capture of lactating female large-eared pied bat along the Cliff Trail on the plateau above the coastal escarpment indicates that maternity roosts for this species are present within the study area. No roost locations were found, but there are many cracks and crevices present on the vertical cliff face below the Cliff Track that are difficult to access and were not surveyed.

The shoreline observations found the targeted bird species to be uncommon, with no nesting activity observed and records primarily represented by the sighting of single individuals. For example, the only record of the little tern was of a single individual fishing just off the Bundeena sea cliffs

in January 2010. Single eastern osprey individuals were encountered along the Port Hacking shoreline west of Yenabilli Point in January 2010 and at Red Jacks Point in March 2010. During this period, single birds were also sighted during calm conditions along the ocean shoreline of Royal NP, such as along the Bundeena sea cliffs, Marley and Wattamolla beaches (M. Schulz unpublished records). In contrast sooty oystercatcher was regularly observed on intertidal rock platforms and adjacent ocean beaches along the Royal NP coastline, with occasional birds observed on the rocky shoreline in the Jibbon Beach area and on the intertidal flats at Bonnie Vale. This species was predominantly encountered in small numbers, with maximum numbers of 11 individuals observed on exposed rock platforms in the Little Marley Beach area in August 2009 and 12 individuals on a reef platform at Bulgo in May 2007.

A number of other shoreline species were recorded incidentally on single occasions, including the ruddy turnstone, kelp gull and the white-fronted tern. Two little penguins were encountered moulting under boulders in a small embayment on Jibbon Head. A number of reptile species were detected during the

Proc. Linn. Soc. N.S.W., 134, 2012

B227

shoreline observations. The broad-tailed gecko was regularly encountered in crevices along sea cliffs south of Wattamolla Beach, while the eastern water dragon was located in the tidal lower reaches of the Hacking River and on intertidal rock platforms in the Bulgo area of Royal NP. In the latter locality, large adults were observed feeding in pools in the upper intertidal zone.

A number of wetland and water-dependant species were not detected by systematic or targeted survey techniques, but only by incidental observations. For example, the eastern snake-necked turtle and Eurasian coot were each only recorded incidentally in the wide lower freshwater reaches of the Hacking River. Similarly the Australian reed warbler, spotless crake and white-necked heron were only recorded incidentally at Engadine Waterhole.

Summary of threatened species recorded during the survey

A total of 26 threatened species listed under the TSC Act and/or the Commonwealth Environment Protection and Biodiversity Conservation Act 1999 (EPBC Act) were recorded during the current survey (Appendix 1). However, only seven of these species were detected at 10 or more locations. The most frequently recorded was the red-crowned toadlet, which uses drains and runoffs on the edge of roads and management trails, including the main sealed roads within Royal NP. The grey-headed flying-fox was recorded in a range of habitats across the reserves, with occurrence varying depending on the flowering or fruiting of key plant species. During autumn 2010, for example, the majority of sightings were made around flowering heath-leaved banksia (*Banksia ericifolia*). The giant burrowing frog, detected at 17 locations all within Royal NP, was probably under-recorded during the survey due to the generally dry conditions. The majority of eastern pygmy-possum observations were of active or killed individuals seen at night on the sealed roads of Royal NP. Similarly, the majority of observations of the Rosenberg's goanna were incidental encounters along walking tracks and roads within the study area. These last two species, although predominantly Dry Sclerophyll Forests and Heathlands inhabitants, were also recorded in Rainforests. Several eastern pygmy-possums were observed along Lady Wakehurst Drive in rainforest in the Hacking River valley and a single Rosenberg's goanna was encountered feeding on ripe fig fruits that had fallen on to the ground in littoral rainforest in Palm Jungle at least 200 m straight-line distance from more open habitats. The remaining threatened species recorded in 10 or more localities were the

large-eared pied bat (which was located in 11 sites in a range of habitats including Rainforests, Wet Sclerophyll Forests and Dry Sclerophyll Forests) and southern myotis (which was recorded at 10 locations the majority of which were on large watercourses).

Species not detected during the survey

An important outcome of the current survey was the failure to locate a number of species that either were formerly known to occur (e.g. green and golden bell frog, stuttering frog, ground parrot, eastern bristlebird, spotted-tailed quoll, parma wallaby and red-necked pademelon); have an uncertain status within the reserves (e.g. brown toadlet, king quail, barking owl, mangrove gerygone, dusky antechinus, greater glider, platypus and water rat); are rare and declining visitors (swift parrot and regent honeyeater); or were considered to potentially be present since they are known from nearby localities or potential habitat is present (e.g. wallum froglet (*Crinia tinnula*), Littlejohn's tree frog (*Litoria littlejohni*) and golden-tipped bat (*Kerivoula papuensis*)). The species listed in this paragraph are now considered not likely to currently be present in the study area, with the exception of some of the bird species that occur as rare visitors (including barking owl, swift parrot and mangrove gerygone) (after Anyon-Smith 2006) and the greater glider which has recently been re-discovered in Royal NP (D. Andrew pers. comm.).

In total 107 species previously recorded from the study area were not located during the current survey (Appendix 2). This comprised seven amphibian, 15 mammal and 85 bird species. The review of previous records and relevant literature, together with results of the current survey, were used to assign a current status to each of these species; the list includes rare visitors or vagrants, sporadic visitors, regular winter-visiting birds, winter-vocalising frogs, species considered locally or regionally extinct, and species with uncertain status.

DISCUSSION

The current study demonstrates the value of dedicated fauna survey, even in reserves that are close to the Sydney metropolitan area, are long-established and have a high volume of visitation. The survey resulted in the location of seven species that had not previously been documented within the reserves, namely common wallaroo, Wilcox's frog, white-plumed honeyeater, lesser long-eared bat, Australasian bittern, eastern grass owl and mainland she-oak skink. The first four species were only located

B228

Proc. Linn. Soc. N.S.W., 134, 2012

on the edge of the study area, while the latter three species were all found in wet heath or sedgelands in Royal NP. An examination of the species detected by the systematic and targeted survey techniques, as well as the incidental observations, indicates that many species were only recorded by a single technique type, or in restricted habitats. This demonstrates that a multi-faceted survey approach, including stratified systematic surveys and targeted surveys, is needed to compile a comprehensive species inventory for an area.

The Royal, Heathcote and Garawarra reserve complex has high vertebrate fauna species richness in comparison with other reserves in the Sydney basin (data from OEH 2012). This high species richness can be attributed to the diversity of environments present. It is fortuitous that the first national park in Australia protected such an important mix of habitats for vertebrate fauna. The systematic survey results showed that the Rainforests and Heathlands vegetation formations each support a distinct suite of fauna. In addition, many species only occur in shoreline or wetland habitats, elevating the number of species present in the reserves.

The vegetation communities that comprise the Heathlands vegetation formation have a restricted distribution in NSW (Keith 2004). Sydney coastal heaths occur on exposed coastal sandstone plateau between Gosford and Garie in Royal NP, with disjunct patches at Jervis Bay and the Budderoo Plateau (Keith 2004). In the central part of their distribution (around the Sydney metropolitan area) they have been almost obliterated by urban and coastal development (Keith 2004). The heaths in Royal NP are an important component of the remaining extent. Royal NP currently supports some of the largest numbers of heath-dependant fauna species in the Sydney metropolitan area, including southern emu-wren, beautiful firetail and tawny-crowned honeyeater (data from OEH 2012). The Heathlands also provide habitat for several species listed as threatened under the TSC Act and/or the EPBC Act, including red-crowned toadlet, broad-headed snake, Rosenberg's goanna, eastern pygmy-possum, New Holland mouse and giant burrowing frog.

The Rainforests of Royal NP and Garawarra SCA lie near the southern limit of the distribution of the northern warm temperate, subtropical and littoral rainforest groups (Keith 2004). Rainforests extend south from the study area along the Illawarra escarpment, but the continuity with the study area is subject to ongoing threats such as urban development. In a regional context the Rainforests in the study area, and the connection with the Illawarra escarpment,

hold conservation significance to fauna species that are dependent on mesic forests, such as green catbird and logrunner. These two species have a restricted distribution in the Sydney basin and are likely to depend on the Rainforests of Royal NP, Garawarra SCA and the Illawarra escarpment for their ongoing survival in the Sydney region. The Rainforests also provide habitat for species listed as threatened under the TSC Act, such as the sooty owl, masked owl and the southern myotis.

The Dry Sclerophyll Forests vegetation formation contains vegetation communities from a wide range of environments within the study area, including relatively dry gully and creekline vegetation, open forest on sheltered to exposed dry sandstone slopes, low woodland on dry exposed ridgelines, and open forest on sand dunes. It is thus not surprising that systematic sites within this formation did not share a high degree of average similarity in bird and reptile species (Average Similarity=31.10 from SIMPER analysis) and that the sites were not found to significantly differ from the Wet Sclerophyll Forests. The Wet Sclerophyll Forests also contained a range of environments, though smaller than the Dry Sclerophyll Forests, ranging from mesic vegetation with rainforest species in the understorey to forests on shale-influenced soils adjacent to urban development. At the formation level, Dry Sclerophyll Forests and Wet Sclerophyll Forests are each widely distributed in the Sydney region (DECCW 2009) and the state (Keith 2004). Many of the species that occur in these habitats in Royal, Heathcote and Garawarra are also widespread through much of the Sydney water catchment lands and much of the greater Blue Mountains (data from OEH 2012). These forests thus do not account for the high species richness of the reserves compared to other areas in the Sydney basin. However, though many of these species are shared with other sandstone reserves, the abundance and density of a suite of threatened species is particularly high in the study area. The study area can be considered a regional 'hotspot' for broad-headed snake, giant burrowing frog, red-crowned toadlet and Rosenberg's goanna (data from OEH 2012). In a regional context, the study area also supports high numbers of eastern pygmy-possum (data from OEH 2012), which primarily occur in Heathlands and Dry Sclerophyll Forests.

Neither the Forested Wetlands nor the Freshwater Wetlands formations were found to support a highly distinctive suite of bird and reptile species based on systematic survey data. Forested Wetlands share many species with the Wet Sclerophyll Forests and Freshwater Wetlands, while the Freshwater Wetlands also share many species with the Dry Sclerophyll Forests and Heathlands (Table 5). Again, however, the diversity of environments encompassed by these formations (and by the Dry Sclerophyll Forests) may have masked the importance of particular habitat features. The Freshwater Wetlands, for example, includes sedgelands, swamps and wet heaths on sandstone ridgetops and slopes, as well as deep open lagoons with reed beds in sand dunes. Systematic sites within this formation did not share a high degree of average similarity in bird and reptile species (Average Similarity=30.08). Fauna species are likely to respond to a finer degree of habitat differentiation than is represented by the statewide vegetation formation grouping. In addition, several species that are known to depend on sedgelands, swamps, wet heaths or lagoons were only recorded once or only by targeted or incidental surveys in the current study, and hence were not included in the analyses, such as eastern grass owl and Australasian bittern. Thus it could easily be argued that the variety of freshwater wetlands present in the study area do contribute to the high species richness of the reserves.

A suite of fauna species is only present in the study area due to the existence of oceanic and/or estuarine shorelines. Many species common along the oceanic shoreline of Royal NP occur up and down the coast, such as the great cormorant, silver gull, crested tern and white-bellied sea-eagle (data from OEH 2012). Other species are rarer along the Sydney coastline. The intertidal rock platforms in the south of Royal NP provide important habitat for species such as the sooty oystercatcher and eastern reef egret.

An important outcome of the current survey and review of previous data was the failure to detect many species previously known to occur. Some of these remain residents or visitors that were simply missed by the current field surveys (Appendix 2). However the lack of records of other species reflects true absences from the study area. Despite the current fauna species richness of the reserves, a range of species are known to have become locally extinct. Additional species that were common in the Sydney and/or Illawarra regions at the time of European settlement, but have since disappeared, are also likely to have once occurred within the reserves but no longer do. The species extinctions, losses and declines have occurred across a range of vegetation formations and other habitats, as follows.

Freshwater Wetlands: Species that have been lost include the green and golden bell frog and ground parrot. These species have both declined across the Sydney and Illawarra regions. The green and golden bell frog was formerly one of the most common frogs in Sydney but is now only known from a small number of localities (White and Pyke 1996; McEntee 2005). The ground parrot was described as "fast disappearing' by Cayley (1923) during his visit to Marley Beach in the early 1920s. It is likely that the black-necked stork (*Ephippiorhynchus asiaticus*) and magpie goose (*Anseranas semipalmata*) also occurred in the study area, but information regarding the distribution and status of these species at the time of European settlement is limited (DECC 2007b).

Watercourses: Both the platypus and water rat are suspected to have been lost from the reserves as neither has been seen since the 1970s, despite considerable search effort. The platypus was last recorded in the Hacking River and Kangaroo Creek catchments in the 1970s, with no recent records reported in a summary of the current occurrence of the species around Sydney (Grant 1998) or in subsequent years (Curtis 2001; T. Grant pers. comm.). Neither species has been encountered over a 25-year period on the lower Hacking River or on the lower reaches of Kangaroo Creek by the operators of the Audley Boatshed (J. Hughes, pers. comm.). Similarly, fish netting studies in the Hacking and Woronora rivers (e.g. Bishop 1993; Bruce et al. 2001) resulted in no captures or sightings of these species.

Heathlands: Species that appear to have become locally extinct include the ground parrot and eastern bristlebird. The former species also occurred in sedgelands within wetland habitats, while the latter species occurred in dense heathlands and was last reported from the region in the 1960s west of Mount Kembla (Chafer et al. 1999). It is also likely that the southern brown bandicoot (*Isoodon obesulus*) formerly occurred in heathland and heathy woodland, and that the long-nosed potoroo (*Potorous tridactylus*) utilised wet heath in addition to dense gully vegetation.

Rainforests: Species that have been lost from Rainforests and associated Wet Sclerophyll Forests with a rainforest subcanopy include the parma wallaby (now considered regionally extinct with the last sighting in the region in 1969 (Robinson 1988)), stuttering frog (last recorded in the Hacking River valley in 1994 (Rice 1995) and has declined throughout the southern part of its range (Gillespie 1996)) and the regent bowerbird (last reported from the study area in the 1920s (Anyon-Smith 2006)). The superb fruit-dove and the rose-crowned fruit-dove are considered to once have been more frequent seasonal visitors but are now only very rarely recorded. Although not documented (e.g. Anyon-Smith 2006), an additional species that was likely to have occurred is the wompoo fruit-dove (*Ptilinopus magnificus*) which was once resident in the Illawarra

B230

Proc. Linn. Soc. N.S.W., 134, 2012

region but has not been recorded since the 1920s (Chafer et al. 1999.). The fruit-doves have either become locally extinct or are now very rare visitors across the Illawarra region with all three species being vulnerable to fragmentation and disturbance (Recher et al. 1995; Moran et al. 2004). A number of species are suspected to have become locally extinct from the reserves; the red-necked pademelon was last reported in the 1980s and the dusky antechinus was last confirmed to be present in 1974. The greater glider was suspected to have been lost from the reserves since the 1994 wildfires, but has recently been sighted on Lady Carrington Drive (D. Andrew pers. comm.).

Wet Sclerophyll Forests with a grassy understorey: The Wet Sclerophyll Forests statewide vegetation formation includes two subformations: Wet Sclerophyll Forests with a shrubby understorey and Wet Sclerophyll Forests with a grassy understorey (Keith 2004). Vegetation communities that fall into the latter subformation are highly restricted in distribution within the study area, occurring only in small patches in residual shale and ironstone caps near Heathcote, Loftus, Otford and Garawarra. More extensive stands were once present on ridges and rises around the adjacent suburbs of Loftus, Engadine, Sutherland and Heathcote (DECCW 2009). These forests may have provided peripheral habitat for a suite of species that were once more extensively distributed within grassy woodlands across the drier Cumberland Plain to the west of the study area (DECC 2007a). The bush stone-curlew was formerly resident in the reserves but is now locally extinct (Anyon-Smith 2006). Other threatened species that are documented to have once utilised this habitat and have not been recorded in recent years (e.g. Anyon-Smith 2006) comprise a suite of grassy woodland bird species including the speckled warbler, painted honeyeater, black-chinned honeyeater and the diamond firetail, while barking owl now only occurs as a rare visitor. Additionally, a number of other species are known or suspected to have been lost from the reserves or today only occur as rare visitors including the peaceful dove, pallid cuckoo, white-throated gerygone, yellow-rumped thornbill, blue-faced honeyeater, little friarbird, white-winged triller, pied butcherbird, restless flycatcher, jacky winter and the rufous songlark. These species would have been largely confined to the Loftus-East Heathcote sections of the reserves. Within these areas some of the species were formerly common. For example, jacky winter was reported as "he should be the first bird recorded" around the National Park Station (Cayley 1923). Other species in this category from the same general area included the restless flycatcher, yellow-rumped thornbill, white-

throated gerygone, white-browed woodswallow and the masked woodswallow (Cayley 1923). None of these birds occur in this part of the study area today.

Shoreline habitats: The shoreline species that were formerly present in the study area have not been documented. Species that probably once used shoreline habitats for breeding, but today only visit in very low numbers, are the eastern osprey, Australian pied oystercatcher and little tern. The eastern osprey was a resident species last century in the Port Hacking area (Hoskin et al. 1991), while the Australian pied oystercatcher and little tern are likely to have bred in areas such as Deeban Spit and other beaches on the southern shore of Port Hacking. There are a number of shorebird species that are likely to have once visited the intertidal mudflats and adjacent shorelines and wetlands of Port Hacking, but now would only occur as extremely rare visitors or no longer visit at all. These species include the pacific golden plover, lesser sand-plover (*Charadrius mongolus*), red-capped plover, hooded plover (*Thinornis rubricollis*), grey-tailed tattler, sanderling (*Calidris alba*), curlew sandpiper (*Calidris ferruginea*), sharp-tailed sandpiper, red-necked stint (*Calidris ruficollis*) and Pacific gull. This is a result of either a national decline in numbers (such as documented for curlew sandpiper and hooded plover), or a statewide decline in numbers (as demonstrated by a dramatic loss in numbers in the Hunter estuary for species such as lesser sand-plover or in the Sydney area for species such as such as sanderling (Hoskin et al. 1991; Straw 1996; Barrett et al. 2003; Watkins 2003; Herbert 2007). The range of the Pacific gull has contracted southwards, with it being common on Sydney beaches in the 1920s but now a rare visitor with most records attributed to mis-identifications of the similar-looking kelp gull (Higgins and Davies 1996).

Wide-ranging species: The eastern quoll was known from the reserves (Robinson 1988), but similar to the rest of the Australian mainland has now disappeared (Jones 2008). The status of spotted-tailed quoll in the reserves is less certain, but it is considered that the resident population that was known from Royal NP in the 1960s and 1970s has been lost (Robinson 1988). There have been no confirmed recent records within the reserves but given recent sightings on the Woronora Plateau (DECC 2007a), Holsworthy Military Area (DECC 2008) and in Coledale (M. Schulz, unpublished record) it is likely that individuals may occasionally wander into the reserves from other surviving populations. A population of koala occurred in the Helensburgh area in the 1940s and was reported to have become locally extinct in Royal NP in the 1970s (Robinson

Proc. Linn. Soc. N.S.W., 134, 2012

B231

1987). A number of recent records of this species exist for the study area, primarily in Heathcote NP and either represent rehabilitated released individuals (WIRES records) or wide-ranging individuals from the Campbelltown population (Ward and Close 2004) that is common along the Georges River, including in nearby areas of Holsworthy Military Area (DECC 2008).

The study area supports populations of a number of species which have declined in numbers across their national range in recent years (Barrett et al. 2003) or across the Sydney Basin Bioregion (e.g. DECC 2007b). These species include the swamp harrier, red-browed treecreeper, rockwarbler, southern emu-wren, tawny-crowned honeyeater, grey currawong, beautiful firetail and the Australian pipit. However, the population trends of birds and other fauna species occurring within the study area is unknown. A number of bird species, such as the topknot pigeon, pilotbird, rufous fantail and black-faced monarch are thought to have declined within the reserves in recent years (S. Anyon-Smith pers. comm.). Similarly, a variety of reptile species have declined in abundance, most notably the yellow-faced whip snake (K. Griffiths, unpublished records), while during the current survey the broad-headed snake could not be located at sites where it previously occurred such as along the coastal cliffs east of Bundeena (R. McLaggan, WIRES and Bundeena resident, pers. comm.). The eastern bearded dragon was common in the Jannali-Sutherland area in the 1960s and was seen in Engadine, North Engadine and also Heathcote NP more than ten years ago but not since (K. Griffiths, unpublished records). Given the lack of recent sightings, eastern bearded-dragon was suspected to have disappeared from the area (K. Griffiths pers. comm.), although during the current survey a single individual was encountered on the edge of the F6 freeway in wet sclerophyll forest with a grassy understorey. The status of extant amphibian species in the reserves is poorly known. Although red-crowned toadlet was recorded in a number of localities during the current survey, this species has declined in numbers and locations occupied most notably in Heathcote NP (R. Wells, unpublished records).

One approach to assessing species at risk of decline in the reserves is to investigate adjacent areas supporting similar habitat. Kamay Botany Bay NP, approximately 6 km north of the study area on the northern side of Port Hacking, supports a smaller area of Heathlands and Dry Sclerophyll Forests than the Royal, Heathcote and Garawarra reserves (298 ha compared to 16,152 ha in the study area)

and is effectively isolated from other reserves with similar habitat due to urban and coastal development. There are no recent records of the following species in Kamay Botany Bay NP though they are likely to have once occurred (Morris 1989; DECCW 2011), and all still occur in the current study area: Freycinet's frog, Cunningham's skink, Rosenberg's goanna, broad-headed snake, painted button-quail, chestnut-rumped heathwren, beautiful firetail, brown antechinus, long-nosed bandicoot, eastern pygmy-possum, swamp wallaby, New Holland mouse and bush rat. The absence of these species from Kamay Botany NP, even given the marked difference in the size of available habitat, could potentially provide an indication of species at risk of decline in the current study area in the future.

This study did not include an investigation of the current threatening processes acting on fauna in the reserves. However, based on observations and interviews made during the surveys and a review of relevant literature, key current threats that require management include fire, feral animals, road fatalities, loss of connectivity, hydrological changes, public disturbance and wildlife poaching. Frequent fires in the Maddens Plains area on the Woronora Plateau have been implicated in the local extinction of the ground parrot and eastern bristlebird (DECC 2007a). A large proportion of Royal NP has been affected by at least three major wildfires over the last three decades since 1974, while during the same time period Heathcote NP was burnt by a single wildfire in summer 2001/2002 (NPWS 2001; Tulloch 2003). The study area potentially faces isolation for some species. Current Rainforests and Wet Sclerophyll Forests habitat connections with the Illawarra escarpment and other reserves to the south are under threat from housing development and habitat fragmentation. Less mobile fauna species in Royal NP are isolated from Heathcote NP and reserves to the west and south as a result of the Illawarra railway and F6 freeway corridors. The effects of isolation are generally gradual, resulting in a slow decline over several generations. It is likely that further fauna species loss will be experienced over time without abatement of these threatening processes. Without the establishment of a regular monitoring program across vegetation formations, particularly those supporting habitat specialists, the loss of species may go unnoticed. It is recommended that ongoing research, monitoring and management efforts focus on species that still occupy the reserves, especially species for which the reserves are significant in a regional conservation context.

B232

Proc. Linn. Soc. N.S.W., 134, 2012

ACKNOWLEDGEMENTS

This project was carried out by the Biodiversity Survey and Assessment Section in the Metropolitan Branch of the Office of Environment and Heritage (NSW). It was jointly funded by the Metropolitan Branch of the Parks and Wildlife Group. Special thanks to the following people for assistance with the field work: Debbie Andrew, Steven Anyon-Smith, Aaron Coutts-Smith, Mike Fleming, Tim Hager, Meagan Hinds, Wendy Kinsella, Manu Martinero, Kylie McClelland, Clare O'Brien, Patsy Ross, Megan Rowlatt, Joe Stammers and Jessica Zichar. We also thank Steve Anyon-Smith for providing information on birds; Anne Carrick for providing information on the birds of the Constables Point area; Richard Jackson for providing information on nocturnal birds; Gary Daly, Ken Griffiths, George Madani and Arthur White for providing information on frogs; Ken Griffiths, John Cann, Andrew Melrose and Henry Cook for providing information on reptiles; Ross Goldingay for providing information on broad-headed snakes; Tom Grant and Jason Hughes for providing information on the platypus and water rat; Harry Parnaby and Glen Hoye for providing details on the bat fauna; Ken Allen for providing location details of bat roosts within Royal National Park; Derek Engel and Rose McLaggan for providing general fauna information; Patsy Ross for providing valuable field logistical and communications support; Debbie Andrew, Bill Sullivan, Kylie Madden and Josh Madden for providing important background information; and Daniel Connolly, Kylie Madden and Debbie Andrew for commenting on an earlier draft of this paper.

REFERENCES

Andrew, D. (2001). 'Post fire vertebrate fauna survey – Royal and Heathcote National Parks and Garawarra State Recreation Area'. (NSW National Parks and Wildlife Service: Audley).

Anstis, M. (2002). 'Tadpoles of South-eastern Australia: a guide with keys'. (New Holland: Sydney).

Anyon-Smith, S. (2006). 'Birdwatching in Royal & Heathcote National Parks'. (NSW Department of Environment and Conservation: Audley).

Barrett, G., Silcocks, A., Barry S., Cunningham, R. and Poulter, R. (2003). 'The New Atlas of Australian Birds'. (Royal Australian Ornithologists Union: Victoria).

Bilney, R.J., Kavanagh, R.P. and Harris, J.M. (2007). Further observations on the diet of the Sooty Owl *Tyto tenebricosa* in the Royal National Park, Sydney. *Australian Field Ornithology* **24**, 64-69.

Bishop, K.A. (1993). 'Woronora River proposed water quality treatment plant freshwater fish study: Woronora River downstream' Unpublished report. (Sydney Water: Sydney).

Blakers, M., Davies, S.J.J.F. and Reilly, P.N. (1984). 'The Atlas of Australian Birds'. (Melbourne University Press: Victoria).

Bruce, A., Growns, I. and Gehrke, P. (2001). 'Woronora River Macquarie Perch survey'. NSW Fisheries Report Series 32. (NSW Fisheries: Sydney).

Cayley, N. W. (1923). The birds of National Park. In: 'Guide Book to the Excursions in the Sydney District'. (Ed. Anon.) pp. 27-29. (Pan Pacific Science Congress: Sydney).

Chafer, C.J. and Andersen, M. (1994). Sooty Owls in the Hacking River catchment. *Australian Birds* **27**, 77-84.

Chafer, C.J., Brandis, C.C.P. and Wright, D. (1999). 'Handbook of birds found in the Illawarra, Shoalhaven and adjacent tablelands'. (Illawarra Bird Observer's Club: Wollongong).

Clarke, K.R. and Warwick, R.M. (2001) Change in marine communities: An approach to statistical analysis and interpretation. 2nd Edition. PRIMER-E, Plymouth.

Curtis, D. (2001). 'Investigation to determine whether Platypus populations exist in waterways of the Royal and Heathcote National Parks'. Unpublished report. (NSW National Parks and Wildlife Service: Audley).

DECC (2007a). 'Terrestrial Vertebrate Fauna of the Greater Southern Sydney Region: Volume 2 – Fauna of Conservation Concern including priority pest species'. (NSW Department of Environment and Climate Change: Hurstville).

DECC (2007b). 'Terrestrial Vertebrate Fauna of the Greater Southern Sydney Region: Volume 1 – Background Report'. (NSW Department of Environment and Climate Change: Hurstville).

DECC (2008). 'Rapid Fauna Habitat Assessment of the Sydney Metropolitan Catchment Management Authority Area'. (NSW Department of Environment and Climate Change: Hurstville).

DECCW (2009). 'The Native Vegetation of the Sydney Metropolitan Catchment Management Authority Area. Volume 1: Technical Report and Volume 2: Vegetation Community Profiles'. (NSW Department of Environment, Climate Change and Water: Hurstville).

DECCW (2011). 'The Vertebrate Fauna of Kamay Botany Bay National Park'. (NSW Department of Environment, Climate Change and Water: Hurstville).

Evans, J. (2000). The fungi in the diet of the Swamp Wallaby (*Wallabia bicolor*) across different vegetation types in the Royal National Park. Hons thesis, University of Western Sydney, Penrith South.

Giles, J.R. and McKenzie, L.B. (1973). 'The ecology of the Javan Rusa in the Royal National Park'. Unpublished report. (NSW National Parks and Wildlife Service: Audley).

Gillespie, G.R. (1996). 'Survey design and management prescriptions for the Giant Burrowing Frog (*Heleioporus australiacus*) and the Stuttering Frog (*Mixophyes balbus*)'. (Arthur Rylah Institute, Dept of Natural Resources and Environment: Melbourne).

Grant, T.R. (1998). Current and historical occurrence of Platypuses, *Ornithorhynchus anatinus*, around Sydney. *Australian Mammalogy* **20**, 257-266.

Hamilton, C.A. (1981). Rusa Deer in the Royal National

Park: diet, dietary overlap with *Wallabia bicolor*, influence on the vegetation, distribution and movements. MSc thesis, University of Sydney, Sydney.

Herbert, C. (2007). 'Distribution, abundance and status of birds in the Hunter estuary'. Special Report No. 4 (Hunter Bird Observer's Club: Newcastle).

Higgins, P.J. (Ed.) (1999). 'Handbook of Australian, New Zealand and Antarctic Birds. Volume 4. Parrots to Dollarbird'. (Oxford University Press: Victoria).

Higgins, P.J. and Davies, S.J.J.F. (Eds.) (1996). 'Handbook of Australian, New Zealand & Antarctic Birds. Volume 3: Snipe to Pigeons'. (Oxford University Press: Victoria).

Higgins, P.J. and Peter, J.M. (Eds.) (2002). 'Handbook of Australian, New Zealand & Antarctic Birds. Volume 6: Pardalotes to Shrike-thrushes'. (Oxford University Press: Victoria).

Higgins, P.J., Peter, J.M. and Steele, W.K. (Eds.) (2001). 'Handbook of Australian, New Zealand & Antarctic Birds. Volume 5: Tyrant-flycatchers to Chats'. (Oxford University Press: Victoria)

Hobcroft, D. and James, D.J. (1997). Records of the Grass Owl from southern New South Wales. *Australian Bird Watcher* **17**, 91-93.

Hoskin, E.S., Hindwood, K.A. and McGill, A.R. (1991). 'The birds of Sydney, County of Cumberland, New South Wales, 1770-1989'. (Surrey Beatty and Sons: Sydney).

Jones, M. (2008). Eastern Quoll *Dasyurus viverrinus*. In: 'The Mammals of Australia'. (Eds. S. van Dyck and R. Strahan). pp. 62-64. Third edition. (Reed New Holland: Sydney).

Kavanagh, R.P. and Jackson, R. (1997). Home-range, movements, habitat and diet of the Sooty Owl *Tyto tenebricosa* near Royal National Park. In: 'Australian Raptor Studies'. (Eds G.V. Czechura and S.J.S. Debus). Birds Australia Monographs No. 3, 2-13. (Royal Australasian Ornithologist's Union: Victoria).

Keith, D.A. (2004). 'Ocean shores to desert dunes: the native vegetation of New South Wales and the ACT'. (NSW Dept of Environment and Conservation: Hurstville).

Keith, D. and Pellow, B. (2005). Effects of Javan Rusa Deer (*Cervus timorensis*) on native plant species in the Jibbon-Bundeena area, Royal National Park, New South Wales. *Proceedings of the Linnean Society of NSW* **126**, 99-110.

Keith, D.A. and Tozer, M. (unpubl.). 'Vegetation map of Royal National Park and surrounds'. (NSW National Parks and Wildlife Service: Hurstville).

Kevin Mills and Associates (1995). 'Fauna assessment of proposed wetland sites in Royal National Park, Engadine, Shire of Sutherland'. (Kevin Mills and Associates Pty Ltd: Jamberoo).

Lemckert, F. and Mahony, M. (2008). Core calling periods of the frogs of temperate New South Wales, Australia. *Herpetological Conservation and Biology* **3**, 71-76.

Lesryk Environmental Consultants (1996). 'Fauna

assessment of proposed fencing programme adjacent to the Illawarra Railway Line between Heathcote and Waterfall Railway Stations'. Report prepared for State Rail. (Lesryk Environmental Consultants: Bundeena).

Lesryk Environmental Consultants (2005). 'Ecological assessment of proposed culvert works'. Report prepared for the Roads and Traffic Authority. (Lesryk Environmental Consultants: Bundeena).

Lesryk Environmental Consultants (2007). 'Flora and fauna assessment of proposed culvert works'. Report prepared for the Roads and Traffic Authority. (Lesryk Environmental Consultants: Bundeena).

Lesryk Environmental Consultants (2008). 'Roadside flora and fauna survey'. Report prepared for the Roads and Traffic Authority. (Lesryk Environmental Consultants: Bundeena).

Lesryk Environmental Consultants (2010). 'Flora and fauna assessment of proposed table drain clearing and culvert upgrading work'. Report prepared for the Roads and Traffic Authority. (Lesryk Environmental Consultants: Bundeena).

Mahood, I. (1981). Rusa of Royal National Park. *Australian Deer* **6**, 15-24.

McEntee, B.A. (2005). An investigation into the feasibility of reintroducing the Green and Golden Bell Frog (*Litoria aurea*) into Marley Lagoon, in the Royal National Park. Hons thesis, University of Wollongong, Wollongong.

Moran, C., Catterall, C.P., Green, R.J. and Olsen, M.F. (2004). Fate of feathered fruit-eaters in fragmented forests. In: 'Conservation of Australia's forest fauna'. (Ed. D. Lunney). pp. 699-712. (Royal Zoological Society of NSW: Sydney).

Moriarty, A. (2004). The environmental impacts of Rusa Deer in the Royal National Park. PhD thesis, University of Western Sydney, Penrith South.

Morris, A.K. (1989). The birds of Botany Bay National Park, New South Wales. *Australian Birds* **23**, 7-21.

Nolan, L. (2006). 'Biodiversity survey report 2006: Royal and Heathcote National Parks'. Unpublished report. (NSW National Parks and Wildlife Service: Audley).

NPWS (2000a). 'Royal National Park, Heathcote National Park and Garawarra State Recreation Area plan of management.' (NSW National Parks and Wildlife Service: Sydney).

NPWS (2000b). 'Biodiversity Study for the Georges River Catchment. Volume 2: Fauna Assessment'. (NSW National Parks and Wildlife Service: Hurstville).

NPWS (2001). 'Draft Fire Management Plan for Royal, Heathcote National Parks and Garawarra State Recreation Area'. (NSW National Parks and Wildlife Service: Sydney).

NPWS (2002). 'Wollongong LGA Bioregional Assessment (Part II): Fauna of the Illawarra Escarpment, Coastal Plain and Plateau'. (NSW National Parks and Wildlife Service: Sydney).

OEH (2012). The Atlas of NSW Wildlife. (NSW Office of Environment and Heritage: Hurstville).

B234

Proc. Linn. Soc. N.S.W., 134, 2012

Ramp, D. and Ben-Ami, D. (2006). The effect of road-based fatalities on the viability of a peri-urban Swamp Wallaby population. *Journal of Wildlife Management* **70**, 1615-1624.

Recher, H.F., Date, E.M. and Ford, H.A. (1995). 'The biology and management of rainforest pigeons in NSW'. Species Management Report No. 16. (NSW National Parks and Wildlife Service: Hurstville).

Rice, J.P. (1995). A survey of amphibian populations associated with permanent waterways in the Helensburgh region of the Upper Hacking River catchment. Hons thesis, University of Wollongong, Wollongong.

Robinson, N.H. (1987). 'Mammals of the national parks and nature reserves between Port Hacking and the Shoalhaven River'. (Illawarra Heritage Committee: Wollongong).

Robinson, N.H. (1988). The impact of European man on the status of mammals in the Illawarra Region. MSc thesis, University of Wollongong, Wollongong.

Rohweder, D.A. and Baverstock, P.R. (1999). Distribution of Platypus, *Ornithorhynchus anatinus*, in the Richmond River catchment, northern New South Wales. Australian Zoologist 31, 30-37.

Schulz, M. (2000a). Roosts used by the Golden-tipped Bat *Kerivoula papuensis* (Chiroptera: Vespertilionidae). *Journal of Zoology, London* **25**, 467-478.

Schulz, M. (2000b). Relative abundance and other aspects of the natural history of the rare Golden-tipped Bat, *Kerivoula papuensis* (Chiroptera: Vespertilionidae). *Acta Chiropterologica* **1**, 165-178.

Schulz, M. (2000c). Diet and foraging behaviour of the Golden-tipped Bat *Kerivoula papuensis*. *Journal of Mammalogy* **22**, 23-33.

Schulz, M. and Magarey, E. (2010). Diet of an Eastern Grass Owl at Kamay Botany Bay National Park, Sydney. *Australian Field Ornithology* **27**,177-178.

Straw, P. (1996). 'Wader population study of Botany Bay and Adjacent Wetlands'. (Royal Australian Ornithologists Union: Victoria).

Triggs. B. (2001). 'Tracks, scats and other traces: a field guide to Australian mammals'. (Oxford University Press: Victoria).

Trustees (1915). 'Official Guide to the National Park of New South Wales'. (Government Printer: Sydney).

Tuck, M. (1971). Javan Rusa Deer (*Cervus timorensis*) in the Royal National Park – habitat utilization and distribution. Hons thesis, University of Wollongong, Wollongong.

Tulloch, A. (2001). Distribution, abundance and habitat use of the Eastern Pygmy Possum, *Cercartetus nanus*, in Royal and Heathcote National Parks, New South Wales. Hons thesis, University of Sydney, Sydney.

Tulloch, A. (2003). 'Post-fire distribution, abundance and habitat use of small mammals in Royal National Park, Heathcote National Park and Garawarra State Recreation Area, New South Wales'. (NSW National Parks and Wildlife Service: Audley).

Ward, S. and Close, R. (2004). Southern Sydney's urban Koalas: community research and education at Campbelltown. In: '*Urban wildlife: more than meets the eye*'. (Eds. D. Lunney and S. Burgin). pp. 44-55. (Royal Zoological Society of NSW: Sydney).

Watkins, D. (2003). 'A national plan for shorebird conservation in Australia'. RAOU Report No. 90. (Royal Australasian Ornithologist's Union, Victoria).

Whelan, R.J., Ward, S., Hogbin, P. and Wasley, J. (1996). Responses of heathland *Antechinus stuartii* to the Royal National Park wildfire in 1994. *Proceedings of the Linnean Society of NSW* **116**, 97-108.

White, A.W. and Pyke, G.H. (1996). Distribution and conservation status of the Green and Golden Bell Frog (*Litoria aurea*) in New South Wales. *Australian Zoologist* **30**, 177-189.

Young, B. and Young, A. (2006). 'Understanding the Scenery: the Royal National Park and Heathcote National Park'. (Envirobook: Sydney).

APPENDIX 1. SPECIES RECORDED IN THE CURRENT SURVEY

Values are the percentage of systematic techniques in which the species was detected that were in the designated vegetation formation. Cells are shaded by the following percentage classes:

Percentages are not presented for species recorded once only; these are denoted by #.

Introduced species are denoted by *.

VERTEBRATE FAUNA OF ROYAL NATIONAL PARK

Common name	Scientific name	Threatened species listed under the TSC Act and/or EPBC Act	Recorded during targeted or incidental techniques only	Recorded during systematic techniques							
				% RF	% WSF	% DSF	% HL	% FrW	% FoW	% SW	% GL
Amphibians											
Bleating tree frog	*Litoria dentata*					#					
Blue Mountains tree frog	*Litoria citropa*					#					
Brown-striped frog	*Limnodynastes peronii*					21.4		28.6	45.7		14.3
Common eastern froglet	*Crinia signifera*			4.2	4.2	35.4	22.9	14.6	12.5		6.3
Eastern banjo frog	*Limnodynastes dumerilii grayi*					#					
Eastern dwarf tree frog	*Litoria fallax*			15.4		30.8		23.1	30.8		
Freycinet's frog	*Litoria freycineti*					83.3		16.7			
Giant burrowing frog	*Heleioporus australiacus*	x				66.7	33.3				
Haswell's froglet	*Paracrinia haswelli*								#		
Leaf-green tree frog	*Litoria phyllochroa*			30	20	43.3			6.7		
Lesueur's frog	*Litoria lesueuri*					100					
Peron's tree frog	*Litoria peronii*					37.5		37.5	25		
Red-crowned toadlet	*Pseudophryne australis*	x				62.5	37.5				
Smooth toadlet	*Uperoleia laevigata*					50			50		
Wilcox's frog	*Litoria wilcoxii*					#					
Reptiles											
Bandy-bandy	*Vermicella annulata*	x									
Barred-sided skink	*Eulamprus tenuis*					66.7			33.3		
Bearded dragon	*Pogona barbata*	x									
Black-bellied swamp snake	*Hemiaspis signata*	x									
Blackish blind snake	*Ramphotyphlops nigrescens*					#					
Broad-headed snake	*Hoplocephalus bungaroides*	x				#					
Broad-tailed gecko	*Phyllurus platurus*			11.1	44.4	22.2	16.7		5.6		
Brown tree snake	*Boiga irregularis*					#					
Burton's snake-lizard	*Lialis burtonis*	x									
Common death adder	*Acanthophis antarcticus*					50	50				
Common scaly-foot	*Pygopus lepidopodus*						20	80			
Common tree snake	*Dendrelaphis punctulatus*					#					
Copper-tailed skink	*Ctenotus taeniolatus*					38.5	53.8	7.7			
Cream-striped shinning-skink	*Cryptoblepharus virgatus*				25	50	12.5		12.5		
Cunningham's skink	*Egernia cunninghami*						100				
Dark-flecked garden sunskink	*Lampropholis delicata*			13.6	18.2	34.1	17	4.5	8	2.3	2.3
Diamond python	*Morelia spilota spilota*			60					40		

B236

Proc. Linn. Soc. N.S.W., 134, 2012

Common name	Scientific name											
Eastern blue-tongue	*Tiliqua scincoides*											
Eastern brown snake	*Pseudonaja textilis*											
Eastern small-eyed snake	*Cryptophis nigrescens*			14.3	14.4							14.3
Eastern snake-necked turtle	*Chelodina longicollis*	x										
Eastern water dragon	*Physignathus lesueurii lesueurii*			17.6	17.6	47						
Eastern water-skink	*Eulamprus quoyii*			19.4	22.2	36.1	13.9		8.3			
Emydura	*Emydura* sp.	x										
Golden-crowned snake	*Cacophis squamulosus*			66.7	16.7	16.7						
Jacky lizard	*Amphibolurus muricatus*			4.3	8.7	39.1	39.1		8.7			
Lace monitor	*Varanus varius*			50	25		25					
Lesueur's velvet gecko	*Oedura lesueurii*			37.5	62.5							
Mainland she-oak skink	*Cyclodomorphus michaeli*						66.7		33.3			
Mountain dragon	*Rankinia diemensis*			50	50							
Pale-flecked garden sunskink	*Lampropholis guichenoti*			100								
Red-bellied black snake	*Pseudechis porphyriacus*			11.1	22.2	22.2	11.1	33.3				
Red-naped snake	*Furina diadema*	x										
Red-throated skink	*Acritoscincus platynota*				1.5	98.5						
Rosenberg's goanna	*Varanus rosenbergi*	x		20	40	40						
Thick-tailed gecko	*Underwoodisaurus milii*			100								
Three-toed skink	*Saiphos equalis*			50.8	34.6	11.5	3.8		15.4	3.8		
Tiger snake	*Notechis scutatus*				50		50					
Weasel skink	*Saproscincus mustelinus*			31.6	31.6	15.8	10.5	10.5				
White's skink	*Liopholis whitii*				12.5	81	6.3					
Wood gecko	*Diplodactylus vittatus*			100								
Yellow-faced whip snake	*Demansia psammophis*			50	50							
Birds												
Australasian bittern	*Botaurus poiciloptilus*	x	x									
Australasian darter	*Anhinga novaehollandiae*	x										
Australasian figbird	*Sphecotheres vieilloti*							#				
Australasian grebe	*Tachybaptus novaehollandiae*	x										
Australian hobby	*Falco longipennis*				#							
Australian king-parrot	*Alisterus scapularis*			42.9	42.9		14.3					
Australian magpie	*Cracticus tibicen*				28.6	14.3	14.3		42.9			
Australian owlet-nightjar	*Aegotheles cristatus*			13.8	27.6	48.3		10.3				
Australian pelican	*Pelecanus conspicillatus*							#				
Australian pipit	*Anthus novaeseelandiae*				50			50				
Australian raven	*Corvus coronoides*			4.8	4.8	23.8	23.8	9.5	14.3	4.8	14.3	
Australian reed-warbler	*Acrocephalus australis*	x										

Proc. Linn. Soc. N.S.W., 134, 2012

B237

Common name	Scientific name			Distribution / frequency grid
Australian white ibis	*Threskiornis molucca*			33.3 … 66.7
Australian wood duck	*Chenonetta jubata*			50, 50
Azure kingfisher	*Ceyx azureus*			25, 12.5, 37.5 … 12.5, 12.5
Bar-shouldered dove	*Geopelia humeralis*	#		
Bar-tailed godwit	*Limosa lapponica*	x		
Bassian thrush	*Zoothera lunulata*			85.7 … 14.3
Beautiful firetail	*Stagonopleura bella*			5.3, 10.5, 57.9, 26.3
Black bittern	*Ixobrychus flavicollis*	x	x	
Black swan	*Cygnus atratus*	x		
Black-faced cuckoo-shrike	*Coracina novaehollandiae*			40.6, 43.3 … 6.7, 13.3
Black-faced monarch	*Monarcha melanopsis*			70, 15, 10 … 5
Black-fronted dotterel	*Elseyornis melanops*			50 … 50
Black-shouldered kite	*Elanus axillaris*			75 … 25
Brown cuckoo-dove	*Macropygia amboinensis*			… 20
Brown falcon	*Falco berigora*	x		
Brown gerygone	*Gerygone mouki*			66.7, 20.8, 4.2 … 8.3
Brown goshawk	*Accipiter fasciatus*			50, 50
Brown quail	*Coturnix ypsilophora*			50, 50
Brown thornbill	*Acanthiza pusilla*			23.6, 19.4, 36.1, 12.5, 2.8, 2.8, 1.4, 1.4
Brown-headed honeyeater	*Melithreptus brevirostris*			85.7 … 14.3
Brush bronzewing	*Phaps elegans*			66.7, 33.3
Brush cuckoo	*Cacomantis variolosus*			100
Buff-banded rail	*Gallirallus philippensis*	x		
Buff-rumped thornbill	*Acanthiza reguloides*			100
Channel-billed cuckoo	*Scythrops novaehollandiae*			28.6, 42.9 … 14.3, 14.3
Chestnut teal	*Anas castanea*			33.3, 33.3, 33.3
Chestnut-rumped heathwren	*Hylacola pyrrhopygia*			37.5, 54.2, 8.3
Cicadabird	*Coracina tenuirostris*			50, 40 … 10
Collared sparrowhawk	*Accipiter cirrocephalus*			50, 25, 25
Common bronzewing	*Phaps chalcoptera*			50, 50
Common myna*	*Sturnus tristis**			50 … 50
Crescent honeyeater	*Phylidonyris pyrrhoptera*	x		
Crested pigeon	*Ocyphaps lophotes*	#		
Crested tern	*Thalasseus bergii*	x		
Crimson rosella	*Platycercus elegans*			28.6, 19.1, 42.9, 2.4, 2.4, 2.4 … 2.4
Dollarbird	*Eurystomus orientalis*			37.5, 12.5 … 12.5, 37.5
Dusky moorhen	*Gallinula tenebrosa*			25 … 25, 50
Dusky woodswallow	*Artamus cyanopterus*			14.3, 85.7
Eastern barn owl	*Tyto javanica*	#		

B238

Proc. Linn. Soc. N.S.W., 134, 2012

Common name	Scientific name		
Eastern curlew	*Numenius madagascariensis*	x	
Eastern grass owl	*Tyto longimembris*	x	#
Eastern great egret	*Ardea modesta*		50, 50
Eastern koel	*Eudynamys orientalis*	11.1, 55.6	11.1, 22.2
Eastern osprey	*Pandion cristatus*	x	#
Eastern reef egret	*Egretta sacra*	x	
Eastern rosella	*Platycercus eximius*		50, 50
Eastern shrike-tit	*Falcunculus frontatus frontatus*	50, 50	
Eastern spinebill	*Acanthorhynchus tenuirostris*	13.3, 12.5, 50	8.3, 8.3, 4.2, 1.4
Eastern whipbird	*Psophodes olivaceus*	24.3, 10.8, 10.8	32.4, 10.8, 10.8
Eastern yellow robin	*Eopsaltria australis*	36, 18, 30	2, 6, 8
Emerald dove	*Chalcophaps indica*	x	
Eurasian coot	*Fulica atra*	x	
Fan-tailed cuckoo	*Cacomantis flabelliformis*		50, 25, 25
Fork-tailed swift	*Apus pacificus*		#
Fuscous honeyeater	*Lichenostomus fuscus*		#
Galah	*Eolophus roseicapillus*		#
Golden whistler	*Pachycephala pectoralis*	55.2, 13.8, 20.7, 3.4	6.9
Golden-headed cisticola	*Cisticola exilis*		#
Great cormorant	*Phalacrocorax carbo*	50	50
Green catbird	*Ailuroedus crassirostris*	100	
Grey butcherbird	*Cracticus torquatus*	60, 30	20
Grey currawong	*Strepera versicolor*	x	
Grey fantail	*Rhipidura albiscapa*	17.5, 27.5, 40	5, 7.5, 2.5
Grey goshawk	*Accipiter novaehollandiae*	60, 20, 20	
Grey shrike-thrush	*Colluricincla harmonica*	12, 16, 36	20, 4, 12
Grey teal	*Anas gracilis*	x	
Horsfield's bronze-cuckoo	*Chalcites basalis*	■	
House sparrow*	*Passer domesticus**	x	
Kelp gull	*Larus dominicanus*	x	
Large-billed scrubwren	*Sericornis magnirostra*	90.8, 9.1	
Latham's snipe	*Gallinago hardwickii*		#
Laughing kookaburra	*Dacelo novaeguineae*	10, 20, 40	10, 20
Leaden flycatcher	*Myiagra rubecula*	22.2, 66.7	11.1
Lewin's honeyeater	*Meliphaga lewinii*	48.1, 14.8, 14.8	3.7, 18.5
Lewin's rail	*Lewinia pectoralis*		50, 50
Little black cormorant	*Phalacrocorax sulcirostris*		#
Little corella	*Cacatua sanguinea*	50	50

Proc. Linn. Soc. N.S.W., 134, 2012

B239

VERTEBRATE FAUNA OF ROYAL NATIONAL PARK

Common name	Scientific name								
Little eagle	*Hieraaetus morphnoides*	x					#		
Little egret	*Egretta garzetta*		x						
Little grassbird	*Megalurus gramineus*						#		
Little lorikeet	*Glossopsitta pusilla*	x				#			
Little penguin	*Eudyptula minor*		x						
Little pied cormorant	*Microcarbo melanoleucos*				21.1		33.3		33.3
Little tern	*Sterna albifrons*	x	x						
Little wattlebird	*Anthochaera chrysoptera*			4.4	8.9	33.3	33.3	15.6	4.4
Logrunner	*Orthonyx temminckii*			50	50				
Long-billed corella	*Cacatua tenuirostris*						#		
Magpie-lark	*Grallina cyanoleuca*						■		
Mallard*	*Anas platyrhynchos**		x						
Masked lapwing	*Vanellus miles*								#
Masked owl	*Tyto novaehollandiae*	x		#					
Mistletoebird	*Dicaeum hirundinaceum*			7.7	15.4	69.2		7.7	
Musk lorikeet	*Glossopsitta concinna*						#		
Nankeen kestrel	*Falco cenchroides*				40				60
Nankeen night heron	*Nycticorax caledonicus*					#			
New Holland honeyeater	*Phylidonyris novaehollandiae*			3.4	3.1	28.8	35.6	20.3	6.8
Noisy friarbird	*Philemon corniculatus*				25	75			
Noisy miner	*Manorina melanocephala*			33.3			16.7	50	
Noisy pitta	*Pitta versicolor*	x							
Olive-backed oriole	*Oriolus sagittatus*			■			16.7		
Pacific baza	*Aviceda subcristata*						#		
Pacific black duck	*Anas superciliosa*				28.6		28.6	28.6	14.3
Painted button-quail	*Turnix varius*				50	50			
Peregrine falcon	*Falco peregrinus*					100			
Pheasant coucal	*Centropus phasianinus*							12.5	
Pied cormorant	*Phalacrocorax varius*		x						
Pied currawong	*Strepera graculina*			16	32	40		8	4
Pilotbird	*Pycnoptilus floccosus*					75		25	
Powerful owl	*Ninox strenua*	x		#					
Purple swamphen	*Porphyrio porphyrio*							25	75
Rainbow lorikeet	*Trichoglossus haematodus*			4.3	17.4	52.2		13	13
Red wattlebird	*Anthochaera carunculata*				18.2	72.7		9.1	
Red-browed finch	*Neochmia temporalis*			11.1	16.7	38.9	5.6	22.2	5.6
Red-browed treecreeper	*Climacteris erythrops*				66.7	33.3			
Red-whiskered bulbul*	*Pycnonotus jocosus**			14.3	14.3		14.3	14.3	28.6	14.3
Rockwarbler	*Origma solitaria*			7.7	61.5	30.8			

B240

Proc. Linn. Soc. N.S.W., 134, 2012

Common name	Scientific name	Data
Rose robin	*Petroica rosea*	#
Royal spoonbill	*Platalea regia*	#
Ruddy turnstone	*Arenaria interpres*	x
Rufous fantail	*Rhipidura rufifrons*	61.5 19.2 15.4 3.8
Rufous whistler	*Pachycephala rufiventris*	25
Sacred kingfisher	*Todiramphus sanctus*	22.2 11.1 33.3 11.1 22.2
Satin bowerbird	*Ptilonorhynchus violaceus*	33.3 33.3 33.3
Scaly-breasted lorikeet	*Trichoglossus chlorolepidotus*	x
Scarlet honeyeater	*Myzomela sanguinolenta*	■
Scarlet robin	*Petroica boodang*	x x
Shining bronze-cuckoo	*Chalcites lucidus*	50 50
Silver gull	*Chroicocephalus novaehollandiae*	50 50
Silvereye	*Zosterops lateralis*	31.3 25 14.6 10.4 2.1 8.3 4.2 6.3
Sooty owl	*Tyto tenebricosa*	x 100
Sooty oystercatcher	*Haematopus fuliginosus*	x x
Southern boobook	*Ninox novaeseelandiae*	7.7 15.4 46.2 30.8
Southern emu-wren	*Stipiturus malachurus*	4.3 39.1 39.1 4.3 4.3 8.7
Spotless crake	*Porzana tabuensis*	x
Spotted pardalote	*Pardalotus punctatus*	3.1 25 59.4 3.1 9.4
Spotted turtle-dove*	*Streptopelia chinensis**	20 20 20 20 20
Straw-necked ibis	*Threskiornis spinicollis*	x
Striated heron	*Butorides striatus*	#
Striated pardalote	*Pardalotus striatus*	■
Striated thornbill	*Acanthiza lineata*	13.9 22.2 40.1 2.8
Sulphur-crested cockatoo	*Cacatua galerita*	21.1 31.6 26.3 5.3 10.5 5.3
Superb fairy-wren	*Malurus cyaneus*	5.3 10.5 10.5 10.5 15.8 15.8 5.3 26.3
Superb lyrebird	*Menura novaehollandiae*	47.1 17.6 35.3
Swamp harrier	*Circus approximans*	50 50
Tawny frogmouth	*Podargus strigoides*	11.1 66.7 22.2
Tawny-crowned honeyeater	*Gliciphila melanops*	7.1 57.1 35.7
Topknot pigeon	*Lopholaimus antarcticus*	33.3 33.3 33.3
Tree martin	*Petrochelidon nigricans*	12.5 37.5 50
Varied sittella	*Daphoenositta chrysoptera*	x
Variegated fairy-wren	*Malurus lamberti*	2.1 16.7 41.7 29.2 6.3 2.1 2.1
Wedge-tailed eagle	*Aquila audax*	x
Welcome swallow	*Hirundo neoxena*	5.7 2.9 8.6 14.3 2.9 8.6 5.7
Whimbrel	*Numenius phaeopus*	#
Whistling kite	*Haliastur sphenurus*	33.3 66.7

Proc. Linn. Soc. N.S.W., 134, 2012

B241

Common name	Scientific name		Values
White-bellied sea-eagle	Haliaeetus leucogaster		7.7, 46.2, 7.7, 7.7, 30.8
White-browed scrubwren	Sericornis frontalis		13.6, 13.6, 33, 23.9, 8, 5.7, 2.3
White-browed woodswallow	Artamus superciliosus	x	
White-cheeked honeyeater	Phylidonyris niger		100
White-eared honeyeater	Lichenostomus leucotis		84.6, 15.4
White-faced heron	Egretta novaehollandiae		50, 50
White-fronted tern	Sterna striata	x	
White-naped honeyeater	Melithreptus lunatus		#
White-necked heron	Ardea pacifica	x	
White-plumed honeyeater	Lichenostomus penicillatus	x	
White-throated needletail	Hirundapus caudacutus		8.3, 8.3, 25, 41.7, 8.3, 8.3
White-throated nightjar	Eurostopodus mystacalis		14.3, 57.1, 28.6
White-throated treecreeper	Cormobates leucophaea		14.8, 40.7, 40.7, 3.7
Willie wagtail	Rhipidura leucophrys		20, 20, 40, 20
Wonga pigeon	Leucosarcia picata		100
Yellow thornbill	Acanthiza nana		50, 50
Yellow-faced honeyeater	Lichenostomus chrysops		6.3, 21.9, 53.1, 9.4, 6.3, 3.1
Yellow-tailed black-cockatoo	Calyptorhynchus funereus		9.1, 90.9
Yellow-throated scrubwren	Sericornis citreogularis		86.7, 6.7, 6.7
Yellow-tufted honeyeater	Lichenostomus melanops		80, 20

Mammals

Common name	Scientific name		Values
Black rat*	Rattus rattus*		#
Brown antechinus	Antechinus stuartii		#
Bush rat	Rattus fuscipes		#
Cat*	Felis catus*		#
Chocolate wattled bat	Chalinolobus morio		17.6, 5.9, 70.6, 5.9
Common brushtail possum	Trichosurus vulpecula		50, 50
Common dunnart	Sminthopsis murina	x	
Common ringtail possum	Pseudocheirus peregrinus		16.7, 8.3, 58.3, 16.7
Common wallaroo	Macropus robustus	x	
Common wombat	Vombatus ursinus	x	
Dog*	Canis lupus familiaris*	x	
Eastern bentwing-bat	Miniopterus schreibersii oceanensis	x	25, 25, 50
Eastern broad-nosed bat	Scotorepens orion		#
Eastern freetail-bat	Mormopterus ridei	x	
Eastern horseshoe-bat	Rhinolophus megaphyllus		35.7, 14.3, 42.9, 7.1
Eastern pygmy-possum	Cercartetus nanus	x	#
Feathertail glider	Acrobates pygmaeus		33.3, 66.7
Fox*	Vulpes vulpes*		#

B242

Proc. Linn. Soc. N.S.W., 134, 2012

Common name	Scientific name			Chart
Gould's long-eared bat	*Nyctophilus gouldi*			10 / 70 / 10 / 10
Gould's wattled bat	*Chalinolobus gouldii*			11.1 / 19.4 / 50 / 8.3 / 8.3 / 2.8
Greater broad-nosed bat	*Scoteanax rueppellii*	x		
Grey-headed flying-fox	*Pteropus poliocephalus*	x		81.8 / 18.2
House mouse*	*Mus musculus* *		x	
Koala	*Phascolarctos cinereus*	x	x	
Large forest bat	*Vespadelus darlingtoni*			12.5
Large-eared pied bat	*Chalinolobus dwyeri*	x		14.3
Lesser long-eared bat	*Nyctophilus geoffroyi*			#
Little bentwing-bat	*Miniopterus australis*	x		
Little forest bat	*Vespadelus vulturnus*			8.2 / 14.8 / 63.9 / 3.3 / 1.6 / 4.9 / 1.6
Long-nosed bandicoot	*Perameles nasuta*			100
Mountain brushtail possum	*Trichosurus cunninghami*	x		
New Holland mouse	*Pseudomys novaehollandiae*	x	x	
Rabbit*	*Oryctolagus cuniculus* *			#
Rusa deer*	*Cervus timorensis* *			28.6 / 14.3 / 14.3 / 14.3 / 28.6
Short-beaked echidna	*Tachyglossus aculeatus*	x		
Southern myotis	*Myotis macropus*	x		60 / 40
Sugar glider	*Petaurus breviceps*			16.1 / 29.1 / 41.9 / 12.9
Swamp rat	*Rattus lutreolus*	x		
Swamp wallaby	*Wallabia bicolor*			6.7 / 20 / 60 / 6.7 / 6.7
White-striped freetail-bat	*Tadarida australis*			18.2 / 18.2 / 63.6

Proc. Linn. Soc. N.S.W., 134, 2012

B243

APPENDIX 2. SPECIES PREVIOUSLY RECORDED BUT NOT DURING THE CURRENT SURVEY

Sources: Atlas of NSW Wildlife (OEH 2012), Anyon-Smith (2006), M. Schulz (unpublished data), Robinson (1987, 1988), Andrew (2001), B. Sullivan OEH staff at Royal NP (pers. comm.).

Introduced species are denoted by *.

Common name	Scientific name	Threatened species listed under the TSC Act and/or EPBC Act	Status in the study area
Amphibians			
Broad-palmed frog	*Litoria latopalmata*		Status uncertain
Brown toadlet	*Pseudophryne bibronii*		Status uncertain
Green and golden bell frog	*Litoria aurea*	x	Locally extinct
Green tree frog	*Litoria caerulea*		Status uncertain
Jervis Bay tree frog	*Litoria jervisiensis*		Winter-vocalising
Stuttering frog	*Mixophyes balbus*	x	Locally extinct
Verreaux's tree frog	*Litoria verreauxii*		Winter-vocalising
Birds			
Apostlebird	*Struthidea cinerea*		Rare or vagrant
Australian brush turkey	*Alectura lathami*		Rare or vagrant
Australian little bittern	*Ixobrychus dubius*		Rare or vagrant
Australian pied oystercatcher	*Haematopus longirostris*	x	Winter visitor
Australian shelduck	*Tadorna tadornoides*		Rare or vagrant
Australian spotted crake	*Porzana fluminea*		Rare or vagrant
Baillon's crake	*Porzana pusilla*		Rare or vagrant
Barking owl	*Ninox connivens*	x	Status uncertain
Beach stone-curlew	*Esacus magnirostris*	x	Rare or vagrant
Black falcon	*Falco subniger*		Rare or vagrant
Black honeyeater	*Sugomel niger*		Rare or vagrant
Black kite	*Milvus migrans*		Rare or vagrant
Black-chinned honeyeater	*Melithreptus gularis*		Rare or vagrant
Black-eared cuckoo	*Chalcites osculans*		Rare or vagrant
Black-winged stilt	*Himantopus himantopus*		Rare or vagrant
Blue-faced honeyeater	*Entomyzon cyanotis*		Rare or vagrant
Brown honeyeater	*Lichmera indistincta*		Rare or vagrant
Brown songlark	*Cincloramphus cruralis*		Rare or vagrant
Bush stone-curlew	*Burhinus grallarius*	x	Locally extinct

Caspian tern	*Hydroprogne caspia*		Sporadic visitor
Cattle egret	*Ardea ibis*		Sporadic visitor
Common sandpiper	*Actitis hypoleucos*		Rare or vagrant
Common tern	*Sterna hirundo*		Rare or vagrant
Diamond firetail	*Stagonopleura guttata*	x	Rare or vagrant
Double-banded plover	*Charadrius bicinctus*		Winter visitor
Double-barred finch	*Taeniopygia bichenovii*		Rare or vagrant
Eastern bristlebird	*Dasyornis brachypterus*	x	Locally extinct
Eurasian blackbird*	*Turdus merula* *		Sporadic visitor
Fairy martin	*Petrochelidon ariel*		Sporadic visitor
Forest kingfisher	*Todiramphus macleayii*		Rare or vagrant
Freckled duck	*Stictonetta naevosa*	x	Rare or vagrant
Gang-gang cockatoo	*Callocephalon fimbriatum*	x	Sporadic visitor
Glossy black-cockatoo	*Calyptorhynchus lathami*	x	Rare or vagrant
Great crested grebe	*Podiceps cristatus*		Rare or vagrant
Grey-tailed tattler	*Tringa brevipes*		Rare or vagrant
Ground parrot	*Pezoporus wallicus*		Locally extinct
Hardhead	*Aythya australis*		Sporadic visitor
Hoary-headed grebe	*Poliocephalus*		Rare or vagrant
Intermediate egret	*Ardea intermedia*		Sporadic visitor
Jacky winter	*Microeca fascinans*		Rare or vagrant
King quail	*Excalfactoria chinensis*		Status uncertain
Little friarbird	*Philemon citreogularis*		Rare or vagrant
Mangrove gerygone	*Gerygone levigaster*		Status uncertain
Masked woodswallow	*Artamus personatus*		Rare or vagrant
Musk duck	*Biziura lobata*		Sporadic visitor
Oriental cuckoo	*Cuculus optatus*		Rare or vagrant
Pacific golden plover	*Pluvialis fulva*		Rare or vagrant
Pacific gull	*Larus pacificus*		Rare or vagrant
Painted honeyeater	*Grantiella picta*	x	Rare or vagrant
Pallid cuckoo	*Cacomantis pallidus*		Rare or vagrant
Peaceful dove	*Geopelia striata*		Rare or vagrant
Pied butcherbird	*Cracticus nigrogularis*		Rare or vagrant
Plumed whistling-duck	*Dendrocygna eytoni*		Rare or vagrant
Red-capped plover	*Charadrius ruficapillus*		Rare or vagrant
Red-capped robin	*Petroica goodenovii*		Rare or vagrant
Red-rumped parrot	*Psephotus haematonotus*		Rare or vagrant

Regent bowerbird	*Sericulus chrysocephalus*	Locally extinct
Regent honeyeater	*Anthochaera phrygia* x	Rare or vagrant
Restless flycatcher	*Myiagra inquieta*	Rare or vagrant
Rock dove*	*Columba livia**	Sporadic visitor
Rose-crowned fruit-dove	*Ptilinopus regina* x	Rare or vagrant
Rufous songlark	*Cincloramphus mathewsi*	Rare or vagrant
Satin flycatcher	*Myiagra cyanoleuca*	Rare or vagrant
Sharp-tailed sandpiper	*Calidris acuminata*	Rare or vagrant
Spangled drongo	*Dicrurus bracteatus*	Winter visitor
Speckled warbler	*Chthonicola sagittata* x	Locally extinct
Spectacled monarch	*Symposiachrus trivirgatus*	Rare or vagrant
Spiny-cheeked honeyeater	*Acanthagenys rufogularis*	Rare or vagrant
Spotted harrier	*Circus assimilis* x	Rare or vagrant
Spotted quail-thrush	*Cinclosoma punctatum*	Rare or vagrant
Square-tailed kite	*Lophoictinia isura* x	Rare or vagrant
Striated pardalote	*Pardalotus striatus*	Sporadic visitor
Stubble quail	*Coturnix pectoralis*	Rare or vagrant
Superb fruit-dove	*Ptilinopus superbus* x	Rare or vagrant
Swift parrot	*Lathamus discolor* x	Sporadic visitor
Tawny grassbird	*Megalurus timoriensis*	Rare or vagrant
Torresian crow	*Corvus orru*	Rare or vagrant
Wandering tattler	*Tringa incana*	Rare or vagrant
White-bellied cuckoo-shrike	*Coracina papuensis*	Rare or vagrant
White-headed pigeon	*Columba leucomela*	Sporadic visitor
White-throated gerygone	*Gerygone albogularis*	Rare or vagrant
White-winged triller	*Lalage sueurii*	Rare or vagrant
Yellow-billed spoonbill	*Platalea flavipes*	Rare or vagrant
Yellow-rumped thornbill	*Acanthiza chrysorrhoa*	Rare or vagrant

Mammals

Australian fur-seal	*Arctocephalus pusillus* x	Sporadic visitor
Dusky antechinus	*Antechinus swainsonii*	Status uncertain
Eastern quoll	*Dasyurus viverrinus* x	Locally extinct
Feral dog*	*Canis lupus familiaris**	Status uncertain
Feral pig*	*Sus scrofa**	Status uncertain
Greater glider	*Petauroides volans*	Status uncertain
Leopard seal	*Hydrurga leptonyx*	Rare or vagrant
New Zealand fur-seal	*Arctocephalus forsteri* x	Sporadic visitor

Parma wallaby	*Macropus parma*	x	Locally extinct
Platypus	*Ornithorhynchus anatinus*		Status uncertain
Red-necked pademelon	*Thylogale thetis*		Locally extinct
Southern elephant seal	*Mirounga leonina*	x	Rare or vagrant
Spotted-tailed quoll	*Dasyurus maculatus*	x	Locally extinct
Water rat	*Hydromys chrysogaster*		Status uncertain
Yellow-bellied sheathtailed-bat	*Saccolaimus flaviventris*	x	Status uncertain

Proc. Linn. Soc. N.S.W., 134, 2012

B247

Population Dynamics of *Xanthorrhoea resinosa* Pers. Over Two Decades: Implications for Fire Management

MARK. G. TOZER[2] AND DAVID A. KEITH[1,2]

[1]Australian Wetlands and Rivers Centre, University of New South Wales, Sydney 2052, Australia.
[2]NSW Office of Environment and Heritage, PO Box 1967, Hurstville 2220, Australia.

Published on 3 September 2012 at http://escholarship.library.usyd.edu.au/journals/index.php/LIN

Tozer, M.G. and Keith, D.A. (2012). Population dynamics of *Xanthorrhoea resinosa* Pers. over two decades: implications for fire management. *Proceedings of the Linnean Society of New South Wales* **134**, B249-B266.

Fire has an important influence on the biota of Royal National Park and is a factor over which park managers exert some control. Fire management guidelines for biodiversity conservation are expressed as thresholds that define fire-regimes associated with elevated risks of extinction that management must aim to avoid. These thresholds strongly reflect fire-interval effects on fire-sensitive (non-resprouting) species. In contrast, the guidelines are less prescriptive about the characteristics of particular fire events (e.g. intensity, season, post-fire rainfall) or competition because the long-term importance of these factors is less well understood. On-going monitoring is required to determine if conservation goals will be met by management actions under these guidelines, or if they should be adapted to counter previously unidentified negative trends. In particular, populations of resprouting species which appear to be relatively resilient to interval-dependent effects must be monitored to detect subtle, but ultimately dangerous declines. We describe population trends in the iconic grass-tree *Xanthorrhoea resinosa* based on observations of over 3000 individual plants over a period of 23 years. We identify divergent population trends predicted to result in either local extinction within 200 years or slight declines depending on rates of mortality. Experimental evidence is presented for a strong impact of competition on survival which, at one of the study sites, led to local extinction following a single fire interval of 17 years. The relative importance of mortality associated with heat shock during fire, the effort of post-fire resprouting and flowering and other factors such as disease and competition are discussed. Our results suggest that a focus on minimum fire intervals alone will not guarantee the long-term persistence of key understorey species and that fire regime thresholds should more directly consider functional groups containing species with low potential for population growth.

Manuscript received 27 February 2012, accepted for publication 10 May 2012.

KEYWORDS: bushfire, fire intervals, fire management, park management, population dynamics, Royal National Park, *Xanthorrhoea resinosa*

INTRODUCTION

The structure and composition of heath communities in Royal National Park vary in time as a function of the interactive effects of fire, the environment and inter-specific interactions (Keith and Tozer 2012). In response, fire managers have adopted a flexible approach with the specific aim of avoiding the extinction of local populations (cf optimising the size of local populations; Bradstock et al. 1995). The key components of this approach are: i) defining groups of species which respond to fire regimes in similar ways (functional groups); ii) identifying fire regime thresholds beyond which species in certain functional groups are likely to decline; and iii) promoting variability in fire regimes in space and time as a means of managing conflicting requirements of different functional groups (Keith et al. 2002).

Central to this approach is a capacity to predict the cause, direction and magnitude of changes in population density. Population changes may be the result of: i) the length of the interval between fires (interval-dependent effects); ii) density-dependent feedbacks (self-regulation); iii) characteristics of individual fires and their timing in relation to seasonal population processes and weather (event-dependent effects); or iv) interactions with other species (Bond and van Wilgen 1996). The length of the fire interval is an important factor regulating the growth, reproduction and death of plant populations, thus interval-dependent effects are relatively easy to translate into management thresholds. In contrast, deriving management guidelines relevant to density-dependent or event-dependent effects is less tractable because the processes are less-well understood, inherently unpredictable or not amenable to management manipulation (Whelan et al. 2002). Dynamics driven by competitive interactions have been largely ignored (Bond and van Wilgen 1996), although recent studies have demonstrated that some understorey species decline in response to competition from overstorey shrubs in heath and shrubland communities (Cowling and Gxaba 1990, Keith and Bradstock 1994, Tozer and Bradstock 2002, Keith et al. 2007a, Keith and Tozer 2012).

The heath flora of Sydney may be classified into functional types based on life-history responses to fire (Keith et al. 2007a; Keith & Tozer 2012). Fire management guidelines for heath in Royal National Park assume that the plant functional type that includes serotinous obligate-seeder species is the most susceptible to local extinction due to interval-dependent effects on reproductive capacity. Fire-regime thresholds specified under the management plan (DECC 2009) nominate successive intervals of less than seven years and intervals greater than 30 years as incompatible with the conservation of these species (Short fire intervals eliminate populations before they reach reproductive age, while long intervals result in senescence and loss of both standing plants and the serotinous seed bank). In effect, the approach to fire management in Royal National Park assumes that on average, density and event-dependent effects on populations of other species are neutral under a variable fire regime and that competitive exclusion of understorey species by shrubs is prevented by recurring fire. Therefore, the risk of local extinction in resprouting species is low, at least for several fire intervals.

We established a demographic study in order to determine if the population dynamics of *Xanthorrhoea resinosa*, a long-lived, resprouting understorey species were consistent with these assumptions. We sought evidence for divergent population trends which may potentially arise as a result of contrasting fire regimes under the current management model. We compared growth, mortality and fertility in populations subject to two short inter-fire intervals (5 & 8 years) with populations subject to a short interval followed by an intermediate inter-fire interval (5 & 18 years) and computed population projections for a range of seedling establishment rates measured in field populations. Our aims were: i) to quantify the potential

for population growth in populations subject to each fire regime; and ii) develop an understanding of the relative importance of factors inducing mortality (eg fire, competition). Our observations were augmented with an experiment in which we manipulated shrub cover in order to measure the effect of shrub canopy on survival.

METHODS

Species and study area

Xanthorrhoea resinosa is a common species occurring in heath and low sclerophyll woodland in seasonally wet sandy soils in the Blue Mountains and coastal sites south from Sydney (http:www.plantnet.rbgsyd.nsw.gov.au, Harden 1993). It has a terminal crown of up to several thousand leaves arising from a woody stem (caudex) which is typically subterranean but may grow up to 1 m above ground. Our study sites were located exclusively in heath on sandstone soils in Royal National Park, 20 km south of Sydney, Australia (Figure 1). Heath is characterised by a shrub stratum of variable cover up to 4 m tall with a semi-continuous groundcover of smaller shrubs and graminoids (Keith and Myerscough 1993, Tozer et al. 2010). Major bushfires occurred in the area in October 1988, January 1994 and December 2001. Study sites were burnt in either one (Garrawarra), two (Garie Trig, Bundeena Road and Jibbon) or all three fires (Wises Track, Maianbar Road and Crystal Pools).

Sampling methods

Six sites (Table 1) were established following a major summer wildfire in 1988, either on shallow, relatively well-drained soils (Wises Track, Crystal Pools, Maianbar Road, Bundeena Drive and Garie Trig) or deeper damp soils (Jibbon, Figure 1). Three sites were subsequently burnt in summer wildfires in January 1994 and December 2001 while the remainder were burnt only in 1994. A seventh site was established on deep, damp soil following the 1994 fire and remained unburnt thereafter (Garrawarra, Table 1). Sites subject to three fires (Wises Track, Crystal Pools, Maianbar Road) were burnt between 11 and 14 years prior to the 1988 fire and were structurally open at the time of the 1988 fire (Table 1). Sites subject to two fires (Bundeena Drive, Garie and Jibbon) were burnt between 8 and 22 years prior to the 1988 fire and ranged in structure from open heath to thicket at the time of the 1988 fire (Table 1).

Two transects (50 – 500 m apart) were established at each of the well-drained sites sampling contrasting scorch levels (high/low) assuming that

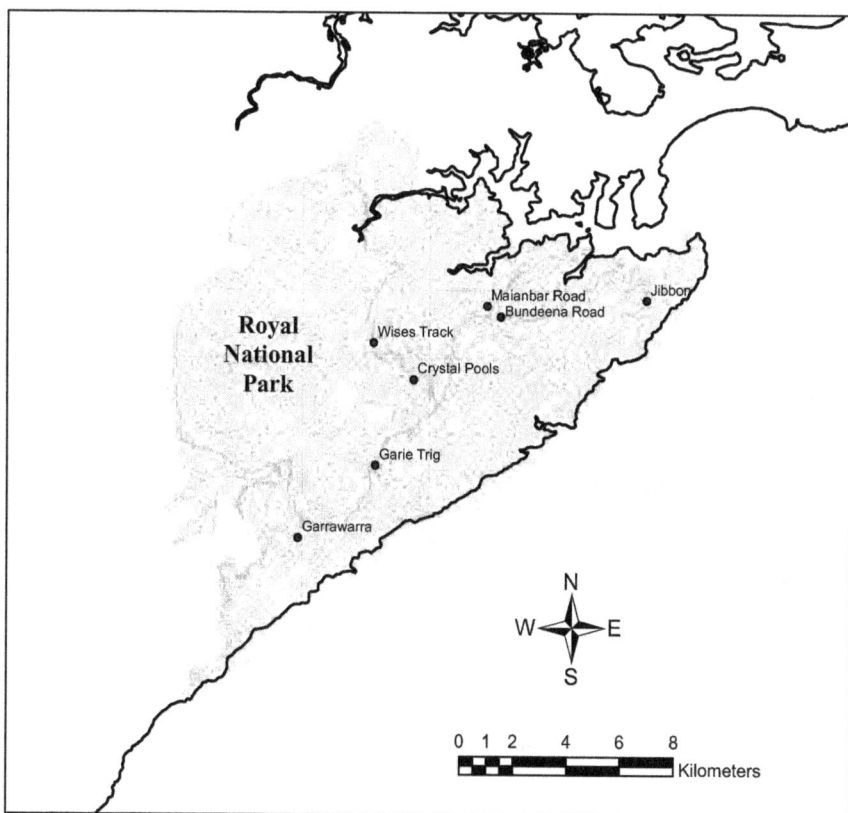

Figure 1: Location of study sites in Royal National Park.

Table 1: Location of study sites and their fire history and structural state prior to the 1988 fire

Site	Grid Reference (GDA)	Interval prior to 1988 fire (years)	State prior to 1988 fire	Burnt 1988	Burnt 1994	Burnt 2001
Wises Track	321085E 6223809N	11 (subpop. 1) 14(subpop. 2)	Open Heath	Yes	Yes	Yes
Crystal Pools	322345E 6222537N	11	Open Heath	Yes	Yes	Yes
Maianbar Road	324565E 6225205N	12	Open Heath	Yes	Yes	Yes
Garie Trig	321229E 6219446N	22	Shrub thicket	Yes	Yes	No
Bundeena Road	324997E 6224808N	20	Scattered shrub thicket	Yes	Yes	No
Jibbon	329486E 6225512N	8 (subpop. 4) 12 (subpops. 1-3)	Open heath and shrub thicket	Yes	Yes	No
Garrawarra	318912E 6216811N	-	Scattered shrub thicket	No	Yes	No

this represented variability in the above-ground heat output of the fire. At Jibbon a pair of transects (10 - 20 m apart) was established in each of four sites (200 – 500m apart) defining a (pre-fire) structural spectrum from open heath (no tall shrubs) to dense thicket. Two pairs of transects were established at Garrawarra. All tall shrub species were removed at the seedling stage from one transect of each pair, and seedlings left in the other to develop into a dense thicket. A minimum of 50 plants were sampled along each transect with the sample increased up to one hundred at most sites in order to increase the number of plants in size classes that were poorly represented. Plants were marked with uniquely numbered brass fire-proof tags attached to stainless steel stakes placed in the ground. A census of all populations was carried out approximately annually in summer from 1989 to December 2011 (Garrawarra was sampled in 2001, 2007 and 2011). Survival, crown size (number of living leaves), caudex height, flowering and fruiting data were recorded at each census except between 1990 and 1994 when crown size was measured on a subset of 15 plants at each transect). The number of capsules was counted on each spike except following the 1994 fire at Jibbon where a sub-sample of inflorescences was counted.

Seedling emergence and survival

Emergence, survival and growth of seedlings were measured at Jibbon in a seed-sowing experiment commencing in May 1990 after the first post-fire seed release. Clusters of 50 seeds were sown in five locations selected randomly at intervals of 1-5 m along each of the eight transects. Clear, square, perspex boxes (30 cm square and 10 cm tall, with open tops and bottoms) were used to reduce secondary dispersal of seeds by ants and surface water flow. The top edges of the boxes were smeared with tanglefoot to reduce access to the seeds by insect predators. Initially the seeds were monitored weekly. Additional seeds were sown to replace those in clusters that suffered high rates of seed removal or predation within 3 months of the initial placement. The perspex boxes were removed after 6 months. A total of 987 seedlings emerged. Survival of emergent seedlings was monitored at decreasing intervals, starting with weekly censuses for the first 3 months, reducing to monthly censuses until 2 years and 3-monthly censuses thereafter. All seedlings were burnt in the 1994 fire, 3.6 years after seeds were sown. Individuals that survived the fire were recorded in October 1994 and subsequently checked at approximately annual intervals.

Seedling establishment rates following the 1994 fire were estimated at the other six sites in 1996, approximately one year after seed release. Seedling density was estimated by counting seedlings in 0.25m² plots located at regular intervals along parallel transects through each population. Sampling continued until the coefficient of variation of the sampling error of the mean was below 0.3 (26-50 quadrats). The same method was used to estimate inflorescence density in 25m² plots (6-18 quadrats). Inflorescences were classified as fertile or non-fertile (no capsules). Capsule density on fertile inflorescences was estimated by measuring the length of the spike and counting the number of capsules on a representative portion (10 – 48cm) or the entire spike. Establishment rates per capsule were calculated by dividing the estimates for seedling and capsule density. Combinatorial errors were calculated as follows:

For $X = A + B$ or $X = A – B$, then $DX = \sqrt{\{(DA)^2 + (DB)^2\}}$

For $X = A.B$ or $X = A/B$, then $DX/X = \sqrt{\{(DA/A)^2 + (DB/B)^2\}}$

Where D denotes the sampling error associated with the respective measurements.

The resprouting capability of seedlings approximately 1.5 years old was investigated following a simulated fire at Garrawarra in May 1997. Plots (25m²) containing 6-20 seedlings were randomly allocated to two defoliation treatments or a control (n=4). The first treatment simulated a moderate intensity fire using a hand-held propane gas torch (see Bradstock & Myerscough 1988). In the second treatment seedlings were defoliated using scissors. Seedlings were monitored weekly for two months then every three months until September 2000.

Population projections

Census data spanning the period 1988-2011 were used to construct a static life-table for each of two fire scenarios (two or three fires). Our preliminary appraisal of the data suggested that the rate of crown growth (leaf number) was geometric but very slow and that a significant proportion of individuals were either static or declined during the observation period. Furthermore, there was no apparent relationship between survival and reproduction and the location of the caudex (aerial or subterranean) and aerial growth in the caudex during the observation period was generally below the error of measurement. Therefore, we set our life-table time unit to the maximum possible (23 years) and used a stage structure based on leaf number alone. Stages were devised such that on average, individuals progressed by a single stage per unit of time (Krebs 2009). We calculated the average annual rate of crown growth for all individuals over 21 years (see below) then applied this to a hypothetical individual commencing with one leaf and growing for 400 years. Standardised to a 21 year time unit, this yielded 20 stages (Table 2) covering the variation in crown-size observed in the sample populations.

B252

Proc. Linn. Soc. N.S.W., 134, 2012

Table 2a: Static life table (part a) for a 23 year time step derived from census data for sites burnt, respectively, twice and three times, during the 23 year study period (see first column). Flowering data are Number flowering (%), number of failed infloresences, average capsule production (+ SEM) and range of capsule counts (Column totals are range with upper and lower bounds). NR = not recorded. Fertility data are seedlings produced per individual (observed range with upper and lower bounds (calculated from lowest rate – SEM and upper highest rate + SEM).

# Fires	Stage	# Leaves	N	Flowering (%) 1988	Flowering (%) 1994	Flowering (%) 2001	Dead (%)	Ann. Surv. (%)	Fertility
1	Sdl.		987	0	0	0	986 (99.999)	74.1	0
2	2	1	1	0	0	-	1 (100)	0	0
2	3	2	1	0	0	-	1 (100)	0	0
2	4	3	2	0	0	-	1 (50)	97	0
2	5	4-5	21	0	0	-	10 (47.6)	97.2	0
2	6	6-7	15	0	0	-	7 (46.7)	97.3	0
2	7	8-11	34	0	0	-	13 (38.2)	97.9	0
2	8	12-16	56	0	0	-	17 (30.4)	98.4	0
2	9	17-24	52	0	1 (2%) 0,NR(NR) NR-NR	-	15 (28.8)	98.5	0
2	10	25-35	45	0	0	-	19 (42.2)	97.6	0
2	11	36-50	56	0	3 (5%) 0,NR(NR) NR-NR	-	20 (35.7)	98.1	0
2	12	51-72	65	1 (2%) 0,48(-) 48-48	10 (15%) 1,102(-) 102-102	-	18 (27.7)	98.6	(0) 0 – 1 (1)
2	13	73-103	55	1 (2%) 0,5(-) 5-5	25 (45%) 0,NR(NR) NR-NR	-	11 (20)	99	(0) 2 – 24 (24)
2	14	104-148	57	4 (7%) 0,268(98) 5-590	22 (39%) 1,1156(-) 1156-1156	-	20 (35.1)	98.1	(0) 1 – 20 (20)
2	15	149-212	67	3 (4%) 0,399(95) 300-590	22 (33%) 0,1247(239) 22-2720	-	21 (31.3)	98.4	(1) 1 – 19 (35)
2	16	213-303	65	12 (18%) 2,869(176) 56-1785	24 (37%) 4,817(180) 56-1785	-	14 (21.5)	99	(1) 1 – 17 (29)
2	17	304-433	35	8 (23%) 0,1190(240) 76-1909	13 (37%) 0,1129(250) 80-2400	-	12 (34.3)	98.2	(1) 2 – 31 (51)
2	18	434-622	32	14 (44%) 1,1905(162) 1105-3080	15 (47%) 0,1412(101) 730-1700	-	7 (21.9)	98.9	(3) 4 – 65 (104)
2	19	623-886	12	5 (42%) 2,1145(718) 10-2280	4 (33%) 0,NR(NR) NR-NR	-	6 (50)	97	(1) 2 – 34 (57)

Proc. Linn. Soc. N.S.W., 134, 2012

B253

Table 2a continued

# Fires	Stage	# Leaves	N	Flowering (%) 1988	Flowering (%) 1994	Flowering (%) 2001	Dead (%)	Ann. Surv. (%)	Fertility
2	20	887-1266	3	0	3 (100%) 0,0(0)0-0	-	0 (0)	100	(3) 4 – 64 (118)
		Tot.	674	(111) 49 - 2213 (3297)	(381) 439 – 6539 (8153)	-	213 (32)	98.4	(1) 1 – 13 (13)
3	3	2	4	0	0	0	0 (0)	100	0
3	4	3	7	0	0	0	0 (0)	100	0
3	5	4-5	29	0	0	0	8 (27.6)	98.6	0
3	6	6-7	35	0	0	0	8 (22.9)	98.9	0
3	7	8-11	34	0	0	0	7 (20.6)	99	0
3	8	12-16	41	0	0	0	9 (22)	98.9	0
3	9	17-24	59	0	0	0	21 (35.6)	98.1	0
3	10	25-35	55	0	0	1 (2%) 0,0(-) 0-0	22 (40)	97.8	0
3	11	36-50	66	0	3 (5%) 0,NR(NR) NR-NR	0	24 (36.4)	98.1	(0) 0 – 1 (2)
3	12	51-72	81	3 (4%) 0,81(48) 4-170	3 (4%) 0,NR(NR) NR-NR	0	22 (27.2)	98.6	(0) 0 – 1 (2)
3	13	73-103	80	4 (5%) 1,412(225) 81-924	14 (18%) 0,NR(NR) NR-NR	0	20 (25)	98.8	(0) 0 – 5 (9)
3	14	104-148	69	6 (9%) 1,297(96) 21-516	19 (28%) 0,NR(NR) NR-NR	0	13 (18.8)	99.1	(0) 1 – 8 (14)
3	15	149-212	71	8 (11%) 0,569(129) 68-1173	18 (25%) 0,545(112) 210-880	1 (1%) 0,2(-) 2-2	12 (16.9)	99.2	(0) 1 – 9 (9)
3	16	213-303	59	9 (15%) 5,672(162) 353-1232	16 (27%) 0,975(156) 211-1720	9 (15%) 6,112(46) 13-210	8 (13.6)	99.4	(1) 1 – 14 (25)
3	17	304-433	80	15 (19%) 2,1017(136) 41-1740	32 (40%) 3,1061(97) 410-1920	8 (10%) 3,478(266) 20-1806	7 (8.8)	99.6	(1) 2 – 26 (42)
3	18	434-622	33	5 (15%) 0,1410(332) 396-2424	11 (33%) (1,343(122) 8-790	4 (12%) 1,227(171) 14-620	2 (6.1)	99.7	(1) 1 – 15 (25)
3	19	623-886	9	5 (56%) 0,3045(1176) 714-7020	5 (56%) (0,3190(1197) 670-6000	0	1 (11.1)	99.5	(6) 11 – 157 (259)
3	20	887-1266	1	0	0	0	0 (0)	100	(0) 0 – 0 (0)
		Tot.	813	(104) 139 – 2075 (2964)	(237) 295 – 4396 (5911)	(5) 10 – 155 (270)	184 (23)	98.9	(1) 1 – 8 (8)

Table 2b: Static life table (part b) for a 23 year time step derived from census data for sites burnt, respectively, twice and three times, during the 23 year study period (see first column). Stage matrix specifies the final stage distribution (%, columns 11-29) by starting stage (column 2).

#Fires	Stage	#Leaves	N	2	3	4	5	6	7	8	9	10	11	12	13	14	15	16	17	18	19	20
2	Sdl.		987							0.1												
2	2	1	1																			
2	3	2	1																			
2	4	3	2						50													
2	5	4-5	21			4.8	9.5	9.5	4.8	4.8	9.5	9.5										
2	6	6-7	15					6.7	33.3	6.7		6.7										
2	7	8-11	34					5.9	5.9	23.5	8.8	11.8										
2	8	12-16	56	1.8					5.4	17.9	25	8.9	2.9	2.9								
2	9	17-24	52							7.7		21.2	5.4	5.4	1.9	1.9		1.9				
2	10	25-35	45								8.9	13.3	13.5	13.5	4.4	4.4						
2	11	36-50	56									5.4	8.9	17.8	12.5	5.4	1.8	1.8	1.8			
2	12	51-72	65								3.1	4.6	8.9	17.9	12.3	15.4	4.6	3.1	1.5			
2	13	73-103	55		1.8		1.8				1.8	5.5	9.2	18.5	16.4	12.7	14.5	10.9	3.6			
2	14	104-148	57										3.6	7.3	9	14.4	7.2	14.4	14.4		1.8	
2	15	149-212	67										1.8	1.8	6	9	16.4	16.4	9	6	3	
2	16	213-303	65										1.5	1.5	1.5	6.2	12.3	18.5	12.3	15.4	4.6	7.7
2	17	304-433	35													2.9	5.7	14.3	20	14.3	5.7	
2	18	434-622	32												2.9		9.4	6.3	15.6	15.6	25	6.3
2	19	623-886	12													8.3			16.7	25	25	
2	20	887-1266	3																33.3	33.3	33.3	
	Tot.		674																			

Table 2b continued

# Fires	Stage	# Leaves	N	2	3	4	5	6	7	8	9	10	11	12	13	14	15	16	17	18	19	20
3	3	2	4	25																		
3	4	3	7		3.4		14.3	28.6	57.1													
3	5	4-5	29			25	14.3	17.2	31	13.8	3.4	3.4										
3	6	6-7	35				25	17.2	22.9	14.3	11.8	2.9	2.9									
3	7	8-11	34			2.9		17.1	11.8	14.7	14.6	11.8	8.8	2.9								
3	8	12-16	41				2.4	5.9	14.3	23.5	23.5	24.4	11.9									
3	9	17-24	59					7.3	22.9	14.7	11.8	11.8	4.9	7.3		1.7						
3	10	25-35	55					1.7	13.8	6.8	6.8	16.9	7.6	9.1	5.5							
3	11	36-50	66						5.5	5.5	11.9	16.4	13.6	13.6	5.5	1.5	1.5					
3	12	51-72	81						1.5	6.1	14.6	16.9	12.7	18.2	14.8	1.5	2.5	2.5				
3	13	73-103	80						1.3	1.2	4.9	24.4	11.9	9.1	19.8	6.2	6.4	2.9	2.5			
3	14	104-148	69						1.4	1.4	5.8	7.6	14	12.3	8.9	11.6	22.9	8.9	8.5	1.4		
3	15	149-	71						1.4	1.4	2.8	1.4	4.3	2.5	14.5	20.3	8.9	6.4	8.5	2.8		
3	16	213-303	59								1.7	1.7	2.8	2.8	8.5	4.2	39.4	14.5	2.9	2.5	1.4	1.7
3	17	304-433	80									3	1.3		1.7	6.8	10.2	28.8	23.7	10.2	3.8
3	18	434-622	33										1.3	2.8	1.3	3	5.1	25.3	12.1	18.2	24.2	30.3
3	19	623-886	9												3	3		7.6	27.9	11.1	19	44.4
3	20	887-1266	1																33.3			100
	Tot.		813																			

a   b

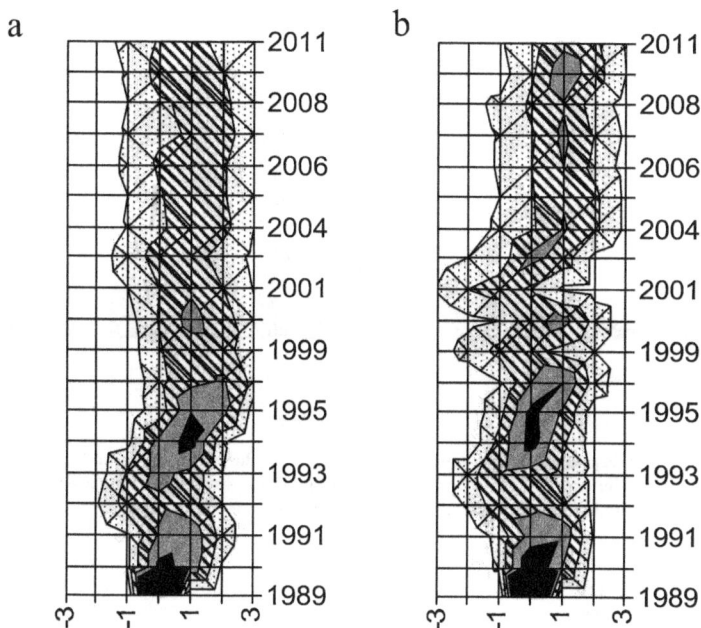

Figure 2: Growth stage relative to starting stage of populations subject to a) two fires and b) three fires. Shading indicates the percentage of individuals smaller than the starting stage (-1 to -3), static (0) or larger than the starting stage (1 to 3) at each census during the observation period 1988 to 2011 (no fill: 0-10%, stipples: 10-20%, diagonal stripes: 20-30%, grey fill: 30-40%, black fill: 40-100%).

The large number of stages meant there were insufficient individuals sampled to construct projection matrices for each site. Therefore sites were lumped according to the number of fires that occurred during the observation period. Transition probabilities were based on initial size recorded between October 1989 and April 1990 (12-18 months after the 1988 fire) and final size at December 2011. The probability of seedling transition to the first size class was estimated from the sample of 987 seedlings artificially established following the 1994 fire at Jibbon. Fertility rates (seedlings per individual) were calculated by multiplying total capsule output for the observation period by seedling establishment rates (as calculated above) and dividing by the number of individuals. Errors in the estimated parameters were combined as described above. Population projections were calculated for the lowest (non-zero) and highest establishment rates recorded across the seven sample sites as well lower (lowest rate – SEM) and upper (highest rate + SEM) bounds (where SEM is the standard error of the mean).

RESULTS

Growth

Crown recovery following fire occurred rapidly and individuals typically attained pre-fire size by the first year post-fire. Thereafter, crown growth became slower and more variable. The proportion of individuals in a stage higher than their starting stage increased through the study, although at any given point, some individuals were suppressed at or below their starting stage (Figure 2), generally those that were covered by shrub canopy (pers. obs.). Individuals burnt three times were more likely to progress to a higher stage than those burnt twice (Figure 3). The proportion of individuals suppressed below the starting stage increased slightly with increasing size although this trend was more pronounced in individuals burnt twice compared with three times (Table 2). All but one of the seedlings raised in 1990 remained static with 1-3 soft short leaves characteristic of the juvenile form until death (< 20 years). The remaining seedling entered

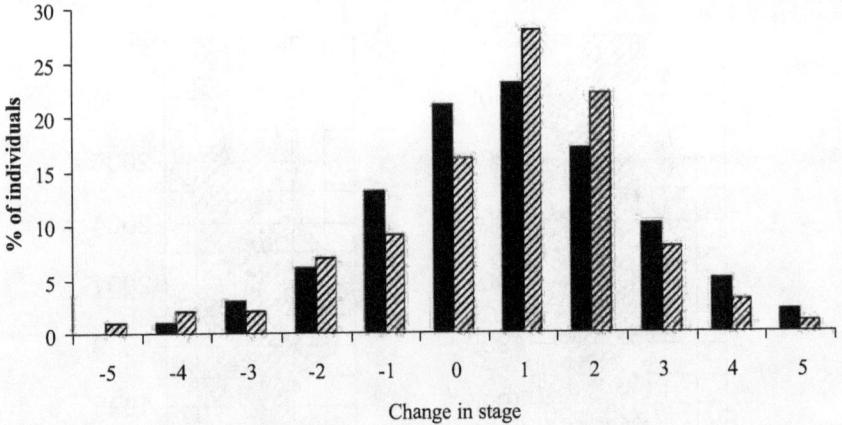

Figure 3: Histogram representing the growth of individuals over the course of the study partitioned by the number of times burnt (dark fill – two fires, diagonal shading – three fires). Data are the stage occupied at year 23 compared with the stage occupied at year one.

stage 1 in 2005 (15 years) and was at stage 8 at the end of the observation period, a rate of progression that was unmatched during the observation period.

Death

The survival rates for established plants over 23 years were 98.4%/year (two fires) and 98.9%/year (three fires), (Table 2). Survival varied among sites: Wises Track (3 fires) and Garie Trig (2 fires) were notable for higher mortality compared with the other sites (Figure 4). Within sites, individuals located

under dense thicket were more likely to die than those located in gaps in the thicket (pers. obs.). Survival during fire was high: only 42 individuals failed to resprout and of these, 15 were in a state of senescence immediately preceding the fire. Survival of healthy individuals during fire ranged from 98.5% (1994 fire) to 99.6% (1988, 2001 fires, Table 3). Survival during the first year following fire was lower than the annual average (94.6 – 97.3%, Table 3, Figure 4). Fire-related mortality (heat shock combined with death following resprouting) affected up to 10% of

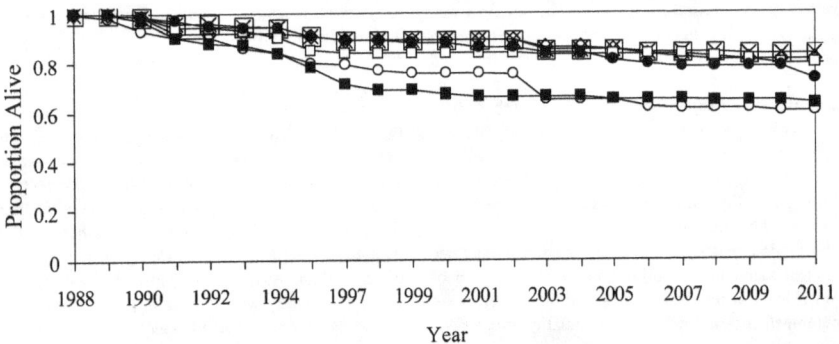

Figure 4: Survival of individuals at each site over the course of the study (o- Wises, X – Crystal Pools, ◇- Maianbar, ■ - Garie, □ - Bundeena, ● – Jibbon). Data are the proportion of the starting population surviving at each census.

B258

Proc. Linn. Soc. N.S.W., 134, 2012

Table 3: The number of individuals recorded alive and well prior to fire (N) and the number failing to resprout after the fire (killed). Post-fire survival applies to all individuals that were alive before the fire and survived up to the next census approximately one year later. The sizes of individuals killed in the 1988 fire were not recorded.

Starting stage	N	Killed	Post-fire Survival	N	Killed	Post-fire Survival	N	Killed	Post-fire Survival
	1988			1994			2001		
2	1	-	100	0	0	-	0	0	-
3	5	-	80	4	0	100	4	0	100
4	9	-	100	8	0	100	7	0	100
5	47	-	98	45	1	95	22	0	100
6	43	-	98	51	0	100	28	0	93
7	58	-	100	60	1	100	25	0	100
8	75	-	95	90	1	99	26	0	92
9	77	-	96	107	2	98	33	0	91
10	55	-	93	90	0	97	25	0	84
11	62	-	94	115	0	99	28	0	79
12	82	-	98	145	0	97	41	1	85
13	64	-	97	133	1	99	33	1	88
14	69	-	100	129	1	98	34	0	97
15	97	-	99	133	6	98	44	0	100
16	105	-	98	132	3	95	45	0	98
17	95	-	99	111	3	97	63	0	100
18	46	-	100	67	2	95	20	0	95
19	8	-	100	20	0	85	5	0	100
20	1	-	100	4	0	100	1	0	100
Total/ Average	999	4 (0.4%)	97.1	1444	21 (1.5%)	97.3	484	2 (0.4%)	94.6

the population in the 2001 fire (Wises Track, three fires), although the only other noticeable fire-related dips below background survival rates were 6% (Garie Trig, two fires) and 5% (Bundeena Road, two fires) following the 1994 fire (Figure 4). Mortality between fires (i.e. excluding the first post-fire year) varied among inter-fire periods (1989 – 1993; 1994 – 2001; 2002 – 2011) and stage classes (Figure 5). Mortality in sites burnt twice was generally higher than in sites burnt three times; the difference was generally greatest in the third inter-fire interval in small plants (stages 6 - 14) but the converse was true for plants in stage 5 and there was no trend for larger plants (stages 15 – 19, Figure 5).

At Garrawarra, 63% of seedlings burnt at age two years resprouted following simulated fire compared with 74% of those defoliated but not burnt. Survival rates over the subsequent year were 13% and 33%, respectively, compared with 74% survival in the control treatment. Of 141 four-year old seedlings alive immediately prior to the 1994 fire 53 (38%) were recorded alive eight months after the fire. There was no sign of the remainder, therefore they were probably killed by fire.

Fertility

Seedling establishment following the 1994 fire varied from zero to almost one seedling per four capsules produced (Table 4). A total of 2719 seeds were

Proc. Linn. Soc. N.S.W., 134, 2012

B259

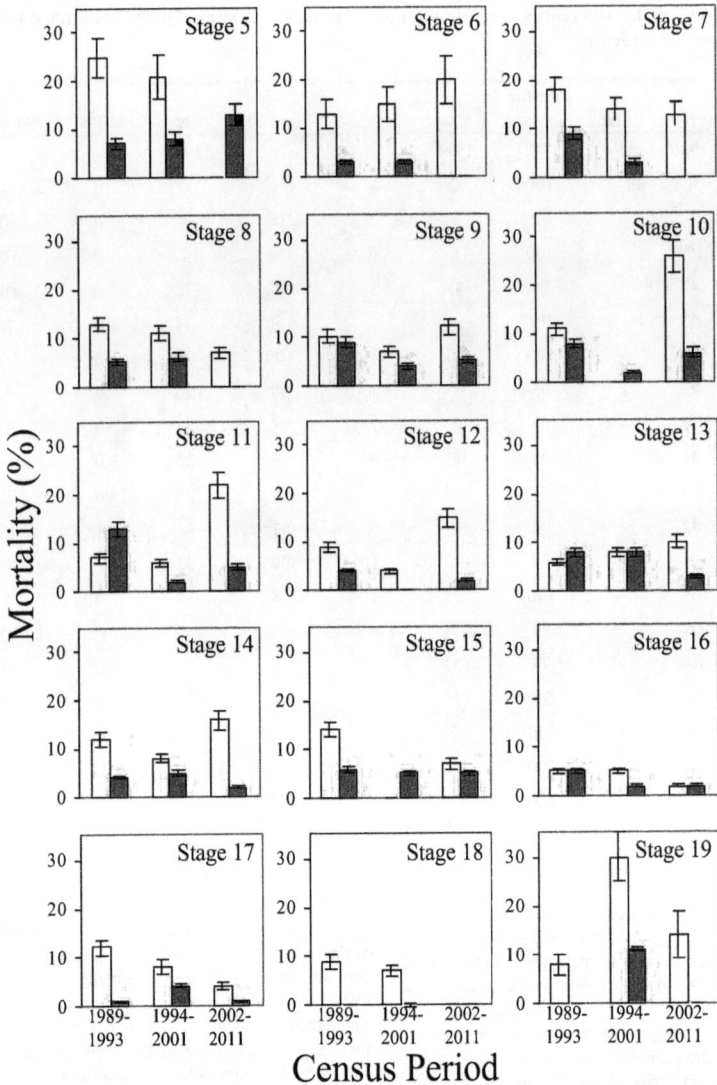

Figure 5: Mortality (%) partitioned by stage (stages 5-19) and fire-incidence (no fill – two fires, grey fill – three fires) during consecutive inter-fire periods during the study. Inter-fire periods (1989 – 1993; 1994 – 2001; 2002 – 2011) exclude the first post-fire year and mortality was calculated using the number of individuals alive at the start of each interval. Populations subject to two fires were not burnt prior to the third interval: in that case mortality for intervals two and three represents the early and later part of a single inter-fire interval.

B260

Proc. Linn. Soc. N.S.W., 134, 2012

Table 4: Seedling establishment as a function of capsule production following the 1994 fire (SEM).

Study Site	Seedling Density (m⁻²)	Capsule Density (m⁻²)	Establishment rate (sdl./foll.)
Crystal Pools	0.85 (0.28)	74(0.2)	0.012 (0.004)
Wises Track East	0	50 (0)	0
Bundeena Road	2.19 (0.99)	48 (0.7)	0.045 (0.038)
Garie Trig	0.57 (0.2)	187 (0.2)	0.003 (0.001)
Maianbar Road	1.04 (0.34)	116 (0.3)	0.009 (0.004)

required to raise 987 seedlings at Jibbon (1 seedling per 2.75 seeds), although more seeds were placed in sites with high rates of predation and following the first census measures to reduce predation were implemented. Reproductive output following the 1994 fire was more than double that of the 1988 fire, primarily because a higher proportion of individuals flowered, but also due to higher capsule production in some of the smaller size classes (Table 2). In comparison, reproductive output following the 2001 fire was negligible due both to the low proportion of flowering plants and the relatively high number of failed inflorescences. Individual fertility increased with plant size because flowering frequency generally increased with size and large plants produced larger inflorescences (Table 2).

Population projcetions

Populations declined to extinction following the projection of the two-fire population matrix through 18 cycles (414 years) under all but the highest of the four fertility schedules. Under the maximum fertility rate the population stabilised at a size of 275 individuals however these were dominated by seedlings with only a single individual occupying each stage from 8 to 20. Raising the highest fertility schedule by a factor of 35 was sufficient to stabilise the population at its current size. Despite having lower fertility overall, populations subject to three fires were predicted to grow, although the rate was sensitive to variation of the mortality rate in the highest stage class, especially when this was reduced below 0.99. Small reductions in survival of individuals in class 20 could plausibly be offset by increased fertility (1.5 – 6-fold), however this effect diminished rapidly as survival was reduced from 0.99 to 0.9, a plausible range based on survival in other classes (Figures 6, 7). In contrast, projections under the two-fire scenario were insensitive to increases in survival and growth of individuals in stages 15 to 20. The divergent trajectories were

thus interpreted to be primarily caused by different mortality rates in the smaller stages. Life expectancy was consistently higher in individuals experiencing three fires compared with two (Figure 8).

Competition experiment

Survival of established plants in artificial clearings at Garrawarra was 98% from 2001 to 2011 with 60% of survivors progressing to a larger stage, 8% regressing and 32% static. Mortality in uncleared treatments was 44% in 2007 (comprising plants in stage 10 or smaller) and 98% in 2011.

DISCUSSION

Population Dynamics

Divergent population trajectories were predicted under the two fire regimes based on our 23-year census of multiple *Xanthorrhoea resinosa* populations. This was primarily due to contrasting patterns of survival which are attributable to at least three main sources: heat shock during fire, early post-fire mortality (probably associated with the effort of post-fire resprouting/flowering) and competition from overstorey shrubs. Relatively few deaths in our study were attributable to heat shock alone, although high rates of mortality have been observed in plants with a large aerial caudex at other sites as a result of caudex damage following very intense or repeated fires (author's unpublished data, Curtis 1998). Total fire-related mortality (heat shock combined with death following resprouting) was significant in isolated circumstances (e.g. 10% mortality at Wises Track following the 2001 fire) however overall, we observed higher mortality in populations burnt twice compared with those burnt three times.

Results from other studies suggest that overstorey competition affects the survival of understorey species such as *Xanthorrhoea resinosa*

Proc. Linn. Soc. N.S.W., 134, 2012

B261

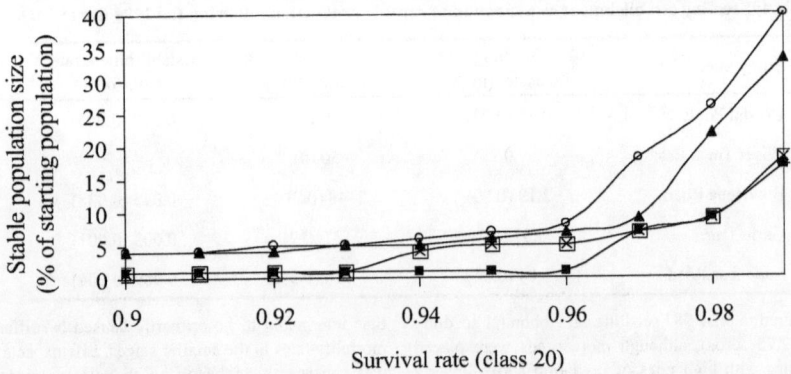

Figure 6: The size at which X. resinosa populations stabilize (as a percentage of the starting population) when projected over repeated 23-year intervals using survival rates derived from populations subject to three fires and the four different fertility schedules described in the text (○- maximum, ▲- high, X – low, ■ – minimum). The graphs show the decline in stable population size as survival of individuals in class 20 is reduced progressively from 99 to 99% (per cycle).

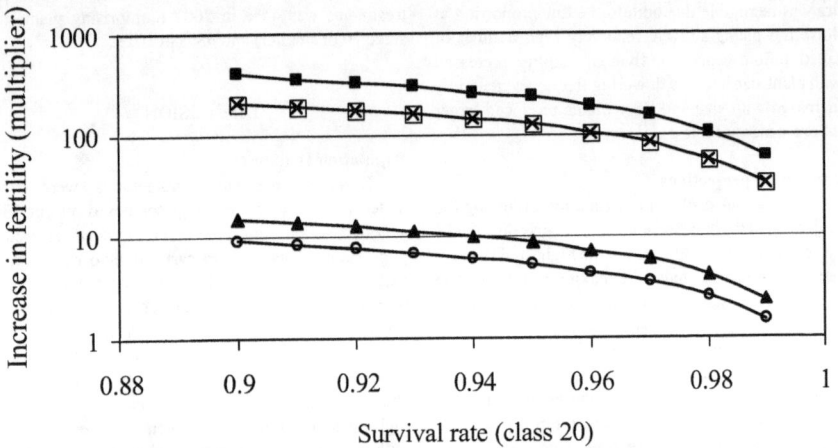

Figure 7: Increase in fertility (multiplier) required to maintain population growth when populations are projected over repeated 23-year intervals using survival rates derived from populations subject to three fires and the four different fertility schedules described in the text (○- maximum, ▲- high, X – low, ■ – minimum). The graphs show the increase on fertility required to maintain population growth as survival of individuals in class 20 is reduced progressively from 99 to 99% (per cycle).

(Keith & Bradstock 1994, Tozer & Bradstock 2002, Keith *et al.* 2007a), consistent with the dynamics of desmium starch storage in the caudex, as described by Lamont et al. (2004) for *X. preissii* in south-west Australia. Desmium starch serves as energy storage and is drawn down during the post-fire production of leaves and inflorescence. In the absence of fire, starch reserves fluctuate seasonally, accumulating over summer and depleting in late autumn (Lamont et al. 2004). Assuming a similar mechanism applies

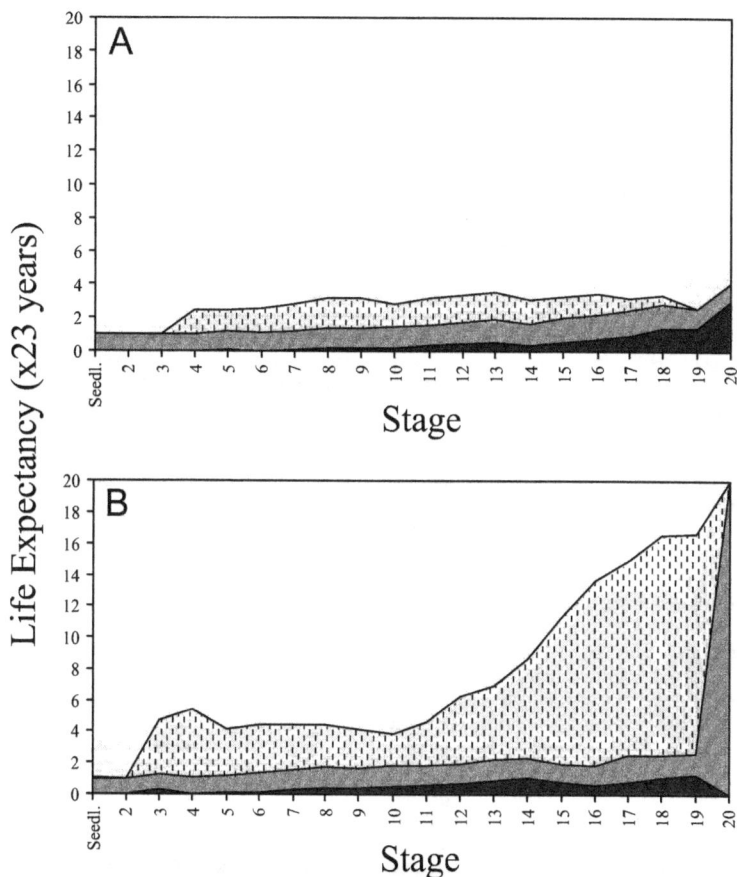

Figure 8: Life expectancy for individuals experiencing A) two fires and B) three fires as a function of starting stage (dark shading – time spent below the starting stage, grey shading – time spent at the starting stage, vertical dashes – time spent above the starting stage).

in *X. resinosa*, it seems probable that depressed crown growth under heavy shading is indicative of photosynthetic deficit, with the effect that progression through the size classes is slowed or reversed. In turn, this may render individuals less fit for resprouting and flowering following fire and more susceptible to death following pathogenic attack. Consistent with this model, we observed a lower overall risk of death among individuals that flowered.

Although the results of our experiment at Garrawarra provide a strong demonstration of the effect of competition on survival of *X. resinosa*, evidence in support of competition as the primary factor driving the dynamics of other populations is more equivocal. While survival patterns during the period 2002-2011 were consistent with patterns observed at Garrawarra (higher mortality in smaller size classes in sites not burnt in 2001), the response was much weaker and the higher overall mortality observed throughout the study in sites burnt twice can not be explained by competition during the period 1988 - 2001. Three factors can be identified which

Proc. Linn. Soc. N.S.W., 134, 2012

B263

complicate the interpretation of our results. First, the pattern of shrub establishment following the 1994 fire was patchy as a result of lower recruitment due to the short inter-fire interval. Thus, competitive pressure on understorey species varied widely within sites, with some individuals subject to dense cover and others growing in open heath. Assuming patchiness was equal across sites then this factor is expected to diminish the expression of the competition effect. Second, our study sites had different histories prior to the commencement of the study: those in the three-fire treatment generally experienced a shorter fire-interval prior to 1988 and were free of thicket, while sites subject to two fires were subjected to a longer fire-interval and varying degrees of competition from thicket (Table 1). Sites subject to two fires were therefore more likely to have experienced the effects of competition prior to 1988 and higher mortality following the 1988 fire may have been a legacy of this competition. Third, attack from pathogens such as *Phytophthora cinnamomi* identified at some of our study sites (e.g. Wises Track and Garie Trig) may have contributed to higher mortality at heavily infected sites thus confounding any response to fire regimes. If sites subject to strong pathogenic attack were concentrated in the two-fire treatment then the argument for dynamics driven by competition is weakened. This does not appear to have been the case since the site with highest mortality was subject to three fires while that with second-highest was subject to two fires. However, it is likely that the presence of *P. cinnamomi* would exacerbate the effects of competition from overstorey species.

Our interpretation of the population dynamics of *X. resinosa* differs from that of Regan et al. (2011), primarily as a result of differing perspectives on mortality. Based on a stochastic model compiled from an earlier version of these population data, Regan et al. (2011) concluded that populations declined more slowly under lower fire frequencies because mortality induced by the combined effects of fire and disease outweighed higher fertility under higher fire frequencies. Our results corroborate this conclusion only when overstorey species are absent, but suggest that the opposite is true when competition from shrub species increases mortality. Regan et al. (2011) interpreted mortality differences among sites as a function of the presence of the pathogen *Phytophthora cinnamomi*, but did not incorporate the effects of overstorey competition into their model. Our observed rates of mortality were lower than in other disease-affected plant populations elsewhere in Australia (Keith 2004; Shearer et al. 2008), suggesting that the impacts of the disease are more subtle than elsewhere (see Keith et al. 2012). Nonetheless, in species such as X. resinosa, with slow population turnover, the effects of slow-acting disease on population persistence can be significant (Keith et al. 2007b). Disease effects manifest primarily by exacerbating the effects of fire early in the fire cycle and may also exacerbate effects of competition later in the fire cycle. Further experimentation is needed to resolve these interactions and their effects on population persistence.

On balance, increased mortality resulting from competition is a plausible explanation for the divergent population trajectories observed in our study sites because competition from overstorey shrubs is likely to have been less intense over the longer term (prior to and following 1988) and was more regularly interrupted by fire in the sites burnt three times compared with twice. Even allowing for the cumulative effect of fire-related mortality and strong inter-site variability in survival there exits a clear trend not easily explained by factors other than fire, although further analysis is required to examine the nature and implications of variation in survival among sites. Conversely, although survival appears crucial to population dynamics, fertility could also be important, especially if rare conditions that promote highly productive recruitment events were not observed during our study period. This hypothesis could explain why populations are apparently susceptible to decline despite having survival rates that are favourably high compared with other members of this long-lived genus (Lamont et al. 2004) and very similar (on average) among treatments.

Increased fertility may result from increased flowering frequency and fruit set, reduced predation and/or higher rates of seedling establishment. Among *Xanthorrhoea* species, flowering frequency increases with increasing plant size (Gill and Ingwerson 1976, Curtis 1998, Ward and Lamont 2000), is highest, and generates the greatest seed set following summer fires (Gill and Ingwerson 1976, Lamont et al. 2000, Taylor et al. 1998), and decreases with the length of the preceding inter-fire interval (Taylor et al. 1998). Flowering patterns in our populations were consistent with those observed in other species. We assumed that the timing of fires during our observation period was optimal for fruit production (authors' unpubl. data). Flowering frequency increased with plant size and experimental burning demonstrated a peak in flowering frequency in *X. resinosa* following summer fire (author's unpublished data). We observed flowering following inter-fire intervals of nine, six and 8 years. Although we observed a high proportion of individuals flowering in populations burnt in one

B264

Proc. Linn. Soc. N.S.W., 134, 2012

short fire-interval, our data suggest this may not be repeated following two or more short inter-fire intervals, possibly due to the depletion of desmium starch.

Since our fertility estimates were based on seedling establishment following the most productive of three observed flowering events (1994), several arguments suggest that increased fertility is unlikely to offset observed mortality rates, particular under the two-fire scenario. First, following the analysis above, we consider that seed output is only likely to increase as a result of an increase in the proportion of plants flowering, and that a doubling of output (from 18% to 36% of all plants) is at the upper end of the plausible range. Second, given the intensity and scale of the 1994 fire (the entire park was burnt) and the large numbers of flowering individuals and undamaged capsules per inflorescence (authors' unpubl. data), we consider that satiation of both pre and post-dispersal predators was likely. Third, there were no obvious weather conditions (e.g. drought) to which we could attribute lower than average recruitment. We conclude that mortality is more important as a limiting factor than fertility because very large increases in fertility are required to offset relatively small differences in mortality. This interpretation is consistent with a strategy of longevity and repeated flowering events as a response to unpredictable reproductive success (Bond & Midgley 2001, Keith et al. 2007b, Krebs 2009).

Management implications

We conclude that local populations of *Xanthorrhoea resinosa* decline or grow depending on the level of competition from overstorey species and the extent to which seedling establishment varies both temporally and spatially. If temporal variation in seedling recruitment is similar to spatial variation in recruitment observed after the 1994 fire, then populations may stabilise or grow under a regime of frequent fires similar to our three-fire scenario (although lower densities are more likely). Conversely, if our measurements of spatial variation in recruitment are indicative of the relative suitability of different sites for seedling establishment then in the long term, the species is likely to contract in range to safe sites (sensu Harper 1977), or sites where overstorey is interrupted such as under *Eucalyptus* canopy, on rock shelves or areas of very shallow soil unsuitable for shrubs. More pessimistic projections may occur under a stochastic treatment of these data, because we have not factored in recruitment failure as observed in this study (although a stochastic treatment would also take into account higher recruitment, hitherto not observed).

This study provides an insight into the consequences for the population dynamics of a range of species known to be negatively impacted by competition from overstorey species (Keith and Bradstock 1994, Tozer and Bradstock 2002). Our results challenge central assumptions governing fire management of heath in Royal National Park in suggesting that a focus on minimum fire intervals alone will not guarantee the long-term persistence of key understorey species. To achieve this goal, fire management must also promote periods and places of low overstorey shrub density. This might be achieved by applying either very short fire-intervals (to interrupt shrub recruitment), under which serotinous obligate seeder species are the most obvious group affected, or very long fire-intervals (causing shrub senescence) under which resprouting shrubs, ferns and both rhizomatous and non-rhizomatous graminoids and herbs are likely to decline (Keith et al. 2007a). While one empirical study has suggested that populations of overstorey shrubs species may be more resilient under high fire frequencies than demographic studies suggest (Bradstock et al. 1992), the implications of local extinction caused by long fire-intervals for species such as *X. resinosa* are potentially more serious. For example, *Banksia ericifolia* has a similar dispersal capability to *X. resinosa* but a much higher capacity for population growth by virtue of rapid growth and maturation. In comparison, *X. resinosa* is likely to require 40 – 160 years to mature and from 120 – 240 years following germination before significant reproductive output occurs (Table 2). Nevertheless, proteaceous shrubs comprise an important habitat and food resource for nectarivores. Further studies are required to establish what spatial and temporal pattern of shrub density is required to promote coexistence of these contrasting species. Meanwhile, we argue that fire regime thresholds should more directly consider functional groups containing species with low potential for population growth.

ACKNOWLEDGEMENTS

We gratefully acknowledge the assistance of the following people in with field work: Elizabeth Ashby, Tony Auld, Ross Bradstock, Nicholas Carlisle, Janet Cohn, Andrew Denham, Richard T. Dutchman, Helga T. Dutchwoman, Murray Ellis, Cathy F. England, Meredith Henderson, Lisa Holman, Simon Hunter, Nathan Kearns, Karen Maling, Lisa Metcalfe, Ben Owers, Vicki Logan, Berin Mackenzie, Mark Ooi, Christopher Pennay, John Porter, Suzette Rodereda, Patsy Ross, Christopher Simpson, John Steer, Elizabeth Tasker, Dan Tindall, Ken Turner and several others (PG, MR, JD, PH, AP, and GN)

REFERENCES:

Bond W.J., Midgley J.J. (2001) Ecology of sprouting in woody plants: the persistence niche. *Trends in Ecology and Evolution* 16: 45–51.

Bond W.J. and van Wilgen B.W. (1996). Fire and Plants. Chapman and Hall, London.

Bradstock, R.A. and Myerscough, P.J. (1988). The effects of frequent fires on recruitment and survival in woody resprouters: *Banksia serrata* and *Isopogon anemonifolius*. *Australian Journal of Botany* 36: 5-31.

Bradstock, R.A., Tozer M.G. and Keith D.A. (1992). Effects of high frequency fire on floristic composition and abundance in a fire prone heathland near Sydney. *Australian Journal of Botany* 45: 641-655.

Bradstock, R.A., Keith, D.A. and Auld, T.D. (1995). Fire and conservation: imperatives and constraints on managing for biodiversity. In : *Conserving Biodiversity – Threats and Solutions* (eds Bradstock R.A., Auld T.D., Keith D.A., Kingsford R.T., Lunney D. and Sivertsen D.P.), pp. 323-333. Surrey Beatty and Sons, Sydney.

Cowling R.M. and Gxaba T. (1990). Effects of a fynbos overstorey shrub on understorey community structure: implications for the maintenance of community-wide species richness. *South African Journal of Ecology* 1: 1-7.

Curtis, N.P. (1998). A post-fire ecological study of *Xanthorrhoea australis* following prescribed burning in the Warby Range State Park, north-eastern Victoria, Australia. *Australian Journal of Botany* 46:253-272.

DECC (2009). Royal and Heathcote National Parks and Garrawarra State Conservation Area Fire Management Strategy. Department of Environment and Climate Change, NSW.

Gill, A.M. and Ingwersen, F. (1976). Growth of *Xanthorrhoea australis* R. Br. in relation to fire. *Journal of Applied Ecology* 13:195-203.

Harden, G.J. (ed.) (1993). Flora of New South Wales Volume 4. New South Wales University Press, Kensington, Australia.

Harper, J.L. (1977). Population biology of plants. Academic Press, London.

Keith, D.A. and Myerscough, P.J. (1993). Floristics and soil relations of upland swamp vegetation near Sydney. *Australian Journal of Ecology* 18: 325–344.

Keith, D.A. and Bradstock, R.A. (1994). Fire and competition in Australian heath: a conceptual model and field investigations. *Journal of Vegetation Science* 5: 347-354.

Keith, D.A., Holman, L., Rodoreda, S., Lemmon, J. and Bedward, M. (2007a). Plant Functional Types can predict decade-scale changes in fire-prone vegetation. *Journal of Ecology* 95: 1324-1337.

Keith, D.A., Tozer, M.G., Regan, T.J. and Regan, H.M. (2007b). The persistence niche: what makes it and what breaks it two fire-prone plant species. *Australian Journal of Botany* 55: 273-279.

Keith, D.A. and Tozer, M.G. (2012). Vegetation dynamics in the coastal heathlands of the Sydney Basin. *Proceedings of the Linnean Society of New South Wales* 134: in press.

Keith, D.A., McDougall, K. and Simpson, C. (2012). Are there spatial patterns in threats posed by root rot disease, *Phytophthora cinnamomi*, in Royal National Park? *Proceedings of the Linnean Society of New South Wales* 134: in press.

Keith, D.A., Williams, J.E. and Woinarski, J.C.W. (2002). Biodiversity conservation – principles and approaches for fire management. In: *Flammable Australia: the Fire Regimes and Biodiversity of a Continent* (eds R.A. Bradstock, J.E. Williams & A.M. Gill), pp. 401–425. Cambridge University Press, Cambridge.

Krebs, C.J. (2009). Ecology: the experimental analysis of distribution and abundance. Benjamin Cummings, San Francisco California.

Lamont, B.B., Swanborough, P.W. and Ward, D. (2000). Plant size and season of burn affect flowering and fruiting of the grasstree *Xanthorrhoea preissii*. *Austral Ecology* 25:268-272

Lamont B.B., Wittkuhn R. and Korczynskyj, D. (2004). TURNER REVIEW No. 8. Ecology and ecophysiology of grasstrees. *Australian Journal of Botany* 52:561-582.

Taylor J.E., Monamy, V. and Fox B.J. (1998). Flowering of *Xanthorrhoea fulva*: the effect of fire and clipping. *Australian Journal of Botany* 46:241-251.

Regan, H.M., Keith, D.A., Regan, T.J., Tozer, M.G. and Tootell, N. (2011). Fire management to combat disease: turning interactions between threats into conservation management. *Oecologia* 167: 873–882.

Shearer B.L., Cran,e C.E., Barrett, S. and Cochrane, A. (2008). *Phytophthora cinnamomi*, a major threatening process to conservation of flora diversity in the South-west Botanical Province of Western Australia. *Australian Journal of Botany* 55, 225-238.

Tozer, M.G. and Bradstock, R.A. (2002). Fire-mediated effects of overstorey on plant species diversity and abundance in an eastern Australian heath. *Plant Ecology*, 164, 213–232.

Tozer, M.G., Turner, K., Keith, D.A., Tindall, D., Pennay, C., Simpson, C., MacKenzie, B., Beukers, P. and Cox, S. (2010). Native vegetation of southeast NSW: a revised classification and map for the coast and eastern tablelands. *Cunninghamia* 11: 359–406.

Ward, D. and Lamont, B.B. (2000). Probability of grasstrees (*Xanthorrhoea preissii*) flowering after fire. *Journal of the Royal Society of Western Australia.* 83, 13-16.

Whelan, R.J., Rodgerson, L., Dickman, C.R. and Sutherland, E.F. (2002). Critical life cycles of plants and animals: developing a process-based understanding of population changes in fire-prone landscapes. In: *Flammable Australia: the Fire Regimes and Biodiversity of a Continent* (eds R.A. Bradstock, J.E. Williams & A.M. Gill), pp. 94–124. Cambridge University Press, Cambridge.

B266

Proc. Linn. Soc. N.S.W., 134, 2012

SECTION B

Papers from the 2011 Linnean Society of NSW Symposium on "Natural History of Royal National Park"

The Linnean Society of New South Wales publishes in its proceedings original papers and review
article dealing with biological and earth sciences. Intending authors should contact the Secretary
PO Box 82, Kingsford, N.S.W. 2032, Australia) for instructions for the preparation of manuscripts
and procedures for submission. Instructions to authors are also available on the society's web page
http://linneansocietynsw.org.au/).

manuscripts not prepared in accordance with the society's instructions will not be considered.

www.ingramcontent.com/pod-product-compliance
Lightning Source LLC
Chambersburg PA
CBHW030913270326
41929CB00008B/677